# Cornish Oasis.

## A Biographical Chronicle of the Fishing Village of

# COVERACK
## ─Cornwall─

by

Cyril Hart

\* \* \* \* \*

"Coverack is indeed an oasis
in a district much of which is stony and desolate".

(The Cornwall Coast, by A.L. Salmon, 1910.)

\* \* \* \* \*

1990

The Lizard Press, Mullion, Cornwall

The Lizard Press, Mullion, Cornwall, England.

2nd. Edition 1994.

Produced in Great Britain by The Lizard Press.
Set in Press Roman

ISBN 0 9516965 1 3
Dewey Class: 942.376

# *FOREWORD*

Coverack is a small fishing village situated on The Lizard, an area that lays claim to uniqueness in a county that itself boasts a character unlike any other in the land.

The name of Porthcovrek was first documented in the year 1262, but the village of Coverack, as it is now known, had its beginnings many centuries before this time. The round houses and cliff castles of Poldowrian and Chynalls can be dated to circa 1500 B.C. The salt works at Lowland Point were most probably worked during the years of the Roman occupation of England, and there can be little doubt that Saxon raiders carried our depredations here during the 9th. century A.D.

Add to these dates the events of more recent centuries and here in this impressive book, the reader can trace three and a half thousand years of village history. All the events recorded here have helped to shape the character of Coverack. Some have affected lives and events far beyond the parish boundaries of this charming corner of Cornwall.

In this well-researched and well-written history of his native village, Cyril Hart gives his readers a scholarly appraisal of Coverack's past, and its place in the pattern of Cornish life - but in so doing he has achieved far more. In recording the more recent history of the village, the author has captured the very essence of history by the use of anecdotes and personal reminiscences of the men and women for whom Coverack has provided birth-place, home and final resting-place.

Here are rebels; heroes; victims; lifeboatmen; coastguards; smugglers; preachers; fishermen; sailors; soldiers; saints and sinners.

This is a rare book for the reader who is familiar with Coverack and Cornwall, or for he or she who would discover something of the heart and soul of a truly Cornish village.

In CORNISH OASIS Cyril Hart has captured the very essence of Cornwall and added a detailed and fascinating page to the historical record of Cornwall.

E.V. Thompson. Cornwall. January, 1991.

# *INTRODUCTION*

After giving a short series of talks in the Village Hall on the history of Coverack since the middle of the last century I was asked if I would write a more comprehensive account of local happenings. Being a native of Coverack, the idea appealed to me but the thought had to be shelved until retirement provided the opportunity.

Cornish Oasis is a fairly detailed look at the way in which the village has grown and at some of the external influences which have affected its development. The story begins when the cove was void of habitation but used by locals living in settlements at the top of Higher Bridge Hill or in the cliff castle at Chynalls. It goes on to the present day.

It has been said that History is the essence of innumerable biographies. This is particularly pertinent when applied to a small village community, so this chronicle pays particular attention to the people who have made the village what it is over the years. One man, or should I say person, does indeed have to play many parts in village life. The same names crop up, decade after decade, whether the subject under review be fishing, farming, religion, rescue, education, recreation, or the activities of mundane village committees serving the social needs of the inhabitants. There has had to be discretion when dealing with smuggling. It is a tale of triumph and tragedy, wrecks and war, work and play, enacted in A.L. Salmon's "oasis".

C.S.H. Falmouth. September, 1990.

# *ACKNOWLEDGEMENTS*

The writing of this book would not have been possible without help and advice from many Coverack people, some of whom have been mentioned in the text. I am especially grateful to the late John Corin, Frank Curnow and David Mason who are from Coverack and St. Keverne and to Peter Harvey from Falmouth. The staffs of the Cornwall Record Office in Truro, the Falmouth Library, the Local Studies Library in Redruth, the Post Office Archives in Glass Hill Street, London, the Public Record Office at Kew, the Royal Institution of Cornwall in Truro and the Telecom Technology Showcase Resource Centre in Blackfriars have all been most helpful and patient in their efforts to provide the necessary documents and books. Finally I would like to thank my wife Eira for her encouragement and help during long hours of research and our friends Len and Peg Husband who helped Eira in the reading and correcting of the original draft.

CYRIL HART

An Index will help readers in their search for information about family members and the social history of Coverack events and organisations. Since publication of the first edition, I have been given details concerning the 'Oasis' which were not known to me before. I am most grateful to the contributors named in the Addenda. I would also like to acknowledge letters of encouragement which have come from Australia, Brittany, Canada, France, Holland, New Zealand and many parts of Great Britain.

CYRIL HART, Falmouth, October, 1994.

# ADDENDA

### Page 8

#### John Sandys and party blown across the Channel.

Jill Newton wrote in March, 1991, to say that she has access to a printed copy of John Sandys' original diary. The account makes it clear that the Le Marque brothers did not know John Sandys and his party when they arrived on the Ile de Batz. However, Sandys was invited to stay with the Le marque family until arrangements were made for repatriation. Jill, who lives in Brittany, told the story in an article in the magazine "France" (Winter 1990) and is publishing a full account of the adventure in French, English, Breton and Cornish.

### Pages 21,22

#### Wreck of the Dispatch, 1809

Diver Kevin Heath, proprietor of the firm "Wreck and Reef Diving" has located a cannon from the Dispatch on the sea bed near the Black head. The Public Record Office has a letter addressed to The Hon. W.W. Pole written on the 24th. January, 1809 by William Luke, he said the Dispatch struck a ridge of rocks a little to the west of Coverack near the Signal Station. The ship went to pieces and as no part of the vessel or stores could be saved, dead bodies were removed by Coverack Sea Fencibles. The granite memorial in St. Keverne churchyard, in common with other contemporary reports, states the Officers and men were lost on the Manacle Rocks. The original marble monument stated that the soldiers perished in Coverack Cove. More facts need to be uncovered.

### Pages 25,26,27

#### Wreck of the Bay of Panama, 1891

The Rev. Arthur Baker has written from Cumbria to say that he has the Board of Trade Silver Medal which was awarded to his relation William Barker for his part in the rescue during the blizzard. Furthermore, Mr. Barker has a letter sent by William to John Barker (Arthur's grandfather) which describes the difficulties he encountered. "Occasionally the whereabouts of hitherto unrecorded mementoes are revealed." (Page 25). This remark prompted the Rev. Barker to write. I hope the "revelations" in the Addenda will encourage other readers to do likewise.

### Pages 72,93,158

#### The Frank Champions

Frank Champion (Junior) has sent me a copy of the citation concerning his father's bravery when his command, the S.S. Bhutan was sunk during the June 1942 convoy from Port Said to Malta. Captain Frank Champion (Senior), a veteran of the First World War, had to order the ship to be abandoned. True to tradition he was the last to leave and had to swim to a rescue ship, although burned about the arms. "Throughout the action he showed cool courage, and his organisation and leadership were responsible for saving many lives." He was awarded the Lloyd's War Medal for Bravery at Sea. By coincidence, Frank met his father in Alexandria just before the convoy departed. The Bhutan had a cargo of 7,000 tons of munitions on board, which was "protected" by a "wall" of flour each side and by a layer of bags above. Two days later R.A.F. Pilot Frank Champion (Junior) had the job of flying to Malta in an unarmed Lockheed Lodestar to evacuate children to Cairo. He now lives in Masseube, France and is engaged in writing his memoirs. They are sure to be fascinating reading.

### Page 223

#### Some significant dates in the Chronicle of Coverack

Peter Hadley (see P.1) has informed me that the earliest radio-carbon dated site in Poldowrian has been found to be dated 5500–5250 B.C., which makes Poldowrian by far the oldest dated site in Cornwall, antedating Carn Brea by about 1500 years. Important traces of Mesolithic habitation have also been found at Polcoverack and elsewhere, but actual radio-carbon datings for these are not available.

# CONTENTS

# CONTENTS

# ILLUSTRATIONS

FRONT COVER PHOTOGRAPH

## COVERACK HARBOUR circa 1906/7

*The sailing ship moored in the quay is the type which used to bring coal, fertilisers and building materials to Coverack. The name Express can be seen on the starboard side. The girl in the foreground is Ruth Lichensteiger, née Ward. Her father, Sidney Ward first visited Coverack when on a walking tour with his wife not long after the wreck of the s.s. Mohegan on October 8th.,1898. Mrs. Lichensteiger is now 90 years of age. Her son, David visited the exhibition in Coverack in 1988 and sent this photo from his home in Victoria, British Columbia.*

## SKETCHMAP OF THE COVERACK AREA

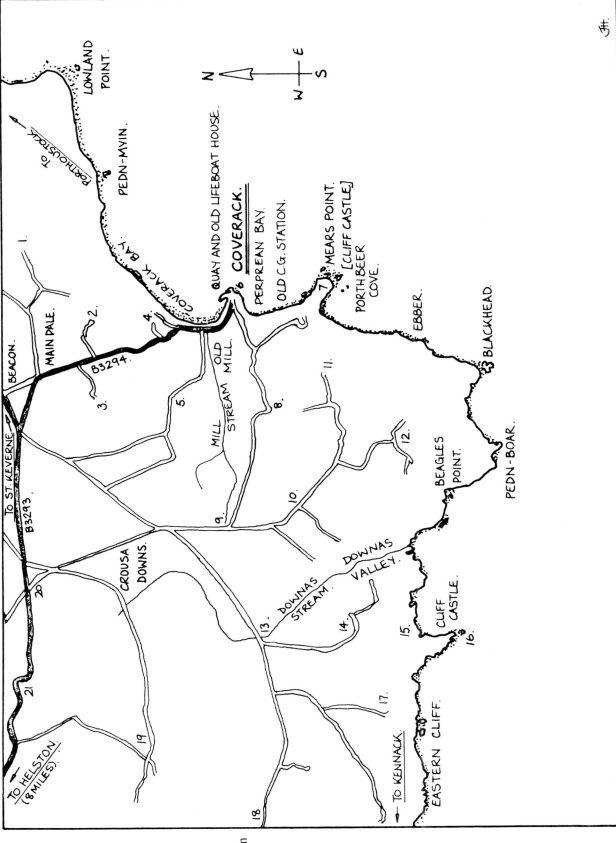

**Key**

1. Trevalsoe
2. Kilter Farm
3. Cowyjack Farm
4. North Corner
5. Polcoverack
6. Watch House
7. Chynalls Farm & Headland Hotel
8. Trevothen
9. Penhallick
10. Pednavounder Farm
11. Trewillis Farm
12. Treleaver
13. Ponsongath
14. Arrowan Farm
15. Borgwitha
16. Carrick Luz
17. Poldowrian
18. Gwenter
19. Trelan
20. Zoar
21. Trelanvean

# BEGINNINGS

Geologists claim that when we go from Paddington to Penzance we travel backwards in time, geologically speaking, at the rate of a million years a mile, our rocks being some three hundred million years older than those found in the South East. The Lizard peninsula is of particular interest to geologists because of the abundance of different types of rock which can be studied there.

The beach beneath Mill Hill below St. Peter's church has been the subject of close study by generations of students because of the extraordinary number of criss crossing 'dykes' of troctolite and gabbro cutting into the bastite-serpentine, all three being cut into by black 'dykes' of epidiorite. We village boys were informed of this by visiting geologists, but to us, the rocks remained a series of fairly smooth, natural dressing 'rooms' where we could dry off after a dip and wash the sand off our feet in a handy pool.

Another reason for the close attention of the geologists is that the only glacial deposit in Cornwall is found in the Lizard area. It is known as 'head' and is a covering of loose stony material which is unfortunately fast disappearing from the cliff tops between the Black Head and Porthoustock, leaving the raised beach as it probably was before the ice sheets. Cornwall escaped the Ice Age proper. Lowland Beach to the north of Coverack is a particularly good example of a raised beach, extending over one hundred acres. It is only a few feet above the high water mark. Salt, a vital commodity in ancient times, used to be extracted from this area. Although the name 'Lowland' is a descriptive one, it should be noted that the Cornish word for salt is 'holan'. 'Lowland' could well be an anglicisation of this word. The salt must have been advantageous to the local fishermen and it was probably used as barter with visiting traders. There is evidence of what is believed to have been a Romano-British salt works in a nearby settlement. The abandoned sandpit used to supply Hayle Foundry with fine sand for casting metal. We must remember that man only started living in Europe some fifty thousand years ago. Britain has been an island for about ten thousand years. It was separated from the continent when the melting water from the last Ice Age filled the area we call English Channel. Geologists consider that the 50 fathom line gives a rough idea of the position of the coast line some 60,000 years ago. This would place the Lizard Head about 15 miles south of its present position, Lands End would have extended to just beyond the Bishop Light off the Isles of Scilly and two inlets would have marked the beginning of the channel which now separates modern Cornwall from Celtic Brittany.

It is humbling to think that this oasis we call Coverack was being formed into a special place all those thousands of years ago and that settlements of people practising an early form of agriculture were to be found around Coverack when the mass of Britain itself could be classed as uninhabited. The Bronze Age hut circles and tumuli on Goonhilly Downs provide evidence of this occupation. Small fields enclosed by stone hedges or drainage ditches with earth mounds are still very much in evidence in the Coverack area. They are relics of the system of agriculture practised since pre-Celtic times. They were constructed in this manner because of the nature of the terrain and the need to protect crops from the strong prevailing winds. The hedges also provided defences against invaders and prevented them from over running the territory at a speed which would have made defence difficult if not impossible. Tumuli are also to be found near Main Dale, (pronounced 'dell' locally). That is the name given to the cross roads on the principal road out of Coverack. Other tumuli are to be found just off the road leading from the Beacon cross roads to Penhallick and Ponsongath and at Carnpessack and Arrowan Common just south of Ponsongath. Mr. Peter Hadley has been responsible for the recent excavation of the Bronze Age 'round house' or hut circle at Poldowrian on the cliffs a couple of miles west of Coverack. He has pointed out that the cliff castle at nearby Lankidden was built by immigrants from Vannes in Brittany called the Veneti. The defences show that they were designed to withstand attacks from the natives and not from seaborne invaders. There is also a cliff castle at Chynhalls or Mears Point which is much closer to the village and might yield interesting evidence of prehistoric settlement. Careful excavation could tell the story of Coverack up to our own time. Drowned shipwrecked mariners are known to have been buried there with their dead horses and cattle as late as the nineteenth century. Sea Scouts used it as a signal station during the First World War and the Home Guard built a strong point there to repel German invaders during the dark days after Dunkirk in the 1940s. Whether the original cliff castle was intended to repel locals or would-be immigrants remains to be seen. I do not think the land to the south of the rampart could have sustained a community for very long, but I remember the sheltered gardens bordering on the cliff at Porthbeer Cove were very productive in the 1930s and it is quite possible that the small peninsula we know today extended further when the cliff castle was constructed. One of the reasons why many 'cove' villages like Coverack are comparatively recent settlements is that the local people preferred to live inland in such places as the site at Main Dale. This gave them a chance to hide or escape when there was a seaborne attack. The marauders, having found no evidence of habitation in the coves, sometimes went away in search of a more accessible objective, leaving the cowering locals secure in their inland settlements out of sight of the top of the cliffs leading from the coves. From the semantic point of view it is very possible that the word Cornwall is derived from the latin based word 'Cornouii', meaning 'those who live in fortified settlements on promontories or headlands'.

Cornish people are proud of their Celtic origin. The Celts are thought to have originated from the lower reaches of the Danube. It is known that they sacked Rome in 387 B.C. and remained there for forty years but it is believed some Celtic settlers arrived in Britain long before that. There seems little doubt that because of its position on the Atlantic seaboard, half way between Brittany and Ireland there has always been a movement by sea of people from peninsula to peninsula. In spite of the hazards of the sea crossings in skin boats, trade was established, goods being dragged overland across the narrowest parts of peninsulas to avoid the rough weather and currents around the headlands. When man began using metals, Cornwall became the source of supply. Later on when the Romans began using the more convenient Spanish metal market, the established routes to Cornwall were used by Christians on pilgrimage to the saints in

Ireland and Cornwall.

There is little evidence of Roman occupation in Cornwall. One villa has been found near Camborne and some coins and artefacts in other places. A number of Roman milestones have been discovered and there is evidence of occupation by the Roman Army in areas where tin workings were an important part of the Roman economy. There is a small square Roman fort at Tregear, near Nanstallon to the West of Bodmin which protected traders and travellers on the overland route to Fowey from local mines and even from Ireland.

The Saxons raided Cornwall in 814 A.D. The battle of Hingston Down near Callington was fought and lost in 838 A.D. when our temporary Danish allies retreated before the Saxon onslaught and put out to sea, reneging on their promise of help. The Cornish put up no further resistance so there was no military or cultural settlement by the Saxons nor by their successors and our former allies, the Danes. This second period of neglect by invaders gave Cornwall some eight hundred years of relative isolation in comparison with the rest of England, allowing the Celtic culture to become firmly established.

The modern visitor to Cornwall should bear these facts in mind when considering Coverack. As the title suggests, Coverack is an oasis, what Chambers' dictionary calls 'a place of rest or pleasure in the midst of toil or gloom'. History has made it so. It is an oasis in a land which itself is isolate. It has been stated that it is in an area which has been favoured by settlers since prehistoric times. However it is not on an actual trade route of the western seaways nor on the Celtic pilgrims' way. It has no parish church yet is only two miles from St. Keverne which as Lankeveran was the religious centre of Meneage and remained a privileged sanctuary where law breakers escaping the vengeance of men could throw themselves on the mercy of God's people '........for with the Lord there is mercy and with Him is plenteous redemption.' (Psalm 130 v.vii). No tin has been exploited in Coverack, nor in St. Keverne parish. The lodes that are there are called 'deaf' by miners and are unworkable. It is a pity in one sense for it used to be said that an acre of mining is worth a parish of farming. A brief account of the existence of copper in the Coverack area will be given later in a section on Smuggling. Tradition maintains that St. Keverne himself laid a curse on the district with the words, 'No metal shall run within the sound of St. Keverne bells.' This was a retaliation for the disrespect of the parishioners. It seems a very unsaintly thing to do, but it is a timely reminder to travellers in Cornwall that they should take note of facts and take a pinch of salt with legendary fiction. Some of the fast growing number of newly settled authors of books on Cornwall have themselves listened to tales told by locals and duly repeated them in their books, blissfully unaware that they are victims of the Cornish wry sense of humour. The Cornish love a good leg-pull, especially if they can keep it going for weeks and weeks. It helps to give them a somewhat perverted sense of superiority, especially when they can dupe a sophisticated 'sawsnek' or English person.

The name Coverack comes from Porthcovrek which was recorded as early as 1262. On the 27th. October of that year, itinerant justices in Lancaveton (Launceston) agreed to allow Richard de Reskymer from Mawgan in Meneage to have some ploughland in Roseneython which was occupied by Osbert Lesor and Dionisia. In return, Richard de Reskymer gave and granted to the couple a part of a tenement which Richard held in Porthcovrek - '........rendering yearly one pair of white gloves or one penny at Easter for all service, suit of Court custom and exaction.' This agreement for the conveyance of land added the proviso that should Dionisia die 'without heir of her body', the tenement would revert to Richard and his heirs. The reason for the exchange of occupation is not known. These friendly agreements were consented to by judges and enrolled in the records of the court. This 'juggling' of local land was carried out some sixty years after King John granted a charter to the Stannaries giving tinners rights of prospecting and about a century before the creation of the Duchy of Cornwall at the beginning of the Hundred Years' War in 1337 when Edward III made the young Prince Edward Duke of Cornwall. The Duchy was the land covered by the estates owned by him in the county of Cornwall.

The Black Prince, as the Duke became known in later years proved to be an absentee landlord but that did not prevent him from raising Cornish money and getting Cornish ships and men to promote the war against France. It should be explained that the new Duke was only six and a half years old when he acquired the Duchy estates. He did not visit them for the first seventeen years of his Dukedom. His officials raised money through local administrators. These local worthies were punished with gaol sentences if they failed to extract the dues from their fellow countrymen When the Duke came to Helston not long after the Black Death, he listened to the pleas of the desperate tenants and made concessions.

I suspect Porthcovrek did not play a great part in the above mentioned events. The village does not appear on early maps. When in 1085 King William sent men to record how much land each holder held, what livestock he owned and its worth, it was noted that the Canons of St. Achebron held eleven acres at St. Keverne, the land being large enough for seven ploughs, with twenty acres of pasture, eight cattle and thirty sheep. The value of the property had decreased from forty shillings when the land was received, to five shillings. These details would not have impressed the officials in Winchester writing in the Domesday book. Perhaps it had the effect of persuading the powers that it would be as well to ignore that part of the Hundred of Winniation or Kerrier as it became known. On the other hand it is interesting to note that Trenance was credited with 100 acres of pastureland while places on the edge of the moorland such as Trelan and Trelowarren were measured in leagues.

The name Covrak, minus the second 'c' is mentioned in the Parish Register in 1588, eight years after Church records began, the year of the Armada. The prefix 'Porth' had been dropped. Toponomy is a fascinating study. Henry Jenner, Assistant Keeper of Manuscripts in the British Museum stated in his 'Handbook of the Cornish Language' that it was easier to criticise other people's derivations of place names than to find better ones. I agree with him. What does Coverack mean? Cove seems obvious. The Cornish for witch is 'gwragh'. The name could mean witches' cove with a little anglicising of the spelling and a quick mutation of the g to c. What a super title for a novel! It could also mean seaweed cove. Wrack is another word for seaweed. The name is most appropriate after certain winds. In fact, local farmers and gardeners have always used the seaweed from Coverack's beaches. There was usually plenty to be had from what is known as Barker's Beach, so called because it lies in front of Prospect Cottage at Sunny Corner which was occupied by the Barker family. There is still a trace of the steep winding cliff path which was used by locals who loaded the weed into panniers strapped to the backs of their donkeys.

In 1337 the Porths or coastal villages of Kerrier from Maenporth to Porth Leven were let by the Duchy of Cornwall for the princely, or should I say, ducal, sum of thirty two shillings. This was reduced to twenty five shillings after the Black Death in 1348 - 1349. At that time, Coverack people were known to be getting income by selling fertiliser to the farmers of the Lizard peninsula. The manure consisted of decayed pilchards, condemned curing salt and sand. It was claimed that because of this the local corn crops yielded 20% above the average for Cornwall. Whether this statement was due to the Cornish love of hyperbole or an actual fact will probably remain a subject for conjecture. What is certain is that some tenant farmers were bound by their leases to fertilise their land. This gave the entrepreneurs of Coverack a ready made local market.

Sir John Killigrew, when pleading to be allowed to erect a lighthouse at the Lizard in 1619, pointed out that ships sailing along the coast were in danger of 'shipwracke' through lack of beacons. Could Coverack mean wreck cove? A legend could soon be fabricated, but there would be no need as Coverack has indeed been a wreckers' cove, or to be more precise, a cove of wrecks. Of course, Coverack got its name before the English language was imposed on the Cornish, so Sir John's spelling is just another of my fanciful red herrings.

Another remote possibility is that Coverack could have come from the name Kaveran, which was how medieval ecclesiastics spelt what we now call St. Keverne. One school of thought is that the word actually comes from an old Cornish word 'cobran', meaning 'one who helps'. This would certainly fit in with the idea of the monastery at St. Keverne being a sanctuary. The pronunciation of the word was said to be 'covrant' - remarkably like the word Coverack. Imagine my relief when I later discovered that from 'covrant' is derived the name of the famous Armorican saint from Brittany, Carentin, who in fact gave his name to Crantock near Newquay. It would be unthinkable for Coverack to be named after St. Keverne. The two villages have always been deadly rivals. I should say keen rivals. It's like saying Redruth is named after Camborne, or Penryn after Falmouth. Even if it were true, historians from Coverack and historians from St. Keverne would rewrite their paragraph on place names for fear that their books would not sell in their own native villages.

A recent book about the Lizard peninsula states that Coverack means hideaway. Like wreckers' cove, it is certainly a name which would fit and the word 'covva' in Cornish means hiding place. Jill Newton may be right, but I prefer the idea that the word Coverack is derived from the word 'goveryk' which means streamlet. The g in this word was mutated to c when the prefix 'Porth' was dropped. I believe the village was named after the farm from whence came the water to drive the corn mill in the village. In 1859 this mill was described in Murray's 'Handbook for Devon and Cornwall' as, '........a little mill, the smallest you ever saw, kept jogging by a tiny rill.' The farm is now called Polcoverack. Porth and Pol are frequently substituted one for the other in Cornwall. Pol can mean pond or pool. It can also mean anchorage. Porth is a harbour, cove or landing place. What convinces me about the word 'goveryk' being the origin of the word Coverack is that there is another Coverack not far away but well inland and nothing to do with a cove. It is Coverack Bridges, near Wendron. It is a village through which a stream called the River Cober (meaning copper) flows to Helston and the Loe Pool.

The stream from which I think Coverack got its name went on flowing through the centuries. There is little evidence of the inhabitants being closely involved in events taking place outside the village subsequent to the first written reference in the thirteenth century to Porth Coverack. It is known for instance, that some Cornish contingents fought at Agincourt in 1415 under a banner showing two Cornish wrestlers in a hitch. Later on in the same century a protest at the levy of crippling taxes resulted in a disastrous 'invasion' of England in 1497. The rebels were led by the St. Keverne blacksmith Michael Joseph through Bodmin, Taunton, Wells, Bristol, Salisbury, Winchester and on to London, gathering supporters on the way. The journey itself was no mean feat in those days of poor roads and unreliable transport. It is not surprising therefore that the citizen army was defeated by the more professional forces waiting for them at Blackheath. Two thousand Cornishmen were killed. They had hoped for support from some Kentish guerrillas but it did not materialise. Michael Joseph, known by the Cornish name of An gof was captured, hanged, drawn and quartered. His head was placed on a stake at London Bridge beside that of his ally and fellow rebel, the lawyer from Bodmin called Thomas Flamank. Whether or not An gof had any friends from Coverack with him is not known, but the Cornish insurgents who escaped from the battle then joined with the Pretender, Perkin Warbeck, who had landed at Whitesand Bay to the north of Sennen Cove and marched to Bodmin where he made a proclamation that he was King Richard IV, the rightful sovereign. The impostor surrendered at the approach of the army pursuing the Cornish rebels. He eventually admitted that he was the son of a Flanders boatman from Tournai on the River Scheldt in what is now Belgium. He was subsequently hanged at Tyburn for his involvement in another conspiracy.

Cornwall, defeated and disillusioned, continued to groan under the heavy burden of taxation. The unfortunate St. Keverne blacksmith was not publicly honoured with a patriot's memorial stone in the village until 1966 when Mebyon Kernow, the 'Sons of Cornwall', had a tablet placed on the boundary wall of the parish church in St. Keverne Square. The inscription is in Cornish for the purists and English for the rest.

The Reformation in the sixteenth century signalled the beginning of the end of the Cornish language.

When protests were made in 1549 by Humphrey Arundell, grandson of one of the leaders of the St. Keverne led insurrection, the sarcastic reply of the officials was that there was no point in objecting to English as the Cornish had never complained about Latin which they couldn't understand either. This time the Cornish rebels got as far as Exeter but eventually had to retreat. Then followed the familiar pattern of hangings, looting and pillaging. The new form of church services was enforced. It seems very possible that some Coverack men were involved in the rebellion. William and John Kilter from Constantine gave their name to Kilter Farm which lies to the right of the main road leading out of Coverack. These men were hacked into quarters at Launceston gaol for their part in leading a mob which killed one William Body in Helston while he was legitimately engaged in removing signs of Roman Catholic worship from the church. The principal leader of the avenging mob was Martin Geoffrey, a priest from St. Keverne. He was subsequently executed in London. Roman Catholicism was associated with the old order and its suppression was seen as another attempt by the English to destroy Cornish culture. H. Spencer Toy, in his 'History of Helston', was of the opinion that the beginning of the fourth verse of the traditional Hal-an-tow song was a reference to the Cornish allegiance to the Virgin Mary and to the rebellion against the imposition of the new Prayer Book. The verse begins:

'God bless Aunt Mary Moses

And all her power and might, O,'

- the reference to Moses, however is still not understood.

By 1560 the Bishop of Exeter relented to the extent that Cornish could be used in teaching catechism in places where English was not understood. I expect he knew this concession would not be needed for very long. A language without a significant literature is bound to decline, especially in a country where those in control speak a different tongue. The historian Carew reported that by the end of the Tudor period few Cornishmen, 'except those beyond Truro,' were unable to understand English. This was in spite of the fact that it was the custom of all Cornishmen to reply, 'Meea navidna cowza a sawsnek,' - 'I speak no Saxonage,' when they were addressed in English by a stranger. Balzac, when doing research for his book 'Les Chouans', on Breton resistance against the French, met with similar language problems in the 19th. century. He complained of the seeming lack of French speaking Bretons. The Celts are a clannish people.

It has already been stated that the village got its first mention in St. Keverne Parish records in the year 1588. This was the year when the largest ever invasion fleet of 130 Spanish ships set out to prosecute the Holy War against Elizabeth of England. Patrol ships were placed in position from the Isles of Scilly to Ushant but what the English were pleased to call a 'Protestant wind' probably did more damage than the waiting patrols could have done. A storm blew up in the Bay of Biscay and put paid to more than thirty Spanish invasion vessels. Over 8,000 soldiers and sailors lost their lives. This was a much greater set back than Drake's attack on Cadiz. Recovery by the Spanish was all the more difficult because they were commanded by the unwilling and unexperienced Duke of Medina Sidonia. The south coast of Cornwall has always been vulnerable to attack by sea borne raiders. It is probable that the original settlement now called Coverack was located in the British village close to what is known as the 'Beacon' field, mentioned earlier. This position was almost certainly chosen expressly to avoid attacks from passing marauders. In 1588, the Beacon itself was ready to be ignited at the first sign of an invasion fleet so that the message from the Lizard could be passed on via the chain of beacons to Plymouth.

St. Keverne parish, like all the other parishes in Cornwall, was able to muster armed men to repel an enemy landing. The parish was divided into 4 'Turns' of unequal size. Turn Bean, which as its name suggests was the smallest, covered St. Keverne Church Town and the coast between Coverack and Porthoustock. Turn Trelan took in the coast line and its hinterland from Coverack village to Kennack. Turn Tregarne guarded the north eastern flank of the parish from Porthoustock to Lestowder and Nare Point, while the north western sector which was called Turn Traboe stretched from Treleague, north of Church Town across country to Dry Tree which is now the site of the Goonhilly Satellite Station. It is interesting to note that the word 'Turn' is not used in this context in other Cornish documents. The word could have originated from the Latin 'quaterni', meaning four men between the ages of 16 and 60 who could bear arms. They were given training every few years and more regularly when there was a threat of an invasion such as the Armada. The following names were among those to be found in the lists of the two Turns which covered Coverack village:

| | | |
|---|---|---|
| John James | - | billman with sling and bag. |
| William Rychard | - | billman |
| John Androw | - | archer and billman |
| Walter Chynalls | - | billman |
| John Tregonyn | - | 6 arrows |
| William Kyverne | - | bow and six arrows |
| William Roskylly | - | archer, bow and six arrows |

These family names, with modernised spelling, are common in the area today. The 'slingers', incidentally, were reputed to be able to hurl stones or lead bullets at an enemy who was 200 yards away. The 'bills' were metal hooks like those used for cutting corn. The hook was mounted on a six foot shaft which had a spike on the end. Men defending their own village with such weapons were not to be treated lightly, though no doubt there were plenty of 'Dads' Army' type jokes going round the parish at the time of the Armada.

A story was told in the area that the year before the Armada a band of Spanish raiders went up the Penryn River to sack the town. The majority of the inhabitants happened to be in the ampitheatre watching a Miracle Play. The raiding party was able to penetrate the town without being spotted. Suddenly the Spaniards heard a deafening roar of hundreds of voices. Thinking that they had fallen into an ambush, the Spaniards took to their heels and rushed back to their boats. In fact, the play in progress was the story of Samson. He had just demolished the temple of Dagon in Gaza, killing himself and 3,000 of his enemies, causing the Penryn audience to bellow their horrified approval and frighten off the invaders at the same time.

This account serves to warn readers to treat stories of the Armada with caution. If one examines the features of some of the native families of Coverack, it is easy to assume that these people are descended from Spanish sailors who were shipwrecked or left behind by a raiding party at the time of the Armada. It may be so but there is no evidence to confirm the assumption. Dolor Point on which the Paris Hotel stands could well be Dollar Point and hint at an Armada Treasure ship lying beneath the waves in the bay. I am more inclined to believe that it got its name from the Cornish word 'tollor', meaning customs collector. The old Watch House still stands on the point. It housed the Customs men who preceded the Coastguards. On the other hand, of course, Dolor Point could mean a place of grief. A number of sailors have lost their lives off Dolor Point and its name could be in remembrance of some well loved locals who perished there. The Dollar Cove at Gunwalloe is so named because a Spanish ship laden with silver dollars lies there beneath the shifting sands. It was discovered by the celebrated Cornish diver and maritime historian, Roland Morris. It is indeed a Spanish treasure ship but it was wrecked 199 years after the Armada. The 'Armada Chest' in St. Keverne Church dates from the period but again no one knows for certain that it came from one of the invading ships. In 1946, Professor C.E.M. Joad spent a holiday in Pretoria Cottage, The Gardens, Coverack. He stayed with Mr. and Mrs. Percy Eustis. He wrote shortly afterwards, 'Here in Coverack one fell asleep without fear, dreamt without alarm and woke without difficulty'. I like to think that apart from the squire's man on watch at the Beacon, Coverack people did just that in 1588. What could the non swearing, non blaspheming, pillaging Spanish sailors possibly gain by disturbing the calm of that quiet oasis? In any case, apart from the fact that outside help could be obtained by lighting the Beacon, always provided it wasn't a wet night, the men on the Muster Roll were on the alert in the Turns.

The defeat of the Armada at sea did not mean that the 'Dads' Army' of the day could relax their vigilance. The Spanish threat remained. In 1595 they were back again. Two hundred men set off from Lorient in Brittany and landed in Mounts Bay, setting fire to Newlyn and Paul. Godolphin arrived with reinforcements and eventually succeeded in driving off the invaders. Drake died the following year and Philip of Spain died two years later. By 1603 Elizabeth was also dead and Tudor England receded into history. Cornwall, which Richard Halliday in his 'History of Cornwall' described as having been 'crushed and impoverished under the Tudor heel,' was still not going to control the destiny of one and all within its boundaries.

The next century saw a divided Cornwall under the Stuarts. Coverack must have been affected by the Civil War in some ways, due to its proximity to Falmouth, but it was still an open beach and could offer few facilities to either side. John Arundell of Trerice commanded the troops of the besieged Pendennis Castle. On his side, fighting for the Royalist cause, were the Vyvyans of nearby Trelowarren, the Bassets, Grenvilles, Trelawneys, Godolphins and Killigrews. Parliament fielded the Robartes of Lanhydrock, who owned land in St. Keverne parish, John St. Aubyn of Clowance near Camborne, Boscawen of Tregothnan and John Trefusis. The Royalists defeated Essex at Lostwithiel in 1644, but Pendennis surrendered honourably in 1646. In 1651 John Grenville and the Royalist garrison were driven out of St. Mary's in the Isles of Scilly. It is said that the Cornish participants of both sides had to be bribed to serve outside Cornwall. Those living on the coast were rightly more worried about poor seaward defences. St. Michael's Mount, Pendennis Castle, St. Mawes and Fowey were all desperate for modern guns and the ammunition to go with them. North African pirates were seen in the Channel and fishermen had to contend with them as well as the press gangs from the Royal Navy. The people who lived inland were afraid that men taken to serve in the Army would mean problems concerning the harvest of the land and the extraction of minerals. The first steam pump was used in Cornwall in 1710. Until steam became established as a reliable source of energy much man power was needed to keep the mines dry. Water was kept out of the mines by men using pumps powered by water wheels and by horses and mules.

There was a certain redistribution of wealth after the Civil War. Land in Cornwall was valued more for its mineral content than its food producing qualities. Miners no longer had to pay coinage nor accept government price fixing, thanks to the rule of the Commonwealth. Tin was much in demand. This resulted in a rapid increase in price as well as the number of mines being exploited. Many 'adventurers' or investors made quick fortunes. Engineers such as Dartmouth born Thomas Newcomen came to the fore, devising more efficient ways of extracting tin. The miners and their families did not derive a proportionate benefit from the boom. There was no organisation of labour. They were in effect self employed, so in spite of protests about wages and supporting food riots, they accepted their lot and tried to top up their meagre incomes by doing some wrecking and smuggling and co-operating with fishermen in exporting tin illegally in fishing boats. It is not surprising that eighteenth century Cornwall proved a ferocious but fertile field for reforming preachers like the Wesley brothers. John Wesley is sometimes called 'the founding father' of modern Cornwall. His influence probably prevented further armed insurrection in that his 'societies' showed how to get things done by forming management committees. These laid down the foundations for future County Councils and Trade Union organisations in addition to interpreting Wesley's exhortations to follow the example of his Lord and Saviour. It meant that a nucleus of working people, accustomed to making decisions democratically were able to assume local government control when the traditional land owning classes lost their local power.

Not long after the upheaval of the Civil War it was difficult to find a Cornish person who could not speak English. By the early eighteenth century Cornish was still spoken in Penwith and in all the 'Porths' between Lands End and St. Keverne. Elsewhere it would have been difficult to find people who spoke the language as their native tongue, especially among the gentry. The latter were beginning to take a more academic interest in the language their servants still spoke to a greater or lesser degree. As there was no literature they could easily refer to, it was a difficult task and all but the genuine academics soon gave up the struggle. If only the gentry had taken the trouble to learn from their own employees, even at this late stage in the decline, perhaps the Cornish language would have continued as a spoken language to this day, giving Cornish irredentists an irrefutable claim to separatism. It is believed that the last sermon to be preached in Cornish was delivered in Landewednack Church on the Lizard peninsula in 1678. The last person whose mother tongue was Cornish died in 1777. Dorothy Jeffery alias Dolly Pentreath was an impoverished old lady, living on the rates and tips given by people who came to hear her speak. She is still remembered because Prince Louis Napoleon Bonaparte became interested in the Cornish language and while on a visit to the county in 1860, he erected a memorial to her in the parish of Paul. The church is now a place of pilgrimage for those who want to revive the language of a bygone age.

By the end of the 18th. century, when the Quay was approaching its first centenary, it was decided Coverack needed protection. Small cannons for coastal defence were placed on Lan Big, which soon became known as the 'Battery'. In 1803 there was a distinct possibility of an invasion of Britain by the French, so Charles François du Perier Dumouriez, former French general and Minister of Foreign Affairs was commissioned, as a former enemy, to survey the defences of the South West and make a report to the British government. Dumouriez was a colourful character and an able general who had been trusted both by King Louis XVI of France and the Girondins after the Revolution. He had been responsible for the conquest of the area which later became known as Belgium. However, Dumouriez became disenchanted when France broke her promise of non aggression and he deserted to the Austrians, eventually making his way to England via Germany and Switzerland. Who better than a former general and secret agent of the King of France to advise the British on preparing defences against a French invasion?

Dumouriez submitted a favourable report on Cornwall entitled, 'Mémoire militaire sur l'Angleterre.' He wrote that it was not probable the enemy would attempt a landing in a country so remote from the capital - one so hilly and easy to defend as well as being a long way from the support of the continent. At this point, Dumouriez flattered his new masters, saying that one should take into account the '........enormous naval superiority' of the English. He added a note of caution. He stated that if France were to be in possession of Ireland, from where the 'enemy' (his own countrymen) would be able to get help and provisions in order to conquer the Cornish peninsula foot by foot and to become established there, the French could turn the difficult terrain to their own advantage. He added a warning that this depended on the French being able to occupy Ireland, arm it against England and thus be supported in the fight against England by the spirit of rebellion and the natural hatred of the Irish for the English. He added a further note of caution to his fanciful hypothesis, namely that if all these events were to come about, a long and costly war would ensue.

The general's survey began at Plymouth. He made it clear that Bodmin was the pivot of the defences of the two halves of Cornwall. He gave a list of coastal batteries which had been placed every few miles along the coast. He made special mention of the approaches to Falmouth from the East and the West:

(The spellings are as in the report. They can be recognised with the help of a modern Ordnance Survey Map.)

'Carrey-Road has to have a naval defence of two or three blockships supported by several small gunboats to defend Maws-Creek and Falmouth Bay. A fort at S. Mawes and the castle at Pendennis which has been restored to good condition, two batteries at Swanpool, one at Pennance Point, one at Mainporth, one at Trerose Point, one at Mawnan, the fort of St. Anthony or Little Dennis is in good condition, a battery at Nare Point, one at Porthalla, one at Porthousestock, one at Coverack-Cove, one at Chynals-point, one at Pedn-boar point, one at Careyloz, one at Poltesca, one at Cadgewith, one at Landewednake, a little encampment at Ruanmajor.'

'All the coast that we have detailed from Plymouth to Falmouth offer two or three difficult but predictable landings places. From Falmouth to Lands End there is none other than Mounts Bay, but it would be the greatest calamity that could befall an enemy, to venture into this country where he would not be able to haul his guns nor his provisions and where the hardy and fierce inhabitants would themselves suffice to halt the enemy and starve him out in a short time.'

Whether or not Dumouriez visited Coverack to inspect the Battery is not recorded but it would appear he was not keen to cross the 'hardy and fierce inhabitants' living west of Falmouth. By the year 1845, Lan Big, or the Battery was described as a meadow, measuring one acre, two rods and twelve perches. It was occupied by Elisha Martin and owned by C.W. Ellis. The guns at the top of the 'meadow' did not appear to have excused Elisha from paying his tithe of two shillings and sixpence for growing the annual crop of hay.

# THE QUAY

Coverack can not claim to have one of the oldest quays in Cornwall, nor can it be said that the quay was conceived by a well known engineer. St. Ives has had a quay since 1481 when the burghers acquired the port from the Duchy of Cornwall. Some three centuries later in 1770 John Smeaton of Eddystone lighthouse fame designed another new pier for St. Ives. Later on he was asked to create what is now called Charlestown harbour. Boscastle, Padstow, Mousehole, Penzance, Falmouth, Penryn and Mevagissey all had quays before Coverack. Most of these ports also had their quays rebuilt in the nineteenth century. This fact allows Coverack to boast that it is one of the few ports using its original eighteenth century quay.

During the seventeenth century the Ellis family, formerly known as Eales, from St. Just in Penwith, had been quietly acquiring property and status. As early as 1629 some land in Sithney and at Trewothen in St. Keverne parish was added to the estate. On the 19th. October, 1719, John Ellis bought land in Coverack itself. It was the parcel known as Chynalls. It was a job lot which had been mortgaged by Thomas Banfield of St. Keverne to trustees who subsequently sold the premises to John Ellis. The transaction included all the land and property still in possession of Banfield and his tenants. The description 'Chynalls' included the part known as 'New Key'. This was probably the land which had been designated for use as a quay. Four years later in 1723 Ellis gave permission for Coverack fishermen to set up moorings to the cliff, or any rock or post, in order to keep the boats safe. This suggests the the quay had not yet been constructed, though as the date carved in stone on the Quay itself is 1724, it may be that it was already under construction when Ellis first gave permission a year earlier.

Large blocks of granite from Penryn, Constantine and Lowertown were brought to the village and local serpentine was used in the construction. To recoup this outlay, John Ellis got local fishermen to enter an agreement which appears to have caused some dissent as only sixteen men signed the document, leaving half of the prepared seals unendorsed. The names on the document were:

| | |
|---|---|
| John Banfeild | John Murrish |
| Henry Banfeild | William Murrish |
| John Cliff | John Rickard |
| David Darnall | James Robearts |
| Nicholas Harris | Nicholas Robearts |
| Nicholas James | William Robearts |
| Thomas James | Francis Sandys |
| John Martin | Richard Williams |

Most of these family names are still common in the locality. My maternal grandmother was a Rickard so perhaps one of my forebears was involved in the agreement.

Ellis exacted a toll of ten shillings for each seine net, seine boat and crew using the quay. Other boats were charged one shilling and sixpence per boat and one shilling and sixpence per man. He was also entitled to receive one sixth of the pilotage dues and one sixth of the profits from wrecks. The latter due was probably profit from salvage. John Sandys signed the agreement but excluded his liability to pay his share of pilotage and wreck dues to the owner of the quay. The fishermen were clearly dissatisfied with the agreement, perhaps because Ellis did not get on with the building of the quay on the western side at 'New Key' known as Coverack and that he would complete the work as soon as possible. This could mean that another arm of the quay was to be built, starting near the Old Post Office, on what is known today as 'Hocking's slip' which is used in summer as a base by boardsailors. Tales have been handed down about the existence of this second arm of the quay but they are only tales. What is certain is that Ellis persuaded the fishermen to agree to increased charges in return for a quick completion of the badly needed shelter for the boats. Seine charges were doubled and other boats had to pay two shillings and sixpence instead of one shilling and sixpence. Five of the original signatories are not on the second document, but there are new names on it. These could be the ones who refused to sign the first document and who now found themselves having to agree to even higher charges in order to be able to pursue their livelihood. The new names were:

| | |
|---|---|
| James Halligey | Christopher May |
| Philip Hicks | John Murrish (Junior) |
| Robert Incledon | Henry Rickard |
| Henry Incledon | Isaac Sedgmore |

Thomas John                   John Thomas

Most of these names are still common in the district.

I sometimes wonder if the great storm of 1703 was the event which resulted in the fishermen of Coverack deciding, after years of living in fear of a repetition of the hurricane, that a quay would be the answer to their fears. It was recorded that in the November storm three hundred ships foundered and eight thousand people lost their lives in a twenty four hour period. A sailing vessel laden with tin and lying near the entrance to Helford River was blown out to sea. The captain and mate had gone up river to Gweek, leaving one seaman and two boys on board. The ship drove before the storm, eventually coming ashore in a creek in the Isle of Wight some 160 miles away. The report seems rather far fetched as the grounding was supposed to have taken place seven hours after the ship went out of the Helford. This means that the vessel travelled at an average speed of 23 knots! I expect tales of the tree-felling hurricane of October, 1987 will be just as wild when they are told in the next century about the jet stream which came from the United States and created a vortex which devastated the south of England. However, that same night in 1703, Henry Winstanley, designer of the first Eddystone lighthouse was swept away while sheltering from the storm in his own timber creation which he had begun building five years before. It must have been a wild night. The following year, Mr. Sandys of Lanarth was returning from Falmouth in his seine boat. He had been to the port to sell some hogsheads of pilchards to a Dutch dealer. He was in company with another Coverack boat which was owned by Thomas Banfeild - no doubt a relation of John and Henry Banfeild who were signatories of the first agreement to pay quay dues to John Ellis. There were some Coverack women on board Mr. Sandys' boat. They had sold their farm and garden produce in the market on the Moor in Falmouth and had gratefully accepted the offer of a lift back by sea. When the two boats, which were attached to each other for safety, had cleared the Manacles, Banfeild indicated that he was having difficulty in manoeuvring because of the line fastened to his craft. The two boats were just off the Great Wrea Rock and close to Lowland Point. Mr Sandys accordingly decided to part company with Banfeild and his men. He told his crew to lower the sails, as he could not beat to windward easily in the seiner. He then ordered his men to ship their oars. The Coverack men in Sandys' boat must have been feeling rather 'fragile' after their stay in Falmouth for they found they were unable to make way and had to hoist the sails again. Then, as so often happens in the area, the wind veered to the north and increased in strength, causing the sails to rip. They lowered them once more and all they could do was to try to keep the seiner into the wind and ride out the storm. Sandys reported later that even the 23' steering oar had no effect when they were on the crests of the waves and they were driven helplessly before the storm. They spent three long nights and four days of misery in the boat before they could reach land. During the whole of this time they were baling continuously and 'calling on God for mercy and pardon'........ Fortunately one of the Coverack women in the boat was an innkeeper's wife. Before leaving Falmouth she had bought twelve pennyworth of white bread and three gallons of brandy to sell to her special customers. She shared this sustenance with the occupants of the boat. Just after dawn on the fourth morning an island was sighted and the party made for it under oars. Fortunately the men still had some strength, thanks to the food and drink supplied by the publican's wife. They landed in the afternoon and met some men who were hunting hares. The hunting party decided that the best thing to do with these 'enemies' who had landed in France was to convey them to the authorities on the mainland. The islanders wanted to rob and beat the survivors but common sense prevailed and the little band of Cornish castaways was put ashore at Roscoff.

Mr. Sandys once more explained that they were a band of innocent travellers who had been blown off course when returning to Coverack from Falmouth. At this point one of the bystanders asked the landowner if his name was Sandys. By an amazing coincidence it transpired that the Frenchman had been shipwrecked on the Cornish coast and given shelter at Lanarth while waiting for repatriation. The French gentleman immediately assumed responsibility for the party and lodged Mr. Sandys at his own home. He arranged for the little band of Cornish people to be declared non combatants. In due course, King Louis XIV was persuaded to give permission for the band to be sent back to Portsmouth with some prisoners of war who were being exchanged. They returned to Coverack some eight weeks after the misadventure began. It was rare that victims of storms had such luck in those days. British prisoners usually spent years in captivity before being repatriated from France. This little band from Coverack was unique. They had been brought to Roscoff in a special way and had been 'preserved from the violence of the seas by the great Maker and Protector of all things', according to Lake's Parochial History. Mr. Sandys' own laconic account concluded, 'I obtained an exchange and returned to my house, much to the joy of my friends who had concluded we were lost.' The usual clandestine way of getting back to Britain was to bribe a French gaoler to look the other way while an escape was effected and then to come back in a fishing boat. Smuggling continued during the French wars. Nothing was allowed to interfere with the 'trade' and smugglers were not averse to bringing back escaped prisoners nor indeed to carrying despatches for agents from either side - provided the price was right.

One can imagine that when Ellis delayed the construction of the new quay, the Coverack fishermen put forward all kinds of reasons to induce him to make haste and they could well have cited the great storms, which some had experienced, as a cogent reason for haste. The fact that the quay was finished and remained in the hands of the Ellis family for two hundred years reveals that the men must have been reasonably satisfied with the deal they were offered.

Ellis did have a rival in Coverack. Perhaps the threat of competition also spurred him on to develop the harbour. On the 11th. of April, 1711, 'in the ninth year of our Sovereign Lady Ann,' John Sandys, Gent, of Lanarth, the intrepid survivor of the Roscoff episode, granted a 99 year lease to his son, Samson Sandys, '........of all that garden or plot of land next adjoining unto Chinalls, ye lands of John Hamm, Gent,' - he occupied Chimbloith. The land was to include '........a cellar, and all houses, courts, courtilages and buildings now built or to be built on ye said garden or plot of land.' John Sandys pointed out that in consideration of the '........natural love and affection which he hath and beareth unto ye said Samson Sandys,' his son could have the lease for £200 which was to be paid to his younger brother, Richard, '........when he shall attain ye age of one and twenty years.'

8

The Ellis quay was finally sold to the newly formed Coverack Harbour Company on the 21st. August, 1920. The principal shareholders were Col. Bulkeley, a local benefactor, the Rev. Gilbert Alfred King and H.G. Thim who lived at Rocklands in Coverack, the former home of 'Inky' Stephens the manufacturer. Gilbert Robertson, a solicitor from Cardiff managed the legal side of the business. The new company afforded the local fishermen and other interested villagers a chance of buying shares in their own destiny. They did not grasp the opportunity with the characteristic charisma of Celtic patriots jealously guarding their autonomy, when the moment came after two centuries of outside control.

When Bowen and Thomas Kitchin's Large English Atlas was published in 1755, 'New Key' was clearly marked in situ. Coverack village was inland, probably because of cartological expediency. Up to the eighteenth century, 'key' was the accepted English spelling. After this time, it gradually changed to 'quay,' taken from the French word 'quai'. The map was claimed to be a new and improved map of Cornwall according to the 'Beft Surveys and Intelligences........ showing the feveral roads and true Meafured Diftances between Town and Town.' There was no road leading to Coverack marked on the map which is to be found in the Bodleian Library, Oxford. Black Head had its Cornish name of 'Peden due' printed beside the English translation. What the modern O.S. Map calls 'Chynhalls' was named 'Dameer Point'. This word could have come from 'dama', Cornish for mother. The local name for Chynhalls is Mears. A story which has been handed down in the village relates that a French vessel foundered off the headland. The crew, together with the captain, his wife and four children, were lost. When a gale is blowing and the moon is full, fishermen claim they can hear the French lady crying for her children. The name Mears supports this legend, whether it is in Cornish - 'Dameer' as on the eighteenth century map, or 'Mère', the French word for mother, which we call Mears. It could be another compelling reminder of the need for a quay to be built at Coverack. Ellis may have been told about it when he was exacting tolls for his unfinished structure. The man himself was described as a 'pewterer' but his father had been elevated to the description 'Gent', by the time he passed on his wealth to his son John who lived in Penzance, not far from his father's place in St. Just.

The quay is now more than two and a half centuries old. It is Coverack's finest monument, there is no other edifice of distinction in the village, but some of the cottages are older. In spite of the difficulties the Coverack men had when trying to get their new landowner to complete the structure, no storm has ever demolished it. The small reef immediately behind the seaward edge of the arc of the pier is its first line of defence. When the breakers are past that they drop into a shallow hollow, losing some of their momentum before they leap up and over the back of the quay. Towards high tide, however, the reef is of little consequence and great rollers come thundering right over the top in a storm, filling the basin to overflowing sometimes, lifting any boats remaining in the harbour higher than the quay platform itself. Then comes the draining of the tiny harbour, sucking everything out towards the Mill Beach, the boats being pulled up with a jerk as their moorings yank at the bollards on the quay. At such times I speculate on the possibility of there having been a second arm of the harbour which was sucked and battered away during some great storm, leaving a stump as evidence until it was adapted as a private slipway. Herbert Dicksee's etching 'Down to the sea' shows a fisher girl going down the steps of 'Hocking's Slip', carrying a bundle of rope. She is preceded by a frisky dog. The artist did his etching from the quay beach and the curve of the slip suggests that it might have continued towards the open sea at one time. Dicksee may have had some knowledge of this and incorporated it in his impression of the harbour, on the other hand, he was a painter of animals and historical genre and could have done the drawing as a way of relaxing on holiday, without having studied his subject to any depth. As I said earlier, the Cornish have a wry sense of humour and the tale which has been handed down could be a gigantic leg pull which is causing a few chuckles in that great fishing village in the sky!

The absence of a second protecting arm means that moorings have to be made fast to some kind of anchor at the western end of the basin. These 'anchors' range from old muzzle loading cannon barrels once used to defend the village, to great boulders and lumps of concrete, all partially buried in the sand and wedged between rocks. The basin dries out just before low water, so I do not know where a suitable entrance could have been placed, unless two overlapping arms were envisaged. The existing arc of the quay is too small for this. A narrow entrance would force large craft to warp themselves in and out. Speculation is pleasant but pointless. It has gone on for years in the village! In 1922 the ketch Heather Bell was unloading coal in Coverack Harbour when an easterly wind sprang up........ Mr Alex. Thomas, one of the young men employed to unload the vessel told me that Skipper Hutchens was advised by some fishermen to telephone Falmouth to get a tug to tow the Heather Bell out of the bay. He decided against this because of the expense to the company. When the wind became a gale the ketch was unable to leave. Everything was battened down and extra hawsers paid out. The sea won the unequal struggle. Two bollards were pulled out of the quay itself because of the violent under-tow in the basin and the Heather Bell was smashed on the rocks between the Old Post Office and the Mill Beach. This ended the seaborne trade of Coverack. Most coal was seaborne up to that date. Cattle fodder, fertiliser and building materials were also brought by vessels of about 80 or 90 tons. There is a story of one 130 ton vessel coming in the harbour and discharging her cargo at spring tide but the name has been lost.

The quay is Coverack. It is the eyes and ears of the village. It is the place to which everyone is drawn. It is the centre of the oasis. Shortly after the sun rises it begins to warm the back of the quay. If you want to catch the last rays of the setting sun the quay is the place to go. Some visitors and indeed, some natives, spend the whole day there, moving round with the sun, observing this microcosm of village life and work while sitting, or lying, or fishing, or playing, or reading, or simply dawdling. Of course the sun does not shine all the time although my faulty memory tries to convince me it did when I was a child. It is well known that Cornwall takes a shower every day and twice on Sundays. Charles Wesley wrote in his journal on the 1st. August 1743, some twenty years after the quay started, 'I saw a strange sight, the sun shining in Cornwall.' He too was given to exaggeration. If you do not believe me, check on his estimates of the number who were attracted to his open air sermons.

Contrary to what some of the glossy tourist propaganda pamphlets might lead you to believe, Coverack quay is not there just for the delight and entertainment of the visitor. It is there, silent and slightly menacing when the men go down after midnight to catch the early tide. It is there, a substantial, welcoming mass, catching the early morning rays of the sun on its yellow lichen covered stones when they get back after a hard night's struggle to earn a living. I do not know if the landpeople who come down to the quay before breakfast, to soak up the atmosphere of the bustling harbour, give a thought to the fact that the men hauling up the catch and loading it on the lorry for transportation to the factory at Newlyn have been toiling all night and are tired out - in spite of their cheery banter. When food was rationed during the second world war, inshore fishermen were allowed food coupons for two breakfasts as it was recognised by the authorities that they were special 'cases'. Today, life is easier for fishermen. They use their engines to drive small capstans for hauling nets and pots and for lifting the catch to the quay. Many have two way radios and use them to keep in touch with each other and with their shore contacts. Wives listen to the channel while they are doing their housework or tending the visitors. Speedy help is always at hand from the rescue services when trouble strikes. Idle quay 'watchers' look puzzled when they hear disembodied voices coming from an empty open boat whose owner has just gone up to the village for breakfast and forgotten to turn off his 'Seavoice'.

Being tiny, the harbour can not be used for sailing, but it is an ideal training space for messing about in boats - woe betide anyone who does make a mess in a boat in Coverack. If you want to board one, make sure you have washed the sand off your feet by skimming them on the surface of the water first - even if you are wearing shoes. The quay is a magnet for all males. Small boys born in Coverack dream of the day when they will be asked to take a boat outside the harbour in order to bring back a fisherman who is anchoring off so that he can go fishing after the basin has dried out. To be qualified for this privilege, you have to be able to propel a boat beyond the quay. The spaces between the boats are too narrow for rowing, so it's a simple matter to pull the boat along by grasping the gunnels of the moored boats. When you get past them you have to start rowing. That is where the fun begins. Most boys start by going in pairs as it is much easier to handle one oar than two. The only problem is that one boy always pulls harder than the other, causing the boat to go in circles. Eventually the pair catch on and work as a team and finally manage to go out a couple of hundred yards or so and gratefully hand over to the fisherman for the return journey. After a while the young hopefuls gradually learn to use both oars. An early problem then is, what do you do if you lose an oar and see it drifting away at an alarming pace? The answer is to learn to scull with one oar over the stern. It is one of the finest ways of developing wrist muscles. If you get too enthusiastic and too vigorous in your figure of eight movements, you can easily topple over the side - which is a good reason for learning to swim before going out in a boat by yourself. Nowadays, most wise mothers fit their children with comfortable life jackets which double as outer garments and that solves the problem. In any case, outboard motors are common and young boys can be seen skilfully conning motorised punts in and out of the harbour, blissfully unaware of the need to be able to 'scully' as we called it.

COVERACK HARBOUR AND COVE HOUSES c. 1920
*Boats with engines are beginning to be in evidence.*
*The large white launch with three port holes is the Barkers' "Cornish Lass"*
*and the large black one is "Inky" Stephens' summer cruiser.*

The harbour makes a delightful swimming area. Successive generations of children have learned to swim there. It is a natural learners' pool. I am sure John Ellis did not realise this or he would have fixed a toll charge for the children! Infants begin by going there to paddle and make sand castles. As they get older they become more daring and go out further and further, holding on to a horizontal mooring rope when they feel the water going past their waists. Before long their natural buoyancy encourages them to allow their feet to leave the sand and splash to the surface. They kick and scream with a mixture of fear and delight. After lots of excursions on the ropes they decide to let go one hand and use it just like the 'real' swimmers do. Soon they are happily dog paddling, keeping close to the trusty mooring ropes, just in case they suddenly lose their confidence. After a while they find they can swim across from one rope to another and then they progress to being able to swim right across the harbour, once they realise that the trick is not to thrash about but to make long, slow movements, keeping their heads above water and breathing through the mouth. Most children love jumping in the water and making a splash, whether they can swim or not. Once they can swim the next step is to join the 'big' boys and girls. When we reached that stage in the 1930s we used to undress in front of the lifeboat house doors, heedless of the fact that if there was call-out our clothes would be scattered to the winds. At a given signal, we would run along the top of the back of the quay and jump off the end. After a while we would try diving. I wasn't very good at that, so I preferred jumping, telling myself that by 'running' in the air I could gain ground for the swim to come. At first we would swim back to the double granite steps. As we became more proficient we would go across to Hocking's slip or round the quay to the lifeboat steps. I always felt that was the coldest swim of all, especially on a flood tide when the water swept round the Dolor Point from Perprean Bay and had not absorbed any warmth from the hot stones on the beach. The big swim was from the head of the pier to the Mill Beach at high tide. You arrived tired but happy. No one minded if you returned quietly on foot or swam on your back in easy stages to the wooden ladder at the end of the pier.

Our real problem as village children was that no one actually taught us to swim. Once we had gained water confidence we could not progress to the more sophisticated strokes. Landlubbers from the cities who came down in the summer could leave us standing or rather floating as they had been taught by experts. That was always a source of envy to me. Some of my contemporaries gave up the struggle quite early and never really learned to propel themselves through the water. I don't know how they had the nerve to go to sea like that but they did. One who was in the Merchant Navy and was not made to pass a swimming test like we were in the Royal Navy, survived two sinkings during the war and consequently still sees no logic in needing to be able to swim. The Coverack Regatta Committee decided long ago that there should be a class of swimming confined to Coverack boys and girls. This was done expressly to encourage the local young swimmers and to prevent them from getting too despondent. The harbour remains an ideal beginners' pool.. Mothers can sit and chat, keeping an eye on their children who play in perfect safety. Our mothers rarely came to see us perform. They were too busy. They knew there was always someone handy with a boathook if you got out of your depth. My sister had to fall in when she was wearing a brand new pink hand knitted dress. She was fished out by Captain Fowler who used his long handled gaff for the purpose. The wool stretched and stretched as Mona was hauled out. Not being six feet in height, that dress never fitted her again. My own worst fright was when I tried to swim under a boat and got sucked up under the keel. It was impossible to swim away from that. I had to grasp the overlapping planks and pull myself out to the surface before I choked. Fortunately it was a clinker built boat and not a carvel with a smooth bottom.

The quay, of course, has had its sad moments. It is amazing how it becomes black with people when a body is brought ashore. Fortunately these events have become more rare as wrecks have decreased in number and people are more safety conscious. After one of our own village boys called George Hayden was drowned quite close to the shore I don't think anyone enjoyed swimming for some time. We began to realise that although we were young, strong and agile, the sea was an overwhelming force, even on a fine day. In spite of this grim aspect, people's love of the sea and of Coverack Bay is such that they request the quay to be their final departure point from this earth before their ashes are scattered on the water. The memorial stone at the top of the slope leading to the quay was given to Coverack to remind everyone of the dangers of the sea and to honour Dick Bowden, former goalkeeper of the village football team, who gave his life in a vain attempt to save his shipmates from R.M.T. Hesperia off the coast of Libya in the last year of the second world war.

Until 1814, nearly a hundred years after the quay was built, there was no public meeting house in Coverack. The first public building was the cottage which is at the top of Sunny Corner next to West House, the nineteenth century residence of Coverack's Chief Officer of Coastguard. The place was purchased by Trustees for the 'people called Methodists' for the purpose of preaching God's Holy Word and would not have been considered a suitable building for profane use. So, from about 1724 until long after 1814, most public gatherings would take place on or near the quay. It was the centre of industry. Behind the quay were fish cellars, some of which to this day bear evidence of the 'cawnsing' or pebbles from the beach which were laid in the central court yard. The uneven floor sloped inwards to a drain in the middle which would collect the oil seeping from the pilchards packed in barrels and kept under pressure while curing. These curing cellars were called penthouses in Coverack. They were sometimes known as palaces in other porths. The narrow track between the Friendship Cellar (now converted into a fine house) and the Paris Hotel is still known as Penthouse Lane by the local people. Dolor House was built on the site of the present Paris Hotel in 1715, just before the quay was built. It was a large thatched cottage with a garden on the seaward side and fish cellars on the landward side. It was not built as a pub. The Saunders family occupied it for a long time and it was the headquarters of a successful seine fishing enterprise. The seine boats used to be pulled up and kept on the present car park on Dolor Point. There was an open space at the top of the slope leading to the quay, where the Fisherman's Rest now stands. Fishermen gathered there when taking a breather or because it was too rough to go to sea. The old men would sit on a huge baulk of wreckwood which was known as 'Parliament Seat' and the younger ones would gather round and listen respectfully to their elders' opinions on current local and national events. Newspapers were relatively expensive and rare. There was a reading room opposite the present Bank House behind the lane leading to the old Post Office. Before it became a reading room it was shoemaker's shop, run by a member of the Barker family. In the summer when everyone was working, the reading room was used as a refreshment place for parties that came from Falmouth on a steamer. Men would go there in poor weather and in the evenings to play cards, quoits and bagatelle. At one time a retired army gentleman used to bring his newspaper and read aloud items of news and politics he had decided were 'safe' to be released. I wonder if he realised that opinions on his censored selections were freely given later on round 'Parliament Seat' and in the pub which was situated overlooking the quay where the public conveniences and telephone kiosk now stand. Ale for local consumption was brewed in the cellar at Jubilee House on the hill behind the old pub. This cellar was also used at one time for purveying meat when butchers came to the village from St. Keverne and the Lizard. The Beer Act of 1830 allowed virtually anyone to sell beer. This was an attempt to persuade poor people to give up their gin drinking habits and turn to the less harmful beer. As there was a clamp down on smuggling prior to the passing of the act and coastguards were beginning to make their presence felt in the area, Coverack men no doubt supported the new legislation with enthusiasm. Some pubs used to have an invitation on a sign over their entrances:

'Come all good Cornish boys, walk in,

Here's brandy, rum, and shrub, and gin,

You can't do less than drink success

To Copper, Fish and Tin.'

Coverack boys would have had to change the last line to:

'To Fish and smuggl'-in.'

No mining of any consequence has ever been done in the area. Although there is evidence that copper has been extracted from two workings near the coast. These are at Beagle to the Kennack side of Blackhead and at Downas, which as its name suggests, is a valley and is best reached by walking down from Pednavounder farm. It is called 'Black Valley' in Cornish due to the presence of lead in the earth.

Since the early eighteenth century, the quay has been the centre of local maritime trading activities, a public forum for the would-be sailors and swimmers. It is more than that. It is a public place where village people have gathered annually to take part in regattas, displaying their prowess in rowing, sailing, swimming, motor boat racing and fun on the greasy pole. Men from other coves come to see if they can carry off the prizes which are low in value but high in prestige. Before they leave for their home porths the visiting teams have a good evening in the pub and part from their hosts on the most amicable terms. Gatherings such as these attract people from all over the district. They come not only to see and participate in the sport but to enjoy meeting old friends. In the evening they sit in companionship on the quay and listen to the local band.

After the arrival of the first pulling and sailing lifeboat, 'Constance Melanie' in Coverack on the 14th. February, 1901, the quay took on a new role. It became the grandstand for the lifeboat christening ceremonies. In bad weather the harbour afforded the boats shelter after a rescue until they could go back on the slip and be winched into the house behind the quay. This tradition began after the first rescue carried out by the 'Constance Melanie' when she brought 16 survivors from the barque 'Glenbervie' into the harbour. Coverack was now on a par with the neighbouring coves. Porthoustock had had a lifeboat since 1869 and incidentally kept a boat there until 1942. Cadgwith and Mullion had a boat in 1867, whereas the Lizard had been saving life with her boat since 1859. Coverack boat had been given to the Institution by Mrs. Constance Melanie Hill of Red Hill, Surrey. The craft was a beauty, a wonderful seaboat, 35 feet in length with a 10 foot beam. She was propelled by twelve oarsmen or by sails. The 'Constance Melanie' was a Liverpool type craft, meaning she could withstand very heavy seas but was not self-righting. Coverack men preferred it that way, reasoning that if she did capsize and right herself, there would be such a tangle of gear that the boat would be unworkable, that is assuming the crew would be able to get back on board after having been thrown in the sea by the capsize. The men were right in that the boat did not let them down during her thirty three years of service and was instrumental in saving 97 lives.

The second ceremony witnessed in the quay was when in August, 1934 the lifeboat 'The Three Sisters' was named. She was a gift from Miss Margaret Quiller Couch of Looe. She was the same type and size as the 'Constance Melanie' but had a 35 h.p. engine which could drive her at seven knots in a straight line without having to tack as the 'Constance Melanie' had to do when she was under sail. The Lizard had had two self-righting auxiliary motor lifeboats since the first world war and not to be outdone by Coverack, acquired a twinscrew motor lifeboat in 1934. Nevertheless Coverack men were very pleased with 'The Three Sisters' and did not reveal any jealousy they might have felt about their friendly 'rivals'.

The last naming ceremony took place on the 10th. September, 1954 when a magnificent 42 foot Watson type lifeboat with twin 48 h.p. Gardner diesel engines was stationed at Coverack. The 'William Taylor of Oldham' only needed eight crew and could carry 75 people in rough weather at eight knots over a distance of 250 miles. She was so named because of a legacy from Miss C.S. Taylor of Oldham. She remained in Coverack until 1972 when she was replaced by an inshore boat which gave five years of service before being considered no longer necessary. The fine lifeboat house over which it was claimed no expense had been spared when it was built at the beginning of the century, has now become a tea room in which you can sit and contemplate the slip down which these fine craft rushed on their mercy missions to the Manacles, the Black Head and beyond.

Now that the lifeboats have gone, the quay is still a public place. It is still the grandstand for regattas and simulated rescues on lifeboat days when demonstrations are given by helicopters from Culdrose Naval Air Station and the Falmouth lifeboat to encourage people to dig deeply into their pockets to support the R.N.L.I.

What better place is there for a religious service? As I have said, the quay is Coverack and Coverack responds wholeheartedly when a service is held on the quay. In 1953 on June 2nd. the Coronation celebrations were scheduled to begin with a combined religious service there. The final firework display and bonfire were preceded by a parade of decorated boats. The Silver Jubilee, twenty five years later, had another united service on the quay. There has always been spontaneous singing there during public celebrations. In August, 1978, the B.B.C. used the quay as an unrivalled setting for Songs of Praise. Treverva Male Voice Choir, Mabe Ladies' Choir, the Coverack Singers and St. Keverne Silver Band led the singing of hundreds and hundreds of people. Such was the popularity of this broadcast that the B.B.C. came again in 1983. These carolares are combined services uniting in song not only the two Coverack Churches but people from all over Great Britain and overseas. They have become annual events during the last two decades and have been organised by a Cornish Bard, J.H. Brock, O.B.E., who is determined that this oasis shall pour forth Christian song to refresh the work weary who come to Coverack for renewal in the summer. People have written from all over Great Britain to show their appreciation of the Coverack Carolares. The memory of the choirs singing Cornish Bard Kenneth Polmear's vesper 'Celtic Benediction' as the sun sets over the harbour with the gaily painted fishing boats bobbing on the silvery sea is not easily forgotten. It serves as an encouragement to all who have witnessed it when they need an uplift to their spirits. It is equally certain that Coverack Carolares are remembered by landpeople in winter when the media give details of a brave sea rescue carried out while they are snugly cocooned in their town houses. They recall the strains of 'Eternal Father strong to save', sung on Coverack Quay to the tune Melita, which itself is the name for Malta, where St. Paul was shipwrecked in A.D.60. At this moment they can identify with the men and women of Cornwall who are always ready to give succour to seafarers.

COVERACK QUAY 1971
*What better place is there for a Carolare?*

One summer's day I heard a man inquiring in a shop about the position of a gravestone in the church yard. I discovered that he was called Black and that his mother had seen Songs of Praise and wanted to know about her father's grave. It turned out that the lady's father, named Ward, was a Coastguard Officer stationed at Coverack and was drowned in February, 1919 off the Dolor Point while attempting to recover a bale of rubber. Petty Officer Ward's grave is easily found as it has a grey War Graves Commission type stone and is close to the front door of the church. Mr. Black told me that his mother was in her eighties and ever since seeing the television broadcast from Coverack had wanted him to check on the state of her father's grave. He finally had an opportunity to do this on visiting the village after Coverack received some publicity in August, 1986. Geoff Cooper, a would-be adventurer, decided to make the quay his point of departure for rowing round the world in his 16 foot Long Liner named 'Water Rat I'. This young man attended the carolare, during which he received the blessing of the people for his voyage. Later on he was seen off by a large crowd of wellwishers. Unfortunately he was ill prepared and inexperienced. His first attempt to leave the Lizard peninsula and a subsequent trial trip were both aborted and he put the rescue services to great trouble when he had to be rescued on each occasion. He wisely decided to abandon his dream. However, in June, 1988 he set out again from Gweek. He got as far as Porthoustock and decided to come ashore for a final picnic with his girl friend. She then watched him leave for France. He managed to go 40 or 50 miles with a following wind but eventually he begged a tow from a French trawler which was making for St. Guénolé in Brittany. His boat was reported to have been holed by an unidentified object and he was said to be suffering from exhaustion and sunburn. Falmouth Coastguards must have felt relieved that he was no longer in their sector. A spokesman said wryly that he looked forward to seeing the oarsman again in 1989.

Meanwhile, the quay remains, waiting for the next drama to unfold. There is no air of expectancy. From time to time, during the summer evenings a drinker saunters down to the sun-trap seat, a pint grasped firmly in one hand and a dainty drink for his spouse in the other. Packets of crisps sprout from his trouser pockets. Suddenly, children appear from nowhere, sensing sustenance at hand. They sit on the warm, comfortable Delabole slate seats, provided as a memorial to Frederick Lyne Pascoe in 1971, crunching happily. They chat noisily, until with some uncanny sixth sense, they feel it is the moment to clamour for a cool ice, topped with Cornish cream. Father shells out some coins and off they dash to the village shop. While mother watches the children till they are out of sight, father slinks back to the Paris Hotel, downs a crafty bonus pint at the bar and comes back to his wife bearing another bribe for her and another pint for himself. In winter, the quay remains dark and brooding, a comforting mass to all who rely on its shelter, but keeping its secret history to itself.

Stories of storms abound in coastal villages. Coverack is no exception. It has already been suggested that the storms at the beginning of the eighteenth century could have been the reason why the fishermen were eager to have a quay to enable them to ply their trade more easily.

To return to the analogy of Coverack being an oasis, this is not meant to imply that the village is immune to storms, no oasis is. It is intended to mean that by comparison it is an oasis when considered in the larger context of Cornwall, Great Britain and the rest of the world. Its very isolation ensured that the great upheavals of the 18th. century had no immediate effect on village life.

Even the social and religious changes caused in Cornwall by John Wesley and his brother Charles in the eighteenth century failed to attract more than a ripple of interest in Coverack until 1814. A building was bought on the 16th. of December at Sunny Corner. According to the deeds it was 'for the use of the people called Methodists in connection with the late Reverend John Wesley, deceased.' In fact, the nearest John Wesley got to Coverack was Helston. He was so taken aback by the hostile reception there in 1745 that he did not return for another ten years, when he reported that the town, 'once turbulent, is now as quiet as Penryn.' He was even more gratified to record in his diary in 1766 that he was able to preach to, 'an exceeding large and serious congregation.' By 1781 he was boasting about Helston and perhaps even taking the credit, for he wrote, 'I scarce know a town in the whole county which is so totally changed, not a spark of that bitter enmity to the Methodists in which the people here have for many years gloried above their fellows.' No doubt some of the Coverack people travelled to hear the preacher who would not have considered it worth a hard ten mile ride to the village in order to preach to so few. Perhaps I am doing Wesley an injustice for he did go to the nearby village of Mullion in 1762 and was pleased to record, 'How tender are the hearts of this people.' What a pity he did not come to Coverack and record his impression for posterity.

The Seven Years War began in 1756 and involved British and French ambitions in what are now called the United States, Canada, India and Bangladesh. It led to the War of Independence which resulted in the loss of the American colonies. It would be surprising if these events caused much comment in Coverack. The French Revolution of 1789 no doubt provided Coverack smugglers with some profitable 'runs', including the transport of a few aristocratic refugees but its influence would not have had a revolutionary effect on the villagers. The impact of the continental revolution was reflected in the new government policy in the 'stormy' century of sending petty criminals to Australia instead of to America so that the urban rabble rousers could not turn the idlers into a threat to Britain's comfortable ruling classes. In 1819 nearly 10,000 people were transported to Botany Bay. At that time 200 crimes were punishable by death. These capital crimes included stealing a sheep and picking a pocket. Ten years later, in 1829, the death penalty was abolished, except in the case of murder. Life in Coverack at that time was indeed marginally more comfortable than life in an overcrowded gaol. However those who were transported for such 'heinous' crimes as stealing a pair of socks could not have found life much tougher than that led by the parish poor in Coverack, except that some of the above mentioned former town dwellers would not have been able to cope as well as the Coverack villagers with country life in Australia. The parish poor would probably have been classed as criminals in a more densely populated area. The treatment of the poor seems harsh to us but local landowners did make an effort to care for their poor and did not always pack them off to prison or worse. Of course it must not be forgotten that a ready source of unskilled labour was needed at peak times and it would not do to send too many people out of the parish.

In July, 1766, for instance, a meeting was held in the house of Sampson Incledon, innkeeper. The name Incledon is carved on a stone in the wall by the back door of the White Hart at St. Keverne. It was reported during the meeting that the poor had become very insolent and troublesome, not only to the overseers but to the rest of the parishioners of St. Keverne. Accordingly, Miles Exelby was authorised to hire a house for a term not exceeding seven years and he was given £6 for rent together with a bushel of barley every fortnight and one shilling and sixpence a week for each person plus £1 and five shillings for clothing. In addition he was allocated an indisclosed sum of money for medicines, care of the poor and for funerals. Miles Exelby must have had a trying time with the insolent troublemakers, for in April of the following year his accounts revealed he had purchased half a pint of brandy 'for the poor', but he stated ambiguously that it was 'taken by the churchwarden' so I consider we can safely assume the brandy was needed by the officials to calm their frayed nerves and that the churchwarden had given his assent, influenced no doubt by the offer of a tot of medicinal brandy.

At this time a child born out of wedlock, known as a 'base child', was inevitably brought up in the care of the parish. No thought was given to the idea of anonymity for the unfortunate child. In 1766 it was recorded by the meticulous Miles that Edward Martin's bastard cost the parish twopence for cochineal and sixpence for syrup of rhubard when he was sick. Edward Martin, the cause of the expense, was taken to Bridewell, as the house of correction in Bodmin had become known. It cost £1, two shillings and sixpence for the three horses to convey Edward Martin to Bodmin. The Guard, Walter Rice, claimed £1, thirteen shillings and five pence halfpenny for escorting him from the Duke's Head at the bottom of Meneage Street in Helston to Bodmin. It had already cost the Parish two shillings and sixpence for Mary Jordan to swear an affidavit that Edward Martin was the father of her child and the expenses for apprehending the irresponsible Edward getting him to Helston amounted to four shillings and sixpence. It must have been a difficult pregnancy for Mary Jordan needed two and sixpence worth of liquor, sixpennyworth of bread and sixpennyworth of tea and butter as well as saffron and Parmeceti candles, Treacle candles, Sugar candles and 'sope' at a cost of one shilling and one penny. The unfortunate girl's luck did not change, for in the following year she cost the guardians of the poor three shillings and ten pence for Liquor candles 'when sick with the small pox.' We can be thankful the society is able to offer unmarried mothers much better support in the latter half of the twentieth century.

When children in the care of the parish grew up, they were literally farmed out under an indenture scheme. In 1780, one Elizabeth Giles was apprenticed to Ann Rogers at the age of seven for a period of fourteen years, or until the day of her marriage. She was bound to serve her mistress 'in all lawful business according to her power, wit and ability and honestly, orderly and obediently in all things demean herself towards her said mistress and all hers during the said term.' It was not a one sided agreement. Ann Rogers, in return for Elizabeth's services, was to instruct her in 'the Art and Mystery of Housewifery and provide sufficient Meat, Drink and Apparel, Lodging and wishing all other things, and not be any way a Charge to the Parish or Parishioners.' That was the criterion. The Parish wanted nothing to do with Elizabeth. What say she had in the matter is open to conjecture. What could a seven year old do in these circumstances? Precious little, I suspect.

There was much discussion in Vestry Meetings about the Poor Houses. During the operation of the Poor Laws they were situated at the Dolly's, Nambol, near Lanarth, Laddenvean and at Rosenithan, (names spelt as in the Rate Books). It is probable that the Poor House at the Dolly's was used for Coverack people. In 1816 it was recorded that Thomas Champion was paid half a year's house rent 'for different paupers at Coverack'. This was no doubt a place which did duty as a Poor House in the village. The house at Laddenvean was a large ten roomed building standing in an acre of ground. It needed quite a bit of money for maintenance. In addition to the normal repairs, the residents sometimes got out of hand, windows were broken and furniture destroyed. In the end it was decided that the building no longer warranted money being spent on it and the property was sold to Edward Lawrance in 1846 for £177 and ten shillings. The idea of building a new Poor House was mooted but the Guardians kept deferring the matter until it was considered not worth mentioning again. The Guardians appeared to do their best to keep people out of the Poor House. It was cheaper to make sure the Parish poor could earn their own living. As mentioned earlier, children were indentured to farmers. Men were given money or materials to enable them to carry on working. A common request in Coverack was for willows to make crab pots. Money for boats was usually given only when the fishermen stated they had already got some money of their own. Some people were given money - though never as much as they asked for - to get a berth on a ship, or to join one of the services. For example, in 1832 Richard Keverne was granted four shillings to go to Plymouth to join the Marines.

Of course, attempts were made to obtain money under false pretences. They were given short shrift. One lady asked for £6 to go home to Worcestershire or failing that, eighteen pence a week to 'go out of the Poor House'. She was granted one shilling and ninepence a week, 'provided she will take herself off from the Poor House but not to leave the Parish.' She was obviously known to the Guardians. Another lady asked for one shilling and sixpence increase of pay because her child was ill. She was refused and told to put her child in the Union House. Another seemingly inhuman decision was made when the Church Rate was fixed at only a penny in the pound. It was: '........in no case the Bastard children shall remain with their mothers. If they do they will forfeit their pay.'

The account of Anne Peters' application for a Bible and a pair of shoes is intriguing. She was granted the Bible but the Guardians held over the decision on the shoes. This seems an odd decision. However, a previous entry in the minutes reveals that she had already asked for just one shoe and some worsted for stockings. It therefore seems likely that the Guardians assumed she had only asked for the Bible in order to get them in a frame of mind to grant the provision of the shoes. Whatever the truth of the matter is, this instance combined with the others which are related, helps us to understand something of the conditions under which poor people had to live in the parish during the nineteenth century.

The Guardians appointed Constables to assist them in their work. A Constable's job included checking that the people who were being helped by the Guardians were in genuine need. They also had to 'send on' poor people who were not entitled to benefit from St. Keverne Parish. Sometimes these unfortunates were given money for the journey back to the parish which was responsible for them. Conversely, local people who were stranded without work or money in another parish were given money to return to St. Keverne. It then fell to the Guardians to recoup the money which they had spent on behalf of another parish. Poor people were not necessarily the responsibility of a parish if they had been born there. They had to prove they were legally settled there. The process of proof of domicile was known as an 'examination'; This was difficult for people who could not read and write as they had to make statements of settlement. These were complicated and depended not only on birth but also on their employment or apprenticeship and on the type of house they rented.

In 1843, Constables were appointed to each Turn:

| | |
|---|---|
| Turn Bean | James Mitchell (shopkeeper) |
| Turn Traboe | James Charles |
| Turn Tregarn | Joshua Williams |
| Turn Trelan | John Roberts (Trevothen) |

It must be remembered that these were not Police Constables in the modern sense. They were local worthies who were paid an annual sum to carry out their duties as and when required. For instance, they were ordered to '........take up all vagrants and others travelling and begging and to put them before a magistrate.' They were also requested to buy handcuffs and post notices warning vagrants of what would happen to them in St. Keverne Parish. This was the Guardians' way of protecting the Poor Rate which they would have to charge if the Parish became swamped with poor people from other parishes. What proportion of the vagrants was unable to read is unknown, but I suspect that those who could read warned those who could not. An indication of the high price the Guardians placed on literacy is shown in the Vestry Minutes for 1831 when Thomas Pearce was paid ten shillings and sixpence a day for seven days for 'taking the population' as a census enumerator. That was a very high rate of pay for anyone in St. Keverne Parish in those days.

The Poor Law Amendment Act of 1834 changed the system of giving aid to the poor which had been in existence since the Elizabethan era. Workhouses were introduced as an alternative to the parishes finding work for the poor to do at a very low wage. This system, of course, pleased local employers who had a ready source of cheap labour at hand. From 1834, the idea was to put able bodied men in the Workhouse. There they were separated from their families. It followed that these poor people would do all they could to stay out of the Workhouses and consequently they were prepared to work for starvation wages and to live in squalid conditions with their families. To be fair, the Guardians of St. Keverne Parish did all they could to prevent the people whose destinies were in their hands from suffering the indignities of the Workhouse and the separation of families which the new Poor Law Amendment Act brought to the poor in town and country. Eventually these conditions led to public outcry after the full implications of the system were highlighted by politicians and writers such as Charles Dickens. It is to the credit of the parishes on the peninsula that with the exception of Manaccan, they did not conform to the letter of the law concerning the 1834 Act. To a large extent they managed their own poor.

A decade or so before the 1834 Amendment Act came into being a statement was made in the Vestry Minutes by Henry Mark, the Chairman of the Guardians. It was that 'Every Labour man shall receive from the Overseers so much wages per day in addition to his wages adequate to his family. No labourer shall have more wages than one shilling per day.' At Michaelmas (29th. September) in 1822 he was pleased to report that he had actually saved £8, eighteen shillings and two pence by his good management. He said of the Guardians, 'They feel confident that from their exertions, more savings may be made, not withstanding the great increasing pauperism and poverty of the times.' He ended his statement with a clarion call not unlike a conference speech made under Thatcherism in the 1980s. 'It will be their study as well as their duty, still to use every exertion to detect imposition, encourage industry and give the aged and deserving poor every comfort and support.' So confident was he of the parishioners' support that he added a rider to the effect that the 'coremen' (term used for a gang of shift workers in a Cornish mine) were assured of having constant work under the new plan. The Chairman's statement was countersigned by John Barker, Richard Pearce, John Roskruge and Thomas Roskruge. In fact, Henry Mark left money to the poor of the parish in 1870. Income from this fund is still being managed by the St. Keverne Relief in Need Charity today.

The Church Tythe Rates provide an interesting list of premises and their occupants in the Coverack or Turn Trelan area during the 18th. and 19th. centuries:

|  | 1721 | 1766 | 1830 |
|---|---|---|---|
| Cowisack | Richard James | Thomas James | James Martin |
| Polcoverack | Henry James | Henry James | John Mildren |
|  | George Harris | Henry Seacomb |  |
| Chimblo | James James | Henry Seacomb | Elizabeth Roberts |
| Chynals | Thomas Banfield | Nicholas Harris | Nicholas Coad |
| Trevothen | Anthony Roberts | John Roberts | Digory Roberts |
|  | Joano Kilter | Thomas Williams | Nicholas Coad |
|  | Mary Trenoweth | William Ralph | Eliz. Pengilly |
|  | Robert Odger | Thomas Hosken |  |
| Porthbean | John James | Mr. Matthew Wills | Jane Matthew |
|  | Thomas Banfield |  |  |
| Trewillis | Richard Courtis | John Rule | Mary Rule |
|  | William Richard | James Copeland | Thomas Bolitho |
|  |  | Thomas Matthew |  |
| Treleaver | William Roberts | John Roberts | John Roberts |

| | | | |
|---|---|---|---|
| | John Nicholas | John Pearce | Dinah Roberts |
| | John James | | |
| Arrowan | Jacob Roskilly | Nicholas Roberts | John Roberts |
| | John Rickard | William Matthew | |
| | | Abraham Gay | |
| | | John Roskruge | |
| | | George Pollard | |
| Bargwitha | Thomas Doubton | William Matthew | Thomas Hocking |
| Carpesack | Mr. Davis | James Downing | Nicholas Coad |
| Gwenter | John Ralph | William Roberts | Ann Pentecost |
| Trelan | Mr. Davis | Richard Lawry | Robert Cock |
| | | Richard Lawry | Samuel James |
| | | | James Roberts |
| | | | Richard Trerise |
| Trelanvean | Mrs. Mary Heano | John James | John Smith |
| Grougath | Hannibal James | Joseph Gilbert | John Harry |
| | Stephen Thomas | John Williams | Henry Mark |
| | | Edward Mitchell | William Pengilly |
| | | Joseph Gilbert | |

The complete list of premises, their occupants and the Tythe Rates they were charged by the Church makes fascinating reading. The same combinations of Christian names are used by the same families over and over again through the years. This makes the task of trying to sort out one branch of a family from another very difficult, especially when some farmers pay tythes for more than one farm. It is comforting to look through the list and become aware of the continuity of the names of people living in the Coverack or Turn Trelan area of the parish. A comparison of the names of the stalwarts defending Coverack at the time of the Armada with those who agreed to pay dues for the 'New Key' and with the above lists will illustrate the point I am making. The farming families have not always remained on the same farms but they are still in the district.

The names of farms have not altered a great deal. The modern Carnsullan at North Corner was spelt Kaersulek in 1285, then Carsulek in 1318 and Carnsulek in 1390. By the nineteenth century it was written Carnsellon and it has not changed much since then. Chynals, meaning 'house on the cliff' was spelt Tynals in 1280 - ty is the older form of chy, meaning 'house' - as shown in the spelling recorded in 1311 which was Chienals. By 1327 it had become Chynals Wyot, the second name probably being that of the resident farmer. Cowisack, the modern Cowyjack, posed a continuing spelling problem for recorders. During the 14th. century it was spelt Kewedick, Kynydic, Kewodyk and Cewesick. By 1720 it was Cowissack and in 1810 it had become Kywedjack which is the phonetic spelling preferred by locals today. The name is believed to mean 'excavated', coming from the Cornish word cowa, 'to hollow', which has kewys as a past participle. Gwenter, meaning 'white land', was spelt Wynter in 1263, Wenter in 1321 and Gwinter by 1720. Mary Wastie, a local artist, has captured the meaning of the name of this area and depicted its isolation by painting a scene showing the road to Gwenter when it was under snow. Arrowan did not alter much, going from Arawon in 1311 to Arrawen in 1652 and Arrawan in 1720 before adopting the present day spelling. This name is not to be found in other parts of Cornwall.

To trace fishing families is not so easy. By and large the Coverack fishermen were not men of substance. Their contribution to Church funds and through them to poor relief was not insignificant. In 1589, just after the Armada, the new Diocesan Elizabethan Bishop's seal depicted a fishing boat with two pilchards beneath it. This indicates the general importance of the tythes paid by the Cornish fishing industry. Tythes were paid in kind at first. Later on they were paid in cash. When the Tithe Commutation Act was passed in 1836, allowing farmers to pay a fixed rent as a tithe, the Coverack men were still paying 1/10th. of the value of pilchards landed there. Fish tithes were not bound by the same laws as farm tithes, but they were duly paid nevertheless. Coverack fishermen did not occupy premises of any financial significance, compared with the local farmers.

In 1830, Henry Saunders was running the Coverack seining industry from Dolor House, which is where the Paris Hotel now stands. He paid one half of the full rate which was the same as the amounts paid by Lieutenant Hodge of the Coastguards and Sir R. Vyvyan who owned a house in the village. The full rate at that time was three shillings and sixpence in the pound. In the Rate Book for 1838, however, Henry Saunders is recorded as having paid four shillings and one farthing for the rates of the Three Tuns Inn at Coverack. The building was actually owned by C.W. Ellis and had an annual value of £13 and ten shillings. In the same Rate Book, Jane Williams of the New Inn, Coverack, paid two shillings and tenpence halfpenny for her pub, which had an annual value of £9 and ten shillings. Paradoxically, Mr. Ellis only paid three shillings and five pence three farthings for the Quay which was valued at £8 and seven shillings per annum. It would appear that Coverack had a lot of hard drinkers who made the Three Tuns more valuable to the Parish Poor Rate than the Quay. The Preventive Station at the Watch House was valued at £4 and ten shillings and paid one shilling and four pence farthing in rates. The smaller Preventive Station at Borgwitha which was owned by William Lory, was only valued at £1 and paid three pence in rates. We must remember that the rates were not paid annually as they are now. The rates were levied when they were needed by the Parish Overseers of the Poor and were sometimes collected three or more times in one year.

The following list gives an idea of the ordinary villagers of Coverack who were charged rates ranging from sixpence three farthings to one shilling and ten pence halfpenny, according to the type of property they occupied. They were listed as having a House, a House and Court, a House and garden or a shop. In the 1838 Rate Book they were charged rates for 'the necessary Relief of the Poor and for other purposes in the several Acts of Parliament mentioned.'

| | |
|---|---|
| James Barker | John Mundy (carpenter's shop) |
| John Barker | Mark Mundy (shop) |
| John Barker Jnr. | John Pearce |
| Richard Barker (shoemaker's shop and cellar) | Nicholas Roberts |
| | William Roberts |
| | William Ralph (shoemaker) |
| Anthony Champion | Simon Roskilly |
| Gro. Champion | Thomas Roskilly |
| Nancy Champion | Peter Rule |
| Henry Coplin | Alice Scantlebury |
| Mark Daniell (cooper's shop) | Jno. Sullivan |
| Beryn Hosking | Beryn Taylor |
| Grace Hosking | Elizabeth Thomas |
| Nicholas Hosking | Hannibal Williams |
| Henry James | Henry Williams |
| Charles Johns | |
| Elizabeth Lory | |
| Elizabeth Luke | |
| John Martin | |
| John Mildren | |
| Thomas Mildren | |

Perhaps it is misleading to consider Coverack as an oasis. True, it seemed to be scarcely affected by the social, political and religious upheavals of the eighteenth century. There were no warring factions of mine owners to affect the villagers, but there was a small, struggling seine industry which was indirectly influenced by wars and international trade. Smuggling declined from the second decade of the nineteenth century. In truth it was a struggle for survival for the majority. One reason for naming this chapter 'Stormy Nineteenth Century' is because of the stormy completion of the change of the country from an agricultural land of hamlets and villages to an urban, industrial centre of empire. It also saw the completion of the enclosure of land which created landless country folk who migrated to the new centres of industry to eke out a living. This change, of course, did not begin in the year 1800. The population of England had doubled from six and three quarter million in 1760 to twelve million in 1820. It was to double again by the end of the stormy century. At the same time, the acquisition of wealth through industry and commerce was becoming respectable.

Communications were vastly improved in eighteenth century Britain by the building of canals. The roads were also improved by the introduction of the turnpike system. Without better canals and roads, the industrial revolution would not have taken place. Two inventions were to revolutionise nineteenth century communications. Watts' steam engine and Richard Trevithick's model road carriage - in effect the early version of Stephenson's Rocket - driven for the first time in 1801 by Lady de Dunstanville and stoked by Gilbert Davies, the Cornish President of the Royal Society. The coming of the age of steam had virtually coincided with the storming of the Bastille in France and the American Declaration of Independence. The latter indirectly encouraged Cornish men and women to go to America in the stormy century when depressions in agriculture and the tin industry forced them to leave their native county. In 1815, Gulval born Humphrey Davy's gift to the nation of the Miners' safety lamp and Illogan born William Bickford's invention of the safety fuse in 1830 were to ensure that sufficient coal was produced to provide the power for industry and transport on land and sea. At the same time as Britain was approaching a period of great prosperity, the country was entering on a period of social and political change. This was partially caused by the use of sweated labour and the overcrowded slums created in the new towns.

There was a trickle of emigration from Coverack in the last century and it has continued to the present time. The fishermen who found life difficult became temporary emigrants. They tended to join the Royal Navy or the Merchant Navy. The merchant seaman were away from the village for long periods but usually discharged themselves from their cargo boats during the summer months and went back to sea when the weather forced them to look elsewhere for a living. The Royal Navy men waited until they either had a pension or had saved up enough money to buy a sound boat with adequate gear, then they returned to the village for good. Some of the other land working emigrants, who went to America or the antipodes, returned when they had saved up enough money to be able to withstand the vicissitudes of village commerce, without going bankrupt. Others remained in the land of their adoption. A few returned for a quick visit to their relations and then went back to their families in their adopted countries.

It has been shown that Coverack people were indirectly affected by social and political change. Living close to the sea, however, they had other storms to weather. Ships without engines are at the mercy of winds and currents. Add to that the inability of navigators to plot an accurate position and one can understand why in 1714 Parliament offered a prize of £20,000 for the discovery of an accurate method of finding the longitude of a ship at sea. The difficulty of doing this is illustrated by the fact that by 'accurate', the government meant it would make the award to anyone who could devise a method which would enable him to bring a ship to a position which was not more than 30 miles from its intended position after being at sea for a period of six weeks. The Board of Longitude had been set up after Admiral Sir Cloudesley Shovell in H.M.S. Association had wrecked his ship on the Gilstone Ledges in October, 1707, causing the ships following in company to ground as well. Over two thousand men lost their lives in this disaster. The winner of the longitude prize was John Harrison. After making four different marks of a chronometer he claimed the award almost 50 years after Parliament's offer. He was finally paid for his Mark IV by a reluctant government, following the testing of his latest chronometer by no less a person than Captain James Cook. By comparing the time the sun reaches its highest point with the time at Greenwich, navigators could now work out how far the ship was East or West of the Prime Meridian. One must remember that it was not until 1884, towards the end of the stormy century, that Greenwich was accepted as the Prime Meridian by other countries. It should also be remembered that each town used to keep its own time. Coverack would have had to rely on St. Keverne time as there was no public clock in the village.

At the beginning of the nineteenth century there were only four lighthouses serving Cornwall. These were St. Agnes in the Isles of Scilly, the Longships off Lands End, the Lizard and Eddystone. Before the century was over, Trevose, Godrevy, the Bishop Rock off St. Agnes in the Isles of Scilly, Round Island, off St. Martin in the Isles of Scilly, the Wolf Rock off Lands End and St. Anthony at the entrance to Falmouth were added to the original four, plus the Seven Stones Lightship between the Isles of Scilly and Lands End. The Pendeen Lighthouse to the north of Cape Cornwall was added in 1900 for good measure.

Now, less than a century later, these lights are nearly all automated. Navigation carried out by using Decca Chains, satellite and radar is so safe that the Trinity House Brethren are proposing to withdraw some of the warning beacons, much to the chagrin of the Cornish inshore fishermen whose small boats are not suitable for carrying expensive, modern sophisticated navigational aids with their necessary alternative back-up systems.

A study of the 'Price of Admiralty' during the years 1793-1815 reveals the following details:

| | |
|---|---|
| Major British vessels lost by shipwreck | 101 |
| Major British vessels lost by enemy action | 10 |
| Major enemy vessels lost by shipwreck | 24 |
| Major enemy vessels lost by action to the British | 377 |

The number of deaths caused by sickness was also in the same proportion when compared with deaths caused by enemy action. The apparent conclusion from these figures points to the fact that the Royal Navy's most effective foes were the sea and sickness. It also seems certain that the Coverack civilian seafarers of that time would have agreed with the implication these figures present.

The first lifeboat to be placed in Cornwall was stationed at Penzance in 1803, some 20 years before the Royal National Lifeboat Institution was founded by Sir William Hillary. At that time the charity was called 'The National Institution for the Preservation of Life from Shipwreck.' It should be remembered that Sir William himself was no mere administrator, he was a leading member of the Douglas, Isle of Man crew and was three times awarded the Gold Medal of the Institution for gallantry. He was involved in the saving of 305 lives during his time as a lifeboat man.

The year 1807 was a year of disasters. The Royal Navy lost twenty seven ships, including the frigate H.M.S. Anson. This ship left Falmouth for patrol duty off Brest on Christmas Eve. A west sou'westerly gale forced the captain to decide to return to Falmouth for shelter, but due to his inability to identify the landfall she had made in thick weather, Captain Lydiard found his ship dragging anchors in Mounts Bay and was forced to run the Anson aground at Loe Bar in order to give the crew a chance to save themselves. About 100 officers and men were drowned but many were saved by means of a rope which Mr. Roberts of Helston took to the wreck by swimming through the surf. This rescue and a subsequent one a few hours later by a Methodist local preacher from Mullion who rightly considered there might still be some survivors aboard the frigate, was witnessed by a young onlooker, Henry Trengrouse from Helston. He decided to apply his inventive mind to a more certain way of getting a line aboard a wreck from the shore and vice versa. The result was a musket with a cylinder fitted to the barrel. In the cylinder was a mackerel line attached to a small rocket. When the musket was fired it ignited the rocket which could carry the line 200 yards. The thin mackerel line was then bent to a larger rope and hauled out to the wreck to be used for pulling the sailors ashore. The Ordnance Board awarded Trengrouse 50 guineas (£52 and ten shillings) for 'the best idea that has yet been suggested'. Twenty sets were ordered to be made for the government. Trengrouse also received 30 guineas and a silver medal from the Society of Arts. There is no record of any lives being saved by Henry Trengrouse's invention as the rocket proved to be too weak for use in storm conditions.

In the course of time, many other inventors adapted his ideas and finally in 1897, William Schermuly won a gold medal for his line throwing pistol. A further glance ahead gives us a brief picture of the outcome of the efforts made to alleviate the sufferings of seafarers who were unfortunate enough to find themselves without power on a lee shore in a storm. By 1928 the Merchant Shipping Act made it compulsory for all ships over 500 tons to carry an efficient line thrower. In 1988, thanks to other developments in providing the mariner with the means of making a safe passage, the Rocket Apparatus and Breeches Buoy used by H.M. Coastguard were made redundant. Records of rescues showed that it was 26 years since the Rocket Apparatus had been used at St. Ives and at the Lizard it had been 57 years. Coverack Rescue Company had already been disbanded. The Rocket Apparatus was used in the rescue during a blizzard of the crew of the Scottish trawler Ben Asdale, at Maenporth near Falmouth in 1978. Unfortunately, when the rocket had been fired and the breeches buoy was being hauled out, the block carrying the rope was jammed and the tripod carried away over the cliff. A Sea King helicopter from Culdrose Royal Naval Air Station at Helston managed to airlift 8 crewmen to safety. Ironically, the helicopter's own winch jammed, forcing the winchman to lower one of the survivors back into the sea in order to clear the blockage and enable the winch to haul the man into the aircraft.

There was an easterly gale at Coverack on the 22nd. of January, 1809, two years after the wreck of the Anson. At about 3 a.m. the troop transport Dispatch struck the Lowlands. She was an old ship which had been hired by the Admiralty to bring back troops from Spain. On board were the 7th Dragoons. Before embarking on the 14th. from Corunna, the troops had fought a rearguard action against the French who had shelled the ship as she was leaving the port. They had been pulled out of the fighting just before Lieut.General Sir John Moore was killed by a cannon shot. He was the man we used to think was as much disliked by his troops as we disliked being made to learn Charles Wolfe's funereal poem. We used to chant.

'We buried him darkly at dead of night.

The sod with our bayonets turning.'

We didn't, or wouldn't, realise that the word 'sod' should have been in the plural, nor that it meant lumps of earth. 'Tobs' were lumps of earth as far as we were concerned. A sod was what we called someone we didn't like. In any case, our erroneous opinion was confirmed by the next verse but one, which began,

'Few and short were the prayers we said,

And we spoke not a word of sorrow.'

We would probably have been much more interested in the poem if we had known of the connection between the brave general and the men who had lost their lives so close to Coverack.

The transport had made good time and the troops were looking forward to going home on leave. Some scandal mongers said that Captain Botley was hugging the shore in the hope of gently beaching the ship in order to make a large claim to the government. It is unlikely that any seaman would choose the Lowland Point for a stranding at 3 o'clock in the morning during an easterly gale. When the ship struck, the soldiers were asleep. The vessel broke up very quickly and it was impossible for the local men to render assistance in the mountainous seas. In addition to the ship's company there were seventy soldiers on board. Their three army officers were, Major Cavendish, son of Lord Cavendish of

Eastbourne, Captain Dukenfield and Lieutenant the Hon.Waldegrave, the son of the 4th. Earl of Waldegrave. In addition there were 34 officers' horses. There were only six soldier survivors: James Clow, Edmund Hall, Thomas Harries, John Ravel the regimental farrier, John Richards and Charles Weeks. Major Cavendish was identified by his brother officer, Captain Treweeke, who by a curious twist of fate, had returned to Cornwall from Corunna in the Barfleur. He had just arrived in Truro from Plymouth when he heard news of the disaster. Captain Treweeke hastened to Coverack with Mr. John Vivian, the brother of Lieutenant Colonel Vivian, who had been a fellow passenger in the Barfleur.

Two hours after the Dispatch hit the Lowlands, the Brig Primrose struck the rocks known as Carn Dhu between Dean Point and Maen Varses. She was a practically new Fowey built ship, bound for Spain with despatches for the generals fighting the Peninsular War. On board were 126 crew and six passengers. Some Porthoustock men set out to rescue the crew. After a horrendous journey they returned to the village with the sole survivor, a seventeen year old lad. Ten days after the wreck the local correspondent's report of John Meaghen's rescue was printed in 'The Western Flying Post', better known in the west country as the 'Sherborne and Yeovil Mercury.' The account underlines what has already been said about the need for an efficient method of rescuing sailors from wrecks:

'........every soul but one perished; and dreadful was the situation of the officers and men at the signal station who heard their shrieks on board but were unable to render any assistance. The lad was saved by clinging to a piece of the mast for several hours until a boat got near him when a rope was thrown to him and blind fortune curled it round his body and he was safely brought on shore.'

The Porthoustock men who manned the boat were the brothers William and Joseph Matthews, Stephen Old, Edward Tonkin, George Tonkin and Bartholomew Tripp. Some of their descendants still live in the area. The first lifeboat to be stationed in Porthoustock arrived some fourteen years later in 1869. Lieutenant Cocke and Lieutenant Withers of the Signal House were also mentioned in a report for their exertions in saving the lives of the men from the two wrecks that night. A signal station had been built at the Black Head at the beginning of the Peninsular War expressly for the purpose of communicating with transports and men of war going to and from Spain. The building was some distance from the Coastguard Look Out Hut. Its chimney and gable end were still standing in 1891 when Mr. H.J. Sincock wrote his first illustrated guide to Coverack.

It is not difficult to imagine the aftermath of the storm. It would appear that on that night over two hundred people were drowned. The 'Sherborne and Yeovil Mercury' again takes up the story:

'The most melancholy spot that ever was or we trust never again will be seen passed through Helston to St. Keverne on Tues. 24th. inst., several wagons to the amount of 50 went through Helston to Coverack and from there with a greater number were conveyed with a slow and solemn step to the churchyard of St. Keverne, the bodies of the unfortunate fellows who had been crowned with honour and glory in the several skirmishes in Spain with the French Emperor's bodyguards, from the edge of the whole sword they had escaped the stroke of death and near the shores of their native country met with a watery grave.' The reporter's account is all the more graphic for its lack of punctuation, which gives it that breathless quality often associated with sensitive people who are the unwilling bearers of sad tidings.

It was not known when the reporter wrote his account that Lieutenant Hugh Williams was one of the sailors who 'met with a watery grave'. He was a Coverack man, drowned in sight of his native village. The villagers were reminded of this in November, 1962, when 91 year old Coverack born Mrs. M.E. James responded to an article in the West Briton about the wreck of the Dispatch. She stated that Lieutenant Williams was her grandmother's uncle.

The memorials are side by side in a plot to the left of the West door of St. Keverne Church. The 'Primrose' memorial is surmounted by a granite Celtic Cornish cross and has the name of the ship's commander at the end of the tribute - James Mein, R.N. Captain Mein's body was taken to Falmouth where he was buried with full military honours. The 'Despatch' has a more grandiose memorial consisting of a granite Christian cross on a two stepped plinth with a large base, presumably covering the burial plot. It mentions only the Officers and men of H.M. VIIth. Hussars 'interred in this plot' who were lost on their return from the Peninsular War. The ship's crew is not included in the citation as they are in the case of the 'Primrose'. It must be remembered that it was not until 1830 that the M.P. for Bodmin, Davies Gilbert, managed to push through an Act sanctioning the burial of shipwrecked mariners at the expense of the county rates. The Church had to meet much of the expense of these two wrecks through the Poor Rates. On this occasion it cost two shillings for 'a journey to Helston for the coroner to hold an inquest on the bodies of the wrecked men.' A further eighteen shillings were spent, 'To 12 men for attending three times on a jury held on the wrecked men by order of the coroner.' The 'going rate' for a coffin at that time in the parish was also eighteen shillings. Over two hundred deaths meant it was an expensive disaster for the Church and the parishioners. The Rev. William Whitehead of St. Keverne had the unhappy task of conducting the funeral services of 104 victims from the wrecks between January 24th. and April 2nd., 1809.

Major Cavendish's body was brought to Helston and placed in an expensive lead coffin which was kept in the church before being removed for family burial. A tablet was erected by the Queen's Own Regiment of Hussars in St. Keverne Church in memory of the drowned dragoons. The memorial was in verse. After describing the unhappy ending of such a fine body of soldiers, it concluded:

'Their mourning comrades feel a moisten'd Cheek,

And bid the Marble their dumb sorrow speak.'

This tablet was later removed from the Church and is thought to be in a private house in Helston. Local people say that the stone was taken by a Mr. Ching to Porthleven for cleaning and repair. It is believed that the work was commissioned by the Regiment which is now mechanised. Countess Waldegrave has been to St. Keverne to see if she can discover the facts as she is writing a history of the family. To date she has not been successful. She told Mr. Frank Curnow a local historian and former Church Warden who helped her in her search, that the Regiment is very keen to get the monument restored to its former position. The present Minister for Foreign Affairs, William Waldegrave, is a descendant of Lieutenant the Hon. Waldegrave who was drowned on the Despatch.

Many of the horses from the Dispatch are believed to have been buried on the Mears Point. Two village boys, John Corin and Archie Rowe found a leg bone of a horse on the beach, not far from the Yellow Rock, when they were playing there during the First World War. The boys' parents explained to them that their parents had told them the horses from the Dispatch had been buried near the beach after the storm of 1809 and that horses' bones were often found there.

All that remains of the Primrose is the gudgeon, which is a large socket in which the pintle of a sailing ship's rudder turns. The gudgeon can be seen on the wall in the vestry at St. Keverne Church. It was found much later by a fisherman named James Cliff. He was made Coxn. of the Porthoustock Lifeboat, 'Charlotte' in 1907 and lived at 'Manacle View', St. Keverne.

'Q', or Sir Arthur Quiller Couch, of Fowey, where the Primrose was built, wrote a superb, ghostly mystery story about the two wrecks. 'Q' gives John Meaghen, the drummer boy, the name of John Christian. He makes friends with a trumpeter, called William Tallifer. He was a survivor from the other wreck. John eventually returns to duty but the trumpeter remains in Coverack. After conducting a ghostly judgment day type of roll call with the drowned dragoons as they formed up on Lowland Point, the former trumpeter dies in mysterious circumstances. To reveal more would spoil your reading of 'Q's' story. It is called, 'The Roll Call of the Reef.' The author captures the atmosphere of the time as only a Cornishman having a life-long connection with the sea could do. It is fitting that Coverack's second lifeboat, the Three Sisters was bought by the R.N.L.I. in 1934 with a legacy from Miss Margaret Quiller Couch of Looe. It is equally fitting that the lifeboat's penultimate port of call when being brought from Cowes to her station by Coxn. William Corin was Fowey. She was refuelled there and shown off to the people whose neighbour, Sir Arthur Quiller Couch was to name the boat which had been given by his relative.

It was reported from Falmouth at the time of the wrecks that a 'great number' of transports arrived there from Corunna within a period of four days. These ships landed soldiers from many different regiments because of the confusion of the retreat. There were also several wounded and sick French prisoners of war brought ashore, most of them belonging to the Imperial Guard. These men had a bleak future in store for them. The Commissioners for conducting H.M. Transport Service had built a prison at Dartmoor in 1806 for the care and custody of 5,000 prisoners of war. When advertising for tenders, the Commissioners had stipulated that the buildings were to be constructed on a 15 acre site out of moor stone 'to be broken from the scattered rocks on the spot, where there is also fine gravel, sand and water.' It is doubtful that the French men who were landed in Falmouth appreciated being transferred to such a place. The compassionate Falmouth people were not unaware of the plight of the prisoners of war. They organised a collection of comforts and money to make the prisoners' lot a little easier when they were taken to their grim moorland prison.

When Coverack people were searching the shore after the storm, papers from H.M.S. Triumph were found among the jetsam. It was feared that she had been wrecked as well. Fortunately she arrived safely in spite of losing some of her upperworks. There was also report of the loss of the transport Phoenix but happily this was also found to be untrue. Another vessel was seen to go down off Mullion Island on the day after the loss of the Dispatch and Primrose. There were no survivors. One body was washed ashore. Not far from the body was a Dutch Bible and some wooden shoes. It may well have been a Dutch ship but the sea has yet to unravel the mystery.

The Manacles continued to take its toll throughout the stormy nineteenth century. Over 50 recorded wrecks occurred in the area during this period. There were almost certainly as many local small craft which were lost and not recorded as well as larger vessels which sank there without trace during violent storms. In spite of the loss of the Dispatch and Primrose, little was done to prevent a repetition of the double tragedy.

Emigration has already been mentioned and will be again. In the 'Hungry Forties' there was a surge of people seeking a better life overseas. This continued into the next decade and beyond. J.B. Willcocks was one of the many shipowners who advertised his passenger ships which went to Canada and the United States in the fifties. His vessels were named Clio, John, Oriental and Siam. The John was a Plymouth barque of 586 tons. She left her home port for Quebec on May the 3rd., 1855 in the late afternoon. She had 279 people on board, including 98 children and 16 infants. There were 16 in the crew which was commanded by Captain Edward Rawle. A fine breeze was blowing and the ship made good time when she got past Rame Head. On the way down channel the mate made several requests to the captain to check the position. The captain was unconcerned and the mate not skilled enough in navigation to be able to prove his argument so he left the responsibility to his superior. The vessel appeared to be too far to the north and consequently the Lizard Head, which the vessel had to clear, was obscured from view. The John was in fact in the 'blind' sector and even when St. Anthony light came into view, the captain did not authorise a large enough alteration of course. By now it was dark and the fine breeze was fast becoming a southerly gale. Before long the barque struck the Manacles at such a speed that she kept her way on and grounded shortly afterwards, close to Lowland Point. One lifeboat was launched with five crew and one passenger on board. The crew managed to get into Coverack and warn the fishermen of the wreck. The Coverack men were unable to sail into the strong wind, so a messenger raced to Porthoustock to give the news of the wreck. Meanwhile, Captain Rawle advised his passengers to stay on board until daylight.

Once more Porthoustock men went to the rescue. They were led by James Hill who was to become the first coxn. of Porthoustock's first lifeboat, the Mary Ann Story. His own crew included his son, also called James, James Connor, a Coastguard, William Matthews, Thomas Pearce and Henry Tripconey. Unfortunately the boats from the shore took some time to find the ship in the darkness. The John had no rockets nor guns to indicate her position. As the wind increased the danger became more apparent. The crew left most of the passengers on the upper deck while they either made their escape in the only lifeboats that were seaworthy, or if they could not get away in them, climbed the rigging. Many of the passengers were swept off the deck by the seas that were breaking over the grounded ship. The more agile of them followed the sailors into the rigging. It was reported in the West Briton on the 18th. May, 1855, that one of the passengers on the John, a shoemaker from Falmouth called Benjamin Skewes, said he was washed off the rigging of the mizzen mast but then managed to clamber on to the mainmast rigging. He hung on there until he was rescued. He added that the children on board gathered on the poop deck. They were washed off by the breaking seas because they were unable to climb the rigging. The crew did not help them. In spite of their difficulties in getting out to the ship in such atrocious weather, the fishermen and the Coverack Coastguards in their longboat saved 91 people. The Chief Boatman of the Coastguards and James Hill were commended by the authorities for their leadership that night.

There is a grave in St. Keverne churchyard which contains 120 bodies from the wreck. When the grave was being prepared close to the grave of the victims of the Dispatch, it is said that the sextons unearthed some soldiers' tunics which were still red in colour after being buried for nearly half a century.

Captain Rawle was accused of manslaughter. The conduct of the crew, all of whom survived, was reprehensible. Little was done to help the passengers get into the unseaworthy lifeboats. Eye witnesses reported to the inquiry that the crew even fought each other for a place in a boat. Andrew Elder and two other crew members were the only ones commended for the way in which they helped the women and children. The remainder did not measure up to the high standard traditionally demanded of British sailors. The captain spent some time in Bodmin waiting for his trial. He was accused of causing the death of Elizabeth Hallet. All eight of her family had drowned. Her body was the only one which was recognisable among the ones cast up on the shore by the pounding seas. The cowardly and incompetent captain was acquitted of manslaughter as the jury could not agree on their verdict. He did serve a sentence for his incompetence as a ship's master, however. It is regrettable that some men from the parish were punished in the same court for looting. As stated earlier, life in the stormy century was tough for the parish poor. The temptation must have been too great. 'Honesty is the best policy' is a splendid maxim. It is a difficult one to follow when one's children lack the basic necessities of life.

According to the Trinity House Buoy Book of 1927, a buoy had been placed near the Manacles in 1838. Four years after the wreck, in 1859, a larger bell buoy was placed in 18 fathoms of water at a distance of 56 fathoms (112 yards) south east of the sunken rock at the eastern extremity of the Manacles ridge. It was secured by three anchors. The buoy was black and had the dreaded word MANACLE painted in white. The cost was said to be £1,100. A small price, even in those days, to pay for the safety of seamen. Commander Lawry of Treleague, St. Keverne had long been campaigning for a light house to warn ships of the proximity of the Manacles. He was a distinguished sailor who had served in the Royal Navy during the French and American wars. He had also taken part in the smuggling blockade, working off the Kent coast and later on more familiar ground off Gerrans and Cadgwith. It needed the deaths of another hundred people to get the authorities to listen to a highly respected local professional seaman. Even then, the Brethren were only able to increase the size of the existing buoy. Unfortunately the detailed records of Trinity House concerning the area were destroyed by fire during the second world war, so full details concerning this buoy are not known. It must be remembered that there were many claims on the Brethren and they had to allocate resources according to the priorities as they saw them in the middle of the stormy century. It could not have been an enviable task.

It is ironic that the Merchant Shipping Act had been passed the year before the wreck of the John. It was in the year of the outbreak of the Crimean War. The authorities were no doubt anxious to avoid a repetition of the loss of ships such as the Dispatch and Primrose which had occurred during the Peninsular War. This time, the French were on the same side as the British. The Act came into force on the first of May, 1855 - two days before the John set sail on her last voyage. Most of the new regulations were ignored by Captain Rawle and by Lieutenant Carew of Plymouth who passed the ship as seaworthy and declared her master and crew to be competent. The Lieutenant resigned his commission after the inquiry.

It is probably not an exaggeration to say that Coverack people appeared to pay more attention to the meteorological storms in the nineteenth century than to those of a social nature. People eking out a living on the coast were not unaware of the devastating effect of storms on their own lives nor on those of their fellow creatures who were unfortunate enough to find themselves close to a dangerous lee shore. It will be seen from records kept by parsons and schoolmasters that these men were preoccupied with the weather and its effect on their respective charges. You will remember that in the eighteenth century Charles Wesley was rash enough to record, somewhat cynically, in his journal, 'I saw a strange sight, the sun shining in Cornwall.' The weather often prevented the schoolmasters from achieving the basic standards laid down by the education boards, which in turn relied on central funds for their very existence. A typical entry in the School Log Books of the period was, 'There being so few pupils present, owing to the weather, it was decided not to mark the registers.'

Gradually Coverack people were caught up in the reforming 'storms' of the nineteenth century. There were not enough inhabitants to attract would-be trade unionists, nor parliamentary reform supporting politicians, to Coverack, but the villagers were not unaware of the social storms that were brewing. The Royal Cornwall Gazette, whose motto was, 'Gwyr yn erbyn y byd' - Truth against all the world - did its best to inform its readers of events in high places.

24

The sort which would sooner or later have an effect on the humblest person in the most remote parish. It should be understood, of course, that in the nineteenth century, before universal education came into being, many people were unable to read and they had to rely on those who could to tell them what was going on outside their immediate environment. In Coverack at that time, the Wesleyan Methodist Sunday School and the Dame Schools provided the villagers with a means of becoming literate.

A letter published in the paper from Fred Marryat on Saturday, March 26th, 1820 stated his regret at not being able to emancipate the borough of Tregony 'from the state of feudal vassalage to which it is reduced'. He warned that when the electors were ready to back him he would put himself forward as their parliamentary candidate once more and he would be found ready to 'espouse the cause of liberty and independence against that of tyranny and oppression.' This sort of revolutionary fervour was typical of the correspondence being published in the local papers early in the nineteenth century. It was too heady for the local inhabitants. Perhaps they feared retribution on the scale of the royal reprisals taken after the rebellion led by Michael Joseph of St. Keverne in 1497. In January, 1821, 110 principal inhabitants of the parish had a loyal address to King George IV printed in the Royal Cornwall Gazette. It began, 'We the Minister, Magistrate and Inhabitants of the Parish of St. Keverne and others the inhabitants of the district of Meneage in the County of Cornwall desire to approach the King of the British Empire under the influence of that loyalty and obedience which the Holy Scriptures enjoin as the command of Him who is 'King of Kings and Lord of Lords........' Having ingratiated themselves they went on to state that even the courts were being unfaithful to His Majesty and that the principles of Magna Carta were at stake. The loyal address concluded by tendering '........the homage of our loyalty and fidelity.' There was thus no doubt about the position of the influential people of the parish as far as Reform was concerned. What opinions the remainder held are not recorded. For good measure the address was also placed in the Church records. This assurance of obedience was to a king who had been acting as Regent to his father, George III. The new king was a womaniser who had married a Roman Catholic widow without his father's consent. The marriage was invalid so the Regent was subsequently persuaded to marry his cousin Caroline of Brunswick, the daughter of his father's sister. It is unlikely that the 110 'principal inhabitants' were as well informed as we are today about the activities of their new monarch. What does appear certain is that the responsible inhabitants of the parish were averse to change, albeit, as events were to prove, the change was for the better.

A decade later when King George IV died, the Times stated, 'There never was an individual less regretted by his fellow creatures than this deceased King. What eye has wept for him? What heart has heaved one sob of unmercenary sorrow?' I wonder if any of the 'principal inhabitants' saw that article and if they did, what were their thoughts on the matter. The fortunes of the monarchy were to change during the remainder of the century.

Of course, there were to be other Reform Bills during the stormy century, allowing a few more of the ordinary men of Coverack to take a small part in electing the Members of Parliament who were to shape their destiny. When the idea of Reform was first publicised, mysterious anonymous correspondents began writing to the press, urging people to think for themselves. They attacked 'those who obtained their seats by purchase.' Other supporters of Reform spoke out boldly. Sir William Jones in his speech on the Reformation of Parliament went so far as to say the the managers of the Revolution did not complete their work, leaving some of the 'feudal poison' behind. He went on to quote Shakespeare's Lady Macbeth, saying, 'We have scotched the snake, not killed it.' For good measure he amplified his meaning in words that would appeal to the ordinary people of our island nation - '........another gale has now sprung up and unless you catch it while it blows it will be gone for ever.' It is understandable that only six of the forty two Cornish M.P.s were in favour of the new Bill which would oust them from their privileged position in Parliament. In the ensuing reorganisation of seats, Cornwall ceded thirty of them to large industrial towns. Voters such as the handful of property qualified voters from Tregony, who had repeatedly returned one generous Member to represent them in the House of Commons now found themselves swimming as small fish in the big sea of a large constituency. Richard Trevithick, Cornwall's idealistic engineer was so carried away with enthusiasm over the triumph of the 1832 Reform Bill that he wanted to build a 1,000 feet high commemorative column in London. It was to have an equestrian statue at the top. Sightseers from the provinces would be carried to the viewing platfrom by an air operated lift in the hollow column. Unfortunately he died in Dartford on the 22nd. April of the following year, leaving so little money that his workmates clubbed together to pay for the funeral.

There were to be two further Reform Bills during the stormy nineteenth century. The Bills of 1867 and 1884 complemented the all important Great Reform Bill of 1832 as it was known at the time. In addition, we must not forget Lord Shaftesbury and the Factory Acts, nor William Wilberforce and the abolition of slavery, nor the all important new ideas of religious toleration. These movements gradually forced Parliament to yield to the demands of the new industrial voters. The influence of these changes on life in the village of Coverack will be reflected in the examination of the work, religion and education of the villagers.

Towards the end of the stormy century, three memorable wrecks occurred. The accounts of what happened are well documented, but around the hard core of truth concerning the stranding of these vessels a persistent folklore has evolved, making it difficult for the casual reader to retain a clear picture in his mind. The newspapers which originally reported the events re-run their stories from time to time. They are popular, intriguing accounts and never fail to evoke a stream of correspondence. Some letters give further information which has been handed down by word of mouth in the families which were involved. Others point out errors in the report which differs from the stories they have heard repeated many times in their own homes. Occasionally the whereabouts of hitherto unrecorded mementoes are revealed. Of course, the local people know who has what, but they never blab about things like that. The Mohegan remained accessible at low tides for some while, so there was a preliminary 'stripping'. The proliferation of sub aqua clubs during the last two decades has resulted in the stripping of the underwater remains of two of these wrecks. Unfortunately this has resulted in the sunken ships continuing to exact their toll of human life from time to time.

The year 1891 is remembered in Cornwall as the year of the blizzard. When reading accounts of personal experiences, I am reminded of Baron Munchausen's highly coloured story of the traveller who was caught in a snowstorm. While making his way through a drift he stumbled against a metal object which turned out to be a weathercock at the top of a church steeple, so deep was the snow. My mother was born on the 19th. March, 1891. She often told us how her mother said one of her first tasks after recovering from my mother's birth was to scrape the snow off the bedroom windowsill. This conflicts with Mr. H.J. Sincock's first 'Illustrated Guide to the pretty and interesting Village of Coverack, Cornwall,' which was published in 1891 by J. Gaskill of 11 Ivy Lane, Paternoster Row, London, E.C. It cost two pence. Henry, or Harry Sincock as he was known in Coverack had been teaching in the village since 1876 and lived at Trevanion with his father, a widower and pensioner of the Royal Marines. Describing the climate of Coverack, the schoolmaster wrote, 'Frost has been unknown many winters, and in the present, (1890-1891) comparatively little has been experienced, and the ground is free of snow (except for a few days during the blizzard in March, and then not more than two or three inches deep - while in other parts of Cornwall at this time the snow was from 6' to 8' deep.)' A few pages further on in the Guide, Mr. Sincock describes the wreck of the Bay of Panama at Nare Point, a few miles to the north of Coverack, beyond Porthallow. He refers to 'the violent wind and blinding snowstorm.' It seems that Coverack really was living up to its reputation of having a Mediterranean type micro climate. The report in Lake's Falmouth Packet and Cornwall Advertiser on Saturday, 14th. March, 1891, confirmed there were drifts at Helston up to 6' and declared that 'the snow is spoken of as a near relation of an American blizzard.'

It is paradoxical that in spite of what Mr. Sincock wrote about frost being unknown, the School Board decided in February to hold their next meeting at Coverack 'as there has been several complaints made about the cold wind coming from the doors.' In addition, although there had been only two or three inches of snow in Coverack, the Board agreed to Mr. Sincock's request for two mats and a shovel at the subsequent meeting in Coverack Board School. Mr. Sincock's colleague in St. Keverne Churchtown Boys' School recorded in his School Log Book on Friday, 13th. March, 1891, 'No schooling since Monday as a snowstorm set in on Monday afternoon and continued nearly for the rest of the week and rendered it impossible for children to come to school.' The Headmistress of the Girls' School at St. Keverne recorded on the same day, 'A fall of snow has again made the roads impassable.' She had also recorded on the previous Tuesday, the date of the wreck of the Bay of Panama, 'Terrible snowstorm - only four present so could not keep school.'

Whatever the absolute truth is concerning the weather in Coverack at this time, it is certain that it was giving problems to the Bay of Panama. She was a fast four masted steel square rigged sailing ship bringing a cargo of jute from Calcutta to Dundee. It will be remembered that just before the beginning of the stormy century, John Harrison had won a prize for a chronometer which would enable a skilled captain to estimate his position to within a 30 mile radius after a period of six weeks at sea. Well, Captain David Wright had been at sea for over 15 weeks and was sailing close hauled up the Western Approaches in an easterly wind which was fast becoming a gale. As is often the case when there is east wind the visibility was poor owing to fog and mist. Having seen no land nor navigation mark for forty hours, and making little headway, the captain estimated that he was off the Lizard. He considered he should let his ship come before the wind and clear the land. Unfortunately the ship was well past the Lizard and the Manacle reef and was driven ashore at Nare Point at 1.30 a.m. on Tuesday, 10th. March. By now a full gale was in progress and the exhausted sailors who had spent days trying to work the ship now had to face the terrors of shipwreck.

Two rockets were fired. Captain Wright, his wife, three of the crew and Second Officer Allnutt who had fired the rockets were washed overboard. The members of the crew who were on deck were then ordered into the rigging by Chief Officer Bullock. No one saw the rockets. It was left to William Nicholls of Penare Farm, who was looking for his lost sheep, to find the ship on the rocks and report it to William Ashley, a Coastguard at Porthoustock. By now it was 2.30 a.m. The gale had worsened and it was impossible to launch the pulling and sailing lifeboat from Porthoustock beach. A message was sent to the Chief Officer of Coastguards at Coverack. He sent Coastguard Allen to get three horses from the farm and the Coverack Rocket Apparatus was hauled through the lanes to Nare. It was a slow, painful process through drifting snow, round and over uprooted trees. It took the Coastguards eight hours to get to the scene of the casualty. Chief Officer John Gibson set up the tripod as near to the level of the ship's hull as he could and fired the lane carrying rocket. Eighteen men were rescued by breeches buoy, thanks to the genius of Helston born Henry Trengrouse. The survivors, fourteen of whom were from the duty watch, were so cold that they had to be carried up the cliff from the Rocket Apparatus. John Gibson was surprised that some of the sailors he could see on the ship had not come down from the rigging to be rescued when the line was made fast. He was told by some Porthallow men that the men were probably frozen to the spars. These fishermen had been at the scene for some time and had themselves tried, unsuccessfully, to throw a weighted line aboard the stricken vessel. In spite of these assurances several of the seafaring men attending the wreck were not happy at leaving the scene before it was certain that no living person was left on board. They could imagine themselves in the same predicament as a survivor unable to draw attention to his plight, so to make absolutely certain that all survivors were accounted for, it was decided to check the wreck. Coastguard James Lewis, Coastguard Boatman William Pond-Fisher and fisherman William Barker from Coverack were hauled out to the Bay of Panama to make a thorough search. No further survivors were found so the line to the wreck was unshipped. It then appeared to some watchers there were now some survivors waving their arms. James Cliff, the fisherman from Manacle View volunteered to swim through the icy seas to double check, but it was decided that in view of the statements made by the three volunteers who had been aboard, nothing more could be done.

The survivors were taken to Penare Farm to warm up, then on to St. Keverne. When the roads were clear they were taken by waggon to Falmouth where they were provided with free railway passes and food for the journey to their homes by Mr. F.H. Earle, the Honorary Agent of the Shipwrecked Mariners Society. With the sixteen survivors travelling home by rail went six men from the Crusader and the survivors from three other ships that had foundered in the storm. They were the Agnes, the Helen and the Dundella. It is not surprising that in the chronicle of events of that week, the reporter from Lake's Falmouth Packet concluded, 'Nothing but anxiety, bad weather and vague reports of almost innumerable shipwrecks.' One of the divers subsequently engaged by a Captain Anderson to salvage the jute cargo from the Bay of Panama was Mr. John George Rowling of 11 Vernon Place, Falmouth. As a waterfront boy he had been a model for Henry Tuke's paintings. Mr. Rowling became one of the foremost divers of the Liverpool Salvage Association.

While the crew of the Bay of Panama was being rescued, another feat of endurance was taking place. Joseph H. James, a butcher from the Old Vicarage, St. Keverne, described in Lake's Falmouth Packet as 'a stalwart young fellow', set out on his pony for Helston. His task was to send a wire to Falmouth, giving news of the Bay of Panama. When he got to Helston, the telegraph wires were all down so he stabled his horse and set out on foot for Falmouth. He had a terrible journey. He became so exhausted that he reckoned he crawled the last one and a half miles on his hands and knees, his face coated with ice. Several times he had to break ice from his eyes. Icicles hung from his ears. The Packet takes up the story:

'More dead than alive he came across a cottage in the occupation of a mason named Combellack. Here he rested until Wednesday morning daylight, then went on and arrived at 9 a.m. and gave the message to Messrs. Broad and Sons (Agents for James Bullock's Bay Line of Bengal Clippers)'

Joe James, or Manacle Joe, as he became known to the people of Coverack when he came to live there, was later given a gold watch by a grateful shipping company. As soon as it was practicable, the Agents sent steamers from Falmouth to look for the wreck. The searchers found the ship deserted. The mainmast had gone overboard. There were six dead sailors tied to the rigging.

Mr. James was not the only person to receive a reward for his deeds on the night of the wreck of the Bay of Panama. As Mr. James was setting out from St. Keverne, James Roberts, the son of the owner of the then Coverack Hotel (known today as Channel View) was leaving Coverack on horseback with the intention of going to the Lizard. He had been asked by the Coastguards to go there to send a telegraph message about the wreck to the authorities in London. Mr. Roberts got to the Lizard in good time, considering the weather. It was not an easy journey. He had to take his life in his hands when negotiating some of the cliff top paths. On one occasion he had to call out a farmer to help him move an uprooted tree before he could continue his journey. A grateful government awarded £5 to Mr. Roberts for his determination in getting the message through. In fact, Mr. Newberry Cox, Postmaster at Falmouth recorded that he sent many important messages to London through the Spanish cables via Spain and France during the time after the blizzard when the lines were down. It is fitting that William Barker, James Lewis and William Pond-Fisher were eventually awarded the Board of Trade Silver Medal for Saving Life at Sea for their part in the rescue they carried out under such hazardous conditions. The bell from the Bay of Panama was placed in the turret of the chapel of ease near the Helford river which is on land belonging to Mr. Pendarves Vivian of Bosahan.

During the night of the wreck of the Bay of Panama, the steamer Helen, which belonged to the Coverack Stone Company, went ashore near Castle Point, St. Mawes. According to Lake's Falmouth Packet of Saturday, 16th. March, 1891, the steamer had her side stove in and six craft belonging to the Coverack Stone Company 'drifted about in various directions.' The blizzard had indirectly made its mark on the village of Coverack.

Seven years after the disaster of the Bay of Panama, on the 14th. October, 1898, the second of the three memorable wrecks referred to above occurred. It seemed all the more terrible as the stormy century appeared to be ending, meteorologically speaking, calmly and normally. Coverack regatta had been held late that year, on the 30th. August. The event of the day was the 32 footer Quay Punt Race. The fine weather had attracted boats from Falmouth. The Minnie Campbell won that race and the Look Out won the 28 footer class. The villagers were no doubt settling down after the busy summer and hoping for another mild winter when the steamship Mohegan struck one of the rocks of the Manacle Reef. Without knowing any of the circumstances, any sailor would tell you that it is not surprising the Mohegan foundered because her name had been changed from Cleopatra when she was still on the stocks. Once again, there were mysteries to be solved concerning a Manacle wreck.

The Mohegan, a practically new steamship of some 7,000 tons, left London on the 13th. October, 1898 - another omen, perhaps, but it was a Thursday, not a Friday. The ship had a crew of 104, including seven cattlemen. Fifty three passengers boarded at Gravesend. The ship then made her way down channel. At 2.30 on the afternoon of Friday, 14th. October the Mohegan requested Prawle Point Signal Station by flag hoist to report that all was well with the ship. She was indeed making good speed. Her engines had been troublesome on her maiden voyage, but there were no mechanical difficulties on this, her second voyage. The weather was mainly clear. The wind was coming from the south east and there were passing rain showers. As in the case of the emigrant ship John, in 1855, the Mohegan was in fact steaming too far to the north. Once more the twin lights of the Lizard were obscured from view as the ship was in the 'blind' sector. Some witnesses from Falmouth said later that she appeared to be heading for the Helford River or Nare Point when she made a large alteration of course as if turning to go back in the direction of Falmouth. She then came on the rocks from 'inside' the reef. It is difficult to pinpoint the position of a ship without the aid of a second cross bearing from the shore, but practised watchers would know whether or not the ship was standing into danger.

What is certain is that if the twin lights of the Lizard had been seen from the ship, the vessel would have lined up on them, passing about a mile south of the Manacles and cleared the Lizard. The chart of the English Channel at that time showed a straight dotted line which began at a point due south of Fowey and ended at the red 'blob' on the Lizard where it was clearly printed 'two Lights F', meaning two lights which were steady or fixed, not flashing. The dotted line had the clear advice 'lights in one' printed at its eastern or Fowey end of the line. This warning could hardly have been missed by a navigator who would have plotted the bearing of Start Point, then that of the Eddystone Lighthouse on the chart.

Unfortunately, no one knows for certain why the Mohegan was on the wrong course. Not one officer survived the wreck. The only other seamen who could comment on the course were the ship's Quartermasters. They are seamen who are employed to steer the ship, attend to the ship's log which records the distance run and generally assist the officer of the watch in the safe navigation of the ship. One surviving Quartermaster of the Mohegan was in fact a qualified First Mate and so more than adequately fitted for his post of responsibility. His name was John W.H. Juddery. He had just joined the Mogehan as an Able Seaman. Mr. Juddery had steered the ship on a West, ¾ North course from ten until noon. When he came on watch again at 4 p.m. he was asked to attend to the log and so did not know what course was being steered. Able Seaman Fred Butt, another surviving Quartermaster, steered the ship from 4 p.m. until 6 p.m. on a West by North course which was passed to him by the Quartermaster he relieved in the presence of the Chief Officer. Mr. Butt passed on the course at 6 o'clock when he in turn was relieved by Quartermaster August, who did not survive. This time the Second Officer was present. An hour later the ship struck the Vase Rock a glancing blow and went on another 3½ cables before hitting the Maen Varses Rocks or 'Voices' as they are known locally. These are two outer or eastern rocks of the triangular shaped reef which has the Carn Dhu at the northern point and the Minstrel at the southern end of the triangle.

Before the vessel struck her masthead lights were seen by the duty Coastguard John Charles May from Coverack. He reported the ship to his Chief Officer, Mr A.T. Jeffery and fired a rocket to warn the ship of her dangerous position. He then lit a blue ground light which burned while he was summoning the Rocket Brigade in anticipation of a casualty. The liner then disappeared from view, being obscured by the Lowland Point and the land rising behind it.

Shortly afterwards the Mohegan fired distress rockets. They were seen in Falmouth by Coastguard Boatman Charles Robert Snell. At the same time the Coastguard Patrolman at Stack Point, which is between Swanpool Beach and Rosemullion Head, also saw what he described as coloured lights in the direction of the Manacle Rocks. Unfortunately it took Mr. Snell an hour to get back to headquarters to report what he had seen. Luckily, however, the liner had also been spotted by a man who was probably the finest seaman on the south Cornish coast at the time. He was James Hill, coxn. of the Charlotte, Porthoustock's second lifeboat, which had been on station since 1886. Mr. Hill realised that the Mohegan was standing into danger and on his own initiative fired the maroon to summon the Charlotte's crew and to tell the liner that help was on the way.

The lifeboat was launched at 7.25 p.m. The spring tide had been ebbing for 1½ hours so the helpers did not have to drag the boat too far over the stony beach to get her afloat. After some time the coxn. burned a white flare to let the shipwrecked sailors know his position and in the hope of a response from the ship. There was no answering light. Eventually the Charlotte's crew rowed through some floating wreckage and then picked up a capsized ship's lifeboat with two men clinging to the bottom. They then discovered two ladies and a dead child beneath the upturned hull. At this point Mr. Hill's suspicions were confirmed and he realised that the wrecked ship was carrying passengers. He burned another flare in the hope of more assistance being summoned by the watching helpers on shore. He then continued his search of the area and came across a waterlogged ship's lifeboat with twenty four people on board. He realised that the ship's lifeboat would not reach the shore in that condition so decided to take the twenty four on board and return to Porthoustock. There was not a great deal of space in the pulling and sailing lifeboat for the sixteen crew, twenty eight survivors and the dead child.

Meanwhile, James Cliff, the Second Coxn. of the Charlotte who had arrived too late to go in the lifeboat was asked by Mr. Edward Roskruge the Lifeboat Secretary to go to sea to help as dreadful cries from seaward were being borne on the wind. Mr. Cliff set out with three Porthallow men, James Bastian, Charlie Bryant and Charlie Tripp. With them was William Pengilly the son of a Coverack man. He was home on leave from the Royal Navy. It was a long pull into the wind but the five men eventually got to the Carn Dhu Rock and then guided by the shouts they went out towards the Maen Varses and found the ship. They could not approach the sunken vessel in their small boat, nor could they take any one on board. After assuring the wretched survivors that help was coming they pulled their small boat back to Porthoustock to give the correct position of the ship. This part of the rescue was not mentioned in the inquiry, but Mr. Cliff gave a full account of it to Mr. P.W. Birkbeck who wrote Mr. Cliff's memoirs for him in 'Down to the sea in ships.'

It is impossible to imagine the full horror of that night. Shortly after the ship struck the rock at 7 p.m., all the lights went out and the crew and passengers were left in total darkness. Those who did not get away in the ship's boats had to wait until the liner's position had been pinpointed by the gallant Mr. Cliff and his crew. Then they had to wait a further agonising couple of hours before the Charlotte came out to take them off. It is not surprising that many more were washed off the ship by the pounding seas and drowned before rescue was at hand. It must be appreciated that these people were not waiting in the shelter of the ship's upperworks. They were clinging for dear life to anything which was still above water. The ship gradually settled down on the rocks until only a small part of the hull, the funnel and four masts were above water. Sheer exhaustion forced many to let go and be carried away in the surging seas.

The darkness was so complete that the Falmouth Lifeboat, under the command of Coxn. Frank Jose, was towed to the scene by the tug Penguin. The lifeboat never actually found the ship. The crew did manage to recover the body of a lady passenger. As time went on, the rescuers realised they had a major disaster on their hands and on receiving the signal for more assistance, the Cadgwith Lifeboat, Minnie Moon was sent for at 9.55 p.m. and the Lizard Lifeboat, Edmund and Fanny was sent for at 11.20 p.m. After a long pull to the scene, the lifeboats remained searching in the area until the early hours of the morning. It was too late. Both Coxns. later declared they should have been called earlier.

Meanwhile the Charlotte had put to sea again after landing the survivors they had picked up. This time the Second Coxn. was on board, so they were able to make straight for the wreck. Mr. James Hill took off sixteen survivors who were still clinging to the rigging and perched on the funnel. The Coxn. was unable to go alongside the sunken ship so Quartermaster John William Henry Juddery of the Mohegan swam to the Charlotte which had anchored off to give the boat some stability. Mr. Juddery then swam back to the ship with a line and the remaining survivors were pulled to the lifeboat. After a further fruitless search in the vicinity for other survivors, the lifeboat returned to Porthoustock.

While all this had been going on, Coverack people had not been idle. The Coastguards and their village helpers were so keen to get to the wreck that they had pushed the cart containing the Life Saving Apparatus up the hill to Main Dale before the horses arrived from the farm. When they got to Dean Point they fired a Rocket. This was at the suggestion of Canon Diggens of St. Keverne. It was realised that as they could not see the wreck from the shore, the wreck would be too far away for a line carrying rocket to be used to carry out a rescue. However, it was felt that the firing of the rocket might give some hope to the wretched people who were clinging to the rigging. In addition, there was the rather forlorn hope that a rocket might evoke an answering flare or light of some kind from the ship of one of her lifeboats, thus revealing the whereabouts of the casualty. In fact, the survivors reported later that the rocket went right over the ship and that it was the first glimmer of hope of rescue they had experienced since the ship struck the rocks.

The villagers of Porthoustock and St. Keverne had not been idle either. They were in the centre of things and had turned out in force to see if they could help in any way. Mr. Edward Roskruge had been the Hon Secretary of the Charlotte for twenty years and was accustomed to organising rescues and giving succour to survivors of shipwrecks. He asked the villagers to open their homes and prepare to give shelter to the survivors. He organised food for the exhausted lifeboat men and the shore helpers. Clothes were procured from St. Keverne shops which had opened up for the emergency. Mr. James Pengilly, the agent of the Shipwrecked Mariners' Society made sure all the survivors were provided with dry clothes and taken to homes where they would be well looked after. The Society was so impressed with Mr. Pengilly's untiring efforts that night and his subsequent caring for the bereaved families that they presented him with an Aneroid Barometer in recognition of his services. The Society spent in all £202, nine shillings and eight pence, which was a considerable sum in those days.

One can imagine the turmoil in the villages on the day after the wreck. Bodies were still being washed ashore. Dr. Leverton Spry of St. Keverne had worked throughout the night, tending the injured survivors, setting broken bones and seeing that the villagers who volunteered to take them into their homes knew how to continue their treatment. The next day the doctor had to continue the grim task of pronouncing life extinct in the bodies that were being cast up on the beaches of the Lizard peninsula. Arrangements for a mass burial had to be made. Some St. Keverne men were engaged in digging a huge grave. Coffins were hastily procured. The Watch House at Coverack served as a mortuary for those who were picked up by the Coverack fishermen and Coastguards. The Falmouth Packet and Cornwall Advertiser told of harrowing scenes in the churchyard at St. Keverne, with relatives recognising their loved ones, kissing their corpses and calling them endearing names. The account concluded '........bystanders turned away awestruck at the spectacle of such misery.' All this while the rain swept down on the gathering, 'the sky dark and threatening, and everything woebegone.'

The indefatigable Canon Diggens who had spent the night of the wreck helping on the shore later chose Acts 27, v.41 for his text at the memorial service. It tells of Paul's voyage to Rome. 'And falling into a place where two seas met, they ran the ship aground, and the forepart stuck fast and remained immovable, but the hinder part was broken with the violence of the waves.' After talking about the 'deep lesson of the brotherhood of sorrow', he concluded, 'That lesson might be taught in the school but it was only truly learned in the hour of trial and at such a time our narrow prejudices, our exclusiveness and petty distinctions all broke down.'

Canon Diggens did not then consider his duty was complete. He campaigned for a lighthouse in the vicinity of the Manacle Rocks. Mindful of the exhausting pull necessary to get the Charlotte out to the Mohegan, he suggested a lifeboat should be stationed at Coverack. In fact, Coverack is particularly vulnerable in a south east gale, but on the night of the wreck of the Pindos in 1912, the Coverack men proved Canon Diggens' point, that even in a south east gale it was possible to launch a lifeboat. Cannon Diggens also pointed out that the Life Saving Apparatus at Coverack had to be hauled up a steep hill before it could travel at any speed to a wreck near the Manacle Rocks and suggested that another set of apparatus should be established at the more central point of St. Keverne. He added that all lifeboats should carry search lights and be able to communicate with shore parties. These points were outlined in a letter he wrote to the Board of Trade after the wreck of the Mohegan.

The Court of Inquiry into the loss of the Mohegan considered all the possibilities that were outlined in Canon Diggens' letter to the Board of Trade and examined the details available from many angles. It concluded that the 106 people who lost their lives did so because of the fact that the Mohegan sank in fifteen minutes and was unable to indicate her position due to a chain of unfortunate circumstances, the main one being the sudden loss of power from her dynamos. The Court recommended that auxiliary oil lamps should be lit at night and be readily available on ships that were lighted by electricity. We are reminded that one of the factors which led to such a high loss of life in the capsizing of the cross-channel ferry Herald of Free Enterprise at Zeebrugge in March, 1987, was the failure of emergency lighting when the main dynamos failed and passengers could not find the escape routes. There are still lesssons to be learned from the loss of the Mohegan.

The Board also concluded that the wrong course was steered after passing the Eddystone. At that time the Variation in that area was almost 18° West. Variation is the difference between Magnetic North and True North. That means that True North was 18° West of Magnetic North. It therefore follows that either the Quartermaster was steering the wrong course and his error was not corrected by the Officer of the Watch, or the Officer calculated the course without making the correct allowance for the large Variation and the Quartermaster obeyed, quite correctly, his instruction. It seems unlikely that we shall ever know the truth as theories are all based on hearsay and there were no survivors who could give convincing evidence.

It goes without saying that Mr. Hill and his crew together with Mr. Juddery the Quartermaster of the Mohegan were highly praised for the vital part they played in the rescue of the 51 survivors. Mr. Hill was awarded the Silver Medal of the Royal National Lifeboat Institution and Mr. Juddery was given the Silver Medal of the Board of Trade.

An air of mystery still surrounds the sinking of the Mohegan. The survivors reported that the Master, Officers and crew behaved in the best traditions of the sea. It was unfortunate that the sudden listing to port of the ship prevented more rockets, which were stored on the port side, from being fired. It was also unfortunate that her wooden lifeboats were smashed to bits. One steel lifeboat got away. The others jammed in the falls. When some were washed ashore after the ship broke up, only one steel lifeboat had a hole in it. All the officers were drowned. But did the Captain really drown? It was reported that a headless corpse dressed in the uniform of a captain of The Atlantic Transport Company-was washed ashore in Caernarvon Bay in January, 1899. Was it Captain Griffiths or did Captain Griffiths, having miraculously survived the wreck, place a corpse on the beach in Wales in the hope that people would assume he had drowned. After all, Caernarvon Bay is a long way from the Manacle Reef. Would a body drift all that way round Lands End, up the Bristol Channel and into the Irish Sea without being spotted? Captain Griffiths had a Welsh name. He could have made his way back to Wales and arranged his own 'drowning'. But where could he have obtained a decomposed, headless corpse for his subterfuge? The idea is probably best left to a highly imaginative creator of local 'legend'! The surviving ship's doctor had testified that Captain Griffiths was in good health and he had told the doctor he was satisfied with the ship's progress and that he had himself overseen the navigation of the vessel since leaving the River Thames. Had he deliberately plotted the wrong course?

In the Register of Burials at St. Peter's Church at Coverack, 'An unknown male person drowned in the S.Ship Mohegan landed at Coverack' is recorded as having been buried on the 30th. October, 1898, more than a fortnight after the wreck. The man's age was given as 'about 35'. It is believed that this man was William Logan Hindmarsh, the Third Officer of the Mohegan. His grave is to be found at the back of the graveyard in Coverack, to the left of the Lych Gate. The inscription on the tombstone reads:

'In affectionate memory of William Logan Hindmarsh, Third Officer of S.S. Mohegan which was wrecked on the 'Manacle Rocks', Oct. 14th., 1898. Interred Oct. 29th., 1898. Aged 30 years.'

The verse dedicated to his memory is:

'He sent from above, he took me

He drew me out of many waters.' (2 Sam. xxii v.17)

At the base of the stone is inscribed:

'This stone was erected by the people of Coverack.

Assisted by the owners of the ship.'

Canon Diggens was the person who performed the burial ceremony and he signed the entry in the register. It does seem odd but nevertheless not impossible that this body should wash ashore in Coverack a couple of weeks after the wreck while the body of the Captain took three months to make its way to Wales.

One macabre story that I've heard many times in Coverack relates how one of the fishermen found a lady passenger with shoulder length fair hair and wearing a lovely evening gown, floating on her back in the sea off Coverack. He hauled her into his boat and placed her in a sitting position in the stern sheets. As the boat was entering the harbour at Coverack the lady's hands, which were adorned with expensive rings, slipped over the side and trailed in the water as if she were testing the temperature of the sea. Thinking that the lady had miraculously revived, the fisherman was heard by the assembled onlookers to utter, 'Won't 'ee speak to me, old girl?'

The Mohegan lies in 12 to 14 fathoms of water. The wreck was inspected by conventional divers in 1912. Hundreds of articles were brought to Coverack Quay where they were put up for auction. At Parc Behan, the Youth Hostel on School Hill in Coverack, the mahogany stairs are those which were salvaged from the liner Mohegan. During the last couple of decades, the ship has been well 'dived' by clubs using very sophisticated equipment. Souvenirs of all kinds have found their way into many homes in the parish. It seems almost certain that no further mysteries lie hidden in the murky depths.

After the wreck, some of the local fishermen got aboard at low water and brought back mementoes. A Porthoustock man was intent on getting a pair of binoculars from the bridge. When he approached the bridge he met a

Coverack man who was a pilot of the stone carrying barges which went into the landing below Trebarveth Farm. The Coverack man had already found the binoculars so the Porthoustock man had to be content with a telescope which had the name Mohegan inscribed on it. The two men did not speak to each other for years after this incident. One of the great grandsons told the writer he had to wait a long time before he could discover why the two seamen always ignored each other. The telescope is still in the possession of a member of the Porthoustock man's family but the whereabouts of the binoculars are not known.

The Atlantic Transport Company did everything in its power to alleviate the pain and grief of the passengers and crew of the Mohegan and their relatives. The company even paid for some of the bodies to be embalmed by Dr. Leverton Spry and taken back to the United States. They were taken across the Atlantic on the Mohegan's sister ship 'Marquette'. The coffins were in packing cases marked 'Machinery' to allay any fears the crew might have had about carrying dead bodies on the ship. The company showed its gratitude to the people of the parish by presenting three new east windows to the church. They bore the inscription, 'To the glory of God and in memory of the 106 persons who perished in the wreck of the S.S. Mohegan on the Manacle Rocks, October 14th., 1898.' The left hand window is a portrayal of St. Keverne and of Jesus stilling the storm. The central window depicts Jesus holding the orb with an inset of His saving St. Peter on the Sea of Galilee. The right hand window shows St. Christopher, the patron saint of travellers, carrying the infant Jesus. It also shows the scene of St. Paul's shipwreck at Malta. A tall Celtic Cornish Cross marks the mass grave which is situated close to the north door of the church. The simple inscription at the base of the cross is MOHEGAN.

THE MOHEGAN, WRECKED ON THE MANACLES, 1898
*This photo is a poignant warning to all mariners.*
*In 1902 the bell buoy was replaced by a can gas and bell buoy,*
*exhibiting a white occulting light.*

The company also presented a drawing of the Mohegan for Mr. Ralph Clayton, the Schoolmaster at St. Keverne, for 'services rendered'. The inquest was held at St. Keverne school in the afternoon of the 17th. October, 1898. On April 17th., 1899, a tea party was held in the school in connection with the ceremony of unveiling the new stained glass windows. The following day, Mr. Williams, the London chairman of the Atlantic Transport Company, visited the school and 'addressed a few words of encouragement and advice to the boys.'

Each time the church bells ring out at St. Keverne, some of the local people remember that Bell No. 5 was placed in the tower by William Neil King of Cincinatti, Ohio. He had it put there in memory of his brother, Worthington King, who was lost, with all his family, on that dreadful night. A new peal of eight bells was dedicated by the Bishop of Truro on the 9th. May, 1907 when the Lord Mayor of London, Sir William Treloar, second cousin of Porthoustock Coxn. James Henry Treloar Cliff, paid a ceremonial visit to the village for the occasion.

The only 'literary' work resulting from the Mohegan that I have found is a narrative poem by W. Quintrell of Camborne. I came across it in a book which belonged to my maternal grandfather, John Pengilly. It was his son, my step uncle, who went with four others in a small rowing boat to locate the wreck. The poem tells the story of the wreck with some accuracy if not with finesse. It ends with a typical Victorian type admonition:

'Unless we heed the rudder,

The rocks will bring us grief

And like this ship, shall perish

On life's great rugged reef.'


The poet expressed the hope in the preface that his poems might be a means of 'inspiring someone to a labour of love in a spirit of greater brotherhood.' It is not known whether his Mohegan poem had any influence, although it has been used frequently as a monologue in the St. Keverne Parish in recent years. What is certain is that the public outcry after the disaster led to the establishment of a lifeboat station at Coverack. This was to change the character of the village. It is for this reason that the story of the Mohegan, which in the main belongs to the history of Porthoustock and St. Keverne is related in this chronicle of Coverack.

The Blackwater born philanthropist, John Passmore Edwards, joined Canon Diggens in the campaign for a lighthouse near the Manacle Rocks. He wrote that he was prepared to build a Manacle Lighthouse in memory of Adams the astronomer. He added that as Adams and Leverrier discovered the planet Neptune he was prepared to build another lighthouse on the French coast opposite, 'so that both should acknowledge with luminous nods the dominant claims of commerce and the brotherhood of nations.' After some discussion at Falmouth, the scheme fell through. The authorities there persuaded John Passmore Edwards that a hospital and free library would be 'more acceptable and useful.'

All was not lost, however. After the wreck of the Paris in 1899, it was with great relief that the Masters of ships about to pass by the Manacle Rocks on their next voyage, read Admiralty notice to Mariners No. 651. It stated:

'The Trinity House, London, has given further notice, dated 9th. September, 1902, that the bell buoy marking the Manacle Rocks has been replaced by a can gas and bell buoy, painted with black and white stripes, without topmark, and exhibiting a WHITE OCCULTING light giving one eclipse every ten seconds.' The charted approximate position of the buoy was not changed. It was still 0.65 cables (130 yards) from the Pen-win Rock. It is impossible to calculate how many lives have been saved by the presence of the light. It is just as impossible to calculate how many lives were lost before the light was placed there. What matters is that a light has been established near the Manacle Rocks.

The third of the trio of important wrecks to occur in the last decade of the stormy century was the Paris. As in the case of the Mohegan, her owners were perhaps inviting disaster as the American Line had changed her name from City of Paris to Paris when they bought her from the Inman Line. Just seven months after the Mohegan disaster, the Paris struck the Little Wrea Rock which is off Lowland Point, about 9 cables (1,800 yards) from the Maen Varses or 'Voices' where the Mohegan foundered. It was Whit Sunday, May 21st., 1899. The Paris was making way down channel from Cherbourg. The sea was calm, but visibility was poor owing to fog and mist. Once more the ship's navigator was at fault.

The 10,669 ton liner with a total of 438 people on board managed to steam across the main shipping lines from Cherbourg and after narrowly missing the Manacle Rocks, struck the Little Wrea just before one o'clock in the morning. Fortunately the ship's distress rockets were seen and Porthoustock Lifeboat, the faithful Charlotte was launched. This time the approximate position of the wreck was known and the lifeboat saw her lights through the mist and came alongside. Although the ship was fast to the bottom, she was not taking in any water and so not in imminent danger of foundering.

Meanwhile the long suffering Coastguards from Coverack, with their faithful helpers, had once more hauled the Life Saving Apparatus out to the Lowlands and got a line aboard the ship so that people could be taken off if a dangerous situation developed. Fortunately, the ship was wedged on the rocks, but safe. A message was sent to Falmouth and in a couple of hours the tug Triton arrived with Falmouth Lifeboat in tow. The two lifeboats then transferred the 366 passengers and some of the non essential crew to the Triton which took them to Falmouth. It was then, in the light of day, when the mist had cleared, that the ship's crew and passengers could see the masts and funnel of the Mohegan sticking up out of the water by the jagged Maen Varses. There must have been many prayers of thankfulness offered when those on board realised how fortunate they had been. What would have happened if those 432 people had been wrecked on the Manacle Rocks does not bear thinking about. As there were no casualties, there was no sensational inquiry. The Court findings gave no hint of mystery, being content with the finding of 'an unaccountable error of judgment' in the navigation of the ship.

It was July before six tugs managed to get the ship off the rocks. Her own kedge anchors were taken by boat and dropped some way astern. By heaving on these with her steam winches, she helped to pull herself off the rocks. The ones which were most likely to impede the smooth slide of the Paris off the bottom had already been dynamited by the divers who had been preparing the ship for refloating.

It goes without saying that while the Paris was on the Lowlands, she became a place of pilgrimage. For once there had been a wreck with no casualties and local people were able to make the visit a pleasant outing. Some went on board and marvelled at the luxurious furnishings and fittings. Coverack born villager Mrs. Agnes Hocking (nee Bowden) told me, when I talked to her about the wreck, that up to the time the Paris hit the Little Wrea, she was not interested in the sea, but when she saw lots of visitors and villagers going out to see the beautiful three funnelled liner, she made her first trip in a boat at the age of ten. She took her dog Nell with her for company. With a sigh she added, 'We used to have lovely visitors then, bishops and people like that.' In an article describing the Whit week end of 1899, a West Briton reporter stated that the wreck of the Paris attracted thousands of people in vehicles of various kinds - 'in spite of wind and weather.'

The Paris, in the shape of the Paris Hotel which was built in 1905, has continued to attract villagers and visitors. The latter can never resist asking the locals how the hotel got its name. Locals have never failed to give an explanation, in return for a little liquid refreshment.

After the Paris was towed to Falmouth she was patched up and taken to Belfast via Milford Haven. She went to sea again in August, 1901 on the Southampton-Cherbourg-New York run. Harland and Wolfe's shipyard had taken away one funnel and provided her with new quadruple expansion engines. The company daringly changed her name to Philadelphia. You will not be surprised to learn that on January 9th., 1914, she got into trouble again. This time she made another acquaintance with the Cornish rocks. She was steaming in thick fog, making for Plymouth when she ran aground near Rame Head. Once more she was lucky. She refloated on the next tide. Once more there were no casualties. The 300 passengers landed safely in Plymouth.

The following year, in 1902, the first wireless messsage was sent from Poldhu in Cornwall to Signal Hill near St. John's in Newfoundland. Marconi, whose yacht Electra used to anchor frequently in Coverack Bay at that time, used the Philadelphia in the same year to continue his experiments. He installed a transmitter and receiver in one of the ship's cabins and subsequently discovered that it was possible to receive a signal from a distance of 2,099 miles at night whereas the daytime range was only 700 miles. In 1917, during the First World War, the Philadelphia was taken over by the United States government and converted into an armed transport. Once again her name was changed. This time it was to Harrisburg. The ship survived the war and in 1920 went back on her old run between America, France and England. After two years she was sold to the New York and Naples Steamship Company. Once more her name was changed - back to Philadelphia. The ship was on her way to Constantinople to collect immigrants for the States when mutiny broke out and she was forced to put in to Naples. She did not go to sea again. She was taken to Genoa and broken up there in 1923. Her luck had finally run out. It was a sad end for a ship that had won the Blue Riband of the Atlantic in 1899.

An interesting sequel to the story of the Paris is that when Mr. R.J. Stewart visited Coverack for the first time he recognised the Paris in a picture he saw at the Hotel. His father had owned a painting of the ship which always hung over his bed. Mr. Stewart knew that his father had been an engineer on the Paris but it was only then that he discovered his father had been wrecked at Coverack. Mr. Stewart has now made his home in the village.

The wreck of the Paris at the end of the nineteenth century forced responsible people to yield to the demands which seafarers and those living on the coast had been making for scores of years. The latter had borne the brunt of the tragedies throughout the stormy century even to the extent of losing their own lives in their attempts to help mariners in distress. The new twentieth century began with a new lifeboat at Coverack and a new light on the Manacle Bell Buoy. Who could have foreseen then that long before the new century was over, Coverack would no longer have a lifeboat? Furthermore, who could have predicted that in 1987, when the government announced an increase in the fee for ships passing lighthouses, the shipping companies would warn that they were considering the possibility of avoiding calls at British ports. The reason for this extraordinary attitude was that their navigational equipment was so sophisticated, they considered lighthouses were no longer essential to mariners.

# THE SIX 'S's

The Six 'S's are salt, seaweed, sand, stones, smuggling and seining. They have played an important part in the development of the village of Coverack and explain to a certain extent why the village can be likened to an oasis. The nineteenth century mingles with the twentieth in some of the subsequent chapters. One could say that in all the essentials the nineteenth century rolled on in Coverack until the first World War and the twentieth emerged as the men were returning to Lloyd George's 'fit country for heroes to live in.'

## Salt

In the chapter entitled 'Beginnings' it was stated that salt was produced at the Lowlands raised beach. There is anecdotal evidence of this ancient activity, backed by the possibility, which has also been mentioned before, of the area deriving its very name from the Cornish language word 'holan', meaning salt. As there is no geological evidence of the presence of salt, the production probably took the form of evaporation of sea water being heated in huge pans. It would have been easy to channel the sea water to the pans as the land is only just above sea level and there would have been abundant furze available to provide the fuel. Today we admire gorse for its lovely, rich yellow flowers. We are inclined to forget that in a poor local community which had no deposits of coal, furze or gorse was used as a fuel. One of the most frequent requests to the Overseers of the Poor from ageing widows in the eighteenth and nineteenth centuries was for a load of furze. The Overseers charged on the expense sheets for the special 'furze gloves' their men used when handling the prickly plant which grew in abundance in the parish. There was also plenty of peaty turf available from Dolly's Field which is reasonably close to the Lowlands. Goonhilly Downs was also a good source of fuel.

The Lowland Point could have got its name simply because it is a low lying raised beach. In spite of the nearby rocky reefs, the headland has always attracted sea borne trade. Traders could have exchanged salt for local stone, thus giving the Lowland Point its connection with salt. In Penlee House Museum, Penzance, is a Bronze Age urn which was unearthed at Dean Point just a short distance North North East of the Lowland Point. The relic is known as the St. Keverne Urn. It contained fragments of human bone when found. This slender evidence helps to support the idea that there was a settlement at the Lowland Point in ancient times. Whether or not commerce in salt was carried on there still remains to be proved conclusively, but as some Lizard pots, thought to have been used to contain salt, have been found on the continent, it does seem likely. The pots are distinctive in that there are black and white particles of gabbro in them. This indicates that they could have been made in the region of the Lowland Point.

After Coverack Quay was built in the early eighteenth century, salt was stored in sheds, or more appropriately, cellars as they were called in Coverack. These cellars were close to the Quay. There is no doubt that salt was imported in considerable quantities up to the final decline of the seining industry early in this century. The salt was brought by sea. French salt was very much in demand for the purpose of preserving pilchards. This was because the pilchards remained in an edible state for a longer period when packed in French salt and the continental customers preferred to eat their prescribed fish before it had deteriorated too much on the long journey from protestant England. It is not generally known that salt was 'smuggled' from salt cellars to locals not engaged in the fishing industry. The seiners were allowed duty free salt. It was inevitable that when times were bad, the cheaper subsidised salt was sold at an advantageous price to their friends and acquaintances by the seiners. This would mean that most of the villagers were implicated, so no one complained to the authorities. When the salt had lost its savour it was mixed with seaweed and sand together with any rotting pilchards available. The revolting mixture was then sold to the neighbouring farmers as a fertiliser. This practice was mentioned in 'Beginnings'.

## Seaweed

The practice of utilising seaweed to manure the land has gone on ever since man cultivated land close to the oceans. Mention has already been made of seaweed being carried in panniers on the backs of donkeys up the cliff from Barker's Beach to the gardens of Coverack. In addition the land now used as a car park close to the cliff at Higher Bridge was used as a storage space for seaweed and sand from the Mill Beach. Rotting fish was added at appropriate moments. Local farmers staked their claims on the spaces by laying straight parallel lines of stones across the ground at right angles to the hill road. The seaweed, which is often called ore weed in Coverack, would be carted to the farms when needed or when there was a lull in the work on the farm. There was a cart track to the bottom of the cliff at the Higher Bridge end of Mill Beach. It was on the eastern side of the small bridge at the foot of the hill. This has recently been eroded by the sea. Present day visitors will note that a load of huge boulders has been dumped over the low cliff by the bridge to prevent further intrusion by the sea.

## Sand

Coverack sand is silver, not gold in colour. It is one of the best types of sand in Cornwall for making sand castles, being coarse enough to bind together to make a definite shape and soft enough to walk on without getting irritating stone particles collecting between the toes. Coverack has the advantage of having two beaches. This means there is always a clear beach available for recreation. When the Mears Beach in Porthbeer Cove has been denuded of sand and seaweed and its accompanying rubbish, the Mill Beach has plenty. Conversely, the Mears Beach has lots of sand and seaweed etc. when there is little at the Mill Beach. This is due to the wind. An easterly gale draws sand from the Mears Beach and the Mill Beach fills with sand. A south westerly gale will put it back on the Mears with plenty of wreck wood

34

and unfortunately plenty of plastic rubbish. Not many people are aware of the Merchant Shipping (Prevention of Pollution by Garbage) Regulations of 1988 which state that the disposal of any plastic into the sea is prohibited, nor that garbage can not be placed in the sea within twelve miles of land unless it has been passed through a grinder. Then the minimum is three miles. When this Act begins to take effect, our Cornish beaches will regain some of their former unspoilt beauty.

In limited quantities Coverack sand is good for the garden, especially when mixed with seaweed. Otherwise, sand has not played an important part in the development of the village, except as a tourist attraction. There was a small supply of sand close to the site of the Wesleyan Chapel. It was dry and unsalted. There is none left.

The sand from the beaches of Coverack is very salt and needs a great deal of washing by the rain before it can be used in building. When it is used before it is clear of salt, mysterious damp patches appear on walls, especially when the atmosphere is humid. This ruins the paint and wallpaper. The only cure is to rebuild the wall. Coverack builders have learned that it is more prudent to get building sand from Gunwalloe or elsewhere and leave Coverack sand where it belongs - on the beach. At one time, builders would prepare a sand pit and a lime pit on a building site and then let the rain do its job of cleansing and slaking for a couple of months or more before commencing building operations. That leisurely way of proceeding has disappeared in the age of instant action.

## *Stones*

The Coverack area is noted for its stones. Geologists come to inspect and take samples from the 'dykes' of troctolite, gabbro and epidiorite which have intruded upon the basic serpentine. The serpentine and the criss crossing dykes do not combine to make an impenetrable bulwark against the sea. On the 17th. February, 1841, a 'Vestry' was held by the Overseers of the Poor and the Waywardens, 'to consult re building cliff at Coverack, lately broken by the violence of the sea.' Notices were duly posted in the village asking people to attend a site meeting. It was decided to get the job done. Tenders were duly received and Walter Nicholls was given the work. He agreed to rebuild the cliff at Coverack with stone five feet thick from the face of the wall to the back. The Overseers were not exaggerating when they said there had been a violent storm. There were three sections to be constructed.

1.          17½ feet long by 12 feet high.

2.          22 feet long by 11 feet high.

3.          23½ feet long by 16 feet high.

The work was to be 'firm and strong and to be inspected by Mr. Richard Trerise of Trevallack.' On condition that a satisfactory job was done, the Churchwarden, Overseers and Waywardens promised to pay Mr. Nicholls £18 for the work he had undertaken. It is pointless to attempt to compare this price with those of today. It is doubtful if Walter Nicholls made much money out of the work. At least he did have employment during the hard winter and could provide work for others. In order to get the job he had to undercut his competitors. William Mitchell in partnership with George Nicholls wanted £23 for the rebuilding of the cliff. James Pentecost's tender was for £25. In October, 1988 it was calculated by Kerrier Council's professional advisers that it would cost £370,000 to renew an eighty metre stretch of Coverack sea wall at the point where the road was most likely to collapse. I wonder what the nineteenth century builder Walter Nicholls would have thought of that? The Cliff at Coverack has always required attention. Storm damage has often been a blessing in disguise, providing much needed money in the village during the winter when work is difficult to obtain.

From 16th. March to the 2nd. May, 1931 storm damage to the cliff at Coverack provided work for my father, grandfather, brother, John White, Bert Carey, Dick Rowe and Percy Eustis. The two masons, my father and grandfather earned one shilling and four pence an hour. The apprentice, my brother George, got eight pence per hour and the labourers eleven pence. The total earned during the seven weeks it took to repair the hole in the cliff was £96, twelve shillings. The haulage costs were £27 and one shilling. This involved the hire of a horse and cart to carry 67 loads of gravel, 18 loads of sand and 36 loads of stone. Five loads of stone came from the Wesleyan Chapel grounds, five were bought from elsewhere (these would be large boulders) and the remainder were from the beach itself. The total cost of the repair was £142, eight shillings and sixpence according to my father's account book.

In the year 1937 another winter storm meant another repair job to the cliff. The masons received the same rate of pay as in 1931 but the labourers received one penny an hour extra and the night watchman, who was Tim Connor, received six shillings and four pence for making sure that no one fell in the hole in the road after dark and keeping the warning oil lamps alight all night. The job lasted from the 29th. March until the 31st. July and kept my father, grandfather and five labourers in work. My father did not name the men working for him. I assume they came and went according to availability. The labour costs were £330, eighteen shillings and four pence. I note that an account rendered had to be sent to the County Council. They paid up, but found my father had overcharged by eight shillings and claimed the money back. This time the firm was mechanised. A lorry was hired for the haulage of the gravel, sand and stone. The cost was four shillings and six pence per hour for the lorry and driver. Ten tons of sand and twelve tons of gravel were bought and the rest of the material for filling the hole was found locally. The cost of the lorry and the wages of the men filling it was the only expense. There was such an amount of lifting gear used in the operation that my father indulged in the luxury of hiring the lorry to carry it to and from his cellar in the old Snell's Coy, seine loft. Usually my grandfather and my father would use wheel barrows or a handcart to carry the wooden scaffolding poles, ropes, pulley blocks and chains to the cliff. They would set the gear up before bringing the labourers to the site, unless one or two happened to be seamen who had the skill to do the square lashings and other knots needed to make the sheerlegs and lifting equipment safe. There was plenty of work in the village in 1937. The water mains were installed, necessitating deep trenches in all the roads and on May 23rd. electricity was switched on in the 'ordinary' houses. Some of the large houses had their own private generators. The villagers were not over enthusiastic about the benefits of the power placed at their disposal. As an inducement for agreeing to have power laid on, they were offered three light points wired free, together with three free lampshades. Many houses made do with three lights for some years and there are still a few free fifty year old glass shades to be seen in use in the village.

CLIFF REPAIRS, 1930s
*Left to Right, Tim Connor, night watchman, Johnny Williams, Cap'n Jim Hart, Mr. Triggs, Council Foreman, George and Tony Gilbert (Mullion), Dick Rowe, Harold Martin*

CLIFF REPAIRS, 1930s STYLE.
*Tony Gilbert and his brother George are seen hauling a boulder up the cliff on the sheer legs. Cap'n Jim Hart is directing operations at the top.*

There have been various attempts to solve the problem of cliff erosion. One scheme, proposed in 1948, was to carve a slice out of the churchyard, cutting through the graves and the War Memorial. The road into the village would then be further away from the sea and not so easily undermined by the powerful undertows created in storm conditions. It is not difficult to imagine the villager's response, especially as surveyor's pegs were placed in the burial ground before any consultation had taken place. Led by the Vicar, the Rev. John Brown, the villagers held a protest meeting. The press was informed and after the 'Daily Mirror' headline 'Village demands, 'Leave dead in peace.' ' was read and discussed in homes throughout Great Britain, the scheme was wisely left in abeyance. Part of the Sentence of Consecration document signed when St. Peter's Church was dedicated on the 20th. August, 1885 reads:

'The said Chapel with the land and site where the same is built ought so to remain FOR EVER........'

The capitals are the author's to illustrate why there was no way in which the County Council could take away part of the church field from the parishioners.

Coverack does not have a council of its own. It is a Ward of St. Keverne Parish. The same councillors are returned year after year and most people are quite happy with this democratic arrangement. However, when something crops up which threatens the routine serenity of village life, there are mutterings and veiled threats. If these warning signs fail to persuade the would-be innovators to abandon their scheme, more positive action is taken and the village people stand solidly together until the threat goes away. To return to the idea of the stone cliff providing financial help in hard times, it must be pointed out that today the monetary aid is only indirect. The use of modern machinery has ensured that there is no need for a local labour force when work has to be done on the village cliff.

At one time there was a quarry in the village itself. The present Methodist Chapel was built in 1861 on '........ all that plot or piece of ground formerly a quarry ........ bounded on the North by the High Road leading into Coverack, on the East by the road leading to a place there called Sunny Corner, on the South by lands of Joseph Saunders and on the West by a sand plot now used by John Roberts and measuring (boundary limits) from North to South about 60 feet and from East to West about sixty feet.' It was leased for 99 years from 13th. February, 1860. The owner was still entitled to 'work, dig, search for and carry away all mines, minerals and metals.' Ralph Arthur Frederick William Ellis, descendant of the builder of Coverack Quay was to be paid five shillings a quarter as ground rent for a Chapel measuring 34 feet in length, 31 feet in breadth and 20 feet in height. It was to have a slate roof and had to be built within twelve months by William Rule Roberts, Farmer, the lessee. The Chapel Trustees were indeed wise men to build their house on a rock as advised in Matthew 7, v.24 as the chapel is in an exposed position on the side of a steep hill.

There was another small quarry at North Corner. When that ran out of stone, rocks were brought down to the quarry by farmers from the hinterland as they cleared rough pasture in the stony, hilly fields for cultivation. Steam stone crushers were stationed at North Corner on the plot of land opposite the Bus Shelter. The machines remained there until after the First World War. Flat bottomed sailing barges would beach at North Corner and load the crushed stone at low water, then they would leave Coverack Bay on the flood tide. Sometimes they were caught there in a south easterly wind and had to be towed to safety by the local fishermen. The latter were much amused when an unsuspecting skipper allowed the carters to overload his barge with heavy stone, preventing it from refloating when the tide came in. There would be a mad scramble to lighten the craft before it was flooded by the sea. Cart horses have been seen actually swimming back to dry land with their carts floating behind them when they have been involved in such an operation.

When the one remaining Coverack stone quarry at North Corner was running out of material, Mr. James Pengilly of Trebarveth Farm decided to supplement the supply by founding the Coverack Stone and Syenitic Paving Company Limited. He began working the stone on his land at the Lowland Point. He supplied huge quantities of small 'rough' stones to St. Mawes, Penryn, Truro, Plymouth and Falmouth Docks. In due course, another enterprise, the St. Keverne Stone Company, installed an 'Artificial Stone Works' at the docks. This produced some of the finest paving stones on the market at that time. The same plant also manufactured concrete bricks from the crushed stone. The bricks had the advantage of being ready for use by builders a fortnight after they were made. The following details taken from Mr. Pengilly's 'Bills of Lading' indicate the extent of the work done by the Coverack Stone and Syenitic Paving Company Limited in the late nineteenth century.

| DATE | VESSEL | CAPTAIN | CARGO | DESTINATION |
|------|--------|---------|-------|-------------|
| 1890 | | | | |
| 3rd. Apr. | Daisy | John Bellmore | 30 tons | Mr. Parry, Polvarth C.,. St. Mawes. |
| 5th. Apr. | Katie | Tregaskis | 43 tons | do. |
| 29th. Jul. | Fanny | X* | 55 tons | do. (from Coverack) |
| 30th. Jul. | Alma | Arthur Trudgon | 60 tons | St. Mawes (from Coverack) |

| | | | | |
|---|---|---|---|---|
| 7th. Aug. | Katie | Tiddy | 45 tons | do. (from Coverack) |
| 7th Aug. | Fanny | Trudgon | 50 tons | do. (from Coverack) |
| 12th Aug. | Helen | J.J. Hallett | 65 tons | Plymouth Corporation |
| 13th. Aug. | Alma | Trudgon | 60 tons | Mr. Parry, Polvarth Co., St. Mawes. |

1890 (cont.)

| | | | | |
|---|---|---|---|---|
| 17th. Sep. | Daisy | Paull | 50 tons | Boat Road |
| 30th. Sep. | Lasso'go | X* | 55 tons | do. |
| 30th. Sep. | Helen | Trudgon | 70 tons | Mr. Chubb, Penryn |
| 31st. Oct. | Lass | Trudgon | 55 tons | Boat Road |

1891

| | | | | |
|---|---|---|---|---|
| 7th. Feb. | Fanny | Profit | 48 tons | do. |

X* indicates the mark of the Captain made on the Bill of Lading. He was unable to sign his name, but was capable of manoeuvring a sailing vessel in those dangerous waters.

* * * *

Note that the skippers were not always in command of the same vessels and that at this time stone was still being taken from the quarry at North Corner. It will be recalled that in March, 1891 on the night of the wreck of the Bay of Panama, the Helen, described as a steamer by the Falmouth Packet, went ashore at St. Mawes. The Helen was probably the sailing barge mentioned in the above list. Six other Coverack Stone Company's craft were set adrift by the storm.

* * * *

In 1798 John Loudon Mc.Adam moved to the Falmouth area where he pursued his experiments in road making. He was paid by the government to conduct trials in order to produce a regular road surface which would enable coaches to proceed at a faster rate. It is interesting to note that John Loudon Mc.Adam came to work in Falmouth officially as a Prizemaster. His job was to represent ship captains who brought captured 'prizes' into Falmouth. He settled in Flushing and remained there until 1802 when the Treaty of Amiens brought the long war between Great Britain and France to a temporary close. Mc.Adam's invention of the use of a top smooth layer of compacted small stones meant that a constant supply of small crushed stones was needed all over the country. What better county than Cornwall to meet the demand? It was not until June, 1886, however, that the West Briton, ever anxious to promote industry in the county, expressed its delight at being able to report that capitalists were investing in '........the invaluable materials obtainable in Cornwall for road making at a mere nominal cost.' Many roads in the Coverack area, in fact, had an even surface because the top layer was of yellow rab which was dug from the Rab Pit at the Beacon. This gravelly yellow clay, though 'messy' for walkers, compacted well and gave wheeled traffic a relatively smooth ride. The pit, when exhausted, was used as a refuse dump until it was full, then it was sealed off with a layer of top soil. The West Briton did not mention this, but announced the formation of the Coverack Stone Company, observing that the hardest stone called syenite (gabbro) was to be found between the Manacle Rocks and Coverack cove. The article also pointed out that before the invention of dynamite, which Alfred Nobel had patented in Britain in 1867, it had been impossible to produce syenite in the form of small crushed stones at an economic price.

For many years until well into the twentieth century it was a common sight to see men at work on large piles of stones which had been deposited by the roadside in convenient lay-bys. These stones were as excavated by the quarrymen and were too large for the top layer of road surfaces, so the men, who were known as 'stone cracker Johns' or 'spallers' hammered and split the stones into the correct size. They were paid by results and received so much per cubic yard. They had to make rectangular piles three feet in height so that the surveyors from the county Highways Department could measure easily the amount of stone that had been prepared. The men had a strange, sinister appearance as they wore metal gauze 'spectacles' to protect their eyes from the splinters. John Loudon Mc.Adam's son William came to Truro from the Office of Roads at Exeter. He was employed to run the Truro Roads which were maintained from funds received from Turnpike Tolls. William improved on his father's 'Directions for the repair of an old road' by ordering the small stones in the top layer to be 2 inches across instead of six as his father had advocated. A story is told about William

McAdam. He instructed his 'spallers' to gauge the size of the prepared stones by making them small enough to put into their mouths. The engineer had problems on one stretch of road where the top layer was not settling down properly. On investigation he discovered that the 'spaller' had such a large mouth that all his stones were too big and were consequently ruining the road surface! The introduction of screening equipment in local quarries gradually forced the 'spallers' to seek other employment in the stone industry.

The turn of the century saw a dramatic increase in stone production. Metalled roads were becoming more popular because of the invention of the internal combustion engine. By 1910, local quarries had multiplied. There was a Dean Coverack Quarry Company, managed by Mr. Fred. Roberts. Mr. George Brook was in charge of the St. Keverne Stone Company and Mr. Henry Roberts looked after the West of England Road Metal Company, Limited. The supply of stone was nearly exhausted at Coverack, so the quarries were developed in the Porthoustock area. Coverack was left to expand as a fishing village and tourist attraction. Around the corner from Coverack the stone companies set up crushing and screening equipment which was driven by gas engines. Compressors for drills, manufactured at Holman's in Camborne, were installed. Bins were built at the cliff edge to contain the processed stone and jetties built for the coasters which came to carry the stone 'up country' and across the Channel. These new workings were out of sight of Coverack but they provided much needed steady employment for the whole parish. The work was hard and frequently dangerous. The stark alternative of unemployment when fishing and farming were poor and berths on cargo vessels few and far between, ensured a constant supply of labour was available to the quarries. In time, some families became 'traditional' employees of the quarry companies. Sons continue to follow in their fathers' footsteps.

Of course, a price has had to be paid for economic security. There are eruptions and scars on the cliffs from Porthoustock to Dean Point. Nature is doing her best to cover the spoliation of the cliffs as the workings become derelict. By taking care it is possible to walk on the seaward side of most of these sites. The Admiralty has taken over Porthkerris. The workers' cottages built there by the quarry company are no more. Before long the industrial archaeologists and environmentalists will probably take over this stretch of coastline which has been ruined by man and restore the devastated areas to their former beauty. Fortunately the National Trust acquired Lowland Point in 1956, thus ensuring that the spread of the quarries westwards towards Coverack will never take place. Some people might consider the devastation a fitting vengeance for modern man to wreak on the coast. We have seen that it has caused the loss of countless passing ships, their crews and passengers, to say nothing of the locals who have lost their lives trying to earn a living from the surrounding sea, or in saving those unfortunate souls who were cast upon the rocks.

Dean Quarry continues to function, providing much needed stone and much needed work. There can not be many National Trust properties like Lowland Point. One can walk eastwards in complete harmony with sea and country across the cliffs from Coverack. On passing the boundary marker of the Trust at Lowland Point, one is confronted with a pole flying a red flag warning of the danger of blasting from Dean Quarry. An accompanying notice explains the times of blasting. This bizarre state of affairs does not deter those who walk the coast. If the time for continuing their walk through the quarry and on to the next stretch of coast is inopportune, they stop and rest, have a snack or take a dip in the shallow sea. There is no need to hurry in Cornwall

Visitors to Coverack frequently express disappointment at not being able to buy locally made stone mementoes of this unique geological area. The serpentine workers of the Lizard have cornered the market in this section of the local tourist industry. Serpentine is so called because of its green colour with veined markings which are similar to the markings on a snakeskin. It is also greasy to the touch. In addition to green serpentine there is much serpentine in the Lizard area which has a reddish-brown hue. The Lizard craftsmen get much of their stone from the Goonhilly Downs area. They used to get it from a serpentine works at Poltesco to the West of Kennack Sands. Mr. Richard (Dick) James Tripp was the last man to work serpentine in Coverack. He was mentioned in Kelly's Directory as early as 1910. He continued his work in serpentine until the 1930s. Mr. Tripp would take a horse and cart and go to Gwendreath Quarry, which is inland from Kennack Sands and just outside the St. Keverne parish area of Turn Trelan. He would spend a long time selecting a load of suitable serpentine. His grandsons, Albert and Norman Carey would often accompany him on these occasions. The stone splits unpredictably and is of little use as a precision building material. In spite of this drawback, skilled workers usually manage to select suitable stones for their models.

Mr. Tripp was a tireless worker and was to be seen during all the daylight hours using his lathe in the tiny workshop. It was situated on the site of the small parking bay, next to the first house on the right, after passing the entrance to the Bay Hotel when approaching the village from the Higher Bridge end. Mr. and Mrs Tripp and their fisherman son-in-law, Mr. Bert Carey lived in these beach side houses with their families. The windows of these houses still have to be protected by shutters from flying stones and other debris which are cast up from the beach by the heavy seas created by Easterly gales.

In addition to respecting Mr. Tripp as a talented worker in serpentine, and as the operator of the stone-crushing machine at North Corner, the village will remember him as the Head Launcher of the pulling and sailing lifeboat, Constance Melanie. He was the subject of a Punch cartoon which was published on the 24th. September, 1924. The cartoonist, George Belcher shows Mr. Tripp as a 'native' in working clothes, giving directions to a 'gentleman' dressed in fashionable plus fours. The two men are standing on the corner opposite the present large car park on Higher Bridge Hill. The village can be seen in the background, complete with passing steamer making smoke. The 'gentleman' is also clearly recognisable as Mr. Willie Arthur Barker, a native of Coverack whose father, Mr. George Barker founded a very successful building business in London, E.1. Mr. Barker in fact suggested the idea of the cartoon to 'George Belcher' who was on holiday in Coverack in 1924. The directions which Mr. Tripp is giving Mr. Barker typify the reply anyone is likely to get from an elderly local. It should be remembered that to a villager the names of local landmarks are often connected with local personalities and they are considered to be common knowledge, needing no explanation. That is why the cartoonist has the following dialogue beneath his drawing: Native (to holidaymaker who has lost his way):

'Yew go downalong what used to be Martin's Field, and then round by where the old mill was afore it was blown down in '94, then you'll see a signpost, but don't yew take no notice of 'ee.'

The Cornish dialect is inaccurate, but the description is plain enough for any English town dweller.

SEPTEMBER 24, 1924.]   PUNCH, OR THE LONDON CHARIVARI.   355

*Native (to holiday-maker who has inquired the way).* "YEW GO DOWN ALONG WHAT USED TO BE MARTIN'S FIELD, AND THEN ROUND BY WHERE THE OLD MILL WAS AFORE IT WAS BLOWN DOWN IN '94, AND THEN YOU'LL SEE A SIGN-POST; BUT DON'T YEW TAKE NO NOTICE OF 'EE."

Reproduced by kind permission of Punch.

I wonder if the cartoonist would have been inspired by another of Mr. Tripp's activities. He was employed as a farm hand when a young man. One of his jobs as a trusted employee was 'walking the horse.' His boss had a pedigree stallion called 'Grenville King'. Mr. Tripp would lead the stallion to any farm which wanted its services. The journey often took the best part of a day because the stallion was required on farms as far away as Zelah on the A30, North of Truro. Mr. Tripp was under strict instructions to walk the animal and not ride it. One assumes the idea was to conserve the horse's energy for the job it had to do on reaching the designated farm. It was Mr. Tripp's custom to spend the night at the farm, then 'walk the horse' to its next assignation the following day.

The above brief 'vignette' of a Coverack worker in serpentine illustrates the versatility which all villagers acquire. Mr. Tripp was not only skilled in handling animals and doing agricultural work, he was a man in whom the local fishermen had complete trust. They knew that he would only let the lifeboat go down the slipway into the teeth of a gale at the right moment. A mistake in timing the waves could mean disaster to the village in that a dozen breadwinners would be lost and the lives of their dependants ruined. One does not choose any kind of man to do a job like that. He has to be special. On the other hand, Mr. Tripp was able to choose the type of serpentine he knew would not suddenly disintegrate after much grinding and polishing on the lathe, thus wasting hours of labour for which there was no reward. The serpentine had to be pleasing to the eye as an ornament and strong enough to be used as a bowl or some other utensil. He knew his stone. He also knew that he had to make enough money out of his craft to last through the long winter when sales were non existent. Like most of the other villagers, he had, as it were, to toss some of the 'S's of this chapter into the air, juggle with them and catch them in order to make life bearable for his family. Mr. Tripp was a challenge to a cartoonist trying to depict village life. It is not surprising that 'George B.' could only illustrate the obvious.

40

## Smuggling

This chapter might well have been entitled 'The Seven 'S's' as the sea is, of course, the dominating influence in Coverack. It provides and it deprives. It is the link by which smuggling was carried on. Smuggling, by its very nature, is a covert operation. People who talk about it openly are usually those who are not directly involved but who wish to air their knowledge of the subject. Rudyard Kipling got it right when he advised in his 'Smugglers' Song', 'Watch the wall, my darling, while the Gentlemen go by!' In other words, 'The less you know about what is going on, the better it will be for you.' The fact that Kipling wrote 'Gentlemen' with a capital 'G' reminds us that almost everyone considered smuggling to be a perfectly reasonable way of combating repressive taxes. Smuggling was called 'Free Trade' and was financed by investors or 'venturers'. They were usually anonymous local landowners who organised smuggling by night and sometimes just happened to be local magistrates by day as well. It was not unknown for parsons to be involved, but there is no evidence of this in St. Keverne parish. Great Britain was the first European nation to set up a financial system which relied on income from taxes on imports and exports instead of from feudal type dues and services. The money financed government departments and was used to prosecute wars with other nations. Wars did not affect the common people to the same extent as they do today. Unless they happened to be in the area of conflict most people scarcely knew their country was at war. The account of Mr. Sandys' adventure in the chapter on 'The Quay' illustrates this point. Smugglers were used by both sides to carry out secret operations during the Napoleonic War. The thought that they might be committing an unpatriotic act did not enter their heads. When in exile on the island of Elba, Napoleon wrote of the British smugglers, 'They did great mischief to your government. During the war all the information I received from England came from the smuggler. They are the people who have the courage and ability to do anything for money.' What Napoleon said is true up to a point. What he did not say was that the 'small time' smuggler supplemented his meagre income by providing a service which was very satisfactory to his customers who were also seeking to avoid paying extortionate taxes on imported goods. It was inevitable, of course, that syndicates like that of the Carter brothers from Prussia Cove would become so successful that the government eventually had to find a way to stop its income from being seriously depleted. It did this by improving customs serveillance of the Channel and the coastline.

There is no doubt that Wesleyans got involved in smuggling. When John Wesley visited St. Ives on Wednesday, 25th. July, 1753, he recorded in his journal, 'I found an accursed thing among them, well nigh one and all bought or sold uncustomed goods.' Wesley would not have been aware of the significance of 'One and All'. The Cornish motto was popularised a century later in 1883 in Dr. Moore's chorus.

'One and All at duty's call

Shoulder to shoulder we stand or fall

On land or sea, where'ere we be,

We Cornish are ready, aye, One and All.'

During Wesley's time in Cornwall, all strangers even from a neighbouring village, were eyed with suspicion. Wesley himself was attacked on many different occasions when entering a town or hamlet, merely because he was not known to the locals. At any rate, two days after his arrival in St. Ives, Wesley was pleased to record that on warning the local men that he would leave if they did not mend their ways, 'They severally promised so to do. So I trust this plague is stayed.' I find it difficult to believe that the St. Ives men so readily abandoned such an important source of income. Smuggling was widespread. Wesley mentioned it again in his journal four years later on the 16th June, 1757 when he was at the other end of the country in Sunderland. He wrote that a few would not stop their activities, '........so these I was forced to cut off.' Two years later when he revisited Sunderland he reported, 'Most of the robbers commonly called smugglers have left us.' Old habits die hard wherever you live. This account serves to illustrate that smuggling was not considered a crime by most people, in spite of the influential Wesley using the word smuggler as a synonym for robber. Smuggling was a way of softening the harsh taxes of an unsympathetic government.

By the time the Wesleyans were established in Coverack smuggling was on the wane due to the introduction of the new style Coastguard Service in the 1820s, so the Coverack 'Society' as the Wesleyans were popularly known, can not be accused of being connected with smuggling - or at least, it was never proved! The infamous so called 'King' John Carter of Prussia Cove was reported to have given up masterminding his highly successful smuggling empire when he became a Methodist. His brother Harry, who took most of the risks, being a sea captain, is supposed to have preached one Sunday on the quay at Roscoff while waiting to leave on the tide for Cornwall with a cargo of contraband. It would appear therefore that religion and Free Trade were not considered incompatible by the top smugglers of the day, in spite of Wesley's condemnation of the unholy alliance. Surely the smuggler's slang word of 'blessings' for contraband has a religious ring to it?

Fifty per cent of spirits drunk in Great Britain at the end of the eighteenth century were estimated to have been smuggled into the country. There was a thriving industry of Dutch Gin distillation in Schiedam. It was produced expressly for sale to British smugglers. Brandy, tobacco, silks and so on were only part of the trade, which was two way. Unstamped Cornish tin was exported illegally to Brittany and the continent beneath cargoes of pilchards. Back came the boats loaded with cognac and other 'goodies'. It was reported from the Channel Isles that Guernseymen considered the Cornish miners relied on smuggled spirits to ward off the rigours of excessive heat, damp and cold encountered in the mines. The Channel Islanders argued that in reality they were providing a health service to miners who could not afford the expensive state 'medicine' in the form of taxed alcohol. Of course, the Guernseymen had a vested interest in Free

Trade. Even the coopers on the island specialised in making half size ankers to enable the smugglers to move their contraband more easily! There is a theory that Cornish men became known as 'Cousin Jacks' because of their predilection for cognac. The name stuck and went to America with the great exodus of miners when the tin mines failed in Cornwall. One can see how our Celtic cousins in France could easily call our smuggling ancestors Cousin Cognac which eventually became shortened to Cousin Jack. It is a fanciful but attractive theory.

The fact that Customs posts were placed at Gweek, Coverack, Cadgwith and Borgwitha, which is halfway between Coverack and Cadgwith, indicates the intensity of smuggling on the Lizard peninsula. It must be pointed out however, that it was still necessary for one Isaac Head to write a letter to local magistrates in 1803 asking for a boat to be stationed at Coverack as apparently no one had been sent to replace the previous officer who had died. The locals were obviously carrying on their illicit trade with impunity. The smugglers did not get it all their own way. They were not popular with law abiding citizens as the whole county was fined if smugglers were not caught when contraband was seized. This reveals that the government knew there was collusion between the smugglers and the general public.

Informers were pardoned by the authorities for giving information leading to the arrest of other smugglers, so their lives were not exactly carefree. Under the terms of the 1736 Act a smuggler could betray his friends and receive £50 a head if two or more were captured. He would also receive a pardon for his own smuggling activities. There was a sliding scale of fines, depending on whether or not the Revenue Officers were injured or killed by the smugglers in a skirmish. The final outcome of a 'dreadful accident' which occurred on board the revenue cutter called 'Fox' in January, 1816 is not known, but the story is worth repeating. The Royal Cornwall Gazette reported that when the 'Fox' was in pursuit of a smuggling vessel not far from Cadgwith, the cutter's mate, a Mr. Owen, tried to fire a warning shot from his blunderbuss over the heads of the smugglers. Unfortunately there was a back fire resulting in Mr. Owen having to have his hand amputated. The newspaper account concluded by stating that in spite of the accident the smuggling boat was captured and taken into Penzance. She had 37 kegs on board and 3 tubs of 'foreign spirits.'

The Royal Cornwall Gazette had also carried a report the previous month about a Customs House boat belonging to the Port of Gweek. It was stationed at Coverack and was commanded by a Captain Thomas. The cutter succeeded '........in taking and carrying into Coverack on Wednesday night a smuggling vessel belonging to that place, having on board 150 ankers of spirits.' (One anker was 8½ gallons). The article added '........the crew of the smuggler escaped in a small boat.' At that time, brandy on which tax had been paid cost about £1 and five shillings a gallon, rum was eighteen shillings a gallon and a dozen bottles of claret cost between £3, twelve shillings and £4, ten shillings, according to quality. A dozen bottles of champagne could be had for £4, ten shillings. The best quality champagne would cost seven guineas (£7, seven shillings) for the same amount. The smugglers would clearly not have made vast fortunes by selling their contraband, but the extra income did mean they could avoid destitution and the ignominy of the Poor House.

There was little pity shown by the authorities for shipwrecked smugglers. On the 17th. April, 1822 it was announced in the Royal Cornwall Gazette that two boats carrying contraband spirits were believed to have foundered off the Manacle Rocks and the crews drowned. Fourteen French fishing boats put into Falmouth at that time owing to 'the very boisterous weather'. No mention was made of any attempt to rescue or search for survivors of the wrecked vessels. It was the smugglers' custom to approach the coast with ankers of contraband already attached to large stones or grapnels. In the event of being approached by a Customs Boat, the cargo could be jettisoned quickly and the smugglers, having lightened their craft, could make their getaway. Alternatively, if they got a warning signal from the shore they could 'lay' a string of contraband in the same way they would lay a string of crab pots and take cross bearings of their position. They would return to the spot when the revenue men had gone and retrieve their contraband. Perhaps the boats which were reported lost in 1822 could not be handled in the heavy seas near the Manacle Rocks because of the weighty cargo. That is another mystery of the Manacles which will never be solved.

The method of leaving contraband cargo to be collected at a later date was not all that popular. In March, 1822 the Coverack and Cadgwith Preventive galleys found 94 kegs of spirits which had been left on the bottom. The cargo was taken in triumph to the Custom House Quay in Falmouth for disposal. The Preventive men used small grapnels called creepers to drag the bottom of the sea. In fact, they used the same technique as the smugglers for retrieving contraband. Large, smooth stones, which have had holes wide enough to take an anchor rope bored through them, are still to be found in use by local fishermen. Abandoned stones are to be found on the bottom in various places round the coast. These were the 'sinkers' painstakingly fashioned by the smugglers for anchoring jettisoned contraband. They were cheaper than grapnels and virtually untraceable if they happened to be trawled up from the seabed by customs officers.

The Coverack smugglers did not always look after their own when trouble broke out. On the 6th. August, 1832, Richard Hosking's wife asked the Overseers of the Poor of St. Keverne parish to allow five shillings a week for herself and two children, '........her husband being taken in a smuggling transaction and put on board a cutter.' - Note once more the commercial turn of phrase. It was a transaction, not a criminal activity. The 'Vestry' was not unsympathetic and Mrs. Hosking was granted four shillings a week. It is possible, of course, that some of the Overseers knew more about this case than appeared in the 'Vestry' minutes. They could have been using public money as compensation for the failure of a 'venture' in which they had been implicated. What is clear about this case is that the smugglers did not ensure Mrs. Hosking did not go short when her husband was apprehended by the Preventive men.

It has already been illustrated that in spite of the determination of the government to reduce smuggling, it continued at a good rate for some years before more efficient means of prevention began to produce significant results. Twenty years after the Love's successful run to Coverack, smuggling had dwindled to a comparative trickle of contraband, thanks to the new Coastguard service, which, having accomplished its first task was then beginning to concentrate more on what has now become its primary objective, the prevention of loss of life at sea.

If you ask Coverack people about smuggling they will tell you about the 'Love'. This craft is not to be confused with the 'Dove' which was a revenue cutter. There was another 'Dove' of 18 tons which was owned by smugglers but she worked the Isle of Wight. The Love was a 26 tonner which plied between Coverack and Roscoff. She was well known to the Revenue officers who had under cover men at Roscoff in order to find out what the smugglers' movements were likely to be. The revenue spies would send warnings of possible landings on the English side of the Channel. There was a steady 'Free Trade' between Roscoff and the South coast. The Love was reported in 1832, ten years after the introduction of the new Coastguard Service, as having brought successfully 125 tubs from Roscoff to Coverack. It seems hardly possible that such a vessel could land a cargo without being spotted. After unloading, most of the cargo was taken to Helston, where the cattle market was the traditional place for disposal of contraband. It seems barely credible, but it's true. The market was not far from the Excise Office in the 'Tavern', now the Angel Hotel in Coinage Hall Street. It was far enough away to allow smugglers to escape should an informer come to the office and subsequently bring the Revenue men galloping down the hill to the cattle market.

It was easy for a large number of men to accompany a cargo on land, especially when there were only a few Preventive men in the area. Being outnumbered, they wisely kept out of the way. Smuggling had got to such a pitch in 1816 that the Royal Cornwall Gazette issued a warning. It stated that the government was determined to put a stop to the practice and would be placing several small vessels of war '........at those parts of the coast where this commerce has been most successfully practised'. It should be noted again that smuggling was described in the paper as 'commerce' not crime. The paper thoughtfully added for the benefit of all and sundry: 'We hear that two troops of the Eniskillen Dragoons have arrived at Exeter, one of which is ordered for Truro.' From that piece of intelligence the smugglers could work out by what date the cargoes had to be landed and dispersed.

The Love became a legend in her time, but of course, there are no official records of her 'runs'. In 1840 the Custom House at Helford was attacked by a gang of men. Contraband which had been confiscated at Coverack a few days earlier was removed from the Custom House by force. Of course, no one knew who these men were. To show there was no ill feeling they left some kegs of spirit in the store as a 'gift' to the customs officers who had intercepted the cargo at Coverack after a landing by the vessels Ant and Exchange.

Since the Love ended her smuggling days, Coverack men have forecast Easterly gales by stating they have seen the ship, manned by a phantom crew, running before the wind to Coverack. Even the gulls utter ghostly cries when the dreaded East wind is approaching. Perhaps they too can see the Love scudding to Coverack from Roscoff and are warning the fishermen to haul up their boats before it is too late. Yes, I agree that this fanciful fiction has no place in a history book, but it does in a history of Coverack. That is why the village is unique. Folk tales are an essential part of local history.

The Corlyon brothers of Coverack became well known for their successful Free Trade activities. It seems that everyone except the Preventive men stationed at Coverack knew when the Corlyons' boat was due to arrive. If the Preventive men happened to be doing a patrol when the boat was due, the day's washing spread out to dry on the Battery would include a bright red shirt. When that was spotted by the smugglers, they would lay off and wait for the red shirt to be removed, signifying that the danger had passed. What explanation was given for hanging out a red shirt to dry when it was raining at the time of the intended landing has not become part of Coverack folklore.

When cargoes were landed, they could not always be spirited away on horseback. It is difficult to discover exactly what happened to the kegs. On approaching Coverack Quay from seawards the Old Post Office stands out as the most likely place to store contraband. The building is perched on the water's edge and has its own slipway. As it was used as a shop, it was easy to hide contraband beneath legitimate goods. It was equally easy for the Preventive men to carry out searches of the most obvious hiding place. Not much evidence has been found of secret passages. If there were any underground stores, they have been blocked up and filled in long ago, leaving no traces.

Charles Lee wrote a fictional account of a Coverack character called 'Paul Carah, Cornishman.' The book was published in 1898 and tells the story of a native of the village who returns after an absence of seven years in the United States. He believes no one will recognise him as his face is hidden behind a fine set of whiskers and he is dressed in foreign clothes. While walking across Goonhilly Downs, Paul Carah hatches a plan to dazzle the simple villagers by telling them tales of lynchings, wolf hunts and prairie fires. As the idea grows, he decides it might be worthwhile hiring the Sunday School and charging six pence a head for giving a talk. He even considers what an impression he will make on the local unattached girls but decides to bide his time on that score and wait for someone who has a dowry to offer. Of course, the villagers recognise the 'stranger' but decide to go along with his legpull, calling him 'Your honour' and letting him get trapped in his own web of deception. When the villagers get tired of Paul Carah, whose physical description closely resembled one of the real villagers called William James Williams, one of Paul Carah's friends advises the other villagers, 'He's been foreign a long time and larned 'ignorance', Liv'en be for a bit, he'll do well by'mby.' So Paul gets lodgings and inevitably turns to fishing, taking 'Dummy' a deaf mute as his mate. Dummy was also based on a real character who had come to the village from Cadgwith. In spite of his disability, Dummy was a fine fisherman and always knew where to get a good catch. Eventually Paul Carah gets into financial difficulties and it is at this stage that Reseigh the shopkeeper who has lent Paul money gets him to agree to meet a French boat and bring in a cargo. Reseigh - obviously a pseudonym for Roskilly, the owner of what is now the Old Post Office - shows Paul how to land the cargo. After dark one evening, the shopkeeper took Paul down the passage to a cellar which was locked. The two men entered. The cellar was stacked with goods which were normally sold in the shop. At the far end of the room was a recess in which a barrel had been placed. Reseigh asked Paul Carah to help him move the barrel. Behind the barrel was a blank wall. Reseigh put his hand in a crevice and gave a tug. A sudden shaft of moonlight flooded the cellar and the two men saw in front of them '........the deserted quay, black against a background of silver moonlit sea.' Reseigh then explained what would happen when a cargo was brought in. A man would be stationed in the cellar and on hearing a signal he would drop a rope and haul up the cargo. When all was placed in the cellar he would push the stone to and no one would be any the wiser. This fictional account stemmed from local gossip about cargoes disappearing into the face of the cliff. It has a convincing ring about it. Charles Lee did considerable research in the village and it seems likely that there is some truth in the description of the secret passage. I hasten to add that there is no evidence of the Roskilly family ever having indulged in Free Trade. It has already been said that smuggling had been virtually eradicated by the middle of the nineteenth century. The Roskilly family started the shop in Coverack in the 1850s. It would appear that Charles Lee studied characters in the village at the turn of the century and used them to describe what was going on in the village during the early years of the nineteenth century. I have already mentioned that Paul Carah was probably William Williams, known to his contemporaries as Billy or Willy B'dall. Other real characters were Jack Sims, thinly disguised as Steve Polkinghorne in the story; Alfred Eustis was called Bob Rowe and the coach driver, Jim Roberts of Trevothen, was called Herklous Rutter, '........a man of autocratic temper and inflexible punctuality.' The name given to Coverack was Porthvean (little harbour), North Corner was East Corner; St. Keverne was St. Kerne and Porthoustock was Porthellick.

It would be unreasonable to expect readers to accept a work of fiction as historical evidence. Nevertheless, in the absence of documentary proof, the book gives an authentic flavour of village life and has been derived from folk tales in the village. Some of the events described in the book have been verified by villagers who were young children at the turn of this century when the book was researched. With hindsight, contemporary works of fiction are often used to mirror the society of a bygone age. Paul Carah, Cornishman, written by a respected Cornish author, is a suitable mirror for nineteenth century Coverack. There are a few treasured copies of the book in the village and some still turn up from time to time at book auctions of sought after Cornish books. When Paul Carah was advertised at the price of six shillings in the December 1898 issue of the short-lived quality 'Cornish Magazine' edited by Sir Arthur Quiller-Couch, a quotation from the London Illustrated News claimed: 'Paul's a living and most amusing human being. He and Mr. Gissing's "Gammon" stand out in pleasant prominence among the humorous figures of recent fiction.' - George Gissing's novels had become popular among a literary elite at that time and the author was being compared with Dickens, but in fact he merely outlined the contemporary social evils and did not campaign for reform as Dickens did.

Let us return to the landing of cargoes in the village. There is physical proof that many old houses have secret hiding places. The obvious place to look is in the roof. When my father removed the thatch from the house on the cliff below the Coastguard station a few years before the second World War, the exposed attic was on a level with the road. A large collection of long forgotten dusty bottles and kegs was revealed to passers by. Unfortunately the liquor was declared undrinkable but it was an exciting discovery for the children in the row as the bottles and kegs could be seen in the roof space when going along the path to the Coastguard Station. The path was on a level with the roof of the house belonging to the James sisters. The find helped to reinforce the stories we had heard about the clever smugglers deceiving the Revenue men and it fired our imagination.

In nearly every small cottage there are three or four planks which can be removed easily from the floor of one of the bedrooms. Ostensibly this arrangement is to allow a coffin to be lowered to the room below. This is because the stairs are narrow and often have a sharp bend in them which prevents the passage of a coffin. The removal of planks also enabled other boxes containing contraband to be taken up to the room above and into the roof space or a secret chamber.

It is a fact that the cob walls of cottages in Coverack are at least two feet thick. It is not surprising, therefore, that the rooms of these cottages seem small in comparison with the impression of size given by the exterior of the cottages. A closer inspection of the bedrooms of some of these cottages will reveal that even allowing for a two feet thick cob wall, the room is smaller than it should be. The reason for this discrepancy in size could be that a secret chamber exists between the wall of the bedroom and the exterior wall of the house. These chambers are large enough to store a good amount of contraband or to hide three or four men for a short while when they wish to escape the attentions of the Revenue men or the Press Gang. Most of these chambers have been found during renovations to the old cottages and are now incorporated in the rooms. Hillside and Tamarisk cottages have both revealed small chambers during renovations. Hillside was, until recently, the property of the Corin family. They are descendants of the Corlyon smuggling brothers. As children we were led to believe there was a tunnel leading from the beach between the Mill and Pedn-myin to a chamber beneath the kitchen of Tamarisk Cottage. One day a few of us tried to find the beach entrance to this tunnel. We had visions of crawling up the tunnel and knocking on the floorboards of Mr. Jimmy Carey's kitchen to give him a surprise. We soon found that digging was hard work and abandoned the idea. In any case, the most direct route to the cottage is via a small stream so it is unlikely that a tunnel would have lasted long in the marshy ground. There was some truth in the tale which fired our imaginations when we were children. Years later, on the 10th. December, 1958, two seagulls got trapped in the chimney of Tamarisk Cottage. Mr. Michael Eustice, a neighbour of Mr. Carey, managed to get one seagull out. The other bit him for his pains and flapped out of sight. Mr. Eustice threw some scraps of food into the chimney and decided to leave the bird there and tackle the problem after the weekend. On Monday morning it was decided to remove the fireplace which was masking the open chimney. Mr. Eustice discovered that the gull had got into a shaft which had been built at the side of the open chimney. The entrance was held up by a stone lintel. The low entrance door to the shaft was in the form of a stone slab which was 'hinged' by a metal rod. The shaft was clean and had been whitewashed some years before. Unfortunately the only contents of the shaft were some rusting brandy cask hoops, lying on the stone slab floor. The shaft led to a recess by the chimney breast in the bedroom over the kitchen.

This recess was backed by wooden panelling which was easily removed. After a thorough inspection of the hiding place, Mr. Carey wisely decided to fireproof the 12 by 12 inch 15 foot length of timber lintel, known as a clavel in Coverack, then the open chimney was blocked by the kitchen fireplace once more. Next to Mr. Carey's house was a cowshed which had a floor of 'bullies' or smooth round beach stones. Mr. Eustice told me that when he stamped on these stones they gave out a hollow ringing sound. He considers that there is a subterranean passage leading from the house and coming out somewhere beyond the old cowshed. It would seem that we should not ignore completely the tales which are handed down in the village. There is nearly always a modicum of truth in them.

We were also told that there was a smugglers' tunnel which led from Downas Beach, which is West of Black Head, to Pednavounder Farm. We searched in vain for the entrance to that tunnel. It is curious how these stories persist. Perhaps they are a subtle means of occupying active children's time in a village where idle hands turn to mischief unless something interesting turns up to occupy their attention. We were required to do some work for our parents but during the school holidays there was always some 'free' time to be whiled away.

It seems possible that the existence of a smugglers' tunnel at Downas is confused with some old mine workings. On the 29th. September, 1751, liberty was granted to drive an adit '........from the water on the West side of Priscan tenement (which divides the same from Arrowan) to the South East corner of Pitwell Croft.' This is recorded in the Bassett Tin and Copper Setts Book of Tehidy. Priscan is also known as Mount Earle. To the East of Downas Valley traces of early 18th. century adits and shafts, a leat and a water mill wheel were found in 1819 by Professor Sedgwick who wrote a book on the structure of the Lizard district. He also stated that there was evidence of workings being reopened not long before his visit, and that there was an adit at Beagle's Point which entered the cliff at sea level. Presumably this is what is known today as Beagle Hole. It is easy to assume that as time went on these disused adits may have been used as temporary storage spaces by smugglers, especially as it appears there was no more money to be made from the copper workings.

In 1966, a smoking chimney in the appropriately named 'Smugglers' Cottage', which is situated a few yards away from the Post Office, led to the discovery of a recess in the cob wall. About 16 feet above ground floor level was a wooden frame holding small twin doors with blacksmith made hoop and twist 'hinges'. The entrance to the recess was about 24 inches square. When the wooden frame disintegrated due to the passage of time, the occupier of the cottage, Mr. David Watts, noticed the gap in the open chimney when he looked up to find out why it was smoking. Unfortunately there was nothing in this recess, so to avoid further problems, Mr. Watts had the space bricked up.

I am confident that in certain houses of the village there are treasured family heirlooms acquired in smuggling days. I am equally confident that there are some 'treasures' remaining in undiscovered hiding places. Family smuggling stories used to be told in hushed tones and were not repeated outside the family four walls. Villagers are less reticent now and are even prone to boasting about smuggling ancestors. Let's hope that accurate information will trickle through and be recorded before facts become so mingled with fancy that they are inextricable. It is sad to think that the greedy modern smugglers of drugs, terrorist arms and explosives will not be regarded by their descendants with the same strange mixture of forebearance and secret pride as the descendants of the 'Free Traders' of the last two centuries look upon their ancestors.

## *Seining*

Seining is the name given to the method of catching pilchards in the 18th., 19th., and early 20th. centuries because of the type of net used. Like mining, the seining industry was a precarious one. Seining depended on the uncertain movements of the shoals of pilchards in the same way that mining depended on the uncertain amounts of tin to be found underground. Both were doomed to ultimate failure because of the amount of capital which was tied up with no guarantee of a reasonable return. Of course, it was impossible to forecast the time of the failure of the seining industry. It was always regarded by the authorities as a good source of income. We were reminded in the chapter 'Stormy nineteenth century' of the fact that in 1836 Coverack men were still contributing 1/10th. of the value of the pilchards landed there as a local tax. The seine fishermen were optimists and were constantly hoping for a good catch which would set them up for the coming winter. They paid their tithes with good grace, or perhaps it was because of ignorance, for as stated in the chapter on 'The Quay' they could have argued that they were no longer bound in law to pay for landing the pilchards. The Church authorities appeared to take advantage of this state of affairs, taking money for the parish when it should have been ploughed back into the seining industry. In any case the seining bosses in large ports were well off and considered able to pay their dues. This was not so in villages like Coverack where resources were limited. Conversely, the church could argue that the fishermen's money was paid back in a form of insurance when they allowed money for boats and nets and other gear to be replaced after a storm.

The following table is taken from a pocket book used in 1852 in Coverack to record Seiners' Wages for the months of August and September. All spellings are as in the pocket book.

SAINERS WAGES IN 1852

| DATE | NAME | AMOUNT | | |
| --- | --- | --- | --- | --- |
| | | £ | s | d |
| August 16 | Abaram Gay | | 5 | 0 |

| Date | Name | £ | s | d |
|---|---|---|---|---|
| | Henry James | | 5 | 0 |
| 15 | Henry James | | 5 | 0 |
| 24 | Henry James | | 12 | 0 |
| | James Mildren | | 2 | 6 |
| | Abaram Gay | | 1 | 0 |
| Septm. 1 | Ricd. Ivey | 1 | 0 | 0 |
| | Wm. Richards | | 1 | 0 |
| | Jams. Mildorn | | 5 | 0 |
| 3 | Henry James | | 9 | 0 |
| 8 | Wm. Richards | | 2 | 0 |
| 9 | Jas. Mildorn | | 6 | 0 |
| 17 | Jas. Mildorn | | 4 | 6 |
| 17 | Henry James | | 3 | 0 |
| 17 | Abaram Gay | 1 | 0 | 0 |
| 25 | Ricd Ivey | | 10 | 0 |
| 25 | Henry Williams | | 10 | 0 |
| 25 | Jams. Mildorn | | 4 | 6 |
| 30 | Exelby in full | 1 | 15 | 0 |
| 30 | Wm. Oates Half Sainer | | 17 | 6 |
| 30 | Wm. Richards | | 1 | 0 |

Work was of a seasonal nature in the seining industry. There was always a plentiful supply of labour available. As long as men could row and heave on a rope they were able to get temporary employment. There were a few men who had, literally, to 'know the ropes'. They were invariably local fishermen who had a stake in the industry. Female labour was used in the preparation of the catch for the market.

The net used was a cumbersome affair. It was about 160 fathoms in length (320 yards) and could be as deep as 8 fathoms, (48 feet). A net of this size would weigh three tons. This included the lead 'sinkers' which were placed on the foot rope causing the net to drop like a curtain into the sea and prevent the fish from escaping underneath the net close to the sea bed. It had to be loaded on to the stern of a long seine boat which was manned by half a dozen oarsmen and a cox'n. In winter the seine boats were kept on the land which is now a car park at Dolor Point, seawards of the Paris Hotel. They can be seen there in many of the old picture postcards of the village. In August, or earlier if shoals of pilchards had been reported in the Channel, these boats would be launched and staunched, (pronounced stanched in Coverack). That is, they were put in the sea and allowed to fill with water by pulling out the plug. The plug was then replaced so that the water would remain in the boat even when the tide was out and the opened dry seams would swell and close up, making the boat watertight. After a couple of tides the boats would be left on the beach with the plug out so that all the water in them would drain away. The plugs were replaced before the tide came in and the boats would then float normally on the flooding tide and were ready for fitting out. They were anchored behind the quay in fine weather so that they could be available for use at all states of the tide. Then the waiting period would begin.

The one employee who was paid by the week, regardless of the catch was the huer or watcher. On the sharpness of his eyesight and his skill in directing the boats to the shoal of pilchards depended the success of the seining season. All the other men were paid shares according to the job they did and the amount of money or gear they had put into the venture. The huer's vantage point in Coverack was on the piece of ground below where Boak House now stands. When he spotted the silvery purple patch rippling across the bay he would shout, 'Hevva! Hevva!' (meaning, 'They are shoaling!'). At the same time he would send a lad down to the baulk of timber at the head of the quay which was known as the 'Parliament Seat' and where some fishermen were certain to be, chatting and waiting for the word. It was important not to lose sight of the fish, for it would be some time before the crews could gather and the little flotilla put out to sea. The crew of the two large seine boats would be rowed out to them in one of the smaller attendant craft. These boats were used to lay anchors and warps and to try to keep the pilchards from getting away. If the shoal came close to Mill Beach the warp would be taken ashore and the catch pulled in close to the beach. One small boat would be used to take messages to and from the shore or to fetch and carry any extra gear that was needed. The seine boats and their crews of six were steered by a cox'n who had a 23 foot long oar for this purpose. One boat would keep the end of the net taut with a warp (small hawser) while the other boat would enclose the shoal, casting the net in a horseshoe shaped movement. The second boat was followed by a smaller rowing boat carrying a stop net which would be laid across the open end of the horseshoe net when the manoeuvre was completed. While the shoal was being blocked in, the rowers in the boat which remained at the open end of the horseshoe would beat the blades of their paddles on the water to confuse the fish which were trying to escape and drive them back into the closed looped end of the net. Pilchards are reputedly susceptible to noise. It was impossible to see the extent of the shoal from sea level, so the huer would direct the rowers by waving bushes or some easily distinguishable object in exaggerated movements to the right or left. Similar signals are still used today for directing small boats to land. They can be found in 'Seaway Code' which is a guide for small boat users issued by Her Majesty's Stationery Office.

When the stop net had closed the way of escape for the fish - forming a chord to the 'circle' as it were - the process of 'tucking' the fish began. This involved casting a small net into the seething mass and loading the fish into the boats. The seiners also used large mauns - wicker baskets with two handles - to dip into the catch and lift out the fish.

As soon as the boats got to the quay or the beach, the harvest was taken ashore, it was carried up to the seiners' cellars in gurries which are wheel barrow shaped containers with two handles at each end to facilitate transport over rocky ground, slipways, mooring ropes and so on. There were three companies which operated in Coverack in the heyday of the seiners. Jigger's Coy, operated in the cellar nearest the quay, behind the souvenir shop which is appropriately named the Seine Loft. This cellar, as mentioned earlier in the chapter on 'The Quay' is the only one which still has bullies or large pebbles laid as a floor to act as a drain to collect the 'train' or oil seeping from the barrels containing the pressed pilchards during the 'curing' process. Friendship Coy cellar was opposite Jigger's Cellar. As also mentioned in the second chapter, it is now a fine dwelling house. This cellar doubled as a coal store for Roskilly's business. It was convenient to carry coal by cart from the schooner in the quay and dump it in the nearby cellar. Snell's Coy, was behind Friendship Coy, in Penthouse Lane, next to the Watch House.

When the pilchards were brought to the cellars they were 'cleaned' or gutted by the local women and girls. They were placed in the barrels in alternate layers of salt and fish. A press stone was placed on the top of each barrel to accelerate the 'curing' process. Fish for local consumption were put in bussas - large earthenware pots - in the same way as in the barrels and then stored in a cool place. When needed the salted fish or 'scrowlers' as they were called in Coverack, were washed free of the salt and boiled or roasted over an open fire on a grid iron made from a length of iron which was heated and bent round a metal bar in a concentric shape so as to resemble an elaborate question mark with the stem acting as a handle for the grid. If you look at the landward end of Jigger's Cellar you will see a squat chimney. This was reputed to have been constructed by a Dutch mason. It was last used by Alfred Eustis in the early part of this century. He had a small anvil and forge at the end of Jigger's Cellar and made grapnels and other bits of metal equipment for the fishermen. He also fashioned grid irons and other simple domestic utensils for special acquaintances.

Some people have expressed surprise at the original length of the seine cellars. They are now divided into small 'lofts'. It must not be forgotten that the cellars were used for the storage of masts, sails and nets. Beneath the floor of Joe and Billy Bowden's cellar which is now the Fishermen's Rest or recreation room was a huge tank. Before the fishing season began, nets would be taken from the top floor of the loft in the Paris yard, through the door which is placed above the ground and strung across the road into the subterranean barking tank in the cellar opposite for a soaking. Nets were soaked in bark to prevent the rope from rotting in sea water. When ready the nets were pulled out of the tank, drained and taken by cart to Carnsullan Farm fields for drying. When they were brought back they were draped over the back of the quay before being loaded into the boats or taken back to the lofts.

There is scant evidence concerning the amount of pilchards exported from Coverack to Italy, France, Spain and the rest of the Catholic continent. It is more than likely that part loads were bought up by larger concerns and collected from Coverack for subsequent transhipment. It is not difficult to imagine that by the time the pilchards arrived at their continental destination, they were not always fit for human consumption. In the 1870s a glut of pilchards led to huge amounts of fish being 'dumped' in Italy. Not surprisingly, demand for the product subsequently lessened. In any case, the rise in the standard of living in Italy meant that the peasants no longer considered salt fish an acceptable diet on their meatless days. The Cornish fishermen began importing natural ice from Norway in an attempt to recapture the market with good quality unsalted frozen fish. The advent of the steam railway halfway through the nineteenth century in 1859 opened up a more lucrative market in the centres of population in the United Kingdom, so the export of pilchards to the continent declined.

It is interesting to note that some pilchards were sent to the West Indies to feed slaves during the Napoleonic Wars when trade with the continent fell off. It was suggested earlier that schooners would call at Coverack for part loads. It is certain that enough fish barrels were needed to warrant the presence of coopers in the village. Mark Daniell plied his trade in the village from the 1840s to the 1870s. He was known as 'Cooper Daniell'. He lived in a small cottage in front of the present day 'Trevanion' and 'Carn Dhu' cottages near the church. One can still see the remains of the foundation stones of the cooper's cottage by the grass verge of the cliff road. The cottage is clearly marked on the 1878 Ordnance Survey map of the village. Mark Daniell made wooden buckets as well as barrels. His house was in a good position as it was close to the spring from which many of the villagers obtained their drinking water. The corner at the bottom of the lane known to locals as 'The Gardens' is still known as 'The Tap'. The water came from a small well and reservoir on the Chymbloth farm land which was behind the present day house called Chymbloth. It is not known if Cooper Daniell cooperated in making special half ankers to ease the burdens of the Coverack smugglers as did the Guernsey coopers. There are no Daniells left in Coverack now but Daniell remains a common name in Cornwall so perhaps more interesting information will be revealed about the Coverack coopers eventually.

Because of the volatile financial nature of the seining industry, the three local companies changed hands frequently. In 1815 a fish cellar capable of holding 400 hogsheads (pilchard barrels) was sold in Coverack by Nicholas and Pearce Johns. In 1824, Joseph Saunders from Dolor House (where the Paris Hotel now stands) and Henry Williams sold the Friendship seine nets, boats and gear. This was not the end of their venture. The family was soon back in business. By 1852, Henry C. Saunders had control of the seining company once more and Joseph Saunders was still being taken on as an 'Extra Man' during the seining season. Henry Williams' name was written in the seiners' pocket book of wages paid in 1852. He was obviously regarded as a man of experience as he earned more than most. No one was ever averse to earning a little extra from seining. Money has never been plentiful in Coverack. The intrepid John Corlyon from the smuggling family was duly recorded as a wage earner in the 1851 seiners' wages pocket book. That year the season went on into November.

The West Briton watched closely the ebbing and flowing fortunes of the seining industry. On the 29th. October, 1885 it was reported that so many pilchards had been caught off the Lizard peninsula that there '........would be no hard times this winter, no complaints of fishermen wanting bread.' The paper went on to say that because there was so much fish, even the folks inland would find 'No lack of the old Cornish supper, 'fish and tates' during the winter.' By the 8th. January, 1891 the paper was reporting a failure of the seining industry, stating that '.......not a single pilchard had been caught by a seine off the Cornish coast during 1890.' It is no surprise to learn that before the next two decades were over, the seining industry had ceased altogether in Coverack.

It has been pointed out already that investment in the seining industry involved leaving capital tied up in boats, nets and gear for some time without regular return. Large companies in St. Ives, Looe and Mevagissey fared better than the small independent companies in villages like Coverack. Barclay Fox of the famous Falmouth Quaker family recorded his visits to Coverack in his diary. He became interested in the seining industry at the early age of 16 when he went fishing in Coverack. He wrote on the 23rd. July, 1833 that there had been a catch of pilchards at Coverack the previous day. Barclay obtained 300 pilchards for baiting a boulter, which is a long fishing line with hooks attached at regular intervals hanging from it. He stated that they had a good catch after using the Coverack pilchards for bait. His uncle, Alfred Fox, had an interest in seining and would call Barclay from his bed to accompany him from Falmouth to Mevagissey where Pilchards had been sighted. In 1846, Alfred Fox organised a demonstration of seining at Swanpool Beach, Falmouth for the benefit of Queen Victoria who was cruising round Cornwall in the Royal Yacht 'Victoria and Albert.' The pilchards obliged and swam into the seine. Unfortunately the warp broke and the pilchards escaped before the tucking process began. I suppose it would be safe to say that Queen Victoria was 'not amused'.

In spite of the uncertainties of seining, entrepreneurs did not give up their belief that money was to be made in the industry. Steam driven seine boats were put in commission in Falmouth early in the twentieth century. The boats were built to operate seine nets of a new type which could trap the pilchards when they were still in deep water. Coverack men were not happy about this. Matters were brought to a head in 1905 after some trawlers had been in the bay and damaged Coverack mens' nets and pots. The large trawlers came so close to the shore that they cut loose store pots containing crabs and lobsters waiting to be sold. The fishermen complained to the County Fisheries Committee but no positive action was taken. The trawlers came again and once more damage was done. This time the Coverack men decided to remedy the problem in their own way. They got hold of some old tree trunks, towed them out to sea and moored them in an upright position beneath the surface of the water by attaching sinkers to them and binding them in a straight line with wire rope. The next time the trawlers came sweeping into the bay their nets became hopelessly entangled in the underwater obstacles. The trawler skippers then had the temerity to complain to Lieutenant Commander Lake, the Chief Officer of Coastguards at Coverack. He promptly mustered his men and went out to clear the obstacles and help the trawler men to untangle their nets. He then brought the tree trunks into the quay. It goes without saying that the Coverack men were very angry at this turn of events. A tug of war ensued, resulting in the outnumbered coastguards having to let go the tree trunks. The Chief Officer of Coastguards then ordered his men to wear their cutlasses for self defence. They were not necessary. The Coastguards were not foolish enough to use cutlasses against their fellow villagers. After a while the tree trunks were once more in position beneath the surface of the water at the entrance to the bay. When the trawlers came in again and once more got their nets fast in the tree trunks, Lieutenant Commander Lake wisely asked the skipper of the Mallard, a salvage vessel working on a submerged wreck at the Manacle Rocks, to come into the bay and clear the trunks by using her steam winches. This operation resulted in the nets being damaged beyond repair. It became obvious that the Coverack fishermen were determined to protect their livelihood. When the Fisheries Committee received a report from the Chief Officer of Coastguards about the incidents at Coverack, they decided it was time to act before real trouble broke out. One can imagine the celebrations in Coverack when the Cornwall Fishery Board introduced a bye-law in 1908 prohibiting trawling within a line from the Guthens (marked Chynalls on the Ordnance Survey map) and Pedn Myin which is the piece of land jutting out into the sea beyond the Eastern building boundary of the village. This bye-law not only protected Coverack seiners, but the crabbers and whiffers as well. The rivalry between the independent longshore fishermen in Cornwall and the powerful deep sea fishing conglomerates continues today. Even the scientifically based quota systems decreed by the European Economic Community, have failed to calm these troubled waters.

Coverack Seine Company was financed by Mr. Claude Hart of the Lizard during the early years of the twentieth century. He invested in a motor driven seine boat. The problem he then faced was finding a mechanic to service the engine. No one in Coverack could do the job. The difficulty was overcome by the fisherman in charge of seining, Mr. John Corin, Cox'n of the Constance Melanie, Coverack's pulling and sailing lifeboat. Mr. Corin was anxious to start using the motor seiner so he mentioned the problem of finding a mechanic to Mr. Barron, the Fisheries Officer when he came to Coverack on his quarterly visit. It so happened that Mr. Barron's son, Jonathan, had just finished serving his time as a motor mechanic apprentice, so it was arranged for him to come to live in Coverack and be the mechanic for the motor seiner. Unfortunately the new fangled motor seiner never proved to be a financial success. There were some practice sorties with the pulling seine boats and long periods of waiting for the decreasing shoals of pilchards to arrive off Coverack, but no sign of any fortunes to be made.

In 1917 an Easterly gale sprang up. The seine boats were high and dry on their accustomed patch of land on the Dolor Point. One large seiner was smashed to bits by the gale and the other, the Lark was damaged to such an extent that she was not strong enough to be used in seining again. Mr. Jimmy Carey used it as an ordinary fishing boat. The era of the Seine Industry in Coverack was over. Two of the smaller seine boats, the Millie and the Beatrice retained their seining colours of a tar black hull with green and white stripes on it. They remained in the harbour under the ownership of Mr. Bert Carey for many years. The Beatrice had a drop keel. When she was getting old, the water started to come inboard through the wooden casing built round the keel. The keel was removed and the casing sealed, allowing the little seiner to finish her days as a rowing boat. Billy Williams, Charles Lee's model for Paul Carah, owned another of the small seining boats. She had a dipping lug sail and moved beautifully through the water. Mr. Williams sometimes took me with him on short fishing trips when I was a small boy. I was always fascinated by the nonchalant way in which he handled the seiner - the hall mark of an experienced seaman. Mr. Williams must have suffered from a heart problem or asthma in old age as he was always puffing and blowing. In my innocence I thought he puffed and blew to help the wind fill the sail.

The amount of hard work Coverack people had to do in order to supplement a very modest wage is a constant source of amazement to modern students of village life. An entry in my grandfather's account book serves to illustrate what Coverack people had to do in order to make a living. The role of the huer or watcher in the Seining Industry has been described already. It was considered in 1902 that the best man for the job of huer in Coverack was John Stephens. He was a Cadgwith man, so he must have been good if Coverack fishermen wanted him to find the pilchards for them. In fact, he was employed by Mr. Hart of the Lizard, the man who was financing the Coverack Seine Company. When pilchards were reported moving towards the Coverack area, Mr. Stephens would walk from Cadgwith to Coverack and remain in the village until the pilchards were all caught or moved on. The entry in James Hart's account book was as follows:

John Stephens Lodgings

| | | |
|---|---|---|
| September 5th., 1902 | Here making preparations for seining. | 6s.  0d. |
| | Commencing seining. | |
| Sept. 22nd. to the 27th. | | 3s  0d. |
| Sept. 29th. to Oct. 4th. | | 3s  0d. |

At the bottom of the page the terms were written:

To pay by the week.

To give notice either side of the week.

You will note that Mr. Stephens worked a six day week and that he spent a fortnight making preparations for seining. Although money was scarce, Sundays were sacrosanct, so John Stephens walked back to Cadgwith on Saturdays, returning on Monday morning. Clashes involving the sabbath keeping Newlyn and St. Ives men with the East coast and Scottish fishermen are well documented elsewhere. Fortunately the problem did not arise in Coverack. Some of the non chapel or church going fishermen would scoff at the sabbath keepers but they did not fish on Sundays.

When Mr. Hart of the Lizard bought the motor seiner for his Coverack company, he was anxious to show it to his wife and friends. Accordingly he arranged for the head seiner, Mr. John Corin to take the boat down to the Lizard. Mr. Corin took Jonathan Barron as motor mechanic and his own son, John and his son's friend, Archie Rowe, who was destined to follow in Mr. Corin's footsteps as Cox'n of a Coverack lifeboat. When the new seiner arrived at Lizard Church Cove, Mr. Hart, accompanied by his wife and some friends came on board and the party went to a sheltered spot along the coast and anchored in order to have a picnic. While the food was being prepared, Mr. Hart offered one of his friends a cigarette. In extracting a cigarette from Mr. Hart's gold cigarette case, the friend accidentally knocked the case from Mr. Hart's hand and the case went overboard and sank. There was consternation as the case was a wedding anniversary present from Mr. Hart's wife. Jonathan Barron then volunteered to dive overboard to see if could find the case which had gone into about three fathoms of water. Mr. Hart instructed the ladies in the picnic party to look steadfastly seawards while Jonathan stripped naked and dived overboard. Young John Corin and Archie Rowe stood still in the bow of the boat, fascinated by this unexpected turn of events. Jonathan managed to retrieve the case at the second attempt and climbed back on board. The ladies continued to look seawards while Jonathan dressed. Nothing more was said. When the picnic was over Mr. Hart went ashore with his wife and their guests and the motor seiner chugged its way back to Coverack.

John Corin Junior told me that when reflecting on this incident in later years, it occurred to him that the divisions between the two classes of people on board the seiner were so clear cut that Mr. Hart, who was not in any way an overbearing, unfeeling kind of man, accepted it as his right to expect Jonathan or someone else to get him out of his predicament. Jonathan Barron, on the other hand, probably considered he had a duty to please his employer regardless of any danger or discomfort and without any thought of any extra reward for his actions. It may well be that Coverack fishermen, although no longer seiners, have only exchanged one type of exploitation for another. It is true that their lives have been made much more bearable by modern technological improvements, but they still face danger and financial ruin from a different source and a different class. What remains unchanged is their optimism and determination to stay in their oasis.

# SOME 19TH. CENTURY COVERACK PEOPLE

The nineteenth century did not end abruptly on the 31st. December, 1899. In Coverack life continued in much the same way as it did during the reign of Queen Victoria, right up to the First World War. Of course, the internal combustion engine put in an appearance on the roads and on the sea. The tourist trade began to exert a greater influence on the lives of the villagers as did the advent of secondary education and the old age pension. Tommy Champion (1796-1874) is a genuinely historical nineteenth century character but the reader will find that members of the Barker and Roskilly families are chronicled in this chapter up to and even beyond the First World War. People can not always be neatly placed into historical century compartments.

## Uncle Tommy, 1796 - 1874

Uncle Tommy is the life story of Tommy Champion. He was one of twelve children. He was born at Poltesco near Kennack and was brought to Coverack when an infant. His father, a fisherman, was drowned at the age of thirty five when his boat capsized off the Dolor Point during a gale. The whole crew lost their lives. The tragedy was witnessed by many villagers, little Tommy being one of the unwilling spectators. Tommy's story was written by a Coverack person, the Rev. John T.T. Halligey, as a tribute to the powerful influence which Uncle Tommy had on his life.

As a result of Uncle Tommy's example and evangelising in the village, Halligey was converted to the Wesleyan following. He married Hester Mundy from Penhallick. She had four brothers, Matthew, Mark, Luke and John - an auspicious beginning for a man who was to become a minister of religion and go to Sierra Leone in 1869 as a missionary. Halligey's story begins with a topographical description of Coverack in the early nineteenth century. There were between seventy and eighty houses at that time and the principal landmarks were the Quay, which was about a hundred years old and the whitewashed Watch House on the Dolor Point. The houses were concentrated along the curves of the two bays which were likened to the concave sides of the Arabic numeral 3 when laid on its back. Other prominent features included a ridge near the Yellow Rock at the end of Mears Point which 'tradition marks as a grave where many victims of the sea were laid'. Apart from the practicality of convenience, we must remember that St. Peter's Church was not built until 1885 which meant that the nearest consecrated ground was at St. Keverne. We should also take note of the fact that in 1830 Davies Gilbert, M.P., first for Helston and later Bodmin, introduced the Act sanctioning the burial in consecrated ground of persons washed up by the sea. This was not altogether popular with impoverished coastal dwellers as the burials were to be carried out at the expense of the County Rate fund. Lambeag (Halligey's spelling) was described as a place for Sunday School tea drinkings - apparently it was not known to him as the Battery when he was a small boy. It may well have been called Lan bregh - small inlet or bay, as opposed to the larger bay on the other side of Dolor Point.

John Halligey tells us little of Tom's childhood apart from the traumatic experience of seeing his father drown and another frightening episode when he witnessed the Press Gang land in Coverack and carry off some able bodied men. One of them was his uncle by marriage. Like most young men, Tommy was attracted to the pub. One night after he had been drinking he was confronted by what he later described as a dragon. This sufficed to turn him into a teetotaller for the rest of his life. Soon after this experience he began visiting the barn at Trevothen Farm which was used as a meeting place before the first chapel was bought at Sunny Corner. It was in this barn that Tommy wanted to give himself to the Lord, but he did not dare declare it in public. After a sleepless night which he likened to steering a boat on the trackless deep, he finally asked his Saviour to come and make him whole.

At the time when Tommy was converted, there were only four ministers in the Helston Circuit which covered Helston, Hayle, Marazion, Porthleven, St. Keverne and Coverack. This made pastoral visitation difficult due to poor communications. Because of this shortage of ministers, lay people were encouraged to evangelise. A Colonel Sandys, who had been converted by Wesley, bought Lanarth estate when he came home from India. One of the first things he did was to build a chapel on the end of the house. He managed to persuade a preacher to come from Helston on Sunday evenings and locals would go to Lanarth to hear him. Among those going from Coverack was a young lady called Mary. Tom also happened to walk to Lanarth to Chapel on Sunday evenings and offered his services as an escort. They were married in 1818. Gradually Tommy cultivated what Halligey called his 'natural gifts' and became recognised as the village pastor. He was the Sunday School Superintendent for twenty seven years and held classes every Sunday morning. Uncle Tommy, as he was called by everyone, was always summoned to a house when there was a problem to be overcome. One day a girl who lived at Cowidjack Farm (Halligey's spelling) was frightened by two tramps who called at the house when she was on her own and demanded money. She was so terrified by this experience that she was struck dumb and remained so for two years. Throughout this time she continued to attend Sunday School and during one never to be forgotten class taken by Uncle Tommy, her speech was restored. Her teacher's comment was 'More things are wrought by prayer than this world dreams of.'

Religious life in Coverack during the nineteenth century was not all fear of hell fire and damnation. It had its humorous side. When Halligey was fourteen he attended a Foreign Missions meeting for the first time. It was held in the chapel which had been bought by a group of villagers led by Colonel Sandys of Lanarth. Early in the nineteenth century it had become obvious that premises were needed in the village. They were obtained eventually next door to the Chief Coastguard's house at the top of Sunny Corner. To honour the visiting speaker at this special event, a temporary rostrum had been constructed by placing planks over the class leaders' pew in the front. The young Halligey was surprised to hear strange noises emanating from beneath the platform. As no one else seemed to be taking notice he assumed the sounds were in some strange way an accepted part of the proceedings. However, as the speaker livened to his subject, the noises increased to such a pitch, that the chairman wisely announced it was time to take the collection, adding that before the plate was passed round they would investigate the space beneath the rostrum. The makeshift floor was lifted and lo and behold, a sheep was seen to be standing in the class leaders' pew. At this point a local farmer stood up and confessed the animal was his. He reminded those present that at the previous year's meeting he had promised to consecrate the firstborn of his flock for the funds of the church to enable it to 'preach the gospel to every creature'. He added that he hoped the voice of the consecrated lamb, now a sheep, would encourage the congregation in their prayers and stimulate their giving. This hilarious appeal had the desired effect and the Foreign Missions meeting was declared to be the best they had ever had in Coverack.

In 1869 Halligey became the Rev. Halligey and he was called to work as a missionary in Sierra Leone. When the minister left Coverack, Uncle Tommy went up the hill to Gate Wynyack with him. While waiting for the conveyance to arrive, Uncle Tommy commended his young protégé to God and wished him good fortune in his work among the heathen. Years later when Halligey had returned from the mission field, Uncle Tommy confided to him that throughout the four years tour abroad, he had gone up to the top of what is now known as School Hill, every Sunday morning before the Bible Class meeting in order to pray for the missionary's health and success in his work.

Not long after Halligey's return Uncle Tommy was taken ill and began to suffer great pain. His second wife, Jane, nursed him through this final illness. As one would expect, a man with such great faith was not afraid. He had faced death many times at sea. After being rescued at Cadgwith on one occasion when his boat capsized he declared that in his moment of peril, when he was caught in the undertow and sucked beneath his own boat, he was not afraid as God was near. His witness, when he was in such great pain, remained unequivocal. He assured the troubled missionary who was so concerned about the suffering his mentor had to undergo, 'If our afflictions were not permitted, the world would be destitute of one of the clearest evidences of the all perfect grace of God which causes us to triumph in our tribulations also.' It is not surprising that Tommy was held in such high esteem by the villagers of Coverack. He truly practised what he preached. His last words were, 'All is well, home is in view.' It should not be supposed that J.T.T. Halligey was in any way patronising to Uncle Tommy. He recorded that when Uncle Tommy commended him to God before setting out for Sierra Leone, 'The sacred influences of my ordination were not more impressive than that season of farewell.'

When the Rev. Halligey returned to Lagos as Superintendent Minister in 1885, some years after Uncle Tommy's death, he was responsible for the building of a Methodist Chapel in that town. The design he used followed closely the plans of Helston Wesley Chapel. When he completed his tours as a missionary, he worked in Bolton, Newcastle and York before retiring to Uxbridge. He continued to visit his beloved Coverack with his wife, formerly Harriet Dunstan of Truro, and their two sons and four daughters. He is remembered for his talks about Africa, when he would wear native costume to add authenticity to his descriptions. He died on the 15th. February, 1924, aged 78. The writer of his obituary recorded that 'he was of godly parentage' and that 'he had a pecularly fine and radiant temperament.' Like Tommy Champion of Coverack, the mentor of his youth, as the end drew near, John Halligey 'frequently spoke of the abounding grace of God and the confident hope of eternal life.'

I have a pocket book for the year 1851. In it a Richard Halligey received 12 shillings as wages for work in Chinalls Garden. At the other end of the book in 1852 the same person was paid £2 and 2 pence Sainers' wages 'in full'. This reveals the humble family connections of the non conformist minister. It explains his reverence for Tommy Champion who educated himself in the evenings after working a pulling and sailing fishing boat during the day. He also managed to find time to act as honorary pastor and counsellor to the village. In another pocket book in my possession it is recorded that on the 20th. April, 1852, Captain James Eastaway landed a cargo of Cardiff coal at Coverack at 6½ pence a bushel. The next day 20 bushels were sold to Richard Halligey for 10 shillings and 10 pence and Thomas Champion bought 40 bushels for £1, 1 shilling and 8 pence. One can not draw any conclusions from such scant evidence but it does help to paint a picture of the togetherness of the community of Coverack at that time. They were all dependent on one another. Their leader was Uncle Tommy, fisherman by trade, saver of souls, pastor, counsellor, educator and friend in time of need. Most of the villagers were involved in several different activities. The same pocket book records that John Rule, Thomas Bolitho, William Exelby, Antony Tripconey, Abraham Gay, William Gay, William Roberts, Nick Coad, Richard Halligey, William Michell, Thomas Lambrick and James Mildren were all employed on Chinalls garden. John Rule's special job was 'making the edge in the cliff'. John Roberts was paid £2 and 5 shillings for 'Carrin salt to the Dowler Cellar' and 7 shillings and 10½ pence for 'Fish carrin' to the same place. His attendance money was 4 shillings and four pence. The Chinalls men were still working at a 'price perposed' by H.C. Saunders. Meanwhile the same men were recorded at the other end of the pocket book as being paid 'Sainer's Wages'. Henry C. Saunders received £10 and 10 shillings as opposed to the £2, 3 shillings and 2 pence general wage paid to most of the others. Mr. Saunders had a larger share as he financed the seining. He was known as a man of property in the village. By 1854, coal had gone up to 9 pence a bushel. Richard Halligey was still buying 10 bushels at a time. The Watch House was having 40 bushels instead of the customary 22. I wonder why?

To put events into perspective it should not be forgotten that at this time there were no more than 18 million people living in Great Britain, according to the 1851 census. The Crimean War was about to begin. Brunel's bridge had yet to cross the Tamar. John Tabois Tregellas wrote, nearly a decade later, in his Cornish Tales in Prose and Verse, 'Cornwall is now the only English County that is not connected by a more or less circuitous line of railway, with the mighty heart of the kingdom.' Perhaps he should have preceded this sentence with: 'Cornwall, birthplace of the inventor of the high pressure steam engine used in locomotives........' In 1880 the Roskilly family was given permission to start the first Post Office in Coverack. One might be forgiven for thinking that the authorities had neglected the small population. The Penny Post had been introduced thirty years before when people were just beginning to use the new fangled envelopes to hold their correspondence. It must also be remembered that State Education was not in force and the number of people able to correspond would not have been very high. However, the villagers must have taken comfort from the fact that they no longer had to rely on someone going to St. Keverne to post letters for them. We should also remember that in the 1850s the Church of England had not yet decided to build St. Peter's in Coverack and the members still had to walk to St. Keverne to worship. Moreover, everyone had to be carried there to be buried. The Wesleyan Chapel which now stands on School Hill was still a pipe dream of the Chapel Trustees and of course, it would be another twenty five years before the school itself was erected at Gate Wynyack where Uncle Tommy had gone each week to pray for the success of the Rev. John Halligey's work in the part of Africa known at that time as the white man's grave. These timely reminders jolt us to the reality of the situation in Coverack. The people were still relatively self sufficient, but were gradually becoming more closely linked to the outside world.

### *The Barkers*

There are records of Barkers living in St. Keverne parish since the 16th. century. Two girls, Ursella and Jane Barker were christened in St. Keverne Church on the 12th. March, 1581. These christenings were followed by those of John on the 24th. October, 1583, Edward in July, 1586 and Penelopie on the 11th. May, 1588 at Armada time. The Barkers were a prolific family and like all families they tended to name their children after their parents, grandparents and other relations. The following list illustrates this point:

1580-1855

| No. of names | Males | No. of names | Females |
|---|---|---|---|
| 37 | John | 50 | Mary |
| 34 | James | 33 | Elizabeth |
| 31 | Anthony | 12 | Jane |
| 20 | William | 9 | Susanna |
| 15 | Benjamin | 7 | Margaret |
| 15 | Richard | 5 | Catharine |
| | | 5 | Loveday |
| 7 | George | 4 | Dorothy |
| | | 4 | Thomasin |
| 7 | Thomas | 3 | Patience |
| 4 | Francis | 3 | Selina |

Other boys' names used were:
Edward, Henry, Joe, Joseph, Lyslie, Michell, Mychaell, Paul, Peter, Nicholas and Samuel.

Other girls' names used were:
Ann, Anne, Celia, Eliza, Emily, Frances, Frannces, Grace, Jone, Maria, Martha, Penelope, Sarah, Sible, Sophia, Syssie, Tabitha and Ursula.

The Coverack Barkers were allied through marriage to the following families:

| The men: | | The women: | |
|---|---|---|---|
| | Boddy | | Boucher |
| | Dunn | | James |
| | Golley | | Roskilly |
| | Lugg | | Sigmoor |
| | Martin | | Taylor |
| | Nicholls | | |
| | Reynolds | | |
| | Thomas | | |

The Falmouth and Budock Barkers married into the following families:

The men: Brabing                                    The women:    Bennetts

Eva                                                                        Collenso

Palmer                                                                   Holman

Pasco                                                                     Sampson

There were also Barkers living in the mining 'triangle' bounded by Helston, Hayle and Redruth. Most of these Barker families lived in Camborne, Gwinear, Phillack, St. Erth, Gulval, Ludgvan and Breage. Other Barkers lived as far away as Padstow, Tywardreath, Fowey and Looe.

The dates at the heading of the list of male and female Christian names indicate that the above details are by no means complete but they do illustrate the ramifications of a village family. Similar details could be worked out for most of the other village families. There is no doubt that in a small community such as Coverack a prominent family like the Barkers was connected with most of the village families.

Not surprisingly, a study of the Barkers in the second half of the nineteenth century shows that the Coverack Barkers had the sea in their blood. They were fishermen, sea pilots and coastguards. In addition there were Barkers who were shoemakers, carpenters and builders. One was a schoolmaster.

The term 'sea pilot' needs explanation. There were various categories. Some were Master Mariners, highly skilled in navigation and ship handling. Others were local fishermen who could guide a ship past the dangers of the approaches to Falmouth. The former were career men and the latter vied with each other for the lucrative privilege of assisting a ship into or our of port when qualified pilots were not available. It goes without saying that small vessels often chose local men they could trust rather than employing the more expensive professional navigators. Falmouth Pilots were licensed from early in the nineteenth century in 1809 when Falmouth became a Trinity House port. Towards the end of the same century a Falmouth Pilot Boat Association was formed. This heralded the beginning of the end of the local village fishermen-pilots and their racing gigs. The growth of the quarries at Porthoustock and Dean Point meant that local pilots from Coverack, Porthoustock and Porthallow continued to guide coasters through the Manacle Rocks until the 1960s. Now, all stone boats are piloted by Master Mariners who are qualified Falmouth pilots. Coverack is still represented by Captain Peter John Langdon who grew up in the village.

From the pilotage point of view, Falmouth Harbour extends from Black Head to the West of Falmouth to Dodman Point which is to the East. In the days of sail, Coverack bay was a good place to wait for ships coming into Falmouth for orders. When they made a landfall at the Lizard, they would receive a message from a flag hoist at Lloyds Signal Station. It is not surprising, therefore, that some Coverack men became pilots. They were not trained deep sea navigators, but they could take a ship past the dreaded Manacles and into Falmouth Harbour. Some of the Barker family were trained pilots in the sense that they could take a ship up Channel or round to the Welsh ports. Others were only capable of doing local pilotage jobs. There was great rivalry between pilot cutters which raced to meet ships coming up Channel. Falmouth Pilot cutters had a large black 'F' on their mainsails so that ships' captains could identify them from a distance. Cardiff Pilots sometimes ventured as far as the Lizard to get the job of taking a ship round Lands End and up the Bristol Channel. Their cutters had 'Cff' marked on their mainsails. Pilot gigs were used to take the pilots aboard the ships. These fast rowing boats were magnificent craft. Modern copies of them are still used in Cove Regattas today. The gig races attract crews from as far as the Isles of Scilly and Brittany. Sometimes a nineteenth century gig is launched for a special race. The Bonnet from the Isles of Scilly was built in 1830. Cadgwith men, under the encouragement of the late Ben Collins, have done much to revive this sport with their new gig 'Buller'. In 1851 the Cadgwith 'Punt' was repaired in Coverack. The claims that hundred year old Pilot Gigs are still in use are, of course, somewhat exaggerated. This is illustrated by the following details written in a pocket book which is in the writer's possession:


ESTIMATE FOR THE CADGWITH PUNT

March 4th, 1851

| | | |
|---|---|---|
| Garbord Plank 24 feet long | 4s | 0d |
| Plank 12 feet | 2s | 0d |
| Floors 5 at 8 pence each | 3s | 4d |
| Footsticks at 8 pence | 4s | 0d |
| Knees - 2 pence | 1s | 0d |
| Rowlock 2 | | 8d |

| | | |
|---|---|---|
| Starn Sheets | 1s | 0d |
| Bottom Boards | 4s | 0d |
| Nails Copper | 5s | 6d |
| Bilgways - | 1s | 0d |
| Bow Strakes 10 Feet long | 1s | 6d |
| | £1  8s | 6d |

The next page reads:

| | | | |
|---|---|---|---|
| Smith Bill - (Blacksmith's Work?) | | 3s | 6d |
| To 8 Days Work at 3/6 | £1 | 10s | 0d (error) |
| Brought On | £1 | 8s | 6d |
| To Boy Wages | | 8s | 0d |
| | £3 | 10s | 0d |
| Iron Nails | | 1s | 0d |
| | £3 | 11s | 0d |

The above account was probably the bill for a refit. It is clear it would not take long to replace the whole craft at this rate! It reminds me of the fisherman's tale about his broom - 'I've had this broom for 20 years and I've only fitted 4 new handles and 5 brushes.'

The rivalry in Coverack between gig crews was so great that for the sake of peace the different crews drank in different ale houses - the Dolor, where the Paris Hotel now stands; Trewolsta which stood on what is now a small car park beside the public conveniences; and Jubilee House which is a dwelling house on the hill leading to the Wesleyan Chapel. It must be appreciated that the gig crews would sometimes have to wait a week or more for adverse weather conditions to change before they could leave the bay and go to the ships lying off which were waiting to go into Falmouth. One can imagine the boredom and frustration which the crews suffered. It is easy to understand how Celtic tempers and old rivalries could 'boil over' under such circumstances.

Barclay Fox, a member of the famous Falmouth Quaker family, gave a good illustration in his journal of the time scale involved in getting a ship into harbour in the nineteenth century. On the 20th. November, 1838, the year of Queen Victoria's coronation, the Captain of the Larkins, an East Indiaman, asked the Falmouth agents to have his sinking ship towed into Falmouth. She had been holed when the Isles of Scilly pilot hit the Nundeep rock when putting her on the course for the approach to the English Channel. The Coverack pilot, Mr. James, went aboard the Larkins in Mounts Bay and took over the ship. He got 30 seiners from Cadgwith to come aboard and pump to keep the water at bay until the ship got into port. The seiners were still pumping while the ship was being unloaded in Falmouth three days after they had boarded her in Mounts Bay. It was fortunate that the East Indiaman got in when she did as her cargo was valued at between £50,000 and £60,000. A gale sprang up shortly after she reached port. It lasted a week. If the Larkins had been caught in that, the ship would undoubtedly have been a total loss.

It was the 15th. December, 1838 before Mr. James and the Cadgwith seiners who were led by R. Rundell got paid. The Coverack pilot, after much arguing, was given £300 for saving the ship and the seiners had £11 each for working the ship, pumping out and unloading the valuable cargo.

On another occasion, after a week of adverse winds, Carrick Roads was full of sailing craft awaiting suitable weather for rounding Lands End. When the wind eventually dropped and changed direction the ships began to leave harbour. Every available pilot was on service. In his poem 'Big Steamers' Rudyard Kipling wrote, 'Pilots are thicker than pilchards at Looe.' On the occasion about to be related, however, there was a distinct shortage in the waters of the Port of Falmouth. Two ships came out of Falmouth as far as Coverack. They stopped and flew a flag requesting a pilot to take them round Lands End. Mr. Barker, the Coverack pilot who lived in the house now named Gunvor, next to the former Bible Christian Chapel, responded to this request, but obviously he could only take one of the ships. In view of the shortage of pilots, Mr. Barker decided to ask one of the Coverack fishermen, Mr. Corin, if he would take the second ship. Mr. Corin was not very keen on the idea and reminded the pilot that although he knew the local waters he was not qualified as a pilot. Mr. Barker ignored this statement and persuaded Mr. Corin to come out and board the ship, saying they could go in company. Reluctantly the fisherman did as he was asked and indeed succeeded in following Mr. Barker to Swansea. Mr. Barker was so delighted that on their return by train from Swansea, he presented Mr. Corin with a

French compass, no doubt expressing the hope that it would encourage the fisherman to learn more about navigation. This compass remains in the possession of the Corin family and is produced when the story is being related to friends.

Of course, sea stories do not always have such a happy ending. Mr. Jim Barker, a fisherman pilot whose daughter Emily married into the Martin family of Coverack, was drowned in sight of home when he was hauling a store pot off the ground at the back of the quay. The red painted Falmouth tug 'Lizard' was coming into Coverack at the time but the crew was unable to save Mr. Barker who had faced danger so many times before as a fisherman and pilot. The sea provides and deprives. It has already been mentioned in the chapter entitled Stormy Nineteenth Century, that another Barker called William was awarded the Board of Trade Silver Medal for his bravery in saving life at sea when attending the wreck of the Bay of Panama in 1891 during the blizzard. Another descendant of the Barker family, Mr. Harold Martin was destined to become Secretary of the Lifeboat and to take part in the epic rescue of the Citrine, which will be related later.

Now let us return to the nineteenth century Barkers. In 1851 we find Anthony Barker, a retired pilot aged 60 living quietly with his wife Elizabeth who was 67. Their unmarried daughter, also called Elizabeth, was 45 and their son Joseph, aged 21 was a Pilot Apprentice. James Barker, aged 68, and living a few doors away from Anthony Barker was described as a superannuated pilot. He had a wife, Mary aged 63 and two daughters. Celina was 25 years old and a dressmaker by profession. She had a younger sister, Jane, aged 22. Her profession is not known. In the same year, there was a James Barker working as a Coastguard in Coverack. He was 43 years old and had been born in Newlyn. He had a wife, Elizabeth, also Newlyn born, and three daughters. Susannah was 13. She had been born while James was serving at Ramsgate. The middle daughter called Jane was 5 years old and the youngest child was 3. She was called Mary.

Another look at the population of Coverack twenty years later, in 1871 shows another Barker, John, who was a superannuated pilot, living with his wife Elizabeth and their married daughter Elizabeth Watts who was a schoolmistress. There was yet another Barker, also a superannuated pilot living in the village with his wife Jane. Another, James Barker and his wife Priscilla lived with their fisherman son, James, aged 19. They had a daughter called Patience who was a dressmaker and another daughter aged 12 called Emily who was a schoolgirl.

Ten years later in 1881 we find William Barker a retired schoolmaster, aged 63, living in Coverack with his Helston born blind wife, Nannie. She was 10 years older than her husband. Mary Barker, the wife of Anthony Barker mentioned above is now a widow in her 90s and described as an annuitant. She was head of the household and had a boarder called Catherine Daniel who was 76. In addition the nonagenarian had a visitor in the house called Mary Pike who was 66. They were waited on by Grace Williams a 40 year old servant. Thirty one year old William Barker, a village shoemaker was at that time living with his married sister, Selina Roebuck who was the wife of a gunner in the Royal Navy. She had a four month old son called John. It is also interesting to note that by this time Emily Barker, the fisherman's dressmaker daughter mentioned earlier is now described as a netmaker and mender. Another Barker, Henry, an unemployed joiner was living in Elizabeth Barker's house with his wife Jane and their two children. Elizabeth was 2 years old and John eleven months. The 19 year old fisherman, James Barker, mentioned earlier was now married with two children - Emily aged 6 and Norah aged 4. Patience Barker the former dressmaker, and daughter of James Barker the fisherman had now become a domestic servant and was working for Joseph Saunders the seiner.

The above account of some of the Barkers living in Coverack in the second half of the nineteenth century is an indication of the influence the Barkers had on village life. When one includes the families into which they married it is easy to understand why the village is in effect one large family. It has already been mentioned that the Barkers were allied to the Roskillys. The latter family is studied in the next section of this chapter. It will become apparent that these prominent families are connected in one way or another with the other village families. This state of affairs explains why people who come from other places to settle in the village sometimes feel they will never be considered as locals, no matter how long they live in the community. That is not true. They are just not members of the village extended family and will probably never understand fully the village family alliances nor the village family feuds.

Many of the villagers begin to realise family connections only when a crisis occurs or there is a wedding or a funeral. That is the time when the elders come to the fore and make statements about relationships which have not previously been common knowledge in the family. When my own children went to Coverack to attend their first family funeral as my representative, they recounted the punctilious care with which the list of the order of precedence of the people taking part in the cortege had been prepared. In fact the sole problem was the rank order of my three children. That was solved by asking them to walk side by side. It avoided giving only one of them an equal ranking with another member of the Hart family. Besides, although mourners usually walk in pairs, it is common to allow siblings to walk side by side. The other surprise awaiting my offspring who had been raised in the Welsh Baptist tradition by their mother was how much of the 'hard stuff' was downed after the funeral by my Band of Hope raised teetotal Methodist relations. My sister had warned the children that funeral processions were carefully scrutinised in Coverack. She told them that behind the closed, twitching curtains of the houses en route to the chapel, due note would be taken of the order of seniority decreed by the elder in charge of marshalling the mourners. There is nothing irreverent in this custom. It is an accepted village activity. The villagers close the curtains as a mark of respect to the deceased and to allow the mourning relatives to be alone with their private thoughts as they file past the cottages. Nevertheless, although all mourners are equal, some are more equal than others as George Orwell might say, so life must go on. It is important to record privately the family order of succession. The knowledge that this order is being observed and that all unorthodox omissions or additions will be duly noted and subsequently discussed, usually ensures an accurate deployment of the mourners. Today, when some members of a village family, through economic necessity, have to live far away from the village, the undertaker, who usually has a pretty good idea of family rankings, works out the list for approval by the time all the mourners have hastened to the village. The increasing practice of cremation and the gradual decline in church and chapel-going are whittling away the dignity and drama of Coverack funerals.

One branch of the Barker family put down its roots in London during the nineteenth century. Mr. George Barker, a Coverack builder decided he would like to establish a city business. George's brother, John, also went to London and set up in the printing business. George Barker established a business in New Road, Whitechapel, in the East End. As time went on the business prospered and other members of the family joined George. The firm's craftsmen specialised in churches, public buildings such as town halls and city pubs. The Barkers became members of the Guild of Painters and Stainers which had its Headquarters in Little Trinity Lane, London. The Barkers were elected Freemen of London. This began a family tradition. A present member of the family, Mr. David Bruce, great grandson of George Barker is a Member of the Guild of Painters and Stainers as well as a Freeman of the City of London. Mr. Bruce works in the chemical industry and is not a member of the firm. His maternal grandfather, William Arthur Barker married Florence Lake who was manager of a large brewery in London's East End, thus establishing a London family link. The name Lake has now become one of the Barker Christian names. Mr. Bruce's uncle was christened William Lake Barker.

George Barker learned his trade as a carpenter in Coverack with John Roskilly who eventually married George's sister, Jane Barker. It was quite natural, therefore, that when William Arthur Barker, George's son took on the business that he would ask his cousin Tom Coad Roskilly to come and join him in London. Tom was John and Jane Roskilly's son. Tom declined this offer and remained in Coverack. He became a much respected village carpenter, builder and undertaker. The business is still flourishing today.

By 1922 the Barker business was flourishing. It was in the August of that year when the Ellis family decided, after two centuries of ownership, to sell the quay and much of the property in Coverack. The London based Barker family grasped this opportunity of re-establishing themselves in Coverack. George Barker had lived in Bank House before he went to London. When he left the village the house was converted to a shop by Mrs. Joe Bowden. She is still remembered in Coverack for her 'appered of nicey' (half pennyworth of sweets) which the village children bought when they were awarded their weekly spending money. Mrs. Bowden used to dance into the shop at the sound of the bell, singing, 'I shall never forget the day that I was born,' or 'After the ball was over.' The Bowdens were very obliging and everyone loved visiting their shop. When Bank House came up for sale, it seemed a fitting memorial to the founder of the family fortunes to buy the house he had lived in for a summer residence. The Barkers also bought the three adjoining cottages. These are still thatched, and are a permanent reminder of what Coverack looked like in the nineteenth century as they are protected buildings. Smugglers' Cottage, which is next door to Bank House was occupied in 1922 by Mary Champion, grandmother of Mr. David Mason to whom I am indebted for much of the information I have gleaned about Coverack families. Mr. Mason's talks on the history of Coverack have been enjoyed by villagers and visitors over a number of years. Other cottages which were purchased by the Barkers were Ocean View, currently owned by Mr. Peter Barker, a Boat Builder and Yacht Surveyor, which is situated a hundred yards along the cliff road from Bank House and a hundred yards further along the road Minstrel Cottage (named after the rock at the Western end of the "triangle" of the part of the Manacle Rocks known as the Maen Varses, Carn Dhu and Minstrel). The latter cottage is now enlarged and includes the small "one-up and one-down" cottage which was attached to the end of it. The Barker family also purchased Rose

THE COVE FROM BANK HOUSE
*This photo was taken before 1910. The boy is probably looking at the "niceys" in the window. Opposite the shop is a refreshment room which was the Reading Room in winter. The Old Inn can be seen with a whitewashed lower end wall. The last four houses in the row were destroyed by bombs in 1942. The lady in the long skirt may have been wearing pattens to keep the hem out of the mud etc. on the unmade road.*

Cottage and Winifred Cottage which are situated on the hill behind Bank House. The latter is named after Mr. Bruce's mother, formerly Winifred Barker.

The cottages which were bought in addition to Bank House were intended for tenancy by Coverack born people. The purpose was to provide rented accommodation for locals at a price they could afford. A condition of tenancy was that one of the tenants should be Coverack born. Another Barker property is Granville House. The building was named after a relation called Granville Barker. In 1907, Jane Barker had her old family house rebuilt. The house is situated opposite the Seine Loft. The foundation stone states: 'This house was rebuilt to the memory of Elizabeth Coad who lived here many years. Stone laid by her daughter, Jane Barker, May, 1907.' The stone is signed, 'George Barker, Builder, London, E.1.' This house is still owned by a member of the Barker family, namely Mr. David Bruce who is mentioned earlier in this chapter. The bricks for Granville were brought to Coverack by sea. It is one of the few brick built houses in Coverack. Rumour has it that the writer's builder grandfather was not pleased to see the bricks being unloaded on the quay as he was at that time in the early stages of setting up in business in the village as a stonemason. The Barkers also brought their own bricklayers to build Granville.

There are two brothers, William and Noel Barker living in Polcoverack Lane in the village. Their father was one of the carpenter Barkers. Their branch of the Barker family is not continuing under the Barker name as their daughters have married and their children have the surnames of their fathers. This branch of the Barker family has kept up the village traditions. William won honour for the school when he came 175th. out of all England in the R.A.F. apprentices exam in 1922. Noel, who has worked on many of the local road improvement schemes as a supervisor, holds an award for rescuing a girl from the surf on the Mill beach during an easterly gale. Both brothers have been lifeboatmen. Their daughters are both qualified teachers. Mrs. Lillian Tutton, née Barker has been working at St. Keverne County Primary School for a number of years and has provided the writer with documents relating to local events.

The alliance between the Barkers and the Roskillys has been mentioned before. On the 19th. March, 1801, Susanna Barker married a William Roskilly. We found the families joining together again at the end of the century when Jane Barker married John Roskilly. These facts reinforce the remark made earlier about the village being one large family. In case non Cornish readers are beginning to think that they could never be accepted in the village, they should take comfort in the fact that in the 1951 census only 69% of the population of Cornwall were found to have been born in the county. In another survey, a random sample taken 20 years later in the 70s, it was found that only 43% of the children in schools were Cornish. In this instance, being Cornish was defined as having been born in Cornwall of parents who had both been born in Cornwall. By now it is almost certain that the above percentages are lower still. Our non Cornish friends can also be comforted by the fact that Mebyon Kernow, the Cornish Nationalist Party accepts people as Cornish if they truthfully consider themselves to be Cornish. This is borne out by the frequent statements made in a variety of regional accents on Radio Cornwall phone-ins by members of Mebyon-Kernow.

Each year the London Barkers would come to Bank House for their recreation after twelve months' toil in London. They motored down and brought their London relations and friends with them. Boating continued apace. The Barkers' motor boat was always painted a bright yellow - and still is - this was at the insistence of 'Grandmother' who wanted to assure herself from time to time that all was well at sea. She knew that yellow was a colour that showed up well on a grey and choppy sea. If trouble occurred, her family would be easily spotted and rescued in the minimum of time. My Auntie Alice Symes was employed as a cook by the Barkers in the summer. She found that it was easy to spot the Barker boat coming in from the Whiting ground or back from a picnic at Beagle Hole. She could then estimate the time of arrival of the hungry youngsters who would be looking forward to a meal when they landed.

Whenever the male Barkers came down to Coverack for a rest, the local organisations always tried to obtain their advice on building matters. It has been mentioned before that some of the Barkers were shoemakers. Their shop was opposite Bank House. It is now a 'summer let' flatlet. When its days as a shoemaker's shop were over it became a Reading Room. Villagers would gather there and if a visiting Barker happened to walk in, his advice would be sought. The minutes of the Wesleyan Chapel contain several references to building problems which were deferred until the Barkers came down for their holiday. The Society Stewards of the Chapel knew they could have the benefit of free advice from an old boy of the village - even if he did go to Church! It is interesting to note in passing that the small Barker building which was above the Roskilly's cow shed, became a centre for the dissemination of information. Mr. Pete Eddy had a wireless and villagers went there to listen to the war news and to gather gossip while Pete worked on until late in the night.

The Barkers have given considerable help to the village people by their attempts to preserve the 'oasis' for the use of the native villagers. Unfortunately the family is no longer a business unit and economic forces have obliged the various Barker owners to either sell their 'protected' properties when they became vacant or to let them to summer visitors in order to pay for the upkeep of the houses and keep them in the possession of the family. This means, of course, that the villagers now have to look elsewhere for properties which have a reasonable rent. There are still a few Coverack born villagers who rent houses owned by the Barker family. There is a good corporate spirit in the present day village and it is to the village organisations that people now look to conserve the oasis. The future appears quite bright as the village is flanked by National Trust properties and the current development of the hinterland seems acceptable.

## The Coverack Post Office, the Roskillys and Others

Roskilly is a name which is more synonymous with Coverack than Barker - that is if there can be degrees of synonymity between people and places. Generally speaking, the Roskillys have had more continuous and therefore a more direct and stronger influence on the village. In addition to being local carpenters, builders and undertakers the

Roskillys have been local farmers, property owners, importers, exporters and perhaps most important of all, they ran the principal village shop and the Post Office.

The name Roskilly is derived from the Cornish words 'ros', meaning heathland and 'kelly' means a grove or copse. The description of a heath with some trees fits conveniently the hamlet of Roskilly which is situated to the North East of the cross roads near Zoar Garage on the main road from Coverack to Helston. It was usual for the inhabitants of a settlement to be known by the place name of the area in which they lived. As time went on the place name was also accepted as the family name of the people living there. As with the Barkers, the Roskillys tended to name their children after their parents, grandparents and other relations. Like the Barkers there have been Roskillys in the area for centuries. It will be recalled from the chapter 'Beginnings' that a William Roskilly the archer, complete with bow and six arrows was on the muster roll of the armed men who were ready to defend Coverack at the time of the Armada. Some three centuries later another William Roskilly was among the first batch of volunteers to leave the Parish to fight in the First World War. There are more Roskillys in the Coverack area at present than there are Barkers. An examination of the current local telephone directory shows there are 206 Barkers of whom 75 live in the Plymouth and South West Devon area. The remainder live in Cornwall. There is one Roskell, one Roskelly, 3 Roskellys and 41 Roskillys of whom 5 live in the Plymouth and South West Devon area. The other Roskillys live in Cornwall. This count is not conclusive, but it does seem to suggest that the Roskillys tend to be a smaller family than the Barkers and to be concentrated in Cornwall. In contrast we shall learn later that the Coverack Roskillys have branches in the United States and New Zealand.

We know that there was an alliance between the Roskillys and the Barkers when William Roskilly and Susanna Barker married in 1801. A son, Thomas Roskilly was born in 1808, he grew up and married. His wife Jane had a daughter called Sarah Jane, then she bore him four sons. One was called William. He was born in 1834. His brother Thomas was born three years later, then came the third brother, John. After the fourth boy, Richard Roskilly was born, another daughter called Susanna was born in 1847. These nineteenth century Christian names of the Roskillys continued the pattern which has come through to the present day.

Mr. Francis Roskilly, brother of the last Roskilly sub Postmaster, kindly allowed me to look at the entries in the Roskilly family Bible. There is an entry in the year 1858. It states, 'William Jas. Roskilly and Caroline were married in the year of our Lord, 1858, January 12th.' Beneath this entry is the poignant sentence, 'Caroline departed this life May 6th., 1858.' How William James Roskilly coped with his grief is not known.

After two years as a widower, William married again. This time it was to Elizabeth Williams who was presumably a widow as she had three children. John and Sampson were aged 8 and 6. They both became carpenters when they grew up. The youngest child was Elizabeth who was only three years old. After two years of marriage, Sarah Jane Roskilly was born and the familiar Roskilly Christian names are in use once more. Silvanus was born in 1862. He lived for just one year. When records such as these are examined, one can understand why funerals and mourning played such an important part in village life in the nineteenth century. They were frequent. No family escaped. The whole village would unite to help the bereaved overcome their loss of a dear one. Infant mortality was high and older people died prematurely because there was at that time either no cure for their illnesses or they could not afford the necessary treatment. Sometimes, of course, the doctor was unable to recognise the illness before it was too late to try to effect a cure. Sanitation was bad in Coverack although the sea afforded the inhabitants a better place for human waste than the streets did for their contemporaries in the towns. Large families living in close proximity in the small thatched cottages passed diseases round their relations. There were outbreaks of diphtheria. Measles was a serious disease and often left people deaf or with defective eyesight. There were outbreaks of cholera in Cornwall. Falmouth suffered badly from it in 1849. Rabies swept through the county in 1878 and at intervals throughout the century there were instances of small pox. Those unlucky enough to get tuberculosis were usually banished to a shed in the garden once people realised why whole families were going down with the disease. This state of affairs was accepted stoically by the people. Many of them sought solace in religion which promised a better life in the hereafter. Individuals like Uncle Tommy Champion in the non conformist churches and the appointed Guardians who dispensed relief paid for by the tithes collected by the established church did their best to support those who were bowed down by adversity. Local benefactors who were usually also local employers did what they could and the doctors like the Sprys of St. Keverne often neglected to send in accounts when they knew the families could not pay.

In the November of 1863, the year that the infant Silvanus Roskilly died, another William Roskilly was born. There followed a sister, Caroline in 1865, then Thomas two years later. He was destined to take over the Post Office from his father. Jabez and Janie Roskilly were born later.

While the 'shop and Post Office' Roskillys were getting established, the farming side continued in the area. Simon and Elizabeth Roskilly worked a smallholding at North Corner. They had a dressmaker daughter called Mary living with them. There were Roskilly farm buildings in the village, behind the shop. The younger members of the Roskilly families who could not be part of the businesses of shop keeping, farming and carpentering went to work on neighbouring farms or as apprentices to other carpenters. Not many appear to have taken to fishing or piloting as one might expect. It is interesting to note that John Roskilly, the son of William Roskilly and Susanna Barker who married in 1801, had a son called John who became a carpenter. In time his son John became a carpenter. The villagers have become so accustomed to having a Roskilly as a carpenter in the village that they still talk of getting Roskilly the carpenter in spite of the fact that the last Roskilly carpenter, Mr. Tom Coad Roskilly, died in 1959 when he was 78. The name lives on in the building firm of Roskilly and Gilbert which was taken over by the late Leslie Gilbert, Tom Coad Roskilly's nephew.

In the year 1840 the Penny Post was introduced to Great Britain by Rowland Hill. This meant that people could send a letter not weighing more than half an ounce to anywhere in Great Britain for one penny. This was in response to popular demand, although the politicians were not keen. It fell to Mr. William Lory of Treleague, St. Keverne, to write a letter in July, 1842 to Colonel Maberly the Secretary of the Post Office, setting out proposals for a postal service on the Lizard peninsula so that the inhabitants could take advantage of the new, improved service. It is somewhat ironic that this should have been necessary when one considers that the people living on the Lizard peninsula had been watching the swift Falmouth Packet sloops carrying mail in and out of Falmouth for the previous century and a half. Most of the inhabitants, however, would have been unable to afford the price demanded before they could take delivery of a letter. The new idea of paying one penny for sending a letter meant that people could keep in touch with relatives who were working away from home and those relatives were no longer forced to refuse deliveries of letters from home because they could not afford to pay for their delivery.

As time went on, Mr. William Lory's letter to Colonel Maberly was acted upon and a Post Office was set up in Commercial Road, St. Keverne. It was to be nearly forty years before Coverack was to have its own Post Office. Meanwhile, mail was taken to Coverack from St. Keverne by any trustworthy person who happened to be going back to the village. Mr. Joseph Higgins, Superintendent of the Post Office in Glasgow, wrote an account of the delivery of Coverack's mail for the Post Office Magazine when he retired in 1918. Joseph Higgins was a boy in Coverack at the time of the Franco-Prussian War in the early 1870s. He used to attend the Parochial School in St. Keverne. His father was Henry Higgins, Chief Officer (Second Class) of Coastguards in Coverack. Joseph was a Devonian by birth, having been born in 1858 at Chisileton. Coming from an 'official' family, Joseph was considered trustworthy enough to be asked to bring the mail from St. Keverne to Coverack. There were not usually many letters, so Joseph got into the habit of delivering them to the houses when he reached Coverack. A retired sea captain living in the village at the time was especially anxious to get his mail as he had The Times newspaper sent by Post. This newspaper had become famous during the 1850s at the time of the Crimean War. This was because of its exposure of the blunders being made by politicians and army commanders and of the terrible conditions under which Florence Nightingale and her nurses had to work under in order to relieve the suffering of the wounded. It follows that in the 1870s The Times was eagerly awaited for its reliable foreign news. People would flock to the Reading Room in Coverack to hear the news read aloud by the captain, who doubtless only read the parts he thought the villagers wanted to hear. The trust placed in Joseph Higgins by the Postal authorities and by the villagers gave him a strong sense of the importance of his honorary task. The prestige Joseph enjoyed prompted his two companions to ask him if he would share the job with them. Joseph refused and one day a fight developed between the boys when they were walking back to Coverack from St. Keverne. 'When the fight was over,' Joseph wrote, 'I had a swollen lip, one of the two had a bloody nose and the other a black eye, but always after that Her Majesty's Mails for Coverack were safe from juvenile highwaymen, bought over on my part by promising the enemy not to reveal the true secret of our wounds.' The job of postman carried no official pay but Joseph was rewarded from time to time, although his father had forbidden him to accept money from the grateful recipients of letters. On one occasion he received sixpence for delivering a letter to a lady whose husband had been at sea for twelve months. Joseph recalled, 'I promptly spent it in pressed dates in Mr. Roskilly's shop.' Sixpence was a fortune for a small boy in those days. In fact, the job did not last very long because the Postal District Surveyor found out about it and Coverack was given a regular service by a Rural Postman. A few years later Joseph Higgins got his reward. His father, the Chief Officer of Coastguards, got to know Mr. Newberry Cox, who was the Falmouth Postmaster from 1856 to 1896 and Joseph was taken on as one of his assistants. It is interesting to note that Mr. Cox was a member of the family which ran the Falmouth Docks. Another member of the Cox family retired to Coverack in the 1920s and did much to promote the Scout movement in the village. He provided needy boys with uniforms and allowed the young people of the village to use the workshop and hobbies room which he established in the present day Cliff Cottage which adjoins Channel View Hotel. When wireless sets were an expensive luxury, Mr. Cox allowed the village children to take turns to 'hark in' on the headphones of the wireless he had installed in the workshop.

As Coverack is not the Churchtown of the parish, it has always had problems in obtaining the same facilities as St. Keverne. The provision of a Post Office proved to be no exception. In 1848 a petition was sent to the Post Master General from Helston regarding the carrying of mail to St. Keverne parish. It went thus:

'Considering the distance walked daily by the Rural Post Messenger between Helstone and St. Keverne and the necessity they are under of providing a second horse in consequence of their having to stop at St. Keverne every alternate night I have no hesitation in recommending your Lordship to sanction Mr. Cresswell's proposition for raising their wages from 10 shillings and sixpence to twelve shillings a week each.' This illustrates the difficulties encountered in keeping a good service going. In fact it was 1872 before Helston became a Head Post Office. At last, in 1880, Volume 202 of the Post Office recorded under entry 6407 that Coverack Sorting Office was established. The Roskillys were in control.

Things began to happen. In 1881 delivery was extended to Gwinter - the name of the hamlet was not spelt Gwenter by the Post Office archivist until 1911 - and by 1882 Coverack had its own Post Messenger and was given a 'Horsekeep' allowance for carrying the mail directly between Helston and Coverack. The mounted postman's days were already numbered, however. In 1889, Minute No. 9974 was sent to London, proposing a 'Mail Cart Service in lieu of mounted post.' The reasons in a subsequent memorandum were as follows:

'The present Rural Post from Helston to Coverack is a Mounted Post and the distance traversed amounts to twenty eight miles a day. (This included St. Martin and St. Keverne). Although the Post Messenger has received the unusually large allowance of twenty four shillings a week for Horsekeep, the work has been of such an arduous nature that it has not been performed in a satisfactory manner and the Surveyor proposes to take the opportunity afforded at present by the retirement of the Post Messenger, to establish a regular Mail Cart Service on the longer portion of the route.'

Six tenders were submitted, ranging from £70 to £135 per annum. The lowest tender was rejected as 'Mr. H. is not a man of means.' Mr. Henry Pascoe's tender for £96 was accepted, the reason given being that he had already been the contractor for the Helston and Lizard Mail Cart Service for ten years and that he had done the work in a thoroughly satisfactory manner. Further details were given in the Memorandum:

| | |
|---|---|
| Distance travelled by the Cart | 22 miles a day |
| Coverack Sorting Office Salary | £9 8s |
| Delivery in village | 2s 6d. a week |
| Delivery to Gwinter | 3s 6d. a week |

In 1895 the 'Coverack and Gwinter Post' was extended and London granted an increased allowance. When the twentieth century began in 1901 Coverack had its very own separate Mail Cart Service from the 1st. June to the 30th. September. This no doubt reflected the increased volume of mail due to visitors staying in the village. There was also a collection started that year by the St. Keverne Postman at Porthoustock at 2 p.m. each day. At the same time London was informed that four St. Keverne men had been cautioned for delivering unposted newspapers on their rounds.

By 1891, the Post Office had been established for over a decade and was advertised in Mr. H.J. Sincock's twopenny guide to Coverack:

MAIL SERVICE

Week Days - one delivery

Arrive 11.15 a.m. Box closed 1.25 p.m.

Parcels received up to 1.20 p.m.

Sundays No Delivery.

By 1911 the service had improved. It was advertised in Kelly's Directory by Mrs. Mary Roskilly, sub-postmistress, as having a delivery at 10.20 a.m. Letters were despatched at 2.50 p.m. The Post Office was by then also a Money Order Office and was a great boon to the wives of Coverack men who were in the Merchant Navy as they could get their husbands' pay without having to travel to St. Keverne. They were also kept in touch with the movements of their husbands' ships. Running a Telegraph Office meant that the Roskruges of St. Keverne and the Roskillys of Coverack had key roles to play when there was a local shipwreck. They were so inundated with calls in 1898 and again 1900 after the wrecks of the Mohegan and Paris that telegraphists were sent on temporary loan to Coverack from the Falmouth Office to deal with the additional volume of traffic. In 1899 it was recorded in the typical official language of the Central Post Office Records:

'Mohegan S.S. extra duty incurred in connection with loss of at Helston and St. Keverne R.S.O.' It added 'Sub Postmistress commended.'

Most of the main towns of Cornwall were finally linked to the main trunk telephone system in 1898, the year of the Mohegan disaster.

It was the William Roskilly, whose first marriage ended when his bride Caroline died only six months after the wedding in 1858, who firmly established the Roskilly business in Coverack. William had a natural talent for commerce. Eventually the shop was set up in the waterside building now known as 'The Old Post Office'. Before becoming a shop it was a dwelling house and inn. It was most probably the main rendez-vous for smugglers and a store for their contraband before the soldiers and customs men got a grip on the Lizard peninsula. After that it must have become the first place to be searched whenever there had been a 'run' which the Revenue men got to hear about. Coverack men were careful not to leave any records of their 'ventures' so it is only possible to speculate, with very few facts at one's disposal. Like all old buildings, the Old Post Office is reputed to have a ghost. Mr. Francis Roskilly wrote about it in a booklet published to commemorate the centenary of Coverack School in 1976. The booklet is called 'Our School Days By The Sea'. Mr. Roskilly was told that '........after a brawl, a smuggler was chained to a ceiling in one of the rooms and was later hanged and thrown on to the rocks below, and that - to this day - when it's full moon, at the hour of midnight, chains can be heard clanging on the rocks below.' In connection with this Mr. Roskilly mentioned that a clome or unglazed earthenware tea pot was found in the roof of the old Post Office when the thatch was replaced by slates. This was a traditional way of keeping evil spirits from entering through the roof of a house. A tea pot used for this purpose used to have a pisky shape baked to the lid to give it added potency.

Reference has already been made to purchases of coal in Coverack by the contemporaries of Tommy Champion. The coal was brought by colliers under sail from Swansea. Occasionally a small steam coaster would come into the harbour and unload her coal. The Roskillys and the Roberts acted as merchants, storing the surplus coal in Friendship Cellar (opposite the Seine Loft) and Roberts' yard which was behind the cottage called Ocean View. When a ship came in the farmers brought their horses and carts to the village and acted as carriers. It was the custom to dump a load of coal in front of the customer's house. The householder would then shovel it up and take it to the coal shed at the back of the house. Fertilisers for farmers, timber and special stone and cement for builders were also brought to Coverack by sea. Unloading was always done at speed because it meant more work to unload the cargo when the vessel was below the level of the quay platform. There was always the danger of an East wind springing up and the collier being caught on a lee shore.

The Roskillys also used their carts for carrying fish, potatoes and other vegetables to the station in Helston. On the return journey the carts were laden with goods for the Coverack shops, local farmers and other private individuals. The Coastguards hired the same carts to carry furniture to and from Cadgwith, the Lizard, Porthallow and Porthoustock, when men were transferred from one station to another. Moving house was a tedious business in those days, especially in poor weather. The children rode on the carts while the older members of the household accompanied the carts on foot.

Roskilly's shop sold all the basic necessities of life. It was a veritable Aladdin's cave. The cows were milked in the shed behind the shop, so it followed that milk and butter and cream were sold in the shop. The cows were brought from the fields through the village twice a day to be milked. There were also a few hens in a yard at the quayside end of the cowshed, so customers could buy eggs from the shop and the occasional chicken or 'boiler'. Most of the villagers kept a few hens and a pig as a standby source of food when times were hard, so there was not a large local trade in poultry, nor eggs, nor pork.

Butchers used to come to the village from St. Keverne and even the Lizard but a small trade in freshly killed meat was done in the village shop. There was a set day for killing. After that there would be carcasses of pigs and sometimes a bullock hanging in the shop. A temporary butcher's counter would be pushed to the centre of the tiny shop floor space. Jointing would be done on the spot. According to village custom, some joints were set aside for favoured and promptly paying customers. One butcher who used to visit Coverack was a fervent Wesleyan. Everyone knew he kept a 'Wesleyan' shelf of choice pieces for the customers of his religious persuasion! I do not think religion was considered by Mr. Roskilly when it came to holding back juicy joints for favourite customers. The fleshy, cloying smell of freshly killed meat was added to the scents of paraffin, candles, calico, wool, tobacco, vinegar, liquorice, spices, cheese, sacks of flour and sugar and all the other foods. It must be remembered that there was no refrigeration and very little packaging in those days. By the time some of the perishable foodstuffs arrived in Coverack they would not be very fresh, so by the time the food was sold it doubtless had an aroma which would not be acceptable to our delicate late twentieth century noses. In addition to the sale of commodities outlined above, the Roskillys also arranged for the collection of eggs and butter from the surrounding farms. They would be taken to markets in Helston, Redruth and Falmouth on the appropriate days. It was no mean feat to assemble the produce the day before market, then get up at three o'clock the next morning and drive the pony and trap to market - a journey of four hours or more in the case of Redruth or Falmouth - then the produce would have to be sold and at the end of the day there was the long drive home, often in the rain. The arrival in Coverack would be after dark, then the trap would have to be put away and the pony fed and watered and stabled for the night. After a few hours sleep it would be time to get up and bring the cows in for milking. The shop would then be got ready for opening. In view of all this routine work it is clear that a large family was an asset to the Roskillys. They employed a number of villagers as well.

The tragedy which William Roskilly the first shopkeeper and business man suffered so soon after his marriage made him a compassionate person. In the shop there was always a large open ledger in which a record was kept of everything sold on credit. Many villagers had cause to be grateful for being allowed to run up a bill when fishing was bad or the breadwinner was sick and unable to work. This service was sometimes abused and sometimes interest was charged but many villagers had cause to be thankful for a sympathetic hearing in their time of need. The following account by the same William Roskilly was lent to me by the late Mr. Albert Carey who was a descendant of one of the victims of:

'A very melancholy accident.'

(The spellings etc, are as written by Mr. Roskilly.)

'Thomas Eustace aged 25 years, his brother Baulden Eustace aged 21 years, Richard Tripp aged 31 years, three fishermen on July 15th., 1867 about 10 o'clock a.m. when they were coming in under sale, the wind blowing from the westward very heavy, a sudden squall took the boat and capsised her and in a moment men and boat were swallowed up in the mighty deep they were seen by several men in and near Coverack. Thomas Eustace leaveing a widow and one child, Richard Trip a widow and three children to mourn there loss, they were men respected and beloved with all there neighbours'.

William Roskilly

This moving story reveals a man quite different from the fictional Reseigh in Charles Lee's book, 'Paul Carah, Cornishman' referred to earlier.

The Roskilly Family Bible records brief details of emigration in addition to marriages, births and deaths. William Roskilly's stepsons, John and Sampson Williams left for New Zealand in September, 1884. Lizzie, William and Janie left on January 16th., 1887, so did Hilda and Frank. These were from other branches of the family. In the following month, Martin, Loveday and Annie-Lizzie May left. The final entry was Sarah who left on September 29th., 1902. William Roskilly the shopkeeper and business man died seven years later on January 21st., 1909. One might question the fact that so many from one family should leave home, especially from a family which was doing quite well in the material sense. There are several reasons. No doubt some were personal such as the desire for adventure and the need to make one's way in the world without the ever present protective but demanding arm of the family. The business could not absorb everyone and the economic state of Cornwall was not good towards the end of the nineteenth century. Almost as soon as the Cornwall Railway had been built in mid century, the company ran 'emigrant specials' because of the mining slump. There were soup kitchens and bread queues for those who stayed behind. This state of affairs did not affect the Roskillys directly, nor for that matter did it force any of the villagers to consider leaving Cornwall because of impossible conditions in Coverack. It is true that pilchards seemed to be deserting the Cornish coast. There were occasional 'gluts' but it seemed pretty clear that the days of profitable seining had passed their peak. Tales of riches to be gained overseas contrasted sharply with the drab conditions existing in Coverack so it is not surprising that some of the young people decided to try their luck.

Returning to the advent of the railway in Cornwall, Coverack people had to go to Redruth main line station for a number of years after the railway reached Penzance in 1865. In 1882, on the 22nd. of March, the first turf was cut for the Helston-Gwinear branch line. It was such an important event that there was a procession from the Bowling Green in Helston up to the Tile House Field. The older and the younger sections of the community were given free teas and there was a grand firework display in the evening. By 1887 the line was completed. This meant that the carrying business of the Roskillys and the Roberts was extended due to more goods than ever being sent by rail. The seaborne trade of coal, fertilisers, timber and building materials continued until the 1920s. From then on these goods came to Coverack by road from Helston Station or they were landed from coasters at Gweek, Penryn or Falmouth and brought to the village by wagon or lorry.

The 1880s emigration of some of the Roskillys was not the first. In 1817 Simon Roskilly, a farmer from North Corner, Coverack, married Elizabeth Matthews. The couple had nine children:

William, Thomas, Simon, Richard, Joseph, Elizabeth, Susan, John and Mary Jane:

The Christian names are typical Roskilly family names. The fourth child, Richard went to work, when he was old enough, at Tralan or Trelan as it is known today. Richard worked for a Mr. Samuel James, a local farmer who was well known for his veterinary skills. Mr. James and his wife Anna had four sons. Jane Rule, daughter of Simon and Martha Rule who lived at Trelan Gate also worked on the James' farm as a mother's help.

In 1842, Mrs. James left Falmouth for New York on the sailing ship Orient. Jane Rule, then aged ten went with Mrs. James to help her look after the baby, John, who was just over a year old. The other James children were aged 3, 6 and 8, so both Mrs. James and Jane Rule must have had a busy time on the ship. It was the custom in those days for the passengers to keep their part of the ship clean and to do their own cooking under the supervision of the ship's passengers' cook. Mr. James followed his family to America when he had concluded his business affairs in Coverack. The family eventually set up their new home in Racine, Wisconsin. Later the James family moved to the Pacific shore of the state of Oregon.

Meanwhile, Richard Roskilly who had been left without a job in Coverack, obtained work with the Shepard family. When they too emigrated to America, he went with them. He was 16 years old. Mr. Hannibal Shepard was married to Elizabeth, the sister of Mrs. Anna James who had taken Jane Rule with her to Wisconsin. When the James family moved on to Oregon from Racine, Jane Rule remained in Racine. She was found work with Mrs. Shepard, her previous employer's sister. It was on her farm that Jane Rule met Richard Roskilly once more. The inevitable happened. The two Coverack people fell in love and got married on the 8th December, 1852 in the Samuel Skews chapel house on Grovean Farm in Racine County. They must have felt at home in that place with a Cornish name.

I am grateful to Mrs. Elva Stark of Salt Lake City for the information about the Roskillys in America. Mrs. Stark is the great grand daughter of the Racine County Roskillys. She wrote an article about the Roskilly-Rule emigration entitled 'Reminiscences from a Rocking Chair' for the Cornwall Family History Society. She subsequently sent me further information about the American Roskillys in response to my giving her information about the Coverack Roskillys. I also sent Mrs. Stark some photos of the quay at Coverack '........where Richard remembered herding the cows.' Mrs. Stark treasures an oil painting of Coverack quay. It was sent her by an aunt who told her that an artist friend of her great grandfather Richard Roskilly painted it from a postcard. Richard and Jane Roskilly knew they would never be able to go to their beloved Coverack again so the painting had great sentimental value for them in their old age. Mrs. Stark described the scene as '........a peaceful scene with a rockwall and sailboats in the cove.'

The village shop is usually a centre for the exchange of news and views. The Roskilly shop was no exception. It was also a Post Office and was a link with the outside world before the days of wireless and when there were few telephones in the village. There are many tales of what went on in Roskilly's shop. Mr. Francis Roskilly told me an amusing story about his grandfather William Roskilly the shopkeeper. In 1888 William went to London on business. One evening when he had finished for the day he went for a stroll. It was at the time when the man known as 'Jack the Ripper' was being hunted by the police for a series of brutal murders which had occurred in London. Mr. Roskilly was picked up and taken to a police station for questioning. After a while Mr. Roskilly realised that in the eyes of the police he was suspected of being involved in the murders of 'Jack the Ripper.' On being asked if there was anyone who could verify his identity, Mr. Roskilly thought of Mr. Barker, the Coverack builder and his relation by marriage. Mr. Barker had set up his building business in Whitechapel where some of the murders had taken place. The police contacted Mr. Barker who gladly confirmed that Mr. Roskilly was the person he had claimed to be and Mr. Roskilly was soon released. This episode became part of the Roskilly family history. When the young Francis Roskilly and his brother Sam wanted to embarrass their Aunt Janie, William Roskilly's daughter, they would ask her to relate the story. Miss Janie Roskilly was a very religious lady and did not wish to be associated with anything as sordid as the unsolved murders of 'Jack the Ripper.' Of course she knew full well that her father was totally innocent but she got very agitated and embarrassed when the two boys would ask her with wide eyed innocence to tell them the story about their grandfather getting into trouble with the police in London! The boys would choose the time and place of asking the question so as to obtain the maximum effect on their sensitive aunt. A favourite occasion was in the shop when there were several villagers waiting to be served and hoping to be able to gather some interesting news to take home with the groceries.

My own grandmother, Mrs. Ann Pengilly worked in Roskilly's shop when she was known as Ann Rickard. Her sister, Alice Rickard also worked there for a while, so inevitably we heard stories about the goings-on in the shop. Mr. Tommy Roskilly, who took over the business from his father William, was a man who loved a joke. He was a very busy man as he had to look after the shop, the farm, the market distribution business and so on. As a person, Mr. Roskilly was somewhat awe inspiring. Not only was he a prominent figure in the life of the village and therefore commanded respect, his appearance sometimes intimidated young people for he only had one arm, having had to have the other amputated after a shooting accident. It was his custom to attach a hook as an artificial aid when he had heavy work to do. One day after doing some work in the cowshed he happened to walk into his shop when it was closing time. He arrived unobserved and unheard at the very moment when one of his young lady assistants was placing a pat of stolen butter in her bonnet. Mr. Roskilly waited until the girl had put the bonnet on and carefully adjusted the strings so that the butter would remain hidden as she walked out of the shop. He then made his presence known and invited the terrified girl to come into the kitchen and have 'a warm' before going home. She could not refuse her employer's invitation, so she followed him into the kitchen and Mr. Roskilly drew up a chair for her, placing it as close the the slab (cooking range) as he could. He engaged the girl in small talk until the tell-tale melting butter started to run down her red cheeks from its hiding place under the bonnet. Mr. Roskilly then told the girl that he had seen all and said he hoped his ruse would teach her a lesson. After this story was 'leaked' round the village, I am confident that there was little petty thieving from the shop for some time after this incident.

Mr. Tom Roskilly was interested in village activities. He was a School Manager and took his duties seriously without being pompous. When he called at the school to sign the registers and see that all was well, it was his custom to bring some 'goodies' such as sweets, fruit or biscuits to give to the children. He was even more popular on some occasions when he asked the teacher to let the children go early because of their good behaviour. Tom was also a chapel-goer. At Christmas it was the custom for the chapel choir to get up early on Christmas Day and sing carols as they walked through the village. The singers always finished their walk at Roskilly's shop, knowing they would be invited indoors to sing to the Roskilly family and share in their Christmas breakfast. Some of the choir members would have been taken on as temporary workers by Mr. Roskilly a few days before Christmas. Their job was to sit at the large kitchen table, plucking chicken and geese and getting them ready for market. For these people, the Christmas breakfast was a little reward for their work as well as their singing.

When the horses which had been requisitioned by the government to serve in France during the First World War were brought back to Great Britain, the government sold them cheaply to farmers. Mr. Tom Roskilly could not resist the temptation to buy a couple of these horses. One of them was a tall chestnut and was used as a light cart horse. One day, Mr. Roskilly's son, William was driving the horse down Higher Bridge Hill when the Coastal Defence guns at Falmouth began a practice shoot. The former war horse took fright and bolted down the hill, going round the sharp corners at high speed. When the horse got to the corner by the present Council Car Park in the middle of the hill, William Roskilly decided discretion was the better part of valour and threw himself clear. It was a wise decision. The horse continued down the hill at a gallop and jumped over the cliff, dragging the cart behind it and killing itself when it landed on the rocks. It was another lucky escape for a man who had survived the horrors of the First World War.

The other horse bought by Mr. Roskilly was little better. He appeared ideally suited to pulling the 'trap' which Mr. Roskilly used for getting about the countryside to see to his businesses. The horse was duly named 'Fleetwing' and was most satisfactory at first. One Saturday, the trap was being loaded with produce which Mr. Roskilly had collected from neighbouring farms prior to going to the butter and egg market at Helston. The horse set off from the shop but when it had gone a couple of hundred yards and was outside the Bible Christian Chapel, which has been converted since to a dwelling house, Fleetwing took fright and started to 'back 'n back' as we say in Coverack. The frightened animal pushed the trap right into a water barrel which was standing on the road to catch rain water from the roof of a house for washing clothes. The horse reversed so violently that it broke the shafts of the light trap and the eggs and butter were splashed all over the road. Naturally this incident attracted a crowd of villagers, among whom was David Mason, then aged nine. It was he who related the anecdote to me. The moral of the story is neatly phrased in Charles Lee's 'Paul Carah, Cornishman'. Paul, guilty of driving a hard bargain, stated: 'All the world do know what a bargain is - two honest men trying to cheat aich other!'

The story of the shell-shocked war horses does not end there. Because of the poor quality of horses available in the area, some farmers got together and formed a 'Meneage Committee.' Representatives of this committee were appointed to go 'up country' and purchase suitable stallions for breeding purposes. These stallions were then taken round from farm to farm when owners who had contributed to the scheme required their mares to be serviced. Readers will recall that Mr. Tripp of Coverack used to 'walk the horse' for his employer. The Meneage Committee stallions were easily identified as they were lead about the countryside, for they always had a white halter. This was presumably a sign of the purity of the stallion's blood. In due course the locals were identifying village philanderers by saying, 'He ought to have a white halter!' The advent of tractors and the use of artificial insemination have put an end to this practice in the Meneage District.

The Roskillys were property owners in Coverack. Mr. William Roskilly had a house built in the lane behind St. Peter's Church. The property was named 'Chymbloth' after the nearby farmland which was worked by Mr. Richard Roberts. The Roskillys also had two large houses in Sunny Corner. They are now called 'Sunnyside' and 'Graham House'. These houses were destroyed by enemy action during the Second World War but have since been rebuilt. The properties were eventually sold, Chymbloth being bought from the Roskillys by Mr. Hannibal James, Sunnyside by Mr. Jack Saunders a descendant of the Coverack seiner and Graham House by Dr. Kempthorne, Mr. Saunders' brother in law. It is interesting to note how the Barkers invested in older village properties for long term renting when they decided to become more intimately involved in village life, while the Roskillys speculated in new properties which were sold again in a fairly short space of time in order to raise capital for the other businesses.

The Roskillys and Barkers were not the only enterprising people in Coverack in the nineteenth century. They have been studied because of the impact they have made on village life. Through them some interesting facets of village happenings have emerged, as illustrated above.

Miss Diggens, sister of the St. Keverne parson lived in Coverack at the turn of the century. She lived with her sister in the former Wesleyan Chapel House at the top of Sunny Corner lane. Like her brother, Miss Diggens was deeply interested in goings on in the parish. She made some notes about John Harris. He was born in 1783 at Trevanion, the house which later became the home of the village schoolmaster, Mr. H.J. Sincock. When a young man, John Harris began trading with the Red Indians in North America. He would take a cargo of items which were valued by the Red Indians and exchange such things as hunting knives, cutlery and other manufactured goods for pelts and furs of all kinds, which he would bring back to England. He is recorded as saying that one cargo of lanterns which he took across the Atlantic was received with great joy by the Indians. Unfortunately there are no details available about the Atlantic crossings made by John Harris, but the following extract from a manuscript of Miss Diggens reveals the nature of this enterprising man:

'In early life he began a small but enterprising trade with America and crossed over in his boat 15 or 16 times. No money transaction passed between them - simply an exchange of goods - they would bring various kinds of skins in return for Harris' wares. He is spoken of as 'an eccentric, but upright honourable man,' as may be proved by the following incident.

'Once when in London he went to an exhibition in which several North American Indians were doing a war dance. He was much interested in watching it when suddenly one of their number recognised him and shouted for very joy, calling him by the name they had given him amongst themselves. All eyes were turned to him - some thought it was part of the performance. So great was the excitement among the natives at seeing their old friend that the stage manager thought it wise to ask him to come down and make a speech. He was particularly good at speech making so raised no objection. Before be began however he was lifted off his feet and embraced in proper North American Indian fashion. In addressing the audience he told how it was he became acquainted with these savage looking people and he accounted for their fondness for him by saying that in all his dealings with them he had never driven a hard bargain.'

During his retirement, John Harris lodged in Coverack with 'Uncle' Tommy Champion and his second wife Jane. He owned the farm properties of Trevalso, near St. Keverne and Chynalls in Coverack. He is buried in St. Keverne Churchyard, in the section to the left of the entrance gate. The inscription on his headstone reads:

'Born at Coverack in this Parish and after a wandering life died in the same village, December 19th., 1874 at the advanced age of 92 years.'

Other families known to have lived in and around Coverack during the second half of the nineteenth century are as follows:

| NAME | LOCATION |
| --- | --- |
| BASTIAN | Village |
| BOUCHER | Village |
| BOULDEN | Village (shop and fishing) |
| BRAY | Treliever Common |
| COAD | Village |
| CORIN | Village |
| CORLYON | Village |

| | |
|---|---|
| CREUSE/CRUZE | Village |
| EUSTIS/EUSTACE/EUSTICE | Village, Polcoverack Common |
| EXELBY | Ponsongath, Treliever |
| HARRIS | Ponsongath |
| HOCKING | Village, Gwenter, Content |
| JAMES | Village |
| JOHNS | Gwenter |
| LAMBRICK | Trevothen Downs |
| LAWRENCE | Trewillis |
| LYE | Village (Inn) |
| MARTIN | Village (Mill), Carnwijack |
| MUNDY | Village, Penhallick |
| PENGILLY | Village, Content, Downas, Pednavounder, Polcoverack |
| RALPH | Village (Mill) |
| RICHARDS | Trewillis |
| RICKARD | Village, Mount Earl, Ponsongath |
| ROBERTS | Village, Poldowrian, Treliever, Trewillis, Trevothen |
| ROGERS | Polcoverack |
| RULE | Chynalls, Trewillis, Trevothen |
| TRIPP | Village, Downas Mill |
| WHITE | Village |
| WILLIAMS | Village, Carnsullan |
| WILLMOT | Trevothen |

It will be appreciated that the above families were not living in the places indicated throughout the whole of the second half of the nineteenth century. There was considerable movement due to tenancies of farms changing and leases of houses running out. It is possible, of course, to illustrate life in and around Coverack during the nineteenth century, by relating the history of some of these families. It is hoped that someone will complement this chronicle by so doing. Details of some of the Coverack Coastguard families are given in a subsequent chapter.

# RELIGION AND EDUCATION

The chapter has a composite title because in the context of this book one can not consider the one in isolation from the other. It has been explained that the first public building in Coverack was the first Wesleyan Chapel house next to the Chief Coastguard's home at the top of Sunny Corner lane. The house was adapted for worship in 1814. The second public building was the new purpose built Wesleyan Chapel which was completed in 1861. The first secular building was the Board School which was finished in 1876. At first, the school was, in effect, controlled by those who had previously had much say in church affairs. In Coverack, church means Church of England and in the nineteenth century, that meant control by a majority of St. Keverne people. The School, being situated at the top of the hill on the periphery of the 'oasis', has not had the same 'physical' effect on the village as more centrally placed schools have in some other villages. The two churches, the Church Hall and Wesleyan Sunday School proved more convenient for village gatherings until the Lambeage Hall was built in 1928. The Fishermen's Rest, a club house at the top of the slope leading to the quay, has been a male preserve until recent times. Of course, the churches and the Board School were not built solely as places for village people to meet socially, although that is an important functional use. Religion and education have combined to bring together those villagers who were not committed to either.

Until Forster's 1870 Education Act was implemented in Coverack in 1876, the Church authorities, working through their Parish representatives and in the main funded by locally raised tithes, organised religion and cheap education in Coverack. In some ways, Coverack was the poor relation of St. Keverne because of its relative remoteness. Porthoustock and Porthallow were similarly deprived.

We have seen that a network of paths from the village and from local farms led to St. Keverne Church. Until St. Peter's Church was built in Coverack in 1885, all baptisms, weddings and funerals took place in St. Keverne, so the paths were well worn. It was not until 1837 that marriages were allowed to take place in Methodist Chapels but because of the fact that in the early days of the Wesleyan movement, its new converts continued to attend the Church of England services as well as those of the Wesleyan Chapels. Long after the chapels and church were built in Coverack, St. Keverne Church continued to be the venue for the three main events in the villagers' lives.

Physically, Cornwall is remote from Canterbury. It was A.D. 803 before Kenstec, a bishop in charge of Cornish church affairs, acknowledged the primacy of the Archbishop of Canterbury. In the 16th. century, the Bishop acknowledged the importance of the Cornish fishing industry's contributions to Church funds by adopting a new seal which included a fishing boat and a couple of pilchards. This gesture made amends for the remarks of a 14th. century Bishop of Exeter, whose diocese included Cornwall. This gentleman declared, on being appointed, or perhaps one should say banished, 'Here I am, not only at the end of the world but even, if I may say so, at the ends of the very end, for this diocese is divided from the rest of England.'

It is perhaps not surprising that it was to be 1876, the year of the opening of Coverack Board School, before the Cornish Bishopric was reconstituted, just in time for the consecration of Dr. E.W. Benson, the future Archbishop of Canterbury, as first Bishop of Truro in 1877. The consecration of the cathedral itself took place ten years later. Cornwall could boast of a city, at last. It is interesting to note, in passing, that one of the arguments in the petition for a Cornish Bishopric that was presented to the Upper House of Convocation in 1863 by the Archdeaconry of Cornwall stated, 'The character of the Cornish population is quite distinct from that of the people of Devonshire and requires peculiar treatment.' The definition of 'peculiar' in this context is, 'exempt from the ordinary jurisdiction.' It took 13 years for the argument to be accepted by the Convocation.

Cornwall was considered remote by Canterbury. In turn, St. Keverne was remote from Truro and consequently had to rely largely on its own resources. The compassion of the local Overseers or Guardians of the poor has already been demonstrated in the chapter on the Stormy Nineteenth Century. It is in the nature of things that St. Keverne was chosen as the best place to house the poor and to educate their children. This fact probably accounts to a certain extent for the successful life of Coverack's 'Uncle' Tommy Champion. He lived from 1796 to 1874. Tommy's formal education had been minimal, but his evangelical zeal and concern for his fellow villagers' material, moral and spiritual welfare enabled him to accomplish so much with the minimum of financial backing and no ecclesiastical assistance. His success, as a member of the non conformist Wesleyan Chapel may well have been a factor in the argument for the setting up of a 'chapel of ease' in Coverack by the Church of England authorities.

It had been possible for poor children to obtain a very basic elementary education in the St. Keverne Parish since the 17th. century. This was due to the charitable foresight of Sampson Sandys of Lanarth and John Hoskin of Tregowris. This charitable foundation, known as the 'Sandys and Hoskin's Charities', exists today.

In the first instance, Sandys bequeathed in 1698 '........the tenement called Chywoon with its appurtenances' together with '........a little cottage and close of land' so that the Vicar, Churchwardens and Overseers could use the rent to '........lay out to a schoolmaster and schoolmistress, both or one of them for the teaching and bringing up of such poor children, whose parents should not be of ability to read and write and for the defraying the charges and in the putting and binding out such poor children to some honest trade or calling.'

Secondly, Hoskin bequeathed in 1770 the '........premises known as the Bowling Green and Dolly Toms in trust for 999 years.' He specified that the rent was to be used by the Vicar, Churchwardens and Overseers of the poor of St. Keverne '........to educate poor children in reading, writing and arithmetic.' He added that the children should not be more than 8 in number and that none was to continue being educated after reaching the age of 12.

The appointed Parish Church executors of the wills and their successors did their best with the income from the land given by Sandys and Hoskin. The charity foundation was the sole source of education for the fortunate few poor children of the parish who were selected to benefit from the charity. It is interesting to note that Sandys had the foresight to insist that having been educated, the children were to be found suitable jobs. Hoskin made sure that the opportunity he was making available was shared by as many as possible by insisting that the pupils left after four years when they were 12 years of age and in theory, literate and numerate. Their illiterate and innumerate juniors would then have an opportunity of attaining a similar level of education. Successive vicars and their assistants were responsible for the spread of education among the poor of the parish until well into the 19th. century when the state was forced to take the responsibility for egalitarian elementary education.

It must not be forgotten that education of a sort was available from 'Dame Schools' in Coverack. One can imagine that not many Coverack children were among the fortunate few able to derive the benefit of a free education from the Sandys and Hoskin's charity foundation, so some of the 'better off' poor of Coverack considered it worthwhile to send their children to a Dame School in order to fit them for a better life. Of necessity, the fees demanded were minimal. In 1833, Bennet Martin, who was to become the miller at Coverack, started a 'Daily School.' His sister, Mistress Looy Martin, who lived on the site now occupied by the house named 'Ar-Lyn', continued with the school which was reported in a return made by the parish officials to central government, to have 44 pupils. In 1865 Miss Martin was paid £4 per year by the Sandys and Hoskin charity for teaching 10 poor children whose parents were unable to afford the fees. The educational standard of Miss Martin's school, which was situated on the site currently occupied by 'Brenda's' shop, must have been quite good. The Dame School at Porthallow was only allotted £3 for the same work, while Traboe Dame School was given £5. Another Dame School was housed in the building which became the first Wesleyan Chapel in Coverack. It seems likely that this was run by a person from the Wesleyan 'Connection', but precise details are not known. It is certain that the Sunday School would have taught reading in order to enable the children to use their bibles.

Religion and education slowly became separate issues. Separate is, strictly speaking, not the correct word to use. Perhaps the word 'different' is more appropriate, for the state included religious instruction in its curriculum, with the proviso that it was 'not distinctive of any particular denomination.' The following sections of this composite chapter will give an account of the progress of religion and education in Coverack from the 19th. to the 20th. centuries.

## Church

While considering the impact of St. Peter's Church on the village of Coverack, it is important to bear in mind that the Church as an institution was in effect the most influential body as far as the day to day lives of the villagers was concerned. The state used the established church to administer much of its social legislation. It is worth noting that in its drive to improve the quality of life for the underprivileged in the inner cities, the Home Office has, in 1989, given a grant of £100,000 for 'Evangelical Enterprise' to help inner city churches care for people in their neighbourhoods. Whether or not this is one of the first steps towards the return to a partnership between Church and State in social welfare remains to be seen, for there are now religions other than Christianity to be considered.

Visitors to Helston Museum which is situated in the former Victorian built Butter and Egg Market behind the Guildhall, will see a glass case in which is a silver trowel with an ivory handle. The inscription reads, 'Presented to William Trevenen, Esq., on the occasion of the laying of the foundation stone of St. Peter's Church, Coverack, April 16th., 1885.' Mr. Trevenen was at that time the Mayor of Helston and he donated the land to the St. Keverne parish church council. The stone itself can be seen on the outside of the eastern or seaward side of the church. Although it is of granite, the stone's inscription is barely legible due to a century's erosion. Beneath the dedication are the letters A.D. and M.C. Presumably these were the initials of the builder and architect who constructed the church for £500. This was a considerable sum, especially in the year which marked the beginning of the decline in the export of pilchards to Italy - ironically it was also the year in which, as noted in the chapter on seining, landings of pilchards on the Lizard peninsula were such that 'a comfortable winter was in store for the inhabitants.'

The church is built on a half acre of land which was part of Chymbloth Farm. At the time of building, William Roskilly was the tenant of this farm. As described earlier, Mr. Roskilly bought a parcel of land on the other side of the path behind the church field for building purposes. The church building itself is of red brick and granite. The original roof was of Welsh slate. The roof had to be refurbished with Delabole slate in 1955 due to the ravages of the weather. The design of the building is in the Early English style which became popular again in the 19th. century. John Pearson's Truro Cathedral, which was consecrated two years after St. Peter's Church, is a refined form of the 13th. century Early English style. The Vicar of St. Keverne in 1885 was the Rev. Meyrick John Sutton, M.A. He was quoted by a visiting acquaintance as calling the style of St. Peter's Gothic, on account of the window heads being all strictly equilateral arches. St. Peter is portrayed in the stained glass window at the West end of the church, as is St. Keverne himself, holding his staff. The building will hold 130 people in its pitch pine pews. This was an optimistic provision with regard to the potential congregation as a contemporary account states that St. Keverne Church only had a congregation of about 20 at that time, although being the parish church, it could hold upwards of 700 people. The pulpit, font and lectern at St. Peter's are of serpentine which was brought from Poltesco, the birthplace of Coverack's Tommy Champion.

After the usual mad scramble to get everything to perfection in time, the church was consecrated by George Howard Wilkinson on Thursday, 20th. August, 1885, only four months after William Trevenen laid the foundation stone. This suggests that the church was nearly finished by the time the stone was ceremonially inserted. The actual consecration service was described in the diary of an anonymous nineteenth century tourist who was staying with the Vicar of St. Keverne. It is the best account available. 'At ll o'clock, the consecration service commences. The Bishop, with his pastoral staff borne before him by the Rural Dean and followed by a large train of robed clergy paces up the aisle with great solemnity. The church is crowded - I act as sidesman and get no seat at all. The choir come from Falmouth for the day and chant the service very well, and the Bishop's address - still more his final benediction (staff in hand) are grand.'

One can imagine the impression this colourful ceremony made on the Coverack villagers who managed to squeeze into the church. Being a villager, I wonder what those villagers of 1885 thought of a total stranger assuming the office of sidesman on such an important occasion. It also appears that the Bishop's sermon was not very inspiring as the benediction was greeted with such enthusiasm by the temporary sidesman. Afterwards, about 200 people had lunch in a room built to take about half that number, according to the diarist. Understandably he complained of lack of room and poor service but he acknowledged that 'All passed off merrily.' Clearly the villagers were not going to let anything mar such a grand occasion in the life of the village. The only room in the village of the size described would have been in the Board School at Gatwynyack, unless one of the Seine Cellars was scrubbed and adapted for the occasion. This seems hardly likely as the critical diarist would surely have remarked on the 'atmosphere'.

The anonymous tourist did not come back to Coverack on the following Sunday to resume his duty as a temporary sidesman. He preferred to remain in St. Keverne where he sketched the Vicar's two collie dogs, Duke and Laddie and mused on the state of affairs in the remote parish in which he found himself. He recorded that Pearson the architect of Truro Cathedral had estimated that £2,000 was needed for the restoration on St. Keverne Church. Coverack was indeed lucky to have been allocated £500 for its new church. He also stated that most of the locals '........in this long neglected neighbourhood' were non conformist and hostile to the Church, adding unkindly that one of the Williams family, althouth reputedly a millionaire, '........won't give a farthing.' This nineteenth century literary tourist is not unlike one or two of his twentieth century successors in that he relied on hearsay and his own superficial impression rather than taking the trouble to find out the true facts of the status quo.

It was February of the following year, 1886, before a licence for marriages was granted to St. Peter's Church and it was to be another year before the new facility was used in Coverack. Mr. Richard James Tripconey married Miss Mary Anna Rogers on the 31st. March, 1887. Twenty four year old Richard Tripp as he was known in the village was described as a labourer at the time. He was also the new village gravedigger. He later became the serpentine worker who is described in the section on 'stones'. His bride was the daughter of John Rogers who farmed Kestalls. This farm probably got its name which means 'castle' because it was not far from the site of the Bronze Age settlement near Main Dale, mentioned in 'Beginnings'. Miss Rogers became the caretaker of St. Peter's Church. At the time of the wedding the entrance to the church was through a stile situated near the house known currently as Chymbloth. Villagers still talk of a red carpet which was laid on the path between the stile and the west door of the church. What a prestigious event for the newly weds. The eighth couple to be married in the church on the 24th. August, 1893 were Harry John Sincock the 43 year old village schoolmaster and Emily Ann Phillips Boyns Barker whose father was described in the register as 'William Barker, Gentleman.' The term 'Gentleman' with a capital G was used to describe a man of superior position in society. He was usually a man of leisure who naturally had enough money to live on without having to work. Mrs. Sincock, née Barker was the agent for Mr. Sandford, a solicitor who owned much of the property in the village that was not owned by the Ellis family. Granite posts marked with the letter 'S' can still be seen in the village. Two are in front of Trevanion, where the Cooper's house was situated. They marked the boundary of Sandford property. Descendants of the 'Gentleman' Barker are still in the village. The Sincocks' son Rex died without issue. More will be written about Mr. Sincock and his contribution to education in the village. Seventy eight marriages took place in St. Peter's Church during the first century of its existence. In the same period there were 500 burials and over 200 baptisms. It should be remembered that marriages and baptisms also took place in the non conformist chapels during the same period. This accounts for the seemingly high number of burials in comparison with the number of baptisms. At the first baptismal ceremony in the new church, the three children of George Cruze and his wife Mary Jane were christened. The service took place on the 11th. December, 1885 when Susan, aged three, her brother John, aged two and her sister Mary, aged ten months were all baptised by the Rev. Meyrick John Sutton. George Cruze, the fisherman son of a Coverack pilot was to become the first Coxswain of Coverack's first lifeboat, the Constance Melanie. His infant son John eventually became the signalman.

The Rev. Sutton remained as Vicar of St. Keverne Parish until 1888 when he was succeeded by the Rev. John Lewis, B.A. He in turn was followed by the Rev. William Alfred Diggens, the man who did so much more for the parish than his office of Vicar demanded. Much has already been said of his efforts towards the prevention of the loss of life at sea. His two sisters lived in the old Chapel House at the top of Sunny Corner hill, so he was quite favourably disposed towards the people of Coverack.

During his term of office Canon Diggens was responsible for encouraging his Coverack parishioners to raise funds for a Church Hall. As early as 1908, Coverack people began fund raising. In August of that year £40 was collected for the building fund by holding a 'Fancy Fair' on Bank Holiday in the newly built Paris Hotel. The proceedings were opened by Miss Vyvyan of Trelowarren. She deputised for her father who was unable to come, but he did send a cheque to Mrs. Kempthorne the cashier to help swell the funds. Entertainment was provided by visitors who were staying at the Headland Hotel. There were also local dignitaries and distinguished visitors present, such as Miss Vivian of Bosahan, Miss Highfield-Jones, Mr. and Mrs. Bittar and party, Dr. and Mrs. Middleton, Mr. and Mrs. Lamb, Mr. and Miss Quick and Mr. Clatworthy. The stall holders and other helpers included Miss Bastian, Mrs. Bonfield, Mr. and Mrs. F. Champion, Mr. A. Collins, Mr. and Mrs. Gibson, Mr. Haines, Miss James, Miss May, Mrs. Miller and Mrs. Sincock. These names are still familiar to Coverack people, as are those of the supporters who gave financial help. The amount of £40 may appear paltry to present day readers. It was about one third of the amount needed for the building. It was a considerable sum at that time and much effort was needed to raise it. Prices in Helston Market in August of that year help to place the relative values in perspective:

Price per pound

Beef 6d. to 9d.                                    Pork or Veal 5d. to 8d.

Lamb 8d. to 10d.                                  Butter            10d.

Eggs were 10 pence per dozen

Coverack was lucky to have fine weather for the 'Fancy Fair'. In addition, all the hotels in the district were fully booked, so people with money to spend were drawn to the attractive event in a new hotel with an unrivalled setting.

After the usual concerts, sales of work, sewing meetings and so on, sufficient money was raised and on Monday, May 8th., 1911, the foundation stone was laid with the traditional ceremonial trowel by Mrs. P.D. Williams of Lanarth. May the 8th. is the date for the Helston Flora, except when it happens to fall on a Sunday or a Monday, which is Market Day in Helston, so all the villagers were able to be present without having to forego the annual jaunt to the Flora.

Monday, May 8th., 1911 was a beautiful day. At the appointed time a procession formed up. It stretched from the West door of the church along the new path to the lych gate in Mill Hill. The children were dressed in white and carried bunches of wild flowers. They followed the St. Peter's Church banner which was proudly borne by Norman Tripconey, the son of Richard and Anna, the first couple to be married in St. Peter's Church. Tom White and his friend held on to the long tassels of the banner in order to steady it as it was carried down the hill. After the children came the two ladies' church choirs. Each member was carrying Arum lilies. Next came the Fund Raising Committee, the St. Keverne mens' church choir, the Churchwardens and visiting local clergy. The procession sang, 'We are soldiers of Christ, Who is mighty to save' as they marched down Mill Hill. The hymn was written, appropriately for Coverack, by a gentleman named T.B. Pollock. After the opening ceremony the congregation went to tea in Mrs. Connor's and Mrs. Bowden's tea rooms in the centre of the village.

Mr. John Williams, the builder from Helston managed to complete the hall by August 3rd, 1911. The cost is not known but it was probably less than £148 10s. which was the amount of the tender unsuccessfully submitted by my paternal grandfather. The door of St. Peter's Church Hall was ceremonially unlocked in August by Lady Jane Vyvyan of Bosahan. The building was to prove a boon to all the village and did not need refurbishing to any great extent until 1987 when once more the villagers not only contributed a great deal of money towards the project but also did much of the initial unskilled work connected with the relaying of the floor of the hall.

The next major fund raising effort by the congregation of St. Peter's, after the building of the hall, was for the provision of a granite Celtic Cross as a First World War Memorial in 1921. Once more the whole village contributed. Ceremonies have been held annually at the memorial by the lych gate ever since. This project was carried out when the Rev. E.C.H.B. Norris, M.A. was Vicar. He remained in the parish for 20 years until 1933. In due course a Church House was built behind the Church Hall. This was used by persons who came to Coverack to rest and carry out the Vicar's preaching duties while he was on holiday. The house was used after the second world war by resident Coverack curates. In 1989 a curate named the Rev. Andrew Wade moved to St. Erme as a team vicar and the Church House, at the time of writing, is being let pending a decision by the incoming Bishop with regard to its future. There is no longer a curate at Coverack.

### *Coverack Wesleyan Chapel*

The first Wesleyan Chapel in Coverack was bought from Anthony Tripconey, a carpenter from St. Keverne on the 16th. December, 1814. He had obtained it from Jacob Lory, Yeoman of St. Keverne, who '........did grant and release to Anthony Tripconey all that dwelling house and garden situated near Coverack Quay' in March, 1812. The joint purchasers of the chapel were Colonel William Sandys of Lanarth, Samuel Cock of Coverack, Simon Roskilly of Kilter, Thomas James of Choon, Peter Rule of Trewillis, James Rule of Coverack, Simon Rule of Bargwitha, John Bolitho of Treveler and John Roberts of Treveler. These family names and places are still familiar in the area today, although the spellings have changed in some instances. It is very likely that the two Simons - Simon Roskilly and Simon Rule were the forebears of the Richard Roskilly and Jane Rule who emigrated to America in the 1840s. Their story has already been told in the chapter on 'The Roskillys and others.' Richard's and Jane's respective fathers bore the same Christian names as two of the purchasers but they would have been in their twenties when the chapel was bought, so it seems more probable that the two signatories of the 1814 identures were either the couple's grandfathers or their great uncles.

The chapel house was bought by the men '........for the purpose of preaching and expounding God's Holy Word therein and other religious exercises provided always that the said persons preach no other doctrines than is contained in Mr. Wesley's notes on the New Testament and the first four volumes of sermons by him published........' Moreover, it was added that if any of the trustees ceased to be members of the society of Methodists, the others would have to '........choose another trustee or trustees in order to keep up the number of trustees for ever........' The chapel house was described as '........all that house and garden situate near Coverack Quay........ and part of the tenement of

Chenhalls........' This meant, in a sense, that religious worship was to be conducted once more in this part of the parish. Ancient chapels, built for the use of parishioners, were placed at Chynhalls, Gwenter, Tregowris and other locations. Details of these countryside oratories were given in a report by Charles Henderson to the Royal Cornwall Polytechnic Society in 1931 after his investigation of original documents giving information about these sites.

Much of the work done by Tommy Champion, as described in the chapter on 'Some nineteenth century Coverack people', was done from the small house at the top of Sunny Corner. It was a much better place than the barns and fish cellars which had been used hitherto but it was not then as splendid as the house it has become in the twentieth century. The roof was thatched and the walls were of cob. The chapel leaders sat on the front pew beneath the tiny pulpit. There were two rows of backless benches behind the leaders, three pews on the right hand side and two on the left. At the back was a diminutive gallery and at the side of the building was a lean-to for the preacher's horse. There was no organ but singing was accompanied by a fisherman member of the congregation who played the clarinet - if he happened to know the tune. One of the clarinettists contemporaries described what used to happen: 'Poor old chap. he was not always equal to the task especially when the peculiar turns, twists, repeats and sundry other features of the old time methods of song prevailed. At those intervals the instrument would be reverently laid across his chest, to unite with the voices again when the tune got into a steadier run.' It is clear that what the worshippers lacked in finesse they made up in fervour for their Lord.

Most Wesleyan chapels came into being as a result of preliminary meetings being held in private houses or other buildings such as barns and fishermen's lofts. Later on the congregations would progress to buildings such as the one adapted for worship in Coverack. Finally when funds allowed, purpose built chapels were acquired. Plans for these chapels were often passed from place to place as the need arose. It is not surprising that the chapels resemble the cottages of the people who worshipped in them, especially when one realises that they were often built by the members of the congregation in their spare time.

The Coverack Wesleyans learned to be self reliant. Sometimes there was a professional preacher from Helston but more often than not the people listened to local men like Tommy Champion. We know that in the eighteenth century Wesley did not find the time to go to Coverack during his tours of Cornwall. Billy Bray, the celebrated miner-preacher was born at Twelveheads near Truro in 1794. He was converted at the age of twenty four when he returned to Cornwall after working for seven years in Devonshire. He began preaching some ten years after the first Coverack Wesleyan Chapel was purchased and he died in 1868 not long after the second Wesleyan Chapel was built in Coverack. He did not visit Coverack but he got as close as Helston. . It seems very likely that some of the villagers went to town to hear him. He drove himself very hard, preaching and building small wayside chapels. He confined his preaching mainly to the mining area in which he worked and to some of the larger towns in Cornwall. Richard Hampton, a contemporary of Billy Bray, known to most people as 'Foolish Dick' was a popular preacher who appealed to Cornish congregations because of his naive form of delivery. He came to Coverack in 1812, two years before the first Wesleyan Chapel came into being. He did a circular tour, visiting Porthleven, Gunwalloe, Cury, St. Keverne, Coverack, Gweek and Constantine. He reported that many souls were converted but did not specify what success he had in the different villages. When he came to Coverack he probably had to preach on the quay or in a fish cellar. Visiting preachers no doubt spurred on the villagers to acquire premises so that they could attract other speakers from 'away' and have a building for regular worship regardless of the weather or the availability of other accommodation.

The Wesleyan congregation gradually outgrew the chapel house at Sunny Corner. In 1860 it was decided to build a chapel on the site of an old quarry at the bottom of Sunny Corner lane. This site has been discussed in the section on 'Stones'. It will be recalled that precise dimensions of the building to be erected were included in the indenture. This time farmer Rule Roberts took responsibility for the chapel and the document was witnessed by miller Bennet Pascoe Martin on the 13th. day of February, 1860. Clearly the Wesleyans were not worried about it being a day of ill omen. The land belonged to Ralph Arthur Frederick William Ellis and his partners and was to be rented at 5 shillings a quarter for 99 years provided the agreement on the building of the chapel was honoured.

No mention of the magnificent new Coverack Wesleyan Chapel being built in 1861 can be found in the contemporary press. Chapel records are not held by the chapel authorities nor are they in the district archives. It seems that news of the event was confined to the 'oasis'. Cornish newspapers continued to report local affairs but gave a wide coverage to national and international events.

The year 1861 was quite momentous in that the American Civil War was raging. Cornishmen working in a gold mine in North Carolina were chased out of the town where they were working, being called, 'You damned Britishers.' The Cornishmen eventually escaped by rowing down the Great Potomac river and returned to Cornwall via New York. One of the escapees reported to the Royal Cornwall Gazette in October, 1861 that, 'Amongst the foremost in ranks in North Carolina are the free coloured niggers,' adding that if the South were to be subjugated it would only be done by crippling their cotton trade. In December of the same year, the popular Prince Consort, husband and first cousin of Queen Victoria, died of typhoid. Albert was 42 years of age. The Royal Cornwall Gazette had thick black vertical lines of mourning between the columns of news. In a lighter vein, a local reporter hailed Flora Day in April as a happy day to anticipate, stating that 'Although the world generally is beginning to despise its old customs, Helston appears determined to keep up its old merry making.' He added that the Rifle Bazaar promised to be a splendid affair. The bazaar was an attempt to raise money on Flora Day in aid of the local volunteer Rifle Brigade. Coverack did get into the news in the edition after Flora Day. The paper reported, 'New potatoes were selling in Helston market on Saturday. Most of them weighing upwards of 2oz each, and grown in the open air by Mr. Thomas Mildren of Coverack, St. Keverne. The price charged was one shilling and as they are ripening fast in that neighbourhood it is supposed that they will be sold at half that price next market day.' Space was also given to the publishing in November, 1861 of Florence Nightingale's 'Notes on Nursing,' in which she pointed out the dangers of women wearing crinolines 'shuffling and waddling through sick rooms, creating a danger of fire by knocking over lamps and candles.' She added that the crinolines were not really modest as, 'A respectable elderly woman, invested in a crinoline, exposes quite as much of her own person to the patient lying in the room as any opera dancer does on the stage, but no one will ever tell her this unpleasant truth.' These unconnected snippets give twentieth century readers a glimpse of life in the year that Coverack Wesleyan Chapel was built. Unfortunately the Cornish papers' 'Local Intelligence' articles did not give any news about the important step forward taken by Coverack Wesleyans.

It may be that one reason for the apparent lack of press coverage of the new building in Coverack was that it was in effect one of the last of its type to be built and accordingly was no longer a newsworthy item. Those chapels which had been built earlier were now too large, because of falling congregations due partly to emigration from the mining districts and partly to a falling off in fervour. Other chapels in the area were built as follows:

| 1814 | Penzance | 1830 | Truro |
| 1815 | Carharrack | 1833 | St. Just |
| 1826 | Redruth | 1828 | Camborne |
| 1839 | Centenary (Camborne) | 1839 | St. Keverne |

The latter cost £2,000 and had to be partially rebuilt in 1906 after a fire.

A glance at the membership recorded in the 'Helstone Quarterly Meeting Resolution Book' gives an idea of the gradual decline in attendance in the years when Coverack Wesleyan Chapel was increasing its membership in the new building.

| YEAR | FULL MEMBERSHIP | ON TRIAL | MONEY IN HAND |
|------|-----------------|----------|---------------|
| 1867 | 2,200 | 148 | £19 7s 7d |
| 1868 | 2,253 | 24 | £ 5 17s 11½d |
| 1871 | 2,050 | 198 | £84 17s 4d |
| 1872 | 1,992 | 13 | £19 6s 6½d |
| 1874 | 1,994 | 282 | £ 9 4s 4d |
| 1877 | 1,519 | 16 | £ 8 14s 6½d |
| 1880 | 1,126 | 266 | £ 2 3s 0½d |

On the 23rd. December, 1873, Mr. Lambrick proposed that St. Keverne district be a self supporting and independent circuit. This motion was seconded by Mr. Pascoe. St. Keverne, Coverack, Manaccan and St. Martin duly combined to become a separate circuit and they were granted £15 from the Helston contingent fund. The Helston and St. Keverne ministers agreed to exchange pulpits every six weeks. The St. Keverne gig was sold and St. Keverne was allocated £1 for horse hire and Coverack 13 shillings. It is interesting to note that in spite of the poor state of circuit funds, the Stewards organised collections for Indian Famine Relief and sent the money to the Lord Mayor's Fund in London. They also collected for Truro Infirmary and made various grants to ministers ranging from £4 to £25 for 'family afflictions'. In those needy times it would appear that balances were kept low so that money could be spent on pressing necessities.

By the year 1893 Coverack Wesleyan Chapel found that it was in need of a larger, committed membership. In due course a special three week long 'Divine Mission' visited the village. The leader was Mr. Vosper, assisted by the Rev. R. Evans and James Bowden from Cury who did an eight mile daily walk to and from the village during the mission. An overall increase of over 30% in membership was reported. This included all the choir and the top class in the Sunday School. Apparently these individuals had been attending chapel but had not become full members. The chapel authorities reported the increase in numbers as 'a matter of gratitude', adding, 'Praise God from whom all blessings flow.' The upsurge proved to be a blessing in time for the 1897 celebration of Queen Victoria's Diamond Jubilee when a special banner was made for the parade through Coverack. The blue banner is still to be seen in the Sunday School room. It was a great day of celebration in Coverack. There are many purple and white celebration mugs still adorning the cottages' china cupboards in Coverack. Yellowing photographs of the Wesleyan Sunday School 'in toto' on the green known as 'the Battery' are tucked away in Family Bibles and rarely used drawers. Included in the photo are some members of Mullion Band proudly holding their shining instruments. The Corin brothers are sandwiched between the scholars, their Sunday School teachers and the recently converted chapel choir. In the foreground on the right is the redoubtable bowler hatted William Roskilly and three rows behind him is his son Tom, standing beside Sam Champion, his father in law fisherman whose own son Frank was to become a submarine commander during the First World War.

Some of the small boys are wearing sailor suits and most of the small girls have straw sailor hats. The ladies have frothy white 'creations' on their heads. Some have 'boaters'. One fierce looking lady is standing apart in the left hand foreground of the photo. She is dressed in black, gloves and all. She is holding a voluminous handbag. It is likely that she was in mourning for a recently departed dear one. Most of the other ladies are wearing white blouses and dark skirts. It must have taken quite a while to assemble everyone for this photograph. The 'frozen' expressions on the villagers' faces give the impression that the taking of the photograph for posterity was a serious business and that the jubilee jollity was not going to be allowed to interfere.

QUEEN VICTORIA'S DIAMOND JUBILEE, 1897
*Photo taken at the time of Queen Victoria's Diamond Jubilee.*
*Bowler hatted Mr. William Roskilly is in the foreground on the right.*
*Note the popularity of straw sailor hats and sailor suits.*

The leasehold agreement made in 1861 only lasted 60 years of the projected 99. Ralph Ellis died in 1915. By 1921 the will had been sorted out. The land on which the Methodist Chapel in Coverack and another Methodist Chapel in Skircoat, near Halifax, Yorkshire had been built was made available for purchase by the respective chapel trustees. In due time the new Coverack agreement was signed by three members of the Ellis family, two other people, the minister of St. Keverne, the Rev. Ephraim Mortimer and the signatories from Coverack Wesleyan Chapel. They were:

| | |
|---|---|
| John Corlyon Corin | Wesley Roberts |
| Annie John | Caroline Rapson |
| Richard Phillip William John | John Rapson |
| James Martin | Janie Roskilly |
| Richard Roberts | Thomas Roskilly |

The chapel building had been extended in the 1870s. It is thought that the work was done by the builders G. Cook and Sons of Rosevear but it has not been possible to confirm this. The chapel was extended and now had three windows on the south side. The gallery had been floored in and converted into an upper chapel. The lower floor was converted into a Sunday School with a side room extension for Society Stewards' meetings and for serving teas at chapel functions. The square granite bases of the pillars which supported the gallery can still be seen in the wooden flooring of the Sunday School. There is a small exterior annexe on the north side of the ground floor which housed the acetylene generating plant used to light the chapel and Sunday School in the period between finishing with smoky but warming oil lamps and the advent of electricity in Coverack just before the Second World War.

It is regrettable that the only minute books of Coverack Wesleyan Chapel which are currently available are those of part of the twentieth century. It has not been possible to trace any records from the last century despite many enquiries to official sources and appeals to inhabitants. The same difficulties were experienced when researching the history of St. Peter's Church committee meetings. Only one half filled note book is in the possession of the St. Peter's Church authorities. The hand written Chapel Minute books which have been made available indicate that finances were never taken lightly. The sums of money involved and the subject matter discussed might appear paltry to readers in the late twentieth century but it is clear from the records that these details were of great importance to the chapel committees. Unfortunately the Minute Books do not begin until 1915 but they are sufficient to illustrate an interesting facet of village life. In general the minutes were written in a neat hand in a cheap notebook. The language is quite formal and correct, reflecting great credit on the elementary education provided in Coverack. At times when the secretary had resigned or died, the Minister himself wrote the minutes. Each Minister clearly took great pains in the unenviable task of maintaining strict neutrality. The following extracts are in the main verbatim. They give an indication of the slow tempo of village life, the wisdom of people elected to posts of responsibility and, of course, some of the petty jealousies and family quarrels which are never far from the surface of a seemingly tranquil community.

October 4th., 1915: Item - to consider damp walls.

Action: The Barker Bros. were reported to be staying in the village and were invited to meet Mr. Hart and Chapel Stewards and give an opinion. This they did in a letter laid before the meeting. After careful thought it was decided to leave the matter for a time as funds were low and demands many.

The question of the damp walls was undoubtedly of concern to the Minister, the Rev. John Nanscawen Broad. In 1907 he was living in St. Mawes and had refused to sign a petition proposed by leading residents of the village, asking consumptive visitors to stay away. He was subsequently pilloried by the Press when newspaper men were investigating the presence of the 'White Plague' or tuberculosis. It was claimed that the disease had been brought to St. Mawes by well to do tourists who were convalescing. The journalists did not draw attention to the crowded living conditions of the locals which created an ideal breeding ground for consumption. Instead they tried to get Mr. Broad to 'confess' that he had been sent to St. Mawes as Minister in order to convalesce from an attack of tuberculosis. He did have some respiratory problems but his illness had not been diagnosed as Tuberculosis. One assumes he found the St. Keverne area a much more tolerant place in which to live.

Tues. 22nd. Feb., 1916: Hymn Books.

It was deemed best to keep hymn books in a box (due to the damp? - author's note). Mr. George Mundy to have sole charge of them.

The following year, in February, 1917, Mr. R. (Dickie) Roberts was asked to convey a vote of thanks to Mr. Mundy '........for the care he took with the books and for the attention he paid in distributing them to visitors and strangers.'

In the same month was an entry which reveals that the often much revered 'good old days' were not always that good:

19th. Feb., 1917: Complaints were made regarding the behaviour of some lads and young men outside the chapel during services. It was decided this should be stopped and after a talk together it was thought that the best thing would be to ask the policeman to come down for a Sunday or two just to warn these disturbers - not wishing to prosecute.

(Many of the fathers of these boys had by this time been on active service in France for two or three years and it was clear that village discipline was not as good as pre war.)

March 14th., 1919: It was agreed that '........all young men who have in any way served in the war were to have tea free at Easter and to have someone on the platform to express gratitude to all these young men.'

(Coverack was returning to normality.)

17th. February, 1921: The Treasurer reported that he had purchased the freehold of the property at Ellis's Property Sale for the sum of £5. He added that the auctioneer and solicitor had promised to make up the Deeds of Transfer free of charge.

A complaint was received from Miss Clara James about the water running from the Chapel on to her property. It was decided to let the matter stand over as the Trustees did not consider it was 'chapel water'.

Miss James let the matter drop for six years until:

24th. February, 1927: Mr. Richard Roberts advised the Trustees to refer to the Highways Surveyor.

(After another year had gone by, Mr. Hart was asked to channel the offending water to a nearby drain. There is no need to hurry in Coverack!)

14th. September, 1928: The Minister, Rev. G.T. Peet proposed '........that Sunday School forms and Chapel property were not to be lent in future for secular purposes.'

(The motion was carried and the ban lasted until the Second World War when it was wisely decided to 'cooperate with other village institutions and share equipment.')

5th. November, 1930: It was proposed that a lavatory be built and that the Chapel be connected to a water supply.

(There were no public mains at that time, they were connected in 1937).

15th. February, 1934: Seven new Trustees were appointed.

| | |
|---|---|
| Edith Carey | Spinster |
| William Corin | Fisherman |
| William Edwards | Farmer |
| Edward Thomas Pearce | Farmer |
| Sidwell Pengilly | Married Woman |
| William Pengilly Richards | Hotel Proprietor |
| Alice Symes | Married Woman |

The Minister, the Rev. H. Gauden asked the Chapel to accept the new Methodist Hymn Book.

(This meant extra expense - more was to follow).

14th. May, 1934: It was agreed to purchase an organ from Chandler's, Redruth, for £14.

(The price was 18 guineas (£18 18s 0d) but £4 18s 0d was to be allowed for the old instrument in the school room).

3rd. June, 1935: Informal Meeting.

Proposed: Mr. Corin, Seconded: Mr. T.C. Roskilly - that we instal ELECTRIC LIGHT in the chapel.

Agreed that Mr. Roskilly and Mr. Corin represent the Trustees at a public meeting to be held in the Village Hall on the 5th. June to discuss prices etc.

(When it was finally agreed to have electricity connected, the usual fund raising began. Special long tablecloths were purchased for the two large tables in the Sunday School, a sumptuous supper was donated by the ladies of the village and everyone who came paid sixpence for the meal. The fund raising must have been very successful because the electric lights were installed. It was to be another 11 years before it was decided to heat the chapel by electricity. The Chapel Trustees, with healthy funds in their possession that year not only saw fit to buy an individual communion set for £2 but also to give £1 to the choir funds for their good work!)

It was decided at the same meeting to send Mrs. J. Corin a letter of thanks for preparing the Dinner Plans. This term needs an explanation:

When visiting preachers came to Coverack Chapel for the two Sunday services, they were invited to a private house for Sunday dinner (always at midday in Coverack) and they also took tea at five o'clock before the evening service. Mrs. Corin had been appointed by the Trustees to arrange a plan of those members of the congregation who were prepared to feed the preachers. This was not an easy task. Some hostesses felt they should be chosen every time for the prestigious task of feeding any ministers who came to the village and as might be expected, some local preachers were more sought after than others. Village gossips would report the contents of the menu provided in a certain house and this piece of information often prompted the next duty hostess to 'leak' information concerning the superior meal she was going to provide. It is known that on one farm there was a special preachers' privy or bucket lavatory which was used only by the people 'on the plan'. At other times the sacred 'loo' was reported to be used to store the farm butter before it was taken to market. The name of the farm with the dual purpose outhouse remains a Coverack secret. What an unenviable task Mrs. Corin and her Dinner Plan colleagues had!

Soon after Coverack had electric power laid on the war clouds were gathering and we read:

10th. September, 1939: 'It was decided to abide by the decision of the quarterly meeting regarding changing the evening service to an afternoon one owing to the blackout.'

There were no meetings recorded for 1940.

1941 passed by and in February, 1942 it was decided to paint the windows of the Chapel and to 'stain' the Sunday School.

On the 17th. August, 1942, the Chapel was hit by bomb blast.

18th. December, 1942: It was decided to consult about the repairs to the chapel damaged by enemy action.

(Clearly there had been other social priorities to be considered before the Trustees could get round to thinking about their beloved chapel.)

Over two years later, on the 31st. January, 1944 the Trustees decided to write to Mr. Nicholls '........urging him to proceed with the repairs to the chapel.' Mr. Nicholls, of course, had been busy repairing houses so that villagers could live in them.

16th. September, 1944: It was reported to the Trustees that the government had paid in full for war damage.

Six years later in 1950 the Kerrier R.D.C. had the audacity to send the Trustees an account for a tarpaulin loaned to cover the roof after the raid eight years earlier in 1942. The Trustees wisely decided to approach Mr. Williams the Clerk to the Council suggesting that '........in our opinion the War Damage Committee should be held responsible for settling the account.' Nothing more is recorded in the minutes but one wonders where that tarpaulin went after the roof was repaired. That is another Coverack secret.

4th. February,1946. There was no mention in the minutes of the end of the war since the last meeting. The Trustees decided, on being asked for a room by Mr. Moses, the Hon. Sec of the Liberal Association, that they could not allow any meetings of a political nature to be held in the Sunday School room. They also decided to ask the British Red Cross to vacate the vestry which had been turned into a First Aid Station during the war. (The Red Cross left and subsequently sent a donation of £3 for Chapel funds as a token of their appreciation of the loan of the vestry.) At the same meeting, Mrs. S. Pengilly asked to be relieved of her duties in order to nurse her son Eric who had returned from Naval service in Motor Torpedo Boats and was in poor health. Mrs. Pengilly was the chapel organist so it was agreed to write to Mr. Francis Roskilly stating '........our need of help at the organ and expressing our hope that he will soon feel able to render assistance in time and take up duties as one of the organists.' (Mr. Roskilly had been a Prisoner of War for 3 years).

Effects of the war continued to be related in the minutes:

1st. May, 1950: It was agreed that the Food Officer could have the use of the Sunday School Room from 10 a.m. to 5 p.m. on May 4th. (The room was probably needed as a distribution centre for ration books. It should be remembered that even sweets were rationed in Great Britain until February, 1953 and that food rationing did not end completely until the 3rd. July, 1954).

21st. February, 1950. A major decision was taken, bringing the Chapel in line with the rest of the denomination. Mr. Eddy Pearce proposed that seat rents should be abolished. Seconded: Miss Edith Carey.

Present day readers will find it difficult to believe that people actually paid rent for seats in the chapel. It was, of course, a regular source of income. Weekly collections were taken in addition to rent payments. People who were visiting the village or could not afford to pay were obliged to sit in the 'Free Seats' which were the ones at right angles to the pulpit. This made sense when all the seats were rented out. It guaranteed a place for regular chapel goers. In any case, the main body of the chapel was usually full on Sunday evenings. Nevertheless the system did reveal those who were less well off in a village where nearly everyone was poor in comparison to the average citizen of the United Kingdom. There they were for everyone to see, the people who could not afford to worship God as others did. It is not considered that this financial discrimination was intended to humiliate but there is no doubt that it did. I can remember one old farm labourer who always sat by himself in a Free Seat while his employer and the farm family sat in a rented one. I used to think the farm worker sat there because he was usually late and did not want to disturb people when he came in. The farming family was a kindly and loving one and would no doubt have been horrified if they had been accused of treating their worker as an inferior person. It was the way of things and evidently not many people were conscious of an injustice being done in the house of God. Of course, by the year 1950 the chapel was never full enough for the Free Seats to be used by passing strangers or visitors and the congregation had adopted a much more tolerant attitude and invited strangers to sit with them.

To return to Mr. Pearce's proposition:

The voting figures reflect contemporary thinking on this matter. Six people agreed and two remained neutral. The wise committee finally agreed to abolish the rents on condition that '........we are released from our payment to the Quarter Board of £9 per annum and also that the Society will promise to hand us over two Sunday collections per year, one if not both to be during the summer quarter.' So you see, the Trustees had an obligation to the Circuit and were not really as bigoted as they probably appeared to their critics in the village.

Before leaving the subject of seating in the chapel I would like to relate the following childhood reminiscence of Sunday evening services in Coverack before the advent of 'street' lights.

It was not always possible to find room to sit in the first pew, which had no 'stall' in front, because people brought lanterns with them and they were deposited on the front seat in readiness for the return home after the service. In fact, I do not think that the front seats were ever rented out because of this practice. One lady member of the congregation invariably came late, bringing her lantern or 'moonbox' with her. The 'moonbox' was a square glass sided lantern with a candle resting in a short tube which was fixed to the centre of the metal base. Most people were in the habit of extinguishing the candles in their 'moonboxes' before entering the chapel. One only had to lift up the top of the lantern and the wind outside usually blew out the candle. As already stated the lady in question was often late and would dash into the service with her candle still alight. The four glass panelled sides of the lantern were held in position by a double wire frame. One of these panels could be slid upwards by pushing on a metal lip which would raise it high enough to be able to blow out the candle from the side. This was quite a tricky business, especially if one had cold hands and the top of the lantern was hot. The lady usually made two or three clattering attempts to undo the top of the 'moonbox' and then would blow several times before managing to extinguish the candle. Then a pungent 'smeech' would waft through the chapel while the hapless latecomer settled down. We looked forward to this distraction while the preacher got the service under way. At the close of the proceedings we were entertained once more by people trying to light their 'moonboxes' in the wind outside the chapel because they were embarrassed at the idea of lighting up before leaving the sanctuary. To give credit where it is due, the lady in question, being by nature a person not to be hurried, was usually prudent enough to light her lantern before leaving!

The above anecdote no doubt seems trivial to non villagers but we enjoyed the repeat performances and it is hoped the story will convey an idea of the atmosphere in the tiny chapel in the days before we became jaded with more sophisticated Sunday evening 'entertainment'.

Visitors and strangers have always been welcome in Coverack Wesleyan Chapel despite the seating system. After the Second World War it became evident that they no longer came to the chapel as a matter of habit when they were on holiday, so in 1953 the Treasurer was authorised to obtain cards to be placed in hotels and boarding houses indicating the times of services. These details had been placed on a board outside the chapel since 1945 but numbers had not increased through this means of advertising.

In 1954 a new 'batch' of Trustees were appointed to make up the losses since the war:

| William Edward Blewett | Bay Hotel | Proprietor |
| Evelyn Clarice Carey | Sunny Corner | Married Woman |
| John Corlyon Corin | Barclays Bank, Helston. | Manager |
| Henry Richard Eddy | 5 Gatewynyack | Shoemaker |
| Emily Barker Eustice | Tre pol pen | Married Woman |
| Horace Eric Pengilly | Pen Dava | Postman |
| Theodore Richards | Treliever | Farmer |
| Winifred Roberts | Riverside | Married Woman |
| Lois Pengilly Tripconey | Boak House | Spinster |

It is worth noting the spread of occupations in 1954. The usual village names are still there.

Easter, 1966:    The new Minister, the Rev. Thomas Shaw was invited to preach at the Easter Service. This is the most prestigious Sunday of the Coverack Chapel calendar.   Each year the Minutes recorded that much discussion ensued before the final choice of speaker was made. Mr. Shaw is a Cornish Bard, in spite of being Manchester born! In 1967 his well known 'History of Cornish Methodism' was published.  He has since published other local church histories and is an accomplished broadcaster. The author is grateful to Mr. Shaw for his advice and help regarding certain Chapel matters.

August, 1968:  Mr. John Brock, organist of Coverack Wesleyan Chapel produced a carolare on the quay at Coverack. As previously described in the chapter 'The Quay', Coverack became nationally famous in 1978 after 'Songs of Praise' was televised there. Paradoxically in the same year, falling numbers of the congregation forced the Trustees to vote for Sunday morning worship only in the Chapel.

### *Organists*

The above excerpts give some idea of the way in which the Chapel was administered. As stated in the opening paragraph of this section, the Minutes reveal much about personalities. We have already seen that it was vital to have organists who were prepared to turn up Sunday after Sunday. It was a continuing problem for the Trustees. The following 'saga' - one is tempted to write 'soap' - taken from the minutes gives an account of the internal machinations of the musicians. Although I am a member of one of the families involved it must be understood that I did not become fully aware of what had gone on until I read the minutes. I was blissfully unaware of the exits and entrances and only then did it occur to me that Shakespeare's line from 'As you like it' could apply to my own father in the literal sense of the quotation: 'One man in his time plays many parts!'

An entry in the minutes on May 15th., 1915 reads, 'S. Hart is enlisting so can not continue at the harmonium.' His place was taken by his sister Hilda and Mrs. Tom Coad Roskilly who later took over her husband's job of Secretary when he in turn went into the army in April, 1918. In March, 1919, my father was demobilised and was asked to resume his post as organist. In 1921 he resigned but was persuaded to remain by Mr. Corin who was sent by the Trustees to ask him to continue as organist. My father continued until 1923 when once more he tried to resign his organist's post and his unpaid job of working the carbide lighting system of the chapel. The Trustees' answer to that was to agree to purchase a new gas generator and ask him to continue. These gas lighting systems were not reliable and we were frequently plunged into darkness during the evening services. This meant that someone - quite often my father or his brother Charlie - would light a wax taper and proceed to the generating room on the ground floor and try to get the lights going again. It was an eerie experience watching the lighted taper being carried through the darkened chapel and disappearing down the stairs to the Sunday School room. The chapel then remained in darkness until another taper was lit or the lighting was restored. While waiting we sang hymns from memory or listened to an extemporary prayer if the preacher was unable to continue the service. To continue the saga: My father agreed to carry on with his technical duties but was adamant about not playing the organ. This occurred in the year in which I was born. I do not know if my arrival influenced my father's decision. In due course, Mrs. Tee, the daughter of the Mays who kept one of the village shops was appointed and Miss Hilda Roskilly and the faithful Mrs. Tom Coad Roskilly agreed to assist when required.

By 1930 my father was back again as organist. The minutes do not reveal how he was reinstalled, they merely recorded at the end of the year 'Mr. S. Hart and Miss Amy Roskilly were thanked by the Trustees for their services as co-organists.' This state of affairs continued until 1932 when Miss Roskilly and Mrs. Pengilly were asked to carry on until Christmas. No indication was given regarding the reason for this but the term 'carry on' gives a clue.

More organists were found as the years went on. They played, resigned and started again as my father had done. During the Second World War while the regular organist Mr. Francis Roskilly was languishing in various Prisoner of War camps, Mrs. S. Pengilly, Miss Joyce Cox (later Mrs. Rushworth) and Mrs. Mavis Hart took over. When they in turn had to leave, Miss Mary Bastian from St. Peter's Church played the Chapel organ - an early victory for modern ecumenism. The trustees were so grateful that on two occasions the Trustees ordered a pound note to be enclosed with letters of thanks to Miss Bastian for her services.

The post war years met with similar problems. Eventually in 1965 the choir became non existent and the current organist, Mrs. Marrick, was given £1 1s 7d from the choir fund 'for any special music which may be required at a future date.' The organ problem was finally resolved when Mr. John Brock, the carolare organiser, offered a free loan to purchase an electronic organ. The offer was gratefully accepted. Once more the Trustees organised fund raising, paid off the loan and, appropriately, Mr. Brock was appointed Chapel Organist. He is still the organist at the time of writing.

### *Finance*

Throughout the Minute Books, details of balances were reported annually. Comparisons with today's prices will not be made because of the difficulty in calculating the amounts in what contemporary politicians call 'real' terms. These are the facts as they were recorded from the year 1915. Once again the intention is to give the reader a brief insight of this aspect of village life as it affected individuals. It is for this reason that details of wages in Coverack are given. These wages were not necessarily the same as those earned elsewhere.

The year 1915 began with a deficit of £2 12s 8d. This was thought to be '........highly satisfactory, considering the heavy expenses of the year.' Two years later in 1917 a healthy balance of £9 0s 0d was reported. It took another 29 years before the balance reached three figures in 1946. The amount was £104 4s 2d. By the year 1979 there was a healthy balance of £386.82p - note the advent of decimal coinage. It began in 1971. The trustees had now become known as the Church Council. Between 1915 and 1979 the insurance value of the Chapel had increased from £500 to £7,000.

The caretakers' or chapel keepers' pay rose from £3 PER ANNUM in 1919 to £16 in 1949. Even so it was a labour of love. In 1919 when the Keeper asked for an increase she stated that she spent one day a week cleaning the Chapel and Sunday School for which she received less than 1s 2d per day. In spite of poor pay the Trustees demanded good work. In 1925 a resolution was passed, warning the then Keeper: '........unless the Chapel be cleaned more thoroughly, steps would be taken to secure another.' This ultimatum reveals that the Trustees were confident there would be someone else willing to accept the poorly paid job. There was always someone who needed money badly and was prepared to be exploited in order to get it. It was not always the desperate need of money which attracted villagers to the job of Chapel Keeper. Sometimes it was a person's desire to do something for the good of the non conformist movement in Coverack. For no altruistic reason I helped occasionally in the cleaning of the chapel. It was simply because my grandmother, Mrs. A. Pengilly, became Chapel Keeper in 1928 and being a small boy I enjoyed pottering about in the empty building doing what I considered to be a helpful bit of polishing or dusting here and there while she did the more demanding chores. By 1931 her salary was increased to £8 - '........inclusive of summer cleaning.' I take no credit for this upsurge in wages.

To help the reader put the finances of the Chapel in contemporary perspective, the following details have been taken from my grandfather's account books of the period in question:

In 1915 my grandfather was paying his masons 7 pence an hour which meant they would receive £1 5s 8d for a full 44 hour week. In the same year my father was paid sixpence a day as a soldier. That amounted to 3s 6d a week. There was also an allowance for his wife and child.

By 1931 masons were earning 1s 4d an hour which meant they would receive £2 18s 8d for a 44 hour week. They were earning the same amount at the outbreak of war in 1939.

By 1946, the wage had increased to 2s 6d an hour or £5 10s 0d for a full 44 hour week.

During the next thirty years or so, wages increased at a fast rate. The 1979 annual balance of £386.82p was approximately the amount a mason in Coverack would have earned in 5 weeks. In 1917 the balance was what a mason in Coverack would have earned in 7 weeks. It would appear from these calculations that people were more generous in 1917 than they were in 1979 - or perhaps the Trustees were more canny in 1917. It is an interesting puzzle.

### Coverack Bible Christian Chapel

The Bible Christian Chapel started in Coverack in 1880. Five years before St. Peter's Church was built and some six years after the first Wesleyan Chapel began. The Bible Christian Chapel had a thatched roof and could seat sixty or more people. There were wooden seats on the ground floor and fixed pews in the small gallery at the back of the chapel, facing the pulpit end. The building is now a private house. Visitors to Coverack will notice a plaque on the wall of this house which is next to Roskilly and Gilbert's carpenters' yard.

It has not been possible to obtain written records of the Bible Christian Chapel in Coverack. Nevertheless those villagers who remember the days when worship was carried on there, do so with great affection. There was always a good relationship between the two chapels. A few village children attended both non conformist Sunday Schools. This entitled them to two prizes a year and two Tea Treats. A small number of villagers also attended both chapels, especially at revival times when visiting preachers would be guaranteed to give a lively 'performance'. Some of the local ladies were known to have 'revival hats' which they wore on these occasions. Whenever a special team of evangelists arrived in the village for the purpose of reviving religion, these ladies would attend, dressed in the finery which had been placed aside for the occasion. When invited to come forward and be converted they would stand up and walk proudly to the front of the chapel, resplendent in their home made millinery and best dresses. They would then confess their need to be 'saved.' This was often a genuine necessary renewal of faith but it provided the cynical young villagers with an interesting spectacle, for in their eyes the conversion was nothing more than a mini fashion parade to the accompaniment of mild histrionics. It is a curious fact that there were usually no men waiting to be converted on these occasions.

In common with the Wesleyan Chapel, the Bible Christian congregation, which included a good proportion of farmers from the district, dwindled after the First World War and in 1936 the Chapel had to close. Most of the congregation then moved to the Wesleyan Chapel. Many of the local country folk attended Ponsongath Chapel, which was built in 1829, as well as the Bible Christian Chapel in Coverack, so on the whole the members of the congregation were not deprived of their only place of worship. The Wesleyan Trustees instructed their secretary '........to write a cordial letter of thanks' to the Trustees of what had by that time become known officially as the United Methodist Chapel. The secretary thanked the former Trustees for their kind gift of £20 towards the electric light. It is presumed that the proceeds from the sale of the building went to central funds.

### Preachers

This is a biographical chronicle but it is not possible to give a detailed account of the preachers who came to Coverack during the period covered by the minutes outlined in the previous section. The writer can only relate his childhood memories of the time.

Some preachers paid special attention to the children in the congregation on Sunday mornings and told a good yarn with a moral which was fairly easy to understand. Others, as I intimated earlier, vitrually read a story from the 'Christian Herald' or 'Sunday Companion' which I had sometimes read before when sitting with my grandmother in Winifred Cottage. She was very deaf and it was not easy to communicate with her so she often passed me her magazine to keep me occupied and encourage me to stay a little longer. If there was a preacher who was unusual in any way he naturally attracted the attention of small boys. One man had a speech peculiarity and it seemed that every time he came to Coverack he told the story of Zacchaeus. We all waited for the moment when Jesus asked the rich little tax collector to come down from what the preacher called the sycamore 'TWEE'. All his Rs were pronounced as Ws. We were fascinated by this and went around imitating the poor man ad infinitum until told off by our elders. It has to be admitted that as far as young people were concerned most of the sermons were boring because they were incomprehensible so we seized on any little idiosyncracy we could to relieve the tedium.

When I grew older I found the Sunday evening sermon a convenient occasion for learning my French vocabulary ready for the weekly Monday morning test. The slim vocab. note books fitted neatly into the Methodist Hymn Book and could be smuggled easily into Chapel. 'Hell fire' preachers were listened to intently because of the theatricals involved rather than the threat of eternal damnation that was surely coming if we did not mend our ways. In the days before television there was very little visual drama available in Coverack, except when we watched home produced plays so it was both unusual and stimulating to see adults gesticulating and proclaiming their beliefs in such an exaggerated manner.

Preachers used to invite members of the congregation to pray. Some older Chapel members had a habit of reminiscing while they were praying and would say such things as, 'I can mind the time (remember) when old John -------- (a villager who had been dead for some years) sat there in his pew with the tears streaming down his face, proclaiming the Lord as his Saviour.' At that moment another man would join in the prayer and add, 'Ess, Ess. (yes, yes) dear soul, I can see 'n (him) now.' Then several others would shout 'Amen!' We would turn round wide eyed half hoping and half afraid that a ghost had appeared in the seat behind us. For the first few times we enjoyed being scared out of our wits, never being quite sure of what we would see on turning round but after a while we became blasé about the whole affair and treated it as just another inexplicable foible of our elders. I am quite sure we did not intend being irreverent, if indeed we were, we just did not understand what was going on and no one thought of explaining it to us.

Sometimes, of course, a good preacher would build a compelling word picture of life in Palestine at the time of Jesus, or relate vividly the trials of the captive Israelites when they were deported. On such occasions we would sit up and take notice and learn in spite of our determination to be able to boast after the service that we were bored and didn't learn a thing. Our preachers had a difficult task to perform.

## Sunday School

Sunday School was in every sense far removed from the school on the hill. With one or two exceptions we could all read fluently so there was no formal learning of the two Rs needed to be able to study the scriptures.

The teachers were our adult neighbours, respected but well known, so we played on their known weaknesses and usually had a pleasant time. We were well aware of the fact that there was one who would allow you to suck sweets during the lesson; another who would let you off catechism if you had not learned it; and another who would give you a sharp tap on the head with his horny knuckles if you did not come up to expectations in either behaviour or learning; yet another who could be persuaded to let us all learn something we already knew and so give us time to fool about during the time allowed for preparation before the test. Learning by heart is one of the facets of Sunday School life for which I have always been grateful. We were made to learn Psalms, important passages of prose and catechisms by heart. This was excellent memory training and gave us all a feeling of pride and pleasure when at last we were able to repeat what we had learned to the satisfaction of our long suffering teachers.

We got to know many hymns by heart as well through constant repetition. It still puzzles me, or perhaps saddens would be a better word, when I see people burying their noses in their books during hymn singing because they do not know the words by heart. To my shame I have never mastered musical notation so I will concede that some of those who look down whilst singing are reading the music so in the interest of harmony I will withdraw the last remark.

Each year we had to learn something special for Sunday School anniversary. That was always difficult because the chosen piece had to be repeated when standing alone in the front row of the choir stalls in a packed Chapel. Those are the moments I choose to forget. The part of the anniversary to be enjoyed was the prize giving. Prizes were awarded to everyone. They were not given for academic achievement but for attendance. The number of Sundays on which you had come to Sunday School was written on a special decorated label which was pasted in the front of the prize book. The value of the prize was calculated according to the number of attendances recorded. At one time the books were chosen by the teachers and had titles like 'Tamsin Rosewarne and her burdens' or 'Daniel Quorum and his religious notions.' The younger scholars were given books such as 'Bible Pictures and Stories' or 'A ride to pictureland. A book of joys for girls and boys'. In time the system was changed and we were allowed to choose our own books from a publisher's list which was arranged in price order. We were very grateful when we were finally allowed to have a say in the choice of our coveted prizes. A recent survey claimed that there are only five books in the average British household. Coverack 'Wesleyan' households are well above 'average' in that case.

Although we attended Sunday School, I do not think we looked on it as a school in the sense that it was a place of education. It was, of course. The implications of the moral training we received stood us in good stead for life in the world outside Coverack. Living in the close community of the village we realised as we grew older that some of our mentors had not cast out the beam that was in their own eyes before exhorting us to remove the motes that were in our young, relatively innocent eyes. However, they were our Coverack people and we accepted them for what they were, changing the metaphor, 'warts and all'. They accepted us in the same way. That is what village life is like. We knew that deep down they were mainly good people giving up their time to help us understand their interpretation of religion and to offer us a way of life which they had found acceptable. At worst we learned to recognise the hypocrites, the saints and the sinners. At best we were shown one way to a meaningful existence.

## Feast

Feast day occurred in November. There were special services conducted by a returned missionary who persuaded the villagers to contribute the money needed to convert the heathen. This has been mentioned in the chapter about Tommy Champion and the Rev. John Halligey. Feast Monday was a mixture of customs which were adapted to changing conditions as the years went by.

The hounds from Cury Hunt would meet in the morning down by the old inn which was beside the present day public toilets in the centre of the village. In the early afternoon the traders from Helston would set up their standings (pronounced 'stannins' in Coverack) and begin selling cheap jewellery, ribbons and combs to the girls, toy cap guns, catapults and marbles to the boys and sweets to everyone. The favourite pre Second World War sweet stall was Mr. Harry Perry's. His brown and cream coloured rock was absolutely delicious. It had a distinctive aroma which pervaded the air for yards round his 'stannin'. I am confident that Coverack people who remember that stall only have to close their eyes to enjoy once more its unique scent.

COVERACK REGATTA Nº 2

"STANNINS" (Feast, Tea Treats, Regattas)
*The stalls were manned by traders from Helston,*
*Mr. Harry Perry's brown and cream coloured "Rock" was delicious.*

When it started to get dark the acetylene pressure lamps would be lit in the stalls and the road from Granville House to the quay would be illuminated by the hissing, flaring lamps. Meanwhile the Chapel service would have started, leaving the stalls to be patronised by the non chapel goers. In the oil lamp days the short early evening service began in daylight and it was considered by the thrifty chapel stewards that it would not be worth lighting the lamps before everyone went down the wooden stairs to the Sunday School for Feast Day Tea, so the service often ended with the congregation singing the last hymn in the dark. By tradition the last hymn was the one written by Reginald Herbert, Bishop of Calcutta in the early nineteenth century:

'From Greenland's icy mountains,

From India's coral strand,

Where Afric's sunny fountains

Roll down their golden sand.'

The hymn goes on to ask:

'Can we whose souls are lighted

With wisdom from on high,

Can we to men benighted

The lamp of life deny?'

This hymn has now been withdrawn from many modern hymn books because of its somewhat arrogant nineteenth century attitude to our fellow beings overseas but it was always sung with gusto in Coverack. When he was home on leave from Africa the Rev. John Halligey would lead Coverack's Feast Monday Service, so it became a very important day in the Chapel calendar. According to those who heard him preach, it would appear that he had a much more practical approach to mission work than that expressed by Reginald Herbert in his hymn.

Feast Monday has always had a special significance in our family. My parents were well aware that most

Coverack people were fully occupied on Feast Day, so taking advantage of that fact, on Feast Monday, November 19th., 1913, when they were both 22 years old they disappeared and cycled to Helston where they were married in secret at the Wesleyan Chapel in Coinage Hall Street. At least they thought their marriage was secret. They returned to Coverack and joined in the Feast Day celebrations. At 3.10 p.m. a telegram was handed in at Helston Post Office. It was addressed to Mr. and Mrs. Stafford Hart, Dowler House, Coverack. It read:

'Heartiest congratulations on your marriage.'

The telegram was unsigned. It was timed as received in Coverack at 3.25 p.m. Someone had seen the happy couple leaving the Chapel in Helston. Within an hour the whole village knew their secret! The give-away telegram is still a treasured family possession.

## Tea Treat

Tea Treats were similar to Feast Days, except that they were held in late spring and summer. The Treats were an important part of village life. This fact was reflected in the Cornwall Education Committee's regulations. Coverack School was allowed to choose 10 half day holidays each year for use on Tea Treat days. Mr. Edward Dunn the schoolmaster recorded the following in the School Log for 1912:

| | |
|---|---|
| 19th. June: | Half Holiday for the United Methodist Church Tea Treat. |
| 20th. June: | St. Keverne Agricultural Show. |
| 25th. June: | Wesleyan Tea Treat. |
| 16th. July: | Bryanites' (Bible Christians) Tea Treat at Ponsongath. 83 present out of 94. |

No doubt most of the absentees were 'Downsers' or farming children who had defied authority and gone to the Ponsongath Tea Treat. Perhaps it would have been politic to request a half day for Ponsongath Tea Treat as well, bearing in mind that the 'Downsers' would be there whether or not they had been granted a half holiday in advance.

| | |
|---|---|
| 18th. July | 100% attendance. |

One can imagine that the 100% was attained after the truants had been suitably punished. Mr. Dunn recorded sadly two days after his triumphant full attendance:

| | |
|---|---|
| 20th. July | 74% present, due to 'Heavy Rain'. |

One can imagine that the truanting Tea Treat 'Downsers' would have taken advantage of the heavy rain on that day just to even the score with Mr. Dunn.

During the evenings preceding the Tea Treats in Coverack the men of the village would be seen building temporary wooden frameworks for floral arches which were subsequently decorated during the evening before the Tea Treat with flowers, tamarisk and pampas grasses. The silvery white leaves of the pampas and their pliable stems were ideal for the formation of arches and the plants grew conveniently in the ground behind the Wesleyan Chapel. At the Wesleyan Tea Treats there was always an archway over the entrance to the Sunday School and another by the steps leading to the Battery where the Tea Treat proper was held. Other arches were built in front of the Bible Christian Chapel and near St. Peter's Church Hall. Some of the big boys would be sent 'wrecking' to get wood for the fire which would heat the water for the tea. Other boys went off in search of dry furze bushes which were used to get a good flame going when hot water was needed in a hurry. A small amount of coal was also brought to the Battery to keep the fire burning steadily once it had been lit. The water was heated in large metal boilers which were balanced on iron grids placed across a temporary stone fireplace, usually situated half way up the slope from the cliff edge. The smoke would then be carried up and away from the tea tables on the level ground below where the Lambeage Hall now stands. The grass on the Battery was cut just before the Tea Treat to make sure that the children could race on the uneven ground without being hindered further by the long grass. In addition this activity drove off any adders which had been lurking in the long grass so that people could come and sit on the ground in safety. It also ensured that if any rain fell, the ground would dry out quickly. Everyone prayed for fine weather on Tea Treat day because rain meant having to hold the Tea Treat in the Sunday School. No one wanted that to happen. While the men and boys were performing their allotted tasks in preparation for Tea Treat day, the women and the big girls would be baking for the adults' tea, getting the crockery ready, pressing the snowy tablecloths and in the privacy of their homes the mothers would be putting the finishing touches to the summer dresses which they had been sewing in secret for the 'coming out' on Tea Treat day.

When the children were let out of school at 12 noon on Tea Treat day, they ran down the hill to their homes, ate a hasty dinner, changed into their best clothes and rushed down to the 'stannins' for a preliminary buying spree before going up to the Sunday School where the procession was forming up.

The bigger boys were given flags on blue poles to carry. A couple of teachers carried the banner at the head of the parade. The banner was strung between two tall poles so that visitors could read the name of the Sunday School as the teachers led the scholars through the village. As soon as the brass band had assembled, the procession moved off to a lively tune. It was the custom to halt outside the house of anyone known to be ill or too old to attend the festivities. The band would then play the person's favourite hymn to show that he or she had not been forgotten. One of the teachers would pop in the house to have a word with the occupant.

'Summer suns are glowing

Over land and sea,

Happy light is flowing,

Bountiful and free.'

was a frequent choice for this occasion. The words summed up Coverack Tea Treats. The second verse seemed to describe it perfectly:

'God's free mercy streameth

Over all the world,

And his banner gleameth

Everywhere unfurled.'

To Coverack's Wesleyan children that was a word picture of a Tea Treat. The hymn writer's metaphor was lost on them as was the meaning of the last two lines:

'Go Thou still before us

To the endless day.'

It was indeed a day the children wanted to go on for ever.

The band usually stopped playing when going up hill - there are no gentle slopes in Coverack - there are hills. The silent march up hill was the moment of glory for some small boy when he would be allowed to beat the marching step on the big bass drum. His jealous friends would try to give a knock in between beats without the drummer noticing them do it, because the drummer would become exasperated and then offer the stick to another young hopeful marching near the drum, thinking that the boy he had chosen was unable to maintain a steady beat. Of course, the drummer usually knew exactly what was going on but he joined in the game, knowing what fun the boys were having ostensibly at his expense.

On returning to the Sunday School, the children handed in their banners and flags and rushed down to the Battery where the long tables were laid in readiness for the 'bun fight' as Tea Treats were sometimes called. Each scholar had a pound size saffron bun as big as a dinner plate. The bun was duly eaten and washed down with smoky 'bonfire' tea. After this unique heavy meal there were races with sweets for prizes. Everyone had something, so there was no problem about who was the fastest. While these races were going on it was the adults' turn to eat while the band played popular tunes. The tables were laid with buttered splits, chunks of saffron cake, fruit cake and tarts. There was always plenty of 'tay' to wash down the meal which cost sixpence. While the adults were preoccupied with their meal, the children would slip away for another visit to the 'stannins' where they could spend their pocket money as foolishly or as wisely as they wished without their parents peering over their shoulders offering good advice.

When the tea things and trestles and tables were cleared away, the elders found a comfortable place to sit overlooking the flat base of the Battery and the young ones rushed about, enjoying the experience of being allowed to stay up late. At this stage the teenagers would organise a game of 'Kiss in the Ring' while the band played on. The girls formed a ring, holding hands. The boys then formed an outer circle and walked round behind the girls. When a boy found the girl he fancied he would place a long 'string' of grass round the girl's neck and kiss her, if she were willing. Then the couple would race round the ring. When they came together again they both joined the inner circle. This procedure went on until there was only one ring left, consisting of pairs of boys and girls. It was understood that if the girl appeared willing to be kissed she would allow her 'shiner' or sweetheart to accompany her home at the end of the evening - parents permitting! If she were unwilling to be kissed she would break away from the grass 'halter' and race round the ring to rejoin the circle of girls waiting for a 'shiner'. The boy would stay in the outer ring and try his luck elsewhere. Unfortunately there were so few older pupils in the Sunday School when the writer reached the stage of being interested in this quaint game, that it had been discontinued, so he has had to rely on his elders for a description of the 'rules'. Former players of 'Kiss in the Ring' have interpreted the 'rules' in many different ways, so he suspects that they were flexible and changed from year to year according to the wishes of the dominant participants!

To return to the Tea Treat. When 'Kiss in the Ring' was coming to an end, and it was getting dark, the younger children were rounded up in their crumpled suits and soiled dresses and taken home to bed by their parents, who literally left the field free for little romances to develop in the gathering dusk. The 'stannins' remained open until quite late, doing a good trade. The stall holders sold 'bribes' to mothers for the little ones being taken reluctantly home to bed. Paired off 'Shiners' bought each other little presents as they strolled home. Fathers going down to the pub bought token compensations for their wives who were caring for their children while they slaked their thirst in congenial surroundings. Tea Treat day really was a Treat from start to finish. Other Sunday Schools sometimes took their scholars away from home for Tea Treats. They tended to be private affairs. Tea Treats in the village of Coverack were public affairs.

## *Easter*

In keeping with the solemnity of the occasion, Good Friday was a quiet holiday in Coverack. By this date, the men had done the spring gardening that was necessary. The 'taties' were 'teeled' and coming up and it was a question of waiting for the next round of gardening chores, so the men would go out while their wives got on with the housework. At one time the men would gather on a flat piece of ground to play marbles. The space in front of 'Parliament Seat' where the Fishermen's Rest now stands was a favourite spot. Circles of 'towns' were formed with marbles, teams chosen and the game would commence. Some of the 'alleys' were of glass with coloured whorls built into them. They were much coveted and the more daring village boys would ask their elders if they could play and would try and win an alley. The public games of marbles gradually died out because it was said that people from 'up country' mocked the marble playing men. It is a pity because the game was ideal for a village where there was no suitable place for skittles or bowls.

Good Friday was also the traditional day for picking 'trig' - winkles - when the tide was out. Some people used to boil them in tins over wreckwood fires on the beach, then eat them from their shells with the aid of a pin. Others would take the winkles home, cook them and pick out the winkles in private. Connoisseurs of small shell fish preferred to go to the Helford River where hundreds of people were to be found picking their Good Friday tea.

When Easter Sunday arrived, people went to chapel to celebrate the Resurrection, secure in the knowledge that a favourite preacher had been planned for what the Trustees' secretary called in the Chapel minutes 'Our special day'. The choir always prepared special music for Easter. Sometimes the special preacher would bring a special soloist with him as an extra Easter treat. On Easter Sunday afternoon almost everyone could be seen out walking if it was a fine day. It was a sign that summer was on the way and it was necessary to show off the new clothes that had been waiting for this occasion. The ladies wore dresses which were often too light for the early spring and little girls gathered daisies and made chains into haloes to adorn their hair. After the 'Easter Parade' it was home to tea and finish off the Hot Cross buns before going back to Chapel for the evening service.

## *Harvest Festival*

At Harvest Festival, Coverack Chapel would be transformed into a veritable cornucopia. Every corner, every crevice, every ledge was utilised to display fruit, vegetables, eggs, jars of honey, pots of home made jam, packets of sugar, salt, Quaker Oats, Oxo, tins of beans, fruit, biscuits, loaves of bread, pats of farmhouse butter, joints of beef, legs of ham, pressed tongue, boiled crabs, lobsters and last but not least a large sheaf of golden corn in pride of place before the pulpit. The gifts nestled in beds of leaves or flowers or straw according to the artistic bent of the person appointed to do the decorating in that particular spot. Perhaps nestled is the wrong word because the Chapel, having been constructed with economy and simplicity in mind, did not have many wide ledges nor deep crevices to hold the gifts so freely given at that time of the year. Many were placed in such a precarious position that they could be dislodged easily by a large passing pasty-eating member of the congregation, or by a wicked youngster intent on creating a disturbance which could not be readily attributed to him, and which would be guaranteed to win him an accolade from his peers when the inquest on the events of the evening was held in the shed of the Council School playground on Monday morning.

The pièce de résistance was a line of juicy apples balanced on the ledge in front of the choir, inviting the ladies to tip them over with their large brimmed harvest hats when they bent forward to pray. Bump, bump, bump down the wooden steps the apples would go, giving little encouragement to anyone who wanted to compose his mind to prayerful thoughts and contemplation. Sometimes, if you were lucky you would see a spider hanging in the gloom above the glare of the acetylene lamp directly above the speaker's head. This would give rise to much speculation regarding the creature's subsequent manoeuvres - especially if the preacher happened to have a shiny bald head which would attract the spider, who like us, knew that such areas were often used as skating rinks by flies. In my own defence I felt I could be forgiven for such irreverent thoughts, as I sometimes found I'd already read the sermon in Granny Pengilly's 'Christian Herald' the week before.

At the end of each pew would be lashed two or three feathery canes of pampas grass which grew in the Chapel garden. If you were sitting at the end of the pew you could gently nudge the base of these canes with your foot and shake some powdery white dust on to the shoulders of the person in front. Should enough dust be displaced it would cause him to sneeze or at least give the visual impression that he was suffering from a sudden attack of dandruff.

As time and the sermon droned relentlessly on and you had counted the apples, the potatoes, the flowers, the packets and tins, added them all up, found the square root, squared it and ended with the total you had first worked out, your thoughts would become more fanciful. Could they will that spider crab to fall out of the withy pot suspended over the organist? If you closed one eye and squinted through the lashes of the other, then you could make the cucumber on the shelf behind the preacher appear to be growing out of his right ear-hole. The possibility of creating a droning monster in a dark suit caught in a cage of plenty was becoming a reality! If you dared move your head far enough without attracting a dig in the ribs from the parents stationed on either side, the preacher could be made to sprout corn from his head, have a bunch of bananas for fingers and spew rosy apples in a straight line right through the open window and across the bay to the Mere's Point. On reflection, I'm sure my parents were aware of my phantasies and were probably indulging in a nostalgic reverie of their own childhood until made aware of my presence by the unnatural angle of my head as it reached sideways to encompass the unsuspecting preacher in the ciliated frame of a half closed right eye.

Harvest Supper was always held in the Sunday School on the Monday evening after the Harvest Festival. Everyone looked forward to drinking smoky tea out of the big white cups and stuffing roast beef, tongue, ham, cold potatoes and pickles which were placed on large white plates which had the words 'Coverack Wesleyan Chapel' printed in a blue circle on the rim. Choice joints had been known to disappear when being carried down the dark wooden stairs which led from the Chapel to the Sunday School. Everyone always knew who had done it. No one ever said the name out loud, except in confidence to a close friend who was guaranteed to reveal the name in confidence to another close friend, so it became a kind of open secret, and the 'confidence' would be passed on in the hearing of the guilty party just for the fun of seeing whether he or she would have the grace to blush or appear confused in some way. The meat course was followed by trifle or tinned fruit and cream and eaten with spoons specially polished for the occasion - you could taste the polish - and each spoon had an identifying twist of coloured cotton round the neck of the handle so that it could be returned to its owner at the end of the evening. I have never been able to work out why we never had fresh fruit for dessert at Harvest Festival time.

The supper was followed by a noisy auction. Our function as small boys was to hide behind a large onlooker and call out a price in a gruff voice in the hope that the luckless customer in front would be forced to pay an exorbitant price for a large, rosy worm eaten apple which looked most attractive from the side away from the auctioneer. We were seldom successful in the ploy, but oh, what bliss when we were!

Curiously, the auction always lacked some choice specimens which had been earmarked by would-be purchasers when they were allowed to have a preview of the produce in the Chapel on Sunday evening. This discrepancy would be explained away by the helpers, or perhaps I should say, 'help themselvers', who would claim that some things had been 'put on one side' because it was well known that they would be too busy clearing up to compete in the bidding. In any case they claimed they were intimidated by the local lads who had a habit of outbidding the adults at a fast pace and then they would suddenly stop and leave the worthy ladies in the lurch, forcing them to pay an outrageous price for a common turnip or a bunch of wilting flowers. This explanation was considered right and proper. In any case, it was all in a good cause, they all enjoyed the Harvest Home and went back to their houses with full tummies and almost empty pockets.

Were we ever asked to consider the plight of the dusky members of our far flung Empire on which we were told the sun never set? Certainly the thought that there were areas of famine and pestilence in need of our help did not register with me. If the message was passed, I did not receive it. I was, to my shame, too occupied with my own thoughts. If those were, as we often like to claim, the 'good old days', before we were mesmerised by the media, what shall we call our present days forty years hence? Today, when in spite of the daily horrendous tales of violence and greed, children in their compassion and unprompted by do-gooding adults come and ask their parents and teachers if they can do something about others less fortunate then themselves. Are Harvest Festivals still necessary to remind us of the good gifts given us by the Almighty, or are they merely a pleasant interlude in the church or pub calendar, intended to make us feel good about the mite we are entreated to offer as our thanksgiving.

Perhaps they are still necessary, if only to make us stop and see ourselves as others see us.

### *Other Harvests, including Wrecking*

It was a source of wonderment to me when I was a small boy that the Wesleyan Chapel was filled mainly with the harvest of the land at Harvest Festival time. Contributions were brought down the hill to the chapel by the 'downsers' - the farmers who were only seen in the village on high days, holidays and at Harvest Festivals. Why was there little evidence of the sea in a village, which to the outside world, was first and foremost a fishing village? To be fair to the organisers, there was usually a withy crab pot slung at an angle from one of the transverse metal expansion rods, which were probably placed in the building as a precaution when the gallery was removed from the chapel to make room for the Sunday School. Sometimes an old fishing net was draped over one of the 'free' seats in front of the choir but apart from an occasional boiled crab or lobster there was not a fish in sight. When I became a little wiser I realised that the congregation would not have appreciated the extra aroma of warm rotting fish in the cloying atmosphere created by the acetylene lamps, added to which was the scent of flowers and fruit, the earthy vegetables and the crowded congregation.

To return to the harvest of the sea. Fishermen, like farmers, do not boast about bumper harvests but they do moan about meagre catches. This does not mean necessarily that when they complain they have had a bad day. It could mean that they have found a good spot and intend slipping back to it when their dispirited competitors have decided to cut their losses and repair to the pub. Today, in spite of sophisticated fish finding devices, fishermen still keep a canny eye on their rivals' movements, not to mention a listening ear. They leave Channel 13 open on their two way radios in the hope that a chance remark by another fisherman might reveal where the fish are to be found.

My fisherman grandfather used to delight in subterfuge. Being a stubborn man, he would often remain over a ground, although the fishing was poor. When he was approached by another lugger and asked about his catch, he would not shout a reply, he would reach down to the bottom boards, pick up a pollack and show it above the gunwale. Then he would slowly and solemnly repeat the process some ten or a dozen times with the same fish, to indicate to his fellow fishermen that he had done well. He would then haul in his lines and make for home, supposedly satisfied with his day's work, leaving the hapless men eagerly fishing the ground in the hope that they would share in what they assumed was old John Pengilly's good fortune. The next time grandfather was approached at sea he would go through the same ritual when he was really doing well. His competitors, determined not to be fooled again would leave him alone and go off to another ground, thinking that old John Pengilly was up to his usual tricks. This manoeuvre would leave the wily fisherman in peace to reap the harvest of the sea in his own good time.

CRABBING OFF COVERACK
*Hauling and shooting a string of pots can be a hazardous job.*
*Alex Symes and his father Ted are seen using withy pots.*

I have never seen a choice piece of wreckwood on display in the chapel as a token offering of the harvest of the sea but I consider it would not have been out of place. Not many people now believe that there really was a deliberate Cornish custom of luring ships on to the rocks, though doubtless it has happened on certain occasions. The legendary prayer probably reveals the situation as it was in the 18th. and early 19th. centuries:

'O Lord, let there be no wrecks,

But if there are,

Please let them be here!'

Most seafarers will perform incredible feats of courage to snatch their fellows from a watery grave. They will also be equally zealous in obtaining the rights of salvage of a rich prize.

Because coastal dwellers did plunder wrecks and lure ships on to the rocks an act was passed in 1713, reinforcing existing legislation on wrecks. It stated, '........where any living creature escapes alive out of a ship, that ship could not be regarded as a wreck, even by those who claimed the right of ownership of wrecks which occurred on their foreshores'. This act was ordered to be read four times a year in all the churches and chapels on the sea coast. It is not known if it used to be read out regularly in St. Keverne Church.

By 1753 wrecking had reached such proportions that another act was passed making it a capital offence to '........plunder, steal or take away, cargo, tackle, provision or part of such a ship whether any living creature was on board or not.' Robert Heath had written in 1750 that because no trees suitable for timber grew on the Isles of Scilly, the inhabitants depended on imports or 'wreck furniture' which was sent by 'the hand of Providence!' The writer even revealed that St. Warna was considered to be the patron saint who sent wrecks to the Isle of St. Agnes. This gives an idea of the attitude to wrecks in the 18th. century.

As far as 18th. century Coverack was concerned, the men appeared to have adopted a compromise in their philosophy concerning local wrecks. On the 22nd. December, 1791, nearly 40 years after plundering wrecks was made a capital offence, the Dutch frigate Brielle hit a rock half a cable (100 yards) from shore about one mile west of Coverack, according to Joseph Banfield who was one of the first men on the scene. The Dutch ship fired her guns as a signal of distress. A small boat went out from Coverack in answer to the signal and brought back one of the ship's officers. He persuaded the Coverack men to launch one of the seine boats which had been laid up for the winter. Joseph Banfield wrote later, '........with great alacrity and activity tho' there was a great sea and they ran some risk of the boats and their lives, very humanely brought all the ship's company together with the soldiers safe to land, excepting only some few who were unfortunately drowned.' This was indeed a heroic feat as the Brielle was carrying 350 soldiers and sailors.

It will be recalled that a John Banfield and a Henry Banfield signed an agreement with John Ellis when the Coverack Quay was built in 1723. It is possible that Joseph Banfield had Coverack connections as he appeared quickly on the scene. He had a vested interest in the Brielle as he happened to be the local Dutch Vice Consul. After the rescue Banfield made an agreement with the Coverack men. He promised to give them one third of the value of the stores and other material that could be salvaged from the Brielle. This was not a bad offer but temptation proved too great for Coverack men. They did go to the wreck to get salvage but all the salvage did not reach Joseph Banfield's men waiting on the shore to recover it. Mr. Banfield complained in a letter he wrote to Mr. Knill of Falmouth on the 28th. February, 1792: '........they took every opportunity they could to throw overboard near the shore as they rowed from the wreck towards Coverack such of the goods as they knew when to creep for and pick up at a future opportunity.' (Creeping meant going back unobserved to the place where the jettisoned goods lay on the seabed and dragging a grapnel along the bottom in order to regain possession of the salvage.) The wreck soon turned into a bonanza for the people of the Lizard peninsula. Banfield recorded sadly: '........they imbibe this idea from their infancy and nothing but some of them being brought to condign (adequate) punishment will remove their delusion.' Banfield claimed his account of the wreck and the subsequent plundering was:

'........a pretty just account of the behaviour of my countrymen.'

The Ladies' Magazine published a more sensational account of the wreck of the Brielle and its aftermath. Six months after the event, on the 6th. June, 1792, the magazine made light of the brave rescue and concentrated on the plundering perpetrated by the locals: '........as soon as she was perceived by the country people they came down with all kinds of weapons they could lay procure and plundered the ship and people of everything they could lay hold of - they even stript the crew of the clothes off their backs.' This was not the only sensational piece of reporting. Banfield found himself defending the actions of the Coverack people in his letter to Mr. Knill, '........as to the accounts given in the papers of their plundering the people of their cloaths as they came on shore I believe it is totally destitute of truth.' He added '........this is a justice I owe to the people of Coverack.' It seems pretty clear that by the summer following the wreck of the Brielle, the brave rescue had been forgotten and the plundering had become a more newsworthy item. Coverack might well bring Shakespeare to her rescue in mitigation:

'The evil men do lives after them,

The good is oft interred with their bones.'

On Friday, the 9th. October, 1846, the Cornwall Royal Gazette announced, 'On Monday last a large fish of the Grampus species was washed ashore at Coverack. It is supposed to be upwards of a ton in weight. On its being cut up for the purpose of extracting the blubber, a young one was taken out which measured about 5 feet in length.' A killer whale such as the one which went ashore at Coverack in 1846 must have been a boon to all Coverack wreckers as it would have been to their primitive ancestors who were always searching for food. In this instance the blubber obtained was rendered down to provide lamp and lubrication oil. It was later on in the nineteenth century that mineral oil was used for these purposes. No doubt 'Steak baleine', a good substitute for beef, was on the menu in the 'wreckers' ' cottages in Coverack for a few weeks after the grounding of the whale provided an unexpected 'harvest'. Five years later in 1851, Herman Melville's whale named Moby Dick was introduced to the literary scene in America. This book was one which graced the shelves of Coverack Council School in the 20th. century. There seems little doubt that the 20th. century Coverack children viewed the whale in quite a different light from that of their mid 19th. century forebears. Whales still get washed ashore on the coasts of Cornwall from time to time. At first there is a rush to get teeth as a souvenir before the Coastguards take them for the scientists in the Natural History Museum. When the flesh starts to decay the environmentalists stir the local council into action and get them to remove the carcass to avoid pollution.'

Houses are often named after wrecks. The cottage in Coverack named Gunvor and the bungalow named Pindos have already been mentioned. Children have also been known to be called after local wrecks. In 1895 the 2,093 full rigged ship Andola was wrecked near Shark's Fin which is an appropriately named rock forming part of the inner Manacles reef off Porthoustock, close to the beach. The ship had been at sea for six months and endured gales for much of that time. On reaching Falmouth she was ordered to go to Hull before the crew could take a rest and once more she encountered gales and after much tacking in the Channel was driven backwards on to the rocks in a snowstorm. Fortunately the Charlotte, Porthoustock's pulling and sailing lifeboat got to her in time to save the 28 men in the crew. The grain washed ashore from the Andola proved good enough for the local chickens to eat. The ship was remembered by one of the Porthoustock men who named his daughter Andola Cox. Mr. Cox's son Fred settled in Coverack and his son Jim became the Auxiliary in Charge of Coverack's Auxiliary Coastguard team.

'Wrecking' in the 20th. century is quite a different occupation. To go wrecking in Coverack is to go along the shore in search of wood or anything else of interest which has been cast up by the waves. Once a piece of wood has been found, it is dragged along the beach and placed above the high water mark, usually at the foot of the cliff or in a convenient hollow a few yards above beach level. There it remains until the water has drained out and it is light enough to carry home. The fact that the wood has been placed in a vertical position at the base of the cliff denotes that it is now someone's personal possession. It is rare for this wood to be lifted by someone else. Of course there were, as there are now, a few known people who would take anyone's wood. They were and are, beneath the contempt of the true 'wrecker'.

This harvest of the sea was an important part of the local economy, as it was in the Isles of Scilly. The wood provided fuel in winter, parts for garden sheds, outside toilets, stepping places in the boggy parts of cliff paths and stiles at the entrances to fields. Naturally more valuable prizes are cast up from time to time - barrels of wine, wooden cases of food and so on. My best find was a knife which had been made in Sweden. It had a wooden barrel shaped handle in which the blade could be concealed when the knife was not in use. I carried this knife on my Scout belt for some time until I lost it when scrambling up a cliff after doing some 'wrecking'. So, although I have never seen jetsam used as a token of the produce of the sea at Harvest Festival time, it was truly a part of what contemporary economists would probably call 'invisible imports'.

Another important harvest for the village was 'the visitors'. They were known as visitors, not tourists nor emmets nor foreigners, those names have a faintly offensive ring about them, whereas the word 'visitor' implies that the person is welcome to come and stay for a while. The visitors were people from 'up country' as we say. They seemed at first sight to be rather superior to us. They appeared to be well off, yet they gladly paid to live in a small cottage that had no indoor sanitation and was lit by oil lamps and candles. I hesitate to say that all visitors were welcome when I was a boy but those who were comely and about the same age as one's self certainly were a welcome change from the limited local 'talent'. I was going to say that most visitors were tolerated but that is not the right word either. Let's say they were accepted and received with pleasure as a welcome addition to local income.

Of course, tourism did not begin in the twentieth century. Coverack was in fact linked with Falmouth by a regular steamboat service in 1876. Messrs. Symons and Sons of the Bar, Falmouth, built a small steamer, named appropriately St. Keverne, for the purpose of taking passengers from Market Strand, Falmouth to Durgan, Helford, Porthallow, Porthoustock and Coverack. The ship had a Board of Trade certificate and it was claimed it would obviate the dangers of boat traffic which had claimed so many lives over the years. The St. Keverne was certainly a boon to local farmers and tradesmen during bad weather. By the year 1884, an article in the West Briton stated that Coverack had been 'well filled with lodgers' and the reporter pointed out that Coverack Pier afforded facilities for a 'safe and dry landing that Cadgwith and the Lizard were in much need of.' The Helford River also got a mention. It had been visited by an unusual number of yachts - '........as many as five having been at anchor there at a time.' I wonder what the reporter would have made of Helford in the long dry summer of 1989 when it was crammed with yachts?

In the same way that farmers get ready for the harvest of the land, the ground for the visitors to Coverack was prepared in early spring. Not long after Christmas, letters arrived asking for accommodation. Calendars were consulted, arrangements made and bookings confirmed. Sometimes the preparation of the ground proved to be a thorny problem. On delivering a letter, the postman, having looked at the postmark and examined the letter as closely as he dared, would announce as he walked into the kitchen with the mail, 'Mrs. Clark from up Bristol do want to stay with you again. She do always come in July, but you told me you was booked up then.' This statement was in fact a hint to the recipient of the letter that if Mrs. Clark couldn't be 'put up' then the postman's wife, or his mother, or his sister, wouldn't mind having her instead. Who was it who said that village folk were simple? Certainly not anyone who had lived in a village.

As the appointed time for the arrival of the visitors approached, bedrooms had to be cleared out and sleeping arrangements doubled up, the family's complaints about overcrowding going unheeded. Being the youngest, I always gave up my room but not always with good grace. I eventually solved the problem of being kicked out of bed nightly by my larger brother during the summer season by saving up my pennies and sending for a one-man tent which was advertised in Gamages catalogue. It cost 8s 6d and I slept in it on the lawn at the back of the house for about three months in every year. The tent had 'Egyptian Cotton' stamped on it. The quality must have been good because years after I had left home, my father unearthed it one day and gave it to me for my own children to play in. It still kept the rain out, although it did not have a fly sheet.

The people who came to stay with us soon became friends of the family and they often talked long into the night with my mother and father. Some of them, like Cecil and Margaret Abbot who came in 1935 decided to make their home in Coverack when they retired. My mother loved to 'quiz' people such as these and reap what might loosely be called a cultural harvest. She longed to know what it was really like to live in a large city and have access to good libraries, go to theatres, visit museums and art galleries. The Abbots were especially interesting as they were connected with the Crescent Theatre in Birmingham. Mr. Abbot worked for the Nuffield Trust and related stories of the prominent people he met during the course of his work. He could even give good advice on how to organise a Garden Party at Buckingham Palace if you needed it! Mrs. Abbot was an accomplished linguist and keenly interested in politics. They were a truly interesting couple.

So, after much hard work during the summer season which lasted until early October, the visitors' harvest manifested itself in chapel. Not in produce on display, waiting to be sold at the auction but in the more subtle forms of a new dress for mother, best shoes for the children or a warm coat for father. This reaping of the harvest still goes on today.

Coverack's present day renown is due largely to the fact that it is an unspoiled fishing village. So unspoiled is it that it only takes half a dozen cars to clog the road to the quay. School Hill, being a one in five gradient easily deters the faint hearted tripper driver. Consequently we tend to get the same faithful people coming to the village year after year. When these people go to seed (or retire) they take root and settle in the eagerly sought after cottages. They are able to pay far more than the young locals who would like to remain in the village. Be that as it may, the 'alien corn' is not all bad as some people would have us believe. Some of it springs up with great gusto, withers just as quickly and dies away into nothing, drifting back across the Tamar to settle once more in the land from whence it came. Other 'aliens', being more circumspect, grow away quietly, give positive proof of their willingness to blend with the indigenous 'crops' and combine with them to make healthy hybrids. Of course it is rare that the state of this human harvest is openly discussed, suffice it to say that it takes two or three decades to be unequivocably acceptable to the locally grown produce, or should I say populace?

If anyone doubts the value of introducing new strains to the human harvests being produced in present day Cornwall, I would refer them to one Robert Stephen Hawker of Morwenstow. In 1843 he suggested that Harvest Festivals should be associated with the Church. This reverend person who wrote our song 'Trelawny' in 1825 was born in Plymouth in 1803 and didn't arrive in Morwenstow until he was 31. Today the memory of this colourful Plymouthian is honoured by all Cornishmen. Not only did he write what has become accepted as the Cornish National Anthem, Trelawny, but also he was the first to invite his parishioners to receive the Sacrament at harvest time 'in the bread of the new corn'. In effect he instigated the modern Harvest Festival. Although Hawker was born on what Cornish folk consider to be the wrong side of the Tamar, what Cornish person would say with conviction, 'Of course, he was all right, but he come from Devon, he wasn't one of we.' I am convinced that a present day Cornish person would rather exercise a little historical licence and be proud to associate himself with this controversial adopted son of Cornwall. After all, did not Boaz say to Ruth the foreigner:

'........heav'n did not mean,

Where I reap thou shouldst but glean,

Lay thy sheaf adown and come,

Share my harvest and my home.'

I like to think that Coverack people are as proud of those who do us the honour of wanting to come and live amongst us as they are of the Plymouthian Robert Hawker.

### Memories

In 1970 a Minister from Penhallick, Coverack wrote an appreciation in the St. Keverne Book of Memories, describing the life he remembered when growing up on the farm. The Minister was the Rev. William John Mundy, then aged 82. He came from Saginaw, Michigan, U.S.A. His letter was so much appreciated that it was displayed again in 1988 at the Coverack Wesleyan Chapel Exhibition which was held to celebrate the 250th. anniversary of the beginning of the Methodist Church in Great Britain. The letter reveals the simple delight Mr. Mundy felt at having been born in the 'Cornish Oasis.' It expresses the thoughts and feelings that must have been shared by many an emigrant from Coverack. I am grateful to Mr. Mundy's niece, Mrs. Evelyn Carey (née Pearce) who kindly lent me the following:

'What a privilege to be born close to the sea, the home, the thatched roof, the blacksmith's shop, the barn, the fields, the downs, the turnips, the rabbits, the blackberries and in the home, mother with her large white apron. On Sundays, roast beef and rice pudding always. During the week, potato pie, pasties, saffron buns, heavy cake and home made bread. How about out neighbours? We never could come out of Mount Earl (a neighbouring farm) without eating a seedy bun or a piece of heavy cake.

'On Sundays we attended 11 a.m. service at Coverack. At 2 p.m. we attended Ponsongath Sunday School. At 6 p.m. back at Coverack again. (This meant that young William John Mundy walked about six miles every Sunday in order to attend Sunday Schools and Chapel.) My father was Sunday School Superintendent at Ponsongath and Class Leader and Choir Master at Coverack. I have vivid memories of Coverack Chapel with its gallery and Mr. Alexander Pengilly preaching. An evangelist, Mr. Udy conducted services at Coverack and it was under his preaching that Mr. Joe Martin joined the Church. What a choir we had when the Treloar family from Treliever was there, with Mr. Will Corin to sing tenor and father and Mr. Joe Martin to sing bass.'

The Rev. Mundy concluded by saying that in his 82nd. year he was returning to the U.S. '........with fond memories in my heart.' One episode that he did not recall was the part he took in a School Concert held at Coverack Board School on December 19th., 1902. He sang a duet with his sister, Janie, called 'Crying Song' and he also took part in a sketch entitled, 'A queer mistake.' It must have been a very important concert as the programme was typewritten and had been specially printed for the occasion by 'Lander, Typ., Helston.' The items included recitations, a pianoforte duet by Celia Rapson and Fred Bowden, two solos, one by my aunt Emily Hart entitled 'I won't be a dunce' and the other by my mother, Edith Pengilly, called 'Foolish thoughts.' The 24th. item was a song, 'Good Night', followed by 'God save the King.' It must have been quite a marathon of an evening in the school on the hill. Mr. Mundy did remember his schoolmaster, Mr. W.J. Phillips. He wrote a piece in 1976 for the centenary booklet of Coverack School, called 'Our School Days by the Sea'. 'He (Mr. Phillips) was blessed with the ability to convey to you through the wonderful and beautiful use of the English language just what he had in mind ........ I believe I was subconsciously led to buy my ticket to the United States by way of the River St. Lawrence, Quebec and Montreal. Before I landed in Quebec it seemed to me I had been there before. Mr. Phillips had made that wonderful hotel Fontenac and the Heights of Abraham in such clear outline that when I got off the Cunard liner 'Ascania' I was thrilled to feel I had been there before.' No schoolmaster could possibly wish for a better memory than that to remain in the mind of a pupil for seventy years.

On the occasion of the United Methodist Church Bazaar which was held in Coverack on the 15th. April, 1914, young church members were invited to submit their favourite sayings for printing in a booklet which was to be sent to church members near and far as a memento of the occasion. The villagers had not forgotten those who had gone overseas. Mr. J.C. Eustice, who was working in Nevada, U.S.A. was sent the following sentimental verse:

'We do not forget you, old friend,

We think of you day by day

And the heart goes out to the wanderer

Thousands of miles away.

And in our merry making

No matter where we be,

We always pledge our faithful toast

To our pals across the sea.'

Coverack is never forgotten nor does Coverack forget.

THE MILL AND THE COVE (circa 1899)
*One of the three Mill Wheels can be seen.*
*Note there is no Lifeboat House and that St. Peter's Hall had not been built.*
*A collier is moored in the harbour.*

### School - Early Days

On the 1st. August, 1876, Ian Smith, Clerk to the St. Keverne School Board recorded that he had that day received on the deed for the freehold of a '........plot of land near Coverack on Trevothen Farm' from L.C.F. Ellis Esq. and W.M. Trollope. The School Board, consisting of the Chairman, E. P. Roskruge, B.P. Martin, Alexander Pengilly and Mr. Coad had met the previous year in March, 1875 to examine possible school sites. The Board subsequently asked Mr. Winn of Helston to draw up plans and specifications for schools at Ponsongath and Coverack. Some of the members of the St. Keverne School Board had previous experience in the management of the Parochial School at St. Keverne Church Town. They decided to abandon the Ponsongath project. There was a Dame School there which was convenient for those whose parents could afford to pay, so the Board laid down that it was not to admit pupils above the age of nine, thus forcing the older Ponsongath pupils to come to the new Board School at Coverack. The Dame School at Ponsongath closed in 1892. The Board applied the same pressure on the Dame School at Porthallow so that the older children would have to go to St. Keverne.

Coverack Board School was eventually built at a cost of £370. Mr. John Roskilly won the contract for the carpentry after submitting a tender for £138. Mr. T.P. Stevens was awarded the contract for the masonry with his tender for £232. John Penhall was engaged to make an iron entrance gate.

The idea of a Board School run by local people using government funds was new to Coverack people, so the Board wisely decided to distribute a copy of the bye laws to the prospective parents so that they would understand their rights and obligations. The Board was allowed a draft mortgage to pay for the building and advertisements were inserted in the West Briton and the Schoolmaster for a first or second certificated teacher for St. Keverne and a 2nd. or third certificated teacher for Coverack - which still appeared to be the 'poor relation' in parish terms. Eventually in August, 1876, Mr. Sincock was offered £70 per annum to come and teach in Coverack. There was an extra inducement of £5 which would be paid out of the grant. Mrs. Barker was offered the situation of sewing mistress at Coverack. She was to teach for four afternoons a week and was to receive in the first instance £10 per annum on the understanding that '........ she may be paid more fully in the future.'

By this time the school in Coverack was nearing completion and was to be received officially by the Board on the 28th. September, 1876 at 4 o'clock. As an afterthought, Mr. William Rowe was commissioned by the Board to make a Master's Desk and blackboards on the 14th. September. He agreed to do this for the sum of £3 18s 9d.

The school duly opened and in the manner of many school administrators the Board belatedly realised that children would need a safer place to play so Mr. Peter Hocking was engaged to level the playground and cover it with stone to the depth of 4 inches at the cost of 14 shillings per load. Mrs. Mary Jane Tripp was then engaged to wash the school twice a quarter and brush it twice a week. She was to be paid £1 10s 0d per annum for this work. By November, 1876 it was realised that the playground needed a boundary wall so Mr. Roskilly was engaged to build it and to fill in the unsightly and dangerous pits nearby from which the stone had been excavated in order to provide stone for building the school. Mr. Roskilly was paid £5 for filling the pits and he was awarded £1 for the damage done to the field - which Mr. Roskilly himself was renting!

Compulsory education was not welcomed by all. Fees had to be paid by the parents. Children were refused admission when their parents got into arrears. As school was compulsory this was a tricky situation so the Meneage District Board appointed Mr. Richard N. Keverne as attendance officer on the 1st. November, 1877. He was engaged for one year in the first instance at an annual salary of £8. The unfortunate man did not complete his first year for on the 22nd. March, 1878 the Board advertised for '........a suitable person to act as the Attendance Officer in the place of Mr. Richard Keverne, deceased.' The cause of his death is not known.

The School Board Minute Book reveals the kind of problems which arose from the implementation of compulsory elementary education. William K. and William T. were warned they were to be summoned for not sending their children to school. Richard N.'s daughter Lilian was to be allowed to attend free for one quarter as her school fees had not bee reduced to one penny a week in accordance with a resolution passed by the Board. Jemima T.'s fee was to be reduced '........on condition of her attending the Inspection on Thursday next and paying two pence for the week that she has not paid.' What lay behind these threats and inducements by the Board is a matter for conjecture but it is obvious that the members did their best to persuade problem families to conform without bringing the full weight of the law to bear upon them. In another entry in the Minutes, Thomas R. was to be informed that '........unless his children be sent to Coverack School immediately he must take the consequences.' As in the case of granting poor relief, the School Board was capable of being compassionate. Mrs. Mc.C. was to be allowed to send her children to school for eight pence per week during the absence of her husband at sea but - '........after that time the case will be reconsidered.'

It became clear that the Board and the teachers were running the school in the manner expected by the authorities for on the 28th. October, 1880 Her Majesty's Inspectors' report on the school was received. The state of the school was summed up as 'Very Good' so a grant of £32 15s 0d was paid to the Treasurer. Mr. Sincock must have been relieved as that meant he would get his £5 'inducement'. In 1889 the Board decided to charge parents on a sliding scale according to the earning capacity of the parents and the ages of their children. The amounts due were as follows:

### CHILDREN OF TRADESMEN AND FARMERS

| | |
|---|---|
| Under 5 | 1 penny per week |
| Over 5 and Under 7 | 2 pence per week |
| Over 7 and Under 10 | 3 pence per week |
| Over 10 | 4 pence per week |

### CHILDREN OF THE LABOURING CLASSES

| | |
|---|---|
| Under 10 | 1 penny per week |
| Over 10 | 2 pence per week |

The government's education department approved the St. Keverne Board's fees, but mindful of its own employees in the area, asked the Board which class of fee it was proposing to charge for Coastguards' children.

The Church of England did not easily relinquish its former control over the education of the poor in the Parish of St. Keverne. In February, 1882 the Diocesan Inspector, the Rev. Atholl, wanted to examine the schools in Religious Knowledge. The Board delayed a decision by allowing the application to 'stand over for the present year.' At the same time the Board asked their Secretary to inform a Mrs. Rowe that her application to open a Private School was not going to be 'encouraged'. The Board School considered it was still too vulnerable to allow criticism of its attainments or opposition from private enterprise. However, four years after the favourable inspection of 1880, it was decided to charge those children at Coverack School who had passed Standard VII the sum of one shilling per week if their parents wished to send them. The villagers were becoming aware of the monetary value of education and the Board was getting more confidence in its ability to provide a satisfactory standard of education.

In 1886 it was decided to build two extra closets for the girls at the cost of £18. The boys had to wait until 1902 for their new ones. The minutes did not state how they managed in the interim six years! These were bucket toilets, but at least the Board was aware of the need for sanitation of sort even though funds would not allow them to be as thorough as they would have liked. In 1887 the Helston Sanitary Authority sent a message to the Board asking them to remind the teachers that they had to give the Medical Officer of Health '........the earliest intimation of any preventable or contagious disease should it occur in the immediate vicinity or in the school.' When there was an outbreak of measles in the village the Headmaster closed the school on the orders of the Medical Officer of Health. He was immediately reprimanded for not first obtaining the Board's sanction. The Board informed him that they considered his action '........ open to grave question' adding that he had exceeded his rights. Mr. Sincock naturally felt he could not serve two masters and in the following month he tendered his resignation at the comparatively early age of 47. He had been Headmaster for 21 years.

There were 30 applicants for Mr. Sincock's job. Mr. W.J. Phillips was chosen by the Board from a short list of three and he was offered a salary of £55 per annum - £15 less than Mr. Sincock had been offered twenty one years earlier. As there were thirty applicants for the post of Headmaster it would appear that the salary offered reflected the state of supply and demand of qualified teachers. As already described in the Rev. Mundy's extract, Mr. Phillips was to prove to be a much loved and efficient teacher. In the same year, Mrs. Mary Jane Tripp was receiving £3 10s 0d as caretaker. This amount was increased to £4 a year in 1899. Two years later Mrs. Tripp resigned and my grandmother, Mrs. Ann Pengilly got the job on being offered £4 10s 0d per annum plus two shillings and six pence for hirings. The number of pupils in Coverack Board School had risen in the interim, this is why the caretakers' wages had been increased.

In February, 1896 tenders were invited for the 'enlargement' of the school. John Roskilly the Coverack carpenter was undercut this time and the contract was awarded to Cook and Son of St. Martin who undercut Mr. Roskilly by £7 and agreed to do the carpentry work for £88. Nicholls and Son from Porthallow were chosen to do the masonry for £131 1s 8d. The extension to the school was the addition of what became the Infants' room and the adjoining cloak room. It can be seen when comparing the sites marked on the Ordnance Survey maps of 1878 and 1906. The work was contracted to be done during the Harvest vacation and Mr. John, a member of the Board, undertook to find a safe place for the school furniture when the masons came to the stage when they would have to cut through to the existing room.

The builders did not keep to the contract. The Board had to get the Helston architect, Mr. Winn to press the tradesmen to complete the large room as early as possible. Meanwhile the Board decided to have 'stops' fixed to each desk to prevent slates from sliding off. They also instructed the carpenter to put an extra leg on the forms (seats) 'as may be required' to prevent the seats from warping with the weight of the pupils. The latter must have been delighted with their extended holiday, for in spite of the terms of the contract it was mid October before the school was ready and even then the Board had to get Mr. Roskilly to mend some desks which had been broken while in store.

The school eventually reopened on the 19th. October, 1896 with a brand new classroom, a brand new cloak room and a brand new Assistant Mistress called Miss Harris who was to receive a salary of £60 per annum. Presumably The Headmaster's salary had by this time been increased from the original £55 but no mention of this was found in the Minutes. Miss Harris. stayed in Coverack until Christmas, 1898 when she was asked to resign. The Board replaced her with Miss A. Stevens of Marazion on January 5th., 1899 at an annual salary of £45, thus saving £15 a year on their salary expenditure. To complete the story of the new extension somehow or other the School Bell went out of action during the Harvest or Summer vacation so Mr. Alfred Eustice, a local fisherman, was employed '........to put the bell in proper order under Mr. John's direction'. I suspect the bell rope had been cut and Mr. Eustice was chosen to do a splicing job. In 1900 the Board went further in their quest for perfection in their provision of suitable accommodation at Coverack School and asked Mr. Roskilly to build sheds in the playground for use in bad weather. They were built for the sum of £16 10s 0d. The school buildings were now complete with the exception of the two boys' toilets which were not built until 1902, as stated earlier.

### Monitors and Pupil Teachers

Coverack School would not have functioned as well as it did if it had not been for a ready supply of keen pupils who were willing to be appointed as Monitors and uncertificated Pupil Teachers. They did not always fulfil their early promise in the school where they had been ordinary pupils, so they were either transferred to St. Keverne School on an exchange basis or dismissed. For example, in March, 1877, Anthanina Barker was transferred from St. Keverne to Coverack as a Pupil Teacher and Dorothy I. Keverne took her place in St. Keverne. Both were paid £5 per year. When

Charles James was engaged as a Pupil Teacher in October, 1880 he was paid £3 for the first year on the understanding that if all went well he would get a rise of £1 per year until he reached a salary of £10 per year. At first Pupil Teachers were indentured in the manner of trade apprentices. In 1882, William R. Pengilly's indentures were cancelled. According to the Minutes of the Board, '........he being about to emigrate to America to his mother's friends in consequence of his father's death.' By July, 1882 Anthanina Barker completed her apprenticeship and the Board cancelled her indentures, confirming that she could remain in Coverack until Michaelmas if she could not find another post. The Board evidently had insufficient funds to pay Anthanina the salary her new status demanded.

Sometimes the parents of children playing truant would put the blame for their children's behaviour on an over zealous Monitor, but the Monitors were invariably exonerated after enquiries were made. After all, Monitors were virtually 'slave labour' as they only received extra tuition in return for the help they gave the teachers, until they had proved themselves, so they were in effect 'not always' paid servants of the Board.

In 1896 when the school had an extended Harvest Vacation, three pupils were elevated to the title of 'Miss' and asked to help start off the new term until the new mistress, Miss Harris, could cope. The promising pupils were named as Miss Roberts, Miss Mundy and Miss Katie Smith. Shortly after the term started the school yard was 'laid' by Mr. James Roberts at the cost of three shillings and sixpence a square yard. He used yellow rab (clay) from the Gwenter Pit. One can imagine the three young ladies, anxious to justify their new status, having their work cut out trying to get the younger children to wipe their boots before entering the new class room. While he was at the school, Mr. Roberts was asked to 'dip out' the school closet pits. The expression used by the Board's secretary leaves little to the imagination! Mr. Roberts was paid the sum of £8 12s 0d for the two jobs. One can not help wondering if it was a coincidence that early in 1897 the school was ordered to be closed for one month, 'there being measles in the village.' Measles was a serious illness at that time. It is easy to understand why the Medical Officer of Health had to take the drastic step of closing the school when it was operating under such insanitary conditions. At the end of the term, Esther Mundy was offered £5 a year to remain as Monitor and Edith Carey was taken on as unpaid Monitor at the same time. Miss Carey soon became a Pupil Teacher at the school and her position of Monitor was filled by Sarah Roskilly who was paid £5 a year, starting in November, 1897. Miss Roskilly was succeeded by Fred Bowden in 1902 and Frank Champion in 1903. The two male monitors were paid £6 a year.

### Twentieth Century Education

When the 1902 Balfour Education Act gave local authorities the power to provide secondary education, the St. Keverne School Board Foundation Charities which had been deposited in Bolitho's Bank, Helston since 1899. From the inception of the School Boards in 1870, the Chairman of the Board had received the income of the charities for use in schools but eventually the Charity Trustees declined to hand over this income because 'Free' education was coming into being. The advent of secondary education provided a new outlet for the charity moneys. After some deliberation it was decided to award an annual scholarship of £15 to pay for secondary school fees, books and travelling expenses to children in St. Keverne Parish in need of financial assistance. In 1902 this money also paid for the board and lodging of pupils who won places at the new Helston Secondary School because they had to remain in Helston from Monday to Friday as there was no daily transport to the St. Keverne parish.

Cornwall County Council continued to charge fees for secondary education until 1944. A small number of children in each educational district won free places each year and local charities such as the Sandys and Hoskin Foundation gave a few extra pupils the chance of winning a secondary education. Otherwise the only pupils to benefit from secondary education were those from the more affluent families in the country. They were the children of landowners, farmers, shopkeepers and others on a relatively high income. Because of the rural nature of Cornwall the town dwelling children tended to benefit more from secondary education than the country children, due to poor but nevertheless costly communications.

Today, fees, books and transport are regarded as a right for all pupils so the money from the St. Keverne Parish Charities is paid into 'The St. Keverne Relief in Need Charity'. The Trustees of this almagamation of charity funds give money to any good cuase deemed to be needing help in order to continue its work.

Several twentieth century Coverack people, including the writer, have cause to be grateful for the foresight of Sandys and Hoskin in providing the means to obtain secondary education before it became universal. Comprehensive education funded by the state has already proved the inadequacy of even that generous provision. The opportunity to acquire a good education is now available for everyone who has the necessary incentive and ability, regardless of family finances.

When secondary education was introduced in the early 20th. century, pupils who wished to become assistant teachers were required to have an academic qualification instead of becoming indentured apprentices. The qualification was known as 'The certificate' and was taken after three years in a secondary school from the age of 14. Helston County School pupils had to go to the Pupil Teacher Centre at Penzance for the examination. They were warned to make sure they had booked lodgings as the exams lasted from Monday to Friday. In 1909 the one hour English Essay Exam had to be sat at 4.15 p.m. after a three hour History paper in the morning and an hour and a half Maths paper in the afternoon. The subjects were:

a)        Is life in the country dull? and if so, how can dulness be avoided?

b)          Dress as an index to character.

These subjects were no doubt considered relevant at the time - as indeed they would have been at the time when the Bronte sisters were developing their writing skills - but one can not help wondering how unsophisticated country bred working class young people coped with these questions at the end of a long day of examinations.

Seven pupils out of the fifteen from Helston County Secondary School (which was in reality a grammar school) were awarded the Certificate in 1909 and were informed by letter that they would be appointed to schools with effect from August 1st. Their pay was £26 per annum. Presumably there were at least seven vacancies in the area for successful candidates.

The pupils who became 'Uncertificated' teachers after passing 'The Certificate' contributed much to elementary education in what became known as 'Council' schools. These assistants were supervised by the teachers who had been to Teachers' Training Colleges and because of the education the 'Uncertificated' teachers had received in the new secondary schools they were able to assimilate the necessary knowledge and develop their own techniques and expertise. They did not teach merely by copying their college trained colleagues as the younger apprentice monitors had to do through force of circumstances.

When the time came in 1911 for Mr. Phillips, the second Headmaster, to leave Coverack School for a better post at Looe, the village made much of his departure. Mr. Phillips and his wife were much loved by parents and pupils. They were presented with a silver egg stand. Two pupils, Jim Lawrence and Annie Carey, as recorded in the School Log '........voiced the feelings of the upper group' and Mr. James Coad spoke on behalf of the 'School Managers' - the original 'Board' having passed into History.

Mr. Edward Dunn succeeded Mr. Phillips as Headmaster. His first entries in the School Log concentrated on the poor attendance due to bad weather. The Log recorded routine happenings such as Canon Diggens from St. Keverne Church and the Rev. T. Hitchon from Helston Wesley Chapel coming to the school a month after Mr. Dunn's arrival to examine the children in Religious Knowledge. By Easter, Mr. Dunn had begun a School Garden in the field behind the school. He had it ploughed so that the boys could dig and rake the earth, making it ready for planting seed. At the end of his first school year Mr. Dunn was pleased to record that Irene Carey had won a free place at Helston County Secondary School. At the end of the following year, 1913, the Log recorded the departure of an Uncertificated teacher, Miss Edith Pengilly, as she had got married on the previous Feast Monday. Women teachers were asked to leave in those days when they got married. She was described as a '........diligent, painstaking, careful teacher.'

### Coverack School at War

On the 4th. August, 1914, Mr. Dunn wrote, 'The gloom of war hangs over the village and children, as Coastguards and Naval Reservists have been called up.' The school closed ten days later for the four week 'Harvest Holidays.' Only 90% of the pupils attended on the last day of term and Mr. Dunn complained, 'War, Harvest and Visitors all seem of more importance than the school.'

The school reopened on the 14th. September. Not long after the beginning of term, Mr. Dunn read a pamphlet to the children. It was written by an M.P. with the most inappropriate name of Sir Joshua Peace. The subject was, 'Why did we go to war?' The Headmaster dutifully recorded in the Log that after his reading the children were '........required to give an abstract of its contents.' Mr. Dunn was a strict but unpredictable disciplinarian. It would have been interesting if he had recorded his comments on the attempt his pupils made on a subject which has occupied the minds of eminent historians for more than seventy years.

By Christmas 1914, two dozen garments had been forwarded to the Queen by the children of Coverack Council School for the Belgian refugees who had escaped to Britain. Her Majesty's letter of thanks was framed and hung in the school for visitors to admire. The classroom wall was gradually being covered with propaganda pamphlets which were being sent regularly to the Headmaster. These pamphlets had emotive titles such as:

'The Prime Minister's Appeal to the Nation.'

'An Appeal to the Nation by the Chancellor of the Exchequer.'

'The King's Message to the People Overseas.'

'The Germans, their Empire and how they made it.'

'The Germans, what they covet.'

Early in 1915, Mr. P. D. Williams, the squire from the Lanarth Estate gave a free tea at St. Keverne for those serving in H.M. Navy or Army. Apparently no one from the Parish had joined the Royal Flying Corps which had been formed in May, 1912. Mr. Dunn did not explain how there were sufficient service men at home to warrant giving them a free tea but he complained in the Log '........several children took advantage of this to be absent in the afternoon.' By March, 1915, a 'Roll of Honour' had been placed on the wall beside the letter from the Queen. It contained thirty names.

The War was not allowed to dominate the teaching. In April, 1915 the Vicar came to school to give an address entitled 'The inscription on a sovereign.' In the following July, it seems that some of the braver pupils decided they would be patriotic and help the war effort by going haymaking. After all, some of the local servicemen were allowed home to bring in the harvest. Mr. Dunn was not of the same opinion and recorded in the Log: 'Some of those absent yesterday morning discovered their mistake, I ween.' He did not state how many stripes the would be patriots had been awarded! These children must have felt they were the victims of an injustice when the Headmaster informed them in the following year that the Whitsuntide Vacation had been postponed until the Hay Harvest, to give them '........the opportunity of assisting in this important work.' Mr. Dunn made no mention in the Log of compensating the children for the punishment he had meted out to them the previous year for their correct interpretation of the part they could play in bringing about a victory.

The war dragged on. In 1916 there was an outbreak of sores in the school and Mr. Dunn wondered if the eruptions could have been '........a relic of the lepers who had originally settled in this district.' Obviously he had heard stories about Lizard Head being a corruption of 'Leper Head'. He did not repeat his theory the following year when there was an outbreak of ringworm at Ponsongath. In the same year there was a terrific storm in Coverack. The school garden shed was blown over, houses were 'unroofed' and boats wrecked. The storm was followed by an outbreak of impetigo, ringworm and diphtheria. This led to the school being closed for a month. In June, 1917 a mysterious rash made its appearance in the village. Mr. Dunn attributed this to the effects of the potato spraying which had been carried out by Charles Roberts of Trevothen and R.J. Tripp from the Mill.

In 1918, the last year of the war, it rained on St. Swithin's Day and only 58 pupils put in an appearance. Influenza was on the increase and once more the school was closed. Miss Carey, the former scholarship girl had by this time become an Assistant Teacher at the school and was temporarily transferred to the Lizard. Mr. Dunn was sent to St. Keverne to take charge as the Headmaster there had died.

It would appear from the above catalogue of school events during the war that Mr. Dunn tried to keep the war in the background as much as he could. He dutifully passed on propaganda messages which doubtless did not greatly interest the children. He was more concerned with trying to cope with the day to day problems which hindered the pupils' progress and so recorded the unavoidable interruptions to their education. When the news of the Armistice came at last, Mr. Dunn waxed lyrical when writing his entry in the School Log. He stated that a telegram had just come, announcing that hostilities had ceased. He concluded, 'This ends the Great War after raging four years and three months. Te deum laudamus.' Four days later on the 15th. November, 1918 he wrote that the school was closing for Coverack Feast. What a lovely Feast Monday that must have been with everyone looking forward to the return of their loved ones.

A year later, Captain Gibson, the son of a previous Chief Officer of Coastguards at Coverack visited the school with Mr. Roskilly and presented each child with a Peace Souvenir Mug. The mugs were a gift to the school from Mr. H.G. Thimm who lived in the house called Rocklands at North Corner.

Mr. Dunn left Coverack in December, 1921. His final entry in the School Log was that he had been given '........a handsome pipe in a case which I greatly value.' Thus ended another chapter in the history of Coverack School.

### Coverack School in the 1920s and 1930s

The arrival of Headmaster Mr. Littlejohns in 1921 ushered in a new era in Coverack School. He had served in the 1914-1918 war and would brook no nonsense. He soon got the school working steadily without any fuss. His comments in the log were brief and matter of fact. The following extracts speak for themselves:

1921-1923

Fire not burning in Infant School.

Haymaking - boys absent.

Mrs. Treloar left.

Miss Curnow arrived.

Attendance unusally good - only four absent.

Much coal used by evening classes.

Mr. Cox very kindly lent his gramophone.

Nelly Brown, Gladys White, Nancy White and T.A. White awarded certificates by the Daily Graphic Scholarship scheme.

Head absent for County Cricket Match.

In October, 1923 Mr. Littlejohns wrote, 'With feelings of profound sorrow and deepest regret I record here the death of

Miss Alice Irene Carey, Assistant for the last five years, an excellent teacher beloved by all. To her sorrowing relatives we extend our heartfelt sympathy.' The former Coverack scholarship girl was indeed a great loss. Her former pupils, now elderly, still speak of her with love and respect. Work went on. Mr. Littlejohns complained occasionally about the effect of the weather on attendance. He took a party of pupils to the Wembley Exhibition in 1924, leaving Mr. Haden in charge. Mr. Haden was known as 'Lew Tink' by Coverack pupils. The following year Mr. Littlejohns proudly recorded: 'Gladys White upheld the honour and tradition of the school by winning the Sandys and Hoskin Scholarship.'

Each year the Headmaster took the children to the new War Memorial on Armistice Day. On the occasions when the Inspector of Coastguards came to Coverack, Mr. Littlejohns took his pupils to hear the Inspector '........lecture the crew on matters related to the treatment of unconscious sailors.' A lucky boy or girl was usually given a ride in the breeches buoy afterwards. Mr. Littlejohns got Colonel Bulkeley interested in the school and invited him to address the children on 'The Empire and its meaning.' Colonel Bulkeley was a kindly man and arranged treatment in Westminster Hospital for villagers who could not get specialist help locally. The Colonel also extended the School Library collection by presenting nineteen new books and a special School Library stamp to encourage children to take books home to read.

Coverack children always did well in the Preliminary Exam which was the first exam taken by children who had reached secondary school age. In 1928 Albert Harvey, Susie Hosken, Pearl Roberts, Teddy Robinson and Phyllis Roskilly passed the 'Prelim'. This test in the 3Rs was taken in the familiar surroundings of the school. The next one, known as the Minor Scholarship had to be taken in the Helston Secondary School in Penrose Road. The occasion often proved too much for Coverack hopefuls who were unused to being made to sit in single desks, supervised by a formidable looking master resplendent in cap and gown. Many of the children were secretly relieved when they learned they had not passed the 'Minor' and could continue their education in friendly Coverack School instead of having to go to Helston every day.

In 1928 Miss Katherine Giles became the first Headmistress of Coverack Council School. She lived in St. Keverne and travelled to Coverack every day. Miss Giles continued the regime of Mr. Littlejohns who had been succeeded for a short while by Mr. Harvey. One of Miss Giles' first tasks was to obtain a new piano. Just like contemporary education committees, the Cornwall Education Committee was not prepared to finance the whole project so Miss Giles collected £17 10s 0d from local subscribers. Mrs. Woodcock a local music teacher kindly organised a concert by her pupils and raised another £4 1s 0½d and at that point the Education Committee relented and paid the rest of the £35 required for the piano by Chandler and Sons of Redruth.

Life went on smoothly in the school under Miss Giles. All the children were proud of her little Austin 7 motor car and the boys vied with each other for the privilege of cleaning it during the dinner hour. Miss Giles continued the night school classes at Coverack and for the first time Coverack pupils were able to learn French. After seven happy years Miss Giles was promoted to the headship of a larger school in North Cornwall. There followed a succession of temporary heads, the last one being Mr. Scantlebury. He was succeeded by a permanent Headmistress, Miss M.P. Stephens, B.A. She was to remain in charge until half way through the Second World War.

COVERACK COUNCIL SCHOOL 1936
*Miss Mavis Stephens, Headteacher, is standing on the left
and the Infants' Teacher, Miss Doris Corin is on the right.
The author is standing on the left of the back row.*

96

While the war clouds were gathering over Europe once more, routine life continued peacefully in Coverack School. It would be foolish to claim that in 'the good old days' there was no crime in Coverack but it is true to say that most people left their doors unlocked and that theft was unusual. An entry in the School Log in 1937 recorded that Alex Symes' bike was taken from the school shed between the beginning of afternoon school and playtime. The bike was eventually found in a lane nearby but the pump was missing. The police constable at St. Keverne was duly informed as was the clerk in the District Education Office. It was an unusual occurrence and merited an entry in the Log so perhaps they were 'the good old days' after all.

One entry in May, 1939 reminds us that the school was under female management. Miss Stephens wrote: 'While I was at home during the dinner hour Miss Corin and the boys dealt with an unwelcome visitor in the boys' yard - a live adder.' This was one of the last of the type of entry which reflects life in a peaceful seaside school. War was declared on Sunday, 3rd. September. The school was closed on the following day so that teachers could prepare for an influx of children. It reopened on the 11th. September. There were already thirteen new children, including ten unofficial evacuees from Manchester and London who had been brought to Coverack by their parents. Two more from Seaham Harbour arrived on the 13th. September, causing Miss Stephens to record, '........this increase has seriously strained our seating accommodation and we are bound to borrow one or two forms.' The pupils in the school had increased by 30% in a few days. It is perhaps as well that the first influx was a drop in the ocean compared with the flood that was to follow.

The part played by Coverack School during the Second World War will be related later in a chapter devoted to the war. The village became involved in what has become known as 'total war' which has been defined as 'war with every weapon at the combatants' disposal, sticking at nothing and sparing no one.' This description is apposite in Coverack's case and it is considered that it would be more fitting to tell the story of the 1939-1945 war in toto rather than separate the school story in a section on Religion and Education.

## *Coverack School Getting Up to Date*

R.A. Butler's 1944 Education Act was actually introduced in the House of Commons in December, 1943. It received the Royal Assent on the 4th. August, 1944 exactly 30 years since the outbreak of the First World War and while the Second World War was still raging.

The Act declared that each Local Education Authority was to be obliged to provide secondary education for everyone. When the Act was implemented, Coverack Council School became Coverack County Primary School. Pupils who did not pass the notorious 11+ Exam which had replaced the Preliminary and Minor Scholarship, were sent by 'bus to the Secondary Modern School in Penrose Road which was in reality the former Helston County Secondary School building. The old H.C.S. had moved into new premises near Helston Station not long before the outbreak of war.

In 1947 Mr. H. Frank Hopton was appointed as Headmaster of Coverack County Primary School with Mrs. Winter and Miss Glasson who came from Cury as Assistants. Like Mr. Littlejohns who had been appointed just after the First World War, Mr. Hopton was an ex Service man. He had been an air gunner and flown on bombing raids and was naturally anxious to leave all that destruction behind and continue with the job he had begun before the war interrupted his career. He was to remain in Coverack as Headmaster for over a quarter of a century and was responsible for bringing the school through the educational and technological revolution of the post war years.

The previous rather fine sounding phrase does not exactly describe the early years of Mr. Hopton's Headship. He had to wait seven years before the Education authorities permitted the school to be wired for electricity, although power had been available in the village since the 23rd. May, 1937. Mr. Hopton also saw to it that the closet buckets were replaced by flush toilets. The playground was properly surfaced to reduce accidents caused by the children rushing about during recreation and in the physcial education lessons. He recorded in the School Log after the School Christmas Party in 1955: '........the benefit of having electric light was much appreciated. In previous years after 3.30 p.m. the light faded rapidly and we had to rely on borrowed oil lamps and end the party at about 4.30 p.m.' As a professional teacher, 'Hoppy' as he was affectionately known by the pupils gave no hint of the daily problems he encountered through lack of resources, he simply stated what a joy it was to be able to provide his pupils with a pleasant party after a hard term's work.

The post war provision of school dinners had a unifying effect on the pupils. At one time the 'Fishguts' or cove children combined with the 'Millrags' or children from the Mill Beach area against the 'Downsers' from the farms and outlying hamlets. The latter often arrived at school wet and bedraggled after their long walk through the pouring rain. At lunch time they had to stay in school and eat cold sandwiches or warmed up pasties which had been heated on the aptly named 'Tortoise' stove in the 'big room'. After the war, many of the 'Downsers' were brought to school by hired cars provided by the authorities, so they arrived dry and ready for a day's work. As dinners were cooked on the premises many children stayed at school all day and the three 'gangs' got to know each other. The school was the better for it. The ancillary workers who cooked and served the meals became a valuable section of the school personnel. They were local ladies and were regarded with great affection by the children not only for their culinary skills and generous helpings but also for their sympathetic attitudes when the young ones became 'upset' during the dinner hour and went to the motherly helpers for comfort. Villagers such as Mrs. Elizabeth Watts, (née Eustice), Mrs. Beatrice Nicholls (née Carey) and Mrs. Elaine Daw (née Eddy) will surely be remembered by Coverack Primary School pupils when some of their teachers have been forgotten.

Mr. Hopton managed to get sports gear provided so that the children could learn the rudiments of different games before transferring to one of the secondary schools. He had to wait until April, 1965 before the field opposite the school was acquired for the use of the pupils. Before that, the neighbouring farmer, Mr. William Roskilly generously allowed the children to use his field free of charge so the pupils were not too deprived. In the same year of 1965 the school ceased to be a Village Library Centre. The County Council had acquired a travelling van to meet the reading needs of the village. The new system was convenient for those villagers who were unable to climb the one in five hill to the school but it meant that the school became that little bit more remote from the village and consequently it lessened its influence on the inhabitants.

In the post war years much use was made of the radio and later the television lessons. They brought the outer world in sound and vision right into the little school in Coverack. The children were able to take advantage of the expertise of dozens of specialists who had virtually unlimited resources at their disposal in comparison with the facilities available in Coverack. Even so, in their book of reminiscences which was published in the school's centenary year, the most abiding memories were of the stories told by a gifted Welsh teacher who presented them with 'Hoppy's magic mintoes' as a reward for work well learned!

Mr. Hopton kept interest in the school alive in the minds of villagers, who were not involved as parents, by holding various fund raising efforts and inviting everyone to school open days when the work being done was available for everyone to inspect and comment upon. In 1973 the pupils, parents and Coverack Women's Institute members planted 58 trees around the school field. It is not easy to get trees to grow on such a windswept site, so the results were somewhat disappointing. The following year Mr. Hopton persuaded the Sandys and Hoskin Trust to grant £30 to the school for extra books. This was just before he retired. It was characteristic of the man who had instilled the love of learning into so many children. On the 17th December, 1974 he wrote his last entry in the School Log: '........for me it was a very moving occasion and I could only express my deepfelt thanks for all the tremendous goodwill, help, cooperation and may I say amazing tolerance given to me through almost twenty eight happy years.' The 'oasis' had worked its influence on yet another immigrant!

Perhaps the best tribute of all was paid to Mr. Hopton in a verse written by one of his former pupils:

'Looking back it's hard to sort,

The work out from the pleasure

But that was Hoppy's trick,

He mixed 'em well together!'

Mr. W. Staple, an expert in computer studies succeeded Mr. Hopton. He too was an ex service man who had spent much time at the nearby Royal Naval Air Station of Culdrose before embarking on a second career as a teacher. One of Mr. Staple's first public duties was to organise a Spring Fayre on the 15th. May, 1976 to celebrate the first hundred years of the school's existence. The second Headmistress, Mrs. Mavis Hart (nee Stephens) was invited to perform the opening ceremony. Many of the village people wore Victorian costume. Old photographs and paintings were put on display to lend authenticity to the occasion. It was a wonderful day. Villagers met school friends they had not seen for decades. A small book compiled by Rachel Roskilly and Pat Harvey for the Parent-Teachers' Association was published for the centenary celebration. It was printed by John Keverne, an old boy of the school. It was entitled 'Our School Days By The Sea.' It is now a treasured and unique illustrated record of an important part of Coverack's social history. It contains the memories of school days written by 83 different contributors who attended the school between the years 1890 and 1975. One would be forgiven for thinking that such a book wallows in nostalgia and does not give an objective view of the facts. That is not so, the school really was and still is a most pleasant place to work. The reader is assured that when the writer revisited the school in 1988 he found the atmosphere as friendly as when he was first welcomed there by his infants' teacher, Miss Doris Corin in 1928.

This chapter could also be called 'Into the Atomic Age' for the presence of radio activity in certain matter had been discovered by Henri Bequerel in 1896, heralding the work which leading scientists like Lord Rutherford were to be doing during the new century. Indeed this chapter could equally be entitled 'Another Stormy Century.' There were to be storms which made the Coverack Lifeboats known to the whole country and beyond. The other storms were the world wide conflicts on a scale beyond the imagination of the generation which became known as the Edwardians soon after the new century began. The political storms were already brewing. It is therefore not easy to name any one event which pinpoints the start of the century. Lake's Falmouth Packet and Cornwall Advertiser got the century off to a good start on Saturday, 5th. January, 1901 by reporting that '........the advent of the 20th. century was solemnised on Monday night by special watch night services in St. Paul's Cathedral, in Westminster Abbey and in many churches and chapels throughout the country.' There was no mention of the fact that during the stormy night of the 31st. December, 1900, one of the upright stones holding up a huge lintel at Stonehenge fell to the ground. Could it have been interpreted by superstitious folk as a fitting end to the stormy nineteenth century? Or even an omen for the twentieth.

The unpopular Boer War was still in progress at the beginning of the century but the end appeared to be in sight, for Kimberley, Ladysmith and Mafeking had been relieved during the previous year. It was to be another eighteen months before the Boers were to surrender and the soldiers could return to Britain. The war seemed very remote to Cornish people although they were accustomed to thinking about far off places because of the fairly constant emigration from the county. The Falmouth Packet saw fit to relate a joke concerning the unfamiliar names which were cropping up in the world news section of local papers:

Intelligent Rustic:     They tell me as 'ow Enery has got wounded in the Transvaal.

Mrs. Gummins:          Lor a mussy me! And what part of 'im might that be?

Simon Bowden from Coverack was feted on his return from fighting the Boers and was presented with a silver watch and chain by Coverack villagers who were delighted that he had returned safely. Simon stayed in the village long enough to complete the work on the iron slipway for the new lifeboat then he returned to South Africa to try his luck in the gold mines.

Gloom settled on the whole country when shortly after the new century began Queen Victoria died on the 21st. January, 1901. Lake's Falmouth Packet front page headlines read, 'Death of the Queen. An Empire mourns.' The details of the Queen's passing were printed in columns between thick black vertical lines. An inner page was devoted entirely to an article entitled, 'Queen Victoria the Good.' She had visited Penzance in the year 1846 and gave a boost to the Serpentine Trade by ordering some serpentine items for her new property, Osborne House, on the Isle of Wight. The people of Cornwall demonstrated their grief in local outward show because not many were able to go to far away London for the funeral of the first reigning monarch ever to visit Cornwall - with the exception of Charles I during the Civil War. Trade in Cornwall was suspended temporarily, sporting events and other entertainments were cancelled and special parades and services held. Downings of Falmouth announced patriotically and no doubt profitably, that '........ in order to give effect to the orders of His Majesty the King and the wishes of the public, we are now showing a full assortment of every description of Black Goods.' The Victorian Age was over.

The new king announced he would be known as Edward VII, not Albert Ist. as his loving parents had hoped. Edward identified easily with commoners, perhaps it was because he was known to be 'a bit of a lad' and people could see that he was an ordinary person with many of the human weaknesses that ordinary people had. He was known as 'Teddy' to the commoners. He was a familiar figure in Cornwall and his popularity there increased as his reign progressed, although his reputation as a kind of elderly playboy, which he gained as Prince of Wales while waiting to become monarch, did not go down well with Cornish moralists.

The new Prince of Wales, the future George V and his wife, the future Queen Mary came to Cornwall on July 18th., 1903. They visited Bodmin, Lostwithiel, Falmouth and Truro. They witnessed the benediction of the nave of Truro cathedral by the new Scottish born ecumenical Archbishop of Canterbury, the Rev. Randall Thomas Davidson. The new Prince of Wales' father, King Edward VII had laid the foundation stones on the 20th. May, 1880 when he was Prince of Wales. While they were staying at Tregothnan House the seat of the Earl of Falmouth, they went to the Poldhu Wireless Station near Mullion. They were shown round by Guglielmo Marconi who had received the first wireless message in Morse broadcast to him in St. John's, Newfoundland from his station at Poldhu on Thursday, 12th. December, 1901. Cornwall has remained in the forefront of long distance communications throughout the century. The cable station at Porthcurno was in use from 1866 to 1970. Bodmin and Lands End Radio Stations - the latter replaced Poldhu - are known world-wide. So is the Earth Station on Goonhilly Downs which began in 1962. The submarine cables also terminate there. In addition there is a Government Communication Headquarters Radio Station near Bude.

After Marconi bought the yacht Electra in 1919 she became a regular visitor to Coverack Bay. She was always a welcome sight and was soon surrounded by rowing boats after dropping anchor. Some of the villagers used to receive little luxuries as well as cash from the crew members in exchange for fresh fish, milk, butter and cream. On one occasion two sisters were given half a cold roast chicken to take home. They did so but to their dismay they were made to throw it in the dustbin because their mother did not trust foreigners. No doubt she had been influenced by reading some lurid novel about white slavers! Marconi himself got on well with the Cornish and told his wife that they had much in common with the Italians from the point of view of temperament and attitude to life in general. His favourite place when relaxing from his experiments was the port of Fowey.

As Coverack stepped slowly into the twentieth century the village itself began to change in appearance. In the year 1900 the increased number of visitors to the area led to the building of the new Headland Hotel in a prime position overlooking Porthbeer Cove or Mears Beach as it is known today. When the hotel site was being excavated, traces of native copper were found. It is fortunate for Coverack that the owners considered tourism a more certain investment. The hotel was not on the grand scale of the international Headland Hotel built a few years previously by Sylvanus Trevail at Newquay, nor did the owners cause similar problems with the locals by building a wall round common land thus depriving locals of its use. Difficulties were to come to light much later in the seventies and eighties when successive owners wanted to make the area surrounding the hotel exclusive to their clients and erected 'Keep Out' type notices. Curiously these warning signs were found at the bottom of the cliffs at Coverack. A period of local protests followed, including a march round the hotel to establish the presence of a public footpath which had been used for generations. The dispute resolved itself eventually when the hotel was converted into luxury flats which Kerrier District Council stipulated were not allowed to be occupied during the winter months. There is now a new path which joins with the coastal footpath. It was a wise move, for now as in the days of Solomon, '........all her paths are peace' in Coverack. To return to the early part of the century; the Headland Hotel was destroyed by fire in 1905. By 1909 it had been rebuilt. The new proprietor, Mr. George Harvey was proud to claim in Mr. Sincock's Illustrated Guide to Coverack that not only was the hotel built on '........a commanding site on one of the most picturesque parts of the lovely Cornish coast' but that it was ideal for '........those who love Fishing, Boating, Driving and Bathing' and furthermore, '........the noted Tariff is made moderate that these pleasures may be within the reach of all.' Mr. Harvey was proud of the fact that Marconi came to dine at the hotel from time to time. Mr. Harvey ran a Horse bus to Helston every Saturday and every other Monday at 1230 p.m. for the convenience of hotel visitors and the villagers. By 1914 he was driving his visitors in a 20 h.p. Model T Ford, registration number: AF 1324.

HEADLAND HOTEL "TAXI"
*By 1914 Mr. George Harvey was taking his visitors to and from Helston Station
in his own Model T Ford, Registration Number AF1324.*

In passing it is interesting to note that since 1891 the guide had gone up in price by 50% and cost three pence. During the same period the population of the village had increased from 192 to 200, an increase of about 4% in comparison. Newquay, the up and coming tourist town of Cornwall which used to be known as Towan Blistra when it was a small fishing village, had increased its population from 2,023 in 1891 to 2,935, an increase of about 45%.

The other new building to herald the new century was the Lifeboat House with its iron slipway. It has already been demonstrated in the chapter on Religion and Education that it is not always possible to consider one aspect of village life in isolation from another. The beginning of the 20th. century was highlighted by the arrival of the Lifeboat, 'Constance Melanie' on the 14th. February 1901, some three weeks after the death of 'Queen Victoria the Good.' It is certain that this village event did much to lift Coverack from the gloom which had been cast over the place by the loss of a loved monarch at the close of the Boer War. In spite of her great age, the Queen had refused to become morbid in her attitude to the losses inflicted on her professional soldiers by the Boer guerrillas. Her comment on the situation has since become a celebrated British rallying call when in danger of losing a battle: 'We are not interested in the possibilities of defeat: they do not exist.' Coverack men were to adopt a similar attitude in their work of rescue during the next seventy five years. The Lifeboat was to have an influence on every village family and every village activity. This will become evident as the chronicle of the 20th. century unfolds.

Behind the new Lifeboat House stood Dolor House. It was the centre of Coverack's seining industry and was occupied by business men like those of the Saunders family which has already been mentioned. The house was built in 1715. It was thatched with the gable end facing the quay and a walled front court yard facing up the hill towards the cove houses. At right angles to the back of the house were the fish cellars and beyond them was the spit of land at the edge of Dolor Point which was used to accommodate some of the large seine boats in winter. This land is now a small car park. Opposite Dolor House were more fish cellars where the Fishermen's Rest room now stands. There was a slipway leading up to these cellars which housed the Coastguards' galley which did duty as a rescue boat before the arrival of the Constance Melanie. At the top of the slip was the huge baulk of timber known as 'Parliament Seat' which has already been described. The quay was as it is seen today with the exception of the stone seats beneath the back wall. The slipway leading down to the quay beach has not changed. There was a 'privy' for the use of fishermen at the side of the Lifeboat House. Behind Dolor House was the Watch House. The top floor was used as a duty room by the Coastguards. The bottom floor contained boat gear and rescue apparatus. Some rifles were also stored there. The floor space was often used as a temporary mortuary after shipwrecks.

In the year 1905 Dolor House was pulled down and replaced by a purpose built hotel with stabling and store rooms in the courtyard. It was named the Paris. The bar soon became the focal point of the village for fishermen and visitors. The hotel also became the first place of shelter for the survivors brought in by the lifeboat - and for their rescuers. The members of the Band of Hope in the lifeboat crew, being teetotal, did not indulge in the alcoholic beverages offered by the Paris.

The Lifeboat House itself looked much the same from the outside as it does now it has been converted to a restaurant. It was a fine purpose built building. As the guide book of 1909 put it, 'The Institution has spared no expense in making the house and slipway as perfect as possible, with every facility for the instant despatch of the boat.' It had cost £1,800 to build the house and slipway. The boat was hauled up the slip stern first by a manually operated winch. This was so that it could re-enter the water bow first. It was held in position in the house by two short wire strops or ropes and a chain containing a Blake slip. When the boat was about to be launched the two strops were removed and the boat was held in place by the chain only. At the appropriate moment the 'pin' was knocked out by the Head Launcher and the boat slid on rollers down the slipway, gathering momentum as it went. In rough weather some skill was needed by the Head Launcher in order to gauge the right moment to 'let her go' so that the boat would not be broached to by a huge wave as she hit the water. It has to be remembered that there were no powerful engines to thrust the boat away from the iron slip and the jagged rocks of Dolor Point - only the muscle power of the crew who had to start pulling on the massive oars to maintain the momentum given by the slide down the slip as soon as she touched the water. Sometimes the Coxswain would decide to ship the masts and sails on the slip before entering the water but this was not possible during a gale as the boat would be blown sideways off the slip on to the rocks beneath. The cork lifebelts and oilskins were slung on racks on each side of the boat when she was in the house. The men's gear was suspended to allow easy access to each side of the boat. The normal headwear was a sou'wester but in fine weather and on ceremonial occasions the crew wore bright red woollen caps, giving them the appearance of being jolly pirates. Above the boat at the seaward end of the house a committee room was built in due course so that the officials could deliberate on the day to day problems 'in situ' as it were.

Looking across the bay from the Quay, the village was 'bare' in comparison with today. It is necessary to study comparative photographs of the village in conjunction with the description which follow in order to appreciate the changes which have taken place. The Mill House was operating and in season carts could be seen bringing grain and loading bags of flour. The lowest Mill Wheel was visible from Polcoverack Lane. Mr. Richard Robers, the miller who had taken over from Mr. Martin, owned the river rights. The development of the village was governed to a certain extent by the fact that the land to the west of the river (the cove side) belonged in the main to the Ellis family and the Sandfords who were mentioned in the chapter on Religion and Education. The land to the east was owned mainly by the Trelowarren Vyvyans and was not parcelled out until after the First World War. Even then, much of the land was rented for Market Gardening and Flower Farming. There was a cluster of thatched houses round the Mill and by the lane leading to Polcoverack Farm. Proceeding along the flat from the bottom of Mill Hill one would pass the houses on the beach road before coming to Gyllyngvase Field, then there were no more dwellings until taking the road leading to the footpath to St. Keverne through the fields. The Bay Hotel had not been built, nor Trerose House. There were the three houses just off the road leading to the St. Keverne footpath. These were the ones now known as the Punt and the Dinghy. There were only three houses actually on the road leading to the footpath to St. Keverne. They were the present day Tamarisk Cottage, Rope Walk - now known as Tregisky Cottage - and Pedn Myn - now known as Tregatreeth. In view of this, one can understand why Mr. Sincock's description in the guide book went thus: '........the part of the village overlooking the Cove is the oldest ........ the view from the Cove is extremely pretty commanding the spacious Bay, with its dark blue rippling waters, bounded by the steep Northern arm of land which terminates in a low tongue of land called the Lowland.' He does not mention the northern end of the village as having houses along the roads and built on the 'steep Northern arm.' There was a rough road leading down to the northern end of Mill Beach. This trackway was used by carts loading stone on to the barges and by farmers and gardeners collecting sand and seaweed. Some of the seine boats which could not be accommodated at the Dolor were taken across the bay and hauled up this road and laid up on the green sward of common land behind the present day bus shelter. The trackway gradually dwindled to a narrow path because of natural erosion and was in constant use until it became dangerous in the late 1940s. It will be recalled that the fishermen used to dry their nets in fields at North Corner. The large pile of huge boulders which has been placed in the cleft close to the corner where the ancient path came to the top of the cliff is a reminder of the need to be ever vigilant regarding the erosion of the seaward defences of Coverack.

By 1914 the northern end of Coverack was showing signs of the housing development which is evident today. Large houses such as Rocklands on North Corner hill and The Croft had been built. Later came the Bay Hotel, Trerose, and Porthgwarra with larger house such as Tregisky and Penmarth on North Corner hill. Then came a good sprinkling of smaller houses and the development of former barns, cowsheds, cart houses and early garages into dwelling houses. The only room available for development now is at the top of North Corner hill in the former market garden fields. It is fortunate that the Nature Conservancy Council has informed the local planning authorities of the fact that Coverack Cliffs are designed as a site of Special Scientific Interest. This means that it is unlikely there will be any desecration of the unique coastal environs of Coverack.

In 1909 Mr. Sincock described the western half of the village thus: '........the portion fringing the Lan Big Bay being much more modern and styled Sunny Corner, a well deserved name and a position much appreciated in the spring of the year'. Of course, the Wesleyan Chapel was situated at Sunny Corner. It might be regarded as an old building by present day people but in 1909 it was not even half a century old and was not thought of as being particularly ancient. The Coastguard houses had been established at Sunny Corner since the early nineteenth century. The present Channel View Hotel was one of the places advertised in the earlier guide as Bay View Cottage and boasted six bedrooms, two sitting rooms and the use of a Pianoforte. Names of previous distinguished visitors such as Mr. and Mrs. C. Napier Hemy of Falmouth were included in the advert. Napier Hemy's paintings of Cornwall's landscapes and seascapes are highly valued today. Hill Crest, Boak House and Parc Behan were prominent. The latter had the stairway from the Mohegan as a special feature of the new building. The gateway to this house is adorned with the remains of the jaw bones of a whale which was washed ashore at the Blackhead early in the century. The horse bus to Helston picked up its passengers at Boak House to avoid having to carry them up the steepest part of School Hill. There were no council houses on the skyline at Gatewynyack, nor in the field below. The Battery had the Coastguard signal mast at the highest point facing seaward and was bounded by a walled garden at the western end. The green was much in use as a drying area for clothes as well as for recreation and public events.

With the exception of the houses at the top of the slope leading from the quay, which were destroyed by enemy action in 1942, the Cove is much the same as it was at the beginning of the century. Mr. James Roberts kept the Coverack Hotel or old inn. He also kept Trevothen Farm and ran a horse bus, post horses, carriages and waggonettes. The latter were used to carry parties of visitors to places of interest around the Lizard and Helford areas. The Cove houses began opposite the present day Seine Loft, filling the space now occupied by the public toilets, telephone kiosk and small car park. The house on the corner opposite the Seine Loft made the turn up towards Sunny Corner very dark and narrow. There is a new house built above the Old Post Office yard, next to 'Archie's Loft'. At the side of the new house there was a hole in the uneven road where carts would shoot down loads of mangolds, turnips and other foodstuffs for the animals which were fed in the yard. This convenient arrangement saved the suppliers the difficult job of carrying the fodder down the steps through the narrow entrance to the Post Office. Bank House was a village shop. The front rooms of several houses along the Cove were converted into Tea Rooms in the summer. Mrs. Connor and Mrs. J. Bowden were well known for their food while Mrs. May's Lodging House on the hill behind the Old Inn which had opened in 1897, the Jubilee Year, boasted five bedrooms on one floor as well as two sitting rooms and a piano. Greystone, situated in the centre of the Cove, was an imposing private house owned by a pilot called Smith. In front of Roskilly's carpenters' yard on the seaward side of the road was a pigs' 'scrow' or sty. This was pulled down much later and Mr. John White had a temporary building there which was used as a shop and café until it was in danger of sliding into the sea and had to be abandoned. There were also small gardens and drying areas on the cliff on the seaward side of the Cove road. Some chicken runs were also perched on the cliff edge as well as some strategically placed private bucket 'privies'. These miniature gardens and structures have long since disappeared - without carrying away any villagers inside them, I hasten to add!

### The Bo-at

In Coverack the word boat is pronounced in two syllables. The first 'bo' is pronounced as in law - 'baw' and the second is an abbreviated et - the e sounding rather like the e in THE bo-at. The bo-at in this chapter is the Lifeboat. We have already seen that there was much lobbying of the authorities by locals after the wreck of the Mohegan and the stranding of the Paris. The officials of the Royal National Lifeboat Institution wisely approached Coverack fishermen and they collectively decided that the crew for the proposed Coverack Lifeboat should be chosen by the seafarers in the village and that the chosen crew should elect their own officers. Mr. George Cruze was duly appointed as Superintendent Coxswain designate with Mr. John Corin as his second in command.

The next step was to decide which type of lifeboat would be suitable for the conditions likely to be met in the Coverack sector. Accordingly the two coxswains were taken on a fact finding mission by the R.N.L.I. officials. First of all they went to Penzance and inspected the Elizabeth and Blanche, a self righter. The Coverack men were quite impressed but continued on their way to St. Ives. Their boat was also of the self-righting type and was not considered suitable. The Coverack men went on to Newquay. Their boat did not appeal either so the two men asked the R.N.L.I. officials if there were any other boats worth considering. The officials told them that there was a new type of boat which had just started her service at Ardrossan on the Firth of Clyde and asked the two Cornish men if they were prepared to go that far afield. They said they were as they still had not found the type they would be happy with at Coverack. It is interesting to note that Porthoustock men always chose self-righting types with the exception of the James Stevens No.17

which arrived in 1900.

When Mr. Cruze and Mr. Corin inspected the Liverpool non self-righting type boat at Ardrossan they knew she was the kind that would suit Coverack men and Coverack waters. She was 35 feet long with a ten foot beam. She was designed to carry fifteen crew - twelve oarsmen, a Coxswain, a Second Coxswain and a Bowman. The two masts carried a jib, a mainsail and a mizzen. There were two drop keels for use when sailing. The boat was of wooden construction and had been made by the Thames Ironworks, Blackwall, which as the name of the firm implies. usually made iron vessels. She cost £907 to build.

In due course the new Lifeboat arrived on the 14th. February, 1901. The cynics and the jealous longshoremen scoffed at her. Being prophets of doom, they wondered how the crew would fare if she capsized. The two coxswains countered this argument by saying that the Liverpool type boat had proved herself in very heavy seas and that in any case they had been told by other lifeboat men that the self-righters were of necessity narrow in the beam. In addition they had a fairly high freeboard at each end which tended to make them difficult to handle and more importantly, to capsize more readily than a 'beamy' boat with less freeboard. (Freeboard is the vertical distance between the top plank or gunwale of a boat and the water line). At the back of everyone's mind were some disasters which had occurred. One had happened off the coast of Lancashire in 1886 - fourteen years earlier - when two self-righting lifeboats from Southport and St. Annes capsized with the loss of twenty seven lifeboat men. Another, closer to home, occurred at Padstow in 1900 when the steam lifeboat, a large moored boat of 31 tons called the James Stevens No.4, capsized with the loss of eight of her crew. The other Padstow lifeboat, the pulling and sailing self righter called Arab lost nine of her oars in the same rescue attempt and the crew had to drift ashore using the kedge anchor and some spare oars. Another powerful argument in favour of a non self-righting type boat was demonstrated by the fact that when men are thrown in the water and the boat rights itself, if they manage to scramble back on board, what chance is there to get hold of the oars, and how could the inevitable tangle of ropes and gear be sorted out to enable the lifeboat to continue her mission? The arguments for and against continued and all waited for the day when the new Coverack 'bo-at' could be tested on service in adverse conditions.

Coverack Lifeboat was bought by the R.N.L.I. with the money from a legacy from Mr. F.E. Hills of Penshurst, Kent. His widow, Mrs. Constance Melanie Hills of Redhill, Surrey presented the money for the boat which was named 'Constance Melanie'. Most people in Coverack pronounced the second name of the boat at 'Me-lay-nee' not 'Mell-a-nee'.

The first call for the services of the new boat was not long in coming. The month of December, 1901 was a stormy one. There was a heavy toll on the East coast. The St. Ives steamer Trefusis was driven ashore at Seaton Carew, West Hartlepool Bay but fortunately the crew was rescued by the local lifeboat and Coastguards. It was in the same stormy month that Marconi received the first Morse message by wireless from Poldhu. His critics claimed he had heard static due to the stormy conditions but of course Marconi soon provided scientific proof of his 'wireless wonder'.

The storms continued into the new year. On Monday, 13th. January, 1902 a strong easterly wind was blowing. The wind was actually South of East which caused a rough sea to get up and mist to set in. It was the very kind of weather Coverack fishermen detest because it often necessitates their having to haul up the boats and leave valuable gear out at sea at the mercy of the wind and waves. Being winter time, not many boats were still down and fishing was almost at a standstill. There happened to be another of those popular school concerts in progress that evening, so a large number of village people had climbed the hill to see and hear the children performing under the leadership of Mr. W.F. Phillips. At about twenty past eight when the show was drawing to a close, a young pupil named Alfred Ernest Rapson was reciting Henry Wadsworth Longfellow's dramatic poem, 'The Wreck of the Hesperus'. a schooner which was wrecked on a reef called Norman's Woe in winter on a dark night during a snowstorm. Suddenly the door of the school burst open and a man shouted that a ship had gone ashore on Lowland Point. Almost at the same time the maroons were fired summoning the lifeboat and Coastguard Rocket Apparatus crews. Within a few moments all the men present in the school had rushed out, leaving the mothers and children to find their own way down the hill to their homes or to watch the first service launch of the Constance Melanie.

By this time a big sea was running but the untried crew of Coverack and the seasoned crew at Porthoustock did not hesitate to man the boats. The distress rockets from the stricken ship had also been seen at Falmouth and the crew assembled there on stand-by. Dr. G. Bryan Daunt, the Hon. Sec. of the Coverack boat recorded that the men were called out at 8.25 p.m. and that the boat was launched at 8.35 p.m. - creating a precedent that was to prove hard to beat.

It was a dark night but the sixteen men on board the Constance Melanie settled down to a long hard pull into the wind with the seas breaking every now and then over the starboard bow. By nine o'clock they were within shouting distance of the 800 ton iron barque Glenbervie which had gone ashore on the part of Lowland Point known as the 'Air Pool'. When the vessel struck the crew swung out the ship's lifeboats on their davits but soon realised they would be unable to thread their way through the unfamiliar rocks in the sea that was running, so they wisely elected to remain on board with Captain Gardiner and wait for the lifeboats which had answered their distress signals. The crew was a mixture of nationalities with a strong contingent of Norwegian seamen.

The ship proved to be 'wedged' in so well that George Cruze the Coxswain could not run alongside and take the crew off because of the heavy sea and the rocks surrounding the Glenbervie. He therefore put down an anchor and warped to within 50 feet of the wreck and took off the crew by throwing a heaving line on board and subsequently pulling one crew member at a time through the breaking water on a more substantial rope to which the heaving line had been 'bent' or attached. The Constance Melanie was held steady during this operation by the anchor and the rowers keeping the lifeboat into the wind by giving way and back watering (pulling and pushing) on their oars. Meanwhile the new Porthoustock Lifeboat, the James Stevens No.17 had arrived on scene and the Coastguards had struggled to the Lowland Point with their horse drawn apparatus and fired a rope across the ship as a supplementary means of rescue. The Porthoustock Lifeboat returned to station and a message was sent to Falmouth telling the Lifeboat crew they could stand down.

When all the 16 shipwrecked sailors were safely aboard the Constance Melanie the crew had to begin the row back to Coverack. The bowman found however that the anchor which had been holding the boat in position during the rescue had fouled and was held fast by a submerged object. He was forced to cut the rope, leaving the anchor, chain and rope on the bottom to be recovered at a later date when the tide was out. After another long row, this time with the wind behind them, the lifeboat entered the quay basin at 10.45 p.m. The seas were too heavy to allow the boat to be hauled up the slip. The shipwrecked mariners were quickly helped ashore and given food and clothing. The Cornish Echo reported later that '........the poor fellows, shivering with cold and drenched to the skin had lost all their belongings but were soon made comfortable by the good people of Coverack.'

**THE IRON BARQUE GLENBERVIE
ON LOWLAND POINT**
*16 men were rescued on the first service call
of the Coverack Lifeboat, Constance Melanie in 1902.*

The men who manned the Constance Melanie on her first service call were:

Superintendent Coxswain:   George Cruze

Second Coxswain:         John Corin

| | |
|---|---|
| George Bowden | William Corin |
| Joseph Bowden | Alfred Eustice |
| William Bowden | Harry Eustice |
| Frederick Carey | John Pengilly |
| James Carey | Stanley Roskilly |
| Samuel Champion | Thomas Roskilly |

Each man received £1 10s 0d in expenses from the R.N.L.I. for the night's work and the six shore helpers who assisted to launch and haul up the lifeboat received four shillings and sixpence each.

The Glenbervie, built in 1866, was known locally before she was wrecked. She had been laid up for a while near Bowyer's Cellars which are close to the new Yacht Marina in Penryn. The 800 ton barque was registered in Glasgow and part owned by her master, Captain Gardiner who had spent £1,500 on a refit in London Docks before setting out on the fateful voyage. She left London on December 19th., 1901 with a general cargo bound for Algoa, Port Elizabeth which is about four hundred miles east of the Cape of Good Hope in South Africa. Due to the December gales which have already been mentioned, a tug took the ship as far as Beachy Head then she made her own way down channel. She passed four miles south of the Eddystone Light at 1530 on Monday, 13th. January, 1902. Captain Gardiner then set a course to clear the Lizard. At 2030 a course alteration was made to clear a red light which was presumably that of another ship as St. Anthony Light did not have a red sector at that time as it does now. In the haze, neither St. Anthony nor The Lizard lights were positively identified. Soon after the course alteration the Glenbervie's lookout reported land ahead. The mate went forward to look but could see nothing. Shortly afterwards the mate 'discovered blackness' as he subsequently described it and shouted a warning to the helmsman to go 'Hard a starboard!' It was too late, the Glenbervie struck a rock and was aground on Lowland Point. It was high water which probably accounts for the fact that the ship had not struck a rock earlier in deeper water. In retrospect, local seamen thought she had followed virtually the same track as the liner Paris in 1899 as she came to a stop within a few hundred yards of the spot where the Paris had grounded. The Glenbervie had the unenviable distinction of being the last sailing ship to be wrecked on the Lowland Point.

By the following Wednesday the sea was fine enough for salvage operations to begin. It was hoped that the local helpers from Coverack and Porthoustock would be able to lighten the ship sufficiently so that she could float off the rocks as the Paris had done. During all the drama of the shipwreck the ship's cat had remained on board. Captain Gardiner was very fond of this cat and offered the Coverack men who were working on the salvaging operation a reward if they could bring the cat ashore. The cat did not want to leave the ship and managed to elude its would be captors. There were plenty of places to hide. The ship was carrying barrels of cement and sheets of corrugated iron in the bottom of the hold, together with some zinc. When the salvors got on board they found pianos and items of furniture floating about in the flooded hold. They were beyond salvage but they managed to retrieve most of the ship's stores and some of the bonded goods the ship was carrying. There were some 600 cases of whisky, 400 of brandy and an unknown quantity of rum in the hold. This necessitated the presence of a Coastguard on board to prevent stealing or 'wrecking' as the locals would have put it in private. In spite of this precaution some of the spirits inevitably found their way into the homes and down the throats of the thirsty locals. Some of their sheds were observed to have nice new corrugated iron roofs not long after the Glenbervie came ashore. The local children also joined in the unexpected bonanza and feasted on ships' biscuits. In the normal course of events they would not have deigned to eat the 'hard tack' but they found it went down well when spread with golden syrup which was to be found in the large tins which were dotted about the local shoreline.

When the Glenbervie's crew was taken to Falmouth prior to going home or joining other ships, they were interviewed in the Royal Cornwall Sailors' Home by a reporter from the Cornish Echo. The ship's mate - '........a grisly grey bearded old sea dog of about 60' revealed that it was the first time he had been shipwrecked in his 46 years at sea. He declared, 'It seems that Providence has arranged matters nicely for the Coverack Lifeboat was placed there just in time for my first wreck.' On the other hand, the Norwegian carpenter told the reporter that he had been wrecked three times in the previous year, two of the occasions being during the last three months.

Unfortunately another gale sprang up at the end of January and the Glenbervie broke up. In the same gale the Italian ship Logaro was lost with all hands off the Isles of Scilly as the St. Mary's Lifeboat was unable to get to her. Nearer home a schooner was driven on to Black Rock at the entrance to Falmouth Harbour and there were many other casualties round the Cornish coast.

Some of the survivors from the Glenbervie were taken in by my paternal grandparents who lived in Beach House next to the Mill. One of these men wrote to them on February 8th., 1902 from the 'Rest for Scandinavian Sailors' at 7 West India Dock Road, in the East End of London. Charles Hernanson told them that four of the crew had to remain in London for 'the protest' about the wreck. He apologised for not writing before, saying he had been unable to get down to writing before the affair was settled. He said that the remainder of the Norwegians in the crew had already left in a Norwegian ship bound for New York. He sent a message from 'the young Finnish fellow' who had embarked on a 'weekly boat.' - 'He sends his best wishes to the family and a big thank you for the kindness shown him when being in your house.' Charles Hernanson continued: 'The jolly carpenter you know took ill when coming ashore and was sent to the hospital and will probably come out next week.' He ended with a delightful tribute: 'My best respects to your servant and to your children and many thanks from us all to you for your kindness to us strangers. A special thank you from me for everything you did for me in your home. It was quite as if I had left my own home and mother when I left yours.'

The correspondence continued for a while. My grandparents were sent a letter from Newcastle on the 18th. August, 1902. Charles said they were loading coal for San Francisco. He thanked them for their previous letter which he had received in Sydney and told them that the ship he was on was called the Howth - 'not like that old ship' - meaning the Glenbervie. It had taken them 119 days (17 weeks) to get to Sydney. They were there on Coronation Day (Edward VII) and the town was beautifully illuminated for the event. He mentioned that the old mate of the Glenbervie was on board the Howth and 'that coloured man that was the steward.' He added that the latter was a very nice man and that he had lost a lot of clothes in the wreck. This time the Norwegian signed himself 'Your sincere friend.' He ended by asking my grand parents to write him c/o The British Consul, San Francisco, California, U.S.A. Unfortunately there is no evidence of the correspondence continuing after this letter.

The saga of the Glenbervie does not quite end there. On August 14th., 1990 the great grandson of Captain Gardiner telephoned the writer from Coverack. He had come to visit the scene of the wreck. He said his great grandfather had stayed with the Roskillys at the Post Office while he was sorting out the salvage and that Mr. Roskilly used to send the Captain a tin of Coverack cream every now and then as a small compensation for his unfortunate introduction to the village. He also told me that Captain Gardiner was one of the traditional nineteenth century seamen who clung to the use of sail for as long as possible. The Captain's own father had been a Captain of a ship which was chartered to transport convicts to Australia in the nineteenth century.

The people of Coverack settled down to being Edwardians. The Boer War had ended, bringing peace of mind to all, especially those who had relatives in South Africa. The School had been enlarged, bringing satisfaction to the parents. Two new hotels had been built and extra refreshment rooms had been opened in the cove in response to the demands of the burgeoning tourist industry. A new lifeboat had been stationed in the village giving contentment to the crew and confidence to passing mariners. The name Paris continued to be an added attraction to visitors to Coverack, not only in the context of the new hotel but because the ship, now renamed Philadelphia, was in the forefront of Marconi's well publicised wireless experiments. Communications by road were improving slowly. The local horse buses continued to take the villagers to Helston. They had romantic sounding names like 'Star of the South' and modern ones like 'Telegraph'. In January, 1904, Mr. H.A.L. Rowe of Helston took out Licence No.101 for his new 6 horse power Bella motor car. No one in Coverack aspired to being a motorist at that stage. There was no petrol station there, although that would not have posed a serious problem as the new automobiles carried spare metal petrol cans on the running boards or strapped on the back. A few motoring tourists ventured as far as Coverack but vehicles propelled by the comparatively new internal combustion engines remained relatively few and far between until after the Great War when motor bus services were inaugurated. These services operated three times a week. Milling stopped in 1907. A new use for the Mill premises was found soon after the war when Mr. Percy Roberts established a garage repair business in them. He also sold petrol. Even so, most of the motor transport which came to Coverack was of the commercial type, bringing supplies to the local shopkeepers and other tradesmen. Mr. Roberts continued the haulage and coal business but it was mechanised. His lorry became a boon to the village of Coverack as farmers became less inclined to interrupt their daily routine to do some carting for the villagers.

STAR OF THE SOUTH
*This photograph was taken circa 1906. The driver is Mr. Willie Richards.*
*Sitting next to him is Mrs. Lily Corin, then Miss Edith Pengilly in white,*
*Mrs. Date, Miss Annie Hart, ?, Mrs. Kate Hart. The small boy looking after the dog*
*is Charlie Hart.*

Just over a year after the wreck of the Glenbervie, Coverack Lifeboat was called out again to Lowland Point on February 1st., 1903. It was another barque, the Clan Graham of Glasgow. This time there was a southerly gale blowing. The lifeboat did not have to take off the crew but she did assist in the salvaging of the vessel by taking hawsers through the rocky shallows to the Falmouth tugs which came to the assistance of the Clan Graham. The tugs managed to get the barque off the rocks and tow her into Falmouth before the rising water in her hold could sink her.

Another year went by. At 6 a.m. on the 7th. March, 1904 the villagers were awakened by the sound of distress rockets exploding overhead. The 1,100 ton Danish steamer G. Koch had come ashore in thick easterly weather right beneath the Coastguard Station in Perprean Bay. She had passed the Coastguard Watch House on her way into the little bay. There was a moderate sea running, the visibility was poor and it was bitterly cold. Fortunately it only took the lifeboat crew a quarter of an hour to row round the Dolor Point to the casualty. Meanwhile the Coastguards had mustered the Volunteer Life-Saving Apparatus Company and got a rope aboard by firing the line carrying rocket over the ship. There were nineteen people on board the G. Koch and they were all taken off by breeches buoy while the Constance Melanie stood by. She returned to the quay at 10 a.m. The sea was too rough to allow the lifeboat to get back on the slip and into the house. She could not manoeuvre easily as she had damaged her rudder when a sea carried her on to the wreck while she was standing by. The grapnel rope which had been thrown over the ship's rail to keep the lifeboat in position while the rescue was being effected, was chafed almost in two by the movement of the two vessels. Repairs were done locally to enable the lifeboat to remain ready for another service during the bad weather.

DANISH STEAMER G. KOCH
*The G. Koch ran ashore in Perprean Bay on 7th. March, 1904*
*Mears Point (Chynhalls) is seen in the background with the three banks of rock*
*extending into the sea. They are known as the Inner, Middle and Outer Clubbas.*
Photo by kind permission of F. Gibson

In fact there was a three year wait before the next call came. This time the Constance Melanie was needed at the Lizard. The liner, Suevic, homeward bound from Australia struck the Brandies Rocks which are part of the Maenheere Reef. The rocks are about five cables (1,000 yards) out from Polpeor Cove where the Lizard Lifeboat was housed. The time was 7.30 p.m. on the 17th. March, 1907. There was a West Sou' West gale blowing which created a heavy sea. Visibility was poor due to fog and rain squalls. There were 524 people on board the 12,500 ton White Star Liner. It soon became obvious that the Lizard Lifeboat, Admiral Sir George Back and the Cadgwith Lifeboat Minnie Moon were not going to be able to cope so the Coverack and Porthleven boats went to assist. It was indeed a mammoth rescue. As far as the Coverack boat was concerned, the first problem was getting to the Lizard in the shortest possible time. Under sail it meant a good seven mile haul, most of the way with the wind 'on the nose'. Under oars it meant two to three hours exhausting work for the crew. Fortunately the dilemma was soon settled for as the Constance Melanie got out past the Guthens rocks she fell in with the Falmouth tug, Triton. She too, was on her way to assist the Suevic and her skipper, known to the Coverack men as 'Whitey', offered the rescuers a tow. This meant that when the lifeboat arrived on scene the men were reasonably fresh for the task of getting the passengers and crew off the Suevic and landing them at the Lizard.

Due to the heavy swell running the passengers had to jump from the ladders on the side of the Suevic into the Constance Melanie when she rose on the crest of a wave. Forty four were rescued in this way, each passenger jumping into the strong arms of Mr. Cruze. The passengers then had to be ferried ashore. The wind had increased by this time, making it impossible to get into Polpeor Cove - one of the Suevic's own boats had already been smashed up there - so the lifeboat went down wind into Cadgwith.

Lake's Falmouth Packet, Cornwall Advertiser and Visitor's List described the aftermath of the rescue as follows: 'Many of the ladies had but scanty clothing and were in a fainting condition when landed after the awful experience they had. They were given restoratives and shown the greatest hospitality by the natives. Fires and hot food were prepared and many of the shipwrecked passengers spoke with gratitude of the hospitable treatment afforded them.'

Of course, most of the rescue work fell to the Cadgwith and Lizard boats who were the first on scene. They rescued the amazing number of 227 and 167 respectively. The Porthleven boat rescued 16. The total of 454 people being rescued in a single operation by boats of the Royal National Lifeboat Institution remains a record to this day. There were no fatalities. The people who were not rescued by the R.N.L.I. boats were taken ashore either in the Suevic's own lifeboats or the rescue tugs Dragon, Eagle, Triton and Victor.

The Constance Melanie returned to Coverack and the crew got on with their normal daily routine. The Lizard men and indeed the Lizard villagers had their daily lives interrupted for some time to come because of the interest the practically new White Star liner had created among the public. It proved quite a boom for local shopkeepers and hotel and boarding house keepers at a time of the year which is normally quiet. In due course of time, six Silver Medals were awarded for the work done that night in March, 1907. They were awarded to lifeboat men Coxswain William Henry Mitchell, Second Coxswain Edwin Mitchell of the Lizard Lifeboat, Coxswain Edward Rutter and the Rev. H. Vyvyan of the Cadgwith Lifeboat. Two seamen from the Suevic were also decorated. They were George Anderson and William Williams. These men carried all the small children down the 40 foot swaying and bumping ladders to the waiting arms of the lifeboatmen going up and down in the great swell.

When George Anderson was interviewed on arriving in Falmouth he modestly told a reporter of Lake's Falmouth Packet that he had only done what any man would do. He was one of the few Suevic sailors who had managed to carry his clothes ashore. He did not leave the ship until the Captain and officers abandoned her, nevertheless he insisted on collecting his clothes first. Presumably in view of the work of rescue he had done that night the officers allowed him the privilege. It was impossible for everyone to collect personal possessions at that time because there would not have been enough room in the rescue craft. Much of the passengers' luggage was brought off later by a Great Western Railway steamer while other ships unloaded the cargo that was salvable. Mr. Anderson explained to the reporter that he only had £7 in wages coming to him and therefore could not afford to lose his gear. This is an interesting revelation of the conditions under which seamen lived in those days. They have never been adequately rewarded for the dangerous work they have to do at sea. Perhaps his comment prompted a grateful Lifeboat Institution to give George Anderson and his shipmate, William Williams a sum of £10 in addition to their Silver Medals.

The story did not end there. It was revealed that it was Captain Jones' last trip after spending forty four years at sea. The Suevic was in fact a day early in reaching the English Channel. On the very evening that she struck the Maenheere Reef at full speed, Captain Jones had been presented with a congratulatory address by his crew and another from his passengers, testifying '........to his good qualities and their confidence in his safe and able seamanship.' It was fortuitous that the ship had been travelling at a good rate although perhaps it is not considered to be good seamanship to do so in poor visibility, for the Suevic stuck hard and fast on the rocks and therefore did not slip back and sink into deeper water. When she struck there was no panic. Indeed the Captain was applauded by the passengers after he had assessed the situation and come down from the bridge to tell them they would all get off safely. He even advised them to go below and get a coffee while waiting for the lifeboats to arrive. As Lake's Falmouth Packet put it: 'British officers and crews are not expected to display symptoms of alarm in the hour of danger and the commander and men of the Suevic did not belie their reputation.'

The final outcome of the wreck was that after the salvors had unloaded the passengers' baggage and cargo they separated the damaged bow from the rest of the hull with a controlled explosion and towed the hull up channel past Coverack to Falmouth for temporary repairs. She was then towed to Southampton where a new bow was fitted. The Suevic continued working as a liner. Finally she became a whale oil factory ship. She was scuttled in 1942 by her Norwegian owners who did not want her to be captured by the Germans.

Life was not easy for the Coverack Edwardians. Work was not plentiful but the people managed somehow. The new buildings provided employment for some during their construction. Others had permanent but poorly paid work on the farms. Fishermen continued their eternal quest for bumper catches. When they did materialise the brief period of prosperity made up for the long periods of interim back breaking unpaid toil. An indication of the difficulties experienced by ordinary people in the early days of the twentieth century is illustrated in part by an item in the West Briton in 1908. The Chairman of the Finance Committee of the Board of Guardians of Helston Workhouse reported that during 1907, 903 tramps 'were relieved'. The Rev. H. Vyvyan also added that the total number of days in which tramps stayed at the 'Union' was 1,092. If the unfortunates stayed more than one day it meant that the Guardians would not have been able to cope with such large numbers.

There are few pictorial records of Coverack to take us back to the Edwardian scene except some family photographs and postcards. Artists did not settle and found schools as they did in Newlyn and St. Ives. We have seen that Napier Hemy favoured Coverack for his holidays but it is believed that he did not produce any canvases devoted to the village. There were a number of lesser known painters who came to the village such as Herbert Dicksee whose 'Down to the sea' has already been mentioned. Harry P. Clifford was another Royal Academician who painted scenes of the village. His watercolour of the village viewed from the Mill Beach glows with the true Coverack light which even expensive modern cameras have failed to reproduce faithfully. Flora Lion, who became a fashionable portrait painter on the London scene, stayed in Coverack in the early 1900s. She painted local characters in oils. After her student days she went on to paint not only society beauties like Liza Lehman and Annie Horniman the founder of repertory in England but also well known public figures such as the composer Sir Edward German. Flora Lion's portrait of her own mother hangs in the Tate. The artist returned to the village in August, 1951 to visit friends made in the early part of the century. It was her last visit. She died in 1958 at the age of 82.

Coverack remained relatively remote during the prelude to the Great War. Individuals from the village such as the service men made forays to all parts of the world as did their forebears in Victorian times. There was also a small trickle of emigrants who went in search of a better life and subsequently relayed details of conditions and current events elsewhere in lengthy letters. Some returned disillusioned, never to stray again. Some, enthusiastic about the new life they had carved out for themselves, came back for a brief period to settle personal affairs and departed once more for their adopted home. Others went away and were never heard of again, while a few remained silent, giving their relatives a great deal of anxiety for some time before deciding in a fit of remorse after many years of absence to write and reveal what had been happening to them.

Today we sometimes stop to wonder at the advances in technology that are being made in our own lifetime. It was not really so different during the prelude to the Great War. It was also a period of rapid technological advance. We have already seen something of the advances made in telephone, cable and wireless communications, the use of automobiles and the transport system. Before the first decade of the new century was over, aviation had developed sufficiently to allow Bleriot to fly across the English Channel in July, 1909. No one in Coverack dreamed that before the next decade was over, aeroplanes and airships seeking German submarines would be flying regularly over the village.

With regard to telephones, it is worth taking a look at the conditions prevailing in the Coverack area at the turn of the century. The National Telephone Company's Directory for the Provinces of 1899-1900 was a slim volume in comparison with those which are in contemporary use. That of 1903-1904 revealed a significant increase in the number of subscribers. The following table illustrates the growth in telephone communication in Cornwall in the early part of the twentieth century. It should be remembered that at the time the Post Office had a telegraph system in operation and the Coast Guards had their own coastal telephone network. Each town had a Public Call Office for non-subscribers.

| | 1899-1900 | 1903-1904 |
|---|---|---|
| Camborne | 13 | 24 |
| Falmouth | 18 | 40 |
| Hayle | 8 | 12 |
| Newlyn | 2 | 2 |
| Newquay | 10 | 29 |
| Redruth | 8 | 15 |
| Penzance | 43 | 70 |
| St. Austell | 25 | 45 |
| St. Ives | 7 | 20 |
| Truro | 18 | 67 |

By the year 1912 the Post Office had taken over the National Telephone Company. Helston had got its own exchange and was no longer listed under Falmouth. The St. Keverne Stone Co. had an office number in Church Street, Helston at that time as well as one in the quarry office at Porthoustock. The number to which faults were reported was Truro 1.

After the 1914-1918 war St. Keverne PBX - Private Branch Exchange - came into being. The first ten numbers listed in the Post Office Directory for 1920 were as follows:

| | |
|---|---|
| St. Keverne 1 | St. Keverne Post Office |
| St. Keverne 2 | St. Keverne Stone Co., Porthoustock. |
| St. Keverne 3 | West of England Road Metal Co. |
| St. Keverne 4 | Mr. P.D. Williams, Lanarth. |
| St. Keverne 5 | Dr. Spry, St. Keverne. |
| St. Keverne 6 | Mr. R. Coad, Treleague. |
| St. Keverne 7 | Rule and Son, Grocers, St. Keverne. |
| St. Keverne 8 | Dean Stone Co. |
| St. Keverne 9 | Mr. Collins, Porthallow Mills. |
| St. Keverne 10 | Coverack Post Office<br>Express Delivery Service 9 a.m. - 7 p.m.<br>(Tuesdays 1 p.m.) |

A Coverack man joined the Royal Navy at the turn of the century. It was the time of the Boxer Rising in China against the European countries which had seized ports and naval bases from the Chinese. They had been weakened after their war with Japan. This meant that Royal Navy ships had to remain on station to protect the recently won British interests. It also meant that Mr. Martin had to do a six year commission on the China Station instead of the usual three.

That long period of time away from home was a severe test of the loyalties of a young sailor towards his family and his country. Being a committed christian, Joe Martin remained faithful to both. Indeed, he made contact with a band of British missionaries working in China. The missionaries were singled out by the Chinese for harsh treatment during those troubled times.

Mr. Martin joined the navy when sailors still wore straw hats. He used to remind Coverack people with pride that he had served on ships which had auxiliary steam power and that when steam propulsion was required, the captain would give the order, 'Up funnel, down screw!' The first British submarine was built in 1901, some fifteen years after the first one was ordered by the French government. Mr. Martin was among the pioneer seamen who served in submarines. He served for some time on B5 which was serviced by the depot ship H.M.S. Forth. For a special treat he would tell his Sunday School class of the time when his submarine crept through the Dardanelles during the First World War. Seven of the twelve submarines were lost in the allied operation which failed in the attempt to help our Russian ally by attacking Turkey. In parallel with the development of the submarine, Mr. Martin and other Coverack men serving in the Royal Navy saw the increase in reliability of steam power and the use of oil fired ships, plus the building of the Dreadnought class of Battleship which was encouraged by King Edward VII. These 18,000 ton ships had a speed of 21 knots and could outgun any ship afloat at that time. One can imagine the proud stories which were told of these revolutionary technical developments when Coverack men came home on leave.

Other changes in the way of life in Great Britain during the prelude to the Great war slowly permeated to the little oasis. Outwardly, visual changes such as new style houses, clothes and so on are evident in contemporary photographs of the village and village people at such times as Regattas and Tea Treats. The roads were not yet smoothed away to accommodate the new motor cars with their solid tyres. The cows' 'pancakes' dotted round the village still caused problems for ladies wearing their best long dresses. A pair of pattens remained in our shed at home until the 1960s, serving as a reminder of the days when ladies fitted each outdoor shoe on to a patten. This was a sole shaped wooden 'platform' which was mounted on struts fastened to an iron ring base. The ladies moved about on these miniature stilts and kept their best dresses out of the mud or whatever happened to be on the roads. Due to the hilly nature of the village and the fact that not many villagers wore dresses which actually touched the ground, pattens had virtually gone out of fashion by the beginning of Edwardian times. The Coverack men of that time adopted Edwardian fashions as the need for new clothes arose, which was not often, because of economic necessity. Some emulated their sovereign in their choice of headgear but the straw boater remained a firm favourite for a long time. The children of the village began to look more like little adults, having stopped wearing the more ostentatious 'best' clothes of Victorian times as these were not easily adapted for everyday wear. The boys were still bowling metal hoops along the uneven, hilly roads of Coverack. These were made in blacksmiths' shops. Later on, when the majority of the forges had disappeared, the local lads started using discarded motor tyres which could be bowled along silently but were not controlled so easily as the metal hoops which had hoopiron rods to guide them.

Throughout this period, the newly made peer, Lord Northcliffe, formerly Alfred Harmsworth, kept warning his readers in the Daily Mail and the Mirror of the growing menace of Germany's plans for economic and territorial expansion. The Royal Navy was working up to a state of readiness as we have seen. Lord Fisher was supported by King Edward VII in his campaign for the introduction of the Dreadnoughts and the king also backed Haldane in his fight against cuts in spending on the professional army. He also encouraged the reorganisation of the volunteer Yeomanry which was soon to be known as the Territorial Army and which attracted a number of Coverack men. It is not known what influence the popular press had on Coverack people. It is suspected they preferred to read the West Briton and the Packet which had a good coverage of national and international news as well as fairly comprehensive accounts of local happenings. Nevertheless, rumours went around Coverack that the travelling German bands which sometimes came to play in the village had orders to save all the coppers they were given and take them back to Germany to provide metal for what became known as the 'Arms Race.' Likewise when the Pindos was wrecked at Coverack in 1912 while taking nitrate from Chile to Hamburg, some locals became convinced the Pindos was part of a master plan for the manufacturing of explosives to be used in the coming war. There was probably some truth in this conviction but it did not prevent Kaiser Wilhelm II, son of Queen Victoria's daughter, the Princess Royal, from sending a reward to the lifeboat men of Coverack as a token of his acknowledgement of their bravery in rescuing the German crew. Neither did the thought that the Germans were about to become their enemies deter the Coverack men from their mission of rescue.

There is no doubt that Coverack people were not as interested in European politics as they were in the old age pension scheme which was introduced by the Liberal government in 1909. Amounts payable ranged from one shilling to five shillings a week at the age of seventy and were a great comfort to the old people. Most of them had earned so little during their lifetime that their meagre savings were soon exhausted when they became too infirm to continue earning money.

I am grateful to Mrs. Phyllis Beattie of Falmouth, whose grandfather, fisherman William Cowls of Porthleven, wrote the following lines in appreciation of the Old Age Pension at the age of 70. The poem was found in Mr. Cowls' note book containing the registered numbers of 'Mackeral Boats', 'Pilcher Boats', 'Half Boats' and 'Crabers' in the port just before the 1914-1918 war. There were 329 boats named in the list.

'I've reached the age of seventy

And say I'll tell you more

My sails are stowed quite neatly

I've reached the weather shore.


And yet I feel the surge of youth

A newness of life in me.

I have a pension now and that

Makes the difference, you see.


The winds may blow a perfect gale,

Make wreckage all around.

No fear of dragging anchor here.

The government is sound.'

These lines express vividly what a few shillings extra meant to one ancient Porthleven mariner in the early part of this century. The sentiments were no doubt echoed by some of the Coverack fishermen as well.

All working people were well aware of the importance of insurance and whatever happened they always drew some comfort from the knowledge that at least they would have a decent burial in Coverack, financed by their own private insurance contributions which they paid regardless of the sacrifice they had to make. It was a matter of pride to 'be put away proper.' I can remember the delight expressed by my maternal grandmother, who had been brought up in this school of thought, when she was told at the age of 90 that she need no longer pay the few coppers a week she had been contributing to an insurance company for her funeral expenses. The company considered she had already paid more than would be needed.

In the same way, the working men of Coverack felt more secure when Labour Exchanges for finding employment were set up and the National Insurance Act started a scheme in 1911 to protect them against unemployment. At first the insurance did not cover all manual workers but it did protect those who lost their jobs through illness. At that time the national unemployment rate was about 6%. This was to increase to 14% in the period between the two world wars.

During the pre war period Mrs. Emmeline Pankhurst began her stormy campaign to obtain votes for women. Balfour's government was not sympathetic to the Women's Social and Political Union. One can understand that the Coverack men adopted a similar intransigeant attitude. Women were not expected to contribute to the masculine deliberations which went on in the reading room and the bar of the Paris. Their place was in the home. Any woman daring enough to protest by chaining herself to a railing in Coverack would probably have been forcibly released before dark in order that she could go home and get her husband's tea! An indication of this kind of attitude can be illustrated by an incident which happened on the last day of the 'Kaiser's War.' Mrs. Willie White and my mother were told that the war had ended. They found this difficult to believe but were informed that if they wanted confirmation they could go to the Fishermen's Rest and see the official telegram for themselves. The two women, whose husbands were fighting in France, rushed down the slope to the recreation room, which is still a male preserve in conservative Coverack. Their excitement was abruptly quelled. Mr. Jimmy Carey was coming up from the quay and on seeing the ladies enter the 'sacred precinct' bellowed in his gruff bass voice, 'What are you two b......y women doing in there?' They told him, but not before verifying the wonderful news. They were forgiven for doing the unthinkable, for Jimmy was a kindly man in spite of his brusque manner and many of his relations were also involved in the fighting.

Coverack has had its fair share of visiting celebrities. One morning in the early 1900s Baden Powell came to the village when he was on a walking tour of the Lizard peninsula. He went into Dolor Cottage and ordered breakfast from my grandmother, Mrs. Ann Pengilly. She often reminded her grandsons of that proud moment if they visited her when wearing their Scout uniforms. As she was profoundly deaf I can not imagine how the conversation went but I'm confident my grandfather had something interesting to say to the controversial hero of Mafeking, who in 1908 founded what has proved to be the largest youth movement the world has ever known. More will be said about the Scouts and Guides in Coverack.

In the years before the outbreak of war, life in Coverack proceeded at its normal pace, barely touched by the changes which were taking place in Britain. Some of the men were lured away from the village by the prospect of a more secure future in the forces, on the railways, in the police or Civil Service. The social reforms to come were outlined in the press by the Liberal and the relatively young Labour Party which had begun the century with two Members of Parliament and by 1910 had forty two. This promise of more security encouraged some young villagers to be more adventurous and move to 'England'. Others considered that the more traditional Cornish way of seeking one's fortune by emigration was a better method of improving their standard of living. The writer's father was one of the latter. He went to Canada on the S.S. Ausonia. He found that there was no work for masons in Montreal in winter and had to earn his living as a worker in a rubber factory during the long freeze-up. He returned in the 'fall' of 1913 as he could not face a second winter as a factory hand.

Not quite so many men were working on the farms round Coverack before the First World War as there were in Victorian times, but it was still 'Rural England' or perhaps it should be 'Rural Cornwall'. The farm labourers were not yet affected seriously by the introduction of mechanisation but there was more competition from overseas which gradually reduced the overall need of labour on the farms. This took some time to permeate as far as Coverack because of the relatively poor transport system which meant that local demand was largely met by local farms. In addition the local growers had found a new market by sending their early vegetable crops to London and the Midlands, so the level of employment of workers on the land reduced slowly. However, the cargo of frozen meat and fruit brought ashore from the wrecked Suevic was an indicator of the changing state of commerce. Life continued to be hard for the majority of the villagers and as mentioned earlier, they were grateful for the improvements in the social sector of everyday life.

We have already seen that the tedium of life in early twentieth century Coverack was punctuated by short periods of intense excitement when the services of the lifeboat were needed. The boards giving details of the Coverack Lifeboats are now hung in the Wesleyan Chapel instead of the Lifeboat House. These boards do not tell the whole story. Sometimes the boat was launched and after hours of searching, returned without having been able to assist the casualty.

On the 21st. February, 1911, exactly eight years to the day after the Constance Melanie went to the assistance of the Clan Graham the lifeboat went to the assistance of a three masted steamer reported to be in trouble off Black Head. Nothing was found. The steamer probably corrected the problem and went on her way without signalling that all was well. The lifeboat crew was at sea for a long time and each man was awarded £1 10s 0d for his night's work. Mr. Phillips the Schoolmaster-Secretary of the lifeboat recorded that the shore signalman had reported the 'inconvenience' of trying to keep his lamp alight in the strong wind when following the boat on shore across the cliffs. The signalman was awarded 4s 6d for his night's work, as was the messenger who did liaison between the Coastguards and the Hon. Sec. of the lifeboat. Visitors to the Wesleyan Chapel in Coverack will note that there is no mention of the wreck of the Danish steamer G. Koch in 1904 on the Constance Melanie's Record of Service Board. This incident has already been described. Perhaps the lifeboat crew felt they had not contributed much to the rescue but I am confident that the Danish seamen were pleased to see the lifeboat standing by while they were being pulled ashore by the breeches buoy. It is important to remember that some of the most arduous operations carried out by lifeboats end without anyone being rescued. Those are the times when the zeal and seamanship of the lifeboat men are tested to the full. They never give up until there is absolutely no hope of finding the people who are in distress, whatever the weather and no matter how long it takes.

The year 1911 wore on. The summer duties of the Roskillys at the Post Office now included handing over letters to callers at the Office on Sundays when there was no village delivery. The area covered by the Coverack delivery men had now been extended to include not only Gwenter but the individual farms situated round about the hamlet. In May, St. Peter's Church Hall was built and put to use as we have already seen. One of the 'outside' events to arouse interest took place at the end of the year when Amundsen reached the South Pole, just beating the ill fated British Expedition led by Captain Scott. Coverack people were to hear all about the expedition after the war when Mr. Patrick Keohane was appointed to Coverack as Station Officer of Coastguards. He was a member of the third sledge team and reached 85° South, getting closer to the South Pole than anyone on the expedition, apart from those who made the final march.

January, 1912 was a stormy month. Gales swept the eastern seaboard of Great Britain. The Liverpool steamer Weston Hall was driven on the rocks in Aberdeenshire during a snowstorm. Fifty three men lost their lives. Nearer home on the 19th. January the barque Gustav went ashore at Portscatho, having parted from the tug Oceana. It was Coverack's turn the following month. The circumstances under which the wreck of the Pindos occurred at the Mears Point were very similar to those of the Gustav. The difference was that the Gustav got off the rocks and was towed into Falmouth for repairs.

## *The Pindos Story*

At about 9 p.m. on Saturday, 10th. February, 1912 the writer's father was coming down the hill past the Wesleyan Chapel with his girl friend when they saw distress rockets soaring into the sky above the Guthens Rocks. The couple dashed down to the Reading Room which was opposite the present Bank House and informed the men who were gathered there for the weekly Saturday night discussion and exchange of news.

The Reading Room was soon empty. One man dashed off to warn the Hon. Secretary and another to fire the maroons to summon the lifeboat crew and the Volunteer Life Saving Apparatus Company. The call was not unexpected. During the afternoon Coverack fishermen had been watching a tug with a sailing ship in tow trying to make her way down channel from Falmouth in an easterly near gale force wind. The fishermen had discussed the situation with the Coastguards and the latter decided to keep a close watch on the situation.

Coastguard Symes was on watch and saw the rockets at the same time as my father and mother and Mr. Symes burned a blue flare in response. He also fired an answering shot from his pistol. Next he informed his Chief Officer, Mr. Toy and Mr. W.H. Bonfield, the Hon. Secretary of the Lifeboat. The Coastguards assembled the Rocket Apparatus crew and the cart horses dragged the wagon to the Mears Point. It was a rough road and the cart had to be manhandled the last few hundred yards.

Meanwhile the lifeboat crew had assembled. The Hon. Secretary and the Coxswain decided they should go at once. They were one crew member short so 15 year old Sandy Pengilly volunteered to take the place of the missing man. The boy's father, John Pengilly had been a member of the crew on the night when the Constance Melanie went to the assistance of the Glenbervie in 1902 when the wind was blowing in the same direction.

On this occasion the Constance Melanie was eased out of the Lifeboat House until she was clear of the doors, then the masts were stepped and the sails hoisted and well reefed (shortened) before being lowered again prior to going down the slip. This itself was a difficult manoeuvre to accomplish for the strong wind could easily have toppled the four ton vessel off the slip if the crew did not maintain control of the sheets (ropes attached to the sails). The seas were sweeping over the back of the harbour wall. The tide was flooding and there was less than an hour to go before high water. The onlookers looked at each other in dismay, they were convinced no boat could live in such a sea which could be clearly seen in the beam of a lamp which was shining on the foot of the iron slipway. Coxswain John Corin coolly counted the breakers as they swept over the slip and when the brief lull came he shouted to Mr. Dick Tripp who was standing by with his hammer. Mr. Tripp, the Head Launcher knocked out the pin which was holding the lifeboat and away she went down the slip into the maelstrom below. Mr. Tripp was heard to mutter, 'Oh God, what have I done?' The boat struck the water on a receding wave and the mizzen sail kept her head into the wind as she got away from the slip. The sails were hoisted and the two keels quickly lowered to give the boat more stability.

The official R.N.L.I. Return of Service form does not allow enough space for a complete account of the way in which the operation was carried out. Mr. Bonfield, the Hon. Secretary who was the steward of Lanarth Estate, completed the relevant sections of the form as follows:

| QUESTION | | ANSWER |
|---|---|---|
| 7. | Direction and force of wind? | S.E. to S.S.E. Whole Gale. |
| 8. | Condition of sea. | Very heavy. |
| 9. | Condition of weather. | Fine to showers and cold. |
| 17, | Was service done under Sails or Oars? | Both. |
| 18. | If under Oars, did Boat pull against wind & sea? | Impossible to pull. |
| 19. | How did the boat behave? | Splendidly. |

The answers were brief and to the point but the implications would have been very plain to any R.N.L.I. official whose job it was to evaluate the report.

It took the Constance Melanie half an hour to reach the wreck. On the way out to the Guthens Rocks, while crossing Perprean Bay the crew were literally under water from time to time when a sea engulfed the Constance Melanie. The men had to hold on while the clearance valves got rid of the water in the boat. It was a pitch black night which made the mountainous seas more terrifying especially as the force of the water bearing down on the men banged their faces against their oars or whatever they clung to when the sea came aboard, knocking out teeth and gashing their faces as well as chafing their hands raw. Nevertheless the boat went on towards the feeble lights of the wreck.

The Coastguards had not been standing idly by. They had fired a line carrying rocket, which in spite of the wind, had literally hit its target. The rocket actually struck one of the masts and the crew of the Pindos started hauling in the whip (rope) which was going to bring out the breeches buoy. As it dropped into the trough of a wave it snagged on a rock and try as they might, neither the seamen on the Pindos nor the Coastguards on shore could clear it. The broken end of the whip was pulled ashore and quickly spliced, then another rocket was bent (tied) on. That one failed to reach its target, so did the next. A fourth rocket went over the stern and a fifth hurtled over the bow but the ship's crew could not get to the lines. It was probably just as well because if the Coastguards had attempted to pull the crew members through the rock strewn thundering surf, the sailors would have been cut to ribbons as the hawser carrying the breeches buoy would not have been taut enough to keep them up above the water while they were being hauled in.

It was at this stage of the rescue that the Constance Melanie arrived on scene. The Coxswain knew that he would never be able to take the boat alongside so he dropped a kedge (stern) anchor and paid out the cable slowly until the lifeboat was about twenty yards from the barque. There was no way of communicating directly with the crew of the Pindos but one brave German realised what the Coverack men were trying to do. He tied a rope round his waist, jumped into the raging sea and brought another rope to the waiting lifeboat. It was made fast and the job of transfer by lifebelt began. Two more Germans were hauled aboard the Constance Melanie before the rescue operation was halted once more. The seas were running so high that it was impossible for a seaman on the Pindos to get into the lifebelt and for the Coverack men to haul him back to the lifeboat. The Pindos crew had gathered in a shelter on the poop deck but the seas were sweeping over with such ferocity that they could not come out on deck to get into the lifebelt.

Up to that moment the rescue was being carried out in almost complete darkness. The lifeboat men tried to keep their oil lamps alight but found it impossible. While the lifeboat was weathering the storm and the Germans were sheltering on the poop deck, nothing could be seen from the shore. A broken oar washed ashore and the watchers began to fear the worst. They were so sure that the lifeboat had foundered that the Coastguards sent another message to Falmouth asking for the Bob Newbon to come to the assistance of their Coverack colleagues.

At this point Mr. May and his helpers arrived on the headland and set up the acetylene lamp which was known in the service as the Imperial Flare Light. One village account regarding the setting up of the light is that the onlookers began to despair of ever seeing the lifeboat men again. A woman cried, 'What shall we do?' The Rev. Fairfax suggested praying. Mrs. Bowden, whose husband was on the boat retorted, 'Damn praying, take the light over to them!' After lighting the lamp with difficulty, the shore helpers managed to illuminate the wreck and they could just make out the Constance Melanie straining at the kedge anchor and riding out the storm. The Bowman of the lifeboat, Alfred Eustis had not stocked the anchor properly. In his haste to prevent the Constance Melanie from being dashed on the rocks, he had not secured the pin in the crossbar or stock of the anchor. This meant that the anchor had no other gripping power than its two flukes, only one of which could bite into the bottom at a time. Fortunately the anchor did hold after slipping for a while and the error only resulted in the loss of the anchor and Mr. Eustis having his leg pulled about it on each occasion he dropped the kedge during subsequent operations.

Shortly after the searchlight lit up the scene it began to rain heavily. This was just what the lifeboat men had been praying for. The sea began to go down slightly and the wind changed direction allowing the men to restart the rescue work. They managed to get the full ship's complement of twenty eight men on board. Then they set out on the return journey.

One of the comforting thoughts at the back of the mind of a lifeboat man when he is on a service call is that there are many people in the area doing all they can to back him up. It has already been stated that the Falmouth Lifeboat had been requested. Indeed, the distress rockets had been seen in Falmouth and the crew of the Bob Newbon was already standing by. She launched at 11 p.m. at the request of the Hon. Secretary of Cadgwith Lifeboat which could not launch because of the weather. The Bob Newbon was a self-righting pulling and sailing boat about the same size as the Constance Melanie. The tug Briton took the Falmouth Lifeboat as far as possible to windward to allow her a straight run down channel. She arrived off the Manacles at 4 a.m. and was in Coverack Bay before 7 a.m. only to learn that the rescue had been successfully carried out after all. The Falmouth men then faced the long trip back to Falmouth in the storm which by then was beginning to go down. The devotion to duty of the Falmouth men that night went unrecorded, except in their own station log. Their seamanship had been tested to the full and had not been found wanting.

There were other men involved that night on the Lizard peninsula. The force and direction of the wind made it quite impossible to launch the lifeboats west of Coverack but the Lizard Volunteer L.S.A. Company set out for Coverack when they got the message that the Coverack Coastguards were having problems with their apparatus. Of course it took some hours before the team of horses arrived with the Lizard Life Saving Apparatus and by then the Constance Melanie had effected the rescue. The disappointed Lizard men then faced the long journey back without having been able to help. The Falmouth and Lizard men's efforts that night were greatly appreciated by the Coverack men. It proves that although they indulged in friendly rivalry during rescue exercises and local regattas, they kept to the Cornish motto of 'One and all' when it was a matter of life and death.

It should not be assumed that the tug Arcona abandoned the Pindos easily. She had battled for some eight hours to keep her tow on course. At 7.30 p.m. she signalled the Pindos asking her to set sails to keep her nose into the wind. The Officer of the Watch on the Pindos, Second Mate Behrena set the foresail and lower topsail but the wind increased and the Pindos began going slowly astern, taking the tug with her. The Arcona eventually had to slip the tow or she herself would have been wrecked. The Pindos, with the added weight of the towing hawser making it impossible to manoeuvre, went on to the rocks. If the tug had released her earlier probably she would have hit the Guthens Rocks broadside on and capsized before the lifeboat could get to her.

The Constance Melanie returned to the harbour at 3.30 a.m. It was impossible to get the boat on the slip in the storm. The ship's crew was taken into the Paris Hotel where they were made welcome by Mrs. Lyle Cuttance whose husband had been out in the Constance Melanie to rescue them. Mrs. May, the wife of the man who had rigged up the new searchlight, had collected an assortment of clothes from the villagers to give to the German sailors. Mr. J. Pengilly from Trebarveth Farm, the representative of the Shipwrecked Mariners' Society came down to the village to organise practical help for the sailors. Those who were not too exhausted began to cheer up and before long were singing songs in German round the piano in the Paris Hotel. Some of the lifeboat men who had also come in for a warm and a much needed drink joined in when they could, despite a few missing teeth.

Later, Coxswain John Corin in describing how the men were rescued, told a reporter from Lake's Falmouth Packet and Cornwall Advertiser: 'We thought we had lost one of the sailors, for just before he left the ship a heavy sea struck her and we lost sight of the man for a minute or two. We gave him up for lost but to our surprise and delight we perceived him again and after a great deal of trouble managed to get him on board.' Mr. Corin went on to tell of the battering the sailors received when being pulled through the rocky waters off the Guthens and explained, I suspect with a twinkle in his eye, for he was a tee totaller: 'Fortunately we had some brandy on board and this revived them. All the time we were in breaking water and thought many times we were going to be swamped. Several of the waves were higher than my house.' - Mr. Corin's house is situated on the hill overlooking the harbour and is still known as Hillside.

The morning after the rescue the crew of the Pindos was taken to Falmouth in hired horse buses organised by Mr. Pengilly. A large crowd assembled in Coverack to cheer them on their way. Lake's Falmouth Packet and Cornwall

Advertisers reported the following week: 'One of the most remarkable and pathetic services ever held at the seamen's Bethel during the twenty five years popular ministry of Chaplain J.C. Badger was that which took place on Sunday evening when the crew of the German ship Pindos and the crew of the steam trawler Maud joined a crowded congregation in thanksgiving for safe deliverance.' The Bethel was a Mission Church in Quay Hill, Falmouth. It had a ship's bow for a pulpit, which was known as the King Edward Memorial Pulpit. There was a sailing ship's wheel behind the pulpit, at the base of the pipe organ which was flanked by flags in the gallery. Seventeen of the crew of the Pindos left the next day for Plymouth where they boarded the President Lincoln for Hamburg.

Many of the crew of the Pindos could speak English and told the Packet reporter their individual stories. One of the sailors called Hans Steffen was only fourteen years old. It was his first voyage. When asked how he liked the job he replied with a smile, 'It is all right, but I must hope for better luck in the future.'

The day after the Pindos was wrecked she began to break up as she was hammered more firmly broadside on to the Guthens Rocks. She was listing to port with her lower gunwale on the seaward side and it became obvious she would never sail again. The wreck was bought for a couple of hundred pounds by Mr. Roskilly who went aboard with a team of Coverack men to remove the stores, sails, gear and any cargo which was still salvable. Due to the water in the hold the Chilean nitrate dissolved and was lost. The once proud ship which had withstood the batterings of Cape Horn was no more. She had been destined never to reach Port Talbot in South Wales where she was to load coal brickets before going on to Hamburg. The Pindos had begun life as the Eusmere and had made some very fast runs from China to Europe. It was the beginning of the end of an era. By 1928 there were fewer than thirty fully rigged ships in the world which were in a seaworthy state.

WRECK OF THE PINDOS ON THE GUTHENS, 1912.
*The day after the Pindos was wrecked she began to break up.*

Today, apart from the R.N.L.I. Record of Service hanging in the Wesleyan Chapel, all that is left to remind the villagers of the wreck is a small bungalow named Pindos which is situated on School Hill, overlooking the spot where she was wrecked.

At the time of writing some of the older villagers can tell you the names of the fifteen Coverack men who went out in the lifeboat that night. Soon they will be forgotten, so here is the list:

Superintendent Coxswain:    John Corin

Second Coxswain:    Sam Champion

| | |
|---|---|
| Joseph Bowden | Alfred Eustice |
| William Corin | Bowden Eustice |
| James Carey | Henry Eustice |
| Cecil Connor | John Hocking |
| Edwin Crews | Alex (Sandy) Pengilly |
| Lyle Cuttance | Stanley Roskilly |

William Williams

These names are as on the Return of Service certified by Mr. Bonfield.

**THE CREW OF THE PINDOS LEAVING FOR FALMOUTH**
*The morning after the rescue the crew was taken to Falmouth
in hired horse buses organised by Mr. Pengilly.
A large crowd gathered to cheer them on their way.*

**CREW OF THE CONSTANCE MELANIE, 1912.**
*From Left to Right:*
*Henry (Harry) Eustice (Stroke), Lyle Cuttance, Tim (Cecil) Connor, Jimmy Carey,
Sandy Pengilly, Edwin Bastian, Stanley Roskilly, James (John) Hocking, John Corin (Coxswain),
Willy Williams, Bowden Eustice, Joe Bowden, Sam Champion, William Corin, Alfred Eustice,
Billy Bowden (Signals).*

Fifty years after the wreck, a letter was sent to the people of Coverack from one of the survivors. For some reason or other the letter was passed to the Porthleven historian, Mr. Frank Strike. Eventually Mr. Strike told the writer's father about it. The latter considered it would be of great interest to the people of Coverack if he could obtain an account of the wreck from the German sailor for a reading at the Coverack Lifeboat dinner which was provided each year by some money which had been left to the village for that purpose by Judge Roxburgh. My father duly wrote to Mr. Paul Tessendorff who had emigrated to America and married an Irish lady. He lived in Redwood City, California. Mr. Tessendorff sent the following account dated January 8th., 1965. It is quoted verbatim from the point where the tug Arcona lost the tow.

'........five minutes later we were on the rocks; the sea lifted us twice after that then the pounding began. I do not remember how long it was until someone noticed us ashore, but my memory recorded the time as 9 p.m. when we hit the shore. It was not too long when we saw lights and people ashore and the first life saving rocket hit our rigging.'

'Perhaps ten more attempts were made but for some unexplained reason then, none of the lines would work. They perhaps got caught in the rocks which are so numerous along your coastline.'

'That's where the lifeboat came in. It was like a ray of sunshine to see that lifeboat bobbing up and down on those twenty foot waves. It was a game of now you see it and now you don't. How those men managed to stay alive is a puzzle to me to this day.'

'The trick now was how do we get the crew off the poop deck without having the waves smash the lifeboat against the Pindos. Better seamanship might have happened in this world but I can not remember hearing of one. The first four times it was jump and swim. That did not work out too well and it was then that the coxswain demanded that the next person bring along a clew line. It was our carpenter, a good swimmer, who volunteered. He made the connection all right, swimming without a lifebelt towards the boat.'

'Thus was saved the twenty eight men of the Pindos on the night of Feb.10/11, 1912 on the coast of Cornwall by the heroic crew of the Coverack Branch of the R.N.L.I.'

'My most heartfelt thanks to those still alive and to those who have passed on and especially to Mr. John Corin the Coxswain of the lifeboat to whom I am indebted that I am still alive.'

'Three cheers to all of you and all the nice people of Coverack who so gracefully received us with some warm clothing after we got under cover.'

'Yours sincerely,

Paul Tessendorff,

Ordinary Seaman member of the Pindos.'

The letter was duly read out at the Lifeboat Dinner on the 20th. February, 1965. It was held in the Paris Hotel where the sailors had been looked after when they were brought ashore. There were only two men still living who had been in the crew that night. They were Mr. William Corin, brother of the then Coxswain and Mr. Jimmy Carey. The Chairman of the evening was Mr. John Corin, son of the Coxswain who won the R.N.L.I. Silver Medal for gallantry shown during the rescue. The Coverack crewmen were awarded an extra sum of money by the R.N.L.I. and as mentioned earlier, the German government sent £50 via the Kaiser to be shared among the rescuers. Some accounts state that Mr. Corin was given a gold watch by the German Emperor to commemorate the rescue. Mr. Corin's son John assured the writer that this was not so.

After the letter was read out the inevitable comparisons were made concerning the different versions of the happenings of that night. It will have been noticed that Mr. Tessendorff's account fifty years after the event differs slightly from that given by the Coxswain and survivors shortly after the rescue. Discipline was very harsh on German sailing ships in those days. When Ordinary Seaman Tessendorff had the temerity to suggest that the ship was drifting astern towards the shore he had his face slapped for his pains. He said in his letter to my father that, 'The captain had no idea where we were, least of all did he know that we were so close to shore.' It would seem that in common with many other wrecks round our coast, the finer details concerning the sequence of events will never be known. The account has to remain incomplete. It would be very interesting to discover the name of the ship's carpenter who brought the line from the Pindos. It is probably recorded somewhere but it is believed he did not receive any official recognition of his bravery.

It is ironic that two and a half years after the episode of the Pindos the rescued and the rescuers had become enemies in theory, due to the outbreak of the Great War. Mr. W.H. Bonfield, the Hon. Secretary of the Lifeboat, became an army Lieutenant and was killed. One of the coastguards, Chief Petty Officer Freathy was killed at the Battle of Coronel, the prelude to the battle of the Falklands, when the old fashioned cruiser he was serving in was outgunned by Admiral von Spee's Squadron. His son was also killed in action in France not long after he had joined the army. Sandy Pengilly, the fifteen year old boy who volunteered to go out in the Constance Melanie when one of the crew members was unavailable, was taken prisoner by the Germans in France in 1918 during an infantry action in which he had a finger shot off. Further comment would be superfluous.

### The Year of the Titanic

1912 was not a lucky year. The Pindos story has been told. That was soon dwarfed by the terrible Titanic disaster which occurred in April. Ten days before the unthinkable happened to the 'unsinkable', a strange wreck occurred at Coverack.

The Corin brothers left the quay very early in the morning on Easter Saturday and rowed their boat in thick fog down towards the Blackhead. Just before 4 a.m. the fishermen stopped and lay on their oars for a break before hauling their pots. They had been looking forward to the freshly baked bread which Mrs. John Corin had packed for them the previous night. Suddenly a clearing in the fog revealed the outline of a sailing ship which was hard and fast on Pedn Boar beneath Treleaver Cliff with all sails set.

The two brothers, John and William rowed in all haste to the ship. They saw that some of the crew were already on the cliff top. On shouting to the sailors the brothers discovered that no one was missing. However, the rising tide was covering the deck and the wooden ship's boats were beginning to break up. It was decided that the younger brother, William should climb up the cliff and after guiding the sailors to Treleaver farm, return to keep watch on the wreck. John Corin hoisted the sail and made his way back to Coverack to raise the alarm, although he knew that there was little chance of saving the Gunvor, as the Norwegian barque was called.

As he approached Coverack Quay, John Corin lowered the sail and rowed in to the harbour where a little knot of people headed by Coastguard Freathy awaited him. The Coastguard had just walked back to Coverack from the Blackhead where he had been on coast watching duty all night. He had seen that John was alone in the boat and fearful that an accident had occurred rushed down to the quay, followed by a few curious early risers who were also anxious to know what had happened. Mr. Freathy was soon on his way back to the Duty Room at the Coastguard Station to inform the authorities of the wreck. John Corin set out once more on the lonely trip back to the Pedn Boar to fetch his brother William from the beach near the wreck and resume fishing.

Meanwhile the crew of the Gunvor had reached Treleaver Farm and awakened Mr. and Mrs. Ivey and their young family. Mr. William Ivey decided that the best thing to do would be to accommodate the 16 man crew in a large outhouse where there was a fireplace. While Mrs. Joanna Ivey bustled about getting cups and plates together and as much food as she could find, her husband lit the boiler fire in the barn and soon had hot water ready for the tea. Some of the men had got pretty grimy after climbing the cliff and they were very pleased to have a quick wash in warm water which was placed in some pans in the barn. It was fortunate that Mrs. Ivey was accustomed to providing for large groups of men at harvest time, so she coped very well with all the extra mouths to feed, except that it was April month and she did not have a great deal of surplus food. Before long there was nothing left to eat in the house.

The Ivey's young son Bert told the writer that he was about six years old when the Gunvor was wrecked. He vividly remembered the household being woken up by the Gunvor's crew. Apparently some of the seamen brought some green coloured half gallon glass bottles of lime juice with them in case of emergency so Bert and his brothers were soon enjoying an unaccustomed early morning drink.

When the news of the wreck spread through Coverack, Mr. Billy May, the lifeboat lamp man and local representative of the Shipwrecked Mariners' Society set about hiring a horse bus to transport the crew to the Seamen's Mission in Falmouth. His father in law, former Coastguard Hill helped him with the customary arrangements which had to be made when there was a wreck. When the sailors had finished their impromptu breakfast at Treleaver Farm they thanked the Iveys for their kindness and set out on foot for Coverack, following their personal belongings which were piled on a farm cart. They were then taken to Falmouth, their original destination.

The villagers subsequently learned that the Gunvor had left Calet Buena in Chile with a cargo of nitrate on the 23rd. November, 1911 and was making for Falmouth for orders. The ship passed the Lizard at 8 p.m. on Good Friday. The sea was calm and the Gunvor was making the approach to Falmouth in thick fog. At 11.30 p.m. Captain Tobiassen became aware that his ship was too close to the shore. The Captain was unable to 'wear' round or turn away from the wind before the vessel struck Pedn Boar rocks with her sails still set.

There was no panic. A couple of sailors calmly placed a long ladder over the bow and clambered ashore to have a look at the rocks below and see what could be done to refloat the ship. A small steamer could be seen passing through the mist so flares made of oily rags were burned in the hope that she might be able to assist but there was no response to these distress signals. By 12.30 a.m. the captain realised that the ship was firmly embedded in the rocks so as she was beginning to bump and grind he gave the order to abandon ship. Those of the crew who had already clambered ashore came back on board to collect all the belongings they could carry and the whole crew made their way to the cliff top, lighting their way with paraffin lamps taken from the ship. There were no casualties except one man who had fallen in the sea on impact. When it was realised he was missing a search was carried out and he was rescued by Second Mate Yoger. The only creature not accounted for was the ship's black cat. She probably managed to scramble ashore across the ladder and make her way to a nearby farm.

Subsequent happenings proved that Captain Tobiassen had made the right decision by leaving the Gunvor because as the tide rose the steel ship broke her back when the hatches lifted off and water entered the hold from the flooded deck. As in the case of the Pindos the cargo of nitrate was lost by the action of the sea water.

There was one English man on board the Gunvor. He was George Kersey, a former schooner skipper from Appledore. Being in his seventies he found Treleaver Cliff a difficult climb so the Norwegian sailors hauled him up on a rope. Mr. Kersey declared later that it was his second shipwreck and added that it was going to be his last for he intended settling down with his wife in Appledore. The Lifeboat and Coastguards were not involved in this incident except that the Coxswain of the Constance Melanie and his crew member brother William were at hand to give the help needed and Mr. Freathy of Coverack Coastguards alerted all the authorities who needed to know about the wreck. When the horse bus carrying the crew arrived in Falmouth a reporter from the Falmouth Packet went to the Seamen's Mission to talk to the crew. In his summing up of the loss of the Gunvor the reporter wrote, 'Fog on Friday defied penetration and unknown and unobserved another fine ship is added to the list of vessels which this winter have met their doom on the rugged coasts of Cornwall.'

Visitors to Coverack will see a cottage in the cove next to the former Bible Christian Chapel which has a plaque on the wall. The cottage has a nameplate from one of the ship's boats of the Gunvor above the door. At the time of writing 'Gunvor Cottage' is occupied by Mr. Peter James the village carpenter and undertaker. The writer is indebted to the late Mrs. Agnes Hocking, Mr. James' grandmother, who told him in a taped conversation in August, 1979 that she went to Treleaver Cliffs on Easter Sunday to see the wreck and while she was there, Mr. Ivey the farmer handed her the nameplate and said, 'Here you are, Agnes, have that.' She added that for a while the name was on the wall just inside the door of the cottage. Some years later when Mr. Henry Harry was collecting the rates after the cottage had been refurbished by Mr. Roskilly the village carpenter and Mr. Nicholls the builder, the rate collector suggested that he ought to put down 'Gunvor' as the name of the house. Mr. and Mrs. Hocking agreed so the wooden nameplate was put outside and the cottage became known as 'Gunvor'. Mrs. Hocking proudly pointed to a photo of the Gunvor hanging on the wall. It was given to her by Mr. Horace Eustice who had obtained it from Mrs. Bonfield the widow of the former Lifeboat Secretary. This is the way in which village history is remembered and cherished by the villagers.

Ten days after the wreck of the Gunvor at Coverack the whole world was stunned by the news of the loss of the 46,328 ton White Star Liner Titanic which hit an iceberg near the Grand Banks off Cape Race, New Foundland while steaming at 20 knots on her maiden voyage to New York. At first there were conflicting press reports. One even said the Titanic was being towed to port. No one wanted to believe the disaster had happened. The passengers themselves refused to believe the ship was sinking. Consequently some of the lifeboats got away from the ship with less than their full complement because passengers did not want to leave. As in most wrecks, there were unsolved mysteries. Indeed the actual position of the Titanic was not verified until the 1st. September, 1985 when an expedition led by Dr. Ballard located the remains of the liner which was standing upright on the ocean floor. It was discovered after the sinking that the Californian had stopped for the night in the ice field and was within ten miles of the Titanic. The Officer of the Watch on the Californian saw the Titanic's rockets and reported them to the captain but as they were not red nor blue and therefore not distress rockets the captain decided not to investigate further after sending a signal by morse lamp and getting no reply. Later, the Samson, a Norwegian sealer also reported seeing rockets but her skipper interpreted them as signals from a warship searching for illegal sealers and promptly left the area.

On the 19th. April, 1912 the Falmouth Packet headline was 'Greatest liner in the World meets disaster - 1,490 persons drowned.' The paper published details of Cornish people who were involved in the tragedy. There was no one from Coverack but there were some from St. Keverne Parish who were known to the villagers. Mr. Jago Smith, an employee of the Transatlantic Post Office was drowned. He was the son of Mr. John Smith, a farmer at Trebarveth. Visitors to St. Keverne Church will see a memorial tablet which was placed there by Mr. Smith's colleagues in the Postal Telegraph Service. Another casualty was Mr. Hayden Sobey, known locally as 'Ike'. He was a quarryman who was emigrating to the United States. His father, Richard Sobey was a well known fisherman and Coast Watcher from Porthallow. Mrs. Stephen Old, formerly Annie Hill, grand daughter of James Hill the much respected Coxswain of Porthoustock Lifeboat was saved from the Titanic. Mrs. Old was returning with her husband to Sacramento, California after a holiday in Cornwall. Unfortunately Mr. Old was drowned.

The Lloyd's Weekly News produced a special issue, priced two pence, called 'The deathless story of the Titanic'. The double centre page of the magazine showed a section drawing of the great liner and gave some statistics which included a list of 'Previous Great Shipping Disasters'. Named in the list was the wreck of the Mohegan which has already been described. The statistics also revealed that there were only sixteen lifeboats on the Titanic. Each was capable of carrying fifty passengers. There were also four collapsible canvas boats. This life saving equipment was for a possible 3,500 passengers. In fact there were only 1,400 passengers on board when the disaster occurred, plus 850 crew members. The centre page list of the magazine also stated; 'Life preservers on board sufficient for all.' The page named 10 millionaires who were drowned. Among them was Colonel J.J. Astor, a relative of the husband of Lady Astor, who became M.P. for Plymouth and was the first lady politician to enter the House of Commons. The dead millionaires represented a capital of £120,000,000.

The loss of the Titanic marked the end of the Edwardian era. The disaster was discussed endlessly. Modern books about it are still almost guaranteed to become best sellers. The events of that tragic night were talked about in Coverack for a very long time. It was referred to whenever Sarah Flower Adams' 'Nearer my God to Thee' was sung in the village. The powerful image of the Titanic's band playing the hymn as the water swirled round the bandsmen's waists and the sound being carried across the still waters to the lifeboats laden with the wives of the men who were still on the sinking ship, caught the imagination - nowhere more vividly than in the Cornish villages where tragedies of the sea were part of the people's daily lives. They realised what could have happened to the Suevic but for the hand of providence and the swift response of the lifeboat men of the Lizard peninsula. They also sadly realised that the lessons of the loss of the Anson, the Primrose, the Despatch, the John, the Bay of Panama, the Mohegan and other ships in the 'Stormy Nineteenth Century' had not yet been properly learned, nor had the potential for good of Marconi's wireless telegraphy been fully realised.

One pleaasing outcome of the disaster was that the following year the first International Convention for the Safety of Life at Sea was held. It was laid down that each ship should have lifeboat space for each person embarked and that lifeboat drills should be performed on each voyage. Another important recommendation was that ships should maintain a twenty four hour radio watch. The tragedy, great as it was, went to the back of people's minds for a while as the prospect of a war with Germany became more and more certain. Some of the young male villagers looked on the prospect as an adventure to brighten the routine of village life and the government encouraged this idea. It will be remembered that Mr. Dunn, writing in the school Log Book, correctly interpreted the implications of the war of attrition that was to follow when he commented, 'The gloom of war hangs over the village and children, as Coastguards and Naval Reservists have been called up.'

## *The Coastguards*

This is a convenient point in the chronicle to give a general account of the Coverack Coastguards. There has been a Coastguard presence in Coverack since the second decade of the nineteenth century. At first the relationship between the villagers and the government men was cool and sometimes stormy. As the Coastguards' duties changed from active prevention of smuggling to coastal defence and prevention of loss of life at sea the two factions merged. Today former Coastguard family names such as Carey, Combe, Cordall, Symes, Watts and White are considered 'proper' local names.

Coastguards or 'gobbies' as they were called were formed in January, 1822. Their prime duty was to stamp out what was known as 'Free Trade'. These activities were described in the section on smuggling. The Port of Gweek (sometimes called Wike in ancient documents) was the centre of local customs activity. In 1812 John Bunny was the Preventive Officer at Coverack. The 'incidents' or expenditure sheet of the Gweek Customs office recorded Mr. Bunny being paid £5 a quarter plus an allowance of £2 10s for his horse and the same amount for his house in Coverack. William Odger, a 'Waiter and Searcher' was paid 7s 0d for his work and his wife got 6s 0d for 'Cleaning the Custom House and going errands this quarter.' When Coverack Coastguards replaced the Customs men in their prevention of smuggling duties, the Coverack Station was still controlled from the Port of Gweek. As late as 1831 Coverack men were still being recorded on the 'incidents' expenditure sheet of Gweek Customs as shown by the following extract:

| | | | |
|---|---|---|---|
| James George | | 6s | 4d |
| H. C. Saunders | £1 | 7s | 2d |
| A. Mitchell | | 18s | 0d |
| M. Daniel | | 6s | 0d |
| Jno. Bennett | £1 | 18s | 6d |

In 1833 the Chief Officer of Coast Guards at Coverack sent a demand to Gweek for 'A Coal Box and sett of Fire Irons for this Station.' The reply from Gweek was that '........they must be purchased in the lowest terms and brought to charge in the ensuing quarterly account - as the whole cost will be small.' The Chief Officer was successful as he recorded on his 'incidents' sheet that he had bought 'Fire Irons for 5s 6d, an Elm Wood Coal Skuttle - Iron Handle 7s 6d.' - and then he triumphantly added a note that the two objects had been 'purchased at 9s 9d.' He had thus saved his masters at Gweek the sum of 3s 3d. It would appear from such attention to detail that as long as the account books were accurately completed the business of catching smugglers could still wait a while.

Up to 1822 the Preventive men were fighting a losing battle against smuggling. We have seen that about half of the spirits consumed in Great Britain at the end of the eighteenth century were contraband. France, a non tea-drinking nation, was actually importing tea for the express purpose of smuggling it to Britain. In London smuggled gin was openly advertised as genuine 'Crowlink Gap', named after the beach in Sussex where it was landed. We have also seen that Napoleon considered British smugglers as what might be termed a native fifth column in his war against Great Britain. It is therefore not surprising that the British government decided to establish a complete coastal blockade of naval ships in 1818. This move was followed on the 5th. January, 1822 by the combining of the men in the blockading cruisers, the Preventive Water Guard and the Riding Officers under the one name of Coast Guard. It was controlled by the Board of Customs. The idea was to coordinate these resources in the fight against smuggling. A 74 gun ship called the Eagle had been based in Falmouth since 1804. In addition to coastal defence her job was to prevent smuggling between Plymouth and the Bristol Channel. When she went to Liverpool in the 1850s her place was taken by the Russell. These relatively unwieldy guardships did very little to prevent the landing of contraband goods but were useful for sea training in addition to coastal defence.

By 1831 the Coast Guard, as it was first named, was made a reserve force for the Royal Navy. Most of the men were former R.N. Officers and ratings in any case. The authorities had been quick to realise that not only was smuggling declining by being confronted with a more disciplined force but that there was a distinct reduction in the bribery and corruption which was prevalent before the Coast Guard was formed. The Coast Guards in the blockading ships were all naval personnel. The shore staff consisted of a mixture of sailors and civilians - Chief Officers, Commissioned Boatmen, Boatmen and Mounted Guards (former Riding Officers). In fact it soon became known that sailors who had served with some distinction were more likely to get into the Coast Guard service than others. Equally the Mounted Guard tended to accept volunteers from the cavalry regiments.

By the year 1850 traditional smuggling on a viable commercial footing had been stamped out but there was still a need for the Coast Guards to keep smuggling down to manageable proportions. In effect this meant that the small enterprises such as those run by the clandestine Coverack smuggling men continued to supplement their tiny incomes by doing occasional 'runs' to Roscoff.

The Coast Guards were placed under Admiralty control on the 1st. October, 1856. Their duties had gradually come to include Coastal Defence. They were indeed a readily mobilised Naval Reserve with sea going experience. Three thousand of these men were recalled to Active Service in the Royal Navy during the Crimean War. Among those mobilised was Coast Guard Anthony Real, aged 36, who was called up from Coverack Coast Guard Station. He served on the Royal George during the war. The other Coast Guard duties in addition to 'protection of the Revenue' were giving assistance to vessels in danger, taking charge of wrecks, operating Life Saving Apparatus and being actively engaged in rescues at sea from their own boats or from the newly formed Royal National Lifeboat Institution's boats. (From 1824 to 1854 it was known as the National Institution for the Preservation of Life from Shipwreck). Twenty seven Gold Medals were awarded to Coast Guards for saving life at sea up to the year 1859. H.M. Coastguard were awarded the R.N.L.I. Gold Medal in 1972 to mark the 150th. anniversary of the founding of the organisation.

The role of the Coast Guards as a Royal Naval Reserve was confirmed in 1845 by the regulation requiring all recruits to the Coast Guard service to agree to serve on Her Majesty's ships if needed. This was followed by a memorandum on the 2nd. May, 1845 setting out proposals for establishing Coast Guard Gun Batteries for Coastal Defence - '........that they may deter the enemies' steam vessels from approaching the coast and afford protection to the coasting trade.' Coast Guards were sent for training and the first squad to pass out was inspected by the Comptroller-General of the Coast Guards in the Marine Battery at Southsea Castle on the 9th. August, 1847. By 1850 the Comptroller-General sent a message stating that he was confident - '........Her Majesty may securely rely upon the loyal efforts of the Coast Guard to aid in any operations which shall be undertaken for the protection of the country.' Falmouth, Fowey, St. Ives and Padstow were refortified in mid nineteenth century. Some Coast Guard Stations were issued with wooden replicas of Coastal Defence guns for drill purposes. Coverack had some early nineteenth century muzzle loaders on the 'Battery' or Lan Big, now known as Lambeage. The 'Battery' had formed part of the defence of the Cornish coast since early in the nineteenth century. This was described in the first chapter. The guns would not have been of much use against the Comptroller's 'enemies' steam vessels.' It is thought that the Coverack guns were used for signalling purposes rather than defence by the mid nineteenth century. That is to say to draw attention to passing ships when there was a message for them on the flag hoist on the signal mast on the Battery. On the other hand, the guns do appear to have been used at some time or other. Some canon balls have been found in the region of the site of the Bay Hotel. This has led to speculation that one of the guns was positioned in that field and the others on the Battery. It is equally possible that the canon balls were found in the field because they were stray shots fired at the village or at ships in the bay. To date there is no firm evidence to support either theory. When these weapons were finally pronounced obsolete they were taken down to the harbour where one can still be seen doing duty as a mooring post on the small quay known as Hocking's slip, where the present day wind surfers congregate when doing their training. The other barnacle encrusted gun barrels can be located at low tide by following the mooring ropes from the granite bollards on the quay to the beach anchorages.

A coastal militia was formed in the mid nineteenth century to back up the army and Coast Guards. The volunteers were mainly fishermen and boatmen and were known as the 'Sea Fencibles'. They were placed under naval command and were to be mobilized in the event of an emergency such as an invasion. They had to attend four drills in every quarter and were paid a few shillings for turning out. The fishermen from Mevagissey, Fowey, Gerrance (19th. century spelling) and St. Mawes obviously regarded this activity as a good source of supplementary income but no records have been found of the Coverack Sea Fencibles. The villagers may have felt it would not be politic to have a naval officer turning up unannounced in the village to check up on the volunteer militia. On the other hand, the naval authorities may have regarded the village as too remote.

In November, 1866 a Rocket Life Saving Apparatus was allocated to Coverack and a volunteer company of villagers was formed to man it under the direction of the Chief Officer of Coastguards. Coverack men were proud to be associated with an organisation which was using an apparatus based on the model invented by Helston born Henry Trengrouse. In fact, Captain William Manby's 5½" brass mortar had been tried before Trengrouse invented his apparatus. It was used to rescue the crew of the brig Elizabeth when she ran aground near Yarmouth in 1807, the year of the wreck of the Anson at Loe Bar near Porthleven which had inspired Trengrouse to design his line throwing rocket. Manby's apparatus was adopted somewhat hastily in 1810 after Parliament had been petitioned, due to a severe gale in which 65 ships were wrecked with the loss of 500 lives. Manby's mortar weighed 300 lbs and could not be transported speedily over rough ground to a wreck. He developed a lighter model in due course. Trengrouse's Rocket was too weak to be of use in a severe gale. However, their ideas were on the right lines so a succession of adaptations of the apparatus of both Trengrouse and Manby followed until Captain Edward Mourrier Boxer's Rocket was adopted in 1865. It was used for the next 85 years.

As the nineteenth century progressed it was becoming evident that by the time the Life Saving Apparatus was hauled to the scene of a wreck it was already too late to effect a rescue. Statistics provided early in the twentieth century showed clearly that if more lifeboats were made available, more lives would be saved:

Lives saved by luggers, Coast Guard Boats and small craft   - 19,706

Lives saved by  Rocket Apparatus and assistance with
ropes from the shore                                        - 17,446

In due course the Coverack horse drawn purpose-built 'Rocket Wagon' was housed beneath the vestry of the Wesleyan Chapel which had been built five years before the volunteer Life Saving Company was started.  This was a convenient place as it was next to the Coast Guard family houses which had been purchased at Sunny Corner.  The Chief Officer lived at the top of the row in West House from where he could survey the activities of his men working on the station.  The Watch House on the cliff edge close to Dolar Point was not vacated until the 9th. March, 1925 when a Duty Room was established in a vacant Coast Guard house.  This building is now a private house, aptly named Chy an Mor - house by the sea.  Three years after the move, on the 26th. October, 1928 the Rocket Apparatus was taken from the cellar beneath the Wesleyan Chapel and placed in a new cart house on Mr. William Roskilly's Penmarth Farm.  This was so that the 1 in 5 slope of School Hill would not have to be climbed if the apparatus were needed outside the village.  The apparatus continued to be housed at Penmarth until the Coverack Rescue Company was disbanded on the 29th. September, 1985.  As time went on much of the equipment was loaded on a hired lorry instead of being taken to the scene in a horse drawn wagon, thus reducing the time lag between the call-out and arrival at the scene of the wreck.

Some of the rescue work done by the Volunteer Life Saving Company has already been described.  It is impossible to separate the roles of the cliff rescuers and the sea rescuers.  It has been seen that they were often complementary.  Inevitably there was rivalry between the land and sea volunteers but in general it was good natured with lots of leg pulling.  Indeed a glance at the names of the villagers involved reveals that some of the Lifeboat helpers were also Coast Guard Volunteers.  It must be remembered that the Volunteer Company was formed thirty five years before the R.N.L.I.'s boat 'Constance Melanie' appeared in Coverack.  Indeed a Lifeboat telephone was not installed until the 1st. August, 1934.  Until that time the lifeboat crew had to rely on relayed information from the Coast Guard, firstly from their private Coast Communication Circuit and afterwards from 1927 on the more efficient public Post Office Exchange System.

Life Saving Apparatus Company practices were popular social events in Coverack.  A Coast Guard Inspector was usually present so the uniformed men were more smartly turned out than usual.  The ropes, rocket launcher and breeches buoy were at the peak of readiness and the volunteers well drilled beforehand.  Each man wore an armband with a number printed on it to denote what duty he had been trained to perform.  The villagers used to take time off work in order to attend the drills and as mentioned earlier, the children were brought from school on some occasions to the Mears Point to observe an important lesson in rescue and artificial respiration.  The wives and friends of the men involved also came to the practices together with the regular Coast Guard families and interested visitors to the village.  It is interesting to note that in the days before searchlights and flares were part of the rescue equipment of the Coast Guards and Lifeboat men, the young people of the village played an important part in certain rescues.  On a dark night the young people who turned out when a wreck was reported would be sent to the farms situated nearest the wreck to get the farm people to bring lanterns down to the beach or the cliff top in order to illuminate the scene.  It is not easy for the modern urban reader to realise just how impossible it is to handle ropes, hammer stakes in the rocky ground and carry out the many tasks required of a rescuer in almost total darkness on a high cliff top in a howling gale.  That is why even the faint glimmer of just one farmer's lantern was welcomed on a dark night and why a concentration  of a dozen lanterns or more, brought down from several farms, made the rescue much more certain to be a success.  Of course, even the concentrated light coming from these lanterns would only amount to a glimmer but it was a great help to the rescuers and brought hope to the shipwrecked mariners awaiting rescue.

An examination of a photograph of a Life Saving Apparatus exercise taken in 1900 just before the lifeboat arrived in Coverack shows a tableau of a rescue drill.  The Rocket has already been fired over the practice mast and the thin rocket line used to pull out the heavier hawser rope attached to a block with a two fathom 'tail' or rope's end on it.  This rope's end was attached to the practice ship's mast so that the hawser could then be used to carry the breeches buoy to and from the wreck.  Attached to the hawser was a 'tally board' with instructions in four languages to help the shipwrecked mariners understand how to rig the rescue tackle.  The tableau in the photograph shows what happened at the landward end of the Life Saving Apparatus.

In the foreground of the photograph is a metal tripod with its legs firmly embedded in the ground.  It was steadied by a block and tackle at the rear and anchored with three metal stakes which were driven into the ground.  The tripod has a large wooden block suspended from it.  This carries the hawser or strong rope on which runs a smaller snatch block carrying the breeches buoy out to the ship on a lighter rope known as a whip.  The young sailor in the breeches buoy is Alfred Gibson, son of John Gibson the Chief Officer of Coast Guards who is seen standing behind the tripod, wearing a naval frock coat and white trousers.

There are two teams of men holding the whips on each side of the tripod.  They are there to haul the breeches buoy to and from the wreck.  A bearded Joseph Bowden from Bank House village shop is holding a somewhat untidy coil of rope.  He was responsible for the safety of the man to the right of him.  This man's job was to go to the cliff edge to assist the rescued sailors as they were hauled to safety.  That is why he was attached to the rope held by Mr. Bowden and why he is wearing a cork lifebelt.  He appears to have decided that a straw boater was the best form of headgear to wear for the task he had to perform.  There were usually 20 men in the complete team.  Five each for handling the Rocket,

Whip, Hawser and Tripod. The man behind the first one holding the right hand whip rope next to the breeches buoy is Billy May who operated the Imperial Flare light at the wreck of the Pindos in 1912. In the rear, behind and to the left of Chief Coast Guard Officer John Gibson is white bearded Sam Champion, a well known Coverack fisherman. He was the signaller. He is holding a bag containing the signal flags which were used to direct operations when the teams were out of sight of the wreck due to the cliff overhang. Standing behind Coast Guard Carey who is dressed in white duck and holding the whip rope in the left hand foreground of the photo is Mr. William Corin. He is in shirt sleeves. He was the father of the first Second Coxswain of the Constance Melanie. Mr. Carey's team is irregularly spaced so that the men and the village children can all get in the picture. The Life Saving Apparatus cart is at the bottom of the slope behind the tripod. Standing beside the cart is the Coast Guard District Officer and beside him in civilian clothes is probably the Divisional Inspector or he might well be an interested visitor to Coverack.

about 1900.

LIFE SAVING APPARATUS DRILL circa 1900
*Note the thatched houses where Channel View Hotel now stands.*

During an actual rescue extra volunteers were often needed to man handle the heavy equipment on rough ground. The Officer in Charge would give each extra man a token. This disc had a ship on one side and a crown on the other. After the rescue the extra volunteer would call at the Coast Guard Station and hand in his token. He would then be paid for his night's work. Volunteers who worked well were asked to become part of the rescue team when vacancies occurred.

After the simulated rescue had been completed the Officer in Charge would select an 'apparently drowned' man and instruct one of the volunteers to carry out artificial respiration on him. The children watched this operation with bated breath because if the 'resuscitation' were not carried out in the correct sequence the unfortunate volunteer would have to repeat the exercise, counting out aloud as he did so. The inspecting officer would then question other members of the team about their duties. When he was satisfied, he usually made a short speech to encourage the volunteers to keep coming to the drills and declared the exercise completed. The cart was then loaded, the horses put back in the shafts and the Apparatus returned to its base at Sunny Corner. When the men got back to the Battery there was a lead throwing contest on the flat space beneath the signal mast. The leadweight was attached to a light rope and was used like a heaving line to make a connection with a vessel from the beach or cliff top when it was not practical to use a rocket. The Inspector usually offered a half crown reward to the winner of the competition. Mr. Jim Lawrence from Trewillis Farm, an ex Royal Navy Stoker and a very strong man often won the prize during the 1920s. He later became a valued member of the Coast Watching team until well after the Second World War.

A permanent simulated ship's mast stood on the Mears Point. The exercise ground was leased from Redruth Brewery for 16 shillings per annum. The Rocket was aimed and elevated so as to drop the Rocket line as near as possible to the mast without actually hitting it as it did on the night of the Pindos wreck. This exercise post was moved to Traboe Cross on Goonhilly Downs in 1950 as the Downs was considered a safer exercise area - it was also cheaper, being leased from Mr. M.P. Williams of Lanarth Estate for 10 shillings per annum.

The volunteers themselves were not paid princely sums for their endeavours. In 1920 they were being paid 3 shillings a drill plus a 2 shilling retainer. By May, 1946 the drills were still valued at 3 shillings but the retainer had increased to 4 shillings and 6 pence. By the end of 1946 post war inflation had increased the pay for each drill to 10 shillings. It had gone up to £2.85p an hour in 1985 when the Coverack company was disbanded.

It will be seen from the following details that men from the village and the farms were involved over long periods of time with coastal rescue. As stated earlier, some were involved at the same time with the shore section of the Lifeboat Service. These men were not called often, but as in the case of the lifeboat men it was usually on a night when the wind was blowing hard and it was pelting with rain. The kind of night when most people would prefer to remain indoors and go to bed early. These men were prepared to turn out and after hours of working, watching and waiting on an exposed cliff top they would go back home wet through. They would have to be about again before dawn to tend their animals or go to their work in the quarry or elsewhere. It is evident from the monetary awards described above that these men did not do this work for gain. If they remained in the service for twenty years they received a Long Service Medal. Some had bars to their medals for extra service. Their role was not glamorous nor self evident. Most of the time they performed their duties out of sight of the village. They formed a quiet band of men who were always ready to give up their time and comfort and take risks to help strangers from the sea.

## SOME COVERACK VOLUNTEER L.S.A. MEN

| DATE JOINED | NAME | LOCATION |
|---|---|---|
| 1913 | Willie Hocking L.S.M.* | Coverack |
| 1916 | William John Richards L.S.M. | Trewillis Farm |
| 1920 | Jim Lawrence L.S.M. | Trewillis Farm |
| 1923 | F. Rook Roberts L.S.M. | Coverack |
| 1924 | Willie Richards | Trewillis Farm |
| 1925 | Fred Pearce L.S.M. | Coverack |
| 1925 | Simon Ivey L.S.M. | Treleaver Farm |
| 1926 | Percy Ivey L.S.M. | Treleaver Farm |
| 1926 | Cyril Roberts | Penhallick Farm |
| 1926 | Edwin Bastian | Granville House |
| 1930 | Casley Chapel L.S.M. | Polcoverack Farm |
| 1932 | John James | Coverack |
| 1933 | David Mason | Coverack |
| 1935 | Percy Richards | Trewillis Farm |
| 1936 | Bert Ivey L.S.M. | Treliever Farm |
| 1937 | Roy Harris Sen. L.S.M. | Penhallick Farm |
| 1937 | Harold Martin Sen. | Channel View |
| 1939 | Leslie Cliff | The Elms |
| 1939 | L. Roberts | Little Treleaver |
| 1940 | S.W. Thomas | Penhallick Farm |

| 1943 | Eddy Pearce | The Haven |
| 1943 | Charles Wilkinson | Granville |
| 1943 | Gilbert Roberts | Poldurian |
| 1946 | Woodrow Pryor | Polcoverack Farm |
| 1946 | Garfield James | Lowland View |
| 1946 | Roy Harris Jun. | Penhallick Farm |
| 1949 | Michael Eustice | Tre Pol Pen |
| 1949 | Leslie Truscott | Rope Walk Cottage |
| 1949 | Harold Martin Jun. | Cliff Cottage |
| 1951 | George James Roberts | Gwenter Farm |
| 1951 | James Cox L.S.M. and Bar | Coverack |
| 1956 | Kenneth Cox L.S.M. | Coverack |

* L.S.M. = Long Service Medal.

The above details are as given in the C.G.12 Log Book for Coverack. It is the only one available at the time of writing. There were other men involved and other awards made. The fact that about half of the L.S.A. men were farmers reflects the close relationship most Cornish people have with the sea, even if they are not sea farers.

### FIRST WORLD WAR COASTWATCHERS
*L. - R. Petty Officer Edward Ward remained in Coverack to organise the Coastwatching while his comrades were at sea. He was drowned off Coverack in 1919, not long after the end of the war. Harry Eustice, Sam Champion and a Swindon Sea Scout acting as Signaller.*

At one time the Coast Guard had three masters. The Admiralty controlled the signallers and the Royal Naval Reserve. The Board of Trade used the service for saving life at sea. The Customs Board still relied on the Coast Guard for duties in connection with Revenue Protection. In addition to those needed as extra muscle in the rescue teams, men were also needed as Coast Watchers, especially in extended periods of bad weather when there were not enough regulars to keep the local lookout huts constantly manned. By the end of the nineteenth century smuggling was no longer a threat to the national economy so there was no fear of local volunteers being in collusion with local smugglers, hence when the Great War began and Coast Guard reservists left the district literally overnight, Coverack men were recruited for coast watching duties. In time they were helped by some Sea Scouts from Swindon of all places. These lads came to Coverack to do their bit for king and country. At that time a local Boy Scout troop had not been formed in Coverack. The Swindon Scouts soon became proficient at signalling by flags and lamp. It was a vital communication link in those days when there were just a few telephones in the parish and wireless was not universal.

In addition to the Coast Guard signal mast on the top of the Battery in Coverack there was a Naval Signal House at the Black Head. It was established there during the Napoleonic Wars and is marked on the 1813 Ordnance Survey Sheet 32 of the Lizard area. The 1891 Guide to Coverack noted that at that time only the chimney and gable end of the house were still standing. By 1914 when coastal patrols were increased there was no shelter for the men who were guarding the shore. These coast watchers followed the coastal footpaths which were blazed, not by chipping off the bark of trees to reveal the white beneath as woodlanders do, but by whitewashing stones at intervals so that the path could be followed at night. This was especially useful during war time when lights were not allowed near the coast.

Since smuggling days Coast Guards carried 'tuck' sticks. These looked like thick walking sticks and were used as such on cliff paths. The sticks had other uses. The crook handle was attached to a rapier like sword which was sheathed in the cylindrical wooden stick. It could be opened with a twist and the Coast Guard could then defend himself on being attacked by smugglers or others who were up to no good on the cliffs. The metal blade was also used to probe sandy beaches and soft soil if the Coast Guard suspected there might be hidden contraband or valuable salvage stolen from a wreck awaiting collection by a local at a favourable moment. The use of these sticks has lessened during this century. They have now become collectors' items. Some elderly Coverack residents have reason to remember the Coast Guard tuck sticks. During the Great War when the Auxiliaries went through the village at night they would rap the windows of cottages to let the occupants know that a light was showing. One can easily understand how the children would be scared on hearing the tip of the tuck stick tapping on the glass. It should be remembered that it was very quiet in the village then. There were no wireless sets, the only sound in the house would be the family conversation and perhaps a sewing machine being turned by hand or the man of the house mending boots. In addition to the tuck stick, Coast Guards used to be armed with a rifle and bayonet or a pistol and cutlass. These weapons were kept in the Watch House on Dolor Point and issued when considered necessary.

Coverack men were accustomed to keeping watch at the Black Head before they went there as auxiliary coast watchers during the Great War. It was a good place for keeping a good look out for approaching shoals of pilchards. While at the point the huers and their runners would while away their time by carving their initials on a rock. It is situated in the lee of the prevailing wind, that is to say to the east of the old Coast Guard Look Out hut which is still standing at the time of writing. There one will see initials and dates carved into the rock such as: R.N.K. 1870: W.C. 1876: W.R.: H.S.N.. There is also an unfinished name which has an unfinished rectangular frame carved round it: S. TRIPCO........ It would not be difficult to work out the families from whom these nineteenth century carvers came by studying the Coverack names which have been mentioned in this book.

When the Great War began, fishermen were recruited to the Coast Watching Service. People like Mr. Fred Carey were especially useful as not only was he from an old Coast Guard family but he was renowned for his skill as a huer. Tim Connor, a fisherman from another Coast Guard family was also one of the watchers at the Black Head. Mr. Connor disliked the idea of staying in an exposed position on the Black Head in bad weather so he persuaded some of the other watchers to build a rough and ready shelter out of turf from Mr. John Rapson's field and rocks from the cliff. A discarded galvanised iron sheet was used for a roof which was held up with wreck wood. The seats inside were also made from wood found on the beach below. The watchers nicknamed their shelter 'Hotel Cecil'. It is not known whether this was in honour of Mr. Connor or the government of Lord Salisbury which had earlier been dubbed 'Hotel Cecil' because it was so full of Cecil's (Lord Salisbury's) relations. Like his namesake, Cecil Connor was very adept at persuading other people to do his will, especially if there were any physical work involved.

By 1915 a purpose built Watch Hut was placed at the Black Head on Mr. William Ivey's Treleaver Farm land. It had a 40 year lease, the sum of 2 shillings and 6 pence being payable each Lady Day, (25th. March). The hut was to remain in operation, with various additions and alterations until 1987 when watches ceased at the Black Head.

The Great War watchers proved their worth in reporting shipping movements and off shore German submarine activity. They were instrumental in getting help to ships which were threatened. Of course they also carried out other duties which made them more aware of the necessity of a Coast Guard presence in Coverack. In consequence a stronger relationship was forged between the fishermen of Coverack and the Coast Guards.

One of the duties of a Coast Guard was to record details of fish landed in the village. This made the fishermen suspect the Guards were acting as uniformed government spies. In reality the statistics were needed to help formulate a policy of conservation of fish stocks round our shores. Eventually in 1951 the job of collecting and forwarding fish statistics was delegated to fisherman Cedric Staples for the princely sum of £2 per annum. Mr. Staples was particularly well qualified to do this clerical chore as he had abandoned a lucrative city appointment in favour of the 'good life' in Coverack.

The reason for the move from the Watch House on Dolor Point in 1925 to Sunny Corner was that in 1923 the Coast Guard service was rationalised. It became known as H.M. Coastguard - one word, not two. Henceforth they were to

127

coordinate all life saving activities by liaison with the Post Office Coast Wireless Stations and the R.N.L.I. Rocket Life Saving Apparatus Companies were still the responsibility of H.M. Coastguard who had the power to hire transport for the carrying of the apparatus to any part of the coast. Mr. Percy Roberts had just started his garage business in Coverack in the old Mill buildings so he became the official carrier, although Mr. Jim Andrews from Content Farm was still retained to bring his team of three horses to exercises and to take the wagon to places which were inaccessible by lorry. The Coastguards themselves now had to become more proficient in semaphore, morse, ship recognition, knots and splices, First Aid and cliff rescue. They also had to have a good knowledge of local tides as well as navigational marks and hazards. Of course, Coastguards had always been expected to be skilled in these activities but the new emphasis meant that recruits to this new branch of the Civil Service tended to be ex seamen and communications ratings rather than ex stokers and Royal Marines as they had been since the beginning of the century.

Of the 2,925 men employed by the Admiralty in the old Coast Guard service, 352 were retained for Admiralty Coastal Signalling and Wireless Telegraphy Stations, 935 became Coastguards under the Board of Trade and 450 went into the Customs Service. This left about 1,200 men who became redundant. The Coastguards were given fore and aft rig, that is they no longer had sailor suits but resembled Royal Naval Petty Officers. The people of Coverack soon became accustomed to seeing Coastguards wearing peaked caps and coats with special brass buttons. Of course, many of them were former Royal Navy Chief and Petty Officers. The Station Officers were recognised by one ring of black braid on the cuff of their coats. The stations flew the Union Flag instead of the White Ensign. The Coastguard did not have their own distinctive flag until 1974. It is a Blue Ensign with a golden Coastguard emblem at the fly (the top corner opposite the small Union Flag).

From 1923 either the Black Head or Porthoustock Look Out was constantly manned so that someone was always watching for signals of distress. Each man had a telephone bell in his cottage so that his help was instantly available in a crisis. It was laid down that the coast had to be patrolled when the stations had been on Thick Weather Watch or Bad Weather Watch. This was to make sure that all was well on the coast. These patrols were aimed at preventing cases like the Gunvor which had run ashore close to the Black Head but was not found until the Corin brothers went fishing. From the 7th. December, 1924 until May, 1951 Gale Warning cones were hoisted on the flagpole at the battery in Coverack to warn passing shipping and local fishermen to seek shelter. The point of the cone faced upwards when a northerly or easterly gale was expected and the point was down when the direction of the gale was expected from the west or south. When a small boy, the writer was convinced by a leg pulling Coastguard that the cone was placed upside down to catch the rain which came from the south west. After 1951 verbal warnings of gales were passed to Mr. Staples the fisherman statistics collector and he in turn would tell his mates. It was hardly necessary because by then everyone in the village had a wireless set and in any case that kind of warning was of no use to anyone who had gone to sea before it was broadcast.

In the same way that much of the work done by the lifeboat men consisted of long hours of searching with no result, so the Coastguards' work was carried out without the villagers realising what was going on. On the 17th. October, 1925 at 5 o'clock in the morning while it was still dark and most of the villagers were still sleeping, Mr. Jimmy Carey, a fisherman, was going towards the quay from Tamarisk Cottage when he saw that a steamer had grounded on Mill Beach in thick fog. He rushed to the Coastguard Station and informed the Officer in charge, Mr. Archie Williams. By the time both men had returned to the cove the steamer had got off the beach and was proceeding stern first out of the bay. She turned as she was disappearing into the fog and set a southerly course. The Station Officer then telephoned the Coastguard on duty at the Black Head and warned him of a possible casualty. As anticipated the ship came close to the rocks at the Black Head and the Coastguard hailed her. There was no reply but the ship went off out to sea.

The following year, again in thick fog, Coastguard Richard Germain was on Thick Weather Watch at the Black Head. He saw a steamer about to hit the rocks so he warned her off and followed her along the cliff as far as Pedn Boar where the Gunvor had gone ashore under similar circumstances. Mr. Germain continued sounding the letter U in morse . . —, . . —, . . —, on his portable klaxon to tell the vessel she was standing into danger. Eventually she too made off but in the direction of Cadgwith. The Coastguard returned hastily to the Look Out and telephoned the watchman at Cadgwith so that he in turn could warn the unknown vessel. These episodes illustrate the prevention work that was going on all the time in Coverack.

The Coastguards continued to perform other duties which one does not normally associate with the job. On the 25th. March, 1933 a damaged white ship's lifeboat was washed ashore in Coverack. The boat was marked Dolius AH1005 of Liverpool. It is curious to note that after various enquiries were made it proved impossible to trace the owners or discover what had happened to the Dolius so the boat was sold for £1 to Mr. Billy May on the orders of the Receiver of Wreck. On the 7th. April the following year the carcass of a 5′10″ long dolphin was washed ashore in the village. It fell to the Coastguard, after taking measurements, to hack out the lower jaw of the unfortunate animal and forward it to the National History Museum in Cromwell Road, London after sending a detailed telegram to the curator. The Coastguards are responsible for sending reports on all fishes royal - the sturgeon, porpoise, dolphin and whale.

As Sea Fishery Officers the Coastguards had to report boats fishing in prohibited areas where there were known to be immature stocks of fish. This was a difficult task to perform. British skippers were fined if reported whereas foreign trawler skippers invariably went unpunished, as they still do today. It called for great diplomacy by the Coastguards who had to work with the inshore fishermen who could see their livelihoods being eroded because the Coastguards were unable to enforce the law. They had to be just as diplomatic when checking on the number of passengers carried by local boats, especially when someone reported a rival for carrying too many people and the charge could not be substantiated. It is easy to see why some of the Coastguards found life in Coverack stressful and moved on as soon as they could.

Coastguard families which came to Coverack were usually quite large. This meant a welcome addition to the school roll in spite of the fact that as previously shown in the chapter on Religion and Education the School Board was not sure in which social category the Coastguard children should be placed when it came to assessing the payment due for their instruction. A new Coastguard family also meant new friends for local boys and girls. In time marriages took place and the Coastguard families merged with the village families.

## SOME NINETEENTH CENTURY COAST GUARDS WHO CAME TO COVERACK

| DATE | RANK | NAME | NOTES |
|------|------|------|-------|
| 1812 | Commissioned Boatman | Thomas Billett | Dismissed 1830. |
|  | Boatman | Jno. Tregidgo | To Blackman, 1830. |
| 1820 | Commissioned Boatman | Edward Day | To Recorder's Quay, 1830. |
| 1820 | Boatman | Wm. Searle | Came from Cadgwith - to Bognor, 1831. |
| 1826 | Boatman | Edw. Adams | Discharged 1828. |
| 1827 | Boatman | John Odgers (Promoted Commissioned Boatman) | To Bognor, 1831. |
|  | Chief Officer | S. Cockburn | To Ilfracombe, 1828. |
| 1828 | Lieutenant | McKenzie | From Ilfracombe. |
|  | Chief Officer | Stephn. Hodge | To Atherfield, 1830. |
|  | Boatman | Dennis Keverne | From Waterford. |
| 1830 | Chief Officer | Morton Alexander | From Lornepoint - (appointment cancelled) |
| 1830 | Commissioned Boatman | Dennis Carey | To Osmington, 1831. |
| 1832 | Boatman | John Edes | To Porthillick 1833 (as Commissioned Boatman) |
| 1836 | C.G. Boatman | Charles Jones | From Porthcawl. |
| 1838 | C.G. Boatman | James Baker | From Ramsgate. |
| 1838 | C.G. Boatman | Richard Wright | From Jack's Hole, Ireland. |
| 1838 | C.G. Commissioned Boatman | James Hales | From Osmington. |
| 1839 | Lieut. | Charles Maclean | (Retired 1855). |
| 1842 | C.G. Chief Boatman | Philip Calf | From Greystones |
| 1843 | C.G. Commissioned Boatman | William Mean | From Sennen Cove. |
| 1843 | C.G. Boatman | Alfred Ford | From H.M.S. Calliope. |
| 1843 | C.G. Commissioned Boatman | William Cattran | From Mothecombe. |
| 1843 | C.G. Commissioned Boatman | John McHenry | From Whitehouse, Ireland. |
| 1844 | C.G. Boatman | David Smith | From Marwood |
| 1845 | C.G. Boatman | Charles Peake | Born Polperro. |

| 1852 | C.G. Chief | Joseph Lake | |
|------|------------|-------------|---|
| 1855 | C.G. Chief Officer | John Page | |
| 1857 | C.G. Chief Officer | John Way Master | |
| 1861 | Chief Boatman | George Gale | |
| 1871 | C.G. | James Barker | |
| | C.G. | James Pengilly | (Superannuated) |
| | C.G. | Edward Jolinson | |
| | C.G. | James Connor | |
| 1871 | C.G. | Patrick O'Keefe | |
| | C.G. Chief Officer (2nd Class) | Henry Higgins | |
| | Chief Boatman | Patrick Murphy | |
| | C.G. | Nicholas Johns | (Pensioner) |
| c.1881+ | C.G. | Samuel Hill | (from Porthallow) |
| | C.G. | James Carey | (from Landewednack) |
| 1894 | C.G. Chief Officer | Albert Jeffers | |

This Officer remained in Coverack until 1901. He was recommended at the Board of Trade Inquiry for his work on the night of the Mohegan disaster in 1898. The following year he was again recommended by the International Navigation Company and Passengers for his work at the time of the wreck of the Paris. These commendations for Special Services were recorded on his service sheet.

NOTE

Many of the men who worked on Coast Guard duties up to the 1840s were not employed full time. Their service sheets indicated where they lived when unemployed so that they could be contacted when required for work.

### A COAST GUARD FAMILY OF 1881

(At Coverack 1874-1891)

Chief Officer John Gibson aged 48 years.

Mrs. Louisa Gibson aged 44 years.

| | |
|---|---|
| William Henry | 19 years (later became a Captain in the Merchant Navy and settled in Coverack when he retired). |
| Marlborough | 13 years |
| Moleana | 9 years |
| Alfred | 6 years |
| Margret | 4 years |
| Ethell | 2 years |
| Alice | 10 months |

Note:    1.  There may have been another child born after William Henry who was away from home at the time when the names were recorded.

2.  Chief Officer Gibson's father and mother, aged 84 and 82 respectively were also living in Coverack at the time.

3.  In the 20th. century Coastguard families have integrated well with Coverack families. In 1951 the station was reduced to Auxiliary status on the 11th. August. The last Coastguard to work in Coverack was Mr. George Philpott. The Coastguard work of the village is now done by local Auxiliaries under the direction of a Sector Officer based in Falmouth.

## SOME TWENTIETH CENTURY COASTGUARDS WHO CAME TO COVERACK

| NAME | RANK | ARRIVED | LEFT |
|---|---|---|---|
| William Brown | *S.O. | 1922 | 1925 |
| Walter Cordall | †C.G. | 1923 | Remained in village after resigning in 1926. |
| Richard H. Germain | C.G. | 1923 | 1928 - to Rame Head. |
| Archie Williams | S.O. | 1925 | 1927 - Resigned. |
| Edward J. Robinson | C.G. | 1926 | 1937 - to Hartland Point |
| John Geering | S.O. | 1928 | 1929 |
| Thomas Stanton | S.O. | 1928 | Transferred to the Lizard after one month. |
| Reginald Bibbings | C.G. | 1928 | 1933 - to Polperro |
| Patrick Keohane | S.O. | 1929 | 1932 - to Looe |
| John J. Combe | S.O. | 1932 | 1935 - to Selsey Bill |
| Edward Marshall | C.G. | 1936 | Not known |
| Harold Tapper | S.O. | 1934 | Promoted to District Officer.  No date. |
| Herbert Scantlebury | C.G. | 1935 | 1938 - retired. |
| Fred C. Day | S.O. | 1935 | to Clovelly.  No date. |
| Wilfred Holland | S.O. | 1936 | Not known. |
| John Saltwell | C.G. | 1937 | to Porthoustock as S.O.  No date. |
| Arthur Perry | C.G. | 1937 | Resigned after 10 months. |
| Walter Bray | C.G. | 1938 | to Portscatho as S.O. |
| Bertie Harding | C.G. | 1941 | 1943 - to Looe. |
| George C. Clogg | C.G. | 1943 | to Portscatho.  No date. |
| James L.B. Jackson | C.G. | 1943 | 1945 - to the Isle of Wight. |
| Noah S. Watts | S.O. | 1943 | 1949 - to St. Anne's Head, Pembs. |
| David Tonkin | C.G. | 1944 | 1947 - Resigned. |
| Thomas C. Bryant | C.G. | 1945 | 1946 - Resigned. |
| Cornelius Reedy | C.G. | 1947 | Transferred to Hope Cove, Devon after 11 months. |
| Robert Edward Bell | C.G. | 1951 | to Portmuck |
| Ernest Rolfe Hunter | C.G. | 1948 | 1949 - to Tynemouth. |

| Victor J. Powell | S.O. | 1949 | Resigned after 6 months. |
| George H. Philpott | S.O. | 1950 | 1951 - Retired and remained in the village. |

*S.O.  = Station Officer

†C.G.  =Coastguard


The average length of stay in Coverack was just over three years. Some Coastguards left within a year and one stayed for 11 years. A few of the above names will appear again in this chronicle.

Returning to the statement about integration of Coastguard and Coverack families, the following short list gives an idea of various 20th. century family connections. It is by no means complete but it illustrates the expansion of the village family as a whole.

| COASTGUARD FAMILY NAME | LOCAL FAMILY NAME |
| --- | --- |
| Carey | Barker, Cox, Eustice, Pearce |
| Combe | Martin, Mason |
| Cordall | Lory |
| Symes | Pengilly |
| Watts | Eustice, Pengilly |
| White | Roskilly, May |

The names in both columns are considered to be local names as is the writer's, whose paternal grandfather arrived in the village in 1888. The Hart family has since become linked with the Pengilly, Rickard and Roberts local families. There is also a link with a Coastguard family of Careys from St. Just in Penwith. It is not known if the St. Just Coastguard Careys are connected with the Coverack Coastguard Careys. The name is associated with Plymouth and the south coast of Cornwall and there are some Irish connections.

In 1939 the Admiralty intervened in the administration of the Coastguard. It had become clear that war was coming so some 900 volunteer Auxiliary Coastguards were recruited to bring what was known as the War Watching Organisation to a high state of efficiency. Once more men from Coverack volunteered to help. After war broke out in 1939 the Coastguard came under the control of the Ministry of Shipping. By May, 1940, after the capitulation of France, Belgium, the Netherlands, Denmark and Norway the Admiralty placed the regular Coastguards under the Naval Discipline Act from February, 1942. Coverack people soon became accustomed to seeing Coastguards in khaki carrying rifles when they went on coastal dawn patrols. In addition to the duties which have already been outlined the Coastguards were now responsible for the detection of landings by enemy agents in remote coves. They carried out this work for some time before the Home Guard became an effective force.

On the 9th. June, 1941 a supplementary wooden Look Out Hut belonging to Mr. A.W. Long of Trenoweth, the local Home Guard commander was transported to Lankidden and manned by Coverack Auxiliaries. The local coast line was once more under surveillance from the same vantage points as it was in smuggling days when there was a customs post at Borgwitha. The Coverack Auxiliaries were keeping watch from the cliff castle built by the Veneti, the immigrants from Vannes in Brittany as mentioned in the first chapter.

It is not a pleasant walk to Black Head nor to Lankidden on a dark night without a torch to light the way, especially when there is a strong wind blowing, but the Coverack Auxiliaries did so regularly during the war years. An additional hazard was that at the back of their minds was the possibility of being surprised by enemy agents or saboteurs. They were not armed and few people were around to see them performing their war service.

### SOME WARTIME COVERACK AUXILIARY COASTGUARDS

| BLACK HEAD | | LANKIDDEN | |
| --- | --- | --- | --- |
| William Richards | Coverack | Eddy Pearce | *Penhallick |
| Jim Lawrence | *Trewillis | Bert Ivey | *Ponsongath |
| Bert Carey | Coverack | Percy Ivey | *Little Treleaver |
| George H. Bowden | Coverack | H. Butler | *Ponsongath |

| | | | |
|---|---|---|---|
| J.E. Genge | Penhallick | G. Roberts | *Ponsongath |
| Hebden Coome | Paris Hotel | Roy Harris Sen. | *Penhallick |
| Charles Wilkinson | Headland Hotel | Henry Harry | *Penhallick |
| | | William Thomas | *Penhallick |

* Farm

Most of these men were too old for the fighting services or were in reserved occupations such as farming. Some of them had fought in the First World War. It will be noted that some of the family names are the same as those who stood by when the Armada was threatening our shores - they are also included in most of the village activities which have been described. This concludes the general account of the Coastguard presence in Coverack. Their involvement in village life will be described as events are chronicled.

Mr. Dunn's entry in the Coverack School Log on August 4th., 1914 reflected the atmosphere in the village when the long feared war actually began: 'The gloom of war hangs over the village and children as Coast Guards and Naval Reservists have been called up.'

Early in the morning, people in the cove were awakened by the sound of cheering. Six CoastGuardswere already piling their kit on to Mr. Roberts' Horse Bus and they were joined by a few army and navy reservists who had been summoned to the colours by the messages received on the Coast Guard Coastal Communication Circuit. When the cheering had died down and the first Coverack men had left for the war the reaction set in. The children missed their fathers, the wives missed their husbands and the remaining village men wondered what they ought to do. The older men joined the Coast Guard Auxiliary Service as described in the previous chapter. Those who were in the lifeboat crew continued with their important voluntary work which was more necessary than ever during war time. In the towns and cities men began flocking to the colours, motivated by a mixture of patriotic fervour and the fear of being branded cowards. Squire P.D. Williams spearheaded the recruiting drive in the Parish. The first Coverack men to volunteer were three Williams: William Henry Harry, William Roberts and William Roskilly. They were given the privilege of being taken to Helston Station in Mr. Williams' chauffeur driven car. After Christmas the Squire arranged for the Duke of Cornwall's Light Infantry Band to give a concert in the Square at St. Keverne. Those already in the forces were given a free tea as were those local men who declared they were ready to go to war. Lots of local children took the afternoon off school to join in the event.

Before long the trenches stretched from near Ostend in Belgium practically to the Swiss frontier. Men coming home on leave soon dispelled any exciting ideas the villagers might have had about modern warfare. Those fighting men had good cause to agree with the American Civil War General Sherman who told his cadets at a military academy, 'There is many a boy here today who looks on war as all glory, but boys, it is all hell.'

By 1916 conscription was needed to replace the huge losses of men on the Western Front. Today we shudder in horror at the thought of 75,000 Japanese being killed at Hiroshima on the 6th. August, 1945. We are inclined to forget that on July 1st., 1916 the British lost 60,000 men in one day's 'wave' attacks on the German trenches. Before the Battle of the Somme ended in November of that year the British and French had lost 615,000 men and the Germans 650,000.

It was not easy for Coverack people, nor indeed any other people, to visualise the appalling suffering endured by those who had gone to war. There was no radio, no cinema, no television. The papers carried few pictures, just details of battles, numbers of casualties and names of prominent people who had been killed. Propaganda saw to it that people on the 'Home Front' did not become too depressed about the progress of the war. The villagers had to rely on letters from the front which were censored, war artists' impressions in magazines and the tales of soldiers and sailors coming home on leave. They usually hid the real truth, knowing people would not be able to comprehend the horrors they had witnessed.

Mr. John Corin, son of the Coverack Lifeboat Coxswain told the writer how his father explained to him the conditions in the trenches in France. One Sunday morning in 1916 Mr. Corin, then aged about 10, was going to the Wesleyan Chapel with his father when Sandy Pengilly, an infantry man, came down the School Hill. He had walked from Helston Station. Mr. Corin Sen. and Sandy shook hands and chatted for a while. When Sandy had gone on down the hill towards his home, young John Corin asked his father why the soldier had mud all over his uniform. His father explained, 'It's mud from Flanders, by son, the men were taken out of the trenches after a bloody battle and sent straight home. They did not have time to clean their uniforms.' There is a wood near Ypres in Belgium which is still known as Bodmin Copse because it was held by the Duke of Cornwall's Light Infantry - a piece of land which is for ever Cornwall.

Coverack itself was not an oasis of calm during the First World War. The conflict at sea was being fought just a few miles out from the village. There was always plenty of shipping activity because of the proximity of the port of Falmouth. The repair yards were taken over by the Admiralty and engaged in converting merchant vessels into Q ships. These vessels had concealed guns fitted. They went to sea in order to lure German submarines into surfacing and firing at what appeared to be an unarmed merchant ship. The Q ship would then uncover her armament and fire back at the U-boat.

The lifeboat continued to play a vital part in village life. Just one year after the outbreak of war, on the night of 5th./6th. August, 1915 a French ship called the S.S. Arthur Capel struck a rock in thick weather off the Lowland Point. She was bound for Cardiff. The Constance Melanie launched and found the French crew preparing to abandon ship when they arrived on the scene. After the Coverack men had assessed the state of the ship, they informed the captain that they could help save the vessel. She was taking water by the bows but the bulkhead was holding so they got the ship off the rocks and she made for Falmouth at slow speed. She arrived safely in the harbour early in the morning of the 6th. August. Another ship had been saved for the war effort by the Coverack men. The board outside the lifeboat house recorded, 'Saved vessel'. There were several incidents of ships being escorted into Falmouth by the lifeboat after being attacked off the coast of Coverack. Sometimes the lifeboat stood by until the stricken vessel was taken over by a tug or a patrol vessel. Most of these operations were not recorded, probably because it was not possible to state categorically that lives had been saved by the action of the lifeboat men.

On Sunday, 16th. September, 1917 a convoy of about 50 ships left Falmouth and made its way down Channel past Coverack. When about half a mile off the Blackhead the largest ship in the convoy, a Norwegian vessel called the

Thomas Krag was hit by a torpedo. It was 6.30 in the afternoon. The convoy continued slowly on its way without scattering. After a short while the Thomas Krag fired distress rockets. The watchers on the cliff were astonished by the fact that although there were no patrol boats near the casualty, not one merchant ship deviated from her course to help the Norwegian vessel. Of course, while this was happening, the crew of the Constance Melanie were rushing down to the lifeboat house, having heard the explosion. The boat was soon launched and on her way to the Blackhead under oars. The Constance Melanie stood by the Norwegian for an hour until a patrol vessel arrived to take her in tow. Two engineers had been killed in the explosion but there were no other casualties. The ship's pumps managed to cope with the water entering the engine room. Before the Constance Melanie left the scene, the Coxswain was asked by the Captain of the Thomas Krag if he would pick up one of the ship's lifeboats which had broken adrift and take it back to port. The Captain had put some of his personal belongings in this boat in case the ship sank after being hit. Mr. Corin retrieved the ship's lifeboat and towed her back to Coverack. By 8.45 p.m. the lifeboat was back on the slip.

Just over four weeks later, on Wednesday 17th. October, 1917 another explosion at sea was heard in Coverack. Shortly afterwards red rockets were sighted about 7 or 8 miles south east of the village. The lifeboat crew assembled once more but as Mr. George Harvey, the Honorary Secretary wrote in his report later on, 'The Coxswain hesitated to launch the boat for some little time as usually patrol vessels are in the vicinity and the weather and sea were moderate at the time.' However when more distress rockets were fired, 'The crew assembled with commendable promptitude and zeal and at once set off.' It was a long row out to sea. The Coxswain's initial appraisal of the situation proved to be correct. When the Constance Melanie reached the ship, which was sinking fast, a patrol vessel informed the Coxswain that they had already picked up the crew and transferred them to another vessel which was going to Falmouth. The Captain, Mate and Chief Engineer of the sinking vessel, which was called the S.S.Adams of South Shields, remained on board the patrol vessel at the scene of the explosion until their ship sank. The Constance Melanie then made for home under oars, arriving back at 10 p.m. The occasions when the lifeboat went out at dusk in response to ships which had been damaged by enemy action were fraught with danger. It was always possible that a German submarine would attack the lifeboat and equally the British patrol vessels were liable to let off a round at the lifeboat, mistaking her for an approaching submarine. The Coxswain was informed by the captain of a patrol vessel on one occasion that they were about to shell the lifeboat when she was identified at the last moment in the gathering dusk. The crew list of the Constance Melanie when she went to the assistance of the S.S. Adams indicates some changes due to some regular members being abroad on active service:

| | | | |
|---|---|---|---|
| 1. | Coxswain John Corin | 8. | Lyle Cuttance |
| 2. | George H. Bowden | 9. | Alfred Eustice |
| 3. | Fred K. Carey | 10. | William Hocking |
| 4. | James Carey | 11. | Joseph H. James |
| 5. | Cecil Connor | 12. | Tom Coad Roskilly |
| 6. | William C. Corin | 13. | Albert Rowe |
| 7. | Ernest Cox | 14. | George Tripp |
| | | 15. | W. James Williams |

The year 1917 proved to be an active one in the war at sea off Coverack. Mr. Fred Carey and Mr. John Corin were on Coast Guard Duty at the Blackhead one afternoon and were watching a small convoy of three coastal sailing ships and a steam coaster approaching from the Lizard. Suddenly a U-boat surfaced close to the ships and commenced shelling. The surprised Coast Watchers immediately informed the Station Officer of Coast Guards so that he could summon help. The Station Officer did not believe at first that a submarine could be so daring as to surface that close to land but eventually the Officer rang Falmouth and a patrol vessel was sent to the Blackhead. It was too late. The submarine sank the three sailing vessels. While the submarine was occupied with the sailing ships the steamer managed to get out of range of the submarine and continued on her way towards Falmouth.

In February, 1915 the Germans announced that they considered the Western Approaches to Britain to be a war zone. They warned all neutral countries that they would sink any ship they found in the Approaches. Two months later the Lusitania was sunk. She was a British ship but among those drowned were 118 United States citizens. This tragedy prompted Woodrow Wilson to warn Germany that any further loss of American citizens due to submarine activity would be considered 'unfriendly'. The warning was virtually unheeded and by 1917 all United States vessels entering the Western Approaches were armed for self defence. By April, 1917, the United States had entered the war. It was not too soon. It was learned later that there remained only six weeks' supply of food in Britain.

The war against German submarines in the approaches to the English Channel was waged from the air as well as land and sea. In 1915 a 320 acre site close to Bonython Plantation, which is situated between Mullion and Garras off the A3083, was taken over by the Admiralty. In June, 1916 the Lizard Airship Station came into being. A large shed 300' long and 100' wide was constructed as a hangar and latticed wooden wind shields erected to protect the airships while they were on the ground outside the hangar. The first patrols began on July 1st., 1916 after some test flights had been conducted. The people of Coverack soon became accustomed to seeing the C8 and C9 cigar shaped dirigibles going up and down over the sea on anti submarine patrols.

Flying an airship was a hazardous occupation. One came down in the Channel off Start Point when it was being flown to Bonython. Three of the crew were lost, the sole survivor being the wireless operator. After this accident the airships were delivered by road and rail until their engines became more reliable. Flight Commander J.G. Struthers became well known for his attacks on German submarines while he was stationed at Bonython. He and his crew spent long hours in the air searching for U-boats. On one occasion on the 22nd. June, 1917 he set out from Bonython at 5 o'clock in the morning for a patrol to Start Point. At 7.30 a.m. he spotted the tell tale green coloured shape of a submarine beneath the surface and called on H.M. Destroyer No.73 to investigate. The destroyer went to the position indicated by the airship and dropped two depth charges. The airship then dropped a 65lb. bomb on the submerged submarine. Wreckage and oil came to the surface but there was no decisive proof that the submarine had been sunk. The airship then went on to rendez-vous with a convoy off Prawle Point in case of further attacks. Nothing more was seen so the airship was recalled at 1125 a.m. Battling against the wind and heavy rain accompanied by thunder the airship eventually arrived at the airfield at 4 o'clock in the afternoon.

The following September a French steamer called Rouang was torpedoed off the Lizard. Flight Commander Struthers was sent to investigate and after a five hour search spotted the conning tower of a submarine moving towards a Falmouth bound convoy. He closed with the submarine and this time dropped two 100lbs bombs which brought a large patch of oil to the surface. The airship was credited with a probable as later on the German H.Q. was heard calling a submarine which did not answer. In the same month airship SS214 had engine trouble while on patrol and was blown across the Channel. After repairs at an air base near Brest she flew back to Bonython a fortnight later.

In 1917 the Airships at Bonython were joined by four Sopwith aeroplanes which did the inshore patrols. These were withdrawn soon after for service in France and were replaced early in 1918 by six DH6 biplanes. These were backed up later in the year by 236 Squadron of the newly formed R.A.F. which flew DH9 Light Bombers. One of the pilots' wives lived with her mother, Mrs. Green at Wyndleshore, Sunny Corner. Mrs. Green's son in law caused quite a sensation one day when he circled low over the Battery and dropped a message for his wife. The village boys also had a 'field day' on another occasion when one of the 'planes dumped its ammunition near Carnsullan Farm in order to gain height and make its way back to the airfield. Lizard Airship Station closed in November, 1918. It had been the most active of the 17 Airship Stations in Britain, having flown 2,845 operational hours. Thus ended a short chapter of the war in the air off Coverack.

Meanwhile the villagers got on with the war in their own way. The fishermen continued to get food from the sea and manned the lifeboat when she was needed. The farmers used every bit of land they could plough to produce more food. The government not only requisitioned their horses for service in France but also the fodder. The school Harvest Holidays were adjusted each year to coincide with the ripening of the crops and service men who could be spared from their wartime duties were granted special leave to come back home and help with the harvest. More and more men were leaving the village to join the forces in spite of the stories circulating about trench warfare and the all out U-boats campaign at sea.

The successes of the German U-boats in their attacks on merchant ships necessitated the rationing of food. As in other lean times, Coverack people managed with their gardens, chickens, privately owned pigs and a bit of private fishing. Bartering went on as it always had done. Young mothers with small families whose husbands were in the forces could not afford to buy their meat rations so they exchanged their coupons for less expensive food for their children. Wrecking provided welcome supplementary food rations at times during the war. When supply ships were sunk off Coverack the villagers salvaged what they could from the wreckage thrown up on the beach. Sacks of flour were washed ashore after one sinking and the locals soon discovered that there was a dry 'core' in the centre of each sack which was unaffected by sea water. Needless to say the good flour was quickly scooped out and taken home. Boxes of tinned food came ashore sometimes and were eagerly pounced on as were some boxes of lard. In 1917 the British steamer Volnay struck a mine off the Manacles. She was laden with food and ammunition from Canada. When an easterly wind got up, Porthallow beach and the surrounding coves were strewn with boxes of coffee, tea, butter, jam, buscuits, tinned meats, cigarettes and all sorts of luxury items which had been in short supply for so long. Needless to say, people from all over the Parish rushed to the beaches to join in the free for all. It is indeed an ill wind that 'turns none to good.'

It is not possible to relate the experiences of all the Coverack men and women who went to the First World War and it is equally impossible to obtain detailed information about the majority of these people. An interesting case is that of Sandy Pengilly. He was the 15 year old boy who filled a vacant place on the Constance Melanie when she went to the wreck of the Pindos in 1912. He gave up fishing when his father died and went away to sea on a sailing collier from Swansea which used to call at Coverack with a cargo of coal. Sandy decided to join the Territorial Army not long after war broke out and after attending drills for a while he joined the Duke of Cornwall's Light Infantry. He was later transferred to the Gloucester Regiment. They were known as 'the Slashers' because of their prowess in bayonet fighting. Sandy was not long in the army before he was sent to France and found himself in the trenches. In April, 1918, the last year of the war his mother received the dreaded notification from the War Office in Alexandra House, London, W.C.2 that her son was reported 'Missing'. By a strange coincidence, one of the last people to see Sandy before he went missing was his brother in law. The two Coverack men met one another unexpectedly. Sandy was given some clean clothing which his brother in law managed to scrounge from the stores. It was some months before it was realised that shortly after this chance meeting Sandy had been taken prisoner. In fact it was July, 3rd., 1918 before any further details were forthcoming. Sandy's officer, Captain H. Proctor wrote to tell his sister that on April 2nd., 1918, 'He was serving in a Composite Battalion and it has been very difficult to get much information as to exactly what happened during the operations. The Battalion was surprised and surrounded by the enemy in the early morning, during a mist, and your brother may have been made a prisoner.' He added sympathetically, 'I hope you may get news of him shortly.'

The full story was learned later when the war ended. Sandy, a Lance Corporal and his companions saw a German patrol advancing in 'No Man's Land' and opened fire, killing the German officer who was leading the patrol. The Germans attacked the platoon of Gloucesters, killing everyone except Sandy who had been shot in the hand. Fortunately for Sandy the German N.C.O. who had taken charge of the patrol had been employed as a waiter in England before the war. He told Sandy he would be spared if he agreed to carry the dead German officer back to German lines. This was done with some difficulty because of the pain of the bullet wound in his hand. The next day Sandy had his trigger finger amputated. He spent the remainder of the war in a prisoner of war camp. When he was released he told his family that one of his jobs was collecting rubbish from dustbins in a small town near the P.O.W. camp. The British prisoners were so hungry that while on their rounds they would collect scraps of food such as potato peelings, leaves of vegetables, bits of bread and so on. When they got back to camp they boiled up all the food they had collected and made a 'soup' which helped to appease their hunger. The food parcels they were sent from home never materialised.

SANDY PENGILLY, standing left, 1917
*Sandy Pengilly: In turn Fisherman, Lifeboatman,
Infantryman, Prisoner of War, Merchant Navy Bosun,
Naval Petty Officer, Sandy sent this photo to his sister
and signed it "Five of the Fore and Aft Slashers".
At that time he was in the Gloucesters, who were famous
for their bayonet fighting. The Regiment wore badges at the
front and back of their caps
as a reward for a famous rearguard action.*

After the war, Sandy went to sea and became a Boatswain in the Merchant Navy, serving on British tankers. He came back to Coverack in the late 1930s and continued fishing. When the Second World War broke out he volunteered for the Naval Patrol Service and took his boat, the Pathfinder to Falmouth. He skippered his own boat, which was used in the Port Examination Service throughout the war. When he was demobilised at the end of the war he went back to Coverack and continued as a lifeboatman and fisherman.

One of the visitors to Coverack whom Sandy used to take fishing was Professor C.E.M. Joad, a controversial and well known radio personality. Dr. Joad wrote a short essay about Sandy for his collection, 'A year more or less.' The essay was entitled, 'The virtues of Sandy P.' He described Sandy as '........a man devoid of envy, spite and malice, content with his lot, nourishing no ambitions above his station, liking his fellows and being liked by them, a man of his word, a man you could trust, above all a man devoid of most of the misery making emotions.' He concluded, somewhat patronisingly, 'How much easier, in short, to be a good man if your life and circumstances are those of Sandy P., than if they are mine.' Professor Joad finally admitted that he was still wondering why so many good chaps are '........ circumstanced like Sandy P.' If only he had talked to Sandy he would have learned such a lot! Perhaps if Sandy had shown him the message he received from King George V in common with other P.O.W.s Professor Joad would have investigated Sandy a little more closely before writing his essay. The message was as follows:

BUCKINGHAM PALACE, 1918

The Queen joins me in welcoming you on your release from the miseries and hardships, which you have endured with so much patience and courage.

During these many months of trial, the early rescue of our gallant Officers and Men from the cruelties of their captivity has been uppermost in our thoughts.

We are thankful that this longed for day has arrived, and that back in the old Country you will be able once more to enjoy the happiness of a home and to see good days among those who anxiously look for your return.

GEORGE R.I.

At last the longed for day arrived. The Armistice was signed. Everyone thanked God it was over, Mr. Dunn recording it in Latin in the Coverack School Log. Villagers flocked to the harbour to see the telegram with their own eyes. They could hear the 'music' of the thanksgiving peal of bells at St. Keverne Church and occasionally the sound of ships' sirens blowing in Falmouth Bay. By the end of the year the first of the returning heroes arrived in the village. The men who came home first were those with the longest service and the most wound stripes.

Each soldier was given 28 days leave and 28 days ration allowance to start him off once more in civilian life. In addition, £22 10s. was placed in the Post Office Savings Bank - 'Less £1 payable on return of the military great-coat (see Army Book 472)'. This was the gratuity awarded for four years of war service and was equivalent to about six months of a private soldier's pay. Two years later, the soldiers were sent their medals with their names engraved round the edges and the Unknown Soldier was buried in Westminster Abbey. The record of the cost of the war to Coverack was seen in graphic form when the 1921 Armistice Day was remembered at the new War Memorial which had been erected in St. Peter's Churchyard at Coverack:

'They died for us. 1914-1918.

Nurse Zoe K. Bryan-Daunt

Navy T.J. Eustace Boatswain

F. Freathy C.P.O.

J. Carey Boy

Army W.H. Bonfield Lieut.

W. Edwards Pte.

F.C. Freathy Pte.

W.J. Hocking Pte'.

In one sense this list was the tip of the iceberg. Those who were maimed in body had to sustain the damage for the rest of their lives. One of the first volunteers, Mr. William Henry Harry lost an arm but he overcame the physical difficulties the loss of a limb entails and lived a full life. Others were to be short of breath for the rest of their lives, as a result of damage done to their lungs during gas attacks. Most were affected in mind and spirit to a greater or lesser degree. These men came together after the 'fuss' surrounding their homecoming died down and held meetings with the common aim of building a better future for their families and the village. They joined a movement called 'The Comrades of the Great War'.

We have seen in the chapter Religion and Education how the returning service men were invited to a celebratory tea at the Wesleyan Chapel. This kind of celebration continued at intervals for some time. A year after the war ended it was the turn of St. Peter's Church to fete the former soldiers and sailors. On Saturday the 22nd. November, 1919 at 6 p.m. the ex service men and their families were settling down at the tables in St. Peter's Church Hall for a celebratory dinner when the lifeboat maroons went off. The sea was smooth but there was a thick fog. As soon as the explosions were heard there was the usual mad rush of men to the lifeboat house and to Sunny Corner where the Life Saving Apparatus was housed. The dinner was forgotten for the time being.

A 4,623 ton American cargo ship, the Hattie Luckenback with 34 people on board, bound in ballast from Rotterdam to New York had struck the Ebber Rocks which lie between the Mears Beach and the Blackhead. By half past six the lifeboat had been launched and was on her way under oars to the Ebber. The Life Saving Apparatus was also being manhandled across the cliffs. It was not needed. The Constance Melanie arrived at the Ebber by seven o'clock. The ship was in no immediate danger as she was fast on the rocks but the captain asked the lifeboat to stand by. After a long wait two tugs arrived from Falmouth at four o'clock in the morning. The Constance Melanie took the tugs' hawsers inshore to the stricken ship. After a while the lifeboat was released from service as the tug captains told the Coxswain that the ship was in no further danger and more tugs were on their way to pull the ship off the rocks. During the hours of darkness Captain A.R. MacDonald had been pumping fuel oil into the sea in an attempt to lighten ship and when daylight came the lifeboat men were dismayed to find the hull of their smart craft was covered in black fuel oil. Rather disconsolately they returned to Coverack, faced with the prospect of having to spend a few days cleaning and repainting the lifeboat. At two o'clock on Sunday afternoon three more tugs arrived and after some sand ballast had been taken out of the ship's hold, the tugs finally got the ship off the rocks at twenty to eight in the evening and she was towed into Falmouth. Thus ended the Peace Celebrations in Coverack. The comments of the ex service crew members of the Constance Melanie were not recorded!

# SETTLING DOWN AGAIN

## The British Legion and Coverack Village Hall

The newly formed Coverack Branch of the Comrades of the Great War discovered that when the Great War was drawing to a close a group of villagers had decided at a meeting that a new Reading Room would make a fitting and practical tribute to the men who had served their country for such a long time.

Not long after the war ended, on January 21st., 1919 a public meeting was held at the Council School to decide on a site and the ways and means of raising money. Captain W.H. Gibson, the son of a former Chief Officer of Coast Guards at Coverack was appointed permanent Chairman and Mr. Edward Dunn the Coverack Headmaster was made Secretary. A committee of villagers was formed for the purpose of fund raising. When £75 had been collected it was decided to purchase a plot of land in the cove on which stood a derelict cottage. The land was owned by Mr. Ralph Ellis of Penzance, a descendant of the man who constructed the Quay in 1724. It was known that Mr. Ellis intended to sell this piece of land, but after further meetings the committee changed its mind. The site was considered to be too small and in the wrong position for a public meeting place. It was felt that the Lambeage or 'Battery' as most people knew it would be a better proposition especially as the Ellis family had always allowed the village ladies to dry their washing there and the village children had played on the Battery from time immemorial. The Wesleyan Chapel also used the green for Tea Treats and other functions. After further meetings to iron out the details, it was agreed to purchase the Lambeage and to use the £75 earmarked for the Reading Room to buy the green.

Meanwhile Captain Gibson the Permanent Chairman had gone back to sea and was known to be trading in China and Japan. He was sent copies of the minutes of the meetings and details of the proposed purchase of land. After a very long wait the committee received Captain Gibson's sanction for the transfer of money for the purchase of the Battery. At last, on the 24th. August, 1922 the deeds which had been prepared by Walter Tyack, Solicitor of Helston were handed to the Coverack Trustees who were:

| | |
|---|---|
| William Brown | Chief Officer of Coastguards |
| William Corin | Hillside |
| Charles Cottrell | Penhallick |
| James Martin | Pednavounder Farm |
| Henry Mitchell | Trelanvean |
| Thomas Roskilly | Post Office |

A clause in the agreement ensured that in the event of a Trustee leaving the district of 'Coverack and Turn Trelan' a successor was to be elected by the inhabitants of Coverack and Turn Trelan.

As indicated earlier the men for whom the land had been purchased did not remain idle when they returned from the Great War. A 'Post' or branch of 'The Comrades of the Great War' was formed with Mr. T.J. Hocking as 'Captain' or Chairman. Chief Coastguard Officer W. Brown as Treasurer, Mr. T.H. Davies as Secretary. The committee members were:

George Martin

William May

A. (Sandy) Pengilly

William Roskilly

L. Tripp

It is curious how the ex service men stuck to the repressive régime of service life at the beginning of the activities of the Comrades. For example on the 10th. January, 1920 the following motion, proposed by the Secretary was carried: 'That a fine of one penny be imposed on any member of our Post who shall be seen in Public in ordinary walking out dress after working hours (between 6 p.m. and 6 a.m.) without his distinctive badge of the Comrades of the Great War on. Any member shall have power to call attention of any other member to prove the case.' It was further stated that not only was this rule to take effect immediately but that any member who contravened the order would be fined a further penny if he did not come to the meeting when summoned to explain why he was improperly dressed! It is clear that funds were needed as the balance in hand at the time was 12s 3d. It would appear that the committee was using a sledge hammer to crack a nut, but in fact the resolution was also aimed at attracting more recruits for the Post by displaying the badge. In addition, they wanted to win the respect of the villagers by their discipline and bearing in public.

Of course these Comrades were aware of the efforts being made on their behalf by the villagers to get premises but they were in immediate need of a meeting place so they asked if they could borrow St. Peter's Church Hall which had been built some three years before the Great War began, in the year of the coronation of King George V. They were granted the use of the hall for three months without charge. A few years later in 1924, when the Comrades of the Great War had changed their name to the 'British Legion', the Vicar, the Rev. Norris unwisely let it be known that the organisation was still not paying for the use of the Hall. In reply, the committee somewhat indignantly passed a resolution proposed by Mr. W.J. Roskilly and seconded by Mr. J. Stevens, 'That the Rev. Norris be informed that the branch pays 12s 6d for each hiring and furthermore held receipts for the same.' The good parson used to deliver his long sermons in a high pitched nasal intonation which was widely imitated by the village boys when his back was turned. What prompted him to make the false accusation is not known, but his undiplomatic remarks brought to the surface the old arguments between Anglicans and Dissenters, the latter reminding the C. of E. villagers that the Anglican Church in Coverack had not yet celebrated its 40th. birthday in Coverack!

The Comrades, who addressed each other as 'Brother' in formal meetings, did not sit back and wait for the grateful villagers to provide them with premises. A Minstrel Troupe was formed by Mr. W. (Billy) May for fund raising purposes. There are still a few fading photos in the village of villagers dressed in Pierrot costumes. Mr. T.J. Hocking, the 'Captain' wrote Mr. Barker to see if the Comrades could borrow the Old Reading Room for their meetings. This is the building opposite Bank House which has now been converted into a holiday flat.

Whist was the abiding passion of the villagers at that time. It was considered that a series of whist drives would be a good money spinner. Accordingly the Comrades commissioned Henry Harry to buy 20 packs of playing cards. Wearnes the bakers of Helston were asked to supply 18lb. of cakes and 8 dozen splits which were to be brought to Coverack by Comrade W.J. Martin. Mr. Frank Rule, the Secretary of the St. Keverne 'Post' agreed to be the neutral Master of Ceremonies at the first Whist Drive which was held in the school. It was an immediate success, in spite of the unpopular rule which stated that children under 16 were barred from the schoolroom while the Drive was in progress and that the committee forgot to get an exemption from entertainment tax from the Excise Officer at Helston. The subsequent Drives went well but it was noted that in bad weather the villagers declined to get soaked to the skin walking up the hill to the school so Comrades L. Tripp and Joe Hart were deputed to 'interview' the Church Committee with a view to using St. Peter's Church Hall again. They were to ask if they could have it free of charge or failing that, if they could have it for half price on the understanding that the Comrades would clean the hall after use. The negotiations were successful but there was a 'very small' attendance at the next Whist Drive and the Secretary of The Old Comrades recorded that this was '........owing to the St. Keverne Old Comrades being prevented from coming by the circulation of a false rumour.' He added that in spite of this, all present had a pleasant evening. Who knows what Machiavellian plots were being concocted in camera in Coverack? Or perhaps St. Keverne? No names were mentioned but it is certain that every Comrade knew who was behind the sabotage of the Whist Drives.

Problems were not all parochial. A letter appeared in the Daily Express regarding wartime canteen profits held by the War Office. This money was supposed to have been handed to Lord Byng for distribution to ex service men through the United Services Fund which was partly controlled by the Comrades of the Great War. The publication of the letter prompted Coverack Post to apply for affiliation to Headquarters in spite of the fact that each member would have to pay twice the normal subscription. Sixpence from each person would have to go to Divisional Headquarters at Truro and sixpence to National Headquarters. It was considered a worthwhile venture because the Post could then get its rightful share of the Canteen Profits which had been stashed away by the miserly War Office bureaucrats. To make sure that the money would come to the members of the Post, a list of all the ex service men in the district was prepared and sent to Councillor Harvey in anticipation of the distribution of the fund. Mr. William Pengilly, a native of Coverack and at that time a prominent Old Comrade in the Camborne Post came back to the village and gave a talk to encourage the men to stand up for their rights. It is ironic that while this scandalous misappropriation of funds by a government department was being sorted out, the new War Memorial Cross was unveiled in St. Peter's Churchyard. The Comrades had collected the considerable sum of £9 10s towards the cost of the Memorial and handed it over to Miss Kempthorne, the Honorary Secretary of the St. Peter's Hall.

In May, 1921 the Prince of Wales came to Newquay to address the Comrades. The Coverack Post could not send a delegate but later on Mr. L. Tripp went to London for the Unity Conference. His expenses were paid by the Post which organised a concert by Mr. Billy May's Minstrel Troupe in the school to get funds. The concert so impressed Mr. Snell of Falmouth who was in the audience that he immediately offered the Comrades a free trip to Falmouth in his Quay Punt. At a meeting on July 5th., 1921 Comrade L. Cuttance proposed that the Post should join the newly formed British Legion whcih had been started by Earl Haig. Comrade L. Tripp seconded. The motion was unanimously carried by the twelve members present. Coverack Post of the Comrades of the Great War was no more.

Remembrance Day, 1921 saw the first service at the Coverack War Memorial. It was conducted by Mr. Stubbs who declared he was honoured to be asked as he was a stranger to the village. After the two minutes' silence Miss Ruby Bulkeley, daughter of Colonel Bulkeley, D.S.O. laid the wreath on the cross. It was from the newly formed British Legion. The wreath was of Palm leaves to represent Victory and assorted local flowers. It was draped in red and blue ribbon. The blue represented the Senior Service and the red the Army.

The newly formed Coverack branch of the British Legion began the year 1922 with a healthy balance of £19 9s 7d. They had a new Chairman, Secretary and Treasurer. They were Messrs. William Martin, Stafford Hart and Tom Coad Roskilly respectively. A Mr. W.J. Harvey from the Plymouth branch came to the first meeting, bringing samples of ciothes and boots which could be purchased at special prices by the Legion members. The Secretary recorded later that everyone was delighted with the idea of being a privileged purchaser and the evening ended with songs and pianoforte solos being rendered by some of the talented members of the new Branch. He added that it was decided that membership fees would be collected at the next meeting. It is assumed that the members had spent all their money on ordering the goods from Plymouth.

The following year at a special general meeting held in St. Peter's Hall on October 25th., 1923, it was decided to adopt the resolution of Headquarters and forward it with a copy of the British Legion Unemployment Manifesto to the new Prime Minister, the local M.P. and the local Press. The men were most concerned that the task Lloyd George had set at the end of the war in his Wolverhampton speech, 'To make Britain a fit country for heroes to live in,' should not be forgotten by their new political masters. Their fears were well founded as they were to find out later when the country wide depression hit Coverack.

After the war the Labour Party became the official Opposition. All men had the vote and every woman over 30, provided she or her husband owned or occupied land with an annual value of £5. This meant that the electorate had doubled since before the war. There was not much political activity in Coverack except the flurries casued by General Elections. Liberals like David Lloyd George and Winston Churchill were popular but because of the traditional Cornish mistrust of Central Government, the villagers preferred to put on pressure locally when they wanted something done. The strike in Glasgow for a 48 hour week, led by Emmanual Shinwell amongst others, did not mean much at that stage to folk who were accustomed to carrying on with a job until it was finished and they did not see how that could provide more villagers with work. Many of the houses in the area went with the jobs and there was little appetite for antagonising employers who could turn families out of their homes.

The British Legion, having shown itself to be a national organisation with some political influence and the ability to raise funds for the relief of ex service men and their families, became a popular organisation. The Coverack Branch was approached by some of the men who had been Coast Watchers during the war to see if they were eligible to join. Advice was sought from Headquarters which replied that they could become Honorary Members. The Branch then decided that for the time being they could not accept Honorary Members. It was to be 1932 before opinions had changed and the former Auxiliary Coast Guards were admitted. These proceedings appear rather trivial to the modern reader but those men who had lived like animals in the trenches and undergone the privations of a man of war at sea could not at that stage be persuaded that the men who had patrolled the coast line should be admitted to their select band of veterans.

Miss Ruby Bulkeley organised the sale of the new poppies for Earl Haig's Fund in 1923 and Poppy Day was declared a great success. Captain Gibson was invited to be the new Legion President. He was second choice. Squire P.D. Williams of Lanarth did not deem it necessary to reply to the invitation from the Coverack Branch, in spite of the fact that at the outbreak of war in a first flush of patriotism he had sent the first three Coverack volunteers to Helston in his chauffeur driven automobile as a mark of respect for those daring young men. That same year the Legion decided to hold a supper and invite wives and children to come as well. Mr. George Dally successfully amended the proposal to include the lady friends of single Branch Members. In the course of time this event became one of the most attractive dates in the Coverack social calendar. Whist was still very popular so a Drive was held to raise funds and the lower age limit raised to 14. The view of the 14 year olds were not recorded but the age was raised to 16 again for the next Whist Drive so presumably the youngsters did not come up to the standards required by the serious whist players of Coverack. Apart from that, the Drive was declared to be a huge success. Forty persons turned up. The prize winners were recorded in the Secretary's Minutes: Nurse F.A. Gidley - 175, Mr. Donald Uren - 160. The Consolation Prize went to Mr. Sam Roskilly of the Post Office. It had already been agreed that each prize should not cost more than two shillings each as the entrance fee was one shilling. Clearly the honour of winning was more important than the value of the prizes.

The Branch Members now began actively considering the possibility of having a club room of their own. The Secretary applied to the United Services Fund for a loan of £95 and the members pledged 3d a week each to clear any other loan which might be necessary to pay the balance on condition that their own loan be paid back when funds allowed. The apparent miserliness of the members reflects the parlous state of their own incomes at that time and shows why they were so concerned about the post war rise in unemployment.

The Branch was given the go ahead and began asking for tenders from local tradesmen. Colonel H.C. Bulkeley and his daughter pledged £5 each on condition that the building remained an ex service men's hut. Village interest was aroused, not all of it favourable. A letter was received from the Wesleyan Chapel Trustees opposing the erection of the Club Room on the Battery as the activities would interfere with divine service. Their fears were allayed in a diplomatic reply to the Trustees and the British Legion wisely asked permission to hold the next Armistice Service in the Wesleyan Chapel. Meanwhile, Mr. Jim Hart, known as 'Cap'n Jim' to the villagers poured oil on troubled waters by allowing the British Legion to meet in his tea room pro tem, thus removing any religious sectarianism from the situation before it could arise.

The village now renewed its interest in the hall. In December, 1924 it was agreed that a Public Hall should be erected on the Lambeage or Lan Bygh as the Cornish language enthusiasts wanted it spelt. The building was to consist of a main hall and two ante rooms, one of which was to be for the use of the British Legion with the proviso that the Legion ante room could also be used by the Trustees for any special occasion. The British Legion would also have the free use of the Hall for Whist Drives, concerts and so on but would pay for the heating and lighting. A most important rider was added stating that the Battery Trustees and the British Legion would '........unite in one body' to assist in raising money for the Hall. This was indeed a triumphal break through in village life. The Battery Trustees were accordingly invited to the British Legion annual supper. Peace had broken out once more in the village. There were members of the Chapels and Church in both organisations and they were to prove capable of working fairly harmoniously with those in the two organisations who had no religious affiliations.

Dr. Daunt was made the new President of the British Legion. Letters were sent to the usual village benefactors. Colonel Bulkeley, Mr. M. Stephens (Inky), Squire P.D. Williams, Dr. Spry and Mr. Cyril Calvert dug into their pockets to help once more. One cryptic comment in the minutes was, 'The letter received by the President from Sir Courtenay Vyvyan was read and left on the table as no one would agree to it.' Once more it is fairly certain that the whole village knew the content of the letter regardless of the fact that it was the concern of the committee but posterity will probably never find out the reason for the reply being so pointedly ignored. However, leaving no possibility unexplored, the officials of the British Legion approached Mr. W.T. Lamb with a view to purchasing his newly acquired former Coast Guard Watch House as an alternative Club Room. This idea was abandoned when Mr. Lamb said he wanted £500 for his property. The British Legion officials now knew they had done the right thing in deciding to work for a Hall on the Battery.

Fund raising now began in earnest in accordance with the agreement made between the two organisations. The story is a good example of a small community's commitment to working for the common good. Mrs. Woodcock, a music teacher, agreed to organise a concert to raise funds. Once more the Honorary Secretary of St. Peter's Hall was approached to see if the fund raisers could hire the hall at a reduced rate every fortnight during the winter months. At the first concert on the 9th. April, 1926, the cost of reserved seats was one shilling and the others cost sixpence. Fund raising continued, punctuated by occasional public meetings called to deliver 'pep' talks to the villagers when interest in the project was flagging. On one of these occasions Mr. Billy May was persuaded to have a notice board outside his shop, Jubilee Stores in order to improve publicity.

As more and more money came in it was decided that a Bank account should be opened and much discussion ensued regarding which three members were to be given the heavy responsibility of signing cheques. This entry in the minutes reflects conditions prevailing in Coverack at the time. Until this stage in their fund raising the money had evidently been kept safe by the Treasurer. There was little likelihood of anyone stealing public money from him. Indeed it was quite usual to leave doors unlocked in the village because theft of that nature was extremely rare, especially in winter when there were no strangers wandering about. Raising the necessary money took a long time. All the funds could not go towards the Hall building. If they were to make money out of entertainment and the sale of refreshments, equipment was needed. Five dozen cups and saucers, five dozen tea plates, one dozen bread and butter plates, two tea pots and three jugs were bought with the proceeds of one Whist Drive. In anticipation of being able to play billiards in the new club room, one set of billiard balls was purchased plus one 15½oz. plain ash cue. Mr. George Dally was appointed to look after the games equipment and he bought some spare tips. Young people living in the last decade of the 20th. century will find it difficult to comprehend the reason for recording such trivial details in a club minute book. Once more it must be remembered that money was scarce and that in addition to looking after their own interests the British Legion Members were trying to live up to the motto of their organisation: 'Service not self.' The spectre of unemployment was never far from the men of the village and the British Legion did what it could to help fellow ex service men and were always looking for ways of raising money in their clubs in order to have ready cash in their Benevolent Fund.

In 1925 one of the Members who tried to start a business when he was demobilised got into debt and the Fund allocated £3 to help and managed to get another £10 from the area council. The relief committee was prudent enough to ask for documentary proof before handing over the money. A local farmer found he could no longer continue working due to ill health caused by war service so the Branch, with the help of Mr. William Pengilly the Coverack born Secretary of the Camborne British Legion obtained a pension for the unfortunate farmer. The Benevolent Committee members were Messrs. J.C. Martin, G. Dally, R. Germain, whose son was killed in an air crash in 1926, Stafford Hart, W.J. Martin and J. Harvey. All of these men knew what it was like to be short of money, consequently they decided that three of the Members who were unemployed should have some money for Christmas, 1926 to help them enjoy what would otherwise have been a meagre festive season. There were, of course, some people who applied and were refused. Their names were also recorded in the minutes. In general the villagers did not apply personally, in fact most of them would not admit they were in need, but their neighbours knew of their plight and proposed relief for them. The names of those who were refused relief were in the main not village people, they were wanderers and tramps, known to the British Legion as 'wayfarers'. They lived off people's good nature. Some of these names were circulated by Headquarters periodically on a list of impostors. It warned kindly country folk not to give help to those who did not need it, thus depriving genuine luckless people.

One entry in the minutes records the necessity of providing a pair of boots for an ex service man in order that he could go to work. Although it is probably better that the state should look after such unfortunate people, it seems certain that the ex service men's peers dealt with their comrades in a more humane fashion than civil servants who were hide bound by rules and regulations made by people who could not possibly know what it is like to be in such straitened circumstances. Between the years 1914 and 1923 the Civil Service had doubled in numbers, just like the electorate. Even as late as 1935 the Women's Section of Coverack British Legion was given 10s 6d by the men's Branch as they had spent their own funds on making garments for unemployed ex-service men. Unemployment was still there. A minute recorded a suggestion that the committee of the Fishermen's Rest be approached with a view to combining forces and buying a full sized billiard table to be housed in a new room to be built beneath the British Legion ante room (where the committee and youth club rooms are in the redesigned building). Not only were the games of billiards and snooker becoming more popular, more and more men were finding they had time on their hands because of unemployment. This phenomenon became familiar again in the 1980s.

The year 1926 saw the beginning of the final 'assault' on the Village Hall project. Colonel Bulkeley's loan of

£300 at 4% was accepted by the guarantors who stipulated it was to be used only for the building. The Colonel was made President, his daughter Miss Ruby was Treasurer to the guarantors and Mr. John Harvey the new Headmaster of Coverack Council School was the Secretary and British Legion representative. Tenders were invited and excavations began on the 'Battery'. The foundations were dug by the villagers in their spare time, then the professional builders, led by Mr. Tom Coad Roskilly and Mr. Stafford Hart took over - some of them had been digging the foundations, anyway. The Hall was completed for the sum of £300. Materials for the foundations, the cost of skilled labour, one hundred wooden chairs, a piano, oil lamps and wooden stage tables were all purchased with money raised by concerts, Whist Drives and public subscriptions.

In August, 1928 the Hall was declared open by the President's wife, Mrs. Bulkeley. She was accompanied by Sir Courtenay Vyvyan (any previous difference of opinion with the committee having been resolved!), Sir Antony Hawke, Sir William Jones, an industrialist who had settled in Coverack at Penmarth, Dr. Daunt, Mr. Frost, and Mr. G.N. Dickinson. These V.I.P.s had all made substantial gifts to the Hall funds. The opening itself was a fund raising event. Villagers attended the first Coverack Fair in the Hall and much money was raised from the raffles, lucky dips, bric a brac stalls and the jumble. In 1930 an Easter Fair was opened by Mrs. Spry, the wife of the highly respected doctor from St. Keverne. At that stage there was still two thirds of the loan to be repaid. Jerry Baker's Savona Orchestra from Penzance was hired to entertain buyers who were served by stallholders in fancy dress. The writer was dressed as a green gnome and tended the bran tub with his cousin who was a black spider! The fund raising went on into the evening when the Savona Orchestra played for a Grand Dance. The Penzance based musicians were perched on the tiny wooden stage tables at one end of the hall which was packed with villagers eager to show their dancing skills to the elderly non dancers who sat on the hard wooden chairs lining the perimeter of the hall. Some young people from neighbouring villages turned up and entered the dancing competitions. Fortunately Mr. Sam Roskilly from the Post Office and his partner, Miss Frances Woodcock the Music Teacher's daughter won the Spot Dance Competition so in spite of some prizes going to strangers, village honour remained intact.

Jerry Baker was still the favourite band leader of the Coverack dancers in 1936. The dances at which he played were always profitable affairs in spite of complaints from the Wesleyan Chapel Trustees whenever he went on playing after midnight on Saturdays. The popularity of Whist Drives did not wane. The minutes reveal that prizes had become more attractive. Geese, chicken, rabbits and large boxes of chocolates were being offered as prizes in the 1930s. In 1936 the St. Keverne Branch of the British Legion was in danger of disbanding so the Coverack Branch invited those who wished to continue to support the organisation to join the Coverack Branch. After 1954 the compliment was returned. Coverack Branch had lost most of its supporters and St. Keverne men invited the faithful Coverack stalwarts to join them. In 1936, however, the strength of the Coverack Branch can be measured by the fact that a 32 seater 'bus was hired to take the men and women to Truro on the occasion of the visit of the new King George VI to the City. The Honorary Secretary was commissioned to produce a card measuring 18" x 12" bearing the name 'Coverack' in 3" letters to let the King know he had loyal subjects in the Cornish Oasis marching past him.

Signs of gathering war clouds were indicated at a special meeting called by the Honorary Secretary, Mr. Harry Snell on October 1s., 1938. The purpose of the meeting was twofold: firstly to discuss the British Legion National Secretary's appeal for volunteers to go to Czechoslovakia on police duties - the Munich Agreement had been signed two days earlier - and secondly to receive details of the Kerrier District Council's plans for Air Raid Precaution personnel. The Committee decided to defer action on both matters until the annual meeting the following week. Captain Roddick and Miss Grace Sturmer, who had been a nurse in Salonika during the First World War and consequently was qualified to be a member of the men's Branch, both moved that in view of the poor attendance, the Secretary should write to all Members urging them to come to the A.G.M., reminding them that if their apathy continued the Branch would have to close. The minutes were signed by the Secretary, Mr. H.S. Snell who became C.O. of the Coverack Home Guard a couple of years later. The Chairman, Mr. Murland Hunter countersigned the minutes. He was a Reserve Squadron Leader in the R.A.F. Balloon Barrage Service and was called up in January of 1939.

Meetings continued until November 3rd., 1939 when two items were discussed. One was the arrangements for the next Whist Drive, which was to be held in the Headland Hotel by kind permission of Mrs. Coombe. The other item was the organisation of the sale of poppies. The next entry was on the 28th. September, 1945. Captain Roddick was once more in the Chair and he announced that the main purpose of the meeting was to get going again, if only out of consideration for the young fellows who would soon be returning to civilian life. The wheel had turned full circle. Mindful of what had happened after the First World War, a Benevolent Committee was formed. Regrettably, as previously stated, the Branch went out of existence some nine years later, but the sale of poppies continued to be organised by Mr. Alex Symes, the son of one of the founder members of the Branch. The same man was one of the principal fundraisers for the Lambeage Hall until his untimely death in 1989.

The Lambeage Hall as it is now known proved to be a blessing during the years of the Second World War. It was used as a classroom for evacuees during the day and as a Y.M.C.A. for use by the Army, R.A.F. and W.R.N.S. personnel who were stationed in the village to man and guard the local Radar stations. In common with many other buildings in Coverack the Hall did not escape the consequences of enemy action. The roof was damaged by shrapnel and on one occasion the blackouts blown in with the windows.

Finally, in 1946 Dr. O.W. Bateman was able to declare that all debts of the Hall had been paid and that the liability of the long serving guarantors would cease forthwith. The Doctor-Chairman then handed a Credit balance of £137 13s 6d to Mr. W.J. Martin, the Chairman of the Battery Trustees. Dr. Bateman paid tribute to the Honorary Treasurer of the Hall and to the Secretary, Mrs.E.M. Hart and thanked them for their many years of service on behalf of the village.

At the time of writing, some forty years afterwards, the Hall continues to function. Great strides forward have been made under the direction of the talented Chairman, Mr. Derek Atherton, the long-serving landlord of the Paris Hotel. Whist has given way to Bingo as a money spinner. The Coverack Singers arrange regular concerts throughout the summer season to raise funds for the Hall and to give tourists an opportunity of being part of an enjoyable village activity. Otherwise unemployed men have learned new skills by modernising the building. The alterations were subsidised with funds from the Manpower Services Commission. The original Hall still stands but is much extended and has a more robust exterior in keeping with modern standards. The villagers have been joined by newly arrived settlers and the new Committee is introducing ideas which are designed to ensure continuity in village affairs. The local Youth Club has a room in the Hall and the young people are encouraged to help raise funds for the building which one day will be their responsibility. The big question is: Will the young people be able to afford to live in the village if they get employment locally?

AN EARLY AERIAL VIEW OF COVERACK circa 1930

*The newly built Village Hall can be seen above Battery Beach,
to the left of the Watch House on Dolor Point (right foreground).
The Mill area is clearly seen with a long bank of seaweed on the
beach.
North Corner, to the right of Higher Bridge Hill, which leads to
the top left of the photo, has few houses in comparison with the
village of 1990.*

# THE 1920s AND 1930s

We have already seen that in common with the rest of Great Britain the people of Coverack wanted to return to the way of life they were used to leading before the war. Of course, in return for the sacrifices they had made they wanted what we are now pleased to call an improved 'quality of life.'

The peacemaking went on for four years. During that time skirmishes continued. There were problems for Britain in Palestine, India and Ireland. Revenge was in the air. The Treaty of Versailles saw to it that the Germans were crushed. This harsh treatment in turn sowed the seeds of vengeance which were to erupt into a second world war two decades later. Apart from the two post war Prime Ministers, David Lloyd George and Bonar Law, these two decades were controlled by two Prime Ministers who alternated in office. Ramsay MacDonald was the dominant man in the 1920s and Stanley Baldwin was more influential in the 1930s up to 1937 when Neville Chamberlain took over.

Some Coverack men were kept on in the Royal Navy after the war as they were needed to man ships which were sent to the various trouble spots. One Coverack man became involved in a rescue mission which was one of the last 'gun boat' diplomacy operations carried out by the British Empire. Since 1917 the Russian Revolution had kept English forces deployed as a gesture of solidarity with an ally. Eventually the British garrisons at Murmansk and Archangel were withdrawn when it became clear that the Red Russians were going to take control. The anti democratic régime was detested by Great Britain and strongly disapproved of by King George V in spite of the fact that Russian Tsar Nicholas II was his cousin, as indeed was German Kaiser Wilhelm II. King George V knew that if Russia withdrew from the war, Germany would then be able to concentrate a vast army against the allies on the western front but in the end events took over. The Tsar and his family were butchered by the revolutionaries in March, 1919. Soon afterwards it was decided to send a naval force into the Black Sea to rescue the ageing Dowager Empress and the Russian Grand Duke Nikolia Nicolaevich who had been the Russian Commander in Chief fighting the Germans and Austro Hungarians in the first year of the war. Able Seaman Charlie Hart from Coverack was on the destroyer Tomahawk which entered the Dardanelles under fire from the Turks. The destroyer did not return the fire and escaped damage by putting up a smokescreen. A company of Royal Marines went ashore from H.M.S. Marlborough which the Tomahawk was escorting and managed to take off the royal refugees who were eventually landed in Malta. The Dowager Empress Marie Fedorovna came to Britain and spent her time with her sister, Queen Alexandra, the widow of King Edward VII in Sandringham and Marlborough House. In 1923 the Dowager Empress returned to her native Denmark and lived on a pension provided by her nephew, King George V of Great Britain. The Grand Duke went to live in Antibes in southern France until his death in 1929. In relating this incident many years later, Charlie told the writer that the most sinister episode of the action was when the Tomahawk anchored close to Turkish occupied Armenia. On shore was a row of tripods. On inspecting them through a telescope it was seen that a body was hanging from the apex of each tripod-gallows. It was a sobering sight the 19 year old Coverack man was to remember all his days.

Back in Coverack, in common with the rest of the country, prices went up. As always, better wages followed too late to cover the increased prices but at least the 1920-22 Unemployment Acts were amended to include the dole. Men were given an increase of 3 shillings to make their pay up to 18 shillings. Women had the same amount extra, increasing the allowance to 12 shillings a week. The children's allowance was doubled from 1 shilling to 2 shillings a week.

The chapter on the British Legion explained how the ex-service men coped with the return to civilian life. Those who wanted a change of occupation started thinking about jobs which were in keeping with the scientific progress being made in agriculture, fishing and transport. It was evident that the internal combustion engine had come to stay. On the 17th. August, 1903, the Great Western Railway company had begun an experimental Road Motor Service to the Lizard from Helston Station, which according to Helston born local historian A.S. Oates,'........clanked, snorted and smeeched' out to the Lizard. Nevertheless in spite of the fact that in theory the open sided Milnes Daimler Wagonettes should have been preceded by a man with a red flag, the buses were popular and people gladly paid 1s 6d for a ride to Helston from the Lizard. After all, it was the first Great Western Railway bus service and the vehicles did get up a speed of 14 miles per hour on the flat! The buses or Wagonettes as they were called had 20 seats in them, ran on solid tyres and used petrol which cost 4d a gallon. By 1919 Kelly's Directory reported that '........several motor omnibuses were being run daily by the Great Western Railway Company, times varying according to season.' Clearly the days of the locally built blue, green and red horse buses were numbered. No longer would Coverack people see coaches '........packed like pilchards in a barrel, swimming outside like flies on a preserve pan.'

Joe Hart, the above-mentioned Charlie's brother, was one of the ex-servicemen looking for a way of making a living after the war. He was a career sailor and had served under Coverack's Captain Gibson. He had married May Roberts the daughter of Mr. James Roberts who owned and drove the horse bus which travelled between Coverack and Helston. During the war. H.M.S. Osmanieh, the ship on which Joe was serving as Second Officer, was torpedoed on her way to Alexandria from the Dardanelles. After spending fifteen hours in the water Joe was picked up and taken to Italy where he spent two months in hospital recovering from a wound in the leg. He was awarded a Mention in Despatches on the 14th. September, 1917. It was not surprising that when the war was over Joe decided to take a break from the sea. He went into business with his father in law. He bought a chain driven, solid tyred Wolseley because the road down the hill to Coverack was very uneven and it was doubtful if the Royal could climb the hill with a load of passengers. The other horse bus was kept in Van House Lane which is on the right hand side when going up Higher Bridge Hill. It lies between the house known as Thornhill and Boundertreath bungalow estate. The horse bus terminus was so situated in order to avoid having to pull a loaded bus up the steepest section of the hill. Coverack now had two forms of motor transport - Mr. George Harvey's Model T taxi service from the Headland Hotel and the Royal. Later on Joe Hart drove a Model T

Ford and a Rover for Mr. Harry (Jan) Tripp. The Rover was beset with mechanical problems and proved a heavy drain on profits.

It was not long before the Great Western Railway Company decided to open up the route to St. Keverne, Coverack and Porthallow. Joe did not have the resources to compete with the G.W.R. and began to look for another way to earn a living. At first the G.W.R. buses only ran two days a week, starting from St. Keverne on Mondays at 9 a.m., leaving Helston on the return journey at 4 p.m. On Saturdays the bus left St. Keverne at 1 p.m. (most people worked until noon on Saturdays) and the return journey commenced at 7 p.m., giving the beer drinking men passengers an opportunity for a quick pint before leaving and the ladies an opportunity to do some late night shopping. As there was no daily service, the village children who had won scholarships to Helston County Secondary School had to find lodgings in Helston. This added greatly to the expenses of the parents of the secondary school children. The daily bus service began in 1926. Meanwhile, in 1921, after much agitation, a bus shelter was placed at the bottom of Higher Bridge Hill. It was erected at the expense of Judge Francis Roxburgh, a frequent and much loved visitor to Coverack.

G. W. R. COVERACK MOTOR HALT, 1921
*This photograph shows the opening ceremony of the Bus Shelter.*

The photograph of the opening ceremony of the bus shelter shows the hut with the name 'G.W.R. COVERACK MOTOR HALT' painted in bold letters on a board across the top of the hut. There are twelve well heeled local dignitaries lined up in front of the shelter, all beaming broadly. Among them is a bearded Judge Roxburgh and Mr. George Harvey the proprietor of the Headland Hotel and the Model T taxi. Mr. Harvey is wearing his favourite plus fours and standing patriotically beneath a large Union Flag which is hanging from a temporary flag pole. A uniformed employee of the G.W.R. is standing apart, on the left of the V.I.P.s By the expression on his face it is evident that he heartily approves of the bus shelter for the villagers. A brass commemorative plaque was screwed to the back of the interior of the shelter. This was stolen some 40 years after the bus shelter was erected. One suspects it adorns a private wall somewhere in Coverack or perhaps in a visitor's house far away from the village. The villagers who love Coverack are optimists and live in hope that one day the plaque will be screwed back on the wall of the shelter for future generations to admire.

Regular travellers have found the shelter useful for over 60 years, not only when waiting to go to Helston but also on their return. When there is an easterly gale in Coverack the seas come up over the Mill road, which is why the villagers who live there have wooden shutters for their windows. Sometimes travellers have to wait for the tide to ebb a little before they can cross the Mill road to their homes in the village. When the storms were particularly bad, Mr. Percy Roberts' coal lorry would be waiting to take people across the Mill road. This meant that the travellers could get home without having to make a long detour through the fields. This was the sort of neighbourly act which was taken for granted in the 1920s and 1930s. Many Coverack mothers were grateful for the safe transport of their children returning from school in an easterly gale. Of course when the seas broke over the road the children loved the thrill of racing across before being drenched by a wave but the adult villagers knew the foolhardy youngsters could easily be sucked into the sea as the water receded from the road and they were always relieved when the children were told to get on the lorry instead. The children still had the thrill of trying to avoid a soaking but they were safe in the lorry.

The increasing use of motor transport in the 1920s created a demand for a garage in Coverack. The Mill at Coverack has already been mentioned. It was quite unique in that the single stream from Polcoverack worked three wheels which were controlled by sluice gates below the upper and middle mill ponds. Mr. Richard (Dickie) Roberts, who also farmed Treleaver had already put off the evil day of closure by the diversification of his business. He was a corn and flour merchant, of course. In addition he had a coal business and did haulage work as well as running his own farm. He was the last miller in Coverack.

Mr. Percy Roberts found the time was ripe in 1922 to establish a garage and haulage business. The spacious Mill complex was an ideal site. Firstly he bought the Lower Mill and took over the coal merchant's enterprise. By a curious twist of fate a collier ketch named the Heatherbell was wrecked in Coverack in the same year as the garage opened. The story has already been told in the chapter on the Quay. The Heatherbell's destruction at the bottom of the cliff between the old Post Office and the house known as Greystones in Coverack marked the end of an era. The Constance Melanie was not needed when the Heatherbell was wrecked as the fishermen were at hand and the crew had no trouble in getting ashore. The vessel had only travelled, or strictly speaking, been carried by the waves a couple of hundred yards from her mooring alongside the Quay. The transport by sea of coal, fertilisers, building materials and other heavy goods was over. The sailing colliers such as the Alpha, the Emma Louise, the Express, the Hero and the Trio which had been calling at Coverack for generations had to find other small ports in which to ply their trade. A few continued to come to the village for a while and occasionally one or two small steam coasters managed to get alongside the Quay and discharge their cargoes. However, a regular service of bringing coal to Helston by rail was already established and safer seaborne deliveries at Gweek combined to put an end to the visits of colliers to Coverack. This meant that Mr. Percy Roberts was able to develop his coal round by collecting coal from from Helston and Gweek and was able to employ his nephew, David Mason as a driver-mechanic when the latter changed from his original occupation of farming. The additional use of the lorry as a mobile platform for the Coastguard Life Saving Apparatus has already been described.

Mr. Roberts did much of the mechanical work of the garage himself. He had been trained by Bickles of Plymouth. He also taught local men the trade. It was impossible in those days for Coverack people to travel to town to get apprenticeship training. One of the first alterations which had to be made to the old mill was the demolishing of the raised floor which had been built to facilitate the easy loading of sacks of flour. In addition to David Mason, another early garage stalwart was Rooke Roberts, a man of many parts. He came from the Trevothen farming family. He had the happy knack of being able to 'turn his hand' to anything. He was gardener, farmer, mechanic, driver, village postman in turn. In his spare time he was bandsman, Auxiliary Coastguard, fisherman, and Parish councillor. Needless to say he was what urban visitors to the village called a 'character'. Indeed he spoke as he acted, slowly and deliberately and resisted change in all its forms. The writer's mother had occasion to translate Rooke's diagnosis of a fault in a car engine one day. Some visitors who were staying at our house took their car to the garage to be repaired. The visitors returned to the house and admitted they were rather puzzled. They could not understand why Mr. Rooke Roberts had told them their car had to be taken out of the country for repair as it had been made in Britain. It transpired that Rooke had told them, 'I'll have to take 'n abroad before I know what's wrong with 'n.' They were quite relieved when it was explained to them that we Cornish do 'belong' to say 'abroad' when we mean 'apart'. In fact, the Oxford Dictionary gives 'widely apart' as one definition of 'abroad' so Rooke was right after all. He generally was.

ROOKE ROBERTS
*Gardener, farmer, mechanic, driver, village postman.*
*In his spare time, Bandsman, Auxiliary Coastguard,*
*Fisherman and Parish Councillor.*

The corn mill was not entirely redundant when the building underwent a change of use. The water power was harnessed to drive a wheel bought from Poltesco Farm in 1931 to work a dynamo which provided domestic lighting and power for the charging of car and wireless batteries. When electricity from the Cornwall Electric Power Company was brought to the village in 1937 and wireless sets became 'radios' which did not need accumulators, the mill power was no longer needed and fell into disuse. The garage and coal business continued for some forty years and was a boon to all local drivers. At the time of writing the various Mill buildings have been converted into dwelling houses and the garage has become a souvenir shop. All that remains of the Mill is its name, a part of a wheel - and the stream.

On the 29th. September, 1923 a 1,600 ton French vessel named Berville, from Rouen, was on passage from Cannes to Newport with a cargo of iron ore. The sea was calm but there was a thick fog. At about 4 p.m. the S.S. Berville ran ashore just to the north of the Guthens Rocks in Perprean Bay, Coverack. The Honorary Secretary of the Lifeboat wrote in his report, '........being particularly calm weather, myself and Coxswain did not think it necessary to launch the boat. Small boats from Coverack had gone out to render assistance. She was refloated and taken to Coverack Bay.' Captain Pierott of the Berville was then advised by the local men to remain where he was for the night. They added they would send out an agent to consult him. This is where the 'plot' thickens. Mr. Billy May, the local agent, asked two brothers, Archie and Dick Rowe to row him out to the Berville which could not be seen from the village owing to the thick fog. While the trio were on their way, the master of the Berville must have had second thoughts about making public the accidental grounding so he decided to weigh anchor and proceed. At 11.15 p.m. the villagers heard a loud bang which came from seawards. Fearing the worst, the Coxswain launched the Constance Melanie and searched the area. When the rowers reached a position about half a mile off the Guthens they saw the Berville. The Coxswain hailed her and asked if she required assistance. The Captain then asked the lifeboat to come alongside. It transpired that while the Berville was creeping out of Coverack Bay she was struck on the starboard bow by a Finnish steamer, the Ugo Bassi which was making her way to Falmouth. This second calamity unnerved Captain Pierott so he asked Mr. John Corin if the Constance Melanie could accompany him to Falmouth. The Coxswain agreed and put the Bowman, Mr. James Stevens aboard to act as Pilot. The two vessels then made their way slowly to Falmouth. They arrived in port, to quote the Honorary Secretary, '........after a very trying time, the fog being so dense.' The Constance Melanie then had a long row back to Coverack, where she arrived at 11.30 a.m. the following day. Needless to say the two boys never found the elusive Berville. After a long while searching for their quarry in dense fog they eventually found their way back to Coverack and deposited a very frustrated agent back on dry land. Apart from rendering assistance to the steam trawler Audrey of Yarmouth off the Manacle Rocks on November 16th., 1925, it was to be five years before the Constance Melanie was launched on service again.

In 1924 a group of village children went with their teachers, Mr. Littlejohn and Miss Cliff to the British Empire Exhibition at Wembley. It was the first time that many of them had crossed the Tamar but their parents thought the financial sacrifice worthwhile. The children were not only taken to the Exhibition and Fun Fair but also went on sight seeing tours during the week they were there. The visited the Houses of Parliament and Westminster Abbey and were fêted by the London Cornish Association. Each child was given a London Cornish badge to commemorate the occasion and made an Honorary Member of that prestigious company of exiles. These badges are to be seen in Coverack. They are sometimes placed on mantelpieces and in glass fronted china cupboards beside other treasured mementoes of the Exhibition. The latter are easily recognised by the Exhibition logo which is an Imperial Lion above the caption, 'Wembley, 1924.'

Meanwhile, life continued in Coverack. Of course, money was always scarce. The fishermen worked at all kinds of jobs to subsidise their meagre incomes. In winter, mending nets, barking and tarring, general maintenance of boats, sails and engines were very necessary occupations as was the painting of boats and making of crab pots with the new withies but these activities brought no money into the family coffers, indeed they cost money which had been saved from the previous season's work. This meant that the fishermen had to supplement their incomes, by going to sea in winter on cargo ships, doing casual labouring for builders and farmers, breaking stones for the County Council and any other jobs which needed doing. They were not entitled to dole money unless they had done enough casual labour to be entitled to it. Labourers digging a new well at the Headland Hotel for the Redruth Brewery Company in June and July, 1922 worked a 54 hour week for six weeks and received one shilling and one penny an hour for their labours. That came to £2 18s 6d per week less 1s 1d for insurance. The skilled masons got 1s 6d an hour for their particular job. We have seen in the section on Stones that in 1931, after the depression, when the cliff wall at the Mill was being repaired, labourers were paid 11d an hour and the skilled men 1s 4d an hour.

Life was not without excitement for the fishermen in spite of the long periods in between the 'call-outs' of the lifeboat. A weather eye was always kept open for shoals of fish that might be tempted to come close to Coverack. In 1927 a school of mullet was sighted. In spite of many separate attempts by Mr. Fred Carey, the most skilled huer in Coverack, to entice the mullet close inshore, the fish remained scattered beyond the reach of the fishermen. Mullet are 'ground' feeders and are attracted to flies, maggots and small crustaceans which are to be found close inshore in the seaweed. Mr. Carey used to disturb these creatures by 'patting' the weed with a paddle from his boat. The theory was that this would give the impression of waves breaking on the shore which would attract the mullet to come and feed off the small creatures which would be stirred up by the breaking waves. This often was sufficient to attract a passing shoal of fish to come on and be surrounded by a net. The mullet on this occasion ignored the supposed presence of their feed and continued to mill about off shore. At last they began forming up and looked as if they were about to come closer but time had passed, it was now about three weeks after the first sighting and the fishermen had lost interest to a certain extent. They were not prepared for an immediate launch. One person in Coverack had not got tired of waiting for the mullet. He was a Cadgwith man. When he saw there was a likelihood of the fish forming up to come shorewards, he telephoned to his mates and they launched their boats already loaded with nets and made for Coverack Bay. Someone saw the 'spy' and realising what was happening, told the local fishermen. There was no time to get the nets ready so the Coverack men did a quick launch and went towards the fish. The Cadgwith men were coming up fast but the Coverack men got to the mullet first and scattered them by throwing stones and beating the water, thus preventing their rivals from surrounding the mullet, which after all were in Coverack territory.

The above somewhat spiteful episode, which was related to the writer by Mr. Bert Martin of Coverack, soured relations between the two coves for some time. Even those who had close relations in the 'enemy' village stopped family visits until tempers had cooled and those involved had time to realise how petty they had been. This story does serve to illustrate, however, the fact that normally passive men were prepared to go to great lengths to protect their source of income. They knew, like Dickens' Mr. Micawber, that when annual expenditure exceeded annual income, the result was misery.

### THREE COVERACK MERCHANT NAVY MEN
*Coverack fishermen have always had to go to sea on Merchant Ships in winter,*
*returning to their boats in spring. L. - R. Dick Rowe, Leslie Cliff, Alex Symes.*

In that same year, 1927, Cornwall Education Committee, whose Chairman was Sir Arthur Quiller Couch of Fowey, produced an Education Week Handbook to commemorate the 25th. Anniversary of the Balfour Education Act which was described in the section on Twentieth Century Education. Mr. Howard Dunn of Mevagissey wrote in the chapter on the history of fishing in Cornwall, 'Men holding widely divergent views lived side by side in fishing villages with strong beer and smuggled spirits in plenty to bring them together, but with no constable to separate them. It is therefore easy for us to imagine that in those long standing quarrels 'regrettable incidents' were frequent.' Mr. Dunn went on to state that, 'Nowadays, fishing steamers and motor boats move steadily out and into harbour. They may not look so 'artistic' but they are safer, faster, more reliable and consequently raise the fisherman's standard of life.' The coves on the Lizard peninsula were still waiting to catch up with modern technology. Anne Treneer, writing on 'Cornishmen and the sea' in another chapter of the Handbook describes Coverack as one of the better known smuggling haunts and reminds readers that, 'Of those who have followed the sea, the fishers have had least glory and most toil.' Coverack and Cadgwith men would have agreed with that, even if they couldn't always agree with each other.

In spite of Mr. Dunn's comments, motor boats were rare in Coverack, which was not as prosperous as the fishing ports which could accommodate larger boats. Apart from the unsuccessful motor seiner, the first motor boat to work from Coverack Harbour was the Pioneer I. She was built by Mr. Joe Roberts for the Corin brothers. The Pioneer I was constructed in the loft over the Headland Hotel stables just after the end of the First World War. When she was ready for launching the gable end of the upper floor of the stables had to be removed so that the boat could be hauled out and taken down the hill on Mr. Roskilly's wagon. The Corin brothers, both lifeboat men, were justifiably proud of their motor boat and spent many loving hours cleaning the 6 horse power Kelvin engine and polishing its bright parts. The next motor boat to arrive in Coverack was a smaller one which belonged to Mr. Billy May the shopkeeper and Agent for shipping. The third was a much larger craft which belonged to Mr. 'Inky' Stephens who lived in the large house at North Corner called Rocklands. She had a powerful Thorneycroft engine in her. The boat was appropriately painted inky black and was looked after by Mr. Jim Stevens the fisherman and lifeboat man. At about this time Mr. Stephens had the stone steps built at the northern end of Mill Beach. This generous gift to the village has been a boon to bathers ever since.

Unemployment in Great Britain gradually reduced after the First World War until the General Strike, then it started to go up again. Circumstances in Coverack were peculiar to the village. When the slump in shipping came about, that put an end to a secondary means of employment and some men had to remain in the village without work instead of signing on for a ship in Falmouth. Tales came back to the village of seamen with Masters' 'tickets' sailing as Able Seamen. Some of the Coverack seamen and fishermen were glad to take work labouring on the farms or repairing the sea wall, as described in the chapter on Stones. Later on in the 1930s the 'Public Utilities' - water, drainage and electricity provided much needed work for local men. The village became a hazardous place to walk when the trenches were being dug for the pipes. Of course, boys being boys, contrived to fall in some of the trenches, usually grabbing two or three mates and pulling them down into the trench for company. It was no fun, however for the older people trying to negotiate the roads on a dark night when they had forgotten to bring a lantern or torch with them. When all was finished, the street lights had a brief moment of glory and were much appreciated and admired. All too soon they were extinguished for the duration of the war. The water mains were finally installed in 1937. In the same year electricity was brought to Coverack by the Cornwall Electric Power Company. Most of the work was done by the Company's skilled work force but some locals were taken on as temporary help.

It was a real joy to have water literally on tap in the houses instead of having to carry pails from the central tap which was situated at the bottom of the lane known to the villagers as 'The Gardens' which connects Chapel Hill or School Hill to the cove road. There were also chutes in Polcoverack Lane and at North Corner. They are still flowing at the time of writing. Drinking water had to be brought to the school at the top of the hill. It was a favourite chore for the 'big' boys who wanted to miss lessons. There are still one or two wooden yokes lying around in village sheds. These were used for carrying two pails at a time from the tap which brought fresh spring water from the field near Penmarth Farm. Some families carried their water in earthenware pitchers which ensured a really cool drink of water was always available in the house on a hot summer's day. Water for washing was usually obtained from the down pipes leading from the launders or gutters on the roofs of houses. At times some people drank this water which was reasonably pure due to the lack of air pollution in Coverack. Some hotels and other large houses had their own wells which were supplied by springs found by local dowsers or water diviners. The communal tap water system had been working in Coverack since 1880 and many people continued to use that water for drinking purposes, not trusting the filtered water from the newly installed mains. In the fulness of time after much media publicity the communal tap at the bottom end of 'The Gardens' was removed some thirty years after the mains water was provided for the village. Even then, in defiance of scientific evidence, villagers went on record as saying that the original spring water was more pure than the mains water.

When running water became available in the village homes, an added bonus was the installation of water closets. Until they were installed, each house had a little shed at the far end of the garden or down under the cliff if the house happened to be close to the sea. In these 'privies' were buckets housed in small wooden cupboards which had a hole over the buckets. The buckets held all the family night-soil or excrement. When nearly full, the contents were put in the 'stink' cart, or 'chocolate' cart, or 'gravy' cart, or what ever euphemism the family used for the wagon which collected their excrement. If the cart did not come the contents were buried in a deep pit in the garden or thrown over the cliff when the tide was high. This practice led to the use of the phrase, 'bucket and chuck it.' All heads of families were much relieved when the chore of disposing of the night-soil was abandoned. So were some of the village boys who were pressed into service when there was no father available or who had to do it as a punishment for bad behaviour. It was not really amusing to have to pay a visit to the privy in the garden or on the cliff edge when it was dark and raining. One wonders how much sympathy some villagers have for the prisoners in our antiquated gaols who have to 'slop out' each morning, for the older villagers remember having to do it as a matter of routine. One of the 'perks' of these outdoor lavatories was that they were a good place to go for a good read in private. Most households used up their old newspapers and catalogues for toilet paper, so there was always some interesting topic to ponder over while in residence.

The installation of electricity was treated with caution by some of the villagers. Tales of shocks and even electrocutions put many off at first. The Cornwall Electric Power Company gave three free electric light points, complete with glass shades as an inducement to have power laid on. Many householders simply accepted the free installation and patiently waited to see if it would be worth while having any supplementary wiring done. It is interesting to note that at about the same time as electricity was brought to Coverack the mains were connected to Lizard Lighthouse, which had started generating its own electricity as early as 1878. This was produced from power obtained from three coke-fired atmospheric engines. The new connection to the mains meant that the fog horns at the Lizard could be worked by electricity instead of compressed air.

In due course, most Coverack houses had lights in every room. 'Slabs' or Cornish coal burning ranges were taken out and replaced by cosy grates. Electric cookers were installed and the coal blackened saucepans replaced by shining flat bottomed aluminium utensils. In a few short years the villagers were being asked to hand over their nearly new cooking pots for recycling into Spitfires and other war machines. Human nature being what it is, some of the lovely saucepans which had been willingly sacrificed by patriotic villagers were surreptitiously taken off the pile awaiting collection at Higher Bridge and placed in homes by householders who had not got round to replacing their old style pots and pans for new ones. This prompted subsequent donors to the war effort to drill large holes through the bottoms of their aluminium pans before placing them on the patriotic pile of expensive scrap. The scrap metal people could not find a use for the cumbersome box irons which had been replaced by electrically operated ones so the heavy irons were put away to reappear a few years later as door stops and items in mini antique displays.

During the two decades between the wars, Coverack gradually emerged from the nineteenth century conditions which had lasted to a great extent until the First World War. After the conflict a garage business began. Motor buses began operating. In 1928 a second delivery of letters was started during the summer season for the convenience of visitors to the village. Five years later in 1933 Ponsongath was provided with its own letter box, thus saving the inhabitants of the surrounding farms a walk to Penhallick to post a letter. In truth, the country Postman, Mr. Joe Martin was always willing to take letters from Ponsongath people to be posted at Coverack. Water and electricity were laid on. A bakery was set up in the village. In 1932 Mrs. Bessie Mason's house, Beach Cottage at the Mill caught fire and was virtually burnt out. When the shell of the house was put up for sale, Mr. Daw who was a returned Cornish emigrant from Detroit bought the property and came to Coverack to live. He set up a bakery with a Dumbrill steam oven from Croydon and eventually had two local men working for him, Edgar Trewin and Charles Dennis. This bakery was a boon for the northern part of the Lizard peninsula. Two vans were used to deliver bread to St. Keverne, Porthoustock and Porthallow and Gillan. Of course, in time, the convenience of a local bakery put an end to much home baking. The people who continued to make their own bread and splits were in the main those who wished to maintain the 'home made' claim to attract discerning visitors. Mr. and Mrs. Daw had two young sons, Frank and Graham who eventually worked in the bakery which continued to function until 1964. Frank, who was a lifeboat crew man for over 20 years then went to work for the M.O.D. at Culdrose Air Station while Graham and his wife Brenda continued the grocery side of the business on the same site as the baker's shop, which used to be Mr. Willie Mundy's shoemaker's shop. The former bakery has reverted to a private house but the history of the village is remembered in the name of Mr. and Mrs. Frank Daw's residence in Polcoverack Lane which is called 'Bakery Cottage'.

Mr. Edward Daw the baker originated from the Lizard. He served in the Essex Regiment in France and Mesopotamia during the First World War and was wounded. On return to civilian life he emigrated to the United States but after working for some time in the mining area near Detroit he returned in 1929 as there was no further work because of the depression.

At about the same time as Mr. Daw went to the States, Joe Hart, the first Coverack Motor Bus driver decided he would try his luck abroad. He had been working with his father in law Mr. James Roberts the Horse Bus proprietor and with Mr. Joe Blatchford from Helston. Apparently Joe Hart concluded that Canada or New Zealand were the most attractive countries for emigration. He could not decide which was the better so he tossed a coin and New Zealand won. He went out ahead of his small family and obtained a job as a mate on a ship for a while. When his wife May and their two children, Arthur and Kit joined him he came ashore and worked at various jobs in 'windy' Wellington before finally settling in Huntly. In 1923 256,000 people emigrated from Great Britain but by 1930 the annual number had decreased to 92,000. It must also be remembered that at that time many emigrants like Mr. Daw the baker were returning due to the scarcity of employment overseas. At the same time, people from Cornwall, the rest of the 'Celtic fringe' and the North of England were moving towards the Home Counties in search of a better life.

Some emigrants from Coverack left the village never to return. One or two disappeared without trace, others kept silent about their life overseas until something happened to induce them to re-establish contact with the old country. Alfred Pengilly, a nephew of John Pengilly the Coverack fisherman went to Charters Towers in Queensland, Australia early in the twentieth century. In 1906, Alfred sent his uncle a New Year's greetings card in the form of a photo of himself, his wife Bessie and their three children. Regrettably the accompanying letter has disappeared but the photo reveals a prosperous looking young man and his family who appear to have settled happily in their adopted country.

Another member of the Pengilly family, James, the brother of the above mentioned John wrote to his sister in law in November, 1924 from Arcadia, California. James was then 83 and wanted news of the family. He began by asking, 'How did you get on in the war?' - which had ended six years earlier - then he went on to ask about Sandy Pengilly whose war service was described in the chapter on the Great War. James said he had moved to California to live with his two daughters, Alice and Ann, because of his health. The town of Arcadia was well named as he went on to describe a pastoral paradise where there were flowers and green vegetables all through the winter. There was a Rose Festival every New Year's Day and the main orange crop was harvested in January. His son Joe worked in Los Angeles and was a partner in an electrical manufacturer's business. His eldest son John worked as a master mechanic for a lumber company in Oregon and the youngest son Richard had a farm and garage at Brooklyn Centre, Minneapolis. His other two daughters were both married to farmers, Sarah living in Wisconsin and Mary in Minnesota. After saying that his wife had died in 1916 he went on to ask, 'Has Coverack improved any? Have many houses been put up?'

In his next letter, James said how pleased he was to receive news of the family in Coverack and to receive papers and pictures. He continued his description of Arcadia, once again waxing eloquent about the fruit and flowers. He also described a local vineyard of 35,000 acres. In addition there were 'chicken ranches' of up to 3,000 hens. They housed mainly White Leghorns and were 'paying a dollar and a half a hen a year'. The following year in 1925 James died on the 25th. May which was his 84th. birthday. His daughter, Alice, sent the news of his death to Coverack. She included some recent 'Kodak Pictures' of the American family. Alice sympathised with the high cost of living in Cornwall and said they had similar problems. She quoted seedless grapes at 5 cents a pound, 3 pounds of raisins for a quarter - which would also buy 6lbs of potatoes. Grapefruit were 2 cents each. She added that her own hens produced enough eggs for the family and left some over for sale. Alice concluded that she did not think she would ever make it to England but that she wanted to keep up the correspondence. As an afterthought she revealed that her brother Joe was in the army during the First World War and was in London 'a while'. She went on, 'When he had a little spare time he went over to Cornwall to take a look at it. He brought father a pin for a souvenir.' What a pity Joe did not come to Coverack. He would have had a wonderful welcome. It is clear that this particular exercise in emigration from Coverack was a success and that the Cornish exiles were well and truly settled, just like the Roskillys and Rules in the nineteenth century.

In April, 1990, two American Pengillys turned up in Coverack in search of information about their forebears.

They were Michael Pengilly and his married sister Ellen Pengilly Patrick. They were armed with a birth certificate of their great great grandfather and the writer was able to inform them that their great great grandfather called Henry Pengilly was born in Breage and that he was farming Content in Coverack in the year 1851. He was married to Susan, nee Thomas whose brother Henry and sister Alice were living with her and her husband at Content. At the time of writing it remains to be seen which of the Pengilly families in the St. Keverne area are related to the New York Pengillys. Like Joe Pengilly mentioned in the preceding paragraph, Michael Pengilly is serving in the United States Army in Europe. It would be interesting to plot the position of all the emigrants from Coverack on a map of the world and compare it with one which plots the migration of other Cornish people.

It should not be assumed that fishing, boating and tourism were the main sources of income in Coverack in the 1920s and 1930s. Reference has already been made to the importance of farming and market gardening. They are complementary to the other sources of income. Indeed, many of the village people found they had to work in all these industries in order to make a living.

We know that until the advent of the internal combustion engine most of the heavy farm work was done by horses and steam engines. During the First World War horses and fodder were taken from all over Great Britain for use in France. Horses continued to be used on local farms up to and beyond the Second World War. Early tractors were not efficient for ploughing steeply sloping fields and an overriding factor was that horses were cheaper to 'run'. Local farms were not large - a 100 acre farm was considered a big one, so at first tractors were thought of as luxuries. Even now some farms share tractors and combines in the same way that they used to share traction engines. There are still some steep rocky fields where harvesting is done with horse power and a man using a scythe in the difficult corners, so the old crafts are being kept alive and are still demonstrated at annual agricultural shows. Farmers treated their horses with much respect. They were well fed and well groomed. They wore smart harnesses and brasses. Of course, these animals were a source of attraction to all children visiting farms. A ride on a cart horse down to the farm yard pool for a drink at the end of the day was a much sought after privilege. If the horses were working close to the Mill Beach in Coverack, the farmer would sometimes take them down for a quick dip in the sea. The obvious pleasure the horses experienced in cooling their hooves and washing their legs communicated itself to any small children who happened to be in the sea at the time. The horses adored being patted by small hands, even if they did not get any titbits from them.

For the really heavy work on farms, steam power was used. Traction engines were brought around the farms for baling hay and binding. Mr. Jack Andrew from Content Farm had an engine which did most of the threshing or 'thrashing' as it is called locally. Another engine seen frequently in the Coverack area was driven by Mr. Ted Jennings. The machine was named Maudie and seemed tireless as long as she was well stoked with coal. Maudie always attracted a small crowd of children who marvelled at the way in which the work was done against the background of a quiet hiss of steam, the 'slap' of the driving belts and the sweet clockwork-like sound of the moving parts. Every time the whistle rope was pulled to announce 'crowst' (snack time) or to call the attention of the farmer to a job that needed doing, the children would shriek in mock fright as the piercing sound always came as a surprise. In between times these iron 'monsters' were used for moving heavy loads such as farm machinery and even large boats. They also were employed in sawing and moving large trees, crushing stone and other jobs which were beyond the capacity of cart horses.

THRESHING AT TRELEAVER, circa 1930
*Mr. Bert Ivey is seen examining the crop.*

Trips to market from Coverack have already been discussed. Butter and cream were made on most farms and marketed locally. Each farm had a shady dairy with slate slabs for keeping the products cool. When making cream the milk was sometimes passed through a separator first or left to stand so that the cream would come to the top then it was separated. The large flat bottomed pans were slowly heated for hours on end. Sometimes farmers' wives placed the cream pan in an even larger one containing water which acted as a bain-marie. The resultant clotted cream topped by a golden crust was a beautiful sight. Coverack children used to be asked the riddle:

'What is black without, white within

Covered all over with yellow skin?'

The answer was, of couse:

A pan of milk with clotted cream on top.'

When the writer was sent on his bicycle to Penhallick Farm to collect cream for his mother's visitors, he was sometimes allowed to lick the spoon when the cream dishes had been filled. That was considered sufficient payment for an errand which took him away from the Quay or the beach on a hot summer's afternoon. Some of the skimmed milk remaining after cream was made was sold at a lower price to people who were prepared to come to the farm for it. This was advantageous for poor families. The rest was fed to the pigs and calves. Skimmed milk was a favourite thirst quenching drink in summer. It is currently gaining popularity again in today's affluent weight watching society. What we would call full cream milk was made into butter and marketed by delivering it in the village or sending it to the factory by lorry. In the 1920s and 1930s there was no bottling of milk for doorstep delivery in Coverack. The milk was poured into large churns and taken round the village in a milk cart or trap pulled by a pony. The farmer delivered the milk to the door in a small can and poured the amount from a pint or half pint measure into the householder's jug. The farmer sold butter and eggs as well. He was usually accompanied by a dog or two. The dogs always knew which houses would be likely to have titbits available and begged for food when the lady came to the door. In the same way the horse knew where the customers were and stopped outside the correct doors without being told by the farmer. The principal dairymen were Mr. Casley Chapple, captain of cricket and football, from Polcoverack Farm and Mr. Grenville Tripp from Boscarnon Farm at Trevalso. The butter was made by pouring the creamy top of the milk into a large wooden barrel shaped churn. The churn was then turned over and over by a handle attached to the barrel. The butter solidified slowly and formed a mass while the remaining butter-milk ran out of the churn and was used for feeding the young farm animals. Turning by hand was a tedious task which was often passed on to the 'granny' on the farm as it could be done sitting down. She would be encouraged from time to time by such questions as, 'Ow's she going?' If the butter was nearly ready she would reply with a sigh of relief, 'She's coming to come.' When the butter was formed it was cooled and washed with running water and shaped by hand into pats by using flat wooden paddles which had a distinctive mould carved on them so that the customer would know which farm had produced the butter. Summer-made butter was always a deep yellow in colour because of the rich grass the cows were eating. It was a paler yellow in winter when they were eating cattle cake and hay. Churning butter was a boring job which was often passed to boys who came to the farm to help. They soon learned to avoid the dairy area and offered to bring in the cows instead, or to chop mangolds, or collect eggs from the hiding places of the free ranging hens.

The Roskilly firm, Mr. Charlie Cottrell and Mr. Dick Edwards used to collect butter, eggs and other produce from the farms round Coverack and take them to market by horse drawn vehicles to Helston and Redruth. When the Mill Garage became well established, the Mill lorry was used to carry the produce. There were other lorries from St. Keverne in competition. As time went on, the milk was collected by factory lorries and the art of churning butter and scalding cream gradually diminished until only a few specialist farms remained able to carry out these skilled processes. Fortunately, at the time of writing there is one such farm at Penmarth in Coverack and another at Tregellast Barton in St. Keverne. They are run by two Coverack brothers, Ben and Joe Roskilly, the sons of Mr. William Roskilly.

Some of the expertise practised on the above farms is due to the influence of Miss Esmé Bulkeley, a daughter of Colonel Bulkeley, a Coverack benefactor. She started a model farm at Tregisky in the early 1920s. Miss Esme, as she was known to all Coverack people, adopted all the latest methods used in dairy farming and became well known as an owner of a pedigree herd. Naturally, she produced high class dairy products under strict hygiene conditions. When the time came for her to expand, Miss Bulkeley moved to Feock, taking some of the local men with her. Mr. William Roskilly managed her farm and Mr. David Mason also worked there for a number of years when a young man. When the transfer to Feock occurred the animals were driven by road. It was a distance of 27 miles. Mr. William Roskilly, Mr. Edwin Bastian and Mr. Percy Eustice drove them at night. They stopped at Mr. Gilbert's farm, Tickantowan near Half Way House on the A394 for one day to water and rest the animals and continued their journey the next night, arriving in Feock at 5 a.m. the following day.

Until after the First World War most of the cattle which were sent to market had to be driven along the road to Helston from the Coverack district. As the 1920s wore on, the specialist drovers of the area were made redundant by the fact that cattle lorries were introduced to ensure that the cattle arrived in Helston market in good condition.

Miss Esme returned to St. Keverne after some years and became a familiar figure in the area. Mr. William Roskilly, her faithful farm manager then started farming at Penmarth in Coverack. Miss Esme's favourite garb was that of a male farmer - dungarees and boots included. She was much admired by everyone not only for her generosity but because she identified with the villagers and did not remain aloof as many people of her social standing are prone to do.

Coverack farmers have always been renowned for their early potatoes. It was the custom to 'teel' or plant them in January or early February, depending on the current weather conditions, so that they would be ready in time for a late Easter or well before Flora in early May. The sunny slopes of the Polcoverack Valley and Higher Bridge Hill were good spots for potatoes as were the small, sheltered, sloping cliff top gardens which were scattered along the shoreline. After the First World War Mrs. Whale, wife of the Headmaster of St. Keverne School went into partnership with Miss Ruby Bulkeley, sister of the lady farmer, and began a market garden on the land to the north of Higher Bridge Hill. Mrs. Whale had been a teacher at Manaccan but was not allowed to continue as a married lady after the war when more ex-service male teachers were available. After some years Mrs. Whale acquired the sole proprietorship of the business and became a well known market gardener, specialising in flowers.

This enterprise provided very welcome casual local employment at picking time as well as permanent employment for local professional gardeners. Later on, Mr. Calvert started a similar business which was operated from Carnsullan Farm and Parc Behan (currently a Youth Hostel). The latter house used to be the home of Dr. Daunt. Mr. Peter Calvert was a successful market gardener. He developed a new daffodil and called it 'Coverack Pride'. Several private gardeners and farmers also sent potatoes, greens and flowers to market via Helston Great Western Railway Station. Coverack became famous for its early violets, anemones and daffodils. Cornish exiles working in London waited eagerly for the first spring flowers. It is said that during the 1939-45 war when transport restrictions prevented flowers from being taken to the cities by train, some growers despatched their flowers in coffins, which had priority and were unlikely to be inspected en route. There is no evidence that Coverack growers resorted to this method of transport, albeit that it is a stratagem which would appeal to the descendants of smugglers.

During the 1920s and 19320s there was a good trade in wild rabbits for eating purposes. In the height of the season, crates of rabbits were piled high on the roofs of the daily buses to Helston. The overflow crates were placed on spare seats in the buses. Passengers would be confronted with the sight of a row of beady eyed dead bunnies suspended by their hind legs and bouncing up and down in slatted crates as they began their last long journey to the markets in the Midlands. It is interesting to note that very small enterprises were able to operate at that time. They were not undercut and put out of business by the large firms. It was a common sight to see a farmer or gardener waiting at the roadside to put just two or three boxes of flowers or a crate of rabbits on the Helston bound bus for onward transit to a large town. It was essential that the produce arrived in good condition and the Great Western Railway Company saw to it that even a small quantity of goods was delivered on time for a fair price. That may be another reason why the G.W.R. was sometimes known as 'God's Wonderful Railway.'

# ENTERTAINMENT IN COVERACK

One need never be at a loss for something to do in Coverack, but because it is in the nature of things, some inhabitants will tell you it is a boring place to live. When all else fails, a walk along the cliffs will produce an interesting diversion to every day routine, especially if one can do a little wrecking along the way. Should you be confined to the house because of the rain, you have no interesting book to read and the programmes on the radio or television do not appeal, it is fairly certain that a short session of staring out of the window will create a pleasurable period of entertainment. There is always something new to notice. Villagers are naturally inquisitive and have an eye for detail whether it be concerned with natural phenomena or man made occurrences. Those who come to the village from 'up country' do not take long to acquire the villager's ability to derive pleasure from a seemingly quiet scene which is in reality in a constant state of change. The sea changes visibly from moment to moment; so does the land but in such minute detail that it requires experience to notice what is happening. Sometimes the movements of neighbours provide an interesting diversion but they do not usually take kindly to that sort of interest and are quick to notice twitching curtains should it be considered politic to take observation from behind them! People are pleased when others join them in village activities.

It is not possible to remain satisfied with walks along the cliff and looking out of the window. Fortunately the changing scenes of nature bring interesting human activities. Harvest has already been mentioned in the chapter on Religion and Education. The sumptuous harvest supper provided for the workers by the Farmers' wives used to be preceded by the ceremony of Crying the Neck when the harvesters gathered in the last field to be cut. Everyone would wait for the farmer to reap the last swathe of corn, when he would shout:

'I 'ave'n, I 'ave'n, I 'ave'n!' ('I've got it!')

Those present would reply:

'What 'ave 'ee? What 'ave 'ee? What 'ave 'ee?'

('What do you have?')

The farmer would answer:

'A neck, a neck, a neck!'

The neck or handful of corn the farmer was holding up for everyone to see would then be plaited into a corn 'dolly' which would be kept until the next harvest. It is believed that in pagan times the last cut of the crop was the home of the spirit of the harvest and that its retention would ensure another good harvest the following year. It is no longer practical to carry out this ceremony because the harvesters are few and the work is done by machines. In order that the tradition shall not be forgotten, special ceremonies are organised by local branches of the Old Cornwall Society. The proceedings are conducted in English and Cornish and are usually followed by a service in the local chapel and a pasty supper in the Sunday School. People from Coverack travel to the nearest ceremony and have an enjoyable evening discussing the harvest with old friends.

## Wrestling

The Battery or Lambeage has been mentioned as a place of entertainment as well as a defendable position for the protection of the village. In addition to being a venue for Tea Treats and Band Concerts it was also used as a natural wrestling ring with spectators sitting on the slopes around the flat area near the cliff. The highlight of the year used to be at St. Peter's-tide in June when crowds came to Coverack for the 'wrassling' as it is still called locally. In Cornish wrestling, all holds are above the waist. Competitors are allowed to grasp each other's canvas jackets to obtain a hold. The Cornish Wrestlers' motto is:

'Gwary teg yu gwary wheg.' - Fair sport is good sport.

Tournaments are still held in Cornwall and matches are arranged regularly with Breton teams. In the nineteenth century, before the building restoration in 1893, St. Keverne Church had a gallery. It was the custom to hang the wrestling trophy in the church gallery for three Sundays before St. Peter's Day. The trophy was a handsome hat trimmed with gold lace. It was the kind which was worn by fashionable young gentlemen of rank during the early nineteenth century. It was offered as a prize because its wearer would then be immune to seizure by the Press Gang on its search for strong young men to be impressed for service in the navy. The Press Gang would not kidnap anyone wearing such a hat for fear of subsequent repercussions from influential aristocratic families. It goes without saying that such a hat was worth fighting for. Miss Diggens, sister of Canon Diggens, the Vicar of St. Keverne from 1896 to 1913 was told by Mr. John Kempthorne of Sunnyside, Coverack that he remembered seeing the hat being hung in the gallery at St. Keverne Church. Miss Diggens was engaged in research for a History of the Parish which her brother was writing. Miss Matthews, who was reputed to be one of the oldest inhabitants of Coverack in 1900 also told Miss Diggens that when she was a girl she saw:

'........hundreds of people coming from all directions at St. Peter's-tide to witness the splendid feats of strength held there.' (the Battery)

It is worth noting that James Polkinghorne the Cornish wrestling champion of the early nineteenth century was born in St. Keverne. He became the landlord of the Red Lion at St. Columb.

## Regattas

A glance at an old photograph taken during a Regatta at Coverack will be sufficient to demonstrate how popular this form of sport was in the village. It was an opportunity for the men and boys to show off their strength and skills in swimming and seamanship. Some of the ladies had an opportunity to display their catering abilities in providing teas for the spectators and competitors. Others showed off their dressmaking skills as they strolled around in their home-made finery. It is believed that a few years after women became emancipated they were allowed to take part in the swimming and rowing races in Coverack.

The evening before the Regatta began the area round the harbour was decorated with flags and greenery. Forms borrowed from the Chapel were placed on the Quay for the band and the Fishermen's Rest transformed into a committee room. The greasy pole was fixed at the end of the Quay and buoys laid to mark the boundaries of the races at sea.

The band was an essential part of the Regatta as it could be relied on to play popular tunes during the inevitable periods of delay which occur in all Regattas. This 'background' music continued throughout the evening long after the sports were finished. Spectators came from far and wide to watch and to renew old acquaintances. Competitors came in their own craft from the neighbouring coves. Pleasure boats came from Falmouth, filled with spectators. The tugs Victor and St. Mawes were regular visitors and could be relied on to add colour to the scene in their freshly painted summer coats.

Before motor boats were used in Coverack in the 1920s the emphasis was on sailing, rowing and swimming. The first event was always the crabbers' race, then followed contests for the other classes of working boats. Most of them had dipping lugs so that the sails could be hoisted well above the gunwale to allow the fishermen to work their nets, lines and pots without being hampered by a boom swinging close to their heads. The Coastguards organised displays and a race between their two rowing galleys. Sometimes there was a race between two teams of young sailors from the training ship H.M.S. Foudroyant which was based in Falmouth. Their gigs were towed to the cove by one of the Falmouth tugs. On occasions the sailor boys brought their own band which added to the enjoyment of the spectators and was much appreciated by the organising committee.

There was a sailing race for the under 14s. In the same way that the modern Coverack boys and girls learn to handle small boats with outboard motors, so those of yesteryear learned to handle small sailing craft at an early age. There was always a critical band of spectators on 'Parliament Seat' or in the small lean-to shelter in Pent House Lane by the Watch House, so the boys in the boats had no opportunity for fooling about unobserved. Girls rarely attempted to learn to sail. When the boys got back in harbour after a sailing session they were soon told of the mistakes they had made in handling the sheets (ropes attached to the sails) and in their tacking and steering to catch the wind. As they became more proficient and knowledgeable, a favourite game was for one boy to handle the boat after leaving the Quay and the other to lie down on the bottom boards. After a certain time had elapsed the boy who could not see where the boat was heading had to tell his companion where he thought they were. This game was an excellent way of learning about the wind in Coverack Bay and contributed to the sailing skills of the Coverack lads which were displayed on Regatta days.

It was mentioned in the chapter entitled Stormy 19th Century that 32' Sailing Quay Punts used to come to race at Coverack. Later on in the 1920s the Coverack Regatta attracted the Sunbeam class of yachts from the port. They gave exhibition races in Coverack Bay and were much appreciated by the villagers who did not get many chances of seeing such beautiful craft. They were 26' in length but only 17' on the waterline due to the raked bows and sterns. They were beautiful boats but expensive. After one or two Regattas during which the dreaded east wind sprang up, making it difficult to beat out of the Bay, the Sunbeams stopped coming to Coverack. It is believed the owners had problems with their insurance companies when the latter learned the boats were being taken round the notorious Manacle Reef to Coverack. The Bay remains a favourite anchorage for visiting yachts in fine weather but only the foolish linger there when there is a hint of an easterly wind.

Working boat races, inboard and outboard motor boat races, rowing and sculling races, together with all types of swimming events remain on the current Regatta programmes but at the time of writing Coverack has yet to revive gig racing. This is a growing sport in Cornwall and would attract a large number of spectators to the village. There are few sailing races, due to lack of local competitors.

One of the most popular 'swimming' events was and is the 'greasy pole'. This is a large pole or mast which is suspended parallel to the water from the seaward end of the Quay. The pole is balanced over the water by lashings and weights on the end which remains on the Quay. A leg of mutton used to be fastened to the free end of the pole which was covered in thick grease. The competitors had to walk along the pole and try to get the leg of mutton before slipping into the sea. This event caused much hilarity as there was always one foolhardy fisherman who, having drunk some 'courage', would think he could get the mutton by running fully clothed along the pole. Sometimes he succeeded, much to the delight of the crowd. It was a difficult task because after each competitor had tried unsuccessfully to get the mutton, the pole would be given another coating of grease. In later years the leg of mutton was replaced by a small flag and recently the competition has changed into a mock pillow fight between two competitors sitting astride the pole. It was mentioned in the chapter on the Quay that there is a swimming race which is confined to Coverack young people.

156

This is in order to encourage them to acquire skill in an essential seaside activity. The haphazard ways of attaining proficiency in swimming in Coverack have been discussed. The Dickenson Cup was awarded to encourage local lads to take part. It has the names of winners engraved on it each year. As is often the case, family names are repeatedly engraved. For example, Horace Eustice won it in 1913, his grandson, Martin Eustice won it in 1971. That predictable continuity is literally the lifeblood of village life. The same tradition applies to the rowing and sculling races. It is not mere chance that boys like Fred Carey who were prominent in village rowing races became the proud possessors of medals for rowing in Fleet Regattas when they joined the Royal Navy. One of Fred's great disappointments was that he lost his rowing medals when his ship was sunk. To return to the swimming: In the open events visitors who had the advantage of being trained by professional instructors did not always sweep the board. One wonders how far some of the Coverack 'natural' swimmers would have progressed if they had been given a formal training. The village youths often outpaced all comers in the swimming events but did not do so well in the diving competitions. One family of visitors who came to the village every year always took an enthusiastic part in the Regatta. They were called Shann. One can understand that because of their outstanding ability in the water they were referred to by the village children as the 'shags'.

**EDWARDIAN REGATTA**

*Ladies showing off their summer dresses while watching the swimming in the harbour.*

*One of the most popular events was the greasy pole.*

*Watching the bathing belles while waiting for a trip in the Lifeboat The ladies were summer visitors.*

*Note a) The steam pinnace and the Falmouth Quay Punt in the background.*
*b) The absence of buildings at North Corner.*

It is not easy to follow the progress of a Regatta because the events have to take place at some distance from the watchers on shore. One race which created much interest was the Land and Sea race because it ended among the land based spectators. Rowing boats were lined up at the back of the Quay with one man at the oars. Another man sat in the stern of the boat. At the given signal the rowers headed for the Higher Bridge end of the Mill Beach. When the boats arrived at the beach the passenger had to leap out, run across the sand and rocks, climb up the cliff and race back along the spectator lined cove road to the finish at the top of the Quay. This race usually managed to generate a great deal of interest and was useful in that it encouraged everyone to approach the Quay in readiness for the last event of the day which usually coincided with the time of High Water.

The last event of the Regatta was Diving for Plates. One of the officials would take a rowing boat and throw about twenty five enamel plates into the water, taking care to scatter them over a fairly wide area. Some of these plates would settle beneath boats which were on their moorings and were not at all easy to find. In the years before the Second World War there was always a battle between local lads for the prize. Two of the 'star' attractions were Albert Harvey and Frank Champion. Both of these young men became fighter pilots. Another well known contender was David Mason who became a Royal Marine. It is curious that Coverack boys usually won this open event. Perhaps it was because they were more familiar with the bottom of the harbour than those from other parts.

It is probably not an exaggeration to say that Regattas are enjoyed more by the participants than the spectators. Since the beginning of the twentieth century the lifeboat has been the focal point of water activities in Coverack. Intervals between events were used to demonstrate life saving techniques. There was always a strong swimmer available to help in a simulated rescue. Visitors were always delighted to take part, especially if they could go down the slip in the lifeboat when she was launched. One of the prominent supporters of the lifeboat was Mr. Howard Armstrong whose family visited Coverack annually for many years. He was a strong swimmer and was only too pleased to be a 'victim' when the occasion demanded. Howard and some other some members of the Armstrong family are buried in Coverack. Howard's widow Dorothy has retired to the village to pursue her hobby of painting local scenes. This is another example of the way in which visitors to the village become part of the community. There is no longer a lifeboat in Coverack but there is a Lifeboat Day when exercises involving helicopters and the Falmouth Lifeboat, Elizabeth Ann are performed in front of a large crowd which willingly gives money for the charity. The Regatta continues to be held annually in spite of organisational difficulties and problems in sustaining the interest of today's sophisticated spectators. It is difficult to picture Coverack without a Regatta.

A glance at the Treasurer's account book for the 1970s gives an idea of the amount of work voluntary officials have to do in order to present a Regatta. The necessary money is raised from the sale of programmes and a collection which is taken when the St. Keverne Band marches through the village to the Quay. It is the custom for the band to be preceded by four men holding a large sheet into which spectators throw money. There is also a small army of helpers with collecting boxes. These people move among the spectators who sit at various vantage points in the village. In addition money is raised from raffles, refreshments and organised events such as dances, whist drives and bingo sessions.

In 1970 the balance remaining in the Regatta funds was £90 8s 7d by 1973 it was £177.65p. The amounts increase every year as do the expenses. Fortunately the list of private donations for the same years shows that many local people and visitors are prepared to subsidise the Regatta as well as work for its success. Included in the list for the seventies is the name of a temporary resident, Lieutenant Colonel John Howard, the man who became famous for leading the attack on Pegasus Bridge on D Day in 1944. Coverack people were honoured to have such a distinguished visitor show an interest in village affairs.

The long list of items of expenditure in the account book includes the use of Halls, the Rest, the Prizes, the Band, the Dance Orchestras and advertising. An encouraging sign of the common wish to make sure the Regattas continue is that the money prizes, which technically speaking make the amateurs into professionals, are handed back to the Treasurer in order to boost funds. The word Regatta comes from a Venetian expression meaning 'a struggle for mastery.' It is hoped that the Coverack people will win the struggle and engineer a return to the days when competitors and spectators flocked to the village in eager anticipation of a pleasant day in the 'oasis'. It is also hoped that the reader will understand that records of the activities of some village organisations have been examined in detail in order to illustrate the degree of effort, co-operation and personal sacrifice which have to be engendered in order to ensure village life continues.

## *Football*

There is no space large enough in the village of Coverack on which a regulation game of football can be played. One might think that Rugby might have been a natural progression from the popular sport of 'wrassling', especially as Cornwall is renowned for its prowess on the rugby field. However, the moment came when there was sufficient leisure time available to the young men of the village to think about organising a team sport and Association Football won the day. Successive Head Teachers of Coverack Council School had encouraged team games including Association Football for many years but the Cornwall Education Committee did not deem it necessary to try to acquire land for a playing field, although there were suitable spaces large enough for children's sports opposite and adjacent to the school building. In due course several influences created the desire for organised football in Coverack. People who came to live in the village encouraged their new neighbours to share in the pleasure of participating in organised sport and helped the formation of a football committee. The wireless with its Sports News and commentaries of important matches, combined with the accounts of games and results which were published in newspapers helped to sustain interest in the project.

Football stars were school boys' heroes. Most small boys dreamed of becoming professional footballers. There was also the remote possibility that a knowledge of Association Football could result in a win on the 'pools' which started in the early 1920s.

A committee was formed and willing lads vied for a place in the team. At first the team wore green and yellow striped jerseys and did quite well. Later on, Mr. Bibbings, an interested Coastguard, persuaded the team to change its strip to dark and light blue quarters. The colours seemed to bring bad luck as the team did not do so well in their new kit. The Coverack Football Team belonged to the Barker Bowl League and went as far afield as Porthleven, Flushing and St. Mawes. The Coverack Team was a runner up in the Charity Cup League in 1932. The hardworking committee included:

| | |
|---|---|
| Reginald Bibbings (Treas.) | Harry Chesterfield |
| Walter Cordall (Chair.) | Billy Eustis |
| S.A.J. Stranger (Sec.) | Willie White |

There were no facilities for changing, nor for showering - it will be remembered that there was no mains water in Coverack in the early 1930s. It was a difficult walk to the field. In spite of this the team had a good following. Home and away teams changed behind the hedge of the field, some players came ready dressed for the game with their jerseys and shorts on beneath their everyday clothes. The local spectators were naturally partisan and stood by the Coverack boys even when they had failed. Fortunately the referees were in the main officially qualified men and naturally they remained strictly neutral, so there were no recriminations after the matches - except some strong arguments between spectators as they walked back to the village through the fields.

The Captain of the team was Casley Chapple, a farmer at Polcoverack. The team played on his father's land, nevertheless he was appointed Captain solely on his merit as a footballer. Others who played regularly were:

| | | | |
|---|---|---|---|
| Noel Barker | (R.W.) | Willie Barker | (C.H.) |
| Dick Bowden | (Goal) | Reggie Carey | (L.B.) |
| F. Liddicoat | (Centre) | David Mason | (R.H.) |
| Tom Pearce | (L.W.) | Percy Richards | (I.L.) |
| Stanley Roskilly | (I.R.) | John White | (L.H.) |

## Cricket

Polcoverack Farm did not have a field which was suitable for cricket but in spite of the hilly nature of the Coverack area it was decided to go ahead and form a Cricket Team to represent the village. Mr. Stranger, the Hon. Sec. of the Coverack Football Team was the farmer at Chynalls in the 1930s and he persuaded Mrs. Coombes, the Manageress of the Headland Hotel to allow the village team to play on the Hotel's nine hole Golf Course which was situated off the road between Penmarth Farm and Chynalls Farm. It was understood that there would be no pavilion available and the team would have to carry the nets, stumps and other gear to and from the field.

In common with the Football Team, the cricketers joined a minor league and played against teams as far away as Camborne and St. Mawes. Many of the members of the Football Team joined the club together with a sprinkling of older village men and some boys who had not left school. Some players came from outside the village. One of them was Jack Rowe the blacksmith from St. Keverne. He was an outstanding bowler. Cricket was so popular in the 1930s that some of the village men would get up at 5 a.m. to listen to the commentary from Australia when there was a Test Match in progress. The game would be discussed later in the shoemaker's shop, the Fishermen's Rest or the Paris Hotel.

A series of three matches was played annually in the month of August against the visitors to Coverack. Not unnaturally when the last match had finished the village team was invited to come to the nearby Headland Hotel to celebrate the end of the series. This was an evening that many local players looked forward to during the year. Tea used to be served to the cricketers during afternoon matches. This was prepared at Sunny Corner Café which opened in July, 1932. The meal was a traditional homemade Cornish tea which had to be carried in baskets up the steep hill to the field. The water was heated in small urns on Primus stoves which were placed behind the golf course bunkers to prevent the wind from blowing them out. Needless to say it was part of the strategy of the home team to persuade the visiting team members to eat as many splits and cakes as possible in the hope that they might affect the performance of the opposing team! That was not the only stratagem used by the village team.

Coverack Cricket Team usually lost to St. Mawes. They rarely managed even a draw. One year the Dare brothers, who claimed to have played for a county cricket team, came for a fishing holiday with Mr. Sid Hocking who ran a launch called the Silver Cloud in Coverack. During the course of conversation one evening the brothers were told of the recurring problem with St. Mawes Cricket Team. The brothers agreed to help the village team. Everyone had to be sworn to secrecy and the brothers went with the team to St. Mawes, travelling under assumed names. Of course, the outcome of the match was not in question and the Coverack players left a bewildered St. Mawes team to ponder over what had gone wrong. This was definitely not 'cricket'. One wonders what kind of pressure the brothers were subjected to before they agreed to help. Now that the secret is out over half a century after the event, one should be charitable and put it down to the irresistable charm of the inhabitants of the oasis.

## *The Sports*

The Golf Course fields were also used for what was known as 'The Sports' before the fields were adapted for use as a Golf Course. This was primarily a day out for the farmers but it was not an agricultural show. It attracted large crowds which in turn drew stall holders, including cheap jacks, from Helston just like the Tea Treats and Regattas. Poles draped with flags were put up round the arena and even a small temporary grandstand was constructed. The athletics attracted competitors from all over the district. The local runners usually did well in these events. Villagers such as Horace Eustice, Sam Roskilly and Alex Thomas not only competed in Coverack but went round to other athletics meetings. Mr. Thomas told the writer how delighted they were when they were able to use spiked running shoes for the first time.

Tug of war competitions were very popular as there were some exceptionally strong men on the farms in the quarries and coves. The village teams were always well supported. Most of the competitors wore hob nailed boots which did not do much good to the turf. The local young men were attracted to the sheaf pitching contests. They had to pitch sheafs over a bar which was hoisted between two upright posts. Sheaf pitching looks deceptively easy. Strong, muscular young men often found they were beaten in the competitions by slightly built farmers who had developed the art through days of tossing sheaves up to the rick at harvest time. There were also clay pigeon shooting contests. In addition to the men who were interested in the marksmanship of the local hunters who regularly went after rabbits, game and birds which damaged the crops, this sport attracted small children who had to be restrained from collecting shattered souvenirs while shooting was in progress.

One of the most interesting events of Sports Day was the amateur horse racing. This attracted a large number of people because opportunities to see horse racing were rare. Sometimes in order to boost funds, the organisers closed the 'tracks' at the end of the afternoon and reopened that part of the field an hour or so later for the riding events. The St. John's Ambulance Brigade from Helston with their vehicle which was called 'Edith Cavell' used to be in attendance as the jockeys sometimes tumbled at the fences. On one occasion a man was killed when he fell during a race. The parade of decorated farm carts provided a colourful spectacle but perhaps the most attractive sight was that of the farm horses who were groomed to perfection. They had beautiful brasses and decorated harness. The cart horses definitely sensed the importance of the occasion and pranced by the applauding spectators in a blaze of colour and a jingling of brasses. When the horses went back through the village late in the evening, wearing the rosettes they had been awarded, they seemed to be saying, 'Look what we've won!' Perhaps sensing a special treat waiting for them when they got back to the farm, they would go at such a trot that the farmers had to run to keep up with them as they were 'led' past the houses.

The Sports moved to Lanarth fields for a short while after the Golf Course became established. In due course, due to falling attendances and other difficulties it was decided not to continue the Sports Days. After a while some Coverack men including John James, Bert Ivey and Alex Thomas began organising a Horticultural Society in Coverack. This annual event has filled the gap in the Coverack calendar left by the Sports.

## *Coverack Horticultural Society*

Not surprisingly Coverack is well known for its Horticultural Shows, which took their present form in 1954. Nearly everyone in the village takes part. The rivalry is good humoured, but qualified neutral judges who live some distance from Coverack are commissioned to decide on the winners of the large number of categories on display. Apart from the Challenge Cup type trophies which have been given by supporters and former officials of the show, or in memory of well respected villagers, the prizes are only worth a few pence. The prestige of winning is considered more important than the value of the prize. A glance at the 1978 Programme shows that there were medals for cookery and a Blue Ribbon for the best exhibit in the Show. Among the cups on offer were:

3 Coverack Horticultural Society Challenge Cups (for Vegetables, the best exhibit and Cookery)

The W.L. Barker Cup (Best sweet peas)

The R. Coad Memorial Cup (for the children's section)

The Rose Carey Memorial Cup (for cookery)

The Hebden Coombe Cup (for vegetables)

The T.C. Foreman Memorial Cup (for onions and shallots)

The G.J. James Cup (for flowers)

The Joan C. Pasco Cup (for flowering plants)

The Penmarth Cup - in memory of H.S. Snell (dahlias)

The list reveals a small slice of the history of Coverack. Each year when the prizewinner's list is read out, the people whose names are on the cup are remembered by those who knew them. It is truly a village show. There is something of interest to everyone. In addition to the garden produce there are wild flower collections, miniature gardens, wine bottling, breadmaking, cooking, jam making, children's art and handwriting. The day brings everyone together. In one sense it demonstrates what happens when the 'country comes to town' in that the farmers and other rural inhabitants come to the village and show what they can do - with a great deal of help from mother nature, of course. Comparisons are odious, but the Show would not be easily outclassed by entries taken from a much larger area. Visitors are always impressed by the high standards achieved. One of the most important reasons for holding the Show is that it is an opportunity for the local gardeners to congregate and discuss the season's results. It encourages everyone to make a success of his or her garden. It is not therefore surprising that the village has received honourable mentions in the annual national Britain in Bloom competition.

## Some Other Entertainments

Entertainment has been defined as 'the action of occupying attention agreeably.' The young people of the village were quite well catered for in this respect during the 1920 and 30s. Until then the Chapel and Church Sunday Schools were flourishing and there was always some kind of learning activity being carried out in the evenings and at weekends. The Band of Hope tried to interest those who were too old to be attracted by the Sunday School type of activity, the main aim being to keep the young men and women away from the 'demon drink'. The Wesley Guild flourished under the direction of a Mr. Pearce who settled in the village when he retired.

After the First World War a Scout Troop was started. Surprisingly, although it had an ex Navy man, Charlie Hart, for its leader, it was a land based troop. Funds were raised, uniforms, tents and camping equipment bought, giving the lads of the village a chance to experience life away from home and to fend for themselves while being safely supervised by a responsible adult. It was not a military organisation, but the training was such that most of the boys quickly attained senior ranks when they joined the forces at the outbreak of the Second World War. A photograph of the troop taken while camping in the Pendennis Castle grounds at Falmouth shows that most of the Scouts in the Coverack Troop were also in the Coverack Football Team. They look a credit to their founder, Baden Powell, who you will remember was one of the early twentieth century tourists to Coverack.

Unfortunately the troop disbanded in the early 1930s. It was restarted in 1935 by George Hart, the nephew of the previous Scoutmaster, who was helped by Mr. H.J. Brittain from Trevallack who was an experienced Scouter and Commissioner. Once more a committee was formed and funds were raised from the profits of Whist Drives, Dances, Raffles and weekly contributions by the Scouts themselves. The funds of the first Scout Troop were handed over by Captain Gibson to the new Treasurer, Mr. Horace Eustice. St. Peter's Church Hall was rented as a club room for one shilling a week. After attending local camps with other troops from the District, the Troop went to the Jamboree on Mount Edgcumbe, Plymouth in 1936 and met the Chief Scout. By the end of 1937 the lack of boys of a suitable age in Coverack meant that the Troop had to be disbanded once more. It was revived briefly in 1945 by Mr. Frank Tonkin and Mr. E. Nicholls and yet again a committee of adult villagers came forward to help the village lads. The new troop met in a barn on Mr. Roskilly's farm at Penmarth. In June, 1945, six local boys attended an investiture ceremony, they were:

Malcolm Brookfield                    Brian James

Douglas Moore                          Ben Roskilly

Joe Roskilly                               B. Stanton

The ceremony was performed by Canon Gotto. The Scouts were addressed by Mr. L.H. Scotland of Trinidad who was serving in the Royal Air Force at that time. Eventually two Patrols were formed, the Seagulls and the Peewits. The new recruits being:

P. Bryant                                   Ken Cox

Graham Daw                              Alex Foreman

Stafford James                          Vernon James

Francis Lang

Some of the new recruits had been members of a small Cub Pack. Unfortunately the Assistant Scoutmaster, E. Nicholls was called for National Service in the Royal Navy and shortly afterwards Mr. Tonkin resigned. The work was carried on for a time by the Hon. Sec. of the adult committee, helped by interested villagers. It 'folded' in August, 1946 due to the combination of lack of interest, a diminishing population of young lads and a distinct lack of committed adult leaders. The troop has not been restarted.

Perhaps the Scout movement would have lasted longer if there had been some Girl Guides in Coverack. Miss Coombe from the Headland Hotel was a keen Guider but there were never enough Guides to warrant a village troop. The few Coverack girls who were interested made up a small patrol of Sea Rangers with girls from other villages, but the troop did not last long enough to become an integral part of village life. There was a Brownie Pack for a while which had Miss Mona Hart for their 'Brown Owl'. She also ran a Cub Pack but they both disbanded in due course. The writer has been unable to obtain any records of the activities of the Guides, Brownies nor the Cubs.

Politics were probably not uppermost in the minds of the young people of Coverack when they joined the "Imps" which were formed in the village in 1931. The Imps were a type of what would be called currently a young Conservatives Club. Miss Sylvia Whale was the Secretary, Mr. John James the Chairman and Mr. Bert Ivey the Treasurer. The club held dances in the Village Hall and at the Headland Hotel. Trips were organised to places of interest and to towns as far away as Plymouth. The present day former members of the Imps will tell you much about the recreational activities when young. It is fairly certain the the political affiliations of most of the native villagers are known to about 90% of the villagers. It is a fact that when fund raising for a political party is being done, most of the gifts of cakes and so on for the coffee mornings are given by the same people who always give something to village activities, regardless of political allegiance. The political coffee mornings are to a large extent social events where villagers can meet to exchange news. A speech by a visiting politician is regarded as an added bonus by supporters of all parties.

A sure way of raising funds for a village project is to organise a concert. This makes certain that the relatives and friends of the performers will form the nucleus of an audience. Empire Day 'drills' and entertainment have already been mentioned, as have the Minstrel Troupes and Pierrots of the same period in the section entitled 'Settling down again'. From time to time, plays were produced which involved much time being spent in rehearsing, building and painting scenery and making costumes. A memorable play produced in the 1930s was called 'Thirty Minutes in the Street', which portrayed the banal happenings in a small town. This meant that the characters had an instant appeal to the villagers who also led seemingly quiet, ordinary lives but who were in fact, quite complicated and interesting characters. A feature of these entertainments was the comments of the audience, especially those of the children who would 'help' the characters on stage as indeed they were used to doing in village life. In one scene of the above mentioned play a person had lost something and when he voiced his thoughts aloud a chorus of children's voices informed him who had picked it up, giving the real name of the person rather than the 'stage' name. This kind of audience participation enhanced the enjoyment of the villagers. On another occasion a lady who had boasted too much about her singing abilities was clapped and cheered repeatedly until after three encores she was too exhausted to give another rendering. She got the message and was careful not to boast again.

Sometimes a drama club came from another town or village and brought new ideas and standards of acting for the villagers to think about. On one occasion the Truro Players performed Charles Lee's 'Widow Woman' in the Village Hall. The widow, named Mrs. Pollard, was on the verge of acquiring a third husband - or perhaps it should be the other way round - for Mrs. Pollard owned a fishing boat, a 'barking' house (for treating nets and ropes) and five cottages. The plot reveals the manoeuvres of the local men who wanted to 'acquire' Mrs. Pollard, who in fact doesn't get married but engineers a happy ending for the relationship between two shy young villagers instead. This type of play was meat and drink for Coverack folk.

At infrequent intervals small professional touring companies came to Coverack. Tom Leslie and his troupe were welcome visitors. The children loved Tom's pet monkey which sometimes took part in the performances. When these players brought a stage version of 'Uncle Tom's Cabin' to the Village Hall, their acting was so effective that some of the audience were driven to shout their protests out loud when the whip was used on the slave. One can call it melodrama but it brought to life a book that was on the shelves of the school library and created a talking point for a week or two after the play.

Tales of far off places were a great attraction to villagers. Missionaries came to tell the congregations about their experiences. There were lantern lectures in local history by people such as Mr. A.S. Oates, the Helston historian as well as by people who had travelled abroad. As mentioned in the section Prelude to the Great War, the Station Officer of Coastguards, Patrick Keohane, went South with Scott when he tried to be the first man to reach the South Pole in 1911. Mr. Keohane was a great favourite. He was in the sledge party with Bowers, Cherry Garrard and Crean, then got sent back with Atkinson, Wright and Cherry Garrard when Scott pushed on towards the South Pole. Small boys in Coverack were fascinated with his Polar gear which was put on display when Mr. Keohane gave talks about his experiences. They were allowed to get in the special sleeping bag and to try out the skis on the wooden floor of the Village Hall. Mr. Keohane settled in Plymouth when he retired from the Coastguards. In 1968 his widow presented a fine model of the exploration ship Terra Nova, which he had made, to the City of Plymouth so that the general public could study it at their leisure.

An explorer named F.A. Mitchell-Hedges lived for a while at Trerose House in Coverack during the 30s. In 1932 he was the discoverer of a previously unknown race of people who lived in the Panama area of South America. He also accompanied Dr. T.W.F. Gann when he discovered the ruins of the Maya city of Lubaantim in British Honduras. In addition to being an explorer he was a big game hunter and held several world records for his catches of giant fish, so he was a respected resident of the fishing village of Coverack. The younger village children held him in awe as he had brought back some shrunken human heads from South America and it was rumoured that the hair was still growing on these unfortunate sacrificial remains. This macabre tale ensured that Mr. Mitchell-Hedges' stories were listened to with great attention.

The village had its own native storytellers as well. Much of the history of the village has been passed on by word of mouth. Indeed, the lack of recorded history of the village makes the writing of this chronicle a difficult, but fascinating task because of the necessity to verify statements by cross checking and obtaining a consensus of the true version of some village events. Some interesting details about village happenings have had to be omitted because of the lack of reliable oral evidence. In addition to the Reading Room, a good place to find out about bygone days was the shoemaker's shop. Mr. George Mundy, a staunch Wesleyan, believed in what has become known as the Protestant work ethic. He used to work late into the night when all other Coverack men had finished. It was inevitable that those whose work was done would find a place to spend a pleasant hour in the company of their fellow villagers. Where better than the shoemaker's shop? Mr. Mundy's assistant was called 'Willie Waxy' by the village children because one day he put some wax on his employer's stool when he had gone out of the shop. Mr. Mundy returned, sat down and continued his work. Some time later when he tried to stand up he found the stool was firmly attached to the seat of his trousers. The village children got the blame for this prank and had to keep out of the shop for a week or two for fear of retribution. The children were deprived of the privilege of listening to the latest stories circulating in the village and got their own back on 'Willie Waxy' by chanting his new nickname outside the shop. It is not known if Mr. Mundy found out the truth about the trick which had been played on him but it seems highly unlikely that he remained in ignorance for long, as he was at the centre of what might be termed the village intelligence network.

The tradition of staying open late at night was carried on by Mr. Henry (Pete) Eddy when he became the village shoemaker in the 1930s. Mr. Eddy was a talented craftsman who came from a well known Porthleven family. He came to Coverack as a postman and eventually started his own business. He was very deft in his movements, his fingers worked like lightning, yet he would carry on an interesting conversation about topical events while he worked, regardless of the intricacy of the task in hand. Sometimes a game of darts took place in his shop which was situated in the former salt cellar in the cove. Later on, he moved to the Old Reading Room opposite Bank House. The wireless was often switched on in the shoemaker's shop at special times. Everyone would fall silent and listen to the news or football results. The village intelligence network had widened considerably since Mr. Mundy's day. In the years before the Second World War, Pete would tune in to Berlin, just to hear Hitler ranting and raving. That was always a cue for all those present to expound their theories about the rise of Germany and to utter warnings about what would happen if war broke out. After all, the Munich crisis occurred just two decades after the end of the First World War and the middle aged men who had fought the Germans then did not want their sons and daughters to go through a repeat performance.

The wireless had become a powerful influence on the lives of all people who lived in remote communities. The first news bulletin had been broadcast in February, 1921. This was followed in June by Dame Nellie Melba's programme of popular songs which encouraged everyone to want to own a wireless. Before long sets were being bought by the people of Coverack who were eager to listen to station 2LO. Reception was much improved in 1925 when Daventry began transmitting on 1500 metres. Some people began making their own crystal sets which were not very powerful so they soon changed to battery operated wireless sets. One of the villagers, George Harvey, son of the former Lifeboat Secretary, made sets for some of the villagers. Aerials were to be seen leading from the houses to clothes poles in the gardens or to nearby trees. It was essential to have a good earth in those days, so many people drove copper spikes into the ground outside their houses. These spikes required 'watering' from time to time to make the sets more efficient by cutting out the 'crackle' and other interference. After John Reith, later Lord Reith, took over the General Managership of the British Broadcasting Corporation, the variety of programmes improved. The first time most people ever heard the voice of King George V was in 1923 when he spoke on the air to open the Empire Exhibition at Wembley, where the Coverack school children had such an interesting time. In 1932, the first Christmas Day message was broadcast to the nation by the King. It served to bring the nation and indeed the Empire, with its self-governing Dominions, closer to the monarchy. Coverack people began to feel less isolated than before. The 'oasis' was becoming more accessible to outside influences. There is no doubt that programmes on current affairs, drama, music, school subjects, religious subjects, and others such as Women's Hour and Children's Hour, had a good effect on all people in remote areas like Coverack where it had been virtually impossible to experience a wide spectrum of cultural activities organised by experts.

In the 1930s attendance at Church and Chapel began to decline. This affected Coverack and other remote communities later than the cities, nevertheless the wireless continued to bring religion into the homes. Families enjoyed singing hymns together round the wireless. The Rev. Canon Dick Sheppard of St. Martin's in the Fields was a favourite 'wireless' preacher. It was not a one way exchange. The broadcasting of the Nativity Plays from St. Hilary have already been mentioned. There were also broadcasts about tin mining, fishing and farming in Cornwall as well as dramatic reports of life in the villages, the lighthouses round the coast and rescues by Cornish lifeboats. Wireless personalities began visiting the county. One of the favourite Children's Hour personalities, Derek McCulloch, who was known as 'Uncle Mac.' to the children of the 1930s used to stay at the Butler's Farm in Ponsongath during the summer holidays. His daughter still visits the village from time to time.

It was inevitable that what has become known as 'canned' entertainment should come to Coverack. There was a cinema in Wendron Street, Helston called the Flora but it was not easy to arrange to see a film there because the Coverack bus left the town before the programme began. Saturday was the only day when a film could be seen and that was an afternoon or 'first house' performance. For many of the village children of the 1930s their first film was shown to them by a Mr. Cope who rented the Old Watch House for a while. He used to invite people to come and view films in his home. Occasionally, if there was a popular film being shown in Helston such as Noel Coward's 'Cavalcade' a special bus was organised to take Coverack people to see it.

In due course it became clear that showing films in the villages on the Lizard peninsula could be made into a profitable business as electricity had been installed in most of the public buildings. A Mr. Barber from Mullion created a 'circuit' and hired Village Halls on a weekly basis. He showed films in Coverack once a week. They were much appreciated by the village folk and those who lived on the surrounding farms. Holiday makers and service men and women stationed in the area also came to these film shows. In time when television programmes were beamed as far as Coverack, the audences began to dwindle and the mobile cinema ceased coming to the village.

At the time of writing, entertainment has become even more sophisticated and video films are beginning to be shown in the Village Hall. They are usually films which have been shot in the area by local enthusiasts and illustrate local history, the work of the Cornish lifeboats and other interesting activities. Extensive use is also made of tape recordings. Visiting speakers are 'taped' so that people who are house-bound can share in the entertainment being brought to the village.

One important day of the year for many Coverack people is Helston Flora Day. The spring dance through the streets, which takes place on the 8th. May, almost certainly dates back to pagan times before the birth of Christ. It is also associated with the legend of St. Michael defeating the devil in a battle for Helston, which resulted in the devil falling into Loe Pool. The alternative name 'Furry Dance' originates from 'feria' meaning Saints' Day or holiday. That is the important part for most people. It is an occasion to take the day off and go to Helston to enjoy the dance, buy a few bargains from the cheapjacks, go to the Fun Fair and meet friends from far and wide. Cyrus Redding in his Illustrated Itinerary of Cornwall, written in 1842, said the day had its social use '........in bringing the poorer classes in contact with the wealthier and keeping up a kindly feeling.' Happily the 'social use' is no longer noticeable but the 'kindly feeling' still persists. It is a day which is looked forward to by young and old. Coverack children who go to school in Helston take part in the dance and that creates an added interest. In the 1920s and 30s most people went to the Flora by motor bus. Like all other country buses on that day it was always crowded. Standing passengers would be instructed by the conductor to duck down when the bus passed the police sergeant's house in Garras, just in case he happened to be looking out of the window. That little bit of excitement only served to act as a 'starter' for a grand day out for the village folk.

### The Fishermen's Rest

The Fishermen's Rest continued to have an influence on the village in the 1920s and 1930s. Although the British Legion set up a billiard table in their room at the back of the Village Hall, the Fishermen's Rest continued to be patronised by many of the males over the age of 16. It was, of course, in an ideal situation. The new Rest overlooked the harbour, was close to the village pub and there was a warm fire in the grate during the winter - something that was lacking in the Village Hall.

The fishermen used to shelter in a lean-to shed in Pent House Lane which leads to the old Watch House on the cliff behind the Paris Hotel. The Rest was the result of a proposal by a group of Coverack men. Mr. Billy May took on the job of organising the provision of a recreation room. A convenient spot was chosen. It was close to the Quay and the newly built Paris Hotel, which was on the site of the old Dolor House. By August, 1908 the Rest was in use. It was reported in the West Briton that a concert was being held in Coverack to pay off the debt. The article also stated that when the debt had been cleared, Mr. May was going to '........place the Rest in the hands of a Committee.'

When the building was adapted from fishermen's cellars it became a focal point of village life. In addition to fostering skill in billiards, snooker, darts and card games. Euchre was the most popular card game. It is a game of skill and patience, which suits the Cornish temperament. The Rest also became an alternative exchange for the spreading of news and information, the emphasis being on the seafaring side of village life. The Rest became the committee room for the all important annual Regatta. When the Ellis family sold its land and property in Coverack, the building itself was leased to the Fishermen's Rest Committee by the newly formed Harbour Company. From the 10th. November, 1938, the Coverack Harbour Company Limited leased the 'piece or parcel' of land on which the Rest was built, plus one cellar (now incorporated in the extension) to the Committee at a rent of £2 11s 0d per annum for a term of 63 years. This meant that the Committee had security of tenure until the end of the twentieth century. The Trustees at that time were S.A. Roskilly, William C. Corin, F.R.I. Roberts, A.J.H. Coombe and Horace Eustice. It remains to be seen what the Trustees of the year 2000 will do when the lease expires.

Miss Esme Bulkeley, the model farm owner, arranged for the cellar to be converted into an extension of the Rest and gave the Rest Trustees a number of shares in the Harbour Company. In 1948 the Rest Trustees were allowed to send a representative to the Harbour Company's meetings, thus enabling them to be informed about issues which might affect the club.

It will be remembered that the Rest was only open to about half of the villagers as ladies were excluded. Even when two ladies entered the room in a high state of excitement to read the telegram announcing the end of the First World War, they were taken to task. As time went on, opinion began to change. On the 27th. May, 1939, when the question of allowing ladies to come into the building was raised once more, the voting was very close. Eight members were against the motion and seven voted for the admission of ladies. At the same meeting, the opening of the Rest on Sundays was discussed. The practice was allowed to continue by the same narrow majority that kept the ladies out. However, it was ruled that no games were to be played on the sabbath, which meant in effect that not many members would use the Rest on a Sunday. By June 1st., 1939 it was decided to allow ladies into the Rest, with the proviso that they were not allowed to participate in games. It is not possible to discover from the minutes of the meeting what the thinking was behind this victory for women's liberation. The Committee must have been motivated by some democratic influence, for on that same evening they decided that seafaring men were to pay their membership fees only when resident in Coverack.

One might be forgiven for thinking that the Committee felt the topics of conversation and the vocabulary used in the Rest were not suitable for lady members. This is not so. The minutes revealed that the Committee was concerned about the general standard of behaviour in the club. The following entries illustrate this clearly:

31.5.1941   Comment was made about the language of a certain member.

30.8.1941   Reference was made about the language of a certain member.

8.11.1941   The bad language of a certain member to be dealt with when the occasion arises.

No doubt everyone in the village knew who the 'certain member' was, but the wise Secretary, Mr. Horace Eustice, did not want to make matters worse by naming the guilty one in the minutes. Clearly the Committee were hoping the inarticulate person would improve his normal vocabulary and not have to resort to meaningless swearwords to express a point. This does not mean, of course, that Coverack fishermen never swore, it simply illustrates that they considered a certain standard of behaviour and speech was necessary in their club if it were to maintain the respect of their fellow villagers.

The Rest Committee were constantly trying to manage the club on a shoestring. The balance at the end of 1939 was £24 0s 5d. Available funds were never more than this amount until after the war when a balance of £39 2s 4½d was in hand. This prompted the Committee to give £2 towards the Peace Day Celebrations in Coverack.

Two on-going problems of the Rest Committee were the leaking roof and the provision of a fire in winter. The roof problem has never been solved. At the time of writing, the Rest roof is still leaking. The water is caught in a make-shift chute suspended over the billard table and is channelled to a firebucket on the floor at the side of the room. The minutes record faithfully the saga of the fire, which was laid by volunteer members of the club. Being prudent men, the Committee spent much time in discussing the fire. After numerous complaints about the laying of the fire, which often failed to ignite, it was decided to pay the caretaker for laying it, in the hope that the situation would improve. He was to receive one shilling extra per month on top of what was grandly termed his 'salary' - no record exists which states the actual salary he received. This decision  pacified the members and the minutes did not include any reference to the fire for a while.

On the 24th. June, 1940, the Committee readily agreed to open the Rest for the newly formed L.D.V. (Local Defence Volunteers) -

'........whilst on duty during stormy weather.' The Committee added a warning to their permission: 'There must be no lighting of the premises.' Whether they were worried about an increase in the electricity bill or breaking the black-out regulations is not clear. Presumably the Germans were unaware that Coverack's sentries were sheltering in stormy weather. In any case, all the local men knew that only a fool would try to come ashore in bad weather in Coverack, so there was little danger of the village being overrun by a landing party. In the following year, when the L.D.V. had been renamed the Home Guard, arrangements were made for the caretaker to hand the key of the rest to Captain Harry Snell of the H.G. so that he could pass it to his sentries if necessary. The Rest Committee thoughtfully provided 6 cwt. of coal for the use of the Home Guard sentries. This gesture of good will paid off, for on the 19th. December, 1942, it was reported to the Committee that the Home Guard was now prepared to pay five shillings per week for the use of the room.

The story of the fires did not end during the war. In January, 1948 the problem of finding someone who could lay a good fire still existed, consequently the Committee decided to allow Willie Hayden free entry to the Rest in return for lighting the fires. Willie proved to be so expert at the task that in July the Committee decided to offer Willie £1 per month as payment for lighting fires every evening from the 1st. October to the 31st. March. The minutes added that no one was to stoke the fire after half past eight each night. By October, however, the Committee had had second thoughts and cancelled Willie's appointment. They had been persuaded to buy an oil heater for £4 2s 6d, which could, in theory, be operated by any member of the club. For good measure the Committee ordered a fixed electric heater to be installed at the other end of the room. They had solved the heating problem. Willie, a most helpful member of the club, presumably had to start paying his subscription again.

During the daylight air raid on Coverack in 1942, a model ship which was kept in the Rest was damaged. The Committee asked the ever faithful Willie Hayden and Michael Eustice to collect from the villagers to pay for the necessary repairs. The 'ship', as the Ariadne was described in the minutes, is itself an interesting part of the chronicle of Coverack. The model was discovered boarded up in a recess of a wall in a cottage at Sunny Corner by the then tenant, Captain Biggs, R.N. She is a 28 gun three masted man of war and was thought to have been made by French prisoners of war, although there is no hard evidence of this. The Ariadne was one of a number of British frigates which blockaded the French Channel ports in 1805. Napoleon had amassed 163,000 men for the invasion of Britain. Due to contrary winds, the invasion had to be postponed and the idea was abandoned after the British victory at Trafalgar. It seems unlikely that French prisoners of war would have made a model of a ship which had played such a part in the defeat of France. She was presented to the village in 1879 by Captain Biggs who asked the Coast Guards to keep it safe. It remained in the Watch House and then was duly transferred to the new Duty Room at Sunny Corner in 1923. During the 44 years at the Watch House, the model had fallen into disrepair, so Coastguard Richard Germaine and his neighbour, Stafford Hart repaired the rigging, rehoused the guns, which were made of bronze, and did all the other small repairs necessary. In due course a public meeting was called and the villagers decided that the Ariadne would be placed in a glass case and kept in the Rest. It was made clear that any villagers who wished to view the ship would have free access to the Rest in order to do so.

A separate Sports Committee used to organise official competitions for the Rest. There were annual Billiard Handicaps, Snooker Tournaments and Darts Tournaments. The Roddick Cup was keenly contested. It was presented by Captain Roddick, a retired Army Officer who lived in what the villagers call 'The Mansion.' The house is in fact named Tregenwyn and is situated next to the village school. There was also a silver cup for the Darts Tournament. In order that these events could take place, as well as matches played against neighbouring clubs, the Sports Committee had to raise funds by organising Whist Drives and Dances in the Village Hall. Members of the Sports Committee carried out all the routine jobs such as looking after the billiard cues, 'ironing' the table and keeping it covered when not in use - and when it was raining. The leaking roof was and is a constant threat to the expensive table. The minutes reveal some interesting facets of village life. For example, during the war, Noel Barker was thanked for voluntarily framing a photo of Winston Churchill which was hung in the Rest. After the war, a minute was recorded, stating that Adolphus Hocking was to have the use of the chair '........as long as he requires it.' Adolphus had been invalided out of the Royal Navy as a result of war service and the compassionate Committee readily offered him the use of a very comfortable armchair. These apparently unimportant details, combined with many others which are too numerous to mention, all go to make up a caring community, which is the essence of village life. At the time of writing the Rest continues to serve the village. It is in constant use for Regattas, Lifeboat Days, Carolares, Coffee Mornings and Local History Exhibitions. The members readily give up their room for these activities and although the club is still in need of funds, it charges very low rents. In return, the various organisations clean up the room after use and cheerfully accept the inconvenience of the leaking roof and other small problems. That is the way of village life.

## THE CONSTANCE MELANIE
## COMPLETES HER WORK IN COVERACK

An account of the episode of the Berville in 1923 was given at the beginning of the section on the 1920s and 1930s. The next significant wreck happened at 8.25 p.m. on the night of the 24th. February, 1928 when the French ship Gap went ashore in a strong East South Easterly breeze - '........with the usual fog', as recorded by Mr. Thomas Roskilly the Lifeboat Honorary Secretary. The Gap, named after a town which is situated about 65 miles south of Grenoble, was an 1,800 ton steamer which was proceeding in ballast from Rouen to Barry. The Coastguards had reported to the Honorary Secretary that the lights of the vessel indicated she was standing into danger, but no distress signals had been fired. Mr. Simon Moyle from St. Keverne had seen the Gap approaching the rocks and informed Porthoustock Coastguards. They fired three warning red rockets to no avail.

The crew of the Constance Melanie assembled and after consultation with Mr. George Harvey, Captain Gibson and other members of the Committee, Mr. Roskilly decided to launch the lifeboat as it was clear that the Gap had now struck the Lowland Rocks. The Coastguard sent the volunteer company round by land with the Life Saving Apparatus in case it would be necessary to take off the crew by breeches buoy. After an hour's hard rowing the Constance Melanie reached the Gap at 10 p.m. It could not have been an easy trip because the lifeboat lost an oar on the way. It was recovered a few days later. Captain Lemouve informed Coxswain John Corin that he and his 20 crew members were not prepared to leave the ship at that stage, so Mr. Corin dropped anchor and waited. After three long hours standing by in the bitter weather, Mr. Corin decided he could do no further good at the Lowlands, so he returned to the Quay. The strength of the wind prevented him from getting back on the lifeboat slip. Mr. Corin was obviously not pleased with the outcome of the night's work, nevertheless the safety of the French sailors was uppermost in his mind, so he sent four crew members round by land to the Lowlands with the lifeboat searchlight so that the scene could be illuminated and the Coastguards and the volunteer Life Saving Company could effect a rescue by breeches buoy without being hampered by the darkness. The Coastguards later recorded their grateful thanks for this thoughtful action.

These are the men who spent hours waiting in the lifeboat, which was swept every now and again by a cold wave of water:

Coxswain John Corin

| | |
|---|---|
| Willie Barker | Gerald Eustis |
| Reggie Carey | Percy Eustis |
| William Corin | W. Fowler |
| William Cliff | Charlie Hart |
| George Dally | Ernie Lambrick |
| Harry Eustice | Sam Roskilly |
| Horace Eustice | Archie Rowe |

It will be noted that some of these men were among those who were members of the Fishermen's Rest Committee, ran the Scout Troop, worked on the farms and in the Quarry or went fishing every day to earn their living. When their night's work of rescue was done they still had to turn up for work as early as they could. They could not afford to take a day off because they would not have enough money to provide for their families at the end of the week. The 'Rewards' from the R.N.L.I. usually came a few weeks later.

The problems caused by the wreck of the Gap did not end that night. The Master and crew were subsequently taken off by Falmouth tugs when it was fully realised the ship could not be saved. Another gale had sprung up and the vessel was turned beam on to the rocks by the force of the wind and waves. The Coastguards and rescue team were waiting to take off the crew by breeches buoy. Luckily, as the tide ebbed, the ship settled more firmly on the rocks and the breeches buoy was not needed. It was then decided that enough was enough and the crew were taken to Falmouth aboard the waiting tugs.

A small salvage crew went aboard the Gap when the sea had died down. Their job was to retrieve as much as they could before the ship broke up. They worked away steadily until the 27th. October, 1928. On that day, eight months after the Gap went ashore, Mr. Potts, the owners' representative rushed to the Honorary Secretary of the lifeboat to tell him that he had just come from the wreck and that as the North East wind was increasing to gale force, he would like the six salvage men on board to be brought off by the Constance Melanie. Mr. Potts told Mr. Roskilly that he had been unable to understand what the men were shouting to him when he was on the shore, but they had hoisted a flag to indicate their predicament. Mr. Roskilly consulted with the former Hon. Sec., Mr. George Harvey. The Gap was no longer their favourite wreck, but they knew it would be prudent to get the men off before dark. It was a Saturday afternoon and the men were readily available, so the crew was summoned by maroons and once more the men settled down to a long hard row out to the Lowland Point. Coxswain John Corin got his craft through the rocks and went alongside the Gap. In spite of the heavy seas he transferred all six men safely aboard the lifeboat, but not before the port side protection 'slipper' had been damaged along half the length of the boat during the operation. Once more, the men settled down to a row back to the Quay. Once more the heavy seas prevented the Constance Melanie from being re-housed, so she was moored in the harbour and put back on the slip at 8 a.m. on Monday the 29th. October.

The crew were awarded 19s 0d. each for their work on this service. The shore helpers received 4s 6d. Noel Barker, the telephone messenger got 1s 0d. In time, Mr. Roskilly received a cheque for £16 8s 0d but returned it for correction as he noticed that the winchman had been paid two allowances of 4s 6d.

Two days after the call out to the Gap, Mr. Roskilly received a message from the Coastguards stating that there had been a collision off the Lizard. The message was followed half an hour later by another communication which said that the collision was 7 miles East of the Lizard, i.e. 3 miles from the Blackhead. After consultation with the Coastguards and Mr. George Harvey, the Hon. Sec. launched the Constance Melanie, Mr. John Corin being once again in command. There was a strong South Westerly breeze blowing, so Mr. Corin hoisted the sails and made for the position off Blackhead. The S.S. Manspool of West Hartlepool, a small coaster carrying china clay had been in collision with the S.S. Horn of Riga, Latvia. The latter sank almost at once. The Manspool lowered her boats and picked up all the survivors she could find. When the Constance Melanie and the Minnie Moon, the Cadgwith Lifeboat searched the sea systematically for three hours but could find no trace of the five men still missing from the Horn so they returned sadly to their respective slipways. The Coverack boat got back at 2.30 a.m., having had to wait off Dolor Point until the bottom of the slipway was covered by flooding tide.

In April of the following year, there was a dense fog at Coverack and at 11 p.m. the villagers heard the siren of a ship which was obviously very close to the shore. Mr. Roskilly the Honorary Secretary and others gathered on the Dolar Point, fearful about what was going to happen, but before anything could be done, a resounding crash told the little knot of people that a ship had gone ashore on the Mears. The Constance Melanie was launched with all speed and Coxswain John Corin soon discovered that a 4,000 ton Greek vessel named Archangelos from the Piraeus had struck the Yellow Rock on the end of Mears Point. There were 33 men on board. After standing by for three hours it became apparent that the ship was not in any danger so the crew rowed back to Coverack. They told the people who had not gone to the Mears to see the wreck that the ship's crew had put a ladder on to the Yellow Rock from the focsle and had made contact with the Coastguards on shore. Fortunately the Archangelos was only carrying water ballast from Dunkirk to Cardiff so there was no problem about lightening the ship. The hole in the bows was plugged with cement and three days later on the 20th. April two tugs pulled her off the rocks at High Water.

It was to be another four years before the Constance Melanie was called out again. This time there were two wrecks within half an hour of each other. There was an East North East wind blowing, accompanied by the usual patchy fog. The Honorary Secretary, Mr. George Harvey was called by the Station Officer of Coastguards, Patrick Keohane at 4 a.m. on the 4th. March, 1932. He was told that a vessel was in a dangerous position in Coverack Bay. Mr. Keohane had seen the vessel approaching Perprean Bay from his bedroom window after being woken up by the noise of the vessel's engines. The vessel had ignored Mr. Keohane's subsequent warning signals of burning rags. Mr. Harvey lived at West House at the top of Sunny Corner lane where Mr. Keohane lived in the Coastguard house. He too, could hear the engines, so he ordered the lifeboat maroons to be fired at once to warn the boat in the bay and call out the crew of the Constance Melanie. Some of the crew were already on their way as they too had heard the noise of the vessel's engines. The lifeboat was launched and by half past four the lifeboat had crossed the bay and was lying off the trawler which had gone ashore in Perprean Bay. She was a few hundred yards where the Archangelos had been wrecked and about the same distance away from the Coastguard Station.

The R.N.L.I.'s all powerful acetylene lamp was carried on to the Mears cliff to illuminate the misty scene. By this time all the village was awake becuase the noisy engines of the vessel were running at high speed. The lifeboat crew could get no response from the trawler, so Mr. Harvey's elder son got a ladder from home and climbed aboard the ship from a rock on the beach. She was a Belgian trawler, No. 0251 of Ostend and was called Omer Denise. Mr. Harvey's son, also named George, stopped the engines and reported to his father that there was no one on board.

In the ensuing quiet the watchers on the Mears cliff saw distress rockets soaring into the air off Lowland Point. As the Constance Melanie could do nothing at the scene of the wreck of the Omer Denise, the Coxswain made for the Lowlands, urging his rowers to make all speed to answer the call. The lifeboat arrived at the Lowlands at 5.45 a.m. to find the S.S. Ocklinge firmly aground. Meanwhile the faithful L.S.A. Rescue Company had left the Mears and assembled on the Lowlands opposite the rocks on which the Ocklinge had come to rest. They soon had a line aboard and set up the apparatus in case it became necessary to get the crew off the ship by breeches buoy. There were 21 persons on board but Captain Driscoll would not allow his crew to abandon ship. The Captain told Mr. Corin that tugs were on the way but that he would like the lifeboat to stand by. After waiting until 2.40 in the afternoon, the Captain informed Mr. Corin that as two tugs were now in attendance, the lifeboat could return to Coverack and that he would call them again if required.

There was an air of mystery about both of these wrecks. The affair of the Omer Denise was soon cleared up. A small boat was seen drifting off Cadgwith at dawn. The Cadgwith Lifeboat was launched and found there were six Belgians on board from the Omer Denise. The fishermen were brought back to Coverack, where they stayed with Mr. and Mrs. Edwin Bastian until it became obvious that the trawler could not be got off the rocks. There were rumours that the boat was fishing inside the three mile limit when she got into trouble but these were never substantiated. The fishermen were friendly and managed to communicate after a fashion with their Coverack counterparts. They could be heard coming along the cove as they wore wooden clogs which intrigued the village children who had not seen this type of footwear before. The Skipper of the Omer Denise, Captain Vanavillez, kept up a correspondence with the Bastian family for some time after he returned to Belgium.

The mystery of the Ocklinge was a little more complicated. She was carrying iron ore from Bilbao to Port Talbot and had just come through the easterly gales of the Bay of Biscay. She had been towed into Falmouth for repairs to her steering gear and had not long left the port to continue her voyage to Port Talbot when she hit the Lowland Point. The Coastguards were puzzled as to how a steamship could have got into that position so soon after leaving Falmouth. The distress rockets were seen by Station Officer J.E. Cogger of Porthoustock Coastguards at 0500, when the Coverack rescue teams were at the scene of the wreck of the Omer Denise. At the same time, Cadgwith Coastguards heard the distress call of the S.S. Ocklinge on their wireless telegraphy set. Rescue tugs from Falmouth also heard the call and Falmouth lifeboat came with them to the Lowland Point and stood by with the Constance Melanie for a while.

Some time later, when it was realised that the tugs would never be able to get the Ocklinge off the rocks at the Lowlands, gangs of labourers were engaged to get the iron ore out of the holds. The sea round the wreck became a dull red in colour for a number of weeks. Finally a small salvage team remained on board to get what scrap they could before the ship broke up. At the inevitable Board of Trade Enquiry after the wreck, Captain Driscoll was imprisoned for making false statements and had his Master's 'ticket' suspended for a year.

The ship's troubles were not yet over. In the month of May, 1933 a square of dirty canvas was seen flying from the stump of the sloping mast of the Ocklinge. One visual form of distress is that of a square flag, having above or below it a ball or anything resembling a ball. Fearing for the lives of the salvage men known to have been on board the Ocklinge for about a week, the Honorary Secretary launched the Constance Melanie and once more another long row in dirty weather to the Lowland Point was accomplished. When the Constance Melanie got alongside, the three men on board said they had only hoisted the canvas as a signal to some local fishermen that they were in need of provisions. Nevertheless, as the weather was deteriorating all the time, they agreed to be brought off. It seems clear that the salvage men did not relish the thought of making the lifeboat men row out to the Lowlands again, should they find their position untenable due to the worsening weather. The Record of Service Board which is on display in the Wesleyan Chapel at Coverack describes the Service more succinctly. It states simply, 'S.S. Ocklinge of Cardiff. Landed 3.'

That was the last service of the Constance Melanie. After 33 years of faithful service she was replaced by a magnificent motor lifeboat, the Three Sisters.

In February, 1934 a headline in the Western Morning News stated, 'Coverack to lose the Constance.' Everyone knew what it meant. The article gave a detailed account of the exploits of the Constance Melanie and her crews. After assuring the readers that the lifeboat was as sound as when she was built, the article revealed that,

'........mechanical advancement has set a limit to the term of service.' Some preliminary details concerning the naming ceremonies of Coverack Lifeboats were given in the chapter on the Quay.

There was, of course, much rivalry among lifeboat stations with pulling and sailing boats when it became known that a motor lifeboat was to become available. Judge Roxburgh had been an annual visitor to Coverack since 1912 and he did much to persuade the Royal National Lifeboat Institution that a motor lifeboat should go to Coverack. The Three Sisters was purchased with the money from a legacy given by the late Miss Margaret Quiller-Couch of Looe. She was a cousin of Sir Arthur Quiller-Couch of Fowey. The boat was named after Maria, Sarah and Margaret, the daughters of the celebrated Penzance physician, Richard Quiller-Couch. The Three Sisters was fetched from Cowes by Coxswain William Corin who had succeeded his brother John as Coxswain of the Constance Melanie in 1931. The crew on passage were George Dally the new Chief Mechanic, formerly 2nd Coxswain of the Constance Melanie; Charlie Hart, Bowman and Signalman; Percy Eustis was the deck crewman. The Lifeboat Inspector was in overall charge. The new boat called at Weymouth on the way to Coverack and just before arriving at her destination she stopped at Fowey. This was a courtesy call. As stated above, the lifeboat had been donated by a Quiller-Couch and the crewmen were anxious to show her off to the people of Fowey whose beloved 'Q', as Sir Arthur was known to them, was such a familiar figure on the Fowey waterfront.

The new lifeboat was built by J.S. White and Company of Cowes. Like the Constance Melanie she was a Liverpool type and to all intents and purposes she was a motorised Constance Melanie, being just 6″ longer at 35′6″ and having the same beam of 10′. She had a motor in a watertight compartment which could drive her at 7.5 Knots for 100 miles. She was fitted with masts and sails, 'just in case'. She was a six tonner, being a ton and a half greater than the Constance Melanie. There were 115 watertight compartments in the lifeboat and she could empty herself in 12 seconds if swamped by a sea. The bill for this came to £3,248, nearly four times as much as the cost of the Constance Melanie.

On a beautifully warm, calm day, Sir Arthur Quiller-Couch came to Coverack to name the lifeboat. In his address he stated that he was sure Cornish men and Cornish women would understand how delighted he was that the memory of his three kinswomen and their love for their county would continue in the tangible form of The Three Sisters. He added that the three ladies came from the same seafaring stock as he did. That was his excuse, he said, for being in Coverack on that lovely day.

THE THREE SISTERS MOTORING AND SAILING

As might have been expected from a distinguished man of letters who had been Professor of English Literature at Oxford University, he reminded his listeners of the legend of the beautiful siren who lured ships to their doom. He warned those present that the lovely waters round Coverack concealed one of the deadliest reefs of England, illustrating the fact by reminding the crowd of the wrecks of the Dispatch, Primrose, John and Mohegan. The R.N.L.I. could not have chosen a better man for Coverack for no one loved Cornwall more than he. 'Q' is quoted in A.L. Rowse's 'A Portrait of 'Q',' concerning his forsaking the chance of riches for the privilege of living in Fowey:

'All happiness must be purchased with a price ........ to breathe clean air, to exercise limbs as well as brain, to tread good turf and wake up every morning to the sound and smell of the sea and that wide prospect which to my eyes is the dearest on earth ........ a man can never amass a fortune.'

The ceremony began with the firing of two maroons, the traditional way of calling out a lifeboat crew to a rescue. On board The Three Sisters, which was moored in the centre of the tiny flag-lined harbour, were Second Coxswain Archie Rowe, Bowman Charlie Hart, Chief Mechanic George Dally, Second Mechanic Willie Eustis and Crewmen Percy Eustis and Harold Martin. They were wearing their bright yellow oilskins, brown lifejackets and red woollen caps. They were supported by the crews of the Lizard and Falmouth Lifeboats whose craft were anchored off the end of the quay. The Superintendent Coxswain, William Corin, was the most disappointed Coverack man that day as he had been taken to hospital some 24 hours earlier. Coverack people were also saddened to think that their friend Judge Roxburgh, who had done so much for the village, had not lived to see the christening of the new boat. The Constance Melanie had already been removed from Coverack and was being used as a pleasure boat at Skegness, where she had already been used to perform yet another rescue when the local lifeboat was out of action.

Mr. P.D. Williams the Squire from Lanarth Estate received The Three Sisters on behalf of the Coverack Branch of the R.N.L.I. and she was dedicated by the Bishop of Truro. After Sir Arthur Quiller—Couch had broken a bottle of champagne over the bow the St. Keverne Band played 'Eternal Father strong to save', the people of Coverack and their visiting friends singing the hymn they all knew by heart with great feeling. When all the lifeboats had gone and the tired children tucked up safely in bed, the great day finished with a Grand Dance in the Village Hall, the proceeds of which were added to the day's collection for the R.N.L.I.

The crew of The Three Sisters had two months to wait after the christening before they were called out. They had to search for an outboard motor boat with four visitors on board. The boat was soon found and towed back to Coverack. The lifeboat continued to go to the rescue of small craft from time to time until the Second World War broke out when services of a sterner nature were demanded of her. Just before the outbreak of war the crew carried out a tricky operation. On the 14th. August, 1939 the Motor Yacht Sigurd of Southampton was reported to be on fire by Watchman Coastguard J.W. Marriott who was on duty at Porthoustock look out. He alerted the Hon. Sec. of Coverack lifeboat but before The Three Sisters could get to the scene, the crew of the yacht abandoned her and left the blazing craft drifting while they rowed towards Coverack. With great difficulty the crew of Three Sisters managed to get a line aboard the burning boat and beached her at the Mill in Coverack, where she burned out as it was impossible to extinguish the flames.

Some of the war time services of The Three Sisters are related in the chapter on the Second World War. She remained on station until 1954. Her post war activities will also be described in context later.

# PRELUDE TO THE SECOND WORLD WAR

The arrival of The Three Sisters in Coverack in 1935 can be taken as a milestone in village life during the years before the Second World War broke out. The boathouse had to be adapted, a fuel store built at the seaward side of the building and a motor winch installed. Mr. George Dally, the full time mechanic, ensured that all went well and set a precedent in keeping the house and boat with its 35 h.p. engine in perfect running order. He had no lack of young helpers eager to polish the brass and to do errands for him.

The year 1935 was an eventful one. Coverack celebrated King George V's Silver Jubilee on May the 6th. by decorating the village with flowered arches and greenery and holding a grand tea, during which each child was given a Silver Jubilee mug. The tea was followed by Sports for the children on the Battery and a Band Concert for the grown ups. The wireless programmes did much to publicise this event. 'Sailor' George did not realise how popular he had become. After driving through the East End of London he remarked, 'I am beginning to think they must really like me for myself.' In June everyone was shocked by the accident in which beautiful Queen Astrid of Belgium was killed. The special mourning stamps were eagerly sought after by the young philatelists of the village. In October the Italians attacked Abyssinia. In due course the Emperor Haile Selassie's family took refuge in Cornwall for a while and forged a link which lasted to the 1980s when a small band of Cornish people did much through Amnesty International and other agencies to secure the release of the Princesses from prison in the country which is now named Ethiopia. Hitler was now well established as Chancellor of Germany. He was beginning to make thinly veiled threats. The Labour Party was opposed to rearmament. Patriotism seemed to have become a dirty word. In 1933 the Oxford Union Debating Society had passed a motion declaring '........that this House will in no circumstances fight for its King and Country.' Not much was made of this in Coverack. Many of the villagers were only too glad to get a regular job in the armed forces and those who stayed at home were too preoccupied in earning their own living to pay much attention to hot headed students. No one really wanted to think about another war.

King George V died in the following year, 1936. Edward VIII abdicated and the Duke of York became King George VI. The people of Coverack did not ignore these events but were probably more concerned with the coming installation of electricity and running water which was due the following year. If the truth were known they were wondering if they were going to be able to afford it. These 'utilities' were considered to be luxuries in Coverack up to the time when they were put within the reach of everyone. It is interesting to take a look at some current prices of luxuries and necessities and note the comparative amounts. On the 11th. December, 1936, the day after the abdication was announced, Thomas Cook was offering four days in Paris at Christmas for £4 10s 6d. inclusive. If you wanted to give a Christmas present to a smoker you could get a Greetings pack of 100 Craven 'A' cigarettes for 5s 0d. A pint of milk was 2½d. and 1lb. of butter cost 1s 3d. A working man's 'best' suit cost £2 which was what the amount which was considered sufficient to keep a small family for a week without spending anything on luxuries. It is easy to understand that ordinary people were not able to give much thought to rumours of war.

The year 1936 saw the demilitarised Rhineland being reoccupied by German troops. The Civil War in Spain appeared to give the Axis Powers and Russia a chance to test their fighting equipment. Two years later Chamberlain won a respite with the Munich agreement. The Royal Navy and Royal Air Force were built up while the British Army appeared to be neglected in comparison. No one was surprised when war was declared on September 3rd., 1939. Indeed the Royal Navy had been mobilised since the 28th. September, 1938, the day before the Munich crisis was resolved temporarily. Army Reservists and Territorials had already left the village during August, 1939. What was happening became more obvious when the Italian salvage ship Artiglio was ordered to leave the area and was escorted to Plymouth with her valuable cargo, by a Royal Navy destroyer. The Artiglio had been engaged for several weeks in getting metal - rumour had it that some of the metal was gold bullion - from a cargo ship which had been sunk off Coverack during the 1914-1918 War. The Italians had made friends with some of the Coverack fishermen and always welcomed them alongside when they came to sell fish or give visitors an opportunity to see a salvage vessel at work. The Italians had nothing to hide and willingly showed people over their ship when conditions were suitable. It was difficult to believe that the Italians were potential enemies.

## *Early Days*

The news of the events related in the last section of Chapter 10 did not go unnoticed in Coverack in spite of the economic conditions prevailing at the time. As indicated, some Naval Reservists went back to sea a year before war broke out and Army Reservists and Territorials were already in camp or barracks on September, 3rd., 1939. The August weather was quite good. There was an increased crop of visitors, probably due to the fact that people had decided it would not be prudent to go abroad that year. The kind of people who were able to stay in hotels in Coverack were the sort who could also afford to go abroad from time to time. The farmers were pleased with their harvest too. The writer was camping at Porthleven during what used to be called the schools' Harvest Holiday and helped Mr. Kitto bring in his harvest in return for a free camp site. After a wet July a bumper crop of blackberries was ripening in the August sun on the cliffs and in the hedgerows. Coverack people were busy going about their normal summer season activities and tried to put the possibility of war breaking out at the back of their minds. Some of the villagers had already promised their voluntary help in the event of hostilities and were wondering how they would cope with more calls on their time for coast watching, evacuation or Civil Defence in addition to their daily work. They considered that this time Coverack would become part of the war zone. They were right. The 'Oasis' would never be the same again.

For the first time in the history of Great Britain nearly everyone in the country was able to hear the elected leader of the country declare war on another country. The sombre words of Neville Chamberlain stunned everyone into silence when he declared:

'I am speaking to you from the Cabinet Room of 10 Downing Street. This morning the British Ambassador in Berlin handed the German Government the final note stating that unless we heard from them by 11 o'clock that they were prepared at once to withdraw their troops from Poland a state of war would exist between us. I have to tell you that no such undertaking has been received and that consequently this country is at war with Germany.'

No cheering was heard in Coverack as it had been when the news of the outbreak of the First World War was received on the Coastguard Coastal Communication Circuit. Some began quietly getting ready for the work they would be called upon to do, others went calmly about their daily business, wondering how they were going to cope. In the evening, just as people were going to Chapel or getting the supper ready for their visitors, or were about to go for their weekly summer stroll through the village to the Mears or the Lowland Point, the King broadcast from Buckingham Palace. He urged his people to '........stand calm and firm and united in this time of trial.' Copies of his appeal were delivered later to every household in Great Britain.

The evening news bulletin on the wireless told anxious listeners that M. Deladier, the Prime Minister of France, had also declared war on Germany as had Mr. Menzies, the Australian Prime Minister. Although it was Sunday, the House of Commons was in session. Churchill had joined the War Cabinet and Roosevelt had declared the neutrality of the United States. The listeners were also relieved to learn that the Air Raid Warning in London had turned out to be a false alarm. It was announced that the National Service Act made all men between the ages of 18 and 41 liable to be called up. Men were to be sent a travel voucher and a 5s 0d pay advance. It was also announced that landlords were permitted to charge the new recruits eight pence for breakfast and five pence for supper when they were billeted on them. The wireless continued to give a stream of advice and instructions which were quite bewildering to people living in remote parts of the country.

The next day, Monday the 4th. September, Head Teacher Miss Mavis Stephens recorded in the Coverack Council School Log:

'Owing to the regretful outbreak of war and in accordance with the circular from the Secretary for Education, the school today closed for instruction. Both teachers attended at the usual times.'

The report added:

'No evacuees arrived yet at Coverack.'

A week later, the next entry in the Coverack School Log recorded:

'School reopened today. There were 13 new children of whom 10 are unofficial evacuees from Manchester and London. Nearly all have parents staying with them. They appear to be well cared for. 57 on books.'

Two days afterwards on the 13th. September, 1939 the log recorded two more evacuees arriving from Seaham Harbour and warned:

'This increase has seriously strained our seating accommodation and we are bound to borrow one or two forms.'

The new children were Jack and Kathleen Davison who were the grandchildren of former Station Officer of Coastguards John Combe. These children stayed with their aunt Mrs. Jenny Mason.

Coverack settled down to the atmosphere of what was to become known as the 'phoney' war. In a curious way people tried to ignore it, in spite of the news of the bombing and German invasion of Poland combined with the massing of Russian troops on her eastern frontier. Everyone was uneasy at not being able to help the Polish allies. The mass of instructions continued to be given out by the government through the media of the Press, Wireless and government pamphlets. The blacking out of windows caused a major problem to villagers. Material had to be obtained from Helston, which meant a journey by bus and the loss of a day's earnings in many cases. By the time the villagers got round to organising a trip to Helston most of the material which they could afford had been snapped up. The ladies of the village then resorted to dyeing old sheets and thin blankets and any other material they found hidden in their houses. Wooden laths were much in demand later on when it was realised that framed blackouts were much more practical than hanging supplementary curtains. Black paint was at a premium when it became obvious that in order to achieve a perfect blackout round the edges of windows it was necessary to paint a black border on the glass. Special blackouts had to be constructed for the village halls, the Chapel and the Church before their normal evening functions could continue. Car headlamps had to be masked. Not many people in Coverack possessed cars so it was not a major village problem. A small slit 4" wide and 3/8" in depth produced a very thin beam of light which made car driving hazardous in the narrow lanes round Coverack. Most of the village cyclists did not bother to use lamps at all. They were used to travelling round the lanes without lights in any case. They only lit up when coming in to the village or when the St. Keverne 'bobby' was known to be on his rounds. Fortunately traffic was very thin so they did not become a danger to motorists. Where the roads were wide enough, white lines were painted in the centre to help motorists avoid bumping into the hedges. There were very few white lines round Coverack.

By Christmas 1939 Coverack people had become resigned to being in a state of war. They were shocked when they learned about losses at sea such as the liner Athenia, the Aircraft Carrier Courageous, the Battleship Royal Oak and the Armed Merchant Cruiser Rawalpindi. They were heartened when the Graf Spee was defeated and eventually scuttled. A number of Coverack men were away at sea and the villagers were very aware of what was happening. The convoys going up and down the Channel were a constant reminder of the dangers involved. Two villagers, Reggie Carey and his brother in law Noel Barker joined the Naval Patrol Service, working from Falmouth. Sometimes their boat came into Coverack Bay. This localised theatre of war gave people a deeper awareness of what was involved in protecting the coast, the fishing fleet and Channel convoys. People were relieved that the war on the western front in Europe had not developed into a wholesale slaughter as it had in the 1914-1918 war. The French called it the 'drôle de guerre' - the peculiar war. The allies were worried by the inevitable defeat of Poland and the attack on Finland by the Russians. It was just as well that no one could predict what was going to happen in the New Year of 1940.

On January 16th., 1940 the village was saddened to learn of the loss of the submarine Sea Horse. The wireless operator on board was 25 year old John Combe, son of the former Station Officer of Coastguards at Coverack. Two of John's sisters had married Coverack men. He himself had recently married a girl from Torry in Scotland where his father was then stationed. The anguish of the family was made worse when the traitor Lord Haw Haw made reference to the submarine and intimated he would read names of survivors. This was in order to keep people tuning in to the German propaganda station.

Shortly after the loss of the Sea Horse another Coverack man was in action at the Battle of Narvik in April, 1940. Petty Officer Fred Carey was a stoker on the destroyer Hardy which was eventually grounded after being hit in the Engine Room by a German destroyer. Fred Carey distinguished himself by joining Lieutenant Commander Mansell in rescuing Chief Petty Officer Styles. Fred himself was wounded but managed to get away from Norway and in time came on leave to convalesce in Coverack. The villagers were proud to have had a representative at Narvik and clubbed together to present an inscribed silver cigarette case to commemorate Fred's safe return. Coverack people had to wait for the publication of Taffrail's book 'The Navy in Action' before they discovered what Fred had done in the action. He was too modest to talk about it.

The month of May, 1940 saw the end of the phoney war in Europe. At first it was fascinating to study the maps which appeared in the daily newspapers showing the rapid advance of the German Army. Senior children in school learned names of places they had never heard of before as battles took place but each day the line on the map showed the Germans were getting nearer and nearer to the coast. All too soon everyone became aware that the Germans were just across the Channel. It was no longer a bad dream. It was a reality. The island nation was about to be invaded. The village became more aware of the gravity of the situation when fishing boats from Porthleven, Penzance and Newlyn passed the village on their way up Channel to take part in the evacuation from Dunkirk. Coverack boats were too small to go that far. Later on, in 1941, Cadgwith men were given a new lifeboat named 'Guide of Dunkirk'. She had been taken straight from the stocks in 1940 to take part in the evacuation. She took people off the beach but had to return to England under a jury (makeshift) sailing rig after her propeller was snagged by a rope.

Just before Brest and other smaller Breton ports were taken by the German Army, Coverack people were amazed to see a procession of small French boats going into Falmouth. Craft of every description were bringing people across the Channel from France. Some sailing boats were so crammed with refugees that people had to stand in the rigging as there was no room on the decks. One motor lifeboat had five rowing boats in tow, each one full of people. Fortunately the weather was fine in Cornwall as it was on the Kent coast. Falmouth was crammed with craft in addition to merchant ships and men of war which had brought exhausted troops across the Channel. Many of the troops had nowhere to rest before they could be taken away by train so they slept in the open on Falmouth Rugby ground. The French civilian refugees were allowed to sleep under cover in the Princess Pavilion, a large dance and concert hall. It was hard to credit that a few weeks before on May 2nd. the gardeners of Falmouth and the Lizard peninsula had been excited by the thought of going to the Pavilion to listen to the well known broadcaster Mr.C.H. Middleton give a talk on 'Gardening in Wartime.' Service men and women coming on short leave to the village from Plymouth told tales of grateful French and Belgian soldiers giving away their buttons and badges as souvenirs to the people who welcomed them to Britain with the traditional cups of tea. One French soldier gave an A.T.S. girl a programme of a Signals Regimental Concert which had taken place on the 21st. April and had been interrupted by a call to arms. The German 'blitzkrieg' had begun on the 9th. April with the invasion of Denmark and Norway but no one seemed to realise that it was going to succeed even when neutral Holland and Belgium were invaded on May 10th. - the day that Chamberlain resigned and Churchill took over. That gives an indication of the swiftness of the German advance. There were all sorts of tales about 5th. columnists mingling with the refugees as well as enemy agents who were trying to effect an entry into Britain during the confusion at the ports. The Coverack coastwatchers were told to be especially vigilant. Not much was said at the time about the valiant First French Army and units of the British Expeditionary Force which fought a rearguard action to allow more than a quarter of a million men to cross the Channel and reform to fight the Germans another day.

After the fall of France the Cornish became uncomfortably aware that German planes were able to cross from Brittany to the county in under an hour's flying time. Civil Defence authorities had been preparing for the possibility of an air attack just before the war. The Air Raid Precautions log for Coverack started on November 19th., 1939. It was an important date for the village. It was Feast Sunday. On that day an exercise was carried out, timed at 1400 hours, 41 2/3 seconds when German planes carrying High Explosive bombs were supposedly sighted travelling over Falmouth at 180 m.p.h. By 1512 two squadrons of fighters believed to be British were heading S.S.W. over the Manacles and duly reported to Helston Centre. A heavy aerial engagement was going on 8 miles south of the Lizard and machine gun fire was heard in the vicinity. What was learned from this exercise is not known.

The next entry was April 7th., 1940. By now, Coverack A.R.P. team was known as Post G2A. This time the practice began at 2136. The Lifeboat Station had supposedly been hit by a bomb. One person was supposed to be injured on being recovered from the debris and there was an unexploded bomb on the beach. The harbour road was blocked and First Aid had to be given by the local Red Cross and A.R.P. personnel. This simulated exercise proved to be an uncannily accurate forecast of things to come, which were far more serious than the practice raid. To return to the log: It continued with entries about routine duties concerning gas masks and other equipment until July 4th., 1940:

| | |
|---|---|
| Yellow Warning | 0820 |
| All Clear | 0902 |
| Yellow Warning | 1415 |
| All Clear | 1430 |

The Yellow Warning told the A.R.P. Wardens that the enemy might well penetrate the area. On July 6th. there was another type of entry:

| | |
|---|---|
| Red Warning | 0740 |
| All Clear | 0902 |
| Yellow Warning | 1130 |
| Red Warning | 1135 |
| All Clear | 1320 |

The Red Warning told the Wardens that the enemy was in the area and that 'sensible' precautions were to be taken. There was no siren in Coverack. The only way of telling the villagers that a Red Warning was in progress was to blow whistles. People do not go round Coverack blowing whistles, even in wartime. The writer's father had by this time become the warden in charge of Post G2A. He decided that if he put on his white tin hat when there was a Red Warning, people would ask him why and he would tell them that a Red Warning was in progress. The usual village 'bush telegraph' did the rest. The news that 'Stafford's got his white hat on', told everyone that the Germans were about. The war in Coverack was beginning to hot up. This will become clear from the next sequence of entries:

| | |
|---|---|
| July 12th., 1940: | I German plane in company with two French planes. |
| | The German plane had heavy black smoke pouring from it. |
| | |
| Aug. 22nd., 1940: | 2138 Red Warning. |
| | Plane over Coverack. |
| | 1 bomb dropped in sea. |
| | 2 bombs reported by Coastguards to have dropped on the |
| | Ebber Rocks near the Black Head. |
| | |
| Aug. 30th., 1940: | H.E. Bomb exploded in Polcoverack Valley. Position |
| | of bomb unknown. |
| | 2155 Fire reported by Mrs. Crowder in vicinity of |
| | Trevenwith Farm - later found to be on Downas Cliff. |

2215 Two explosions heard.
2250 Captain Crowder, G.S. Hart and Mrs. Hunter on
scene at Penhallick.
Bomb crater 200 yards from cross roads.
High Tension cable crossing road damaged.

The next day it was discovered that 5 bombs had fallen in the fields, one in a croft and one in the road.

**SHRAPNEL FROM BOMBS DROPPED ON COVERACK**
*This table was set up on the steps leading down
to the sheds and privies in front of Trewolsta, the Old Inn.
The provocative notice was tempting fate as this very spot
received a direct hit in August, 1942.*

There was a lull until October 9th. when there was a Red Warning at 1955. A plane dive bombed the village. It was reported that 2 H.E. bombs and 12 incendiary bombs had been dropped. One unexploded bomb was reported by Casley Chapple to have been dropped in Polcoverack Valley. This was subsequently found to be a false alarm, but three bungalows were evacuated as a precaution until it was verified. When the reports of the other bombs were checked out it was found that six bombs had been dropped between the Bus Shelter and Miss Bulkeley's garage, shattering windows and damaging telephone wires. Twenty five houses had bomb blast damage. Three houses belonging to Dr. Blackwood, Captain Gibson and Mr. Jimmy Carey were badly damaged. One bomb landed on the Mill Beach opposite the Bay Hotel. It did no damage. It was fortunate that no villager was seriously injured in this raid but the report also included the fact that one bomb landed in the churchyard and dislodged tombstones. Some villagers were more indignant about that bomb than those which had narrowly missed the houses at North Corner.

A new problem presented itself on October 19th.

2300 Gas alert. All Wardens warned.

The writer's father had experienced gas attacks during the First World War. They had clearly made a lasting impression on him. He claimed that he and his comrades had avoided being badly gassed by urinating on their spare socks and tying them round their mouths and noses as they had no gas masks. It is easy to imagine my father's dilemma when the warning came to Coverack. If he used the Gas Warning rattle the villagers might panic but if nothing happened they would laugh him to scorn and ignore any subsequent and possibly genuine attack. In the event he decided to play a waiting game. It paid off. Nothing happened. The authorities were clearly shaken by the false alarm. The next day the log recorded the arrival of 175 Contex fittings and 1 roll of tape. My father noted tersely: Total now received for the Coverack area: 425. He had been waiting a long time for these supplies. Authorities can move swiftly when it is for real!

The problem of protecting the village from a gas attack gave more trouble in one sense than the bombing. One might argue that it would never be worth while to gas the population of such a small village. That is true. It would also seem not worth while to bomb such a widely scattered community - but it was done - possibly the village was used as a dumping ground for embarrassed German pilots who could not face the Falmouth barrage, nor the embarrassment of returning to base with a full load of bombs. We shall never know the answer. These arguments did not alter the fact that the people had to be protected and the log is full of reports about fitting gas masks. Babies grew up and had to progress from the incubator type which had a bellows operated by the child's mother, to the Mickey Mouse Type which appealed in a bizarre way to very young children. Next the child graduated to a Small, then a Medium and finally to a Large size. Masks were always being damaged, dropped in puddles and lost. Wardens could not put civilians on a charge for exposing themselves to a horrible death! The gas mask wearers themselves often let it be known that they thought the compulsory gas masks were just another of the government's ploys to make life even more unbearable during war time. Those who absolutely refused to be fitted out said quite cheerfully that the consequences of a gas attack were so horrifying that the best policy was to ignore it and hope it would never happen. The Wardens felt that adults could make their own decisions but they made sure the children were protected by going round the schools and keeping the gas masks in good working order. It truly was a labour of love, the work took a long time but they received no payment for A.R.P. work by day nor by night.

Winston Churchill revealed in his War Memoirs 'Their Finest Hour' that on the 14th. July, 1940 he sent the following message to General Ismay: 'It seems to me very important that everybody should be made to look to their gas masks now........it may well be that Hitler has some gas designs on us........action should be taken at once.' He could have taken comfort from the fact that at least Coverack was prepared!

176

It goes without saying that the villagers were unaware of much of the foregoing routine A.R.P. work which went on in Coverack. Many were too involved with other activities to give it much thought. After the fall of France an invasion was expected. Fortunately Hitler became preoccupied with defeating the French Army and went against the advice of his generals who wanted to go ahead and attack England straight away before the French Army was completely defeated. This delay gave Great Britain the chance to prepare defences against invasion. Operation Sealion, the invasion of Britain by the Germans never took place.

A brief account of the Early Days of the Second World War in Coverack would not be complete without another reference to the village children. The end of the year 1940 was fast approaching, accompanied by an Easterly gale in Coverack. Of course, it was only natural that some of the boys should go wrecking at low tide to see what the gale had brought them. They came across a metal cylinder which appeared unusual so they rolled it along the beach and finally decided to load it on an old pram and take it to the Coastguard Station.

The Coastguard on duty told them to take the metal cylinder down to the scrap heap at the Mill Garage. The boys set off through the village, exhibiting their find to anyone who was prepared to stop and admire what was going to be their contribution to the war effort. The object was duly dumped with the other scrap but after a few days the boys noticed that the ungrateful scrap dump owner had put their precious find back on the beach, presumably because it had no apparent value. In view of this, the boys decided to gather some wreck wood and get rid of the object by lighting a fire under it.

At this point a villager saw what was happening and told the boys to leave the object alone and then he reported the find to the writer's father. He inspected the cylinder and 'phoned his A.R.P. H.Q. telling them of his suspicions. The following day a Royal Navy Bomb Disposal Unit from Falmouth arrived and took the object away. The sailors had recognised that it was a shell which fortunately no longer had a nose cap which contains the fuse. When the Bomb Disposal lorry arrived at Goonhilly Downs the sailors unloaded the shell and blew it up. No doubt the village lads were disappointed that the sailors did not arrange the explosion on the Mill Beach, but at least it was an exciting end to the year 1940.

## The Home Guard

The 'phoney war' was over. The Battle for Britain had started. The country was expecting an invasion. There were not enough troops to go round so it was decided to have concentrations of professional 'Leopard' troops ready to be sent anywhere if an invasion began. This meant that additional soldiers would be needed for continuous local defence. Anthony Eden proposed that a band of Local Defence Volunteers be raised and called for men to join. The volunteers were asked to enrol at the local police station.

This was just the opportunity Mr. Alex Thomas of Penhallick had been waiting for. He had had a boyhood ambition to join the Army but his father would not give permission so on the 14th. May, 1940 he decided to go to St. Keverne at once and register. He was the first volunteer to arrive at the policeman's house. The embarrassed constable had to admit that he had not yet been issued with the necessary official forms but he took details and in due course Mr. Thomas became a member of the L.D.V. A number of men who had served in the Great War joined, as well as lads who were too young to go in the forces or were in reserved occupations such as farming. They were a motley crew but the ex-servicemen of the village soon showed the raw recruits what was required.

Mr. Harry Snell and Mr. Edward Daw were appointed officers in Coverack village. They were both First World War veterans. Mr. Alex Thomas became the officer in charge of the Penhallick and Ponsongath contingent. The Officer in charge of the Meneage area was Colonel Long from Trenoweth. Drills were held in the Coverack Village Hall. The 'old sweats' taught the recruits to form fours until someone pointed out that the modern army drilled in columns of three. This was rather puzzling, for the L.D.V. had been told that their primary purpose was to deal with paratroops, saboteurs, enemy troops who would most likely be in British Army uniforms and Fifth Columnists. The expression 'Fifth Columnist' had been coined during the 1936 Civil War in Spain to describe the extra 'column' of supporters the enemy already had living in the country being attacked. The Fifth Columnists in the European countries overrun by the Germans had created havoc and confusion and the authorities did not want to see a repetition of that should the Germans land in Britain. It seemed to the Coverack L.D.V. that if troops now marched in columns of three, surely they should have been asked to look out for Fourth Columnists - not that anyone thought there were any Fifth, or Fourth Columnists lurking in Coverack. It was all very confusing so the local volunteers just did what they were asked and hoped the authorities knew what they were doing because the volunteers did not.

At first the members of the L.D.V. wore their own clothes and khaki armbands with the letters L.D.V. printed in black on them. They armed themselves with whatever they could find. Their weapons ranged from stout sticks, old bayonets from the First World War and beyond and miscellaneous types of shotguns - to some wicked looking farm implements reminiscent of the 'bills' carried by the defenders of Coverack during the Armada invasion scare which was described in the chapter entitled Beginnings. One or two recruits brought obsolete guns for which they had no ammunition but the weapons inspired confidence in both the Volunteers and the villagers who were not aware that there were no cartridges available for the guns.

Some rifles arrived after a while. They were somewhat primitive. The writer, who was in the 5th Form of Helston County Secondary School at the time, was eventually presented with a long rifle and thirty bullets. On inspection it was discovered that the rifle was of French origin and had been manufactured in 1870 during the Franco-Prussian War. It had been brought into Falmouth by a French refugee. After instruction I was allowed to fire one round at a piece of wood floating in the sea off the Battery. I missed but was told to save the other twenty nine bullets for the 'b....y Germans.' In time, khaki uniforms were issued. Coverack people found the army boots were the most welcome part of the uniforms. Sergeant Pete Eddy of the L.D.V. and the village shoemaker was kept busy putting hob nails into the boots to prevent them wearing out too soon. The forage caps were not so popular. The men with thinning hair found them rather draughty so they usually wore their own headgear when on duty at night. They looked faintly ridiculous to some of the servicemen stationed in the district but the Volunteers were not concerned about that.

In November, 1940 the Local Defence Volunteers were re-named the Home Guard. Churchill was not very keen on the word 'Local', he considered it was 'uninspiring'. After all, it was a Guard for the Home. Perhaps the term 'Local' should have been retained. The local men in the Home Guard would soon detect a stranger in their midst. No German in Coverack would be able to pass himself off as a 'friend'. On one occasion a grumpy local Home Guard got fed up hearing the replies of 'friend' when he challenged people who were moving about during his duty night. Finally when a car drew up in response to his challenge and the occupant said he was a 'friend', the exasperated sentry replied, 'Everyone's a b....y friend tonight, get out and let's 'ave a look at 'ee.' The driver meekly got out and proved he was the Senior Officer of the R.A.F. Radar Station travelling in civilian clothes. The Home Guard was unimpressed but allowed him to continue on his way.

There was no lack of enthusiasm in the Coverack area, although guard duties were irksome to men who had been working all day in the open air. The village was defended by men who kept watch on the Dolor Point (unless it was raining and blowing a gale, when they would be in the Fishermen's Rest), Higher Bridge, Lowland Point, Mears Point, Lankidden, various cross roads and other strategic points. Some field training was done on the Golf Course at the Headland and in time, night exercises went on in conjunction with soldiers from the East Yorks Regiment who were stationed in the area to guard the Radar sites at Treleaver, Penmarth and Goonhilly Downs.

The stories about the Home Guard in Coverack are legion. It is interesting to read what the village children thought about their defenders in the School centenary book, 'Our Schooldays by the Sea.' A true story that is not generally known is related here. Some of the Home Guards were still at school. Two schoolboy cousins were detailed to be messengers and as such were based at the Coverack Post Office. They were allowed to sleep on camp beds in the Post Office kitchen if there were no messages to be run. The Officer in Charge also sat in the kitchen, ostensibly awake, so that should the telephone ring he could answer it. At times the Officer would drop off to sleep and begin snoring. That was the signal for one of the boys to go to the kiosk outside the Post Office and ring St. Keverne 10, the Post Office number. The two boys would then witness the awakening of the Officer and his attempts to answer the non existent caller. On one occasion they tied his bootlaces together while he was sleeping and then rang the Post Office. Needless to say the messengers enjoyed the spectacle of the Officer standing up and falling over when he tried to dash into the sorting office, but they did not dare repeat the trick!

It is interesting to note that the Post Office building was used as a Head Quarters for the Home Guard in the same way that it is believed to have been used as a key building when smuggling was part of the way of life of the villagers of Coverack. This was mentioned in the section on Coverack Post Office, the Roskillys and others.

D COY. HOME GUARD OFFICERS AND WARRANT OFFICERS
*Seated left, Mr. E. Daw, behind him Mr. Alex Thomas,*
*next to him, seated, is Mr. Harry Snell.*

The Home Guard was literally a 'Dad's Army' and as such was open to good natured ridicule but there was a serious side to their work and they were a force to be reckoned with. Certain local men kept Mills Bombs and ammunition in their sheds, everyone knew this but no one went to the sheds to play the fool and no one talked about it. When the standard of efficiency in the Home Guard had reached a certain level, the Duke of Cornwall's Light Infantry training school instructors gave the Home Guard a battle innoculation course at Kennack. Mr. Alex Thomas recounted to the writer that when he went to train at Kennack he had to advance to a position from where live bullets were being fired a foot or two above his head. The instructor assured him that there was no need to worry as the training allowed for a 4% casualty rate. At the other end of the scale, so to speak, one middle aged gentleman's wife always accompanied him on sentry duty because she did not trust him out of her sight at night. There is no record of her having accompanied her husband on a battle innoculation course!

There were no concrete pill boxes built in Coverack. Strong points were constructed from local stone and turf in places such as the cliff above Porthbeer Cove, or Mears Beach as it is known today. The reader will recall that this is the site of a Cliff Castle, so it was the obvious place to set up a defensive position. A strong, wide wall was constructed between the Fishermen's Rest and the Lifeboat House to prevent the easy landing of vehicles from the harbour slipway. Some of the more accessible cliffs were festooned with barbed wire to impede the advance of agents or enemy soldiers. These defences were cleared at the end of hostilities by Italian prisoners of war.

The road out of Coverack from Higher Bridge was considered to be a prime target for would be invaders landing on Mill Beach, so in time the Home Guard were provided with a small searchlight and a machine gun with armour piercing bullets to defend the position. When military equipment was being assembled in 1942 for Operation Torch, the invasion of North Africa, Coverack had to give back its light and its gun. Rumour persists to this day that the Cabinet had, in any event, decided to abandon Cornwall if the Germans landed there as the lines of communication would have been too long to keep open. To date, no one has discovered written proof of this but some Coverack people consider that it is one of the reasons why their Home Guard had to give back their most effective weapon, in spite of the fact that there was still a very real danger of a landing being made in the village.

There were two invasion scares in Coverack. One was attributed to an A.T.S. typist in an Army H.Q. in the Midlands who sent a signal with a mistake in the coding. This led to the Army and Home Guard standing-to until the small hours. Mr. Alex Thomas recalled that the reality was such he was ordered to withdraw his guards from Lankidden. He sent a messenger on a bicycle to tell the two Home Guards to leave their post and join the platoon at Ponsongath, from where they had orders to retreat to the Radar Station on Goonhilly Downs should there be a landing and they were unable to repel the enemy. They were to defend the station for as long as possible. After a while, the bicycle messenger returned to Ponsongath saying that the guards were no longer at Lankidden. Mr. Thomas was in a quandary. Had the guards already been captured by the invaders? Were they lying wounded or even dead on the cliffs? He decided that as their officer he had to go and find out. He went cautiously to the guard post and to his relief he was challenged by a voice he knew so well. The two men informed him they had not seen the messenger but they had heard the gate to the field creak and knew someone had opened it. No one came, so they had a scout round. They found nothing so they continued with their guard duties until Mr. Thomas arrived. Mr. Thomas brought the two men back with him to Ponsongath. He concluded that the messenger must have taken fright and retreated with all speed when he made a noise opening the gate. Anyone who knows the area can sympathise with the person who was not prepared to go down to the cliff top at Lankidden in pitch darkness when a German landing was expected at any moment. One can imagine the relief of the Home Guard when the fault in the signal was eventually discovered and they were told they could go home.

It is small wonder that Captain Goldsworthy, the Chairman of St. Austell Rural Council was reported by the West Briton on the 1st. July, 1940 as saying, 'It is muddle, muddle all the time', when discussing A.R.P. and L.D.V. organisation. His comment seems to reflect the general opinion of local government in Cornwall at that time. A fortnight later another West Briton headline declared:

'Sale of cream may be prohibited.'

It is fairly certain that this headline provoked as much local comment as the previous one. Some Cornish people call cream 'white meat'. To be without it was unthinkable. No one denies there was muddle. What is amazing, is that out of the muddle emerged two organisations which were to prove invaluable in due course. Coverack was no exception.

The second invasion scare came one night in November, 1943 just seven months before the Second Front. There was a typical thick November fog blanketing the sea. The Auxiliary Coastguard on duty at the Lowland Point heard ship's engines close by, then the sound of anchor chains running through hawse pipes accompanied by Germanic sounding orders. He not unnaturally assumed that a daring landing was about to take place under cover of the fog. Accordingly he informed the Station Officer of Coastguards at Porthoustock, who in turn informed the Flag Officer in Charge at Falmouth, who in turn informed the Army authorities. In accordance with pre-arranged instructions the Coastguard on duty was told to cut the telephone wires, remove all confidential papers and evacuate the Look Out Hut. This was done speedily. Meanwhile the East Yorks Regiment sent a large body of men to St. Keverne with some armoured units. The St. Keverne and Coverack Home Guard were called out and the men told to load their weapons. Coverack men went to their posts and St. Keverne men were placed in position under the command of the full time soldiers in and around St. Keverne. No one could move in or around the villages without being challenged. It is doubtful if even a scavenging fox or badger could have got past the Home Guards who were in the parts of the area which the East Yorks were less familiar with. If the animals had tried the road to St. Keverne from the coast they would have been frightened off by the sound of a large body of men marching down Tregellast Hill at half past midnight. Some of the local quarry men who were also Home Guards had the job of preparing mines to blow up the roads in key positions. These men were accustomed to handling explosives and would have done a good job. Fortunately they did not lose any of their charges that night.

By the time all the troops were in position and everyone in the villages was wide awake, wondering if the Germans would get a foothold, daylight was approaching and the fog was beginning to lift. After a while, all became clear. A Dutch ship was anchored off Dean Point. It was part of a convoy which had wisely anchored before approaching Falmouth in thick fog. This time the scare was due to the omission of a coded message giving details of the convoy's intentions. The Home Guard could not win!

There are two interesting Coverack footnotes to the story of 'The invasion that never was,' which was the title given to an eye witness account of the night's activities at St. Keverne written after the war by Mr. Willie Moyle for the Sunday Pictorial. The British Red Cross ladies of Coverack were told to assemble at their First Aid Post in the vestry of the Wesleyan Chapel that night. One volunteer nurse was challenged on her way to the Chapel. She became frightened and said to the sentry at the road block, 'Please don't point that gun at me.' The reply was swift and reassuring: 'Don't 'ee worry, Miss, 'ee isn't loaded!' The A.R.P. Wardens of Coverack were also called to duty that night and they too were stopped at a road block. It was noticed that one of the Home Guard manning the post had removed his scabbard from his belt and put it on his fixed bayonet. On being asked the reason, he told the Warden, who had fought in France during the Great War: 'I polished 'n last night and I don't want for 'n to get rusty.' It was obvious that the thought of an invasion was less worrying than the thought of having to clean the bayonet again the next day. It had not occurred to the guard that a scabbard bayonet would have been of little use had he been forced to attack a German with it - or perhaps he realised it was a false alarm - after all, who, in his right mind, would try to invade Cornwall by coming through the Manacles in a thick fog?

In hindsight it is easy to laugh at the Coverack Home Guard. Indeed it was easy to do so at the time. A good laugh was welcome in those dark days. When people made fun of the voluntary services it did not necessarily mean they were being critical. They knew they would probably not do any better if they were faced with the same situation, but they did enjoy the discomfiture of their fellow villagers when they got into a predicament, without being malicious about it.

An entry in the Coverack Red Cross Case Book at 1130 a.m. on the 29th. July, 1942 no doubt conceals an interesting story but unfortunately the writer has not been able to discover what really happened. The description reads: 'Mr. C. Wilkinson, H.G., Granville, Coverack: 2 wounds on leg caused by bullet discharged nearby. Applied dressing and bandages and sent to Dr. Spry.' As far as is known, Charles Wilkinson was the only member of the Coverack Home Guard to be wounded by a bullet during the Second World War.

There seems no doubt that one enemy landing did take place at Coverack. It was the custom during the war for Coastguards to come home from a night watch along the clifftop from the Black Head instead of taking the shorter path across country. This walk was known as 'The Dawn Patrol'. One morning a Coastguard noticed that undergrowth and furze had been disturbed, so he went down the cliff to investigate. He soon found a concealed inflated raft which contained some emergency rations and a First Aid Kit of German origin. He left the raft where it was and reported his find to the Station Officer on his return to Coverack. After a while the raft was brought to the Coastguard Station and later transported to Naval Headquarters in Falmouth. Not many village people were made aware of this find. No mention of it was made in the Press. The raft could have been hidden by a German agent who was hoping to return to the spot, go out to sea and meet a German submarine. No one came back to the spot where the raft was hidden, so evidently it had not been placed there by a local wrecker who would most certainly have taken his prize home in due course. It does therefore seem likely that a German effected a landing near the Black Head during wartime. There are two thousand miles of British coastline. Perhaps it was considered by someone in the German High Command that Coverack was the most unlikely place where an intruder would be detected. One day someone might find a reference to the incident in the German archives.

It has not been possible to consult a written record of the official activities of the Coverack Home Guard. It is a pity. It is hoped that Falmouth Home Guard veterans will not mind if the writer quotes from their granite memorial at Stack Point, Falmouth. It is dedicated to those who:

'After their day's work nightly patrolled this coast, armed and vigilant against German landings. Thus they watched a hundred dawns appear across these great waters which form our country's moat.'

It is a most appropriate description of the activities of all the coastal Home Guard contingents.

### Evacuees

We have seen that some evacuees arrived in Coverack just as war broke out. They did not cause any major problems as they were accompanied by their mothers or stayed with friends and relatives in the village. Nine months later everything seemed to happen at once. Refugees came flooding into Falmouth from Brittany, fishing boats went off to the beaches of Dunkirk, Local Defence Volunteers were called for and more evacuees arrived from Enfield. Due to the seriousness of the situation, there was no Flora Day in 1940 so it was decided to have a half term holiday on the 14th. May. We saw in the last section on the Home Guard that on the 14th. May, volunteers for the L.D.V. were called for. In view of the gravity of the situation, schools were asked to reopen so that children could be occupied and readily accounted for. It is nor surprising that on Tuesday, 14th. May, the day after Whit Monday, for one reason or another, parents and children did not respond readily to the appeal to return to school. Miss Stephens, the Headmistress of Coverack School spent Whit Monday at her home in Roche. In response to the Government's appeal she got up at 6 a.m. on Tuesday to drive to school. On the way she picked up a teacher who was returning to St. Keverne School. The two teachers arrived in St. Keverne at 8.40 a.m. but no one was at the school. On arriving at Coverack, Miss Stephens found ten children waiting. Not to be outdone, she went down to the village and 'rounded up' another nine. By the afternoon there were twenty four present, which was exactly half of the number on roll. As usual there was no real sense of urgency in Coverack.

It was a different situation in London and the Channel coastal towns close to France. People there were being asked to leave their homes and school children were being evacuated. School was the obvious place for them to be so that they could be organised. Sunday the 26th. May, 1940 was declared a National Day of Prayer when special prayers were said for 'the Government and those who command our fleets and armies ........ peoples invaded and oppressed ........ the victory of right and truth; that it might be not long delayed.' Everyone became more acutely aware of the plight of the country and consequently more determined to keep the enemy out. Three weeks later Coverack was told to prepare for the arrival of evacuees.

On Monday the 17th. June, 1940 Miss Stephens wrote in the Coverack School Log:

'In order to give the billeting authorities time to prepare the school as a reception centre for the evacuees expected this evening we opened school at 1.15 and closed at 3.40.'

Meanwhile buses were sent to Camborne station to fetch the children. Some Coverack men and women went to the station to escort the children back. A few of the off duty East Yorks soldiers volunteered to help as well. The Women's Section of Coverack British Legion brought cakes, milk and tea to feed the evacuees children while arrangements for billeting them were being made.

Miss Stephens and her volunteer helpers did all they could to prepare for the children's arrival and the Billeting Officer, Mrs. E.M. Hart had to send messages to the village families to warn them of the impending arrival so that they could prepare beds and food, etc. Village volunteers went by bicycle, motor bike and car to the farms. Not many people had telephones, so it was a mammoth task. There was no time to argue nor to get agitated. Preparations had to be made at once, yet no one knew how many were coming, their age range or whether they were boys or girls or how many of each.

Some volunteers were already tired. There had been Red Warnings at 0300 in the early morning and those involved in that had not been to sleep since as they had their normal daily work to do. Miss Stephens recorded in the School Log for that day:

'Unfortunately it was nearly 9 p.m. before the children reached Coverack and many were asleep. As we have no lighting or blackout it became apparent that only the barest essential details required by the Billeting Authorities would be obtained that evening. I decided to close the school on Tuesday in order to give opportunities to both parties to meet and discuss anything necessary.'

The next day, the five teachers met, including the Teacher in Charge, Miss B.S. French from Southbury Road Girls' School, Enfield. The assistant teachers decided to visit each child billeted in the village and to get the 61 children to come to school at 2 o'clock that afternoon. Miss Stephens took Miss French round the farm billets as it needed local knowledge to find them. After seeing to the immediate needs of the children and giving them as much reassurance as possible, it was decided that afternoon to accept the offer of the Village Hall as a temporary daily meeting place and to start work again the following day at 9 o'clock. A week later, on the 25th. June, it was recorded that a chair had to be borrowed from a villager as another evacuee had arrived. That demonstrates how difficult it was to accommodate the extra children in a small village. Fortunately the weather was fine and some lessons such as Drawing were taken on the Battery where there was no problem about seating on the dry grass.

The school on the hill was bursting at the seams, metaphorically speaking, so Mrs. Roddick from 'The Mansion' invited the girls to do their needlework on her lawn and kindly kept an eye on them while the teacher and the boys were 'digging for victory' in the school garden. It had always been the custom to sell the produce from this garden in the village and this source of reasonably priced fresh food was much appreciated by the people of the village in war time.

The school windows were about five feet above ground level, tall and narrow, nevertheless as it seemed possible that a bombardment of some kind might take place, Miss Stephens decided that it was time to take steps to protect the children from possibly flying splinters of glass. She recorded in the School Log:

'As wire netting seems unobtainable, the Senior Boys and I pasted butter muslin over the lobby windows.'

The lobby was where the children would go in the event of an air raid or shelling from the sea. These 'matter of fact' entries in the School Log serve to indicate the conditions under which the village children and their evacuee friends were being educated in the days after Dunkirk. The disruptions were no doubt a welcome break for them but they must have caused much irritation to the teachers who were trying to keep everything as normal as possible so as not to impart to the impressionable children the seriousness of the situation.

Coverack settled down to 'host' its evacuees. Most of the villagers realised what an emotional upset it had been for the Enfield children to have been taken away from their families and placed in the homes of strangers. Accordingly the people of Coverack did all they could to make the children feel at home. As already described, it was late when the children arrived in Coverack. The evacuee teachers knew their children. The Billeting Officer knew the villagers, but case conferences could not be held on each child in a school with no light and no blackout at 9 o'clock that night. This meant that the children had to be hastily allocated as their teachers brought them forward. The farmers' wives were given their children first as they had the greater distances to travel. Mrs. Hart had to ignore requests from some people for children who appeared to be cleaner and better dressed. She was determined the school room would not be turned into a village cattle market. The children were allocated swiftly and in as kindly a manner as possible, bearing in mind the number and sexes of the local children known to be in the host home. A few spinsters found themselves having to cope with a child for the first time in their lives as did some childless couples. There were inevitable problems after a while which meant some 're-shuffling' of the children but on the whole the children settled down remarkably quickly as did their foster parents. Before long the village children were playing happily with the evacuee children and the older boys and girls were happily finding new girl and boy friends.

There is a Coverack Close in Southgate, Enfield. It would be pleasant to think it was so called because of the wartime connection between the two places, but the Borough Local History Officer, Mr. Graham Dalling says that there is no known historical link between Southgate and Coverack and that the most likely explanation for the name is that a Council official named the Close after spending a holiday in Coverack.

The School Log went on recording routine happenings. German 'planes were now coming over during daylight and the A.R.P. Wardens informed the teachers when they were in receipt of a Red Warning so that children could get behind the wide, protective Cornish hedges when they were working out of doors or in between the lobby walls when they were in school An interesting entry was recorded among the routine details on the 1st. November, 1940:

'For the first time on record the salary cheques failed to arrive by the usual post.' The report added: ' - a particularly 'aerially' active day and night no doubt caused the delay.' The war had become routine as well.

Air Raids on Plymouth were getting heavier in early 1941. On the 13th. January, 25 German aircraft attacked the city and dropped 106 High Explosive Bombs in addition to thousands of incendiaries. The raids continued and on the 5th. March it was decided to evacuate those children who still remained in the city. It was not too soon as will be seen later. This time there was a precedent to follow and improve on concerning the reception of evacuees in Coverack. Seventy six children accompanied by nine teachers and adult helpers came to the village. By now, some Coverack cottages had been rented by the billeting authorities. Among them were properties known as Ar-Lyn , South Cottage, Tolverne, and Curgenven Cottage, the former Wesleyan Chapel. Parc Behan on School Hill was being used as a Hostel under a Warden whose name was Evans. The children billeted there were those who had medical or psychological problems with which Coverack families would have found great difficulty in coping due to their comparatively meagre resources.

Before the Plymouth children arrived the Billeting Officer had been able to go round the village and give details of the possibility of more evacuees arriving. The preparatory organisation was going smoothly when without warning the powers that be decided to send the 76 extra children. The list in the Billeting Officer's Evacuation Register records a potential of 117 extra billets. It was just as well that there were more billets available than for the 76 who came from Plymouth because on the 26th. May, twelve more came from Bristol, with no teacher and they had to be housed as well. Of course, some of the second batch of villagers who had agreed to help in the emergency were elderly and not in good health. They were not called upon, except for a short while, until younger, healthy foster parents could be found.

The Plymouth children were tired and grubby when they arrived. The short journey had not tired them greatly, they were worn out through lack of sleep caused by nights spent in shelters. Some were dirty because they literally had to evacuate their bombed homes and had not been able to get many clothes together before leaving. Fortunately the American Red Cross had sent some clothing to Coverack and the needy children were given these garments to wear while waiting for some to be sent by their parents. As more and more American parcels found their way to Coverack the evacuees began to covet the comparatively expensive clothes and the attractive American styles. It was not a one way process. The children helped others as well. The boys and girls in Coverack School, which now had a hundred and fifty on the roll, were encouraged to make limb pillows and other small appliances used in hospitals caring for the wounded.

The Plymouth children came to Coverack not a day too soon. A fortnight after they arrived in the village the King and Queen toured the devastated parts of Plymouth on the 20th. March. They talked to the people and did a great deal to boost their morale. The people needed that little uplift to their spirits that very night. An Air Raid began at 8.30 p.m. when German pathfinding aircraft dropped thousands of incendiaries on the city. The bombers followed and aimed High Explosive bombs at the conflagration. The Germans came again the following night. The result of the two night's attacks was a death toll of 336 and 20,000 houses and shops damaged or destroyed. The Germans returned again in April and killed another 590 people, damaging and destroying a further 16,000 buildings. One can imagine the thoughts of the little ones in Coverack when they heard about these raids. Indeed, the flashes from Plymouth could be seen in the sky from Coverack on occasions. The teachers and foster parents kept the children as busy as possible to prevent them from dwelling on the news and did all they could to compensate for the absence of the children's parents and families.

Although the children were in Coverack they were not immune to German raids. In fact some of them witnessed an attack at sea soon after they arrived as will be seen in the next section. They were also involved in an air attack on the village. This will also be described later.

Mrs. S. Hart, billeting organiser (right) and Mrs. A. Symes showing evacuees from Plymouth, now at Coverack, some of the gifts of clothing sent by the American Red Cross.

PLYMOUTH EVACUEES RECEIVE AMERICAN RED CROSS GIFTS
AT COVERACK
*Reproduced by kind permission of the West Briton*

### *1941 and The Three Sisters*

The services of The Three Sisters were not called on during the early years of the war. This gave the new shore and boat crew members who had replaced men who had joined the services a chance to get used to the vital work of the R.N.L.I.

The first call of 1941 came on the 20th. March, eighteen months after the outbreak of the war. The reader will remember that this was the day when the visit of the King and Queen to Plymouth was followed by the biggest blitz the city had experienced up to that time. Some of the Plymouth evacuees living in the cove were out of doors that same evening at half past seven when gunfire was heard out at sea. Station Officer of Coastguards Harold Tapper was on duty and immediately informed his Divisional Officer that a ship was being attacked by a German bomber in a position two or three miles South East of Dolor Point. Many of the villagers had heard the gunfire and ran down to the Dolor to find out what was happening.

Mr. W.F. Tremelling the Honorary Lifeboat Secretary came to the Dolor as did the members of the Lifeboat crew. They were readily available as their day's work was done.

The easterly wind was quite light, the sea choppy with the usual misty conditions which often accompany the East wind. Mr. Tremelling wrote in his report:

'The Coxswain and Secretary of the Lifeboat had under observation a steamer approaching from the East with 'planes in the distance apparently coming from the French coast. When over the steamer the 'planes dropped in all five bombs and then machine gunned the crew as the men were in the ship's lifeboats. As soon as the first bomb hit the steamer I told the Coxswain to launch. This was done with promptitude. The lifeboat reached the men in the boat just as the vessel sank.'

The vessel was a 1,500 ton Polish ship called Cieszyn from Gydinia, a port on the Baltic. She was in ballast on her way to Swansea from Falmouth when attacked. As soon as the Three Sisters got alongside the ship's boat some of the ship's crew who had jumped into the water when the ship sank were transferred to The Three Sisters. They were very cold and wet. They were most grateful for the brandy which was offered to them. Coxswain Archie Rowe put a lifeboat crew man aboard the ship's lifeboat and took it in tow.

The Three Sisters rescued twenty seven men in all. The Master was called Captain Mikosza. There were twenty four other members of the ship's company and two D.E.M.S. ratings from the Royal Navy. The latter were the ship's gunners who had tried to defend the vessel. Some of the Poles were wounded. One was a stretcher case and two others also needed treatment at Helston Cottage Hospital. Other members of the crew had their superficial cuts treated when they landed at 8.42 p.m. The complete action had taken just over an hour.

The writer witnessed the whole affair. It was unreal, hearing the explosions after seeing the puffs of smoke and the splashes of the bombs and bullets. No one in the village doubted that all who could be saved would be saved by the lifeboat crew. On arrival at Coverack the bewildered Polish seamen were met by a crowd of villagers, all of whom were anxious to help and to find out what had happened. When it was realised they were Polish, at the back of everyone's mind was the thought that these poor fellows who were already separated from their loved ones, had once more lost all their possessions. This time it was while fighting in defence of the very country which they had vainly hoped would keep the Germans out of their own fatherland. None of these sentiments could be expressed because of the language difficulties.

When the seamen landed it was dark. No lights could be shown because of the blackout regulations. As each man came up towards the Paris Hotel from the Lifeboat House he had to duck in order to avoid hitting his head on the crank of the winch. The waiting villagers, anxious to warn the sailors, shouted, 'Mind your head, my 'andsome!' or 'Look Out!' or 'Duck!'. The writer got the impression that the Poles thought they were being shouted a greeting. Most of them smiled and then bumped their heads as they walked into the winch crank. It was an unfortunate introduction to Coverack for them after all they had been through.

The Polish seamen were given some dry clothing and something to eat and drink and the uninjured men were taken back to Falmouth in transport arranged by the Shipwrecked Mariners' Society. The Coastlines Agent was there to represent the Polish owners of the vessel. After hosing down the lifeboat and refuelling, the crew returned home to await the next call. The members of the crew of The Three Sisters who rescued the Polish seamen were:

Coxswain Archie Rowe*

| | |
|---|---|
| George Dally | Willie Eustis |
| Horace Eustice* | George Hewitt |
| Percy Eustis | Sam Roskilly* |

* Captain Mikosza of the Cieszyn was to meet these members of the crew again in 1958 when invited to pay tribute to Coxswain Archie Rowe in a 'This is your Life' programme.

The Germans were over the village again the next night and every night until May the 7th. without a break. It was the period of the Plymouth blitz. Explosions were reported coming from every direction but Coverack was not harmed. On March the 29th. a German 'plane attacked a mine sweeper which was patrolling 2½ miles South South East of Coverack, not far from where the S.S. Cieszyn was sunk. The Coverack Lifeboat men gathered, thinking their services might be needed again, but being better armed than the Polish steamer the minesweeper drove the 'plane off and carried on with her work.

On April 30th., 1941 a pear shaped mine was washed up in Perprean Cove beneath the Kissing Gates. One of the Royal Navy Bomb Disposal Team sent to deal with the mine cut his hand and had to be treated in Coverack. The following year the writer was on watch aboard H.M.S. Pathfinder in the South Atlantic. My companion was Able Seaman Rouffignac from Newlyn. We began talking about Cornwall and when Rouffignac learned I was from Coverack he told me about the incident. I subsequently discovered that my mother had treated his injury as she lived a few hundred yards from the spot where the mine had washed in. Such is the long arm of coincidence.

On May 21st., 1941 a land mine was dropped at Chywoon Farm just off the road to St. Keverne from the Dollies cross roads. It caused quite a sensation. Many villagers went to visit the spot. Another pear shaped mine came ashore at Mill Beach at the same time. This was promptly dealt with by the Falmouth Bomb Disposal Team. These incidents all served to keep everyone in Coverack very much aware of their proximity to the war. The village was part of it. The activity was right there on people's doorsteps in a manner of speaking.

At 7.25 a.m. on the 17th. June, 1941 Coverack Coastguards informed Mr. Tremelling the Honorary Secretary of the Lifeboat that a torpedo boat had gone ashore at Downas Cove, just west of the Black Head. There was a light easterly wind, accompanied by fog. Some of the regular lifeboat crew and helpers had already gone to work so Coxswain Archie Rowe assembled a scratch crew and set off for Downas. By 8 a.m., in spite of a thickening fog, Archie had found M.T.B. 45, which was called Naraya. She was manned by a Polish crew. She had been observed striking the rocks by Mr. Eddy Pearce who was an Auxiliary Coastguard at Lankidden. On trying to get off the rocks, the vessel had damaged her propellers. There were 11 people on board.

The Coxswain put crewman Horace Eustice aboard the M.T.B. to avoid possible communications problems and proceeded to pull the vessel off the rocks. She came off quite smoothly on the rising tide and The Three Sisters settled down to a long tow. After a while, Horace semaphored one word - RUDDER - to the Lifeboat. He had noticed the rudder of The Three Sisters had not been lowered and consequently was not deep enough in the water to give the Coxswain complete control over the steering of his craft. The fault was quickly and quietly remedied, the fog hiding any blushes, and The Three Sisters continued on her way. The reason for the rudder being hoisted above the keel of the Lifeboat was to prevent it striking the slipway when the boat was launched. No one in the crew had carried out the routine activity of lowering the rudder after launching. As the sea was relatively calm the lack of rudder control had not affected the progress of the Lifeboat until she took the Naraya in tow.

The slow journey to Falmouth was uneventful except for being challenged by the Port Defence of Falmouth just after coming through the Manacle reefs. The Three Sisters was given permission to enter port and after putting the Naraya alongside a jetty, the Lifeboat refuelled and made her way back to Coverack. The crew landed, tired and hungry at 7 p.m. Another small ship had been saved to carry on the struggle against the Germans.

The scratch crew on this occasion were:

Coxswain Archie Rowe

| | |
|---|---|
| Jimmy Carey | Cyril Hart |
| George Dally | Jim Lawrence |
| Horace Eustice | Dick Rowe |

On June 25th., 1941, a German 'plane was shot down. It fell into the sea off Porthoustock. Coxswain Archie Rowe rescued the sole survivor. The German had been in the water for some hours during the night, when Archie, who was going out fishing, heard his cries for help. After a short search, Archie found the airman and pulled him aboard his fishing boat Bessie. The airman gunner was about twenty years old. Archie brought him to Coverack and placed him in the Fishermen's Rest where he was looked after by the Home Guard on duty. When the news of the survivor of the 'plane crash got round, several villagers who were early risers went down to gawp at the real, live German. They went away quietly, realising he was just like one of the village boys who had joined up to fight for his country and now found himself in a predicament as a prisoner of war in a strange land. The young man was given a hot drink and after waiting in the Fishermen's Rest for a couple of hours he was taken away by the civil police.

Two days later at 0319 on the 28th. June, bombs were dropped at the Black Head. The A.R.P. Wardens went to the scene via Treleaver Farm to inspect the damage. Fortunately there was nothing worse than some wrecked telephone lines. The Coastguards at the Black Head kept drums containing oily waste which were placed in lines not far from the Look Out. On receiving instructions they would light the contents of the drums to simulate a flare path. The aim was to fool the Germans into thinking that they were over Predannack Aerodrome. The Coastguards were not very keen on this idea but their reward came when the bombs landed harmlessly on the moorland or in the sea instead of on a military target.

The summer of 1941 wore on. Falmouth seemed to be the centre of attraction regarding both German bombers and German E Boats. Gunfire was frequently reported at night right into the autumn. On one occasion tracer bullets fired from the sea set alight the grass on the Lowland Point, causing the Home Guard to prepare for another landing until it was established what had happened. On the night of the 7th. September, so much shrapnel fell in the Zoar area that visiting A.R.P. Patrols were instructed, somewhat needlessly, to keep their steel helmets on.

The following month, on the 6th. October, bombs fell again in the Coverack area. Reports were conflicting but as there was no evidence of any damage the Wardens came to the conclusion that all the bombs had landed harmlessly on the beach. During the night of the 19th. October, the Coastguards reported that a 'plane had crashed into the sea off Lankidden. Once more The Three Sisters was launched. She returned at 0205 the following morning and the Coxswain had to report sadly that the crew had found some wreckage of a British 'plane but could find no survivors. A wheel from the aircraft was found at the Black Head after daylight, but again there was no sign of any survivors. A week later on the 27th. October the Coverack Wardens' Post G2A reported seeing an aircraft crash into the sea beyond Lowland Point at 0755. It was a Hudson which hit the water four hundred yards east of Porthkerris, near Porthoustock. Fortunately fisherman T. Smitheram was at hand and rescued two men from the Hudson. They were Flight Lieutenant Blanche and Flight Lieutenant King. Mr. Smitheram transferred the survivors from his boat to a passing minesweeper and they were taken to Falmouth. It should not be forgotten that fishermen played a vital role during wartime in the saving of lives. They were often on the spot and able to rescue survivors of ships and aircraft. They were non combatants but faced the dangers of attack by enemy ships and aircraft. One day Coverack fisherman Jimmy Carey was fishing off the Lowlands with his daughter Edith when a German bomber circled their tiny craft. Fortunately for the Careys the pilot decided that a nearby armed trawler was a more worthy target and went off out to sea and attacked it instead.

The year 1941 would not be complete without a further reminder of the presence of evacuee children in the area. Some of those who came to Coverack were selected to go to Helston County Secondary School at the age of 11+ in the same way as the village children. Flora Day of 1941 happened to be in the middle of Helston War Weapons Week when everyone was urged to put as much money as possible into National Savings and War Bonds. It was not possible to hold the top hatted midday dance for obvious reasons but after much debate it was decided that the Children's Dance would take place. It was to start at noon from the Guildhall Chambers and would be led by the Mayor. Children under the age of 9½ were not allowed to take part as it was felt that the dance organisers could not be responsible for them if there were an air raid during the dance. After much heated debate and many pleas from parents and children to allow those under 9½ to take part, the dance went ahead as planned. The West Briton reported a Helstonian as commenting that the children could be safely relied on to carry on the old custom '........until victory comes.' The newspaper also stated that an evacuee had written home to London to tell her mother that she was '........learning the Cornish Lambeth Walk.' Whether she was a Coverack evacuee or not is not known but one can imagine the puzzlement of some of the evacuees' mothers on reading that their children were being taught to dance in and out of the houses as their contribution to War Weapons Week. That was probably considered more abnormal than the worrying news from the children that they had been hearing bombs go off at night and that they had seen a ship sunk by enemy 'planes.

### *1942 and the Year of the Coverack Blitz*

Most of the people in the village were glad to see the end of the year 1941. The war was not going well anywhere and the villagers were getting tired. The conflict was now world wide. The Japanese had attacked Pearl Harbour on the 7th. December, 1941 which meant that the United States was at war with Japan. Great Britain was also at war with Japan. Germany had subsequently declared war on the United States. The Japanese were advancing on Singapore, the relatively new naval base which could not defend itself from a land based attack. In the last two months of 1941 the Royal Navy had lost the Cossack, Ark Royal, Barham, Repulse (Britain's newest battleship) and the Prince of Wales. In those days, people in our island nation, especially those living in seafaring towns and villages, considered naval losses such as these to be little short of disaster. Nevertheless life had to go on and Coverack proceeded into 1942 at the usual slow pace.

In the volunteer Coverack emergency services, the New Year began with Exercise 'Pilchard'. It involved aeroplanes, all of which for the purposes of the exercise were to be considered hostile, with the exception of the Lysander. It was a full scale exercise. There were to be gas casualties as well as people wounded by air attack. Those 'affected' by gas were to be labelled as 'stripped and treated for liquid gas'. Houses were to be 'evacuated' because of unexploded bombs and were to have notes attached to the doors stating the number of people who had been moved because of the danger. 'Enemy' troop movements had to be reported to the Home Guard of the military authorities. To make matters worse, or realistic, depending on one's point of view, messengers were not to be allowed to use motorised transport. The instructions ended by saying that one third of the Wardens had to be on duty all night and added that a report had to be sent by Monday's post to the Head Warden, Mr.H.W.F. Garland who lived at Caynham House, Mullion. One can imagine the hilarity and the frustration these instructions caused among the three Coverack Wardens. How would the people in the village react to having labels pinned to them stating that they had been stripped? There were no strippers in Coverack! After re reading the instructions, common sense prevailed and in the event bureaucracy at the Report Centre was pacified with the terse statement from Coverack: 'No incidents in this sector'. A comprehensive true account of aircraft movements over the village was telephoned to Control throughout the day. The list of 'planes included three Hurricanes making a series of dives over the Headland Hotel at 1546 on the 3rd. January. This was intended to impress the powers that be. They were probably not aware that this was a common occurrence in the village. Pilots frequently flew close to the building because some of their W.A.A.F. and W.R.N.S. girl friends were billeted in the hotel. By 1750 on the same day a report was sent to the Warden's Post from the Coverack Home Guard saying, 'The war is over.' The control centre was asked to confirm this, which they did and the Coverack volunteers thankfully packed up and got on with their daily jobs.

The real war of 1942 continued. More bombs were dropped at the Black Head and at Zoar. Plenty of gunfire was heard at sea. On February 14th., 1942 the Home Guard reported enemy surface craft in the area again. Post G2A of the A.R.P. recorded in the Log that on the 19th. February the wardens were presented with two pairs of ankle boots - between three people - and one lamp refill - for three lamps - so the war did not seem to be going too well on the supply front. It bucked up a little in March when a Gas Detector Board arrived and two greatcoats - for three people. A bomb, minus its detonator was washed ashore on the 29th. April and the Coastguards arranged for its disposal. There followed several reports of air crashes and bombings, all of which turned out to be false. Perhaps that is why on May 20th. at 2145 a message was relayed to A.R.P. personnel to be on the look out for parachutists dressed in civilian clothes. Whether or not they would be carrying their parachutes was not made clear. Perhaps it was just as well the Wardens kept most of the information to themselves so as not to spread alarm and despondency. After the warning about civilian parachutists there were quite a few entries recording enemy planes passing overhead. Bombers were easily identified because of their pulsating, droning sound.

On the 5th. May a message came from Mr. Gilbert the Officer in Charge of the Report Centre in Helston stating: 'Disregard sealed orders before 1100 hours.' It seemed to the puzzled Wardens that they would have to disregard unopened sealed orders anyway, until they were told they could be opened. A further message arrived to clarify the initial one, saying that after 11 o'clock they were to act on the orders and that the Post might be visited by a military officer whose instructions were to be obeyed. This message gave the impression that something important was about to happen. The Senior Warden accordingly asked permission to appoint another temporary Warden. This request was granted, so he asked Captain Roddick from 'The Mansion' to help. He readily agreed. The Senior Warden was also given permission to recruit Mr. Percy Eustis as a temporary Despatch Rider and he was allocated half a gallon of precious rationed petrol.

The exercise, for that was what it was, began in earnest the next day. It was code named 'Carp'. Enemy troops were supposed to have landed at Lowland Point and were advancing in a North Westerly direction towards Point 343. Percy Eustis was sent off on his motor bike to take a message about the landing to the Report Centre at 1047. He returned unharmed at 1145. The British Red Cross and W.V.S. were mobilised and all the volunteers stood by expectantly, wondering what 'Carp' was going to demand from them. To their surprise nothing happened. At five past midnight, more than twelve hours after the exercise began in such a dramatic fashion, the real enemy was overhead and the long drawn out exercise fizzled out as the Germans remained in the area until 2 a.m. The exercise name 'Carp' seemed appropriate. The organisers must have expected the participants to find fault with it. It was not a good idea to assemble everyone and then do nothing, especially when the volunteers had leave to their paid jobs in order to attend.

Sporadic enemy activity continued over and around Coverack until the next exercise, code named 'Bezants', began on June 20th. Sealed orders were again the order of the day. Schools were theoretically closed, the enemy was supposedly in the area, refugees were said to be jamming the roads and false messengers were employed to throw everyone into confusion by delivering spurious orders. Coverack came through this exercise without undue stress and Mr. Percy Eustis was awarded another half gallon of petrol for his motor bike which he had used to deliver genuine messages.

On July 7th., one more greatcoat arrived at the A.R.P. post, one pair of gloves, two suits of battle dress, four chevrons and one lady's hat, labelled 'to try on'. The three Wardens, Mr. Henry Brittain, Mr. Stafford Hart and Mrs. Annette Hunter were called to a parade at Helston two days later and were inspected by the Duke of Kent. It proved to be one of the last public appearances of the Duke in this country. He was killed on Active Service on the 25th. August, 1942.

The day after the parade in Helston, the Germans were back over Coverack. On July 12th., the Post Log reported explosions at 0300. Bombs were dropped at Penlee that day but fortunately the Lifeboat Station was not hit. The Coastguards reported a hostile 'plane crashing into the sea but nothing was found. Red Warnings came to Coverack every day until the 7th. August then there was a ten day respite. This unusually long 'lull' proved to be ominous. The next entry in the Coverack A.R.P. Post Log is Monday, August 17th., 1942 - a day which is as important to the village of Coverack as the 'blitz' is to the towns of Plymouth, Coventry, Dresden, Hamburg and countless other communities.

It was a beautiful summer's day. A day for going to the beach. A day for going out in the boat. A day for a picnic. A day to forget the war and enjoy the 'oasis'. Some Coverack people planned to take advantage of the weather while they did their morning chores and set out after lunch to enjoy themselves and give the children a treat.

Mrs. Harding Eustis of Pier View, Coverack had planned to spend the afternoon with her daughters. While she was preparing the picnic she sent Rene and Lillian to play on the Battery and her other daughter went out in the rowing boat Seagull with her cousins Joan and Harold Martin. Harold Martin (Junior) takes up the story:

'We were off Dolor Point when with no warning at all the 'planes came in, practically at sea level. We saw they were German. One bomb went through Mrs. Hunter's house, one hit the road behind the Chapel and bounced behind Hill Crest, another hit the road where the toilets are now and destroyed four houses. The fourth bomb fell in the sea between us and the Paris Hotel. On seeing this we were very frightened. I got under a bottom board and the girls got under the stern seats. One of the four 'planes machine gunned us but luckily missed.'

When the bomb hit the houses in the Cove, Mrs. Eustis who lived in the house nearest the harbour, was just finishing packing up a picnic. She was in a hurry because she did not want to be late getting back from the beach. Suddenly she felt the force of an explosion, which lifted her up and threw her under the stairs. That probably saved her life. She told the writer on the 21st. August, 1988, just a few days after the 46th. anniversary of the raid that her mouth was full of dirt and she could not breathe, nor could she see. She lay still for a while and then heard Archie Rowe, the Coxswain of The Three Sisters calling her. She managed to make a sound and Archie dug down through the debris to her. When he and the other rescue workers had pulled away some of the heavy stones and pieces of wood, Archie cleared her mouth and eyes and gave her a drink of water. He then asked her to wait as they had to move some more masonry before it would be safe to get her out. Harding said she knew then that it was going to be all right. Archie was known for his great strength and courage and would lead the villagers, including her own brother Eddy Bastian, to her. The next thing she remembered was being carried on a stretcher through the village. It was a great feeling of relief, for her three daughters were walking beside her. They were unharmed. She was taken to Porthgwarra at North Corner, which had become a temporary refuge for the victims of the raid. After a couple of days Mrs. Eustis was moved to Tamarisk Cottage to be looked after by her relatives, Mrs. Alice Carey and her husband Jimmy.

It is not difficult to picture the scene in Coverack before the bombs dropped. It was indeed a typical summer's day. The Mill Beach was filling up, the village boys and girls were swimming, out in boats or 'mucking about' around the harbour. Two young lads, Joe and Ben Roskilly had just come down from Penmarth Farm to spend the afternoon in the village when the four Focke-Wulf 190s came tearing in. Joe takes up the story:

'We could see the aircraft very low over the village, the Swastika was clear on the tail plane and the pilot's head could clearly be seen. Dark objects were seen falling away from the 'plane. A Plymouth evacuee told us to lie flat beside the boats. We were unaware that they were bombs........ There appeared to be a lull and most of the party made their way up the slipway to the Paris Hotel. For some unknown reason I made for Sam's slip (leading to the Post Office). It was then that the bomb on the road above exploded. I must have been stunned by all this but I do remember the sea across the harbour mouth bubbling with machine gun fire........ Archie Rowe was working in the loft below the Post Office. He came to my rescue. I had been quite badly cut and was bespattered with blood. Archie took me into the loft until he was sure all was quiet and then up to Alice Dally's to clean me up. I think they both thought Mrs. Stafford Hart would be more able to deal with my problem. Archie guided me over the rubble and set me off to Sunny Corner. (It was at this moment that Archie must have joined in the search for Mrs. Eustis.) By the Chapel I was met by my anxious parents. Mrs. Hart was inundated with casualties so I went home.'

Joe Roskilly was very close to the Post Office where his grandmother lived. The building is now known as 'The Old Post Office'. Mrs. Hilda White the daughter of the Post Mistress was at home when she heard the 'planes coming. She rushed to get her three year old son John. A Helston Postman, Mr. Harry Williams tried to stop her going up the road as he sensed what was about to happen but Mrs. White dashed on. Both she and her son were killed outright. Mrs. Roskilly, Hilda's mother, pushed a visitor customer under the Post Office counter. They both escaped injury. The front of the Post Office-Shop was badly damaged. Some time later, builders found machine gun bullets in the roof when they were carrying out repairs. This was the second tragedy in 1942 for Mr. Jack White, a Chief Petty Officer in the Royal Navy. His brother Bert, also a Chief Petty Officer, was killed by the Japanese when H.M.S. Hermes was sunk in April. Mr. White now had to cope with the loss of his wife and baby son through enemy action and to comfort his motherless daughter, Rosemary.

Leslie Albert Chambers, a four year old evacuee from Ashford Crescent, Enfield was also killed by the direct hit on the Cove. His six year old brother was hit on the back of the knee by a machine gun bullet. It is difficult to imagine the feelings of the Chambers family who had taken government advice and come to Coverack in order to protect the children.

The preliminary report in the A.R.P. Log for Post G2A in Coverack recorded: 'Four H.E. Bombs were dropped on the village before the Red came in. The raid resulted in many casualties - 4 fatal, 4 seriously injured, 16 slight. Mrs. Hunter, our lady Warden was killed outright through a direct hit on her house.'

Mrs. Annette Hunter was talking to her friend Mrs. Roddick on the telephone when the bomb hit her house. It was fortunate that the Warden's telephone in Wyndleshore, a few hundred yards from Mrs. Hunter's house was not put out of action. The news of the raid was telephoned immediately to the Report Centre in Helston. The Post Log states:

'I sent the S.O.S. to the Report Centre in Helston and all services concerned were on the spot in a short space of time. Also the Military, R.A.F., W.A.A.F.s and W.R.N.S. did excellent work to relieve the sufferings of the bombed out people.'

Once the call for help was made the Senior Warden had to organise the work of rescue and give succour to the distressed villagers. This is when the training in the much maligned 'exercises' was justified. As an experienced builder, Mr. Hart was able to ensure that the rescuing of people from the damaged buildings was not impaired by over enthusiastic helpers who could easily bring down tons of masonry on the trapped people. All the difficulties envisaged in the various exercises happened. The volunteers were well trained and prepared. Telephones went out of order. Water and electricity were cut off. This was fortunate in one way because people could not get shocks from trailing wires. Luckily fires did not take hold, so little water was needed, though of course there was plenty available from the sea. The ceiling of the First Aid Post in the Chapel Vestry had come down, so the room could not be used as a Casualty Clearing Station. It was natural for the villagers to converge on Wyndleshore for help so the dwelling house became a dressing station. Fortunately Mrs. Hart and her local helpers did not have to attend to all the injured. Dr. E. Leverton Spry and his wife arrived from St. Keverne as did the District Nurse. After a while an A.R.P. Ambulance Party arrived from Falmouth, then the R.A.F. Medical Officer from Treleaver Camp, an Army Doctor and medical orderlies from the Headland Hotel, so people were able to have individual attention. A Mrs. Wells from the Isle of Wight, who was an A.R.P. helper on holiday in Coverack also came to help. There was indeed no lack of volunteers before the afternoon was out.

LIST OF CASUALTIES (from A.R.P. and B.R.C.S. Logs)

KILLED:

| Leslie Albert Chambers | Aged 4 | Evacuee from Enfield |
| Annette Bamford Hunter | 46 | Coverack A.R.P. Warden Jan. 1938 - Aug. 1942 |
| John Herbert White | 3 | Coverack |
| Hilda Mary White | 38 | Coverack |

WOUNDED - these are in the order dealt with by the First Aiders, according to the apparent severity of the wounds.

| NAME | AGE | ADDRESS | INJURY |
| --- | --- | --- | --- |
| Mrs. Nora Chard | 58 | Melvia | Eye |
| Mrs. B.M. Hocking | 70 | Hill Crest | Chest |
| Mrs. M. Hocking | 38 | Hill Crest | Eyes |
| Francis Peacey | 12 | Evacuee | Leg - M.G. bullet |
| Mrs. Harding Eustis | 36 | Pier View | Face, Head, Badly shocked |
| Mrs. Mabel Eustis | 65 | Harbour View | Head and arm |
| Mrs. Rawle | 40 | Hill Crest | Head |

| Miss Clara James | 86 | Melvia | Face and arms |
|---|---|---|---|
| Mrs. T.C. Roskilly | 60 | Carpenter's Shop | Neck, badly shocked |
| Stanley Chambers | 6 | Trewolsta | Back of knee - M.G bullet |
| Tony White | 7 | Gloster Cottage | Head (not serious) |
| Michael Robinson | 16 | Hill Crest | Eyes |
| Mrs. Robinson | 50 | Hill Crest | Superficial cuts |
| Mrs. Keast | 70 | Luxulyan | Superficial cuts |
| Mr. Henry Eddy | 40 | Bethune | Several cuts. Sprained knee. |
| Mr. L. C. Barker | 46 | Hill Crest | Slight cut on face |
| Miss Jenny Bastian | 54 | Rose Cottage | Cuts on Head |
| Joseph Roskilly | 10 | Penmarth Farm | Badly cut fingers - M.G. bullet |
| Graham Daw | 11 | The Bakery | Injury to foot - M.G. bullet |

This is not necessarily a comprehensive list. Some people who were treated by other First Aid personnel could have been recorded in their own Case Books. The account of the Coverack 'blitz' is not yet complete but at this point some readers who experienced bombing in cities may be wondering whether the term 'blitz' is justified. The word of German origin means lightning. The raid was certainly very rapid. It was fortunate in one respect that it did not happen at night because the rescue and clearing up operations would have been seriously hampered by the lack of electricity and the blackout. The water and drainage systems would have been out of action for a much longer period. The conditions created by darkness, the spreading of fires and the inability of large towns to restore services made the blitz in populous areas harder to bear. As it was, the services in Coverack were restored very quickly by men who were rushed into the village. The four deaths, though devastating for the Coverack and evacuee families, may also appear to be a small number when compared with casualties in densely populated areas. However, the four people killed in Coverack, which had a population of about three hundred at the time, represent a casualty figure of 1.33%. Plymouth civilian dead numbered 1,172 which is a rate of .53% out of a population of 220,000. These figures give some indication of the impact which the blitz had on the village in comparison with Plymouth. The fact that everyone in the village knew the deceased very well thrust the whole village into mourning. It was a major catastrophe, as were the blitzes on large towns and cities.

During the summer of 1942 the school teachers in Coverack volunteered to supervise children in order that parents and foster parents could carry on with their jobs and voluntary war work activities without having to worry about occupying the children. As the four Focke-Wulf 190s came in over the sea towards the village, Miss Winifred Motton, a teacher from Plymouth was doing her stint as a volunteer. The School Log takes up the story:

'On the first day of the second period of voluntary attandance, the school building and Hall were slightly damaged by enemy action - windows out and plaster shaken down in the school building, windows out and a hole in the roof of the Village Hall.

'Twenty seven children with Miss Motton were forced to shelter under a wall on the way to the beach during the bombing, but fortunately there were no casualties among this number. Miss Jury came to the children immediately and with Miss Motton brought them back to the school building. After about half an hour's sing song, four children from farms were sent home and the remaining twenty three (all hostel children) were taken to the hostel to prepare for temporary evacuation as that building was also damaged.'

The School Log then gave details of the children's injuries which have already been listed. The next entry is for the day after the raid:

'August 18th., 1942: Miss Jury opened School but no children attended. I was unable to telephone Mr. Williams (The District Education Clerk) as all 'phones were out of order. Miss Jury and I went to Lanarth Hostel, where Parc Behan children had been evacuated, to give any assistance we could. We spent the day playing games etc. with the children.'

'The Sandys and Hosken Charity Exam was postponed as Coverack children were suffering a bereavement.'

The statement in the School Log regarding the miraculous escape of the children under Miss Motton's care was indeed a very brief summary of what happened. Miss Motton told the writer that she was leading her children down the path known as 'The Gardens' when she heard the roar of engines and on looking out to sea saw the German 'planes actually lower than the roof of nearby Winifred Cottage. She shouted to the children to lie down and flung herself to the ground, expecting to feel a bullet in the back at any moment. At this point Miss Motton, a peace loving lady, added that if she had had a gun she would have killed the pilot of the nearest 'plane whom she saw quite plainly. The little file of twenty seven prostrate children was showered with dust and earth from the hedge and nearby telephone wires were strewn in the path. When the 'planes had passed some of the children got up and ran away before Miss Motton could gather them together. Those who heard her commands got up and followed her to Winifred Cottage. She opened the door and asked Mrs. Pengilly if she could leave her children there while she went off in search of the others. Winifred Cottage was in a shambles, soot everywhere and the ornaments from the mantel piece lying on the floor. Mrs. Pengilly understood by lip reading that Miss Motton wanted her to look after the children for a while, so she opened her arms and ushered them in to the parlour. It was clear to Miss Motton that Mrs. Pengilly had not understood what had happened outside but there was no time for explanations. She dashed down the Gardens to the village and began rounding up the children. She met Miss Jury, her fellow evacuee teacher from Plymouth and they managed to find all the missing children who mercifully were unharmed, then the teachers returned to Winifred Cottage, collected the bemused children and took them up the hill to the school.

One can imagine what might have happened if the 27 children with Miss Motton had been on the beach when the Germans machine gunned it. There were already a number there. They had all practised in school what they had to do in the event of an air raid, so they all lay down where they were when the machine guns began firing. Stafford James was on the beach, in front of his house, Lowland View (now the Harbour Lights Café). When the 'planes arrived, Stafford was unable to move very fast, so another Coverack boy, Brian James (no relation) lay across him to protect him. Stafford has never forgotten this courageous action by Brian.

Shirley Brookfield (later Mrs. Bernard) was a schoolgirl in Coverack at the time of the raid. She now tells her story:

'My 'growing up' years were spent with my parents and brother Malcolm in Coverack during the 1940s. My father had bought Channel View Hotel as a private house and we were living there on the fateful day of August 17th., 1942. The day dawned bright and clear and a sun touched Coverack promised fun and freedom for the children of the village. My playmate next door was Rosemary Hunter, who had the Sun Room attached to her house as a play room. On this particular day we had intended to play there with another friend, Jean Lang, whose family lived at Chynalls Farm. Our plans were spoiled by Jean's parents who decided to take her to Helston on a shopping trip. Rosemary and I decided to spend the afternoon on Mears Beach instead. This necessitated my telling Mrs. Hunter, Rosemary's mother a lie. I told her my mother was coming with us to the beach, so she willingly gave permission for Rosemary to come with me. We set off for the beach. My mother thought we were still in the playroom next door.

'The tide was out. I remember the exact rock we were playing near when we heard muffled thuds from some explosions and felt the beach vibrate. We were startled but not unduly so as we were used to gunfire at sea and put it down to that. Not long afterwards, however, a W.A.A.F. came running down to the beach, calling that the village had been bombed. She told us she would take all the children up to the Headland Hotel where she was stationed as we were not to go along the usual path home. On reaching the brow of the hill above the beach we were stunned to see that the village was covered in a grey-white cloak of dust and that Rosemary's house was flat to the ground.

'My mother now arrived, shoeless and distraught. Her shoes had been blown off by the blast as the bomb destroyed the two houses next to ours and she had run to the Mears, convinced that Rosemary and I were victims of the bomb which had killed Rosemary's mother but hoping against hope that we might have gone off to the beach. My mother then dashed back to the village to look for my brother Malcolm who had gone to the harbour. He had escaped the machine gunning and been taken to the Paris Hotel where he and the other children were given lemonade to drink. Rosemary and I went up to the Headland Hotel and were taken to the games room. Some time afterwards Rosemary was called from the room and the news broken to her by her father that her mother had been killed.

'I was later taken to Chynalls Farm. The Lang family had by then returned, so I stayed there the rest of the day. Mrs. Lang said we could stay the night but we didn't. I remember a very uneasy night spent listening for the juddering engines of German 'planes.'

Mr. Murland Hunter, a Squadron Leader in the Royal Air Force, had gone down to the village to buy some pickling vinegar for his wife when the bombs dropped. As soon as the dust settled, he naturally went to help those nearest to him. It was not until someone came and told him that his own house had been hit that he went home to discover that his wife had been killed. As described earlier, he then had to tell his daughter, Rosemary and his son James. When he grew up James became a Master Mariner and eventually was appointed as Superintendent Staff Coxswain of the Royal National Lifeboat Institution. He held this position for 11 years and was closely involved with the development of the Mersey Class Lifeboat. He had to retire early owing to ill health, and died in 1989.

It is hoped that this account of the 'blitz' will give the reader some idea of the impact it made on the village. Memories are fading but some of the village people who were there consented to tell the writer about their experiences, or related stories to him which had been told to them by friends and relatives. The writer took care not to revive painful memories and that means there are some parts of the event which have not been told. For example, it was felt that it would not be wise to ask Mrs. Harding Eustis to tell her story. However, on one of the occasions I visited Mrs. Eustis, who was a family friend, she began, unprompted, to talk about the raid. It was on August 21st., 1988, four days after the

46th. anniversary of the attack. When Mrs. Eustis was convalescing at 'Uncle Jimmy's' in Tamarisk Cottage, she managed to walk to the end of her bed one day and saw her face in a mirror. It was black and blue. She could hardly recognise herself. She then bent down and looked out of the low bedroom window across the Bay. She saw the space where she and her neighbours, including her husband's mother, had been living and then saw the tarpaulins on the damaged roofs of the nearby properties. She realised for the first time what a narrow escape she had had. The thought of it made her feel ill and confused all over again. She called to her Aunt and asked her, 'Where has Coverack gone, Auntie?' Mrs. Carey came up the stairs and helped her back to bed. It was six weeks before she could face walking again. Mrs. Eustis also told me that if she had left the house at the time she intended, she estimated she would have been very close to Sunny Corner. She also added, with a wry smile, that a few days before the raid, Mrs. Hunter the A.R.P. Warden had called to ask her husband Percy if he had any tools he could lend in the event of having to dig people out of a bombed house.

One can imagine the thoughts of the villagers who were some distance from the village when the bombing occurred. Joyce Cox (later Mrs. Rushworth) was working in the Headland Hotel Garden as a member of the Women's Land Army when the attack occurred. She dashed down to the village to her family. She recalled that everyone was moving about, frantically trying to account for children, relatives and friends who had not made contact. Many were so worried that they had not stopped to think that their relations were busily helping victims and clearing houses and roads. Alex Symes was a couple of miles away at Trelanvean Aerials Radar site when the bombs dropped. He too dashed home to Winifred Cottage to see if his mother and 80 year old grandmother were all right. He found that the bed room ceilings had come down but otherwise all was well apart from some broken windows upstairs. His mother was at her sister's making tea for the injured but his grandmother was at home. She was covered in soot and complained about the dirty chimney. Being profoundly deaf, she did not know there had been a bombing raid, but because she had had a visit from the evacuee children, she asked her grandson if the St. Keverne Band was in the village for a Tea Treat as she thought she had heard the drum! It was a blessing that she had not gone out and seen the devastation behind her house before her grandson could explain what had happened. Alex returned to his war service in the Merchant Navy shortly after the raid. It was not his first experience of enemy action. His previous vessel, the Cable Ship Faraday was attacked three miles off the coast when picking up the Pilot off Milford Haven on March 26th., 1941. The two Junkers 88s sank the Faraday. Alex managed to get away in one of the ship's lifeboats before she went down and returned to Coverack dressed in borrowed clothes, two days after leaving Falmouth in the fully loaded cable ship. Before leaving the village to go back to sea once more, Alex acted as a bearer to the victims of the raid.

For some time after the raid on Coverack, soldiers manned a machine gun on the roof of Boak Bungalow which overlooks the harbour and the cove. The men were posted there to deter any further attacks on the village. This new form of defence for the village had the desired effect because the gun was not fired in anger and was withdrawn when it was thought that the Germans were not going to stage a repeat raid.

It can be argued that the Germans attacked Coverack because of the presence of a Radar Station at Treleaver, though why children were machine-gunned on the beach still needs explanation. There were aerials at Trelanvean, Dry Tree and Pen Olva at the Lizard. The Ground Control at Treleaver was in direct telephone contact with regional control at Bath. Between them, the Radar plotters were able to 'home' in on approaching raiders and direct the intercepting 'planes from Predannack and other Cornish aerodromes to the Germans.

At Treleaver there were two Leyland lorries, back to back. Inside were R.A.F. men and women operators whose job it was to scan their screens and follow the progress of the Germans and their attackers. Two R.A.F. men sat on a saddle, pedalling away to turn the radar scanner. It was feared that there might be a reprisal raid on a radar station in Cornwall as some Canadian commandos had attacked a German Channel Coast radar station in order to steal a vital piece of electronic equipment which the British 'boffins' needed to examine. As a consequence, it was decreed that the W.A.A.F.s were to be locked in their lorries at Treleaver at night. How this was supposed to deter determined German commandos was not satisfactorily explained. There were, however, some soldiers from the East Yorks Regiment stationed nearby. They were supposedly guarding the W.R.N.S. operators in their communications vans situated near the Headland Hotel. They were monitoring German communications.

In the aftermath of the air raid some unwelcome 'residents' manifested themselves in Coverack. Mrs. Walker of Cliff Cottage, next door to Channel View Hotel, told the Brookfields, her neighbours, that when all had gone quiet, she looked towards the Coastguard Station and saw dozens of 'blitzed' rats pouring down the path in front of her house towards the beach, apparently looking for new homes. For some time afterwards there was also a plague of fleas in the village. Fleas abound in thatched roofs. They too evacuated their habitat after the blast and sought pastures new to the discomfiture of the locals. Visitors to the village in the autumn were amazed at the candour of their hosts who told them not to be alarmed if they found fleas on their persons. True to traditional village humour, the Coverack people did not add that it was 'because there is a war on' - the customary method of explaining away problems in war time - until the visitors had scratched around for a while and were secretly wondering why they had been so unwise as to spend a holiday in a village abounding with fleas.

There are other humorous anecdotes arising from the bombing of the village which are still told from time to time, such as the one of the lady who kept asking why the Germans did not go and bomb the English. When Harold Martin (Junior) was asked by the writer about the time following the raid, he recalled that when he rowed back to the harbour after being machine gunned, he understandably forgot there was a 4lb. pollack in the boat. On going back to get it, he remembered being outraged that 'Somebody or some thing had taken it.' He was compensated, however, for when he and his sister were searching round the harbour they were handed the name plate of their former house,

'Trewolsta', which had been destroyed by the bomb. The plate still adorns the Redruth house of his sister, Joan Martin (later Mrs. Truran).

Some extracts from a letter, written just after the blitz in 1942, to Mrs. Lily Blanche, a regular visitor to Coverack from her friend Mrs. Hayden, wife of the former landlord of the Paris Hotel, illustrate the feelings of a well respected villager. The writer is grateful to Mrs. Sue Smith for permission to quote from the letter which was written to her mother.

'........you will be shocked to hear that we have had a visit from the beastly Hun about a month ago on the Monday afternoon which left our little village a sad wreck........'

Mrs. Hayden described the damage and told Mrs. Blanche about the casualties whom she knew, including one of her favourite village characters, Tim Connor, of whom she wrote:

'Poor old Tim is gone back to the Institution. He was cut a bit........' She continued, 'We never, as you know, get a warning of any kind and so one's nerves don't get a chance to get a bit braced to meet whatever may come.' Mr. Lewis Hayden was a fisherman as well as a pub landlord, so Mrs. Hayden described the harbour in some detail - '........luckily the motor boats escaped but some of the smaller ones were damaged. Poor old Billy May's antique ship (now called the Seine Loft) is finished and the Granville looks awful but I don't know for certain if it's condemned or not . ...... you can imagine the awful business of digging and finding what they could.' She then described the parts of the cove where the houses were completely destroyed and named the people who were killed - '........of course I know this is happening everywhere, but living in these defenceless little villages we are more or less like one family, sharing everyone's joys and sorrows ........ you know what I mean ........ the old thatched roofs stood it fine, of course the old ceilings suffered but not one old thatch moved, it wouldn't have been so good though, if we had fire bombs.'

Mrs. Hayden expressed the feelings of the village by continuing, 'Well my dears, we don't want another experience like that, but we can assure you that if ever we get a chance to have our own back, my word we shall be there. Could have brought the blighters down if we had a gun on the Dolor, in fact we could almost touch them they were so low.' She added that the Germans '........tried to machine gun 'Mother Dally', she being outside getting her rations from the van. She managed to get back and wasn't hit, neither the bungalow.' She concluded by saying that Mrs. Dally was shaken by the experience but that she was '........full of vim and vigour now, I can assure you.' She ended the letter,

'Love and best wishes to you both and the dear children.' She signed the letter 'Auntie Hayden', the name by which she was known to the children.

A year afterwards, in September, 1943, Mrs. Hayden wrote again to Mrs. Blanche to tell her of the death of Tim Connor, who will be described later, she said she felt Tim '........wasn't really happy and grieved a lot about Coverack' - and added that he was only ill for a day or two. After giving more news of the village she wrote, 'The village is still full of the forces, not a bit like our old Coverack. The war news is good, isn't it? I wish this year could end it but I am afraid it will go on longer yet.' After asking about Mrs. Blanche's children, Sue and Bill, she added that she still had Enid, her niece as an evacuee, but that the other one had gone back to Plymouth and ended her letter by saying, somewhat wearily, that it was '........much quieter with one.'

Mrs. Hayden knew that Mrs. Blanche lived in a village called Brockham Green, Surrey and that she would understand the feelings of the Coverack people. Later on Mrs. Blanche's own roof was blown off by a flying bomb and her family had to live temporarily in an old gun emplacement. Such are the effects of total war.

### *Flight Lieutenant Albert Harvey, D.S.O.*

A biographical chronicle of Coverack would be incomplete without a mention of one of her better known 20th. century 'sons'. It is appropriate that his story should follow the account of the bombing of the village, for he is part of it.

That afternoon, Albert or 'Dingo' as the boys of the village affectionately called him, was patrolling in his Beaufighter from Predannack Aerodrome when his radio crackled into life and he heard one of his mates calling to say that he had three Focke-Wulf 190s on his tail. He added that they had just bombed a village. The harassed pilot gave his position as 'West of Point 11'. Albert then knew it was Coverack, where his mother was living. He put the Beaufighter into a steep dive and before long he was over the village. He could see a cloud of white dust rising round a tall column of black smoke. Albert went low over the village and was much relieved to see that West House, his boyhood home, was apparently intact. The former Wesleyan Chapel house next door was damaged but he saw that the two houses below that had been destroyed by a direct hit. (Mrs. Hunter, the A.R.P. Warden had been killed in one of them).

Albert and his Radio Observer, Bernard Wicksteed were directed to make 'sweeps' to try and make contact with the FW190s but were unable to find them. When the patrol was over, Albert flew back over Coverack to take another look at the damage, before landing at Predannack. He rushed to a 'phone and found to his great relief that his mother was safe. He was both saddened and angered when he was told of the deaths of his fellow villagers. Albert was known as 'Len' to his colleagues. Being Cornish and named Harvey it seemed natural for them to name him 'Len' after the Cornish champion boxer. Knowing how 'Len' loved his native county, they left him alone that night to help him to come to terms with the idea of Coverack being bombed. Albert's Observer wrote later in his biographical account, 'Father's Heinkel', that while waiting in the dispersal hut that evening for another call to go up and intercept German 'planes, 'Len' sat brooding. He added, 'If I was a German I should have hated to meet him just then.'

PILOTS AT PREDANNACK DURING THE SECOND WORLD WAR
*Albert Harvey is standing 2nd. from left.*
*The Lizard peninsula was defended by American, Australian, British,*
*Canadian, Czech and Polish Air Force pilots and in this case*
*one from the Fleet Air Arm.*

Everyone was aware of Albert's prowess as a pilot. Two months previously on the 7th. June, 1942 he had won their admiration for his skill. He was directed to intercept a bomber which was approaching a convoy off Trevose Head. Albert soon spotted a twin engined Heinkel 111 travelling East. It was flying so low that its slipstream was sending up spray from the sea. Albert dived after it and the Heinkel began firing at him from the upper turret, while taking sharp avoiding action. Albert returned the fire. The German was now firing from upper and lower gun turrets. He manoeuvred to a position 500 feet behind and below the He.111 and gave a four second burst which put the German's lower turret out of action. He was about to give a further burst when the Beaufighter's starboard engine struck, sending out a plume of thick, oily smoke. The German 'plane was now right in front. His port engine was on fire and began emitting black smoke. The Observer saw it blow up and bits flew off in all directions. By now the Beaufighter was above the German who again began firing from his upper turret. Albert turned away to starboard and because his own engine had packed up he missed with his next burst. However, he got behind the German and gave another two second burst. He could not see the results as bits were flying off the German 'plane and his own windscreen was covered in oil. Albert climbed higher and opened his side window to clear the oil off the windscreen with his gloved hand. As soon as he could see through it he dived after the Heinkel again and opened fire. This time the German did not fire back. He passed over the German 'plane. It was just a blur through the oily windscreen. He was now in trouble himself, so he asked the Control Room to see if they could follow the German on their radar and turned for home. His one remaining port engine was failing and the radio packing up.

The Beaufighter started losing height and when they got in sight of land, it became clear that they were going to have to ditch. Albert was strapped in for the bumpy landing but his Observer did not have time to fasten his belt nor to clip on his dinghy before the aircraft cartwheeled into the sea. Bernard Wicksteed was taken down under water with the aircraft. Fortunately he managed to free himself and surfaced to find his pilot treading water and blowing up his dinghy. Bernard called out and Albert swam over to him. They both tried to get in the dinghy which immediately capsized. By this time, the Observer was getting very tired so Albert persuaded Bernard Wicksteed to get in the dinghy while he swam behind, pushing it along.

Progress was painfully slow in the dark but they could see the flashing beacon of Portreath Aerodrome in the distance. After a while, Albert managed to get in the tiny dinghy and hold up its covering sheet to act as a sail while Bernard used the hand paddles to steer. They had to stop at intervals and change over. They tried to eat their emergency rations to give them more energy but found it impossible as they had swallowed so much salt water they could not eat the dry, hard chocolate.

By half past four in the morning, after managing to avoid rocks on the way, they reached the surf off Samphire Island. This was the most dangerous part of their uncomfortable journey. The dinghy capsized once more. Albert was washed off and had to swim for the shore. Bernard clung to the dinghy and was washed up on the beach with it. The two men shouted, but could not find each other in the dark. After a short rest, Albert called out that he was going to get help in the hope that Bernard would hear him and stay where he was. Albert climbed the cliff of the cove where he had landed. It was between Samphire Island and Carne Island. He made his way to a farm. The farmer's son dashed off to get help for Bernard. Albert learned later that his Observer was too exhausted to climb the cliff but because of the noise being made by the surf had not heard Albert shouting that he was going to get assistance.

On finding out that he was only half a mile from the Operations Room at Tehidy Barton, Albert set off without waiting for the farmer's wife to make him some tea. When he arrived, still dripping wet, he told the startled Controller that Mulet 32 (The aircraft's call sign) was reporting back for duty! Meanwhile the farmer's son had contacted a party of Royal Marines who soon found the Observer and took him to safety.

In completing the account of the action, Flying Officer D.L. Walters, the Intelligence Officer of 600 Squadron added:

'Pilot Officer Harvey commented that he was greatly cheered throughout the combat by the carefree, if at times unprintable comments of his Observer (Radio) from the back seat.'

What the Intelligence Officer did not say was that from his position in the aircraft, the Observer could not see what was happening in front, nor below, so he did not realise until after each attack how close Albert had got to the enemy before opening fire. If he had, his comments would have no doubt been even more colourful.

When it became obvious that the Beaufighter had crashed, two lifeboats were sent to search for survivors. Planes from Predannack flew over the area, all to no avail. The airmen had their whistles, which were of no use to them under the circumstances, but their torches were lost in the crash. The writer is most grateful to Albert Harvey's son, Peter Harvey, who allowed him to read the Pilot's Log Book. Albert's comment in the Log after the loss of the 'Beaufighter Mark VIF No. X7946 A1 Mark IV Cat. E' was:

'Got a little wet.'

This 'wetting' qualified Albert and his Observer for membership of the exclusive 'Gold Fish Club' which was open only to air crew who had crashed into the sea. The badge depicts a goldfish apparently diving into a rolling sea.

The story is not yet finished. What is perhaps more incredible than the miraculous escape is that after a drink of rum and a good sleep, Albert flew back from Portreath to Predannack at midday. He landed, put on his civilian clothes, cycled twenty miles back to Falmouth and by late afternoon was taking his turn at selling cigarettes in his Market Strand tobacconist's shop which his wife and father were looking after while he did his service in the R.A.F.

Of course, the Falmouth Packet got to know about the shooting down of the German 'plane and printed the story on the 12th. June, 1942 with the headline: 'Falmouth Pilot's courage - got Heinkel and rescued his Observer.' The final paragraph of the article read: 'P.O. Harvey arrived home on Wednesday but declined to say anything about the incident to a Falmouth Packet representative.' That was the Albert Coverack people knew. The Cornish Echo had more luck in their search for a story. Their reporter had the good fortune to interview Mr. Harvey (Senior) because his son 'had gone to Coverack'. Mr. Harvey told the reporter that his son was 'very close about his exploits' and that the family knew little more than what was revealed by the Air Ministry, but he did tell them all about Albert's swimming activities when he was a boy in Coverack.

A week after the newspaper articles, Albert Harvey was awarded the Distinguished Service Order for his gallant exploits and his Observer, Bernard Wicksteed, got the Distinguished Flying Cross. They were the first pair to escape from a ditched Beaufighter.

No one in Coverack was surprised when Albert Harvey was awarded the D.S.O. He was known as a 'dare-devil' but they were highly delighted that a Coverack man was going to be honoured by the King. Even after all that, things did not go smoothly for Albert. He was summoned to the Palace but the letter went astray, probably through enemy action, and he had to go to Buckingham Palace on the 19th. October, 1943 and so missed being honoured with his Observer.

Years afterwards, it was suggested that the Heinkel 111 which Albert claimed to have shot down was in fact a Junkers 88 D5 which belonged to the German Long Range Reconnaissance Group. The aircraft are similar to look at, especially in the dark. The crew of four in the German aircraft were less fortunate than the Beaufighter's crew. The bodies of the German pilot and the Wireless Operator were found but not those of the Navigator and Air Gunner.

A month after winning the D.S.O. and a month before Coverack was bombed, Albert Harvey and his Observer Bernard Wicksteed were again airborne in another Beaufighter at 3.20 on the morning of the 8th. July, 1942. They had just passed to the Ground Control of Treleaver, Coverack, when a 'bandit' or enemy aircraft was reported approaching the area from the North. Ground Control decided guided the Beaufighter on to the 'bandit' which took sharp evasive action and escaped. However the Beaufighter regained radio contact and caught sight of the exhaust flares of the German 'plane against the early morning black clouds. Albert followed the German and on entering a clear patch obtained a perfect silhouette of a Heinkel 111. He was even able to see details such as the 'cutout' of the trailing edge of the wing and the individual exhaust outlet holes. Albert closed to wihin 150 feet and gave the enemy a four second burst from below. The Beaufighter was armed with four cannon and six machine guns. The German did a steep climb and returned the fire, then he dived again wih Albert after him. Albert fired another burst and once more observed strikes on the port side of the German aircraft. After another burst the Heinkel went into a vertical dive, side slipping into a thick rain cloud which the flames of the German aircraft lit up from within. The Beaufighter then lost contact with the enemy. After circling for a while Albert returned to Predannack Aerodrome, landing at 0400.

On debriefing, the Intelligence Officer estimated: 'One Heinkel 111 probably destroyed.' It was discovered after the war that on July 8th., 1942, the Germans recorded no loss of an aircraft from Dinard but a damaged Junkers 88 landed there. It had sustained 25% damage and the Air Gunner had been killed. Some authorities consider this also might have been the 'plane which Albert Harvey had intercepted. On the other hand, this time, Albert's statement about the clarity of the silhouette, the 'cutout' of the wing which the Ju 88 did not have and the exhaust outlets, combined with the ensuing conflagration observed when the German dived through the rain cloud seem to point strongly to the fact that it was a Heinkel 111. It also seems improbable that the German could have made the journey of 130 miles back to France from a position 25 miles South of the Lizard. Perhaps another entry on another page of German archives will be discovered one day to confirm the assessment of Flight Lieutenant D.L. Walters, the Duty Intelligence Officer of 600 Squadron at Predannack. His judgment was supported two days after the event by Pilot Officer Pyper the Controller at Treleaver who stated that he swept the vicinity with his radar scanner for several minutes after Albert had last fired at the aircraft, but - '........nothing appeared on the tube.'

Whatever the truth might be, Albert's work that morning must have been some consolation to him while he reflected on what happened in the Coverack bombing a few weeks later, when his own mother had been so close to being killed. At least Albert had fired at Germans who could fire back and he had not machine gunned children who were playing on a village beach a long way from any military installation. Coverack people knew that Albert was stationed at Predannack and took comfort from the fact. They knew he would not be wanting when an attack came. Albert had given a few villagers 'joy rides' when no one was looking. Alex Symes told the writer that when Albert took him up he showed him the fishing grounds from the air and then swooped low over the village so that he could see his house. He was so low that he was able to recognise some friends who were standing on the quay.

It was indicated earlier that Albert was known as 'a bit of a dare-devil' in the village. The young people enjoyed his pranks and used to congregate in the shed outside his home at West House, Sunny Corner, Coverack. Albert had interesting hobbies such as keeping pet snakes, making canoes, and racing home made wooden 'butts' - 'boy-powered' go carts for racing down Coverack hills. He was always tinkering with wireless sets and engines, as was his elder brother, George. He delighted in playing tricks on younger boys, who in turn enjoyed trying to outwit him. One day he hit on the idea of connecting a bucket of water to an accumulator. He then dropped a shiny sixpenny bit in the bucket and told a group of kids that whoever retrieved the sixpence, could keep it. The money represented more than a week's pocket money so there was no lack of volunteers. After several shocks, fortunately without harmful consequences, we told him in the traditional village manner to keep his money. Nevertheless we kept going back to see him because there was always something interesting happening in the shed.

Albert Harvey went to Plymouth Grammar School but did not manage to get into the R.A.F. before the war. He was mad about flying so he contrived to have some lessons and was accepted for air crew not long after war broke out. He joined the Initial Training Wing of Cambridge University on the 25th. May, 1941. After Pilot training in Tiger Moths he went to Cranwell. He joined 600 City of London Squadron and was posted to Predannack after combat training. He was very much at home there, of course. Some of the R.A.F. ground crew and mechanics were also local. Jack Gilbert of Helston was a Leading Aircraftman Engine Fitter at the aerodrome. He told the writer that he remembered seeing off Albert Harvey and Bernard Wicksteed in their Beaufighter on the night when they got 'a little wet' and how relieved everyone was when the news got round the Squadron that the two men had got safely back to land.

One could regard Albert Harvey as a Flying Home Guard for Coverack. Many people from the village used to wish they could 'get back' at the Germans for what they were doing but that was impossible. They therefore had to be content in the knowledge that at least some of the local lads were still in the area and able to hit back on their behalf. Albert was one of them. In due course he was posted away from Cornwall. A farewell party for 600 Squadron was held in the Officers' Mess at Polurrian Hotel, Mullion on the 31st. August, 1942. It was also a special celebration for 'B' Flight, whose pilots toasted Albert's winning of the D.S.O. which had been gazetted a couple of months earlier on the 20th. June. The W.A.A.F.s from Treleaver were also invited to the party to thank them for their help in tracking the enemy aircraft which 600 Squadron had dealt with so successfully during their stay at Predannack. At the end of the war Albert Harvey had been credited with shooting down five enemy aircraft and five VIs - self-propelled flying bombs. He flew over 900 hours in Beaufighters, Blenheims, Mosquitoes and Spitfires.

Albert never lost his spirit of adventure. When he returned to Falmouth after the war, in March, 1946, he became interested in shark fishing and turned a hobby into a business venture. He also became a noted gunsmith and an acknowledged expert in ancient firearms. He did not forget his country upbringing. He befriended and protected local badgers and for a while he managed to get some to walk about with him. Whenever Coverack people visited his shop he always had time to stop for a chat and exchange news. He rarely mentioned the war and most of his customers had no idea they were being served by a hero. He died at the relatively early age of 63 in 1981, his beloved wife having predeceased him. His son Peter has carried on with the business and has himself become an expert in small arms and country matters.

## 1943 - 1945

After the Coverack blitz in August, 1942 the village settled down to recover from wounds and shock, repairing the damage and adjusting to life without the familiar faces of those killed in the raid. Invasion was still a real threat as was demonstrated when from Friday, September 4th. to Monday the 7th., Falmouth Coastal Defence guns had continuous daily practice. Coverack A.R.P. and Home Guard were told this would happen so that there would be no false rumours or panic when the gunfire commenced and continued throughout the weekend. In November, the School Log recorded that arrangements had been made regarding school closure in case of invasion. A message would be sent by 'phone via Mrs. Roddick who lived next door to the school in Tregenwyn (The Mansion). Failing this, the news would come by special messenger.

The Coverack Wardens were disappointed at the public response to an Exercise code named 'Thun' on September 12th., 1942 when sinulated fire bombs were dropped at the Mill Garage, the Post Office and the Coastguard Station. There was also a supposed delayed action bomb at Little Ship 'Police Station' where Mr. Fred Pearce the village Special Constable lived. The area was cordoned off but in spite of the experience of the blitz during the previous month the wardens and the police could only prevail on one villager to go to the Rest Centre. The written report on the exercise concluded it was a 'regrettable sign of indifference.' Perhaps it was too soon after the raid and the implications of not being prepared for another attack had not yet been realised. The only reaction to a practice gas alert when rattles were sounded out of doors was the immediate response of the school children. The village adults ignored it. The Germans continued to fly over the area almost every night until the end of 1942 but they did not attack the village.

The Germans changed their tactics at the beginning of 1943 and began flying over the village in daylight. They kept up their daytime sorties from France until April 14th., when just after midnight the village was awakened by heavy naval gunfire coming from the direction of the Manacles. This was accompanied by machine-gun fire and the sharp crack of pompoms. Amidst all this noise, two torpedoes ran aground and exploded harmlessly on White Beach near the Lowland Point. The village was lit up by starshells and once more the emergency services stood by while destroyers at sea drove off an E-boat attack on a convoy leaving Falmouth. The convoy continued ponderously on its way and Coverack continued its slumbers. The services of The Three Sisters were not needed that night but two days later she was called out to investigate a raft floating off Coverack. The lifeboat recovered a Carley float which suggested that one of the ships in the convoy had been damaged or sunk but the naval authorities did not confirm nor deny this theory.

Three days later on the 20th. April Coverack School announced proudly that Brian James, Michael White and Betty Williams had passed the exam for Helston County Secondary School. The following month, on the 2nd. May, a party was held at Sunny Corner Café to celebrate the second anniversary of the arrival of the Plymouth evacuees. The number of Plymouth children in the village was decreasing roughly in proportion to the intensity of the raids on the city. It was not yet safe enough to warrant the children's return as was proved by the raid on the 13th. June, 1943 when twenty aircraft attacked the city, killing thirteen people and damaging three thousand houses. That year Coverack School managed to contribute £111 in savings to the Wings for Victory Week appeal. The village total was an incredible £2,750 which represented about two weeks wages for each villager.

The summer of 1943 passed without undue incident. The Germans took to flying over the village each day at breakfast time and again at dusk but they continued to leave it alone. Everyone carried on with normal day to day life, trying not to pay too much attention to tales about such interesting events as the clandestine movements in and out of the Helford River by agents and saboteurs crossing to and from France, making preparations for the coming landing on the other side of the Channel. American troops began to be a familiar sight in the area, though not many came to Coverack. Those who did were usually people trying to trace relatives of their families who had emigrated long before to the U.S.A Coverack people were lucky in comparison with those living in the South Hams in Devon. They had to leave their homes by December 20th., 1943 to allow the United States troops to use their lovely Devon villages and beaches as a practice battleground. They were not allowed back until the following October.

At Christmas that year, the Vicar, the Reverend Stephen Pulford urged his parishioners to thank God for '........preserving our land from invasion by a blaspheming, God defying enemy', adding dolefully that he thought it reprehensible that '........many in our own parish slight the God to whom they owe their very safety and security.' He ended his Christmas message by asking '........those who escaped both the last war and this to pull their weight in prayer for those who are fighting for their protection.' The Parish Church accounts showed that the recent repairs to and the replacing of the Weather Vane cost £28. It was strongly rumoured that the Home Guard had used the vane for target practice, so perhaps some of the part-time soldiers dug in their pockets to produce £90 on Gift Day for Church Repairs.

The Reverend Kinchin, who was the Methodist Minister for the area also sent a message to his flock. He gave thanks for the good harvest of 1943 and pointed out that the Bengal famine could be averted by sending food from America and Australia where there was plenty. He also considered it was ironic to thank God for the harvest of barley and sugar beet which was being '........wantonly wasted in the manufacture of alcoholic liquor.' He declared that the leaders of the Methodist Church were pressing for the rationing of such essential food supplies to the brewers. He continued, quite correctly, that over indulgence in alcoholic drink was sabotaging the war effort. The Minister supported his argument by revealing that some young girls in the Women's Auxiliary Air Force had been found 'prostrate and helpless' in the road, resulting in a farmer having to lend a wheel barrow to transport the foolish girls back to camp.

The comments by the two religious leaders of the parish in the 1943-44 'Church Messenger' no doubt caused some caustic comments as well as nods of assent and murmurs of agreement when local people read them. The 'Church Messenger' was reflecting points of view freely written in a democratic country which was, in effect, fighting for the four freedoms outlined in Franklin D. Roosevelt's speech of the 6th. January, 1941. The good pastors did not want to see them eroded further before the fight for the freedoms had finished.

The year 1944 began quietly. The Germans did not bother the local defences until the 5th. January when they flew swiftly over Coverack, probably on reconnaissance. A new type of British smoke float was washed up on North Corner Beach on the 19th. January and was dealt with by the A.R.P. Wardens and the Coastguards. In February the passive defence volunteers were warned about a new 15 kg. oil bomb which the Germans had started using and were told to tackle it from behind in the usual way. It was one of the last directives about enemy activities.

On the 1st. March, 1944, the Coverack A.R.P. Post was warned that United States Forces would be carrying out exercises for the whole of the following week and that Assault Craft would be used. This marked the beginning of the build-up for the invasion of Normandy. U.S. Army soldiers were in evidence in country lanes. They even prevented locals from approaching the American camps unless they could prove they had a legitimate reason for doing so. From time to time large formations of American Flying Fortresses were seen high in the sky, winging their way towards France. The propaganda war was also stepped up. Some leaflets destined to be dropped from British aircraft over France landed on the Battery in Coverack, probably because of contrary winds and air currents. The messages were double folded and measured 8½" x 5½". They were printed on flimsy wartime economy paper. The headline was in bold red type:

'Les Alliés et la France.'

The leaflet was an attempt to explain to the French living in France what had happened while the preparations were being made to open a Second Front and drive out the Germans. The text of the article was a translation from 'The Spectator' dated the 5th February, 1943. The introduction stated that '........in spite of all the efforts of the enemy and his vile propaganda', Great Britain had never ceased to consider France as her ally and that the complete restoration of France was one of the principal aims of the United Nations. The article sympathised with the dilemma in which the French found themselves, pointing out that it would be madness to condemn France for the 'errors' of 1939 and 1940. It confirmed that the common aim of both General de Gaulle and General Giraud was the restoration of France, although they expressed it in different terms.

In spite of an increase in the strength of defence of the Falmouth area, the Germans still managed to get through and bomb the docks and town occasionally. A German parachute mine went astray and landed in a field near Lanarth House on the 31st. May. It exploded and the blast damaged the temporary evacuee school. The building had to be closed for a while right at the beginning of term, after the Whitsun break. Miss Jury, the Plymouth evacuee teacher was sent to Coverack School to help cope with the overflow of displaced children and Miss Badge went to Sithney to assist there.

A week later the allies landed in Normandy on Tuesday, June 6th., 1944, when the moon was full. Coverack people were not surprised. A few days before 'D' Day the authorities had declared a five mile strip of land from the coast facing France to be a prohibited area. They also knew 'something big' was about to happen when they counted over eighty ships lying off the land. Three or four days after the landing in Normandy the villagers spotted three battleships on the horizon and during the whole of the next day, the windows of the cottages in Coverack rattled continuously, accompanying the deep rumble of gunfire coming from many miles away, up Channel.

The Germans came over the village again at 10.30 on the evening of June 13th., 1944. That was the last time a Red Warning was recorded in Post G2A Log Book. It lasted twenty minutes. After that date, normal routine A.R.P. activities continued until the end of the year. No entries were made after December 14th. On April 30th., 1945 the entry was:

'Wardens discontinued patrols and reporting and signing the register.'

They had received over 700 telephone alert calls since the Post opened. The voluntary workers were at last able to do anything they wanted in their spare time.

The rest of the village had already started making plans for peace as the war receded from Cornish shores. When Victory in Europe was declared on Flora Day, May 8th., 1945, down came the blackouts in Coverack, on went the lights. Bonfires were lit on the Battery and in the Mill Gyllyngvase Field. Some hastily constructed 'guys' in the forms of Hitler and Hirohito went on the fires and rapidly disappeared in the flames to the great satisfaction of those watching. The village people began dreaming of the return of their loved ones and the child evacuees still in the village began dreaming of home. There were many private celebrations in gardens and front 'parlours', where they sat down to a meal which had been concocted from the rations they had pooled for the occasion. The celebrations were somewhat restrained. One villager told the writer that when she heard the news on the wireless she went to a cupboard in which she kept some flags for celebrations. When she was hanging the Union Flag out of the bedroom window one of the fishermen passed the house on his way to the quay. He gave her such a disapproving look that she pulled the flag back into the house after he had gone by. She then thought of some of the Coverack service men, including her own brother, who had been in the European theatre of operations and had by this time gone to join their comrades in the Far East, and she knew it was too soon to start believing that it was all over. There were many such private reservations about the revelry going on in the village. The entry in the Coverack School Log reflects this. It states simply, on the 8th. May, 1945:

'Closure for V.E. Day' - adding for future generations which might not understand the abbreviation - (Victory in Europe).

People did not have long to wait before the Atomic bombs were dropped on Hiroshima and Nagasaki on August 5th. and 9th. respectively. Then came V.J. Day (Victory over Japan) on August 15th., 1945. At last the villagers could look forward to the return of the men and women who had been away for so long. This time the flags came out in force and the village was decorated with greenery like it used to be for the tea treats. There were prizes for the best decorated houses and a fancy dress parade for the children. The very young ones had never witnessed such unrestrained enjoyment before. The whole village looked forward to a new Britain.

The War Memorial in St. Peter's Churchyard honours those who did not return:

1939 - 1945

| | |
|---|---|
| Master at Arms | Frank Bonfield, Royal Navy |
| Able Seaman | Richard Bowden, Merchant Navy |
| Boatswain | John Cruze, Merchant Navy |
| Chief Petty Officer | George Herbert White, Royal Navy |
| A.R.P. Warden | Annette B. Hunter |

As in the Great War, others returned from Prisoner of War camps or military hospitals, their health and minds damaged by the service they had performed for their country. Some did not live long after they returned to their beloved county of Cornwall for which they had sacrificed so much.

# POST WAR COVERACK

## Settling Down Once More

V.J. Day or 'Victory over Japan Day' came during the school summer holidays so there is no special written statement in the Coverack School Log. Officially the war was over and Coverack people could get on with enjoying the summer and savouring the anticipated return of the service men and women. Of course, the dangers confronting ships and seamen round the coast did not cease at once. Lieutenant Commander L. Hill, R.N.V.R., who was in charge of minesweeping off the Lizard told a Falmouth Packet reporter on the 31st. August, 1945 that the day before V.J. Day his flotilla had found 124 mines in twenty four hours. One of the skippers, Lieutenant Coxall of Fleetwood told the reporter that a few weeks before a vessel had been blown up off the Lizard with the loss of seventeen lives. The tragedy was the result of a mine exploding during a sweep. Local fishermen who were at sea during that period will no doubt remember seeing some of the following vessels which were engaged in this hazardous work:

Benbecula, Finesse, Hazel, Knight Hawke, Longa, Minolta, Monimia, Mount Keen, Oronsay, Rosevean and Rowan - the latter was adopted by the St. Ives Borough. Some of these ships returned to their normal role of fishing when they were released from Admiralty service. Mines and torpedoes were being trawled up by Cornish fishermen more than forty years after the end of the war, so the dangers have not yet passed.

In general the country did not want to return to the 'good old days' as many people did at the end of the Great War. Both the civilians and the returning service men and women wanted to eradicate the spectre of unemployment and an uncertain future which had haunted them in the period between the wars. They were persuaded by the newly elected Labour government in July, 1945 to look forward to a Welfare State where they would be looked after 'from the cradle to the grave.'

Once Peace was established events happened at a bewildering speed. Not many had realised the full extent of the horrors which had been perpetrated by the Nazis in concentration camps until service men and women returned home with their stories, the Press published photographs and the Nuremburg trials of the German War Criminals in November, 1945 revealed what had been going on. It was only necessary for Coverack people to look at those who had been Prisoners of War in the Far East and in Europe to understand what privations they had endured. Even then they could only guess at what had happened. People like Jack Cordall, a Coverack Merchant Navy man had spent some years a prisoner of the Japanese and Francis Roskilly, who was taken prisoner in North Africa seemed content at first to lean on the wall by the harbour and look out to sea when they returned to Coverack. No one wanted to impede their recovery by asking distressing questions though no doubt their families had some idea of the experiences they had undergone.

The village boys who had grown up during the war found that they too were needed by their country for National Service. Some went to Palestine and witnessed the troubled emergence of Israel in 1948. Others went to Kenya or Malaya or to the Korean War in 1950. Some of these National Service men were the schoolboys who had been given the following personal message from King George VI on the 8th. June, 1946:

'Today, as we celebrate victory, I send this personal message to you and all other boys and girls at school. For you shared in the hardships and dangers of total war and you have shared no less in the triumph of the Allied Nations. I know you will always feel proud to belong to a country which was capable of such supreme effort; proud too, of parents and elder brothers and sisters who by their courage, endurance and enterprise brought victory. May these qualities be yours as you grow up and join in the common effort to establish among the nations of the world unity and peace.'

The older boys who received this stirring message from the King did not have long to wait before they were called up and in the course of their duties had to prove they had the same qualities as the older members of their families.

It is probably not an exaggeration to declare that Coverack people were affected in the same way as all other inhabitants of Great Britain by the sweeping changes brought about through the new system of Social Security, the National Health Service and the nationalisation of coal, gas, electricity and transport. The effect on the village was gradual and beneficial to those in the lower income groups of the village - which meant the majority. In the same way, the dismantling of the Empire and the build up of the Commonwealth were accepted by the villagers as inevitable and overdue. Many of the war time service men and women had been appalled when they saw at first hand the conditions under which the majority of the people the 'Third World' British Empire countries had been living. They sympathised with their desire for independence. They did not feel threatened by the incoming tide of immigration in Great Britain as work was not plentiful in the Coverack area and the immigrants made for the centres of indsutry where there was a better chance of earning a living.

Reconstruction of the village began before the war ended. Building materials were in short supply as was skilled labour but in due course repairs were effected and the two houses at Sunny Corner rebuilt by Mr. Stafford Hart. He was the Warden who had the unhappy task of checking the buildings after they had received the direct hit which killed his fellow Warden, Mrs. Annette Hunter.

It was decided not to replace all the houses in the cove which had been blown up. The bombed site was levelled, the road widened and the narrow corner leading to School Hill extended to enable large vehicles to go up and down. Before the war most of the lorries which negotiated the corner scraped the sides of Pier View house as they started the climb. The site of the house formerly named Melvia which was behind Pier View, between Granville House and Hillside remained empty until 1990 when a private house was built in the gap for Mr. Derek Atherton the Chairman of the Lambeage Hall Committee and popular retiring landlord of the Paris Hotel.

The site of Mr. Tim Connor's house next to South Cottage remained vacant until 1985 when 'Mariners' was built there for letting to summer visitors. Tim Connor's house was one of the village 'sights' before it was bombed. Tim was a fisherman of Coastguard stock and an accomplished raconteur. The latter accomplishment served him well when he was in need of a drink in the Paris and did not have much money with him. His audience saw to it that his throat did not go dry when he was telling them a story about village happenings. When his wife died in 1916 he decided that his house and his person would remain as she knew them, in that he stopped cleaning his house, nor did he wash until it was absolutely necessary. When the curtains of the house disintegrated they were replaced by festoons of cobwebs. Inside there was chaos, a jumble of furniture and all kinds of old household items covered with thick layers of dust. A glance in the doorway would reveal a few strings of mackerel hanging from nails in the passage way. The mackerel were in various stages of decay and some of the 'strings' held perfect skeletons of the fish. One can imagine the smell which emanated from the cottage on hot days. Visitors were fascinated and were to be seen peering in the windows and heard making all kinds of unkind comments. The village people loved Tim. They understood him and did not badger the authorities to come and fumigate and clear up the mess. The village children were attracted to the old man who had a wonderful fund of stories and would sit whittling away at a piece of wood, creating a model boat before their very eyes while he told outrageous accounts of his imaginary life before he stopped working! He once told the writer that he was a General in the Artillery. I could not believe this and persisted in an explanation. No amount of childish questioning could catch him out, he had an amusing answer for everything. In the end he said he was a 'General Nuisance' and that he had spent the war shelling peas and I finally understood he had been pulling my leg. The village children used to ask him personal questions regarding the fact that he rarely washed. Some of the boys were probably envious of his bravery in risking the wrath of others by staying dirty. He used to tell them that he had a bathe every week but because he was black all over no one ever saw him going down to the harbour after dark. When he got tired of the children's company he would raise a grimy hand, crook his fingers and say 'Claws will get you!' and the children would run off, shrieking with laughter. If you were sitting on the edge of the quay looking into the water and having a quiet daydream he would sneak up behind and 'claw' the top of the head, saying 'Claws 've got 'ee!' and give you the fright of your life. He was indeed a lovable character. In the end it took the might of the German Air Force to convince him that he could not go back to his house which he had to vacate when he was cut by flying debris and had to be taken into care. There was no lack of village people ready to help him. Mr. Pete Eddy, his shoemaker neighbour, saw to it that he was as comfortable as he could be. It was said he took his fleas with him when he convalesced and gave the authorities quite a problem. He was taken to an old people's home which was in reality a 'Workhouse' in Helston. When he got better he managed to come back on day visits to Coverack and would be invited to come have a meal with friends who were pleased to welcome a 'sanitised' Tom into their homes. He died in 1943, less than a year after the bombing. It is indeed difficult to decide where a brief, incomplete biography of such a 'character' should come in this chronicle of village life. Many people have been mentioned who have made a significant contribution to community life. What did Tim do for it? Perhaps it is not what he did - though as we have seen he was a coastwatcher during the first world war - it may be that he was important for the reactions he triggered in orther people. As already mentioned the children loved him when they learned not to be afraid of him. He was always treated with respect by villagers and he brought out the good in some who might otherwise not have felt compassion for an unfortunate person. Village people still smile when they speak of him and regret his passing. As the house which is built on the site of his old home is called 'Mariners' it will serve as a reminder of a well known Coverack character who spent much of his life on the sea. (See photo, p.36).

A public lavatory, complete with clock and village notice board, was placed on the site of Harbour View, Mrs. Mabel Eustis' house, which stood next door to Tim Connor's property. Mrs. Eustis was renowned for her cooking, especially her Cornish splits. She used to let her sitting room to Lloyd's Bank once a week so that the village people could conduct their financial affairs without having to spend half a day travelling to Helston. Barclays Bank had a similar arrangement with Mrs. Maisie Cordall who lived at Tremorvah, near the old Post Office. The remaining space formerly occupied by the Old Inn - Pier View and Trewolsta - became the site of the telephone kiosk which used to be outside the old Post Office. The remainder is used as a small car park for most of the year. Unfortunately the District Council was unable to build up the cliff in front of the site to road level. This is regrettable because the extra space could have served as a small belvedere for the use of villagers and visitors wanting to view the harbour. Instead, there is a dangerous, slippery glass slope above the cliff wall. This green has to be kept in good order by voluntary labour. The existing level space, though inadequate, is the most used viewing area in Coverack, the Quay excepted.

Since the war a huge tree has been erected every Christmas in Coverack in the space next to the public lavatories. People come from all over the Lizard peninsula to view the illuminations and join in the festivities. The tree and the attractive illuminations are financed in the usual way from profits of local functions and public subscriptions. On the chosen evening at Christmas, Santa Claus arrives on a sleigh drawn by a donkey. A short dramatic presentation of the nativity is given by Coverack School. Every child who comes to the tree is given a small present. There are hot chestnuts and other Christmas delicacies for the adults and the evening is rounded off with carol singing and items contributed by St. Keverne Band. It is a truly village affair - simple, enjoyable and an opportunity to meet old friends in pleasant surroundings. Somehow or other, no one seems to notice the toilets in the centre of all the activity! The site is again in demand on Christmas Day when people gather to watch the annual swim from the harbour in aid of charity.

The panorama from the prime view point changes in the summer. It becomes the best place for watching the activities on the quay, the movements of the local boats. especially the races on Regatta Day and the Search and Rescue exercises on Lifeboat Day when the R.N.L.I. Committee erect stalls and sell souvenirs to the hundreds who come to the village and congregate along the cove. It is again the focal point for those who come to listen to Band Concerts on the quay and the singing at the Carolares. Perhaps one day the District Council will heed the pleas of the Poll Tax payers and find a way to extend the site as far as the sea wall for the benefit of all. A similar set of circumstances applies to the magnificent cliff repairs which have been carried out near St. Peter's Church. After representations from villagers the engineers relented and allowed small niches to be left in the parapet of the cliff wall for flowers which beautify the cliff top, but the villagers were unable to persuade the designer to construct a safe viewing platform for which they would provide several public seats from village funds. The views from the cove of the harbour, beaches, the Lowland Point and beyond to the Manacles are spectacular in nearly all weathers but the majority of people have to content themselves with leaning on the cliff wall to watch, while traffic moves along the cove road a foot or two behind them.

Apart from the council houses built in Gatewynyack at the top of School Hill there has been no attempt made to house villagers who can not afford to buy their own houses. Most of the private post war building has been in the North Corner area of the hinterland. There is still some designated building land behind houses already bordering the main road out of Coverack. This land is to the west of Higher Bridge Hill. A Kerrier Rural District map drawn in 1977 clearly outlines a conservation area which covers a rough semi circle, the centre is at the western edge of St. Peter's Churchyard and the circumference extends inland from Perprean Cove round to the Bay Hotel.

The 1944 Butler Education Act was welcomed by the village. It meant that children over 11 years of age had to travel to Helston every day. They were educated in the building formerly occupied by the Helston County Secondary School. Some children did not like having to travel by 'bus and some parents felt their children were having a second class education in an old building. The Grammar School pupils had better facilities and a smaller teacher-pupil ratio. The village parents were right in some respects, nevertheless it was a step forward and presented more opportunities to the village children. The new school soon earned the esteem of parents from all over the Lizard peninsula. More recently Comprehensive Education has come to Helston and the Lizard peninsula has its own Comprehensive School at Mullion for pupils up to the age of 16. They go on to a Sixth Form in Helston or to Cornwall Technical College at Pool.

The Royal Navy Air Station at Culdrose near Helston was commissioned as H.M.S. Seahawk on April 17th., 1947. The Satellite Earth Station at Goonhilly was opened in July, 1962, among the prehistoric settlements, mentioned in the first chapter - Beginnings. These establishments have contributed much to the post war economy of the village in that limited, secure employment has become available to certain locals. Small numbers of people from 'up country' have come to live in the village and the surrounding countryside. They commute to their places of work and send their children to Coverack School. In general they make useful contributions to village life while doing their 'tour' of duty. Some remain when they retire or come back to the village and settle when they stop work. They can be considered to have replaced the Coastguards who were the 'official' temporary residents until August, 1951 when the Coastguard Station was reduced to Auxiliary status.

### *The Three Sisters Completes Her Work*

After the 1939-1945 war, life in Coverack continued to be centred on the lifeboat. The Three Sisters and her crew were admired by the visitors in the summer and the villagers continued their support whenever it was asked for. The speeches at the annual Lifeboat Dinners provided by the Roxburghs were always faithfully reported in the West Briton. Enthusiasts pasted the cuttings in their scrap books for future reference.

The first call after the war came at 6 a.m. on the 3rd. February, 1946 when Mr. Ernie Coombes, the Auxiliary Coastguard on duty spotted a distress rocket above Trebarveth Beach, near Lowland Point. The ship in trouble was the Motor Vessel Fauvette of London. She was bound for Falmouth with a cargo of ammunition and had run aground on a falling tide in poor visibility. The Coastguards called out The Three Sisters and sent the Life Saving Apparatus by lorry to the scene. The lifeboat proceeded to the wreck and stood by. The crew of the Fauvette fired their own rocket line ashore and the waiting Coastguards attached their own Whip and Hawser to it and sent out the breeches buoy as a precaution. After a while the tide had receded sufficiently on the shallow shore to enable the crew to clamber down a ladder with their belongings to the rocks below. There were 17 men on the ship. She was in no real danger, having 'nudged' her way on to the rocks so the Coastguards removed their equipment from the vessel and returned to the station. This proved to be the last time that their Life Saving Apparatus had to be put aboard a wreck in Coverack. After a long wait The Three Sisters was released from duty and returned to the slip to get ready for the next call. A fortnight later the Fauvette was hauled off the rocks on a convenient tide and towed safely into Falmouth by the salvage vessel Kinross.

The next call came on the 16th. July, in the following year, 1947. At ten minutes to one in the morning it was reported to Mr. Sam Roskilly, the Honorary Secretary of the Lifeboat that a Coverack fisherman, Mr. Sid Hocking, had not returned from a fishing trip in the Silver Cloud. The Three Sisters was launched and a search commenced towards the Lizard. After a while the S.S. President reported that she had found the Silver Cloud, which had broken down, and that she was towing the fishing boat into Newlyn Harbour with Mr. Hocking and his two passengers on board. The Three Sisters made for Coverack and the boat was put back on the slip at ten to four in the morning. Mr. Hocking returned to the village in the Silver Cloud the next day. He had to put up with some good natured leg pulling from his fellow fishermen in the Lifeboat crew for some time after that episode.

The Three Sisters continued to answer distress calls from small boats which were lost or had broken down and to rescue people who managed to get cut off by the tide on the cliffs round Coverack. In spite of repeated warnings from fishermen, Coastguards and the media some visitors never seem to accept the fact that the tide rises and falls.

The next important wreck at Coverack occurred in the year of the Festival of Britain on the 4th. November, 1951, just three months after the last regular Coastguard had ceased doing duty at Coverack. Auxiliary Coastguard Roy Harris was on duty at the Blackhead Lookout during a Sou' Sou' Westerly gale when at two o'clock in the morning he saw distress flares and heard a siren sounding. The Mina Cantiquin of Gijon in Spain had come perilously close to the cliffs and appeared to be out of control. Mr. Harris acknowledged the distress call to let the sailors know they had been seen and then telephoned the Volunteer in Charge of Coverack Auxiliary Coastguards, Mr. Rooke Roberts and the Honorary Secretary of the lifeboat, Mr. Sam Roskilly. At 0210 the village was rudely awakened by the explosions of three maroons calling out the Lifeboat crew and the Life Saving Apparatus Company. By this time the Mina Cantiquin had struck the rocks beneath the Black Head and was being pounded by the seas. However, before the L.S.A. Company could transport their equipment to the scene the wind and sea lifted the small 750 ton vessel off the rocks. Now rudderless, she began drifting and was being blown out of control towards Chynalls Point. Mr. Roberts and his crew made for the headland where the Greek steamer Archangelos had stranded in 1929.

Meanwhile The Three Sisters had launched at 0325. It was low water and the sea was described as 'heavy'. The Lifeboat arrived on scene just as the Mina Cantiquin was approaching the jagged rocks of the Mears Point (Chynalls Point on the Ordnance Survey Map). It was clear to Coxswain Archie Rowe that the seventeen people on board the steamer would have no chance of survival once the ship hit the rocks in the darkness. The S.S.W. gale had increased in force and it was raining heavily. On shore Mr. Roberts and his team watched and waited, wondering if they were going to be able to get a line aboard the ship in the howling gale and trying to estimate where she would strike. Archie made up his mind about what he had to do. In the words of the subsequent report of the Honorary Secretary, 'The crew had to be taken off the ship before reaching the rocks, this was done in a most commendable manner. The seriousness of the situation is shown by the ship being driven ashore in Coverack Bay and becoming a total wreck half an hour later.'

Coxswain Archie Rowe took The Three Sisters to the lee side of the Mina Cantiquin, which had seas washing right over her. The Lifeboat was rising and falling in the broken sea. When in the trough she was feet below the deck of the little steamer, then she would lift up and go high above her guard rails. The Spanish seamen knew what they had to do by seeing the gestures of the waiting lifeboat men. Eventually one man jumped when The Three Sisters rose on the crest of a wave and after what seemed an age, all seventeen of the crew were pulled aboard the Lifeboat in turn on successive waves as she rose level with the steamer's deck. The Three Sisters was by this time in danger of being thrust ashore herself but the sturdy 35 h.p. engine responded to the thrust of power demanded of it and Archie steered away from the ship and left the scene as quickly as possible, with all the survivors on board. By 0320, less than an hour after leaving the slip, Archie and his crew had brought the seventeen men to safety in Coverack.

The crew members that night were:

| Coxswain | Archie Rowe |
| --- | --- |
| 2nd. Coxswain | Reggie Carey |
| Bowman | Sandy Pengilly |
| Chief Mechanic | George Dally |
| 2nd. Mechanic | George Hewitt |
| Crewman | Noel Barker |
| Crewman | Percy Eustis |

After the news of the rescue of the crew of the Mina Cantiquin was reported in the newspapers and on the radio, Coxswain Archie Rowe and the Honorary Secretary, Sam Roskilly received many letters from members of the public. Sam Roskilly had one from a lady who enclosed a 3/6d. Postal Order '........to help pay for the petrol used in the lifeboat during the rescue.' The lady added that she hoped to be able to send another 3 shillings and sixpence after Christmas.

A sequel to the rescue also received much publicity. The Mina Cantiquin had a dog on board and many people reported having seen the dog moving about on the ship when she was ashore. Archie Rowe was an animal lover himself. Coverack people who lived near the harbour always knew when Archie's fishing boat was approaching the quay as his dog, which accompanied him on fishing trips, would start barking in anticipation of getting back on dry land when the boat was some hundreds of yards away. Consequently Archie made two trips to the wreck in order to find 'Pedro', but he was not successful. The dog's body was eventually washed ashore. For some years afterwards an anonymous lady sent a small gift to the Coverack Lifeboat Fund each Christmas in memory of the Spanish dog.

Some five months later on the 17th. April, 1952 Captain Rafael Bobadilla, the Spanish Naval Attaché in London came to Coverack and presented a well deserved Silver Medal of the Spanish Lifeboat Society to Coxswain Archie Rowe. He also gave Diplomas to the rest of the crew, with the exception of Sandy Pengilly. He had become ill and died a fortnight before the ceremony. His son Eric Pengilly, who was himself destined to win posthumously the R.N.L.I. Silver Medal for Bravery, received his father's certificate from the Attaché.

The ceremony took place in the Village Hall before invited guests and proud villagers. It was a truly village occasion. In seconding a Vote of Thanks given by Major Perkins, Mr. Murland Hunter got carried away by his enthusiasm and in conclusion stated he hoped '........it would happen again next year.'

Everyone laughed heartily, then stopped, hoping the Spaniards had not taken offence. They need not have worried. Consul Captain Juan de Tornos replied, 'Not only as Consul for the region but also as an old sailor, I take off my hat to you all.'

Afterwards in the bar of the Paris Hotel, which the landlord had decorated with all kinds of advertisements for Spanish sherry, Archie Rowe and his second in command, Reggie Carey replied with one voice when asked what they wanted to drink: 'Rum and Shrub, please.' That is the favourite drink of many Coverack fishermen. Far from being offended at the men not asking diplomatically for a Spanish Sherry, the Spanish diplomats ordered the same unfamiliar drink for themselves as a salute to the men who had rescued their compatriots. Their respect for the Coverack men did not end there. A few months later a Spanish Naval Officer and some Spanish Lifeboat Society representatives came to the village and spent some time discussing and exchanging ideas about rescue with the Coverack crew.

COVERACK'S TWO MOTOR LIFEBOATS
*The William Taylor of Oldham is seen at the slip,*
*with the helpers preparing to receive her.*
*The Three Sisters is anchored off, waiting to leave Coverack.*

The Three Sisters was not needed again for over a year, when she was called out in July, 1953, just over a month after the coronation of Queen Elizabeth II, to a French yacht called Mont Joie II which had got lost and had run out of fuel while making for Falmouth. This was the last service The Three Sisters performed. A year later she was replaced by a brand new craft which was the pride of the R.N.L.I.

### The William Taylor of Oldham and the last Coverack Lifeboat

The Three Sisters was twenty years old when it was decided to send the latest 42' Watson Type Lifeboat to Coverack. She was built at Littlehampton. She had steamed right round mainland Britain before coming to the village. The William Taylor of Oldham arrived on Saturday, 24th. July, 1954 at 3 a.m. The reason for this unusual time was that the crew were eager both to show off their new boat and to get back to their families. Instead of calling at Salcombe on the way as had been planned, they completed the voyage in one leg. No one was awake when they arrived so they went round the Bay for a while until they could see signs of movement on shore. News of the arrival of the William Taylor of Oldham soon spread round the district. Hundreds of people gathered in the cove and on the quay to see Coxswain Archie Rowe bring her in.

The Three Sisters was already at anchor in the Bay. She was about to be sold to Messrs. Stevens and Paynter of St. Ives. The Boat House and slipway had been adapted to take the new boat which was 6' 6" longer than The Three Sisters. The new craft was hauled up the slipway while the engineers who had installed the new winch and the builders who had extended the lifeboat house were still available and able to make any last minute adjustments necessary. In the afternoon the William Taylor of Oldham was launched again on exercise after the crew and a group of V.I.P.s which included Commander Greville Howard the M.P. for the St. Ives constituency, had been entertained to tea in the Paris Hotel.

The new boat was a real beauty, the first of her kind to come into the service of the R.N.L.I. She was capable of carrying 75 survivors - 100 in fine weather - and could list to an angle of 98$^{O}$ without capsizing. She was powered by twin 4LW 48 h.p. Gardner diesel engines which were housed in a watertight compartment. This meant that the engines would work when the boat was under water, if necessary, though that situation seemed unlikely to arise as she had 10 water tight compartments and 150 watertight and airtight buoyancy cases built in. The double bottom ensured that in the event of the lifeboat striking a rock when on service, no water would enter the engine compartment. She was capable of a speed of 8 knots and had a range of 250 miles which she could cover at full speed without re-fuelling. An important part of her equipment was a radio telephony set for communication with casualties and Coastguards. She also had a loud hailer and a powerful searchlight. The line throwing pistol kept on board could carry a rope 200 yards, even in a gale. The boat's generator provided power for the electrical equipment mentioned above, the navigation lights and the masthead signalling light. The cost of the £24,000 craft was met by a legacy from Miss Clare Selina Taylor of Oldham.

Coverack people had to wait until Friday, 10th. September, 1954. The day before the big event, the lifeboat helpers had lined the quay with tall poles from which the Lifeboat flags were flying. Strings of International Code flags decorated every building near the harbour. A strong wind was blowing from the South West, resulting in rain for most of Friday morning which continued until just before the beginning of the naming ceremony when mercifully it gradually ceased and the wind dropped a little. The Cadgwith Lifeboat, Guide of Dunkirk, came into the harbour and moored near the William Taylor of Oldham. The two Lifeboats made a brave sight, dressed overall, the flags stretched out in the breeze and the men in their yellow oilskins and red woollen caps which had been knitted and presented by the Coverack Women's Institute. A special platform had been erected on the Quay. The Boat was dedicated by the Assistant Bishop of Truro, the Right Reverend J. Wellington who was assisted by the Methodist Minister of St. Keverne, the Reverend H. Garner and the Vicar of the Parish, the Reverend John Saunders. Mrs. Greville Howard, the wife of the St. Ives constituency M.P., then named the boat 'William Taylor of Oldham', using a bottle of wine. The villagers joined in the singing of 'O God, our help in ages past' and 'Eternal Father, strong to save.' The new Lifeboat then took distinguished guests and some villagers for trips round the Bay. The passengers had an opportunity of seeing how the boat reacted in stormy weather. On occasions like this, Coxswain Archie Rowe always enjoyed turning his craft into the wind so that spray would come aboard and encourage his passengers to dig a little more deeply into their pockets when the collection box was taken round by a member of the crew. It was estimated that it would cost £1,000 a year to maintain the William Taylor of Oldham so it was essential to get contributions from every possible source.

The first crew of the William Taylor of Oldham:

| | |
|---|---|
| Coxswain | Archie Rowe |
| 2nd. Coxswain | Reggie Carey |
| Bowman | Noel Barker |
| Chief Mechanic | Michael Eustice |
| 2nd. Mechanic | George Hewitt |
| Crewmen | Frank Daw |
| | Percy Eustis |
| | Cedric Staples |
| | Alex Symes |

It was unfortunate that the Bowman was not able to be on board the Lifeboat for the naming ceremony. He had just come back from hospital so he watched the proceedings from the Fishermen's Rest.

Ten days after the colourful christening ceremony of the William Taylor of Oldham she was launched on her first service to the 14' dinghy named 'Anne'. The small boat's outboard motor had broken down and she was spotted drifting off Lowland Point. Five minutes after the maroons were fired the Lifeboat was sliding down the slip with 2nd. Coxswain Reggie Carey in command. When the two people on board the Anne were rescued about four miles out from Coverack they were '........in a distressed state,' according to Reggie Carey but after a warm drink the two visitors left Coverack to go back to London. The middle aged man and his female companion declined to give their names to the rescuers, saying there were 'business' reasons. It was gratifying to the Lifeboat men that the grateful couple handed over a generous donation for Lifeboat funds before leaving the village. The interested onlookers were left to speculate on anonymity, as fertile imaginations got to work.

Two months after the first service the William Taylor of Oldham had the grisly job of landing two bodies from the coaster Carpo of Rotterdam. Some days earlier during a heavy South Westerly gale which later went round to the South West, the tanker Casino radioed that the lights of a small vessel she was following had disappeared. The master of the tanker considered the vessel had foundered. The crew of the William Taylor of Oldham prepared to launch. The seas were sweeping across the slipway. It was pretty obvious that the boat would capsize if she were to hit the water at the wrong moment. Then came another message from the Casino saying that she had seen men in a ship's lifeboat and some in the sea. The shipwrecked seamen were nearer to the Lizard than Coverack so Coxswain George Mitchell went out in the Lizard Lifeboat in appalling conditions to go to the rescue. Coverack men were told to stand by. After an exhausting search the Lizard men found nothing and returned, worn out from their night's battering. Some time later, the Clan Maclean called Lands End Radio to say she had spotted wreckage and bodies in the water off the Lizard. Coverack Lifeboat was launched and after a search found two bodies in lifejackets. The men had roped themselves together in order to maintain contact. They did not appear to have been dead for very long. On searching the flotsam near the bodies for clues, the Coverack men confirmed that the wreckage had come from the Carpo. She had been taking coal from Swansea to Amsterdam. It is almost certain that this was the ship which the Casino had seen on the night of the storm. No further bodies were found and the William Taylor of Oldham returned to Coverack with the sad remains of the two Dutch crew members.

COVERACK LIFEBOAT MEN, 1950s.
*L. - R. Jimmy Carey, Coverack's Grand Old Man of the sea, began his service in the*
*pulling and sailing boat in 1902 at the wreck of the Glenbervie and took an active part*
*in the work until just before his death at the age of 83 in 1962.*
*Sam Roskilly, Secretary; Archie Rowe, Coxswain; Percy Eustis, Bowman; Frank Daw,*
*Crewman and First Aider; Cedric Staples, Crewman; Reggie Carey, 2nd. Coxswain;*
*Alex Symes, Crewman; Michael Eustis, Chief Mechanic; George Hewitt, 2nd. Mechanic;*
*Eric Pengilly, Helper; Sinclair James, Helper; Fred Carey, Head Launcher; Noel Barker,*
*Helper/Crewman.*
*Twelve of these men were awarded medals or certificates for saving life at sea.*

The William Taylor of Oldham continued her role of rescuing people from pleasure craft, fishing boats and rocks when they were cut off by the tide but she did not go on service to another ship until 1956 when the name William Taylor of Oldham dramatically became a temporary household word in Britain. A northerly gale was raging when at 0102 in the morning of the 2nd. January, 1956 Porthoustock Coastguard received a relay of a radio message from Lizard Coastguard saying that the Motor Vessel Citrine was sinking because her forward hatch had stove in. A minute later the Watchman, called Mr. Rogers, reported red flares from the stricken ship which was three miles East of the Lizard. The Lizard and Coverack Lifeboats were called out at once to go to the Citrine which was bound for London from Llandulais with a cargo of limestone. As soon as the maroons went up in Coverack many villagers rushed to the Lifeboat House. Two of the crew, Reggie Carey the Second Coxswain and Michael Eustice the Chief Mechanic had to come on their bicycles from North Corner. Archie Rowe the Coxswain and George Hewitt the Second Mechanic were ill, so Reggie Carey took command and Harold Martin and Alex Symes volunteered to make up the crew. (See photo above).

The northerly wind was so strong that when the Chief Mechanic opened the huge front swing doors of the Lifeboat House he could not keep the north door in position at first. When he opened the south door it carried him with a rush to the side of the slipway and he had to lash it to a railing. The crew got aboard and the William Taylor of Oldham was on her way with a full crew twelve minutes after the maroons had been fired. That in itself was no mean feat, considering the fact that the crew and helpers had to wake from sleep, dress and rush to the Lifeboat House. The helpers prepared the boat for launching, the crew donned their oilskins and lifejackets, received their orders and got aboard the boat.

When the William Taylor of Oldham reached the Citrine the Master, Captain Donald Calder, informed the two lifeboat coxswains that he was going to beach his vessel on Kennack Sands, so the Lizard and Coverack boats stood by. one on each side of the ship. She was now down by the bows, consequently when she got nearer the shore her bow hit the bottom. The crew began to abandon ship, using the ship's port side lifeboat. Seven men were flung into the water as the waiting lifeboats closed in. The Lizard Lifeboat, skippered by Coxswain George Mitchell picked up three of the men, including the captain. One man had jumped clear from the stern. Alex Symes threw him a heaving line and pulled him aboard while his colleagues were pulling the other three out of the water. Meanwhile there were three men still aboard the coaster. The situation was now desperate. Reggie Carey went in bow first over the stern of the sinking ship. The three remaining men grabbed the Lifeboat's lines and held on while the Lifeboat bumped the poop and the ship sank beneath them. The suction was so great that the bow of the William Taylor of Oldham went under as far as the bow fender before the built in buoyancy tanks lifted her clear and her engines drove her away from the Citrine while the Lifeboatmen struggled to get the ship's crew aboard and into shelter. One of the shipwrecked mariners actually managed to tie himself to the Lifeboat's lifeline and the knot had to be cut before he could be taken to safety. The elderly man whom Alex Symes had pulled aboard was obviously suffering from hypothermia so Acting Coxswain Reggie Carey sent a radio message to the Coastguards, asking for a doctor to be ready to treat the man and his shipmates on the Lifeboat's arrival at Coverack in half an hour's time.

Michael Eustice, the Chief Motor Mechanic took the elderly man under the canopy to the control seat and wedged him in so as to warm him up gradually. Michael offered him a sip of rum, which was kept on board for such emergencies. The man drank it gratefully and said, 'Lovely stuff!' Michael continued to keep him on the seat with one arm while he handled the engine controls of the bucking lifeboat with the other. After a while the man, whose name was Duncan Mercer, closed his eyes and drifted off to sleep.

It was low tide when the William Taylor of Oldham returned to Coverack. The state of the tide and the bad weather prevented the Lifeboat from getting back on the slip so helpers Ben Roskilly and Vivian Carey took Dr. Freddy Blackwood out to her in a rowing boat which had to be launched from the beach at the harbour mouth. Ben Roskilly injured his chest in helping the doctor aboard the tossing Lifeboat. Dr. Freddy, as he was affectionately known in Coverack, took a look at Duncan Mercer and told the Chief Mechanic that there was nothing he could do as he had died quietly during the return trip. One of the Citrine's crew told a villager later on that he understood Mr. Mercer was a retired ship's cook. His son was the regular cook-steward of the Citrine but as his daughter in law had just had a baby, the proud grandfather arranged to give his son the rare opportunity of spending Christmas at home with his family by taking his place temporarily on the Citrine. The writer has not been able to confirm this unhappy story. The doctor treated the other men for cuts and bruises and sent one of them to Helston Cottage Hospital for further examination. The rest of the rescued crew were ferried ashore by the helpers and given hot drinks and dry clothing in the Paris Hotel which had opened early in the morning to receive the men. True to form the villagers had once more brought down their gifts of dry clothing and food to the Paris Hotel for the shipwrecked mariners.

The next day Coverack had become the centre of attraction for the press. The Daily Sketch headline read:

'Coxswain Courageous Dares and Saves.'

The Evening Standard printed:

'Channel Rescue Drama as Ship Sinks in Gale.'

This was followed by:

'Seven leap into lifeboat after clinging to wreck.'

- an understandable literary exaggeration.

The Daily Mail headline was:

'Courage of Reggie Carey.'

- it showed a picture of Reggie Carey at the helm with Alex Symes and Harold Martin in the stern sheets as the Lifeboat was coming alongside.

As it was low tide the Lifeboat could not get back on the slip for a while so Reggie and the other fishermen went to work on their nets and boats. Frank Daw went back to his bakery and Harold Martin went on his postman's round.

The members of the William Taylor of Oldham's crew were:

| | | |
|---|---|---|
| Acting Coxswain | Reggie Carey | Fisherman |
| Acting Second Coxswain | Noel Barker | Road Foreman |
| Chief Mechanic | Michael Eustice | R.N.L.I. |

| | | |
|---|---|---|
| Acting 2nd. Mechanic | Cedric Staples | Fisherman |
| Acting Bowman | Frank Daw | Baker |
| Crewman | Harold Martin | Postman |
| Crewman | Alex Symes | Fisherman |

In recording the sequel to the rescue, Porthoustock Coastguard Log reads:

'0416 - Coverack not housed but Ready for Service.'

The Lizard Lifeboat was also Ready for Service after she had landed the three survivors she had plucked from the sea, refuelled and was made shipshape once more. In the manner of newspaper stories, the reporters had seized on the sensational side of the rescue. The work done by the Lizard and Cadgwith men had been described in an almost matter of fact way. Coverack men knew that without the presence of the Lizard boat there would probably have been more than one fatality that night.

The following week, on the 10th. January, the annual Lifeboat Supper was held at the Paris Hotel. It was paid for by Sir Ronald Roxburgh, the son of Judge Roxburgh who had worked so hard to get a motor lifeboat for Coverack during the 1930s. The Honorary Secretary, Mr. Sam Roskilly began his report by paying tribute to the Lizard Lifeboat Coxswain, George Mitchell and his crew, saying that the Coverack Lifeboatmen were very pleased indeed to have worked with the Lizard crew during the rescue of the men from the Citrine. He added that Coverack men had always shown the greatest admiration for the courage of the Lizard men. Sam reported that over 100 congratulatory letters had been received, including ones from the Lifeboat Stations of Cromer, New Brighton, Tynemouth and Wallesey. In mentioning Cromer, Sam Roskilly was no doubt thinking of the time in 1941 when six ships from the same convoy all piled on to the Middle Haisborough Sands off Cromer. Coxswain Henry Blogg had twice 'nudged' the Lifeboat H.F. Bailey over the submerged deck of the S.S. Oxshott to rescue the 16 men clinging to the funnel. To have a letter of congratulation from such a station was praise indeed.

The Honorary Secretary concluded his report by quoting from a letter sent by Sir Ronald:
'Your praises are now ringing out all over England. You must be a proud gathering tonight.'

A few months later Reggie Carey was awarded the Bronze Medal of the R.N.L.I., '........in recognition of his seamanship, initiative and courage.' The medal was presented to Reggie by the Duchess of Kent in Central Hall, Westminster on Wednesday, 16th. March, 1956. Later he was also given the Maud Smith award for the bravest act of life saving for 1956.

After the night of the wreck of the Citrine there was a period of inactivity as far as the Coverack Lifeboat was concerned. On January 15th., 1958 another Lifeboat Dinner was held in the Paris Hotel under the presidency of the new Chairman, Mr. John (Jack) Corin. It was a night made for reminiscences, triggered by the fact that Jack, as he was called by all the villagers, was the son of John Corin, the first 2nd. Coxswain of the Constance Melanie. Jack's knowledge of the Cornish Lifeboat Service in general and the Coverack Lifeboat in particular was encyclopedic. His uncle, William Corin, the third Coxswain of the Coverack Lifeboats was his Vice Chairman so there was no problem regarding knowledge of the work which had been done by the Coverack Lifeboats. Committee member Stafford Hart stated that there was no disputing the fact that the Coverack Lifeboat was a world-wide 'household name' and that the William Taylor of Oldham was the 'Pride of Coverack.' Coxswain Archie Rowe, in replying, stated:

'We shall always do our best whenever we can and I know the fellows here are willing to go, but one good thing is we don't get many calls.'

In one sense his words were prophetic for they hinted at the decreasing need for a Lifeboat. Among those who were to need the William Taylor of Oldham was Archie himself. A section of a later chapter will be devoted to this Coxswain.

The Coverack Lifeboat was called out 23 times between 1959 and 1972, and was credited with saving 26 lives. During this time Reggie Carey had succeeded Archie Rowe as Coxswain and he in turn was followed by his cousin, Vivian Carey who is the Harbour Master of Coverack at the time of writing. Vivian is currently earning his living as a fisherman. Before buying a boat he spent some years at sea in the Merchant Navy. He is one of three Coverack born men who are earning their living by fishing. Having been a Lifeboat Coxswain, Vivian is very conscious of the need for boat users to go to sea properly prepared. He offers them good advice when asked and is largely responsible for making the Quay and its surrounds a place of which the Harbour Company and the villagers can be proud. Before the William Taylor of Oldham left the village, Reggie's son Derek became the 2nd. Coxswain. He too is a professional fisherman. The third Coverack born man is Paul Watts. He is the grandson of Horace Eustice who, as the reader will recall, was a much respected Coverack Lifeboatman, professional gardener and one time athlete. Paul's other grandfather was the Station Officer of Coastguards at Coverack and his father served in the Royal Navy for a while, so he comes from an authentic seafaring background, as do the two Careys.

On May 30th., 1972 the William Taylor of Oldham was withdrawn from Service and replaced by a fast inflatable Class D Inshore Life Boat (I.L.B.) which became known as the 'Rubber Duck'. It was a boat for young men, designed especially for the kind of work the William Taylor of Oldham had been doing in recent years, that is rescuing yachtsmen, inshore fishermen, swimmers and cliff climbers cut off by the tide. The William Taylor of Oldham's Chief Mechanic continued to care for the outboard motors of the Rubber Duck, but due to the nature of the work, the need for instant availability was paramount. A team of young men was assembled and trained. When an emergency arose, the first trained helmsman and the first trained crewman to arrive at the Boathouse went on the rescue mission. Former William Taylor of Oldham Lifeboat Crewman, Ben Roskilly was the man who led many of these missions. He was the most experienced member of the team and not disqualified by age from continuing his voluntary Lifesaving work as were some of the former Motor Lifeboat Crew Members. Ben told the writer that on one occasion when a large yacht got into difficulties in the Manacles area he had great difficulty in towing her back to Coverack. He said that at that moment he was wishing he had the power of the William Taylor of Oldham available to him! During the five years in which the Inshore Life Boat was stationed at Coverack, 8 lives were saved.

Some Coverack Inshore Life Boat Helmsmen and Crew Members:

Lyn Harvey

Ian Ladbrooke

Chris Price

Barry Richards

Ben Roskilly

Chris Sharp

Peter Tutton

It will be noted that some of these names are not from 'traditional' village families. These newcomers have moved to the village because of their work. They have taken a valuable, active part in village life and are, of course, present day Coverack people.

Many and long were the arguments over the loss of the William Taylor of Oldham, the 'Pride of Coverack'. In the end it was hard, economic reality which forced the Royal National Lifeboat Institution to decide the issue. There were faster boats at Falmouth and the Lizard. The helicopters from Culdrose Air Station were proving their worth in carrying out speedy rescues, aided by a vastly improved system of communications with Coastguards and casualties. It was decided in 1977 that even the 'Rubber Duck' could be dispensed with. The village still regrets the passing of the era of the Coverack Lifeboats. To date an alternative unifying force has not arisen to fire the enthusiasm of the people in the way that the presence of a Lifeboat did for more than three quarters of the twentieth century.

Benjamin Disraeli wrote, 'Read no History, nothing but Biography for that is life without theory.' This challenging statement has some merit. Where would a village be without its 'characters'? They are part and parcel of village life. They do not have to be great administrators, nor intellectuals, nor heroes, nor saints, nor sinners. The pace of village life usually allows them to be themselves. They are valued and accepted in the community for what they are, '.......warts and everything.' They make the village what it is. It seems appropriate that the final chapter of this biographical chronicle should mention in a little more detail some of the people who have done much to make Coverack what it is. It will also include others who have not yet been mentioned.

It should be pointed out in advance that the writer is acutely aware of the fact that too few ladies from the village are mentioned by name in this book. Most of the modern village women, just like the previous generations of village women, have been busy bringing up children, providing a pleasant home life for them and their husbands and supplementing the meagre family income by 'taking in' visitors or doing other paid domestic service. That is the reason why many women have not come in to 'prominence'. They are always there, so much part of village life that they tend to be taken for granted. Yet it would not be a gross exaggeration to declare that village life is a matriarchal society. 'Ask Mammy.' 'Tell Mammy.' 'I'll tell Mammy.' These are the stock phrases of the male parents. On the whole the men are content to let 'Mammy' manage the young families. When the family grows up, 'Mammy' becomes 'Mother'. The husband often becomes a kind of oldest child, controlled by a wife who contrives to give him the impression he is in control of everything. Of course, village husbands will vehemently deny this but will secretly acknowledge it to be true.

There are exceptions to this as there are to every generalisation about human beings, just as there are fierce, or gentle, maiden ladies and crusty, or genial bachelors who make up an important minority section of the village. They are the ones who do all the social chores that the family men and women do not have time to do. The women take a housewifely pride in the appearance of the village and goad their men into keeping it an attractive place where people can live happily in reasonable harmony one with another.

In public life, men go to committee meetings while their partners carry on with their work at home. At the meetings the men cheerfully commit their partners to doing much of the voluntary work needed before village functions can take place. Frequently the ladies who are present at these committee meetings are unanimously voted into the honorary post of Secretary or Caterer or some other 'office' which entails much unseen, tedious work. The confidence village men have in placing ladies in control of village affairs is illustrated by the fact that at the time of writing Coverack has a Parish Councillor who is also a District Councillor and is the first woman County Councillor from the village. Mrs. Pippa Englefield is the grand daughter of Mrs. Whale who pioneered flower farming in Coverack. This industry was mentioned in the chapter on the 1920s and 1930s. In private family life, when the men leave the village, it is the mothers, wives and girl friends who keep the men in touch and keep things going while they are away. Foremost in the exile's thoughts is the 'head' of the family. A glance at the tattoos which sailors have done in foreign parts confirms this statement. 'Mother' is the most popular name injected indelibly beneath the surface of their forearms.

When Sir Arthur Quiller-Couch was asked to write a recruiting propaganda notice during the 1914-1918 war, he addressed his appeal to Cornish women, not the men. He told the ladies, 'It is your image your man will take with him.' He enlarged on the theme by saying that the England the man is defending is his home which to him is his England. Sir Arthur knew his Cornish men. He knew they would not leave their families unless their wives were in agreement.' He knew who ruled the home he called 'England'.

## *Archie Rowe  1905 - 1963*

By now readers will have become familiar with the name of Archie Rowe in the chronicle of Coverack. He began his part time work of rescue as an oarsman in the Constance Melanie. He was mentioned in the account of the wreck of the French steamer Gap in 1928. He became Coxswain of The Three Sisters at the age of 31 in 1936 when Coxswain William Corin retired. Though one of the youngest Coxswains in the country at that time, Archie was acknowledged as a competent seaman by men many years his senior. Readers will remember how he went without hesitation to rescue the Polish seamen from the bombed steamer Cieszyn in March, 1941, regardless of the presence of enemy aircraft over the Channel. Ten years later in November, 1951 he was awarded the Silver Medal of the Spanish Lifeboat Society for his bravery in rescuing the crew of the Mina Cantiquin. Dozens of other people had cause to be grateful to Archie for saving their lives in minor incidents round the coast. It is not surprising therefore that Archie Rowe came to be considered as a candidate for the popular television documentary, 'This is Your Life.'

Archie was persuaded to go to London to see a lawyer on behalf of his recently widowed sister, Mrs. Hilda Fry, who lived in the capital. While Archie was staying in the city, Mr. Willie Barker of the London branch of the Coverack Barker family invited Archie to go with him to a show. He took him to a television theatre where the compère Eamonn Andrews found Archie in the audience and led him on to the stage which had a blown up photograph of the Paris Hotel, Coverack as a backcloth.

Three weeks before, Ray Marler, a B.B.C. researcher, his wife and six year old son had come to Coverack in the month of March, posing as a family of early visitors. In spite of the usual village grape-vine, Archie remained unaware of what was happening while his friends were interviewed and arrangements made for them to come to London to appear on the show. As Eamonn Andrews unfolded the story of Archie's life, which was written in the well known Red Book, people from Coverack came on the stage and told of their personal memories of Archie's activities.

Mrs. Edith Hart told of Archie's life as a pupil in her Council School class and her husband Stafford related how he gave Archie his first job as a builder's labourer, knowing full well that Archie's first love was the sea. Pete Eddy the village shoemaker added that it was he who persuaded Archie to leave Coverack and go deep sea fishing so that he could get enough money together to buy his own boat. Then came a succession of village school friends; Sam Roskilly the Post Master, Harbour Master and Honorary Lifeboat Secretary told of Archie's fine seamanship and fortitude in the face of danger: David Mason, Gerald Eustis and Horace Eustice all added their testimony and Clifford (John) White gave him the honorary title of 'Uncrowned King of Coverack.'

Archie found the glowing tributes of his fellow villagers most embarrassing. He sat, sweating under the glaring, hot lights, clearly wishing he had never come to London. Then to his surprise, Eamonn Andrews brought Captain Mikosza of the Polish ship Cieszyn on to the stage. The Captain had been found and flown from Vancouver for the programme. After his thanks for the wartime rescue had been expressed, the Spanish Captain Rodriguez of the Mina Cantiquin entered and told his version of Archie's bravery in a storm. Next came a young lady from London called Doris Rau who thanked Archie for rescuing her when a schoolgirl after being cut off by the tide. Finally the compère presented Archie with a bound copy of the story of his life and the programme ended.

The Coverack villagers had a marvellous time in London. They had an opportunity to visit places of interest and were paid two guineas a night each in addition to their expenses. None of Archie's friends really enjoyed the actual appearance on the stage to the full. They were terrified of 'drying up' and not being able to remember what they wanted to say about Archie. In spite of their fears, the show went well. It had the ring of sincerity which has not always been evident when some show business types have been chosen as 'victims' for the programme. At the party after the show, Archie declared that he had been 'double crossed', adding, 'I shall have something to say when I get back to Coverack.'

All the Coverack people present knew that Archie would revert to his usual taciturn self when he got back and that secretly he was quite pleased at being tricked, once the ordeal in front of the cameras was over. The villagers also suspected that he would rather take the William Taylor of Oldham into another storm to rescue shipwrecked mariners than face another ordeal by television.

COXSWAIN ARCHIE ROWE 1905 - 1963
*"This is your life" programme, 14th, April, 1958*
*L. - R. Sam Roskilly, Edith Hart, David Mason, Captain Rodriquez, Gerald Eustis,*
*ARCHIE ROWE, Stafford Hart, Captain Mikosza, Doris Rau, Horace Eustis,*
*Clifford White and Pete Eddy.*
*(Copyright photo by permission of the B.B.C.)*

After the programme, Archie became a minor national celebrity. The whole village had watched the programme. Those who did not possess television sets were invited into neighbour's homes to see the show. Many relatives and regular visitors to Coverack had been informed of the impending programme and they in turn told their neighbours and friends who had heard about the village so there was a ready made audience before it went on the air. Archie appears to have been one of the few people connected with Coverack who was not a party to the secret.

That summer many people came to Coverack in the hope of meeting the modest hero who had been dubbed the 'Uncrowned King of Coverack.' Archie did not allow this unwanted publicity to affect him. He continued his work of fishing and piloting 'stone' boats (coasters carrying stone for the roads) through the Manacle Rocks to the Dean Quarry and like all Lifeboat Coxswains, he rarely left the village as he never knew when the call for his services would come.

Archie's appearance on 'This is Your Life' was not his first experience of being before the cameras. A feature film called 'Born of the sea' was made in Coverack and in it, Archie was none other than the Coxswain of the Lifeboat who rescued the sole survivor of a shipwreck. He was a baby boy. The child was brought up by a kindly village girl, who, in true romantic style, fell in love with the man who had rescued her adopted child and married him. Several of the villagers had parts in the film including George Carey, Alex Foreman and Cedric Staples, the Coverack Lifeboat 2nd. Mechanic. Many of the villagers were used as 'extras'. A long while after the filming was completed, the village was deserted one afternoon when almost everyone went to the Flora cinema in Helston to a special viewing of 'Born of the sea.'

In July 1963, Archie was invited to a Garden Party at Buckingham Palace as one of the distinguished representatives of the Royal National Lifeboat Institution. One week later, on a fine afternoon, with a light North Easterly wind blowing, Archie was on his way back to Coverack after piloting the loaded British coaster Aseity through the Manacle Rocks from Dean Quarry when he was taken ill. Freddy Bastian, a Coverack man working at the quarry had noticed Archie's boat was on a dangerous course and apparently out of control. Mr. Bastian ran for help. Mr. Henry Prior, another quarry worker called out the Coverack Lifeboat and put out in his rowing boat to see if he could help. By this time Archie's boat, Bessie III had foundered on a rock near the Little Wrea and the Coxswain had begun swimming from rock to rock in an attempt to reach the shore. Although shocked and confused after having some kind of blackout, Archie's first thought was to warn Henry Prior of the danger in bringing his dinghy too close because of the rocks and told him to keep back. He eventually managed to get ashore with the help of Mr. Bastian and two other quarry workers, Edward Waters and Noel Curtis.

As the William Taylor of Oldham approached the rocks the lifeboat men recognised bits of wood from Archie's boat, Bessie III which were floating along on the water towards them, being driven by the northerly wind. When the lifeboat had edged in as far as possible, Mr. Prior ferried two crewmen, Ben Roskilly and First Aider Frank Daw ashore. The 2nd. Coxswain, Reggie Carey had already realised the seriousness of the situation and radioed for a helicopter from Culdrose. It landed a few hundred yards from the spot where the Mina Cantiquin had been wrecked on the night Archie had won the Silver Medal. Before Archie would allow himself to be put in the helicopter he told his rescuers that he wanted to be taken home and not to hospital as they advised. To make absolutely certain there was no misunderstanding, Archie looked at the pilot and warned, 'No b....y games!' Frank Daw and Ben Roskilly got Archie into the helicopter and Archie and Frank were flown to the Old Golf Course near Penmarth Farm. Frank Daw borrowed a Land Rover from the farm and drove Archie to his home at Pen Glas. No one ever argued with Archie when he had made up his mind. Later that day he had what must have been another heart attack and died at home.

A gloom was cast over the village when the news of Archie's death was announced. Being a national figure, the B.B.C. put a short item about him in their news bulletins, including the overseas service. Alex Symes, who had been on several rescue missions with Archie, heard of his friend's death while listening to the news on board a tanker in the Red Sea. Tributes came from far and wide. At the funeral, six lifeboat coxswains were in the procession with Admiral King from the Lizard Lifeboat Committee, the local Member of Parliament and the Captain of Culdrose together with R.N.L.I. officials, Coastguards, representatives from shipping companies and of course, all the village. Archie's crew members acted as bearers. After highlighting the important events in Archie's life, the Reverend John Saunders said in his thanksgiving address, which was reported in the West Briton: 'Archie Rowe was a man of the sea who looked the part, sturdily built, his florid complexion typical of those who had been out in the deep in fair weather and in foul. To be seen in Coverack any day walking with carefree steps from the village to and from his boat, he was taciturn but always helpful. He was part and parcel of the life of the village.' His grave overlooks the spot where the sea finally claimed him.

### Cap'n Jim Hart  1867 - 1949

Before proceeding to the final section on twentieth century characters it is considered appropriate to include a person who links the nineteenth to the twentieth century. As will be seen he was not village born yet he and his family became accepted as villagers just like the Coastguard families, the Culdrose families, the Goonhilly workers' families and other 'immigrants' who settled because of their idyllic dreams, or more probably, economic necessity. Cap'n Jim was neither a Captain nor a native Coverack character. Like many Cornish men he was dubbed 'Cap'n' because he was good at his trade and more importantly, an employer of men. As he was the writer's grandfather it is hoped the reader will accept that the details for this extended study were readily available and that combined with the writer's memories, they portray a personal but reasonably accurate picture of a Coverack character who spans the two centuries. (Photos p.36).

According to the Hart family bible, James Hart, my great grandfather, was born on the 22nd. September, 1833 during the reign of William IV. It was the year when Slavery was abolished in the British colonies. It was also the year after the Reform Act was passed, which resulted in the number of Members of Parliament returned by the Royal Duchy being reduced from 42 to 12. Certain householders were given the vote and the monopoly of the franchise which had been held by landowners was broken. What effect these momentous events had on the Hart family was not recorded. James was the son of Elizabeth and William Hart. The latter, my great-great grandfather was a gamekeeper on the Clowance Estate near Camborne which was then owned by the St. Aubyn family. Because of the literary appearance of

Mellors, the gamekeeper in D.H. Lawrence's 'Lady Chatterley's Lover', I suppose the title of gamekeeper might encourage some people to conjure up all kinds of erotic images regarding my great-great grandfather. I am sorry to disappoint them. I can find no evidence to support the theories. William Hart was described as a gamekeeper in the 1841 census returns and in addition to my great grandfather, James, who was eight years of age at the time, there was Elizabeth who was six, Thomas, four, and Jane who was only two. In the next census in 1851, William was listed as an agricultural labourer. Whether this was demotion because of some misdemeanour - I leave it to the students of the mores of gamekeepers to suggest what the misdemeanour could have been - or whether the census enumerator did not consider that the occupation of gamekeeper was bona fide according to the instructions he had to follow, remains a subject for conjecture. I can tell you that William and Elizabeth had added John and Mary to their family during the decade and that my great grandfather, who was then seventeen, had become a working man. Like his father, he was described as a labourer. On the 22nd. July, 1854, James Hart married Christian Bawden, rather hurriedly I imagine, as their first child, Elizabeth Jane was born on the 6th. November in the same year. Francis arrived in 1857, Kate in 1859, Grace in 1863, 'Embley' - spelling later substituted in the family bible for 'Emily' - in 1865. The sixth child, James Henry Hart, my grandfather was born on the 20th. April, 1867. He used to joke in his later years that he could never understand why he had to share his birthday with Herr Adolf Hitler.

This second generation of the Hart family of the Victorian Age was still not complete. James Henry was followed by Joseph two years later in December, 1870, the year of the Franco-Prussian War. His mother, Christian, died in childbirth, but Joseph survived until the following July. James Hart evidently needed someone to look after his large young family, so three years after his first wife died, he married Mary Jane Dunn from Sithney. James Henry, my grandfather found that he had a baby step-sister to look after by the time he was seven years old. She was named Minnie Langdon Hart and was to become a much loved great aunt of my own family. Her sister, Esther Ann arrived in 1875 and another one, Christianna, a year later. It looked as if girls were going to dominate the second family, but a baby boy, Thomas William was born in 1877. He lived for only two years. Another boy, John Dunn Hart, was born in the year that Thomas William died. The third boy of James Hart's second family, Arthur Hart, was born in June, 1882. He lived until the following February, 1883.

At this time my great grandfather was nearly 50 and perhaps it was fortunate that no more children were born. He was classed as Farm Bailiff at Clowance Farm in the 1881 census and therefore had a considerable amount of professional as well as family responsibility. He had already fathered 15 children. That was not bad, even by Victorian standards. It must have been obvious to him that his wife's health would be affected if she bore him any more children. Birth control and family planning are 20th. century terms and I doubt if knowledge of such practices was available in Crowan in the latter half of the nineteenth century. Although the idea was put forward by Jeremy Bentham in the late eighteenth century, in 1876 a Bristol publisher went to gaol for selling a book entitled 'The fruits of Philosophy or The Private Companion of Young Married People', so the climate of opinion was still not favourable to protecting families by educating them in methods of contraception. However, James Hart's second wife lived to a good age in spite of everything. She died in 1923, her husband pre-deceasing her at the end of the first world war.

In view of his position in the family, it is not surprising that James Henry, the seventh child of a family of fifteen decided to leave the crowded family home as soon as he could earn a reasonable living and seek his fortune elsewhere. He chose to come to Coverack. I believe his choice was influenced by the fact that a certain Catherine Gilbert, who was born at Carnmenellis, but had worked at St. Hilary and Crowan, was working at that time as a domestic servant at Polcoverack Farm. She was an orphan and had been placed in domestic service to avoid living in a workhouse.

On the fourth of February, 1890, Catherine Gilbert (pronounced 'Jilbert') the daughter of James Gilbert, omnibus coachman, deceased, married my grandfather, James Henry Hart at Helston. It is interesting to note that they married at the Wesleyan Methodist Church in Coinage Hall Street. This building has been described by Professor Nicholas Pevsner as 'the only eyesore in Coinage Hall Street.' In spite of that worthy gentleman's condemnation, the couple's three sons and their daughter Hilda all made their way, in secret, at different times, to the same church to get married. It follows that my paternal grandmother became a redoubtable matriarch. All her children who reached adulthood felt that it was wiser to present her with a 'fait accompli' when it came to the question of choosing a marriage partner.

When my grandfather first arrived in the village, he went into lodgings, working as a stone mason and gradually setting up a business. After his wedding he went to live at Content Farm which is on the main road leading out of Coverack to St. Keverne and Helston. Exactly one year after the marriage, my father was born on the fourth of February, 1891, the year of the great blizzard in Cornwall. By August, 1900 there were five children and the family moved to Beach House by the mill stream. My father, George Stafford now had a brother, Joseph Henry, a sister, Emily Ellen, who was to die of meningitis at the age of twelve, another sister, Hilda, aged two and a baby brother, William James Charles. It will be seen that the family Christian names of the 18th. and 19th. centuries have carried on into the 20th.

After the first world war when the surviving children had grown up, my grandparents moved a few yards to Lowland View, now known as the Harbour Lights Cafe. At that time it was part of a cluster of houses known as Rock Alley. The couple finally settled in Crowan Bungalow which my grandfather built. It is situated a couple of hundred yards upstream from Beach House in Polcoverack Lane which leads to the farm from where my grandmother was married.

I relate these seemingly uninteresting moves, because as I stated earlier, my grandmother was a formidable lady. In addition to the property in Coverack my grandparents owned a village shop and a house in Crowan. The house in Crowan was called Coverack and one of the houses in Coverack was called Crowan. These names illustrate a sort of love-hate relationship in my grandmother's mind between the two villages. Whenever she was in one place she hankered after the other. Grandfather, or Cap'n Jim as he became known in the villages, was like putty in his wife's hands. She was a diminutive person and like so many small people, she made up for her lack of stature by developing a will of iron which few would dare gainsay. When she decided to leave one village for the other, she went. It was not a simple operation of packing a few items, putting them in a hatch-back and driving off, as we would do today. It meant organising a horse and cart to take all the essential bits and pieces and then it was necessary to hire a gingle, or two wheeled trap, to convey the children who were to accompany my grandmother. Mr. Percy Eustis confided to me in later years that he marvelled at the way in which my grandmother's furniture held together after those twenty mile excursions on rough roads. He was well qualified to judge as he was employed when a very young man to drive the cartload of possessions to Crowan from Coverack. That meant an early start from home and a late return long after dark. Percy complained that Dicky Roberts, his employer, still expected him to be up in time to do the milking the next morning. I suspect the youngest of Mr. Roberts' employees always drew the 'short straw' when it came to electing someone to transport my grandmother to Crowan!

In spite of the way in which Cap'n Jim pandered to his wife's slightest whim, the adoring, amenable husband did not appear to be like that in the eyes of other people. At times he had as many as a dozen people working for him. They were tough chaps. Some of the casual labourers were merchant seamen from the village, having an enforced spell ashore, but even they would go to great lengths so as not to incur his wrath. Cap'n Jim was a big, strong man with a fiery red beard and hands like shovels. However, he did not control his men by brute strength but by example. He worked hard himself and expected others to do the same. I believe some of his employees felt ashamed if he found them wanting. It was almost as if they had committed a sin. His congregations likewise felt uncomfortable when he touched upon a raw spot in his preaching, which needless to say was usually of the hell-fire and damnation variety. He had a loud voice and when he got 'carried away' by his zeal it was quite frightening, whether it was in chapel or on the building site.

Even the Methodist ministers held Cap'n Jim in awe. He had a healthy disdain for motor transport, especially transport which entailed making someone work on his behalf on the Lord's day. When he was planned by the circuit superintendent to preach at a distant village, he would get up early and walk, carrying a large black umbrella to keep the inevitable rain from ruining his best suit. He would not cause expense by taking advantage of the hire car which was available for him and refused point blank to use it. When he reached his sixties he finally agreed to accept motor transport, grudgingly admitting that he might as well use it, seeing that the car would also be used to pick up other preachers in the area and was not laid on specifically for him. The patient ministers had been trying to get this message across to him for years but he had refused to see reason. Perhaps his prowess as a dowser had something to do with the strange effect he had on people, although he would never abuse his God given power nor play on people's fear of the supernatural.

Cap'n Jim decided to retire when he was about seventy years of age. He stuck it for a while, then meekly asked my father who had taken over the business if he could come back. After consulting the doctor, my father agreed that Cap'n Jim could work for a few hours each morning. It was the opportune moment as the second world war had not long begun and labour was getting scarce. In addition, my father was liable to be called out on A.R.P. Warden's duty at night and Cap'n Jim would be a useful addition to the tiny workforce. Cap'n Jim worked on quietly right through the war under the watchful eye of his son. When I left the Royal Navy a year after the war ended, my father was rebuilding two houses next to the Channel View Hotel at Sunny Corner. They had been destroyed by enemy action in 1942. I went to help when I was on demobilisation leave and was given the job of supplying my grandfather with concrete for laying the floor at the back of one of the houses. There was no mechanical mixer so the work had to be done with a Cornish shovel or banjo as the miners call it. Buckets of concrete had to be carried into the house after mixing, and dumped in the right position. Then my grandfather would screed it. I can assure you that although he was in his late seventies, my mate and I were hard pressed to keep up with my grandfather and I at least was supposed to be fighting fit.

It was fortuitous that Cap'n Jim was a dowser or water diviner as well as a builder, for the two occupations are often complementary. They were especially so when Cap'n Jim was young, as local farmers would not speculate on new buildings unless there was water at hand for the cattle, nor would they use capital on piping water when it could be had in situ by sinking a well. When he was asked to go to a farm to find water, Cap'n Jim usually got the job of sinking the well, probably because the farmer reasoned that if no water was forthcoming, he wouldn't have to pay for the inaccurate prediciton of the dowser.

Whenever dowsing was under discussion in our house, which was usually when an interested visitor was present, my father used two of Cap'n Jim's 'triumphs' to illustrate the activity. My grandfather was asked by the Redruth Brewery to find a suitable source of water for their Headland Hotel at Coverack. This was before the mains water was piped to the village by Kerrier Council in 1937. My father, who did not have the gift of water divining, accompanied Cap'n Jim to help him mark out the course of the water. This was not a simple job. The most likely stream was traced from Chynalls Farm to the Helford River. Just before they got to the south bank there was a sudden deviation in the underground course of $30°$ but the stream resumed its northerly direction when it reached the edge of the river. By this time, Cap'n Jim was unwilling to abandon the search for the source, so he got a boatman to row across the river. He sat amidships with his dowsing rod and directed the boatman to row in a northerly direction. To test the width of the underground stream beneath the river he would dowse to port and then to starboard every few yards. He found the best response was always when the boat was pointing in the direction indicated by the rod from the centre of the boat. The two builders landed and went on following the subterranean stream through Trebah and Mawnan Smith, asking farmers for permission to cross their land. Finally they arrived at Treliever Cross and Cap'n Jim declared himself satisfied, much to my father's relief. They had covered a distance of over ten miles as the crow flies, but in fact they had covered over twice that distance on foot, in addition to the boat trip. I never did discover what the boatman thought of the antics of his passengers. Fortunately the terrain was quite familiar to my father as he had worked on the building of a hospital in Falmouth (now the day centre for Age Concern) before the first world war. He used to walk from Falmouth to Coverack and back each weekend, carrying six of his mother's pasties in his haversack on the return journey. These were for consumption during the week in Falmouth.

One of the reasons for taking such care in following the stratum of the course of water was that when it was tapped at first, it was found to be polluted. This was serious. Normally Cap'n Jim would not go to such lengths to find the source of the supply because he could judge the strength of the flow by the movement of the dowsing rod. He wanted to verify his feeling that the water was indeed not only a viable amount, but that it was pure. The fact that it had come such a distance underground indicated to him that it should be clean water. The well which he had already dug measured 8' x 8' and was 52' deep with a cutting below it running East and West which was 5' x 4' and 80' in length. It is ironic that after Cap'n Jim had constructed the well and obtained a plentiful supply of water, the analyst employed by the Redruth Brewery should have found it to be impure. This worried Cap'n Jim. He discovered eventually that at nearby Chynalls Farm they were, like everyone else in the village, using bucket lavatories, but that unlike the rest of the village, what was euphemistically called the 'chocolate cart' did not call at the farm to collect the human waste. Accordingly, the farmer tipped it into a deep pit, covering it with a layer of earth each week. This waste was seeping into the underground course of water which Cap'n Jim had so painstakingly diverted into the hotel reservoir. After some deliberation it was agreed to install a flush lavatory at the farm. Earthenware pipes were laid down to Polgravel Beach in Perprean Bay which assimilated the raw sewage. Three months later when a further sample of the hotel water supply was analysed it was declared to be pure; moreover, it was found at a later date to be more than adequate for the hotel's needs. Dowser Jim was right after all!

The second of Cap'n Jim's 'triumphs' to be related to admiring audiences in our house was the story of his talks to students at the Camborne School of Mines. He had been known to help locate workable lodes and in view of his success he was invited to give demonstrations. He used to show how he would commence testing an area by walking North and then South, using a metal 'Y' shaped rod, holding the 'forks' in gloved hands to prevent his hands from being burned by a sudden rotating movement of the soft iron rod. He would use wet cloths for protection when dowsing for water as they were more effective than leather gloves. It was confirmed that Cap'n Jim's pegging out of the tin bearing strata usually coincided with what geologists had discovered by more scientific means. During one celebrated question and answer session in the lecture room he was asked if there was any tin below the spot where he was standing. He tested with his divining rod and said, 'I should say there is a pretty lot of metal under this room in which you are sitting.' His reply was greeted by laughter and applause as the students had hidden a large lump of tin bearing ore beneath the lectern. On another occasion when he was demonstrating, the rod reacted so violently that it snapped, going off like a shot from a gun. That group of students did not need further proof of the strange power that can come into the hands of a dowser. Afterwards, my grandfather was informed by one of the students that in the Middle Ages dowsing was regarded as a form of witchcraft and that he would have been burned alive for practising. His reply was that he never used his divining rod until he had asked God's blessing on the work he was about to do.

Many people continue to use scathing remarks when it comes to appraising the work of dowsers - except those who have cause to be thankful for their work. They are not usually the sort of people who advertise their powers, they prefer to become known by having their skills passed on by word of mouth. There are only a couple listed in the current 'Yellow Pages' Directory. One of those who is also a well driller states categorically, 'No water - no pay.' You could not have a better offer than that. There is still a hint of mystery about their powers - one man advertises himself as a 'water doctor', but I have not made enquiries about the services he offers. They may have nothing to do with divining. What is true is that diviners or dowsers are gratefully if not scientifically recognised by civil engineers and builders as people who can be of service to them. When my brother George was serving in the Far East during the second world war, he had occasion to use his gift of dowsing in order to find water for his Royal Artillery unit. After finding water on a few occasions, he came to realise that he was the only sergeant whose boots were always cleaned each night and whose washing was invariably done without his having to chase the 'dhobi wallahs' who did the laundry. After discussing this with his mates, he eventually came to the conclusion that the Indian mess boys were not going to risk displeasing a 'sergeant sahib' who could get water out of an arid camp site by waving a metal 'wand' about.

The 1970 version of the Encyclopaedia Britannica stated that extensive scientific investigations of the divining rod have proved that it does not react in any way to the underground presence of water, oil, metals or any substance. It went on to declare that the movement of the rod can be the result of muscular fatigue and that it sometimes happens where water is later discovered, adding that 'there is no causal connection between the two.' Other writers such as Guy Underwood discount the idea that dowsers track underground streams, saying that it is merely water under pressure trying to force an outlet from a network of lines which dowsers find. With regard to the rod itself, Uri Geller, the celebrated demonstrator of psychic phenomena, said that after being introduced to dowsing by Sir Val Duncan, Chairman of Rio Tinto-Zinc mining corporation, he found it preferable to abandon what he called the 'twig' method and simply stretch forth his hands, palms down, and wait for the feeling of pressure which he likened to the resistance felt when trying to place magnets of opposite poles together. I do not know what to believe. I do know that results are obtained by those who have the gift and that each person operates in the way that obtain results for him.

As far as Cap'n Jim's water divining operations in the 'oasis' of Coverack are concerned, he did not have much difficulty in the northern half of the village. In the 1920s Colonel H.C. Bulkeley, C.M.G., D.S.O., war veteran and benefactor of the village, decided he would build a farmhouse for a model farm on land at Tregisky, which is on the right hand side of Higher Bridge Hill as you leave Coverack from the Mill Beach Road. It was among the first of the more sophisticated dwellings to be constructed in Coverack for 'up-country' people who wished to have secondary residences in the village. In fact, this building was for the Colonel's daughter, Miss Esme, who became a highly respected dairy farmer in the course of time. My grandfather was awarded the contract. Local stone was brought from Main Dale by Mr. Jack Andrew of Content Farm, where my grandfather started his family life in Coverack. The house was lit by a special gas 'engine' which was brought from London where the Colonel lived at 19 Gloucester Square. some of the gas piping is still in evidence in the house. Provision was made for a dairy on the right hand side of the entrance and accommodation for the herdsman, Mr. William Roskilly on the other side. His two sons are leading dairy farmers in the district today. When Col. Bulkeley was inspecting the new building one day he asked my grandfather if it was possible to have a well near the house. The reply was that the Colonel only had to choose the spot where he wanted it and that would be the place where it would be dug. The Colonel was a little mystified at this, nevertheless he walked to a spot near the back of the house and said it would be a convenient place. Cap'n Jim took a pick and before he had gone down more than a couple of feet he had struck water. What he had omitted to tell his customer was that he had already discovered the field was a virtual watershed, as indeed anyone could see by looking at an Ordnance Survey map of the area. Anyway, the good Colonel was suitably impressed and the well was eventually placed where he wanted it to be. This anecdote illustrates the fact that much of the mystique of dowsing can be removed by the application of practical knowledge and common sense.

The account books used by my grandfather when he was building up his business in Coverack reveal that he was prepared to tackle most jobs. Transport was poor in the Coverack area at the turn of the century. Most tradesmen were of necessity obliged to accept jobs for which they had received scant training, as there was no one else available within walking distance. The entries are for people who did not pay as soon as the work was done. It is not surprising that Ralph Ellis was one of the people who went 'on account'. He was the descendant of the builder of the quay and an absentee landlord. The family had acquired land in Surrey which needed to be looked after. Mr. Ralph Ellis was an important customer for the new mason at Coverack and the work done for him was given a special section in the account book as details had to be copied out and sent away for chekcing before payment could be made. My grandfather did repairs at Trewothen, the farm which was bought by the Ellis family in 1629, almost a century before the quay was built by John Ellis. There was work done at Treleaver and Penhallick as well. These farms were part of the Ellis 'empire' as well as the cellars and some cottages in the village proper. The cellars needed frequent repair as they had been constructed more than a century before. Some of the men employed on them were the tenants of the buildings, so the work tended to be well done.

The first entry in the book is dated 29th. June, 1889. Mr. William Corin got my grandfather to do 1/4 day of whitewashing and paid him 1/6 (one shilling and sixpence) for it. What is significant is that this association with the Corin family was to last up to the present day. When the Corins were bombed out in 1942 they spent six weeks with my grandparents until their house was made habitable again. My grandmother was only too happy to be able to offer help to her old friends. Mr. William Corin's nephew, Mr. John Corin, an octogenarian at the time of writing, has told me many tales about the Coverack of the days of his youth. He is a fine raconteur and has contributed much to the preservation of the social history of Coverack by his talks on radio and television as well as to the St. Keverne Parish Local History Society.

Cap'n Jim employed a number of different people from the village. They were not skilled masons but mainly fishermen or farm labourers who needed work at different times such as when it was not possible to go to sea or when little work was available on the land due to the season of the year. The following names appeared consistently in the account books from 1889 to the end of the first world war.

| | |
|---|---|
| James Barker | James Lawrence |
| Fred Carey | John Pengilly |
| George Casley | Richard Richards |
| George Cruse | Sid Roberts |
| Henry Hewitt | William Trevaskis |

These names are still to be found in and around the village. John Pengilly was my maternal grandfather. Henry Hewitt and George Casley set up their own building firms later on.

A more detailed glance at some of the work carried out for Ralph Ellis Esquire as he was termed in the book, shows what sort of work was done for him:

1892:

| | | | | |
|---|---|---|---|---|
| Oct. 18th. | George Cruse | 1 day building doorway | 3s | 6d |
| 21st. | | ½ day repairing pier | 2s | 0d |
| 21st. | J. Barker | ½ day | 1s | 3d |

The difference in status between the men is revealed by the wages paid: Two years later, masons were still getting 3s 6d a day and labourers 2s 6d. Hours are not mentioned but sometimes an extra sixpence for a day's work or 6d less for a day indicates that the day was longer or shorter than usual. My grandfather earned 3s 6d on January 18th., 1893 for cutting coins (cornerstones) for the Pigs' House on Ellis' Farm at Trewothen. This settlement is now known as Trevothen. He was back there again on the 20th. finishing the coins and for half a day he charged 2s 0d instead of 1s 9d, so I assume he worked a little extra time. On the 31st. he spent 3/4 of a day and charged 2s 8d., which was ½d more than an exact 3/4 of a day's work. Ellis accepted these calculations, as he did for work done on February 2nd. when Cap'n Jim went back again with James Barker and charged 3s 0d for a ½ day for the two of them. This meant 1s 9d for the boss and 1s 3d for the labourer! Young readers must remember that there were 12 pence to a shilling or else they will find the calculations difficult. Materials do not figure largely in the account book. Ellis was charged 2s 6d for 75 slates for roofing at Trewothen and when my maternal grandfather spent a day working for Cap'n Jim, 'building up' the Barking House and using a barrow of lime in the process, Ellis was charged 7s 6d. There was no mention of any other materials used. The 'Barking House' was where the fishing nets were treated with bark dye to preserve them when immersed in sea water. When work was done at the back of the quay, my grandfather would enter '1 tide' instead of 1 day for a day's work. He charged for a day but it often meant getting up early to be able to work at low water and it was often necessary to wo work on after the normal hours in order to get finished before the tide came in.

As far as I know, my grandfather did not advertise that 'distance is no object' when seeking customers. It must be remembered that not only did he have to walk to the place of work, he also had to carry his tools and materials. When stone or sand were involved, he would hire a horse and cart, otherwise he would carry or wheel what he needed for the job. In addition to going to the different parts of the Ellis estate, he went all over the parish and beyond its boundaries. I note that two days before my father was born in February, 1891, my grandfather was working at Penhallick, only a mile away from the village, but he would have been incommunicado. He wisely stayed in the village for the next week while his wife was coping with the new baby. Then he spent two days working at Trevithian near Lanarth. Two days at Lanarth Gate and the next day at Penhallick. This meant walking for an hour each day before starting work. It also meant an hour's walk home, sometimes in the rain, when tired out at the end of the day. In June of the same year when it was presumably fine weather, he went to Trevenwith, near Kennack Sands on one day, Trewillis, a mile across the fields the next day, Banger's Hill, just past Trelanvean Farm on the way to Helston the next, then after a relatively easy day building a wall in the boys' playground at Coverack School, he went off to Penhallick again and finally finished the week repairing the cart house at Kilter Farm, his old home. It is no wonder he scorned transport when it was offered by the Methodist minister for his preaching days. It must have been relatively easy to walk a few miles to a chapel and preach compared with walking a few miles and then doing a hard day's physical work.

Some entries, taken at random, reveal a little of the social history of the time. In June, 1903, Cap'n Jim paid my other grandfather in kind, giving him some 'tar, corks and manure' for the 5s 1½d he owed him. Ralph Ellis, rich man that he was, did not prove averse to paying grandfather 15s 0d on account on one occasion and leaving a balance of £3 1s 11d to be paid the following month. Cap'n Jim charged one shilling for fixing the bell rope of the school in February, 1905. The children were not all angels in the 'good old days' and someone had cut the rope to save being told off for not hurrying to school when the warning peal was given.

In 1909 a new farm house was built at Gwenter by Cap'n Jim for R.J. Kempthorne, Esq., who was quite satisfied for my grandfather to write out the estimate in the back of the account book and sign it. The price was £142 4s 0d using brick and omitting the plastering, or £126 16s 8d using granite, with ten pounds off if he did not do the casting. The piggery was to cost £34 12s 0d. His tender for St. Peter's Hall, dated January 27th., 1910 was £148 10s 0d. He was not successful. On one occasion when he was working at Lanarth he was asked, on August 30th., 1898, to bring a small bottle of brandy with him. He duly charged 1s 3d for it. The customer had run out by September 27th., as Cap'n Jim brought a 4s 11d bottle on that day. I hardly think the squire would have charged him with this errand, on the other hand I consider the need must have been medicinal as my grandfather would not have connived at any secret drinking by one of the servants at the house! Farmers often asked him to bring small items of grocery when he came to work for them. These were always recorded and charged on the building account, but no service fee was involved as it probably would be today. One entry might cause eyebrows to rise incredulously. On June 6th., 1908, Cap'n Jim wrote, 'Myself, washing Ark - 4s 0d.' Religion had not affected his reason, the 'Ark' was the name of the one time chapel, turned Sunday School at St. Keverne. By 'washing', he meant a cement wash to waterproof the walls. There is no entry recording that he repaired a leak in the 'Ark'!

By 1913, Cap'n Jim was charging 5s 0d a day for his labour. He built a closet for the Rev. Sir Viyell Vyvyan, Bart., at Carnsullan Farm, making a profit of £2 1s 4d. This was the first time he revealed any profit in his account book. When the war was over and my father took over the accounts, he did double entry book keeping and the pattern of work, materials and profit becomes much clearer. It must have been my father's job in the last year of the war as a quartermaster in the Royal Artillery in France which prompted him to update Cap'n Jim's business methods. However, in spite of his evident lack of expertise, clerically speaking, Cap'n Jim made a profit in most of his ventures and became a man of village property in a very modest sort of way.

My grandfather was a stern but kindly person. When I was a small boy I enjoyed 'helping' him, especially when he was fixing up a gadget for the house during his leisure time on Saturday afternoon. There was always something which needed to be repaired or replaced. He wouldn't buy anything new if he could make it 'do'. I remember his spending a long time one Saturday afternoon, beating out an old spoon he had found into a suitable implement for my grandmother to use when pricking out seedlings. I suppose that today one would smile at Cap'n Jim's naivety as one can buy a plastic tool for that purpose for a very small sum and avoid spending one's valuable time on such trivia. But what does one do with the time saved? I believe Cap'n Jim's 'make do and mend' sessions were therapeutic and contributed to his longevity. His favourite answer when I asked him why he was doing some intricate job which needed a great deal of thought to achieve what appeared to me to be a minimal success was, 'They who went schemy must louster, my son.' By this he meant that if people won't (we say went instead of won't) put their minds to a problem, they will have to work someone elso to do the thinking for them if they need something they can not produce themselves. Of course, everyone has to do this to a greater or lesser degree. However, in the final analysis you might as well enjoy thinking hard about a problem, solve it with enjoyment and possibly save some money at the same time. It is much more satisfying to apply one's mind to a job, than to be poorly paid for doing some repetitive task which demands little concentration, lots of physical effort and leaves one with a sense of frustration when the job is completed. This is a simplistic philosophy but it worked. Grandfather would illustrate it with the well known tale of a lady who asked a carpenter to come and fix her front door which would not remain shut. He came, examined the lock, gave the door a sharp tap with his hammer and it closed with ease. When the bill came, the lady protested as the carpenter had written, 'To repairing door, £1.' The carpenter submitted another account:

| | | |
|---|---|---|
| 'For repairing door with hammer: | | 6d |
| For knowing where to hit: | 19s | 6d |
| Total: | £1 | 0d |

The lady paid the bill without further protest.

The dialect word 'schemy' which Cornish people use may have come from the Cornish language noun 'skyans' - meaning 'knowledge, sense, understanding.' I do not think 'schemy' used to mean 'to be crafty and underhanded' in the way some people use it today.

As a family we were always invited to our grandparent's house on the day after Boxing Day. We did not look forward to the 'treat' with enthusiasm as we had to spend much of the time sitting still. We always had to keep quiet for the news on the wireless. Cap'n Jim had one of those early wireless sets in a lovely polished wooden cabinet, whereas ours was a cheap affair made by one of our clever neighbours, George Harvey, who was known as 'Pepper' to the villagers because of his fiery coloured hair. In those days it was my job to take the accumulators to Mr. Richards at the Bay View Hotel to be charged. You had to be careful not to swing the accumulator, making the acid leak out of the terminals and spill on your stockings and shorts, causing holes to appear which then had to be explained when wash day came round. The dry High Tension Batteries were obtained at the Mill Garage or from Mr. Billings who had a shop in Helston and came round the village to repair radios and sell batteries and spares. He was a former Radio Officer in the Merchant Navy. High Tension Batteries were expensive and were used until you could hardly hear the transmissions. Even then, before they were discarded, the aerial would be checked to make sure there was no loose connection, then the earth wire which was attached to a copper stake which was driven into the ground outside the house, would be watered, just like a plant, to ensure that it was doing its job properly. Then, if the sound was still weak and distorted, there was no alternative but to buy another battery as that was obviously the source of the problem.

It was always a point of honour or perhaps I should say pride that at Christmas both types of battery had plenty of 'juice' in them. This was because of the special broadcasts such as the King's Christmas Day message and the Nativity Play which came from St. Hilary. The church is dedicated to the one time pagan saint and was damaged by twentieth century iconoclasts, yet it was chosen by the B.B.C. to bring the message of Christmas to the nation through the medium of local drama. I did not understand the controversy raging about the church of Father Bernard Walke, but I was immensely proud that Cornwall was broadcasting to the whole country and that we could hear it on our wireless. We also liked to listen to 'Carols from around the world' and tried to imagine what the singers looked like. That was part of the magic of Christmas, as were the reports from intrepid interviewers who had gone by lifeboat to deliver Christmas fare to the lighthouses off our coast. It would not do to have those long awaited treats fade away at a crucial moment through lack of power, especially as there were always a few friends present who did not have a wireless set and had been invited to share our pleasure.

There was a gramophone in grandfather's house as well as a wireless. We didn't have one so we enjoyed listening to records at the post Boxing Day party. Unfortunately, Cap'n Jim fancied himself as a flautist and sometimes considered we would prefer listening to his flute playing. Who were we to question that decision? There was a china figure on the mantelpiece of the sitting room of our grandparent's house. There were two rustic children on a seesaw and we reverted to blowing at them surreptitiously to see if we could start the figures moving while the adults were concentrating on the musician, whose beard was more of a hindrance than a help when it came to playing the flute!

The party food was invariably cold ham and pickles, followed by apple tart flavoured with cloves and covered with clotted cream. If we were still hungry after that there was usually some cold Christmas pudding which was quite nice if there was any cream left to go with it. The highlight was being able to drink a large cup of strong tea. My mother did not approve of tea and she wouldn't let us drink anything until we had finished eating, even then it had to be milk or water for me as I was supposed to have what she called an acid stomach. Mother didn't dare question Granny Hart's decision to give us tea right at the beginning of the meal so we drank up gratefully, filling our stomachs so that we could not do justice to the food. Looking at it from the point of view of parents of a large family, by giving children tea, which was relatively cheap, ensured there was enough for everyone without having to spend more money than was available on the dearer food. Fortunately the 'entertainment' took place before the meal. Afterwards we kept eyeing the clock and looking out of the window to see if ayone was going along the cliff road. This was because there was always a social at St. Peter's Hall after Christmas and although it was Church and not Chapel, we were allowed to go if we had not disgraced ourselves during tea. I suspect it gave our elders a chance to discuss happenings which were not for our delicate ears, but we were only interested in escape so that we could run and shout without restraint - or at least I was - my brother and sister who were quite a few years old than I probably had more intimate social matters on their minds. I would not like to give the impression that my grandfather was an ogre in the eyes of a child. He was simply the sort of person no one would want to displease. I have been told that during the second world war some mothers whose husbands were in the forces used to take their children along to Cap'n Jim for a dressing down when they had been naughty. Nevertheless, all children who knew him always greeted him cheerily when he walked through the village.

Grandfather lodged with Harry Harris at Carnsullan Farm, Higher Bridge Hill for a while when he was a young man. As he was an aspiring Wesleyan local preacher, Harry used to ask his lodger to say the Grace at mealtimes. While the adults concentrated on the prayer, with eyes reverently closed, the children would pull faces and lark about in silence, eyes fixed on their elders in case they suddenly opened their eyes. At dinner one day, Harry's son became more daring than usual and moved the form on which the children sat at the table. This resulted in their falling backwards when they were told to sit down at the end of Grace. Their laughter soon ceased when banished by their father from the kitchen and told they would have to do without their meal. Some forty years later, 'Uncle Harry Harris', as he was known to the White family in Coverack, returned to the village from America where he had lived since the early part of the century. He met his friend, Cap'n Jim in the Mill Hill by the lych gate and said, 'It's Jim, isn't it?' Grandfather, who by then was suffering from cataracts, did not recognise the face, but the voice told him who it was and the inevitable period of reminiscence began. Eventually, Harry reminded his friend of the incident at the dinner table, saying he considered he had probably over-reacted. Grandfather thought for a moment then replied, 'Well, Harry, they never did that again, did they?' One can imagine the two men being lectured by a modern student of sociology on the lasting bad effect of such a punishment. One can equally imagine the advice having little effect on the old gentlemen. The adults were saying 'Thank you' for the dinner, the children did not appreciate it, so there was no point in their having it. R.L. Stevenson's rather cynical comment reflects the reality which Harry had to cope with in the domestic situation:

'It's very nice to think

The world is full of meat and drink,

With little children saying Grace

In every kind of Christian place.'

Cap'n Jim Hart died at Christmas in 1949. He was 82. The day before Christmas Eve it was decided that the slate floor in the back kitchen of Crowan Bungalow needed a wash, so grandfather went ahead and did it to please his wife, Kate. That was his last loving chore. He had a stroke shortly afterwards and died peacefully on Boxing Day with his beloved Kate, who was also 82, singing hymns to him. He had been planned to take the service at the Methodist Chapel in Coverack on Christmas Day, but it was not to be. As the Rev. L. Harrison said to the packed congregation at his funeral, 'He was firm and resolute, with a kindly, ready humour, gladness of heart and a spirit of goodwill to men.' Cap'n Jim would have been flattered, but pleased with that.

### Contemporary Characters

Without further mention of some Coverack people who are living in the village at the time of writing, this account might lead some readers to conclude that it is a nostalgic lament for people, customs and activities long since vanished from the village scene. It is intended to be a chronicle of the development of the village up to the recent past. One hopes it will be of service to those who are interested in the 'oasis' in the wider context of Cornwall, Britain and indeed the world. In addition one hopes that the narrative does not give the impression that the village is suffering from a gradual process of decay. The reader might well be tempted to ask, 'Where have all the flowers gone?' - meaning not just the natural flora but also the 'real', village people like the Barkers, the Roskillys, the Martins, the Pengillys, the Whites, the Richards and so on. The answer is that some are still there and that others have joined their ranks to form a band of contemporary villagers.

What of the Roskillys? Francis Roskilly has had to move to Helston for health reasons but he and his sister Phyllis still visit the village whenever they can. Francis has the unenviable distinction of having been a prisoner of war of the Italians, the Germans and of the Russians, albeit for only fourteen days due to general confusion and mistaken identities at the end of the war. Some five months after the blitz on Coverack in 1942, Francis was being held as a prisoner of war at Medina, near Milan when he heard that Coverack had been bombed. Francis told the writer that he had a premonition that all was not well with his family but he had to wait another month before the chaplain sent for him. The Padre told him gently that his sister Hilda and nephew John had been killed by the Germans. Later on, Francis was moved to Germany. He saw some of the allied devastation of Dresden but that was of no comfort to him. On his release at the end of the war, Francis had the good fortune to be sent to a hospital which was in the charge of Miss Grace Sturmer,

218

a former Coverack resident who herself had served as a young nurse in the Great War. Francis was sent to Trewidden Convalescent Home near Penzance and eventually was able to return to Coverack. Because of his war service, Francis was offered a place in the Chelsea Hospital in 1989. He declined. He could not leave Cornwall even for the attractive comforts of such a caring organisation. He prefers to remain independent. Mr. Jack White, Francis' brother in law, whose wife was killed by the bombing, is a member of the Coastguard White family. He has long since retired from the Royal Navy and lives in Coverack as does his grand daughter, who has married a 'new' villager. In old age, Jack devotes most of his time to nursing his second wife, formerly Dorothy Hocking, a nurse from Coverack. Whenever he can, he still spends some time in painting scenes of the village as described earlier in this book.

Two nephews of Francis Roskilly, Joe and Ben are very much village people. Joe has moved to Tregellast Barton Farm, St. Keverne but he still plays an active part in Coverack affairs. Ben Roskilly is also a farmer - and former Lifeboatman. He and his wife Georgia are both very active in village affairs and are great favourites with young people from 'up-country' who come to camp on their farm.

In July, 1979 it was announced that the American 78 ton space workshop 'Skylab' was about to re-enter the earth's atmosphere and break up. Moreover, it was calculated that debris might well land on the Lizard peninsula. Overnight a notice appeared on the window of Raymond White's Cove Shop announcing that he had a supply of tin hats for sale at 50p each. It did not take long for Raymond White to guess that his friend Ben Roskilly was up to his old tricks, so Raymond stuck another notice beneath the advertisement saying, 'Sorry, all sold out.' Customers were advised to telephone a St. Keverne number during the night hours for further information. The number was that of Ben Roskilly. Some people took the affair seriously. Reporters arrived in the village seeking information about the tin hats. Raymond White showed them a collection of shiny ice cream tins, which would be mistaken for cylindrical tin hats if one did not look too closely at them. Being a very obliging village shopkeeper, he kept the empty tins in his store room and gave them to his customers when they asked for one, as they were very useful for all kinds of domestic purposes. A local councillor criticised the Americans and the County Education Office sent special instructions to schools on the Lizard peninusla. The officials did the right thing, as there was indeed a possibility of objects landing in the area, though whether or not an old ice cream tin would have afforded the children protection from an object hurtling down from outer space is another matter.

On being questioned, Raymond White told a reporter that he was merely the selling agent and that the reporter would have to see a 'person' who was at that particular time attending the board meeting of a local treacle mine. An article in the Daily Telegraph for the 11th. July stated:

'Whether Mr. White and his friend are enterprising business men or practical jokers remains to be seen.'

The two village 'wags' kept the joke going for some time. Gullible visitors went hither and thither in search of safety. Knowing villagers sat back on their chairs in the sun and enjoyed the fun.

Raymond White has now left the village but his father Clifford White, affectionately known as 'John Bull', has now retired from his green grocery business and continues to take part in public village affairs. He too is known for his humorous anecdotes of village happenings. The writer is grateful to Clifford and his sister, Mrs. Gladys Harling for taking part in long conversations with him.

What of the Barkers? It has already been stated that Granville House is still owned by a member of the Barker family, namely David Bruce, who is to be seen on holiday each year. He goes out to sea daily in his yellow painted 'Cornish Lass', keeping alive the tradition of the seafaring Barkers. Other members of the London branch of the Barker family come down whenever they can to spend time in the village.

Another family, which has connections with the Barkers, namely the Martin family is very much in evidence. One of the oldest of the contemporary villagers is Harold Martin, Senior - former Lifeboat crewman, Honorary Secretary, fisherman and village postman. His son, Harold Martin, Junior, is an electrical engineer at Culdrose and part time fisherman. He lives with his family in the village, as does Harold (Senior's) brother, Bert Martin. Visitors to the village will sometimes see Bert tidying the Churchyard. He is carrying on the tradition of service to the village. He has retired from the voluntary job of Special Constable. Bert began his working life as an apprentice blacksmith at Tregowris, he then joined the Royal Navy. He spent much of the war on Atlantic convoys and was Mentioned in Despatches when serving on H.M.S. Albrighton which made a number of clandestine raids on the French coast. Bert lives with his wife Rosie, former telephonist and wartime 'lines-person' for the G.P.O. She came to Coverack with her father when he was appointed Station Officer of Coastguards at Coverack. The Martins' children have moved elsewhere as have so many young Coverack people but perhaps they will return and settle one day.

Brothers Noel and Willie Barker, both former Lifeboatmen have been mentioned a number of times elsewhere. They live in quiet retirement and are respected members of village organisations. Their daughters have been committed to educating the children of the district. The family had connections with the Bouldens and the Coplins, well known nineteenth century Coverack names which are no longer part of the village scene. They are also allied through marriage to the Carey and Roberts families.

What of the Careys? The reader will recall that they are branches of the Coastguard Carey families. The name will remain part of the history of Coverack. People will remember the bravery of Fred Carey at the Battle of Narvik and that of his brother Reggie at the wreck of the Citrine. They will not forget the brothers' outwardly irascible and inwardly caring Uncle Jimmy Carey, veteran fisherman, Lifeboatman and very popular raconteur. The Careys are still well represented in the village. Reggie's son Derek continues fishing as does his former Lifeboat Coxswain and cousin, Vivian Carey who is currently Harbour Master at Coverack. Vivian's brother Norman and his two sons still do some fishing and are involved with many facets of village life. Norman is retired and has the important voluntary task of looking after the finances of the Village Hall, which remains the social centre of public village life.

Many of the engines of the cove boats are currently maintained by the former Chief Motor Mechanic of the William Taylor of Oldham. These engines could not be in better hands. Michael Eustice trained as a mechanic at the Mill Garage in Coverack. He then spent three years in the Royal Marines as a vehicle mechanic, attached to No. 42 Commando. After returning to Coverack and spending a while as a crew member of The Three Sisters, Michael was appointed as Chief Mechanic of the William Taylor of Oldham. He did special training on Gardner diesels in Manchester, then went as a 'travelling' mechanic working at Bideford, Minehead and Clovelly on Lifeboats which needed engine overhauls. He stood by the William Taylor of Oldham at Littlehampton before she came to Coverack. The success of the rescue missions of the William Taylor of Oldham is in no small way due to the quiet efficiency of her trained engineer and his assistant mechanics, who ensured the engines were always ready to drive her through heavy seas. We have seen that now the village no longer has a Lifeboat, Michael continues to look after engines but perhaps more importantly, he is seen every day on his postal rounds. He is no ordinary postman. He delivers mail but he is also sick visitor, confidant, bringer of news, good and bad and general messenger to housebound villagers - both Coverack and adopted. He does much of this work after his round has finished when he can use his spare time to go back to those whom he has identified as in need of some kind of help. His attitude epitomises that of the true villager as does that of his sister, Mrs. Elizabeth Watts who has been the School Cook and is always at hand to help elderly or sick neighbours.

There are many names which are no longer known in the village, except to older natives. The Corin fishing family originated from Gulval. A descendant of the Corin family lives in the village and another in Falmouth. There are no male descendants known to the writer but the late Mr. John (Jack) Corin's daughters live in the western counties.

Another name which is no longer represented in Coverack is that of Eustis. Percy Eustis, that stout hearted quarryman, Lifeboatman and indefatiguable helper of all in need was the last male representative of the family in Coverack. Much has already been written about Percy. His daughter Lillian continues to live in the village. Her husband Ken and his brother Jim Cox, are grandsons of local Lifeboatmen and both are former Auxiliary Coastguards as has been shown before.

There are no longer any Pengillys in the village but there are branches in the parish. John Pengilly, lives at Newlyn. He is the grandson of Sandy the former fisherman, Lifeboatman and ex P.O.W. and son of Eric, the Coverack Lifeboat man who was awarded posthumously the Silver Medal when Coxswain-Mechanic of the Susan Ashley, the Sennen Lifeboat. Eric took part in the search for the survivors of the Union Crystal in November, 1977. He had served as a Petty Officer Motor Mechanic in Motor Torpedo Boats during the war. He was no stranger to rough weather. The morning after the launch to the Union Crystal in 1977, Captain Watson of Sennen said, 'We saw the bow go under and the stern come out, then of course she stood on end..... it looked like a man trying to handle a fractious horse.' That was praise indeed for the Coverack born Coxswain. Not long after the Union Crystal affair Eric became ill and died of pneumonia. His friends said that the sea had finally done what the Germans had failed to do in countless skirmishes. He was buried in Coverack, just before his 54th. birthday. The grave overlooks the beach where he learned to swim and the Bay where he learned to sail and fish.

The Symes family too, has gone from Coverack. Ted Symes, the Merchant Navy Boatswain, veteran of two World Wars, his son Alex, Lifeboatman, fisherman, Merchant Navy man, survivor of two sinkings during the war and ex Ministry of Defence Policeman, were descendants of the Coastguard Symes who alerted the village when the Pindos was wrecked in 1912. Geoffrey Symes is currently a Sergeant of Police in the Devon and Cornwall Constabulary. He comes back to Coverack whenever he can and goes fishing. His sister Pauline resides with her family in nearby Helston.

The Daw family, who like the Careys, Eddys, Harts, Symes, Whites and many others came to Coverack from elsewhere and are still in the village. Graham is responsible for the village water and sewage and his wife Brenda runs the shop at the Mill which can supply almost everything a villager or a visitor might need. Frank Daw, former Baker and long serving Lifeboatman has retired from his work at Culdrose Air Station. He served with the 14th. Army in 681 Squadron, R.A.F. in India, Burma and Hong Kong during the war. He takes a keen and active interest in village affairs as does his wife Elaine who works in the village school. Elaine's sister Maureen, former popular dispenser of drinks at the Paris Hotel now caters for the workers at Goonhilly Earth Station.

What of the 'Downsers' - the farmers and countrymen living outside Coverack? They are still to be seen making their regular visits to the village (in cars, not carts!) and catching up on the latest news from the cove dwellers. People like the Bastians, the Bowdens, the Butlers, the Hockings, the Iveys, the Moores, the Richards, the Thomases, the Tripps and Tripconeys. In addition to news from the country they bring, as they have always done, some choice vegetables, free range eggs, clotted cream and other country fare for a chosen few. They take back fish in frails or some other village delicacies as well as some tasty bits of gossip. Of course a number of new 'Downsers' have moved into former farm houses and barns and become 'naturalised' in the Coverack countryside. Among them, as indicated earlier, are ex Naval personnel from Culdrose like Lieutenant Commander Mike Wastie and artists like Mike's wife, Mary. Like many other comparative newcomers, their family has been brought up and educated in the area.

These are some of the people who can be seen going about the village at the time of writing. There are many others. The writer would like to apologise here and now for errors and omissions. It is only possible to name those who are known to the writer and his village acquaintances. They are but an example of the village and countryside families.

It is almost certain that if the reader wishes to extend his knowledge of Coverack he will be directed to Mr. David Mason. David and his wife Jennie have been mentioned already in this book. David has become a popular village oral historian and has been kind enough to spend some hours with the writer, guiding him through the intricacies of Coverack happenings and Coverack family relationships. It is believed that this is the first attempt to record a chronicle of Coverack and it is hoped that it may serve as a starting point for a more detailed study of the village.

In case the reader is wondering what has happened to the Harts, one member of the Hart-Pengilly family currently resides in the village. Miss Mona Hart, M.B.E., former Captain in the W.R.A.C. lives in a cottage in the cove. After a busy life in the Army in war and peace and at St. Loyes School of Occupational Therapy in Exeter, she devotes much of her leisure to raising funds for the R.N.L.I. which is not surprising as her father, grandfather and very nearly all her uncles and cousins have been Coverack Lifeboatmen. Some other Harts are to be found in Falmouth, Nanpean, Roche, St. Just in Penwith, Plymouth, Exford (Somerset), Barrow in Furness, Sussex, Swansea and Huntly, New Zealand.

# *THE 21st CENTURY*

Within a decade of completing this chronicle, Coverack will be entering the 21st. century, some seven centuries after the name Porthcovrek was first recorded. The village will no doubt continue to be a unique environment, an oasis for its regular visitors from 'up-country' and an abiding memory for its enforced emigrant exiles. As the 'oasis' enters the last decade of the 20th. century there are fears that it will become a 'ghost' village. In winter nearly fifty of the cottages are empty, waiting for summer visitors to occupy them. This situation causes many problems. Local young people are faced with the tantalising sight of an empty house which they would love to be able to afford to rent permanently so that they could bring up their families in their native village. They usually have to leave, not only to find a home but also to find work, so it is not just a problem of cost. The two village shops find the winters are hard. Their customers are halved in number and the ageing resident population has to accept increasing prices due to lower turnovers. In spite of this gloomy state of affairs, Coverack born villagers will continue coming back to the village and those who made their first acquaintance with the village, perhaps unwillingly, through force of circumstances, will struggle to stay in the area when the time comes to move away. This has been the experience of many strangers who have come to Coverack, as seen during the course of this chronicle. There are more, like George Stone and his sister Doreen who were evacuated to the Butlers' farm in Ponsongath from St. Peter's Primary School in Plymouth in 1941. George mentioned this to the writer when they were introduced on a ship in the Aegean Sea. He returns to Coverack whenever he can. Margaret Wilcox (now Mrs. O'Brien) was also evacuated to Coverack from Plymouth. She is now a writer and lives in Christchurch, New Zealand. In 1990 she returned to the village for a short visit and then went to Plymouth to see her former teachers, the Misses Jury and Motton. There are others like Colleen Upton (now Mrs. Rogers) who came to Mrs. Martin at Little Polcoverack as an evacuee from Enfield during the war and has remained in the parish ever since. Coverack does indeed have connections throughout the world as has been seen in the chapters which mention emigration. The village will no doubt continue to draw people to it and even keep some of them there perhaps in spite of their better judgment. There are no better words than those which the Cornish miner poet, John Harris wrote after visiting Kynance for the first time, that can be applied, with equal fervour, to Coverack:

'O Cove enchanting! much is said of thee,

But of thy beauty, half has not been told.'

222

B.C.

| | |
|---|---|
| 5500–5250 | Earliest Radio carbon dated site in Cornwall is at Poldowrian. |
| c.1500+ | Round Houses and Cliff Castles – Poldowrian and Chynalls. |

A.D.

| | |
|---|---|
| 43–410 | Possibly Romano-British salt works at Lowland Point. |
| 814 | Saxons raid Cornwall. |
| 1262 | Name Porthcovrek recorded. |
| 1337 | Duchy of Cornwall created. |
| 1497 | Cornish Rebellion led by Michael Joseph and Thomas Flamank. |
| 1533 | Reformation began, leading to suppression of Cornish language. |
| 1588 | Spanish Armada. Covrek mentioned in Parish Church Register. |
| 1629 | Eales family acquires Trewothen. |
| 1642–1648 | Civil War. |
| 1703 | Great Storm. |
| 1715 | Dolor House built. |
| 1719 | John Ellis bought land in Coverack (alias Chynalls). |
| 1724 | Coverack new key completed. |
| 1755 | New Quay (Coverack) marked on Thomas Kinchin's Map. |
| 1803 | Petition for Customs Boat at Coverack. |
| | Dumouriez survey of Coastal Batteries. |
| 1809 | Wrecks of Dispatch and Primrose. |
| 1814 | House purchased at Sunny Corner for Wesleyans. |
| 1822 | Coast Guard Service set up. |
| 1837 | Queen Victoria succeeds to throne. |
| 1850 | Roskilly's shop opened in Coverack. |
| 1855 | Emigrant ship John wrecked. |
| 1858 | Bell Buoy placed at manacles. |
| 1862 | Coverack Wesleyan Chapel built. |
| 1866 | Coverack Volunteer Life Saving Company established. |
| 1876 | Coverack Board School built. |
| 1880 | Bible Christian Chapel began in Coverack. |
| | Coverack's first public water supply. |
| | Coverack Sorting Office opened. |
| 1885 | St. Peter's Church built. |
| 1887 | Queen Victoria's Golden Jubilee. |
| | May 8th. First Train arrived in Helston. |
| 1891 | The year of the blizzard. Wreck of Bay of Panama. |
| 1898 | Wreck of Mohegan. |
| 1899 | Wreck of Paris. |
| 1901 | Lifeboat Constance Melanie arrives in Coverack. |
| 1902 | Wreck of Glenbervie. |
| 1905 | Paris Hotel built. Headland Hotel destroyed by fire. |
| 1907 | Milling ended in Coverack. |
| | Wreck of Suevic at the Lizard. |
| 1908 | Fishermen's Rest built. |
| 1909 | Old Age Pensions began. |
| 1911 | St.Peter's Hall built. |
| 1912 | Wreck of the Pindos. |
| 1914–1918 | The Great War. |
| 1917 | Thomas Krag torpedoed off Coverack. |
| 1919 | Wreck of Hattie Luckenback. |
| 1921 | Bus shelter opened in Coverack. |
| 1928 | Coverack Village Hall built. |
| 1929 | Wreck of Archangelos. |
| 1932 | Wrecks of Omer Denise and Ocklinge. |
| 1935 | Bible Christian Chapel closes. |
| | Lifeboat The Three Sisters arrives. |
| | King George V's Silver Jubilee. |
| 1937 | Coronation of King George VI. |
| | Mains Water and Mains Electricity come to Coverack. |
| 1939–1945 | Second World War. |
| 1940 | L.D.V. (Home Guard) formed. First Air Raid on Coverack. |
| | Evacuees arrive in large numbers. |
| 1941 | S.S. Cieszyn bombed and sunk off Coverack. |
| 1942 | Blitz on Coverack. |
| 1945 | Victory in Europe. Victory over Japan. |
| 1948 | Old Post Office closed. |

| 1951 | H.M. Coastguards finish work at Coverack (Regulars). |
| | Wreck of Mina Cantiquin. |
| 1954 | Lifeboat William Taylor of Oldham arrives. |
| 1956 | Wreck of the Citrine. |
| 1972 | William Taylor of Oldham replaced by Inshore Lifeboat. |
| 1977 | Coverack Inshore Lifeboat withdrawn. |
| 1986 | Coverack Auxiliary Coastguard team disbanded. |

## *BIBLIOGRAPHY*

Ashley Maurice  England in the 17th. Century
Balchin W.G.V.  The Cornish Landscape
Beresford Ellis P.  The Cornish Language and its Literature
Bowen E.G.  Britain and the Western Seaways
Douch H.L.  The Ellis Family & Toll Charges on Coverack Quay
Douch H.L. (Editor) Cornwall Muster Roll
Flett J.S. & Hill J.B.  Geology of the Lizard and Meneage
Hadley Peter  An Outline of Pre-history
Halliday F.E.  A History of Cornwall
Hay D., Lineborough Peter, Thompson K.P.  Albion's Fatal Tree
Henderson Charles  Notes from Essays in Cornish History
Jenkin Hamilton  Cornwall and its People
Joad C.E.M.  A year more or less
Lee Charles  Paul Carah, Cornishman
Noall Cyril  Wreck and Rescue round the Cornish coast
Noall Cyril  Cornish Seines and Seiners
Padel O.J.  Cornish Place-Name Elements
Plumb J.H.  England in the 18th. century
Polsue J.  Lake's Parochial History of Cornwall
Quiller Couch A.T.  The Roll Call of the Reef
Quixley R.C.E.  Antique Maps of Cornwall
Roskilly Rachel and Harvey Pat (Editors) Our Schooldays by the Sea
Row Joseph Hambley  Cornwall Feet of Fines
Rowse A.L.  Tudor Cornwall
Shaw Thomas  A History of Cornish Methodism
Spreadbury J.D.  Impressions of the old Duchy
Stockdale F.W.L.  Excursions Through Cornwall 1824
Strike Frank  Cornish Shipwrecks
Teague Dennis and Peter White  Airfields of South West England
Thomas Charles  The importance of being Cornish in Cornwall
Thomson  David  England in the Twentieth Century
Thomson David  England in the Nineteenth Century
Thorn Caroline & Frank (Editors) Domesday Book 10
Toy H. Spencer  The History of Helston
Wakelin Martyn F.  Language and History in Cornwall
Webb William  An Official History of H.M. Coastguard
Wicksteed Bernard  Father's Heinkel

# INDEX

Note: The spelling of names in this index is in general as recorded on documents used in research. Family Christian names tend to be repeated in succeeding generations. Where possible distinctions have been made, by additional information about the person, e.g. domicile, profession, relationship to a more prominent family member. Family History enthusiasts should refer to Census Returns, Church Registers etc., especially when researching names which have alternative spellings, such as:
Eustace, Eustice, Eustis, Pengelly, Pengilly, Tripconey, Tripp.

225

228